Veni Creator Spiritus

A Theological Encyclopedia of the Holy Spirit

Veni Creator Spiritus

A Theological Encyclopedia of the Holy Spirit

by

Michael O'Carroll, C.S.Sp.

A Michael Glazier Book
THE LITURGICAL PRESS
Collegeville, Minnesota

*To the Sacred Alliance of
the Hearts of Jesus and Mary*

A Michael Glazier Book
published by
THE LITURGICAL PRESS

Cover design by Sudabeth Balakhani

Typography by Brenda Belizzone, Mary Brown, Laura Burke, Phyllis Boyd LeVane, Connie De La Cruz.

Distributed in Ireland and Great Britain by Dominican Publications, St. Saviour's, Dublin 1, Ireland.

1	2	3	4	5	6	7	8	9	10

Library of Congress Cataloging-in-Publication Data
O'Carroll, Michael.
   Veni Creator Spiritus : a theological encyclopedia of the Holy
Spirit / by Michael O'Carroll.
     p.   cm.
   "A Michael Glazier book."
   ISBN 0-8146-5785-0
   1. Holy Spirit—Dictionaries. 2. Catholic Church—Doctrines-
-Dictionaries.   I. Title.
BT121.2.0335   1990
231'.3.'03—dc20
                                          90-33910
                                             CIP

Contents

v

Foreword

This work is my response to the appeal of two Popes, whom I profoundly respect, Paul VI and John Paul II, for serious research and publication on the subject of the Holy Spirit. As I try to show in different articles, very much has been done in this area in very recent times, in the decades since the Council. The increasing literature facilitates the labours of every new worker in the field. Whether we are entering on an age of the Holy Spirit, in the acceptable sense of that word, is the Lord's secret. Should he have so decided, then many have been preparing for such a happy future.

We have now left for good the age of *The Forgotten Paraclete*. Historians of the Church will, in the perspective of time, assess what we have gained. On all sides one sees a certain eagerness, attuned to different human needs, types, groups, institutions, to meet the Spirit, to seek his inspiration, his comfort and his strength. Those interested in the reformed liturgy may be heartened to note the frequency with which the Holy Spirit is mentioned in the Liturgy of the Hours according to the Roman rite; this is especially remarkable in the prayers of intercession.

I wish to acknowledge with gratitude my debt to the authors of works which have facilitated my study: Fr. Y.-M.J. Congar's three volumes, *I Believe in the Holy Spirit*, a comprehensive treatment of the subject by one of the theological giants of the age; Fr. G. T. Montague's very fine biblical study, *The Holy Spirit*; all those who contributed to the international congress which, on the suggestion of John Paul II, was organised by the rectors of the Roman Universities and Pontifical Institutes to commemorate the sixteenth centenary of the Council of Constantinople, and the fifteen hundred and fiftieth anniversary of the Council of Ephesus.

I deem it an honour and a duty once again to thank the librarians of the centres where I have done the reading necessary for the various articles in my work: Milltown Park, Dublin; Les Fontaines; Chantilly; the Bibliotheca Bollandiana, Brussels. I belong to a religious congregation which is under the patronage of the Holy Spirit and the Immaculate Heart of Mary. With the appearance of this book I complete fifty years in the community at Blackrock College, an institution which has been known to many through its students whose names, for different reasons, are known around the world. Nowhere else could I have prepared and achieved the written work I have done here in the "Castle". For this I must thank my fellow religious over the years. We trust in the help and protection of our Patroness, Our Lady of Victories, to whom the College was dedicated by the founding French fathers on their arrival in 1860.

I am once again indebted to Dr. J. Craghan, who read the whole manuscript and gave me most precious, detailed advice. I thank Fr. Kilian McDonnell, O.S.B., for similar help.

I offer a special word of thanks to my publisher, Michael Glazier, a model of sensitive cooperation and professional skill.

Michael O'Carroll, C.S.Sp.

Abbreviations

AAS	*Acta Apostolicae Sedis*
AB	*Analects Bollandiana*
ACW	*Ancient Christian Writers*
AHSI	*Archivum Historicum Societatis Jesu*
ANCL	*Ante-Nicene Christian Library*
ASS	*Acta Sanctae Sedis*
Atti del Congresso	*Credo in Spiritum Sanctum. Atti del Congresso Teologico Congresso Internazionale di Pneumatologia*
BB	*Biblica*
BT	*Bibliotheca Trinitariorum*
BZ	*Byzantinische Zeitschrift*
CBQ	*The Catholic Biblical Quarterly*
CCCM	*Corpus Christianorum Continuatio Mediaevalis*
CCSG	*Corpus Christianorum Series Graeca*
CCSL	*Corpus Christianorum Series Latina*
Congar, The Holy Spirit	Y.-M.J. Congar, O.P., *I Believe in the Holy Spirit*, 3 vols., 1983
CSCO	*Corpus Scriptorum Christianorum Orientalium*
DACL	*Dictionnaire d'Archéologie Chrétienne et de Liturgie*
DBS	*Dictionnaire de la Bible Supplément*
DCath	*La Documentation Catholique*
DHGE	*Dictionnaire d'Histoire et de Géographie Ecclésiastiques*
DNB	*Dictionary of National Biography*
DS	*Enchiridion Symbolorum*, Denziger-Bannwart, Schönmetzer
DSp	*Dictionnaire de Spiritualité*
DTC	*Dictionnaire de Théologie Catholique*
EC	*Enciclopedia Cattolica*
ECQ	*Eastern Churches Quarterly*
EL	*Ephemerides Liturgicae*
Eph Carmel	*Ephemerides Carmeliticae*
EstEc	*Estudios Eclesiasticos*
EstTrin	*Estudios Trinitarios*
ETL	*Ephemerides Theologicae Lovanienses*
Fliche and Martin	A. Fliche and V. Martin, *Histoire de l'Eglise*
GCS	*Die griechischen christlichen Schriftsteller der ersten drei Jahrhunderte*
Greg	*Gregorianum*
Handbuch	*Handbuch der Dogmengeschichte*, ed. M. Schmaus, A. Grillmeier, L. Scheffczyk, Band II, 1a,1b, Franz Courth
HTR	*Harvard Theological Review*
ITQ	*Irish Theological Quarterly*
JTS	*Journal of Theological Studies*
Kelly, Doctrines	J. N. D. Kelly, *Early Christian Doctrines*, 1958 and later ed.
LNPF	*Library of Nicene and Post-Nicene Fathers*
LTK	*Lexikon für Theologie und Kirche*
LumV	*Lumen Vitae*
Message, The	*Message of the Fathers of the Church*, 3, *The Holy Spirit*, J.P. Burns, G.M. Fagin, Wilmington, 1984
Montague, The Holy Spirit	*The Holy Spirit, Growth of a Biblical Tradition*, G.T. Montague, S.M., New York, 1976

NCE	*New Catholic Encyclopaedia*
NRT	*Nouvelle Revue Théologique*
NT	*The New Testament*
NTS	*New Testament Studies*
OCP	*Orientalia Christiana Periodica*
OR	*L'Osservatore Romano*
OT	*The Old Testament*
PG	*Patrologia Graeca*, Migne,
PL	Migne, *Patrologia Latina*
Quasten	J. Quasten, *Patrology*, I,II,III, Washington, D.C., 1950-60
RAM	*Revue d'Ascétique et de Mystique*
RB	*Revue Biblique*
REB	*Revue d'Etudes Byzantines*
RHE	*Revue d'Histoire Ecclésiastique*
RHPR	*Revue d'Histoire et de Philosophie Religieuses*
RSPT	*Revue des Sciences Philosophiques et Théologiques*
RSR	*Recherches de Science Religieuse*
RT	*Revue Thomiste*
RTAM	*Recherches de Théologie Ancienne et Mediévale*
RTL	Revue Théologique de Louvain
SC	*Sources Chrétiennes*
SCON	Constitution on the Liturgy, Vatican II
SE	*Sciences Ecclésiastiques*
ST	*Summa Theologica*
TDNT	*Theological Dictionary of the New Testament*
TheolSt	*Theological Studies*
Theotokos	*Theotokos*, M. O'Carroll, C.S.Sp., Wilmington, 1982
Trinitas	*Trinitas*, M. O'Carroll, C.S.Sp., Wilmington, 1987
TZ	*Theologische Zeitschrift*
VS	*La Vie Spirituelle*
ZKT	*Zeitschrift für Katholische Theologie*
ZNW	*Zeitschrift für die neutestamentliche Wissenschaft*

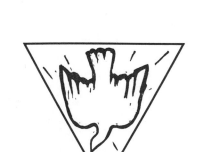

A

ACTS OF THE APOSTLES, THE

The Acts of the Apostles[1] has been called the "Gospel of the Holy Spirit," so much does the Spirit dominate the contents. There is an affinity with St. Luke's gospel, understandable in the common authorship of the two works. Altogether there are fifty-one explicit mentions of the Spirit, of which thirty-five occur in the first twelve chapters. Indeed it can be urged that separate consideration be given to the first two chapters, which give primacy to Pentecost (qv), its immediate prelude and direct aftermath.

The prelude is narrated thus: "In the first book, O Theophilus: I have dealt with all that Jesus began to do and teach, until the day when he was taken up, after he had given commandment through the Holy Spirit to the Apostles whom he had chosen. To them he presented himself alive after his passion by many proofs, appearing to them during forty days, and speaking of the kingdom of God. And while staying with them he charged them not to depart from Jerusalem, but to wait for the promise of the Father, which, he said, 'you heard from me, for John baptized with water, but before many days you shall be baptized with the Holy Spirit.' So when they had come together they asked him, 'Lord will you at this time restore the kingdom to Israel?' He said to them, 'It is not for you to know times or seasons which the Father has fixed by his own authority. But you shall receive power when the Holy Spirit has come upon you; and you shall be my witnesses in Jerusalem and in all Samaria and to the end of the earth" (1:1-8).

The Ascension of Jesus then took place and the Apostles returned to Jerusalem. Peter proceeded at once to the election of one to replace Judas. His first words to the assembly—about a hundred and twenty—were: "'Brethren, the scripture had to be fulfilled which the Holy Spirit spoke beforehand by the mouth of David'" (1:16). Then after the lot had fallen on Matthias and the apostolic college

was again complete in the number twelve, all was ready for the great event, the theophany, which has some similarities with theophanies of the OT, notably the noise or sound and the wind as accompanying elements: "And suddenly a sound came from heaven like a rush of a mighty wind, and it filled all the house where they were sitting. And there appeared on them tongues as of fire, distributed and resting on each one of them. And they were all filled with the Holy Spirit, and began to speak in other tongues, as the Spirit gave them utterance" (Acts 2:2-4; see article Pentecost).

A great pivotal event in salvation history is passed. And the keynote for the story of the early Church, as Luke sees it, is struck; he sees the time of salvation as especially dominated by the Spirit. Immediately Peter explains the meaning of the event to the startled onlookers. He begins significantly by evoking the words of the prophet Joel on the outpouring of the Spirit: "'And in the last days it shall be, God declares, that I will pour out my Spirit upon all flesh and your sons and daughters shall prophesy, and your young men shall see visions, and your old men shall dream dreams; yea, and on my menservants in those days I will pour out my Spirit; and they shall prophesy'" (Acts 2:17-18).

Peter went on to recall the " mighty works and wonders and signs " which God did through Jesus of Nazareth, his death by crucifixion and the fact that God " raised him up. " The important testimony comes later: " This Jesus God raised up and of that we all are witnesses. Being therefore exalted at the right hand of God, and having received from the Father the promise of the Holy Spirit, he has poured out that which you see and hear. " For David did not ascend into the heavens; but he himself says, "The Lord said to my Lord, sit at my right hand, till I make thy enemies a stool for thy feet. Let all the house of Israel therefore know assuredly that God has made him both Lord and Christ, this Jesus whom you crucified" (Acts 2:22,

24, 32-36). Here from the first moment of the Church we see Jesus, Lord, inseparably united with the Spirit. This union should be normative henceforth; they are to remain inseparable.

This too is clear in Peter's reply to those who asked him and "the rest of the Apostles, 'Brethren, what shall we do?'": "And Peter said to them, 'Repent, and be baptized every one of you in the name of Jesus Christ for the forgiveness of your sins; and you shall receive the gift of the Holy Spirit'" (Acts 2:37, 38). The important Chapter 2 of Acts ends with a brief description of the first Christian community, the nascent Church, "devoted to the Apostles' teaching and fellowship, to the breaking of bread and the prayers"; the break with Jewish practice is sensitively stated: the neophytes were "attending the temple together," but "breaking bread in their homes." "Breaking bread" is of course the accepted description of the Eucharist.

If the Spirit and Jesus are inseparable in being, the author of Acts feels free to emphasize certain things in regard to one and the other: charismatic gifts of tongues and prophecy are attributed to the Holy Spirit (Acts 2; 10:46; 19:6), healing and casting out of demons are associated with the name of Jesus (acts 3:6, 16; 4:7, 10, 12, 30; 16:18; 19:13, 17). This may be because tongues and prophecy come from within the Christian body, those already committed to the name of Jesus and who know what Paul would recall to the Corinthians, "Therefore I want you to understand that no one speaking by the Spirit of God ever says, 'Jesus be cursed!' and no one can say, 'Jesus is Lord,' except by the Holy Spirit" (1 Cor 12:3); on the other hand healing and casting out demons are specially meant for those not yet drawn into the body of believers, who do not know how to call on the name of Jesus, Lord. This would have been exemplified in the cure of the cripple at the beautiful gate of the temple (Acts 3:1-10).

It is the life of the Church (qv) that Luke records in Acts and what he has to say of the Spirit is in this context, whereas Paul thinks of the Spirit, especially in his effects on the interior life of the Christian. Important moments and decisions are marked by the Spirit's action. This is very evident in the further narratives of a descent by the Spirit. When Peter and John were released from custody they rejoined their friends and prayed: "And when they had prayed, the place in which they had gathered together was shaken; and they were all filled with the Holy Spirit and spoke the word of God with boldness" (Acts 4:31).

Here the Spirit intervenes to confirm the strength of the community in the first moment of adverse pressure. There is a somewhat intriguing case in the story of the Samaritans evangelized by Philip; his mission had been accompanied by remarkable signs: "Now when the Apostles at Jerusalem heard that Samaria had received the word of God, they sent to them Peter and John, who came down and prayed for them that they might receive the Holy Spirit; for it had not yet fallen on any of them, but they had only been baptized in the name of the Lord Jesus. Then they laid their hands on them and they received the Holy Spirit" (Acts 8:14-17). The delay here between baptism in the name of the Lord Jesus and the gift of the Spirit after the laying on of hands is a discussed problem: Catholic theologians use the text, i.e., v. 16, as evidence of the sacrament of Confirmation (qv); Pentecostals invoke it in favour of baptism in the Spirit (qv).

Here, as in the other descents of the Spirit, the presence of an apostle is deemed necessary. Thus in the crucial case of Cornelius, the first notable Gentile to come to the Church, Peter was in the house of the centurion and had spoken of Jesus of Nazareth, "anointed with the Holy Spirit and with power," telling of his saving mission: "While Peter was still saying this, the Holy Spirit fell on all who heard the word. And the believers from among the circumcised who came with Peter were amazed, because the gift of the Holy Spirit had been poured out even on the Gentiles. For they heard them speaking in tongues and extolling God. Then Peter declared, 'Can anyone forbid water for baptizing these people who have received the Holy Spirit just as we have?' And he commanded them to be baptized in the name of Jesus Christ" (Acts 10:44-48).

Back in Jerusalem from Caesarea Peter explained and justified his action thus: "'As I began to speak, the Holy Spirit fell on them just as on us at the beginning. And I remembered the word of the Lord, how he said, "John baptized with water, but you shall be baptized with the Holy Spirit." If then God gave the same gift to them as he gave to us when we believed in the Lord Jesus Christ, who was I that I could withstand God?'" (11:15-17).

In the last such incident Paul figures: "While Apollo was at Corinth, Paul passed through the upper country and came to Ephesus. There he found some disciples. And he said to them, 'Did you receive the Holy Spirit when you believed?' And they said, 'No, we have not even heard that there is a Holy Spirit.' And he said, 'Into what then were you baptized?' And they said, 'Into

John's baptism.' And Paul said, 'John baptized with the baptism of repentance, telling the people to believe in the one who was to come after him, that is Jesus.' And on hearing this they were baptized in the name of the Lord Jesus. And when Paul had laid his hands upon them, the Holy Spirit came on them; and they spoke with tongues and prophesied" (19:2-6).

Acts records also several instances of Spirit speaking: 1:16; 8:29; 10:19; 11:12; 13:2; 19:1; 21:1; 28:25.

The Spirit also intervened to prevent preaching in certain areas: "And they went through the region of Phrygia and Galatia, having been forbidden by the Holy Spirit to speak the word in Asia. And when they had come opposite Mysia, they attempted to go into Bithynia, but the Spirit of Jesus did not allow them" (Acts 16:6-7).

The life of the Church in the early years grew on witness (Acts 1:8). In assuring this witness, as Luke makes clear, it was especially the Spirit that acted. And the cosmic dimension of the Church was his achievement. Already in the very first gathering after the Pentecostal descent, the multinational character of the crowd was a hint of the end of Jewish exclusivism, a notion of universality outlined. Universalism as an ideal marks his gospel. In Acts it becomes a reality, the opening of a new era in the religious history of humankind. The Church which came forth from the side of the dying Christ, as some of the Fathers liked to think, has taken on a corporate existence among men. A link between the theophany of Pentecost and the ecclesial event was the gift of tongues (qv). It was a sign to some extent perceived by the bystanders, who seemed to form some kind of cohesive assembly since Peter was able to speak to them all at once.

The two essential elements of the Church through the ages to come were discernible, a common faith and the voice of authority. The apostles were seen in an important, indispensable role. The Acts deal largely in the second half with the mission, journeys, teaching, and passion of Paul (qv). Paul never mentions Pentecost. He was an Apostle because he had seen the risen Jesus, and was called by the Spirit. His important role in the growing Church was manifest at the council of Jerusalem, whose message was to include these words, "'it has seemed good to us, having come to one accord, to choose men and send them to you with our beloved Barnabas and Paul, men who have risked their lives for the sake of our Lord Jesus Christ. We have therefore sent Judas and Silas, who them-selves will tell you the same things by word of mouth. For it has seemed good to the Holy Spirit and to us to lay upon you no greater burden than these necessary things'" (Acts 15:25-28).

Even in Acts, sufficient insight is given to Paul's personal life to know what is manifest in his letters, his docility to the Spirit: "Now after these events Paul resolved in the Spirit to pass through Macedonia and Achaia and go to Jerusalem, saying, 'After I have been there, I must also see Rome'" (19:21); "And now, behold, I am going to Jerusalem, bound in the Spirit, not knowing what shall befall me there; except that the Holy Spirit testifies to me in every city that imprisonment and afflictions await me. Take heed to yourselves and to all the flock, in which the Holy Spirit has made you overseers, to care for the Church of God, which he obtained with the blood of his own Son'" (20:22, 28). "When we were staying for some days (in the house of Philip in Caesarea) a prophet named Agabus came down from Judea. And coming to us he took Paul's girdle and bound his own feet and hands, and said, 'Thus says the Holy Spirit, So shall the Jews at Jerusalem bind the man who owns this girdle and deliver him into the hands of the Gentiles'" (21:10, 11). Those who tried to dissuade Paul from going to Jerusalem failed.

Eventually Paul went to Rome. Thus the universality of the Church is symbolized geographically; the message of Christ has been heard in the capital of the world. A first decisive phase in the Church's historical existence is marked off.

The Acts gives us a theology of history and a history of theology. Thinking to a purpose has begun on the divine message which came from Christ, which Christ himself was. It was thinking constantly stirred and animated by the Spirit of Christ.

---

[1]Cf. for bibliography, with general commentaries, A.J. Mattil Jr. and M.B. Mattil, *A Classified Bibliography of Literature on the Acts of the Apostles*, NTTS 7, Leiden, 1966; *Jerome Commentary*, 165, *New Catholic Commentary*, 821a; H.B. Swete, *The Holy Spirit in the New Testament*, London, 1909, 63-109; H. Von Baer, *Der Heilige Geist in den Lukas-schriften*, BWANT III/3, Stuttgart, 1926; F.H. Foakes Jackson and K. Lake, *The Beginnings of Christianity*, IV and V, London, 1933; H.J. Cadbury, *The Book of Acts as History*, London, 1955; L. Cerfaux, *La communauté apostolique*, 2nd ed., Paris, 1953; G.W.H. Lampe, *The Holy Spirit in the Writings of Luke, Studies in the Gospels. Essays in Memory of R.H. Lightfoot*, ed. D.E. Nineham, Oxford, 1955, 145-200; H. Conzelman, *The Theology of St. Luke*, London, 1960; J.H.E. Hull, *The Holy Spirit in the Acts of the Apostles*, London, 1967; J.P. Charlier, *L'Evangile de l'enfance de*

l'Eglise, Brussels, 1966; D.M. Stanley, SJ, *Kingdom to Church* in *Mission and Witness*, ed. P.J. Burns, SJ, London, 1965; J. Borremans, *L'Esprit Saint dans la catéchèse évangélique de Luc, Lumen Vitae* 25 (1970), 103-122; E. Rasco, *Jesús y el Espiritu, Iglesia e "Historia"; Elementos para una lectura de Lucas, Greg* 56 (1975), 321-367; G. Haya-Prats, *L'Esprit force de l'Eglise, Sa nature et son activité d'après les Actes des Apôtres,* Lectio divina 81, Paris, 1975, bibl.; G.T. Montague, SM, *The Holy Spirit* 271-301; Y-M.J. Congar, The Holy Spirit I, 44-47; *TDNT*, VI, 404-415.

AD FOVENDUM IN CHRISTIANO POPULO, 18 APRIL 1902

A Letter sent to the Bishops of the Catholic Church in the name of Leo XIII (qv).[1] With it went a copy of the Pope's Encyclical, *Divinum illud Munus* (qv). The present document is therefore a reminder of the former. The Bishops are again informed of the Pope's teaching on the Holy Trinity, but especially on "the marvellous presence and power of the Holy Spirit," teaching contained in the Encyclical; they are also reminded that preachers and those with the care of souls were strongly urged to convey "most diligently and fruitfully" to the Christian people all that relates to the Holy Spirit. As Pentecost was again approaching, the importance of the preparatory novena was stressed. The letter corrected a misunderstanding sometimes found, that the indulgences granted by the Pope were for the first year. They were perpetually in force. The hope of the Pope was for "the speedy achievement of Christian unity," a good about which he was deeply concerned

---

[1]Acta Leonis XIII, VIII, 103-104.

ALLIANCE OF THE TWO HEARTS

Mighty events in the life of the Church enlighten us on important truths.[1] In 1986 the Philippines went through an experience that was interpreted by many as a political miracle. In February, in the wake of presidential elections, a group of army men led by Fidel Ramos, with the support of the Minister of Defence, Ponce Enrile, broke with the Marcos regime. Civil war threatened when the Cardinal requested by Ramos, made an appeal to the citizens of Manila to go on the streets and keep the armies apart. Everything was done under the sign of Our Lady of Fatima, whose statue was everywhere in the streets during the days of tension. Peace came suddenly and credible stories of Our Lady's intervention, in one casean apparition, were current. The Philippine hierarchy noted that the event had occurred during the special Marian Year which they had declared for the bi-millennium of Our Lady's birthday.

With the relevance of the Immaculate Heart of Mary (qv) to the situation there soon went the thought of the Sacred Heart of Jesus, particularly as at that time Pope John Paul was speaking from time to time of the two Hearts: it was he who first used the phrase "Alliance of the Two Hearts." Cardinal Sin representing the Philippine Bishops had set up a steering committee in Rome in October, 1985, to plan an international symposium to meet in Fatima, in the following year, with this subject as its theme. Speakers well qualified agreed to deal with the subject from every aspect: I. de la Potterie, SJ, on the biblical basis; D. Fernandez, CMF. on the Fathers of the Church; T. Koehler, SM, on the Middle Ages; A. Calkins, on the seventeenth century; M. O'Carroll, CSSp, on the nineteenth and twentieth centuries; A. Chupungco, OSB, on the Liturgy; C. Pozo, SJ, on mystical theology; C. Schönborn, OP, on speculative theology; R. Laurentin on the Teaching Authority. The symposium duly took place with the very warm encouragement from the Holy Father—he sent a message to the symposium members through Cardinal Sin and addressed them in a special audience in Rome when they went to the Vatican to deliver the entire dossier of the symposium.

The particular aspect of the subject relevant to the theme of the present work is the intuition that emerged from all the research and discussion. The unifying bond between the Hearts of Jesus and Mary is the Holy Spirit. As René Laurentin said: "John Paul untiringly refers to the Holy Spirit" in his effort to establish a theology and profound anthropology of the Hearts of the Mother and her divine Son. A typical passage from the Pope: "'Through the work of the Holy Spirit, the humanity of Christ, Son of the eternal Father, took shape in the womb of the Virgin of Nazareth. Through the work of the Holy Spirit the Heart took shape in this humanity, the Heart which is the central organ of the human organism of Christ, and at the same time the true symbol of his interior life: his thoughts, his will, his sentiments. Through this Heart the humanity of Christ is, in a particular way, the temple of God, and at the same time, through this Heart it remains open to men and to all that is human.'"[2]

There is, as the papers given to the symposium made clear, a continuing thread of thought through the ages on the two Hearts. The concept of the

Hearts of Jesus and Mary embodying the new covenant as disclosed by the biblical investigation of Fr. de la Potterie calls for further reflection. The Fathers gave us a particular insight which will serve through the ages as a framework for thought on the partnership of Jesus and Mary: she is the new Eve at the centre of the new creation. The theologians, homilists, and mystics of medieval times can be cited in evidence of a more explicit awareness of the theology of the heart: Helfta is a name that comes to mind. The seventeenth century was a golden age with the writings of St. Francis de Sales and St. John Eudes a treasury which may be enlarged from the works of Cardinal de Bérulle and Fr Jean-Jacques Olier.

The devotional life of the Church, the determining ideas of religious founders, charismatic figures and heavenly apparitions need to be studied and weighed in the modern age. The two Hearts were the inspiration of a spiritual writer such as Joseph de Gallifet, SJ (1663-1749), a religious founder in the days of the French Revolution, Pierre Joseph de Clorivière, SJ, (1735-1820), and another soon after, Marie-Joseph Coudrin (1768-1837); they appear on the Miraculous Medal, of which a thousand million copies were distributed before the death of St. Catherine Labouré in 1876, with what beneficial results we know. The chain of events linked with Fatima which continues to the present time began with heavenly intimations to the children on the Hearts of Jesus and of Mary: "they are attentive to the voice of your supplications" and later "the holy Hearts of Jesus and Mary have merciful designs on you."

Two great theologians of the nineteenth century saw the importance of joining the cult of the two Hearts, M.J. Scheeben and J.H. Newman. One Pope before John Paul, Pius XII, in his Encyclical on the Sacred Heart of Jesus, could write thus: "But if from their devotion to the august Heart of Jesus riches more abundant are to be poured out upon the Family of Christians, and indeed upon the entire human race, then the Faithful must see to it that to this devotion of theirs is linked indissolubly devotion also to the Immaculate Heart of the Mother of God. For in the eternal Will of God the Blessed Virgin Mary has been joined indissolubly to Christ in the accomplishment of man's Redemption, in such a way that our salvation has proceeded from the charity of Jesus Christ and his bitter sufferings, together with the love and sorrows of his Mother most intimately associated thereto. This being so, it is altogether fitting that the Chris-

tian People, who have received the divine life of grace from Christ through Mary, should, after paying their rightful homage to the Sacred Heart of Jesus, also render to the loving Heart of their heavenly Mother the corresponding debt of filial loyalty, love, gratitude and reparation. Entirely in keeping with the above-mentioned disposition of God's most sweet and wise Providence is the memorable form of Consecration by which we ourselves solemnly dedicated Holy Church and the whole world to the sinless Heart of the Blessed Virgin Mary."[3]

All these intuitions and aspirations may be incorporated into the synthesis here suggested on the basis of John Paul II's teaching. It is in the theology of the Holy Spirit that we shall obtain the full justification for the union of the two Hearts and a hard-core thought structure for the whole theology of the Heart. In religious contexts, especially the sacred ones we here contemplate, some authors adhering rigidly to the mental categories of the Graeco-Roman world, which have nobly served Christian theology, tend to marginalise the theology of the Heart. This leads to a cleavage between theology and the life of the Church, which means loss. Thought structures serving divine revelation must have the flexibility of life which derives from mystery. Excessive rigidity means fossilization. There must be recognition for the wholeness and multi-dimensional reality of the Heart. In the past it may have been taken in a superficial, exclusively sentimental, even superstitious sense. From biblical times on it has depth upon depth of meaning. In it we touch the centre of the life of the God-man, the fountain of life to us, the exemplar of heroic conduct, the mainspring, dynamic force of the vast scheme of universal salvation. Closely modelled on the Heart of the most perfect man is that of the noblest, most powerful, most compassionate of women. All under the constant guidance, the sensitive and plenary enlightenment of God's ever active Spirit, he who is the fullest outpouring of almighty love and mercy, God concentrated in Gift to man, his small creature. But a creature called to divinization.

---

[1]Full dossier of the Fatima Symposium published by Bahay Maria, Manila, *The Alliance of the Two Hearts*, 1988; M. O'Carroll, CSSp, "The Alliance of the Two Hearts," *Doctrine and Life*, 38 (1988), 234-241; *Toward a Civilization of Love*, International Symposium, 1981, Ignatius Press, 1985; [2]Angelus, 27 June, 1982, *Osservatore Romano*, English tr., No. 741, p. 2; [3]Tr. C.T.S., London.

AMBROSE, ST., DOCTOR OF THE CHURCH (c. 339-397)

Author of the first formal treatise on the Holy Spirit, *De sancto Spiritu*, [1] by a writer of the Latin Church, A. deals with the subject in other works incidentally. In the *De Fide*, wherein he treated of the Incarnation, he affirmed the unity of power, Godhead, operation in the Holy Trinity; the three Persons are one God and the unity comprehends the whole of the divine being.

There is no dominant logical plan in the work and the approach at times seems apologetic: defence of the truth against current heresies. A. is determined to set beyond all question the divinity of the Spirit, and his equality with the Father and the Son. As to operation he writes thus: "When any divine operation, whether of the Father or of the Son or of the Holy Spirit is treated of, it is not referred only to the Holy Spirit, but also to the Father and the Son, and not only to the Father but also to the Son and the Spirit." [2] "And not only is the operation of the Father, Son and Spirit everywhere one, but also there is one and the same will, calling and giving of commands, which one may see in the great and saving mystery of the Church.... As then God the Father called the Church, so too Christ called it and so too the Spirit called it saying: 'Separate to me Paul and Barnabas for the work to which I have called them.' 'So' it is added 'having fasted and prayed they laid hands on them and sent them forth. And they being sent forth by the Holy Spirit went down to Seleucia.'" (Acts 13:2ff). So Paul received the apostleship by the will not only of Christ, but also of the Holy Spirit and hastened to gather together the Gentiles. [3]

A. insists that the Father, Son and Holy Spirit are of one nature and of one knowledge. [4] "For our knowledge proceeds from one Spirit through one Son to one Father and from one Father through one Son to one Holy Spirit is delivered goodness and sanctification and the sovereign right of eternal power." [5]

The Spirit is called Lord, which word signifies God: "Who, then, is the Lord, who makes us increase and abound before God and our Father at the coming of the Lord Jesus? He has named the Father and has named the Son; whom then has he joined with the Father and the Son except the Spirit? Who is the Lord who establishes our hearts in holiness. For holiness is a grace of the Spirit, as too, is said farther on: 'in holiness of the Spirit and belief of the truth.' Who then do you think, is here named Lord, except the Spirit?.... For the Spirit descended in the likeness of a dove, that he might both bear witness to his wisdom, and perfect the Sacrament of the spiritual laver, and show that his working is one with that of the Father and the Son. And that you should not suppose that anything had fallen from the Apostle by oversight, but that he knowingly and designedly and inspired by the Spirit designated him Lord, whom he felt to be God, he repeated the same in the second Epistle to the Thessalonians, saying: 'But the Lord direct your hearts in the love of God and in the patience of Christ' (3:5). If love be of God and patience of Christ, it ought to be shown who is the Lord who directs, if we deny that the direction is of the Holy Spirit. But we cannot deny it, since the Lord said of him: 'I have yet many things to say unto you, but you cannot bear them now. But when he, the Spirit of truth, shall come, he will lead you into all truth' (Jn 16:12, 13). And David says of him: 'Thy good Spirit shall lead me into the right way' (Ps 143:10). See what the voice of the Lord uttered concerning the Holy Spirit. The Son of God came, and because he had not yet shed forth the Spirit, he declared that we were living like little children without the Spirit. He said that the Spirit was to come who should make of these little children stronger men, by an increase, namely, of spiritual age. And this he laid down not that he might set the power of the Spirit in the first place, but that he might show that the fulness of strength consists in the knowledge of the Trinity. It is therefore necessary either that you mention some fourth person besides the Spirit of whom you ought to be conscious, or assuredly that you do not consider another to be Lord, except the Spirit who has been pointed out." [6] A. then invokes 2 Cor 3:15-17, somewhat as did St. Basil (qv) in a similar argument.

Earlier in the work A. had focussed attention on the Holy Spirit as Creator: "And who can deny that the creation of the earth is the work of the Holy Spirit, by whose work it is renewed? If they desire to deny that it was created by the Spirit, while they cannot deny that it must be renewed by the Spirit, those who desire to divide the Persons must maintain that the operation of the Holy Spirit is superior to that of the Father and the Son (which is far from the truth). For there is no doubt that the restored earth is better than it was created. Or if, at first, without the operation of the Holy Spirit, the Father and the Son made the earth, but the operation of the Holy Spirit was joined on afterwards, it will seem that what was first made required his aid, which was then added. But far be it from anyone to think this, namely, that the divine work should be believed to have a change in the Creator, an error brought in by Manicheus."[7]

His principal argument on the question was based on the role of the Spirit in the Incarnation: "But why do I delay with matters not to the point? Let them accept a plain proof that there can be nothing which the Holy Spirit can be said not to have made; and that it cannot be doubted that all subsists through his operation, whether angels, archangels, thrones, or dominions. The Lord himself, according to the flesh, whom the angels serve, was begotten by the Holy Spirit coming upon the Virgin (A. quotes Mt 1:20; Lk 1:35). The birth from the Virgin was, then, the work of the Spirit .... So, then, we cannot doubt that the Spirit is Creator, whom we know as the author of the Lord's incarnation."[8] Again he concludes from Paul's injunction to serve the Spirit (Phil 3:3). "So, then, when the Apostle says that we ought to serve the Spirit, and also asserts that we must not serve the creature but the Creator, without doubt he plainly shows that the Holy Spirit is Creator, and is to be venerated with the honour due to the eternal Godhead. It is written, 'You shall worship the Lord your God, and him only shall you serve' (Mt 4:10)."[9] He deals with objections that could be made from metaphors like 'Finger of God,' invoking the use of God's Right Hand for the Son.

A. believes that the Holy Spirit, as to his temporal mission, proceeds from the Father and the Son.[10] He it is who sanctifies. A. brings out this in many ways in the *De Sacramentis*. It is not all water, he says, which heals, but water, which has the grace of Christ, heals. "There is a difference between the element and sanctification, between the act and efficacy. The act is accomplished with water, but the efficacy comes from the Holy Spirit. The water does not heal if the Holy Spirit has not come down and consecrated this water."[11]

A. makes an interesting point in regard to the Baptism of Jesus: "Christ came down, the Spirit came down also. Why did Christ come first and then the Spirit, when the customary rite of Baptism demands that the font be first consecrated, and then he who is to be baptized goes down into it. For when the priest enters he at once exorcizes the creature which the water is, then he utters the invocation and prayer so that the font be sanctified and the eternal Trinity be present, while in the case of Christ he went down first and the Holy Spirit followed him. Why? So that the Lord Jesus should not, as it were, appear to need the mystery of sanctification, but that he should himself be the one who sanctified, and that the Spirit should sanctify too. Thus Christ went down into the water and the Holy Spirit came down as a dove. God the Father, in turn, spoke from heaven. There you have the presence of the Trinity."[12]

The Spirit gives stability in Christ and A. delays on the sevenfold gift that follows the "signaculum": "The spiritual sign about which you heard in today's reading, follows, for after the font, perfection must be achieved, when at the priest's invocation the Holy Spirit is poured out, the Spirit of wisdom and understanding, the Spirit of counsel and of strength, the Spirit of knowledge and piety, the Spirit of holy fear, which are as the seven virtues of the Spirit. Doubtless all the virtues are related to the Spirit but these are in a way cardinal, the principal. What is as important as piety? What is as important as knowledge of God? What is as important as strength? What is as important as the counsel of God? What is as important as the fear of God? As fear of the world is weakness, fear of God is great strength."

"Such are the seven virtues, when you receive the seal. For as the holy Apostle says, the wisdom of Our Lord has many forms and the wisdom of God has many forms. Likewise the Holy Spirit is manifold, he who has a wide variety of virtues. Hence he is called the God of virtues, which can be said of the Father, the Son and the Holy Spirit."[13] For 'virtue' we now use 'gift,' and 'cardinal' has become technical. But the sacramental spirituality here expressed by A. complements beautifully the doctrine developed in the treatise on the Holy Spirit. The image and likeness lost by sin is restored by the Spirit.

---

[1]Text of *De Spiritu Sancto PL* 16, 703-815; English tr. *LNPF* II, 10, 91-158; Cf. Th. Schermann, *Die griechischen Quellen des hl. Ambrosius in LL III De Spiritu Sancto*, Munich, 1902; F.H. Dudden, *The Life and Times of St. Ambrose* 2 vols., Oxford, 1935; W. Seibel, *Fleisch und Geist beim hl. Ambrosius, Münchener Theologische Studien*, 14, Munich, 1958; E. Dassmann, *Das Leben des hl. Ambrosius*, Düsseldorf, 1967; id., *Die Frömmigkeit des Kirchenvaters Ambrosius von Mailand*, Münsterische Beiträge zur Theologie, 29, 1965; C. Granado, S.J., *El Espiritu Santo y los Profetas en san Ambrosio de Milan*, Granada, 1979; id., *Actividad del Espiritu Santo en el Antiguo Testamento segun San Ambrosio de Milan*, in *Atti del Congresso*, I, 235-241; P. Smulders DSp, IV, 1, 1276-78; *Message of the Fathers*, 142-149; [2]*De Spiritu* I, 3, *LNPF*, p. 98; [3]*Op. cit.*, II, 10, p. 101-102; [4]*Op. cit.*, II, 11, p. 129; [5]*Op. cit.*, II, 12, p. 131; [6]*Op. cit.*, III, 14, 95-100, p. 149; [7]*Op. cit.*, II, 5, p. 119; [8]*Ibid.*, [9]*Ibid.*, p. 120; [10]I, 11, 120, p. 109; [11]*De Sacramentis*, I, 15, SC 25, p. 68; [12]*Op. cit.*, I, 18, 19, p. 70; [13]*Op. cit.*, III, 8-10, p. 96-98; cp. VI, 9, p. 140f; *De Mysteriis*, 42, op. cit., p. 178.

ANGELS

"In the earthly liturgy, by way of foretaste, we share in that heavenly Liturgy which is celebrated in the holy city of Jerusalem toward which we journey as pilgrims, and in which Christ is sitting at the right hand of God, a minister of the sanctuary and of the true tabernacle (cf. Apoc. 21:2; Col 3:1; Heb 8:2); we sing a hymn to the Lord's glory with all the warriors of the heavenly army; venerating the memory of the saints, we hope for some part and fellowship with them; we eagerly await the Saviour our Lord Jesus Christ, until he, our life, shall appear and we too will appear with him in glory (cf. Phil 3:20; Col 3:4)."[1]

With these words Vatican II sought to revive or give vital awareness to a truth which had been an influential element of Christian consciousness, the unity of angelic and redeemed human society. In God's creative plan there was not separation or partition between the world of angels and humankind. He did not intend humans to live through their salvation history, with but occasional and fortuitous encounters between them and the myriad hosts of angels.

One of the works which preceded Vatican II in this doctrine was Erik Peterson's *Le Livre des Anges*. The author patiently analysed Revelation IV and V to show that according to Scripture there is worship offered to God in heaven by the angels and the blessed. But through the mediation of the 'elders' (Rev 4:10) this worship is related to the Church on earth. The divine office of the heavenly Jerusalem, which is described in Revelation, comprises the singing of the *Sanctus*, victory hymns, psalms (ch. 19:6), the 'new ode,' and also, as Chapter 19 shows, the singing of the *Alleluia*. Finally, the heavenly worship has also acclamations: 'Amen.' There is then no doubt but that we are dealing with a liturgy; the numerous cultic formulas prove it. Our thesis, then, that there is worship in heaven in which the Church on earth participates, is confirmed by Scripture."[2]

Erik Peterson goes on to show from an analysis of liturgical texts that all the liturgy of the Church on earth must be understood as a participation in the worship of the angels. This truth has its completion in his finding that the angels take part in the Church's liturgy, as in his analysis of the role of angels in the mystical life. Both ideas are also argued with much evidence by Cardinal Daniélou in his work, *The Angels and their Mission*.

We are led to consideration of Christ's primacy over the angels, the final satisfying explanation of their liturgical role. For he is the centre of all liturgy. "Christ" says St. Augustine "is Head of the whole city of Jerusalem, which counts all the faithful from the beginning to the end, with the legions and armies of angels added to them, that there may be one city under one king, one province under one emperor, happy in unending peace and salvation, praising God without end, blessed without end."[3] The idea is elaborated by M.J. Scheeben (qv). Christ is, as all theologians admit, king of the angels. "Can we not go further" he asks "and assume that the idea of the head is verified in a still richer sense in Christ's relations to the angels? ... Is it not in the highest degree fitting that the God-man, as the first-born of all creatures, should be, by power and might, the principle of the supernatural dignity and consecration, grace and glory, of the angels as their head? Do not the angels too acquire a much higher dignity, a closer union with God, by this dependence on Christ, than they would have in virtue of the simple grace of divine sonship? ... Hence the re-establishment of the angels, which was accomplished when the Incarnation actually took place, can mean only that their sanctity was now deeply and firmly rooted in the foundation which God had pre-ordained from eternity, and was adorned with the crown by which it was to receive its final consecration."[4]

If the great theologian's opinion be accepted, we must look for an elaboration of the Spirit's role in the angelic world. It is the Spirit who communicates to those dependent on Christ the grace won for them by him. If the Incarnation is the foundation "pre-ordained from eternity," then the Spirit was eternally foreseen as a direct benefactor of the angels. For the Incarnation was achieved by the Spirit (Lk 1:35).

Jewish Christian theology was seeking some understanding of this association: the name of Michael the archangel was given to Christ and that of Gabriel to the Holy Spirit.[5] A more purified theology is discernible in the Annunciation narrative. It is Gabriel who communicates to Mary the message about the Spirit: an intimate bond must be assumed between the messenger and the Spirit. Though the angel motif is found in the infancy narratives (Mt 1:20; 2:19; Lk 1:19; 1:26; 2:9-14) and in the Resurrection (Mt 28:2-8; Mk 16:5; Lk 24:4-7; Jn 20:12, 13) and Ascension (Acts 1:10, 11) narratives, there is no mention of angels in the account of Pentecost (qv). The absence does not affect the general truth which has far deeper justification and wider ramification. The Spirit governs the whole world of angels; he acts directly on the angels, dispensing to them what is theirs in the predestined order of God's creation, guiding them, giving them the spiritual energy needed for their supernatural life and tasks; ensuring especially the total harmony between humans and angels, binding all more profoundly to Christ, who holds the primacy in the entire universe.

St. Fulgentius of Ruspe (qv) was explicit on the Spirit's influence in the angelic world.[6] Among the Fathers, however, it was St. Basil who developed the idea most satisfactorily: "But there is no sanctification without the Spirit. The powers of the heavens are not holy by nature; were it so there would, in this respect, be no difference between them and the Holy Spirit. It is in proportion to their relative excellence that they have their measure of holiness from the Spirit. . . . It results that, if by your argument you do away with the Spirit, the hosts of angels are disbanded, the dominions of archangels are destroyed, all is thrown into confusion, and their life loses law, order and distinctness. For how are the angels to cry 'Glory to God in the highest,' without being empowered by the Spirit? . . . . How could the Seraphim cry 'Holy, Holy, Holy' were they not taught by the Spirit how often true religion requires them to lift their voice in the ascription of glory? Do 'all his angels' and 'all his hosts' praise God? it is through the co-operation of the Spirit. Do 'thousand thousands' of angels stand before him, and 'ten thousand times ten thousand' ministering spirits? They are blamelessly doing their proper work by the power of the Spirit. All the glorious and unspeakable harmony of the highest heavens both in the service of God, and in the mutual concord of the celestial powers can therefore only be preserved by the direction of the Holy Spirit."[7]

---

[1] *Constitution on the Liturgy*, art. 8; for theology of the angels cf. St. Thomas S.T. Ia qq 50-56; Francis Suarez, S.J., *Summa Theologiae de Deo rerum omnium Creatore*, pars secunda, Lyons, 1620; Erik Peterson, *Le livre des anges*, Paris, 1954; J. (Cardinal Daniélou, S.J., *The Angels and their Mission*, tr. D. Heimann, Westminster, Maryland, 1957; DSp I, 580-625, J. Duhr; NCE, I, 506-519; T.L. Fallon, J. Michl, S. Tsuji, A.A. Bialas; A. Vonier, O.S.B., *The Angels in the Teaching of the Catholic Church*, ed. G.D. Smith, London, 1946, 248-87; G.R. Régamey, *What is an Angel?* Faith and Fact, London, 1960; A. Heising, *Der Heilige Geist und die Heiligungdér Engel in der Pneumatologie des Basilius V.C.*, ZKT 87 (1965) 257-308; [2] *Op. cit.*, 41; [3] *Enarr. in Ps.* 36, S. III, PL 36, 385; [4] *The Mysteries of Christianity*, 402, 3; [5] J. Cardinal Daniélou, S.J., Paris, 1957, 171-180; [6] *Contra Fabianum*, XXVIII, CCSL 91A, 810; PL 65, 786; [7] *De Spiritu Sancto* XVI, 38, LNPF 8, 24.

ANNUNCIATION, THE[1]

"And the angel said to her, 'The Holy Spirit will come upon you, and the power of the Most High will overshadow you; therefore the Child to be born will be called holy, the Son of God'" (Lk 1:35). "And Mary said, 'Behold, I am the handmaid of the Lord, let it be to me according to your word.' And the angel departed from her" (*Ibid.*, 38). Very much has been spoken and written through the ages on these verses of Luke's gospel, from the whole dialogue of the Annunciation, which Père Benoit, O.P., the great French biblical scholar, considered the nucleus of the whole gospel. From these words all Christian tradition has concluded that the Spirit did descend on Mary, though the fact is not mentioned, that she did then conceive a Child, though this is not stated either. Her fiat in reply to the angel's promise is deemed affirmation of the fact. Many questions arise in regard to Our Lady's role in the whole event. Here we are dealing with the narrative, as it relates to the Spirit of God.

In biblical terms we are at a starting point. As the Annunciation narrative is part of the infancy gospel of Luke, attention must be given to the immense difference between the content of this narrative and that of other passages recording his action: "In Lk I-II the Spirit which in turn fills the precursor, Elizabeth, Zechariah, Simeon (1:15, 17, 41, 67; 2:25, 26, 27) is obviously the OT Spirit of prophecy; he makes John the Baptist a new Elijah; he informs Simeon about the imminent coming of the Messiah; he impels Elizabeth, Zechariah and Simeon *to speak*. The Spirit who intervenes in 1:35 for the virginal conception of Jesus is *the creative Spirit, the source of a new economy*, the same One who will intervene in the public ministry of Jesus and will show himself powerfully at Pentecost, the One of whom Is 32:15 already spoke (cf. the intervention of the Spirit and of power from on high in Lk 1:35; 4:1; 4:14; 24:49; Acts 1:8; 10:38). Attached by the infancy narrative to the ancient economy, the Virgin Mary bears within her, thanks to the action of the creative Spirit, the very source of the new economy."[2]

What was the significance of the Spirit's descent? A great Orthodox theologian, Sergius Bulgakov (qv) puts it thus: "Thus the descent of the Holy Spirit in the Annunciation was not merely related to the divine conception and child-birth and after it had been accomplished, the human essence of Mary was not deprived of grace (which constitutes the principal heresy of Protestantism, strangely lacking in awareness of the mystery of the Mother of God). The Virgin Mary remained, even after the birth of Christ, in the force of the Annuciation, that is of the Holy Spirit's presence. She was not a mere instrument in the hands of Providence for the purposes of the redemption, but, being a human personality, she was the subject of the divine conception, to the degree that she participated in it. The Holy Spirit did not abandon her after the birth of Christ but remained forever with her in the full strength of the Annunciation."[3]

Can we make this thought more explicit and conclude from the teaching of Vatican II (qv) that there was a visible mission of the Spirit at the Annunciation? Such is the opinion of H.M. Manteau-Bonamy, O.P. In the Constitution on the Church the Council taught that Mary had been "fashioned by the Holy Spirit into a kind of new substance and a new creature" (art. 57). It spoke of Mary "prayerfully imploring the gift of the Spirit who had already overshadowed her in the Annunciation." (art. 59). There are suggestive theological references to the Spirit in the passages on the Mary Church typology and the apostolate.

But doctrine in these passages is more embryonic than plenary. Fr. Manteau-Bonamy contends that in the document on the missionary activity of the Church, *Ad Gentes*, published during the fourth session of the Council, a great step forward was taken. "The Council, putting Pentecost and the Annunciation side by side, invites us to consider that the Holy Spirit truly descended in person on Mary at the Annunciation; and this coming signified by the Shadow of the 'Glory of God,' of the 'Shekinah' took concrete form in the Virgin who was at that very moment pregnant with Christ. The Council insists in the text of the Decree *Ad Gentes*: 'For it was from Pentecost that the "Acts of the Apostles" took their origin. In a similar way Christ was conceived when the Holy Spirit came upon the Virgin Mary.... Thus too Christ was impelled to the work of his ministry when the Holy Spirit descended upon him at prayer.' The meaning of this text of the Decree *Ad Gentes* is, without any possible ambiguity and quite explicit. The statement from *Lumen Gentium* recurs. As it is a 'visible' mission of the Holy Spirit on the Apostles on the day of Pentecost, and, before that, on Christ at his Baptism, it is also really a 'visible' mission of the same Holy Spirit on the Virgin with Child at the moment of the Incarnation. The Church does not innovate. But we must recognise that, at least in the Latin Church, from the beginning of scholasticism, nearly a thousand years ago,

no one had dared state so explicitly that there was a 'visible' mission of the Holy Spirit on the Virgin in the moment of the conception of Christ. Theologians were happy to say after St. Thomas: 'The visible mission of Christ (at his Baptism) revealed an invisible mission accomplished not then but from the beginning of his conception.'"[4]

The idea of a visible mission at the Annunciation, if it is valid, raises very acutely the question of a personal relationship between Mary and the Spirit. The Spirit would not merely have acted in her; he would have come to her in an act of self-communication without parallel, apart from the mystery of the Spirit in the life of Jesus Christ, the God-man. No other creature was taken into such intimate union, association, partnership with a divine Person.

A particular aspect of this relationship centres on the Immaculate Heart of Mary (qv). It is a subject with many facets, as different titles suggest. Spiritual writers, notably St. Louis Marie Grignon de Montfort, and St. Maximilian Kolbe, Popes Leo XIII, Pius XII, John Paul II, (qqv) have called Mary spouse of the Holy Ghost. Vatican II preferred the title 'Sanctuary of the Holy Spirit.' Theophanes of Nicaea (qv) spoke of Mary as the image of the Spirit. Leonardo Boff, O.F.M., known for his forthright views on liberation theology, speaks of Mary as "hypostatically assumed by the Third Person of the Trinity." He sees in this union the fullness of God's revelation of the feminine.

There is an immense call to reflection on the meaning of the Spirit's descent as an event in itself, as a revelation of the Spirit, as that which includes all other self-communication by the Spirit, as Mary's fiat included the entire free offering of humans to God.

---

[1]For bibl., cf. M. O'Carroll, *Theotokos,* "The Annunciation," 29-32 "Spirit, The Holy," *ibid.,* 329-333; R.E. Brown, *The Birth of the Messiah,* Garden City, NY, 1977, 286-329; R. Laurentin, *Les évangiles de l'enfance du Christ,* 1982, passim; articles in present work on Bulgakov, Sergius, Vatican II; [2]A. Feuillet, P.S.S., "L'Esprit Saint et la Mère du Christ," in *Etudes Mariales* BSFEM 25 (1968), 56, 57; [3]*Le Paraclet,* Paris, 1946, 238, 39; [4]*La Vierge Marie et le Saint Esprit,* (Commentaire de 'Lumen Gentium,') Paris, 1971, 15-16.

ANSELM, ST. DOCTOR OF THE CHURCH (1033-1109)[1]

While in exile or absence from the see of Canterbury A. went from Rome to Bari to attend a council, 1098, attended by eastern bishops. In a remarkable effort at dialogue he tried to lead them to acceptance of the Latin doctrine of the *Filioque* (qv). Two years later he completed a work embodying and expanding the ideas there expressed, *De Processione Spiritus Sancti*. His general Trinitarian doctrine is assumed. In the earlier chapters of the book A. treated his subject speculatively, later he tried to extract the doctrine from biblical texts. He inherited the theory of relations from St. Augustine (qv). There is no patristic argument because A. did not know the Greek Fathers and the Greeks did not know the Latins.

A. develops adequately what is held in common by Greeks and Latins. It is from there that he advances to enforce his own thesis. After explaining the difference between the Son coming from the Father by being born, *nascendo*, and the Spirit by procession, *procedendo*, he goes on: "It must therefore be concluded by every incontrovertible necessity—if what I have already said that what we hold with the Greeks be true—that the Son is of the Holy Spirit, or the Holy Spirit is of the Son. But it is clear from Catholic faith that the Son is not from the Holy Spirit. For God is not from God save by being born as Son or by proceeding as the Holy Spirit. But the Son is not born of the Holy Spirit. If he is born of him he is the Son of the Holy Spirit, and the Holy Spirit is his father. But neither one nor the other is father or son. The Son is then not born of the Holy Spirit. Nor is it any less certain that he does not proceed from him. For he would be the Spirit of the same Holy Spirit. Which is explicitly denied, since the Holy Spirit is said and believed to be the Spirit of the Son. For he cannot be the Spirit of his own Spirit. Wherefore the Son does not proceed from the Holy Spirit. In no way, therefore, is the Son from the Holy Spirit. It follows, then, by incontrovertible reasoning that the Holy Spirit is of the Son as he is of the Father."[2]

A. wishes to forestall any kind of objection. "The Holy Spirit is from that in which the Father and Son are one, that is from God, not from that in which they differ from each other. But since God from whom the Holy Spirit is, is Father and Son, for this reason he is truly said to be from the Father and Son who are two. And since the Father is not before or after the Son, or greater or less than him, and one is not more or less God than the other, the Holy Spirit is not from the Father before (being from) the Son, nor from the Son before (being from) the Father, nor is he greater or less in his existence from the Father than in his existence from the Son, nor more or less from one

than from the other.... And if it is said that the Holy Spirit proceeds (literally 'is') principally (*principaliter*) from the Father, as if he were more from the Father than the Son, this is not to be said with the idea of differences mentioned. But since the Son has what he is from the Father, it is not improper to say from the Father, from whom he has being, he has it that the Holy Spirit should be from the Son.... Wherefore as the Father is not more God than the Son, though the Son has his being from the Father; likewise the Holy Spirit is not more from the Father than from the Son, though the Son has it from the Father that the Holy Spirit should be from him."[3] A. explains that "principaliter" used of created things signifies greater; but not in divine reality.

A. did not understand the eastern formula, *a Patre per Filium* which St. Thomas (qv) would be prepared to accept, which was given approval at the Council of Florence (qv). He would have heard of this from the Greek bishops whom he met at Bari, but he dismisses it: "Nor can it be understood how they can show that the Holy Spirit proceeds from the Father through the Son, as they say. Since the Father and the Son do not differ in the unity of the deity, and the Holy Spirit does not proceed from the Father save from the deity, if it is the same deity of the Son, it is impossible to understand how he proceeds from the deity of the Father through the deity of the Son and not from the deity of the Son, unless it is said that the Holy Spirit does not proceed from the deity of the Father, but from his fatherhood, nor through the deity of the Son, but through his sonship—but that idea suffocates itself in its own stupidity."[4]

A. speaks likewise when he comes to criticize the image of the source, the river and the lake, used by St. John of Damascus (qv) also inadequate in the eyes of St. Gregory of Nazianzus (qv): the source refers to the Father, the river to the Son, the lake to the Holy Spirit. The lake comes from the river, as the Spirit from the Son. To the obvious point that the lake comes really from the source through the river, A. replies that this is too material a view and things are different in the deity; one cannot speak of the Son other than of the Father, for he is in the Father and does not differ from him in essence. The source, the river and lake are three, but the water is one and this is the image of the deity.[5]

A. gives an interesting interpretation of Jn 20:22: "After the resurrection we read that the Lord 'breathed' on his disciples and said to them, 'Receive the Holy Spirit.' What does this breathing mean? We know that the breath which then came from his mouth was not the Holy Spirit. We do not for this reason believe that this breathing took place without some mysterious meaning. How can it be more properly and suitably understood than that he acted thus so that we should understand that the Holy Spirit proceeds from him? It was as if he said. As you perceive this breath by which, as imperceptible things can be signified by those that are perceptible, I signify to you that the Holy Spirit proceeds from the depths of my body and from my person; know thus that the Holy Spirit, whom I signify by this breath, proceeds from the secret (depths) of my deity and from my person. For we believe and confess one Person of the Word and of man, and in that two natures, namely divine and human.["6] A. goes on to dismiss subtle misinterpretations of the text he is commenting.

On Jn 15:26, "Whom I shall send to you from the Father," A. writes: "(This) cannot mean anything but: I and the Father shall send? The Son is the name of the one who said: 'the Father will send in my name.' 'The Father will send in my name' is therefore nothing other than: the Father will send in the name of the Son. What therefore is 'the Father will send in the name of the Son' but: the Father will send as if the Son were sending, so that in the sending by the Father is understood the sending by the Son. When he says "whom I shall send (to you) from the Father', how are we to understand it?"

A. argues subtly to conclude, "The Father is understood to send when the Son says 'I shall send from the Father.' What then is 'I shall send from the Father' but I shall send just as if the Father were sending, that there may be one and the same sending by me and the Father. When therefore the Son is so careful to show that there is one sending by the Father and himself, so that the Father does not send except when the Son sends, and the Son (sends) only when the Father does so, what can this mean or how can it be understood save that the Holy Spirit has no different relation to the Father than to the Son, is not more of one than of the other? Wherefore it is extremely difficult, indeed impossible, to show how he does not proceed from both (*ab utroque*),"[7] A. seeks to eliminate every possible misunderstanding. The Spirit is not more from the Father than from the Son; since we are talking about eternity there is no question of interval. He reassures the reader that every important truth in regard to the Holy Trinity—as he sees things—is intact. On certain

aspects of his thinking he is very Latin, proceeding—as his cherished master Augustine—from consideration of the essence, rather, than did the Greeks, from the Persons or hypostases. "He is interested," writes Fr. Congar, "in the divine essence and does not take the hypostases as his point of departure. The notion of 'person' seems to have perplexed him. He does not, therefore, make a very clear distinction between their principle *quo*, their nature and their principle *quod*, the person in the processions. However much we have to admire him, there is always a feeling that there is need to go beyond his thinking. He would himself have agreed with that sentiment."[8]

---

[1] Works: critical ed. F.S.Schmitt, II' Rome, 1940, *De Processione Spiritus Sancti*, 177-279; cf. B. Bouche, *La doctrine du 'Filioque' d'après S. Anselme de Cantorbéry, Son influence sur S. Albert le Grand et St Thomas d'Aquin* (dissertation), Rome, 1938; C. Vagaggini, *La hantise des 'rationes necessariae' de St. Anselme dans la théologie des processions trinitaires de St. Thomas. Spicilegium Beccense*, I (*Congrès international du IXe centenaire de l'arrivée d'Anselme au Bec*, Le Bec-Helloiun, Paris, 1959, 103-139; R. Perino, *La Dottrina trinitaria di S. Anselmo nel quadro del suo metodo teologico e del suo concetto di Dio* (Studia Anselmiana 29), Rome 1952; P. del Prete, *Il concilio di Bari nel 1098*, Bari, 1959; J. Hopkins, *A Companion to the Study of St. Anselm*, Minneapolis, 1972; R. Evans, *Anselm and Talking about God*, Oxford, 1978; J. Bainvel, *DTC* I, 2, 1327-1360; *DTC* XV, 1709-1711; Y.M-J. Congar, O.P., *The Holy Spirit*, III, 96-102; cp. St. Augustine, *Tract in Joh.*, 99, 8, *PL* 35, 1890 and *DeTrin.*, XV, 27, n. 48, *PL* 42, 1095; [2] *De Processione . . .* I, 185; [3] XIV, 212, 213; [4] VIII, 202; [5] IX, 203-205; [6] V, 194; [7] IV, 192; [8] *Op. cit*, 100, 101.

APHRAATES (FOURTH CENTURY)

Known as the "Sage of Persia" A. is the first ecclesiastical writer from his people.[1] He relied entirely, as far as scholars know, on the Bible as his theological source, which gives interest to his theology, in particular of the Holy Spirit. His faith in the Trinity was explicitly formulated. He did not in his Demonstrations express a systematic doctrine of the Spirit. He frequently wrote of various aspects of his activity, without entering into speculation on the inner Trinitarian life of the Persons. He did speak of Christ receiving the Spirit from the Father, of the Spirit sent by Christ, of the Spirit of the Father promised by Christ. The Spirit was given to the prophets, he was breathed into man, he rested upon Christ. In the order of salvation, A. sees manifold action by the Spirit. He is received in Baptism, grace is received from him, and he it is who moves the body to its resurrection. The Spirit protects man, he is to be loved, and with the Father and the Son, praised. One lengthy passage in the Demonstration on Persecution comments on Lk 12:11; "This was the Spirit who spoke through the mouth of Jacob to Esau, his persecutor; the Spirit of wisdom who spoke before Pharaoh through the mouth of Joseph, who had undergone trials, the Spirit who also spoke through the mouth of Moses (qv) in all the portents which he effected in the land of Egypt; the Spirit of knowledge which was given to Joshua, the son of Nun, when Moses imposed his hand on him, and the peoples who pursued him were absorbed and almost totally extinguished, from before his face; the Spirit who uttered psalms through the mouth of David, through whom he sang, as he stirred Saul, his persecutor, harassed by a worthless spirit; the Spirit who covered Elijah, through whom the latter restrained Jezebel, and Ahab, his persecutor; the Spirit who spoke through Elisha, and prophesied, announcing to the king, his persecutor, things to happen in the future; the Spirit who was vigorous through the mouth of Micaiah, when he confuted Ahab, his oppressor and said to him, 'If you return in peace, the Lord has not spoken by me' (1 Kings 22:28); the Spirit who strengthened Jeremiah to take a bold stand, that he should, through him, take hold of Zedekiah; the Spirit who guarded Daniel and his brethren in the land of Babylon; the Spirit who saved Mordechai and Esther in the place of their captivity."[2]

---

[1]Works, ed. J. Parisot, ed. R. Graffin, I, 1904, II, 1907, Patrologia Syriaca; cf. J. Parisot, DTC I, 1457-1463; J. Ortiz de Urbina, S. J., *Patrologia Syriaca*, Rome, 1958, 46; [2]Demonstration XXI, ed. J. Parisot, 983, 986; cf. esp. *Aphraate le Sage Persan,* tr. M.J. Pierre with Intro., bibl. notes, SC 349 (1988).

APOSTOLATE, THE

The succinct definition of Vatican II is memorable: "For this was the Church founded: that by spreading the kingdom of Christ everywhere for the glory of God the Father she might bring all men to share in Christ's saving Redemption; and that through them the whole world might be brought into relationship with him. All activity of the Mystical Body directed to the attainment of this goal is called the apostolate, and the Church carries it on in various ways through all her members." (*Decree on the Apostolate of the Laity*, 2). The theme of the apostolate runs through several Council documents. Thus in the *Constitution on the Church* we read: "The apostolate of the laity is a sharing in the salvific mission of the Church. Through Baptism and Confirmation all are ap-

pointed to this apostolate by the Lord himself. Moreover, by the sacraments and especially by the Eucharist (qv) that love of God and man which is the soul of the apostolate is communicated and nourished" (art. 33). "The various forms of the apostolate should be encouraged. Close collaboration and the coordination of all the apostolic works under the direction of the bishop should be promoted in the diocese as a whole or in parts of it." This is the directive given to bishops. (*Decree on the Pastoral Office of Bishops in the Church*, 17). Priests are reminded that "The other sacraments, and indeed all ecclesiastical ministries and works of the apostolate are bound up with the Eucharist and are directed towards it." (*Decree on the Ministry and Life of Priests*, art. 5). Future priests "should also be carefully taught how to inspire and encourage apostolic action among the laity, and to promote various and more effective forms of apostolate . . ." (*Decree on Training of Priests*, art. 20). In the *Decree on the Means of Social Communication* we read: "All the members of the Church should make a concerted effort to ensure that the means of communication are put at the service of the multiple forms of the apostolate without delay and as energetically as possible, where and when they are needed. They should forestall projects likely to prove harmful, especially in those regions where moral and religious progress would require their intervention more urgently" (art. 13).

The passage on the apostolate or apostolic activity in the *Decree on the Up-to-date Renewal of Religious Life* had its genesis in the confrontation, if conflict is not too strong a word, within the preparatory commission, then within the conciliar commission, between two different views. One was held by the monastic members, the other by the active religious. Earlier draft decrees, schemata drawn up, reflected the monastic outlook and were found inadequate by the active religious, almost irrelevant to what had become an acute problem for them: how to reconcile the claims of religious observance with the urgent demands of apostolic activity, how to engage thoroughly in works of the apostolate and cultivate the spiritual life needed in a religious.

An important literature had so stressed the need for the interior life as to obscure the very nature of the apostolate. Phrases like "the heresy of good works" and "the dangers of the ministry" could easily convey the idea that only the perfect, those advanced in the interior life, could safely undertake work for souls, which is the essence of the apostolate. It was not unlike the heresy that only the perfect could communicate daily, which was to forget that only by communicating could one become perfect. If the apostolate is intrinsic to the Christian vocation, if it is the end or purpose of Christian life in its fullness, then it must be a participation in the very mission and lifework of Jesus Christ. It must be understood at the level of the deepest spirituality and must have its warrant in the very mystery of the redemptive Incarnation of Christ. An attempt was made to express the effects of this truth for apostolic religious in the Decree: "In these institutes, apostolic and charitable activity is of the very nature of religious life, as their own holy ministry and work of charity, entrusted to them by the Church and to be performed in its name. For this reason, the entire religious life of its members should be imbued with an apostolic spirit, and all their apostolic activity with a religious spirit" (art. 8). This was an attempt to end the dichotomy, to eliminate the sense of spiritual schizophrenia which haunted sincere, generous souls. A similar problem in the life of many priests was thus solved by the Council: "Priests will acquire holiness in their own distinctive way by exercising their functions sincerely and tirelessly in the spirit of Christ" (art. 13).

When the universal call to the apostolate is mentioned there may be confusion. Pius XII once said that not all Catholics are called to the organised apostolate. He could not say they were not called to the apostolate without repudiating the central theses of his great Encyclical, *Mystici Corporis Christi*. A Christian as a member of the Body is responsible for his fellow members, however in the circumstances of his life and personality he may discharge that responsibility.

In the choice of means, in the scope of activity, in the solution of the problems which are bound to arise, the apostle will be dependent on the Spirit of Christ whose essential mission he is seeking to further. He may benefit by the extraordinary graces which the Spirit distributes for the good of the Body (see art. Charisms).

Vatican II in its teaching on the Blessed Virgin reveals a profound dimension of the apostolate: "The Church, therefore, in her apostolic work too, rightly looks to her who gave birth to Christ, who was thus conceived of the Holy Spirit and born of a Virgin, in order that through the Church he could be born and increase in the hearts of the faithful. In her life the Virgin has been a model of

that motherly love with which all who join in the Church's apostolic mission for the regeneration of mankind should be animated" (Constitution on the Church, art. 65).

Akin to this thinking is the passage in Paul VI's (qv) Apostolic Exhortation, *Evangelii Nuntiandi*, on the Spirit, without whom evangelization will never be possible. "It is in the 'consolation of the Holy Spirit' that the Church increases. The Holy Spirit is the soul of the Church. It is he who explains to the faithful the deep meaning of the teaching of Jesus and of his mystery. It is the Holy Spirit who, today just as at the beginning of the Church, acts in every evangeliser who allows himself to be possessed and led by him. The Holy Spirit places on his lips the words which he could not find by himself, and at the same time the Holy Spirit predisposes the soul of the hearer to be open and receptive to the Good News and to the Kingdom being proclaimed" (art. 75).

The Pope had recalled the Spirit's role in the external manifestation of Christ's mission, in his mandate to the Apostles (Jn 20:22), as it is described in the Acts of the Apostles (qv). Paul VI echoing the Synod of 1974, has a firm recommendation on the subject to pastors and theologians, and the faithful—"they are to study more thoroughly the nature and manner of the Holy Spirit's action in evangelization today" (*ibid*).

Pope John Paul II (qv) has much to say about the Spirit in his Apostolic Exhortation, *Christifideles Laici*. His teaching here has relevance to the apostolate: "One and the same Spirit is always the dynamic principle of diversity and unity in the Church ... Church communion then is a gift, a great gift of the Holy Spirit to be gratefully accepted by the lay faithful, and at the same time to be lived with a deep sense of responsibility. This is concretely realized through their participation in the life and mission of the Church, to whose service the lay faithful put their varied and complementary ministries and charisms." The Pope then quotes from his own homily which he gave at the concelebrated Mass for the close of the episcopal synod in October 1987. These words have their interest: "The Spirit of the Lord gives a vast variety of charisms, inviting people to assume different ministries and forms of service and reminding them, as he reminds all people in their relationship in the Church, that what distinguishes persons is *not an increase in dignity, but a special and complementary capacity for service . . . .* Thus, the charisms, the ministries, the different forms of service exercised by the lay faithful exist in communion and on behalf of communion. They are treasures that complement one another for the good of all and are under the wise guidance of their Pastors."[1]

As an example of a profound spirituality of the apostolate and how it is related to the Holy Spirit one may quote the convert Jew, Francis Libermann (qv). On the meaning of the apostolate he writes: "The apostolic life is really the life of love and holiness which the Son of God led on earth, through which he sacrificed himself continually to the glory of his Father for the salvation of the world."[2]

On the Holy Spirit, which in the patronage of his society was linked with the Immaculate Heart of Mary, Libermann wrote thus: "To introduce its members to deep and genuinely holy, devotion and to afford a source and powerful means of sanctification, in the fulfilment of the duties of private, common and apostolic life, the Congregation consecrates them specially to the Holy Spirit, author and perfector of all holiness and inspirer of the apostolic spirit, and to the Immaculate Heart of Mary, filled beyond measure by the divine Spirit with the fullness of holiness and the apostolate, sharing most perfectly in the life and sacrifice of Jesus Christ, her Son, for the redemption of the world. This dual devotion is special and distinctive to the Congregation. (The members) will find in the Holy Spirit, who lives in their souls, a source of interior life and an all-powerful principle of that perfect charity, which is the soul of zeal and of all other apostolic virtues. They will consider the Immaculate Heart of Mary a perfect model of faithfulness to all the holy inspirations of the divine Spirit, and of the practice of the interior virtues of the religious and apostolic life. In this Heart they will find a refuge to which they will have recourse in their labours and their sorrows, to it they will open their hearts with childlike trust in their moments of weakness and temptation."[3]

In the sphere of the lay apostolate the present century has seen a very remarkable example of enlightened devotion to the Holy Spirit. The Legion of Mary was founded on 7 September 1921, by a layman, Frank Duff, deeply influenced, despite initial distrust, by the classic of Marian spirituality, *Treatise on True Devotion to the Blessed Virgin Mary* by St. (still at the time Blessed) Louis Marie Grignion de Montfort (qv); Frank Duff knew very soon that, as regards a basic idea in the work, Mary's universal mediation

of grace, he was also in a powerful contemporary current of Marian theology associated with Cardinal Mercier. The association spread throughout the Church rapidly, taking root in over 2,000 dioceses, growing massively in Third World countries, Zaire for example, the Philippines and especially Korea, where its progress is directly linked with the sensational numerical expansion of Catholic life and membership—the number of Catholics has doubled to two million in five years!

The Handbook of the Legion, which has been translated into scores of languages including those most widely spoken like Spanish, Russian and Chinese, sets very high standards for its members and from the very early days aimed to instill in them a profound theology—the founder wished to build on bedrock. The doctrine of the Mystical Body, then beginning to emerge from a phase of partial oblivion, was set forth with clarity. But especially the role of the Holy Spirit was given a prominence which was unique in Catholic literature of the time.

The Holy Spirit dominates the iconography of the Legion. When the Roman vexillum was adapted for use at Legion prayer meetings, the eagle was replaced by the dove, symbol of the Spirit; a similar pattern was used elsewhere. Much more surprising was the formula enjoined on the member entering the Legion, when his/her probation was complete. Many would have expected the formal engagement, the legionary "promise," as it is called, to name the Queen of the Legion, or, after the example of St. Louis Marie Grignion de Montfort, Incarnate Wisdom as the object of dedication. The Holy Spirit was chosen; the background is related in the article on Frank Duff.[4]

[1] *Christifideles Laici*, ed. Veritas, Dublin, art. 20, pp. 52, 54; quotation from the synodal homily, *AAS* 80 (1988) 600; for bibl., *The Lay Apostolate* in Papal Teachings, ed. Solesmes, tr., St. Paul, Boston; L.J. Cardinal Suenens, *La Théologie de l'Apostolat*, Bruges, 1952, new ed., Brussels, 1988; id., *A New Pentecost*, London, 1975; *Handbook of the Legion of Mary*, Dublin, 1964 and later ed.; F. Duff, *The Spirit of the Legion of Mary*, Dublin, 1948; id., *Mary Shall Reign*, Dublin, 1961; id., *Walk with Mary*, Dublin, 1967, esp., The Cenacle, 84-92; id., *The Woman in Genesis*, Dublin, 1976, esp., *The Woman clothed with the Sun*, 176-184; Mary and the Holy Spirit, 274-287; id., *Victory through Mary*, Dublin, 1982, esp. The Mystical Union of Mary with the Holy Spirit, 264-278; F. Cuttaz, *DSp*, I, 773-790; [2] *Règle provisoire de la Société du Saint Coeur de Marie*, Amiens, 1841; [3] *Notes et Documents relatifs à la vie et à l'oeuvre du Ven. Francois Marie Paul Libermann*, Paris, PP du St. Esprit, X, 567; [4] *Handbook of the Legion of Mary*, 1964, 52.

ARIANISM

It is generally taken as an offshoot of Arianism that the divinity of the Holy Spirit was rejected.[1] From the extant writings of Arius himself, the following can be found to refer to the third Person of the Trinity. St. Athanasius (qv) quotes him in *Oratio I contra Arianos*: "For the Son, too, he says, not only knows not the Father exactly, for he fails in comprehension, but he knows not even his own essence;—and that 'the essences (subsisting realities) (*ousiai*) of the Father and the Son and the Holy Spirit, are separate in nature, and estranged and disconnected and alien, and without participation of each other,' and in his own words 'utterly unlike from each other in essence and glory, unto infinity.' Thus as to 'likeness of glory and essence' he says that the Word is entirely diverse from both the Father and the Holy Spirit."[2]

The second passage is from the profession of faith written by Arius on his own behalf and on behalf of Euzoius to the Emperor Constantine. Therein we read: "We believe in one only God, the Father almighty; and in the Lord Jesus Christ, his only-begotten Son, who has been begotten of him before all ages. God the Word, by whom all has been made, both what is in the heavens and what is on earth; who came down and took flesh, suffered and was raised, went up to heaven and will come to judge the living and the dead. And in the Holy Spirit, and in the resurrection of the flesh, and in the life of the world to come, and in one only Catholic Church of God, which stretches from one end of the world to the other. We have received this faith from the holy Gospels from where the Lord said to his disciples: 'Go, teach all nations, baptizing them in the name of the Father and the Son and the Holy Spirit.' If we do not believe that and if we do not truly receive the Father and the Son and the Holy Spirit, as the whole Catholic Church and the Scriptures, according to which we believe everything, teach us, let God be our judge now and hereafter."[3]

As the historian Sozomen pointed out, this document was an exercise in diplomacy by a man who did not wish to miss a big prize, return to the fold backed by the powerful Emperor.[4] It skilfully avoided the doctrinal innovations of the heresiarch. He kept rigidly to the Gospels as his warrant. There is not a suggestion of the theological turmoil of the previous decades, of the conflict over the *homoousion* and the decision of Nicaea.[5]

In general, Arianism, to which many other factors besides the personality of Arius contributed, affected development of the doctrine about the Holy Spirit considerably. Denial of the divinity of Christ, the core of the heresy, rigorously implied denial of the divinity of the Holy Spirit. Exclusion of the Son from the inner being, eternal and unchangeable, of the godhead automatically sealed the Father from any other equal communion of person. For all that we know about the Spirit came from the Son incarnate and all that the Spirit would be and accomplish among us was related to divine power fully possessed by the Son.

As Newman (qv) held, the age in which Arianism flourished gave scope to controversy." Arianism was but the continuation of a series; and, if it was more formidable and eventful than Paulianism or Montanism, this was because it had so large a field to act upon, and so few external hindrances to impede its course.... It was natural then that the first age of the emancipated Church, even more than the age that followed, should be a time of eager, perilous, and widespread controversy; nor need such a phenomenon really perplex us, as if the brave martyrs and confessors of the Diocletian era had the evil destiny of giving birth to a generation of misbelievers; for the Arianism of the fourth century was not a popular heresy. The laity, as a whole, revolted from it in every part of Christendom. It was an epidemic of the schools and of theologians, and to them it was mainly confined.... The classes which had furnished martyrs in the persecutions were in no sense the seat of the heresy."[6]

Radical questioning of revealed truth thus became a luxury, an intellectual hobby almost, of the cognoscenti. Questioning entered the theology of the Holy Spirit, after the Church had closed the debate about the Son—which did not lead to immediate general agreement. Moreover, the Council of Nicaea in its creed had been terse on the subject of the Spirit: "And we believe in the Holy Spirit." There was no need to apply the *homoousion* to him, as agitation had not arisen. It soon would and another Council, Constantinople I, (qv) would eventually deal with it.

[1]Cf. J. Wolinski, *La pneumatologie des Pères grecs avant le Concile de Constantinople I*, in *Atti del Congresso*, I, 142ff; R.P.C. Hanson, *The Holy Spirit in Creeds and Confessions of Faith in the early Church*, ibid., 294-301; *Trinitas, Arianism*, 17-23, bibl.; *Arius*, ibid., 23-28, bibl.; E. Boularand, *L'Hérésie d'Arius et la foi de Nicée*, Paris, 1972; [2]*LNF*, IV, 309, 6; [3]E. Boularand, *op. cit.*, 62, 63; [4]*Hist. Eccl.* II, 27, *PG* 27, 1009D; [5]For the documentation cf. *Trinitas* j. cit., esp., 25, 27; [6]*Newman's Tracts, Theological and Ecclesiastical*, 2nd ed., 1881, *Causes of the Rise and Success of Arianism*, 143f.

ART[1]

There are two products of Christian art in which we should look for an effect of the Spirit's action, Oriental Icons and the Gothic cathedrals of the West. The religious inspiration is practically explicit in each; of course we should add many individual artists like Fra Angelico, whose search for divine guidance and strength in their artistic work was incessant. If we take the Icons and the Cathedrals it is therefore not in an exclusive sense, but by way of illustration generally acceptable.

How does the Spirit enter into the life and work (qv) of an artist? In a secularized world the question may appear pointless. Even in the history of religious art, outside Christian societies, Islamic to take one instance, what relevance can the Spirit's action have?

There are no simple answers to these questions. Art as the creation of things beautiful, brings together certain elements which may be related directly or indirectly to the Spirit of God: the materials needed, the design which will be realized, the imagination and skill which will fashion the materials to embody the design. Over all there is a conception of beauty in itself as an idea and in its embodiment in whatever medium the artist chooses.

Work, expenditure of psychic, nervous and physical energy is part of artistic production; Michelangelo is possibly the unsurpassed performer in this respect. Has anyone ever poured out such energy in creative action? Whether he, and others like but not equal to him, came directly under the influence of the Spirit depended on the degree of interior fidelity to the impulse of grace. This in turn demanded a spiritual outlook wherein the whole of life was deliberately regulated by faith in the Spirit and a will to seek and follow his guidance and help. Anyone can seek to inform his lifework by such an outlook, a carpenter, a road engineer, a chef, a bricklayer, a welder, a chimney sweep. One of the greatest existential exponents of the Spirit's action in this century was a dressmaker, Francisca Javiera del Valle.[2] All these and those in thousands of other occupations, have their work in common with the artist. The bricklayer and the dressmaker may succeed in consecrating their manual work, which may be barely a craft with little demand on imagination or skill, to a degree unequalled by any artist. Two village carpenters did so.

We leave the work aspect to consider the content of the output. Here too some distinctions must be borne in mind. A purely religious subject may be treated by an artist, painter, musician, sculptor, from a purely human motive—just as, in a different world, a brilliant sermon may be delivered by one who barely believes what he is saying and has no idea of practising it. Artists are prone to egoism, which leaves no room for the Spirit. Those who hire artists are prone to the profit-motive, which leaves little room for him, with less hope of conversion. The story of religious shrines all over the world is a record of effort, at times almost futile, to keep commercialism at bay.

Do supreme artistry and purest religious idealism never meet? They surely did in St. John of the Cross who was a poet's poet and a saint's saint; they almost certainly did in Dante, as they did in Fra Angelico. And with some confidence we turn to the Icons and the Cathedrals. Icons are works of art, but of a very special kind. Personal style, so marked a feature of art, is here at a minimum. The genre and mode of representation are fixed. But to carry out the execution a kind of religious apprenticeship is necessary. The objective is a sacramental, a stimulus not only to piety but to theological reflection: S. Bulgakov's work (qv) *The Burning Bush*, had as its starting point the Icon of Our Lady of Novgorod. What is here related to the Spirit is the element of prayerfulness stirred by such products, the sense of a supernatural presence. The rigid artistic limitations imposed on the maker of an icon do not impede the action of the Spirit, for the end in view determines the spiritual character of the work.

There has been, doubtless, exaggeration about the mystic inspiration at the origin of the medieval cathedrals. When such excess is removed we have still works of astonishing artistic beauty and power the origin of which is riveted to the divine. Do they and all other works of Christian art participate in the divine? Fine art aims at the creation of beautiful things, and God is supreme beauty, the source of all beauty. All that has excellence derives from him, excelling only through participation as he does through his essence.

The problem of the Christian artist is to give personal meaning to this relationship between creature and Creator, to bring it to life in his work. Thus will be answered the challenge implicit in the very words Christian art. Thus also the long awaited opening of Christian thought, especially theology, towards beauty, would begin. It is clear that only through a profound assimilation of the human person to the Holy Spirit, *Spiritus Creator*, can this be accomplished. He it is who makes divine beauty live in human workmanship, for he controls all that descends from the divine to the human, directs it, makes it fruitful in proportion not only to the human potential involved, but beyond it through his creative bounty.

The Old Testament contains a revealing passage on the role of the Spirit in artistic production. Thus Moses (qv) who was himself a "prophet" (Deut 18:15), singularly favoured by the Spirit, was instructed on the making of the Ark of the Covenant: "The Lord said to Moses, 'See, I have called by name Bezalel the son of Uri, son of Hur, of the tribe of Judah; and I have filled him with the Spirit of God, with ability and intelligence, with knowledge and all craftsmanship, to devise artistic designs, to work in gold, silver, and bronze, in cutting stones for setting, and in carving wood, for work in every craft!" (Ex 31:1-5). Reporting this to the people Moses added, "And he has inspired him to teach, both him and Oholiab the son of Ahisamach of the tribe of Dan" (*Ibid.*, 35:34).

_____

[1]Cf. A.G. Sertillange, O.P., *L'Art et la Morale*, Paris, 1899; P. Gardner, *The Principles of Christian Art*, London, 1928; L. Brehier, *L'Art Chrétien*, Paris, 1928; M.S. Gillet, *Le Crédo des artistes*, E.I. Watkin, *Catholic Art and Culture*, revised ed., 1947; B. Champigneulle, *Problèmes de l'art sacré*, Paris, 1951; C. Costantini, *L'istruzione del S. Uffizio sull'arte sacra*, Vatican City, 1952; J. Monchanin, *De l'esthétique à la mystique*, Tournai, 1955; H. Read, *Icon and Idea*, Cambridge, Mass., 1955; J. Maritain, *Art and Scholasticism and the Frontiers of Poetry*, tr. W.J. Evans, New York, 1962; G. Van der Leeuw, *Sacred and Profane Beauty, The Holy in Art*, tr. D.E. Green, New York, 1963; esp. A. McNicholl, O.P., *NCE*, I, 859-861; *Catholicisme*, I, 869-878; P.M. Leonard, in *DSp* I, 899-904; L. Gillet, *Histoire artistique des ordres mendicants*, Laurens, 1912; Louis Hourticq, *La vie des images*, Paris, 1927; P. Gaultier, *Le sens de l'art*, 1925; M. Brillant, *L'art chrétien en France*, L. Ouspensky and Vladimir Lossky, *Der Sinn des Ikonen*, Basel, 1952; article Moses in the present work; [2]Cf. *About the Holy Spirit* by this author, Houston, Dublin, 1981.

ATHANASIAN CREED

In the first part of the Creed, which deals with the Trinity the divinity of the Holy Spirit is asserted, and his equality with the Father and the Son, as is the *Filioque*. (qv) Full text and bibl. in *Trinitas*, s.v.[1]

_____

[1]*Op. cit.*, 29-31.

ATHANASIUS, ST. (295-373)

The renowned defender of the doctrine of the Incarnation A. without elaborating a dogmatic theory, either in the manner of the Cappadocians or the much later Scholastics, laid down a firm doctrine of the Trinity: "There is then a Triad, holy and complete, confessed to be God in Father, Son and Holy Spirit, having nothing foreign or external mixed with it, not composed of one that creates and one that is originated, but all creative; and it is consistent and in nature indivisible, and its activity is one. The Father does all things through the Word in the Holy Spirit. Thus the unity of the holy Triad is preserved. Thus one God is preached in the Church, 'who is over all' (Eph 4:6), and through all, and in all'—'over all' as Father, as beginning, as fountain; 'through all,' through the Word; 'in all,' in the Holy Spirit. It is a Triad not only in name and form of speech, but in truth and actuality. For as the Father is he that is, so also his Word is one that is and God over all. And the Holy Spirit is not without actual existence, but exists and has true being. Less than these (Persons) the Catholic Church does not hold, lest she sink to the level of the modern Jews, imitators of Caiaphas, and to the level of Sabellius, Nor does she add to them by speculation, lest she be carried into the polytheism of the heathen."[1]

The passage is from the *Letters to Serapion*, his friend and disciple. For Serapion's benefit he was refuting the heresy of the *Tropici*, an Egyptian group who denied the divinity of the Holy Spirit. Preoccupied with the Arian question in all its ramifications and side-effects, he had dealt with the Trinity but briefly in the *Discourses against the Arians*.[2] He now addressed himself to the problem raised by the *Tropici*. He used two approaches to show their illogicality: the parallel between the Father Son Dyad and the Son Spirit Dyad: if one implied equality so did the other; and the unity of the divinity and unity of the Triad: if there were three and one was not divine there was no Triad, or trinity. That was a polemical approach. His essential argument, which like the two points mentioned, was supported by much appeal to Scripture, was in line with the Alexandrine doctrine of divinization or participation in the divine.

On the parallels *and the imperative of the Triad* he writes: "But it is right that, in some way, (as they themselves say!) we should make a careful reply to those who have been deceived about the Spirit. We might well wonder at their folly, inasmuch as they will not have the Son of God to be a creature—indeed their views on this are quite sound! How then have they endured so much as to hear the Spirit of the Son called a creature? Because of the oneness of the Word with the Father, they will not have the Son belong to things originated but rightly regard him as Creator of things that are made. Why then do they say that the Holy Spirit is a creature, who has the same oneness with the Son as the Son has with the Father? Why have they not understood that, just as by not dividing the Son from the Father they ensure that God is one, so by dividing the Spirit from the Word they no longer ensure that the Godhead in the Triad is one, for they tear it asunder, and mix with it a nature foreign to it and of a different kind, and put it on a level with the creatures? On this showing, once again the Triad is no longer one but is compounded of two differing natures; for the Spirit, as they have imagined, is essentially different. What doctrine of God is this, which compounds him out of creator and creature? Either he is not a Triad, but a dyad, with the creature left over. Or, if he be Triad—as indeed he is!—then how do they class the Spirit who belongs to the Triad with the creatures which come after the Triad? For this, once more, is to divide and dissolve the Triad. Therefore, whilst thinking falsely of the Holy Spirit they do not think truly even of the Son. For if they thought correctly of the Word, they would think soundly of the Spirit also, who proceeds from the Father, and belonging to the Son, is from him given to the disciples and all who believe in him."[3]

In the First Discourse against the Arians A. emphasizes the importance of the Triad: "For if the Word is not with the Father from everlasting, the Triad is not everlasting; but a Monad was first, and afterwards by addition it became a Triad; and so as time went on, it seems what we know concerning God grew and took shape. And further, if the Son is not proper offspring of the Father's essence, but of nothing has come to be, then of nothing the Triad consists and once there was not a Triad but a Monad and a Triad once with deficiency, and then complete; deficient, before the Son was originated, complete when he had come to be; and henceforth a thing originated is reckoned with the Creator, and what once was not has divine worship and glory with him who was ever. Nay, what is more serious still, the Triad is discovered to be unlike itself, consisting of strange and alien natures and essences. And this, in other words, is saying that the Triad has an originated consistence. What sort of religion then is this, which is not even like itself, but is in process

of completion as time goes on, and is now not thus, and then again thus? For probably it will receive some fresh accession, and so on without limit, since at first and at starting it took its consistence by way of accessions. And so undoubtedly it may decrease on the contrary, for what is added plainly admits of being subtracted. But this is not so: perish the thought; the Triad is not originated; but there is an eternal and one Godhead in a Triad, and there is one glory of the Holy Triad. And you presume to divide it into different natures; the Father being eternal, yet you say of the Word which is sealed by him, 'Once he was not,' and whereas the Son is seated by the Father, yet you think to place him far from him. . . . For if the doctrine of God is now perfect in a Triad, and this is the true and only religion, and this is the good and the truth, it must have been always so, unless the good and the truth be something that came after, and the doctrine of God is completed by additions."[4]

A. sets forth his essential argument thus: "He, therefore, who is not sanctified by another, nor a partaker of sanctification, who is himself partaken, and in whom all creatures are sanctified, how can he be one from among all things or pertain to those who partake of him? If by participation in the Spirit, we are made 'sharers in the divine nature' (2 Pet 1:4) we should be mad to say that the Spirit has a created nature and not the nature of God. For it is on this account that those, in whom he is, are made divine. If he makes men divine, it is not to be doubted that his nature is of God."[5]

St. Basil (qv) would not use the word *homoousios* about the Spirit and in this he was followed by the Council of Constantinople (qv). A. thought otherwise: "If the Holy Spirit is one, and the creatures many and angels many—what likeness can there be between the Spirit and things originate? It is obvious that the Spirit does not belong to the many, nor is he an angel. But because he is one, and still more, because he is proper to the Word who is one, he is proper to God who is one, and consubstantial with him (*homoousios*). These sayings (of Scripture) concerning the Holy Spirit by themselves alone show that in nature and essence he has nothing in common with or proper to creatures, but is distinct from things originate, proper to and not alien from the Godhead and essence of the Son; in virtue of which essence and nature he is of the Holy Triad."[6]

Quoting Ps 104:29-30 which ends "You send

forth your Spirit and they are created, and you renew the face of the earth," A. writes: "Scripture expressing itself thus, it is clear that the Spirit is not a creature, but that he has a part in the act of creation: for the Father creates all things through the Word in the Spirit, and things created by the mediation of the Word, hold from the Spirit through the Word the strength to be."[7] A. quotes Ps 33:6 in justification. He goes on to list a string of quotations showing the Word to be inseparable in action from the Spirit—his exegesis might not necessarily command agreement from all.[8] He then strengthens his case by invoking St. Paul's well-known Trinitarian formula in 2 Cor 13:13, and the word of the angel to Mary in Lk 1:35.

A. appeals likewise to the indwelling of the Spirit: "Thus also the Spirit dwelling in us, the Father and the Son will come and take up their abode in us (Jn 14:23); for the Trinity is undivided and its divinity is one, and there is only one God (who is) above all (and acts) in all, and (is) in all. That is the faith of the Catholic Church, (qv) for it is in the Trinity that the Lord founded and rooted it, saying to his disciples: 'Go, teach all nations, baptizing them in the name of the Father and of the Son and of the Holy Spirit' (Mt 28:19). If the Spirit were a creature he would not have ranked him with the Father, for fear the Trinity would not be consistent, if some alien and different being is ranked with it."[9]

Sergius Bulgakov thought that A. was dyadic, not triadic in his theology of the Trinity: A. speaks in one passage, possibly two, of the Spirit possessing the same proper condition towards the Father as does the Son. The passages already quoted contradict such a view. More important is the great Alexandrian's answer to the question: Does the Spirit proceed from the Son? He does say that the Holy Spirit proceeds from the Father.[10] He does not say explicitly that the Spirit proceeds from the Son. But certain passages leave the interpretation a possible one: the Spirit proceeds from the Son, or from the Father through the Son: "For the Son does not merely partake the Spirit, that therefore he too may be in the Father; nor does he receive the Spirit, but rather he supplies it himself to all; and the Spirit does not unite the Word to the Father, but rather the Spirit receives from the Word. He, as has been said, gives to the Spirit, and whatever the Spirit has, he has from the Word."[11] "His Gift (the Spirit) who is said to proceed from the Father because through the Son who is confessed from (as coming from) the Father, he is resplendent, and is sent and is

given."[12] "For the Father creates all things by the Word in the Spirit, since where the Word is, there too is the Spirit"—already quoted. H.B. Swete (qv) thought it impossible to understand the splendour of the Spirit through the Son as anything less than essential dependence. This idea A. shared with the Greek Fathers of the fourth and fifth centuries, an idea often hinted or implicit, not expressed in the terms which the *Filioque* controversy of later times would prompt.

---

[1]English tr. Letters to Serapion, *Letters Concerning the Holy Spirit*, C.R.B. Shapland, London, 1951; French tr. J. Lebon, *SC* 15, 1947; bibl. *Theotokos*, 37-38; cf. H.B. Swete, *The Holy Spirit in the Ancient Church*, London, 1916; T. Schermann, *Die Gottheit des Heiligen Geistes nach den griechischen Vätern des IV Jahrhunderts*, Freilburg i. Br., 1901, 47-89; C.R.B. Shapland in *op. cit.*, 34-43; P. Galtier, *Le Saint Esprit en nous d'après les Pères grecs*, Rome, 1946, 117-134; J. Wolinski in *Atti del Congresso*, I, 145-152; J. Quasten III, 20-79; P. Smulders, *DSp*, IV, 1, 1262, 63; *Handbuch der Dogmengeschichte*, 138-147; *BT* I, 154-159; [2]*Ep. ad Serap.*, I, 15, Shapland, 134-6; [3]*Ep. ad Serap.*, I, 2, Shapland, 65, *Message of the Fathers*, 99-100; [4]*Or. Arian.*, I, 6, 17-18, *LNPF*, IV, 316, 17; [5]*Ep. ad Serap.*, I, 23, 24, Shapland, 123-26; [6]*Op. cit.*, I, 26, *Message of the Fathers*, 108; [7]*Op. cit.*, III, 5, Lebon, 169; [8]*Ibid.*; [9]*Ep. ad Serap.*, III, 6, Lebon, 171, 72; [10]*Ep. ad Serap.*, I, 20; cf. infra; [11]*Or. Arian*, III, 24, *LNPF*, 406, 7; [12]*Ep. ad Serap.*, I, 20. A. Laminski, *Der Heiligen Geist als Geist Christi und Geist der Glaubigen. Der Beitrag des Athanasios von Alexandrien zu Formulierung des Trinitärischen Dogmas in vierten Jahrhundert*, Leipzig, 1969.

ATHENAGORAS (2nd Century)[1]

An Apologist, who wrote his *Plea* (or *Embassy*) *for Christians* to be presented to Marcus Aurelius and his son Commodus, on the occasion of their visit to Athens in 176. Therein he defended Christians against charges of atheism, Thyestian banquets and incest. He was the first Christian philosopher to defend the doctrine of the Trinity. The essential passage is: "I have given sufficient proofs that we are not atheists, but hold God to be one, unbegotten, eternal, invisible, suffering nothing, comprehended by none, circumscribed by none, apprehended by mind and reasoning alone, girt about with light and beauty and spirit and power indescribable, creator of all things by his Word, their embellisher and master. We do indeed think that God has a Son—please do not laugh at the idea of God having a Son. This is not a case of the myths of the poets who make the gods out to be no better than men; we have no such ideas about God the Father or the Son. The Son of God is Word of the Father in thought and power. All things were made through him and after his fashion. The Father and the Son are one, the Son being in the Father and the Son in the Father by the powerful union of the Spirit—the Son of God is mind and Word of the Father. Now, if in your exceeding great sagacity, you wish to investigate what is meant by the Son, I will tell you in brief. He is the first-begotten of the Father. He did not indeed come to be, for God was from the beginning, being eternal mind, and had his Word within himself, being from eternity possessed of a Word; but he proceeded to become thought and over the elements of undifferentiated nature when all the material elements were like a substrate in quiescence and the heavier elements lay mixed with the lighter. The Spirit of prophecy agrees with this account saying, 'The Lord made me in the beginning of his works' (Prov 8:22). Then again this same Holy Spirit who works in those who utter prophecy, we call an outflow from God flowing out and returning like a ray of the sun. Who then would not be amazed hearing those called atheists who call God Father and Son and Holy Spirit, proclaiming their power in unity and in rank their diversity."[2]

A. could not give a developed theology such as later ages would provide, for development takes time and the working of many factors. He could not think in concepts or mental categories which had not yet been used in theology, nature, personality, circumincession (*perichoresis*), nor see the problem arising out of the unity of God which he proclaimed, and the Son and Spirit co-existing with the Father. Apart from the dangerous word "rank" he has been accused of subordinationism in his general theory.[3] His formulation of the Trinitarian belief as he held it and his explicit idea of the Spirit are singular in his age. He was a vital thinking link between the Gospels and theologians.

[1]Works *PG* 6, 887-1024; English tr., *ANCL* 2, 1867; *Oxford Early Christian Texts,* W.R.Schoedel, 1972; *ACW*, 23, J.H. Crehan, S.J., 1956; R.M. Grant, *Athenagoras or Pseudo-Athenagoras, HTR* 47 (1954), 121-29; L.W. Barnard, *Athenagoras, A Study in Second-Century Christian Apologetic, Théologie historique,* 18, Paris, 1972; J. Quasten, I, 229-236; *Message of the Fathers,* 28, 29; *Trinitas,* 41; *Handbuch der Dogmengeschichte,* 47-52; [2]*PG* 6, 908, 9; [3]Cf. G. Aeby, *Les missions divines de Justin à Origène,* Fribourg, (Switzerland), 1958, 23.

AUGUSTINE, ST., DOCTOR OF THE CHURCH (354-430)

A first text from the mighty Doctor of the West, whose thinking would dominate Latin theology for eight hundred years and influence it down to our time—witness Vatican II—almost gives the impression that even in his time the Spirit was the unknown God. He noted that much had been written on the Father and the Son, on the different problems that arise in the theology of the first two Persons of the Trinity. He finds a dearth of such literature on the Holy Spirit. "The Holy Spirit, on the other hand, has not yet been studied with as much care and by so many great and learned commentators on the Scriptures that it is easy to understand his special character and know why we cannot call him either Son or Father, but only Holy Spirit, save that they preach that he is the Gift of God, so that we may believe that God would not give a gift less than himself. But they refrain from preaching that the Holy Spirit is born as the Son of the Father, for this Christ alone is, nor from the Son as the grandson of the Father, nor nevertheless, that he owes what he is to none but the Father, from whom are all things."[1]

A. would not have been ignorant of the treatise on the Holy Spirit by his spiritual father, Ambrose (qv), nor of the wrtings of the Cappadocians. He felt the need for more. He wrote these lines in 393 and thereafter was constantly at work on ideas about the Holy Spirit. They are found in several works, especially, in most developed form, in his large work on the Trinity. He was engaged on this work for some twenty years. Its impact on all subsequent Latin thinking on this subject has been incalculable.

A.'s doctrine on the Trinity must be assumed beyond a typical passage: "This Trinity is of one only and the same nature and substance: neither less in each than in all, nor more in all than in each; but it is as great in the Father alone or in the Son alone as in the Father and the Son together, and as great in the Holy Spirit alone as in the Father, the Son and the Holy Spirit. Nor did the Father, that he should have a Son from himself, lessen himself, but he so begot from himself another self that he should remain wholly in himself and that he should be in his Son as great as he is in himself alone. Likewise the Holy Spirit is wholly from one still in his wholeness, not going before the one from whom he proceeds, but as great with him as from him; nor does he lessen him by proceeding, nor bring increase by adhering to him. And all are one without confusion and three without division."[2]

On the distinction of persons A. carried forward an idea already possessed, relations as the basis: "Wherefore though there is a difference in being Father and Son, there is no difference in the substance, for they are not so named in reference to the substance, but in reference to a relation, which relation is not an accident, since it is not changeable."[3] That the persons are thus constituted does not lessen their separateness and their autonomy. He does not thereby claim to have emptied the mystery: "If we are asked what are the three, human language labours under great insufficiency. The answer has been 'Three Persons,' not so much to answer as not to refuse an answer."[4]

A. has one difficulty with this theory of relations as constitutive of persons. Father and Son are obviously correlative, but how can there be a correlative for the Holy Spirit? If the Spirit comes from the Father and the Son being their bond, communion between them, how can the two be the correlative opposite? A. sees the solution in the concept of the Spirit as Gift: "There should be no anxiety, since we have spoken of the Holy Spirit in the context of relation; not the Trinity itself but he who is in the Trinity, that there is no word corresponding to him as a correlative.... We speak of the Holy Spirit of the Father, but not inversely of the Father of the Holy Spirit, lest the Holy Spirit would be taken for his Son. Likewise we speak of the Holy Spirit of the Son, but not of the Son of the Holy Spirit, lest the Holy Spirit would be taken for his Father.... For many things relative it happens that there is no corresponding word to express the correlative. For example what more obviously expresses a relation than 'pledge'? It refers to that of which it is the pledge and a pledge is always the pledge of something. If then we speak of the pledge of the Father and of the Son (2 Cor 5:5; Eph 1:14) can we speak inversely of the Father of the pledge and of the Son of the pledge? When we speak of the gift (*donum*) of the Father and the Son we cannot speak of the Father of the gift or of the Son of the gift, but to have here a reciprocal response we speak of the gift of the giver and the giver of the gift; here we have current language, in the other case not so."[5]

Donum is A.'s most frequent name for the Holy Spirit.[6] It came to him probably from St. Hilary of Poitiers (qv) whose ideas are assimilated in his thinking.[7] On the Spirit as *donum* he writes thus: "For the love which is from God and is God, is rightly called the Holy Spirit, through whom the charity of God is spread in hearts and by this the whole Trinity dwells in us. Accordingly the Holy Spirit, since he is God, is most properly called the Gift of God (Acts 8:20). What else is this Gift if it is rightly understood but charity, which leads to God, and without which any other Gift of God does not lead to God? Does it need to be proved that the Holy Spirit is called the Gift of God in Holy Scripture?"[8] A. then quotes a number of texts which, as he interprets them, make his question a rhetorical one: Jn 7:37-39; 1 Cor 12:13; Jn 4:7-14; Eph 4:7, 8.

Caritas is sometimes put forward as the essential idea of A. on the Spirit. From a Neo-Platonic influence and Marius Victorinus (qv) came the idea of the Holy Spirit as the communion (*communio*) of the Father and the Son.[9] "The society of the unity of the Church of God outside which there is no forgiveness of sins is the proper work of the Holy Spirit, the Father and the Son co-operating, because the Holy Spairit is, in some way, their society. The Father is not possessed in common as Father by the Son and the Holy Spirit, for he is not the Father of the two; and the Son is not possessed in common as Son by the Father and the Holy Spirit, for he is not the Son of the two; but the Holy Spirit is possessed in common by the Father and the Son, for he is the only Spirit of the two."[10] "The Father and Son wished us to have communion (fellowship) between ourselves and with them by Him who is common to them, and to bind us in one by this Gift which both possess together, that is the Holy Spirit, God and Gift of God. It is in him effectively that we are reconciled with the divinity and that we take our delight in it."[11] When, therefore, we speak of the gift of a giver and the giver of a gift, we are clearly expressing their relationship. Hence the Holy Spirit is in a certain sense the ineffable communion of the Father and the Son. It is perhaps on this account that he has been so called, because the name is appropriate to both the Father and the Son. For he is called properly what they are called in common, because the Father is a spirit and the Son is a spirit and the Father is holy and the Son is holy. In order that the communion between them might be signified by a name which is appropriate to both, the Holy Spirit is called the Gift of both. And accordingly the Trinity is the one God, alone, good, great, eternal and omnipotent. It is itself its unity, deity, greatness, goodness, eternity and omnipotence."[12]

A. concentrates on the idea of the Spirit as love, charity: "As the only Word of God is specially called by the name of Wisdom, although in the universal sense both the Holy Spirit and the Father himself are wisdom, so the Holy Spirit is specially called by the name of Love, although in the universal sense both the Father and the Son are love. But the Word of God, that is the only-begotten Son, has been plainly called the Wisdom of God by the mouth of the Apostle where he says, 'Christ, the power and the wisdom of God' (1 Cor 1:24). But we find that the Holy Spirit has been called Love, if we carefully examine a statement of John the Apostle. For, when he said, 'Beloved, let us love one another because love is of God,' he immediately added, 'And everyone who loves is born of God, and knows God. He who does not love does not know God, for God is love' (1 Jn 4:7-8). He here revealed that God is called that love which he says 'is of God.' The God of God, therefore, is Love. But because the Son is born of God the Father, and the Holy Spirit proceeds from God the Father, the question is rightly asked, of which of them should we rather take it to be said here, that God is love? For the Father alone is God in such a way that he is not of God. Therefore, the Love which is God in such a way that it is of God, is either the Son or the Holy Spirit. But in the following verses after speaking of the love of God (not that by which we love him, but that 'by which he first loved us, and sent his Son as a propitiation for our sins' 1 Jn 4:10), he exhorts us to love one another, so that God might abide in us. Then, because he had said in unmistakable terms that God is love, he wanted to speak more plainly on this subject at once. 'In this' he said, 'we know that we abide in him and he is us, because he has given us of his Spirit' (1 Jn 4:13). Therefore, the Holy Spirit, of whom he has given us, causes us to remain in God and God in us. But love does this. He is, therefore, the God who is Love."

"Finally, a little later, when he had repeated and used the identical expression, 'God is love,' he immediately added, 'He who abides in love abides in God, and God in him' (1 Jn 4:16). From this, he had said above, 'In this we know that we abide in him and he in us, because he has given us of his Spirit (1 Jn 4:13). When God the Holy Spirit, therefore, who proceeds from God, has been given to a person, he inflames him with the love for God and his neighbour, and he himself is Love. For a person does not have the power to love God, except from God. Wherefore a little later he says, 'Let us love him, because he first loved us' (1 Jn 4:19). The Apostle Paul also says, 'The charity of God is poured in our hearts by the Holy Spirit, who has been given to us' (Rom 5:5)."[13]

"My love is my weight, it is that which bears me whither I am borne"; this is a famous phrase from

A. The love by which we are raised up to God, in whom we find our rest, is the Holy Spirit, "the Gift" he says in the Confessions "in whom we enjoy rest, in whom we delight."[14] Transferring this to the divine life he writes: "That indescribable embrace of the Father and the Image (the Son) is not without enjoyment, charity, joy. Therefore that love, delight, happiness or beatitude, if indeed it can be expressed properly by any human word, is called enjoyment concisely by him (St. Hilary of Poitiers), and is in the Trinity the Holy Spirit, not begotten but the suavity of the begetter and the begotten, who inundates all creatures with his immense liberality and abundance, according to their capacity, that they should preserve due order and accept their condition."[15]

A. knows how the missions (qv) of the Persons are related to the processions (qv): "As therefore the Father has begotten, the Son is begotten; thus the Father has sent, the Son was sent. But in the same way as the one who begot and the one begotten are one, so are the one who sent and the one who was sent; for the Father and the Son are one (Jn 10:30). Thus also the Holy Spirit is one with them; for these three are one. For as to be born for the Son is to be of the Father, so for the Son to be sent is to be known in his origin from the Father. And as for the Holy Spirit to be the Gift of God is to proceed from the Father, so to be sent is to be known to proceed from the Father. Nor can we say that the Holy Spirit does not proceed from the Son; nor is it vain that we call the same Spirit the Spirit of the Father and of the Son. Nor do I see what else he wished to signify when, breathing on the face of the disciples, he said, 'Receive the Holy Spirit' (Jn 20:22)."[16]

A. established the *Filioque* (qv), the procession of the Holy Spirit from the Father and the Son; its entry into the Liturgy (qv) and the controversies which arose in subsequent ages are different matters. All the time the weight of such passages as these was there: "Nor was that physical breath proceeding from the body with the meaning of bodily contact, the substance of the Holy Spirit, but the proof by appropriate expression that the Holy Spirit proceeds not only from the Father but from the Son. For who is mad enough to say that the Spirit he gave when he breathed is different from the one he sent after his Ascension (Acts 2:1-4)? For there is one Spirit of God, the Spirit of the Father and of the Son, the Holy Spirit who works all things in all."[17] "It must be confessed that the Father and the Son are one principle, not two, of the Holy Spirit; but as the Father and Son

24

are one God, and in regard to the creature, one Creator and one Lord, thus in regard to the Holy Spirit they are one principle."[18] "If therefore I say that the Holy Spirit proceeds from the Father and the Son, why does the Son say, 'He proceeds from the Father'? (Jn 15:26). Why, do you think, except that he is accustomed to refer to him, from whom he himself is, whatever is his own?"[19] "Wherefore he who can understand the timeless generation of the Son from the Father, should also understand the timeless procession of the Holy Spirit from both (*de utroque*)."[20]

A. applied his doctrine of the Holy Spirit in his writings against the Donatists and the Pelagians. All good things in the Christian life are attributable to the Spirit; on predestination he wrote: "From the beginning of his faith, this grace makes each one a Christian; the same grace made that Person the Christ from this beginning. The one is reborn by the same Spirit from whom the other was born. The same Spirit forgives our sins and preserved him free of all sin. God certainly knew that he would do this. The predestination of the saints is most clearly manifest in the Saint of saints.... Jesus was predestined, then, so that the one who would be son of David according to the flesh, would in power be Son of God according to the Spirit of holiness, since he was born of the Holy Spirit and the Virgin Mary."[21]

The student advancing through all the Trinitarian riches of A.'s writings will particularly note the notional triads with which he seeks to explain the mystery, the different designations of the Spirit.

[1] *De Fide et Symbolo*, IX, 18, 19, *PL* 40, 190, 191; for works of A. cf. E. Portalie, S.J., *A Guide to the Thought of St. Augustine* (tr. of art. *DTC* I, 1903, 2268-2472), London, 1960; 401-406 for editions add *CCSL*; English tr. *LNPF*; Fathers of the Church, esp. 45 *On the Trinity*, S. McKenna 1963; cf. F. Cavallera, *La doctrine de St. Augustin sur l'Esprit Saint à propos du 'De Trinitate,'* *RTAM* 2 (1930), 365-387, 3 (1931), 5-19; J.-L. Maier, *Les missions divines selon St. Augustin*, Fribourg, 1960; B. de Margerie, S.J., *La Trinité chrétienne dans l'histoire*, Paris, 1975, 159-172; E. Bailleux, *L'Esprit du Père et du Fils selon St. Augustin*, *RT* 77 (1977), 5-29; Y.-M. Congar, O.P., *The Holy Spirit*, I, 77-84; III; *Message of the Fathers*, 165-198; *DSp*, IV, 1, 1279-1282, P. Smulders; *Trinitas*, 42-45; *Handbuch der Dogmengeschichte* 189-209; *BT* I, 169-184; [2] *Epist.* 170; *PL* 33, 749; [3] *De Trin.* V, 5, 6, *PL* 42, 914; [4] *De Trin.* V, 10, ibid., 918; [5] *De Trin.* V, 12, 13, 919, 920; [6] Cf. F. Cavallera, *op. cit.*, 368-370; [7] Cf. P. Smulders, *op. cit.*, 1279; [8] *De Trin.* XV, 18, 19, 32-33;1083; [9] For several texts of Marius Victorinus, cf. B. de Margerie, *op. cit.*, 162 and nn. 181, 2, 3, 4, 5, 6; [10] *Sermo 71*, XX, 33, *PL* 38, 463, 4; [11] *Ibid.*, XII, 18, 454; [12] *De Trin.* V, 11, 12, *PL* 42, 919; [13] *De Trin.* XV, 17, 31; [14] *Confessions*, XIII, 9, 10, *PL* 32, 848d, 849a; cf. De *Civitate Dei* XI, 28, *PL* 41, 341-42; *CCSL* 48, 348; Ep. 11, 4, *PL* 33, 76, 77; *CSEL* 34, 1, p. 28; *De fide et Symbolo, j. cit.*, 192; *De Trin.* XV, 26, 47, *PL* 42, 1094; [15] *De Trin.* VI, 10, 11, ibid., 032; [16] *De Trin.* IV, 28, 29, 908; [17] *De Trin.* ibid.; [18] *De Trin.* V, 14, 15, 921; [19] *Tract. 99* in Jo. *PL* 35, 1890; [20] *De Trin.* XV, 26, 47, 1094; [21] *De praedestinatione sanctorum*, XV, 31, *PL* 44, 982; For complete tabulated list cf. E. Portalie, *op. cit.*, 134, 135.

AUTHORITY[1]

The exercise of authority in the Church has been often influenced by the values, patterns of government, techniques of power within given cultures. This is understandable in the light of the laws of social development, of church membership in certain areas living on diminished or badly informed faith—if the level of faith over a fixed area is low then the ideas dictating conduct, personal or social, will be highly influenced by those of the prevailing secular mentality; they may be directly borrowed and given a veneer of something like Christian living. Anyone with some intelligent reading in Church history may illustrate these generalizations easily and plentifully: legalists obsessed with rules and regulations, administrators obsessed with immediate results, sometimes of a purely worldly kind (examination results, financial yield in fund-raising), feudal masters intent on the paraphernalia of office ... the Church has seen them all and many other variations on the theme of power.

The Law of the Spirit (qv) suggests, even prescribes, a very different outlook and attitude. The soul of the subject whom one with authority commands is himself subject to the law (qv) of the Spirit. How to reconcile the claim of the Spirit on each, the superior and the subject, is a problem not always solved happily for the reasons already given.

One more profound reason is failure on the part of those in authority to seek the light and strength of the Spirit. The model is Jesus Christ and he summarized his ideal in the word service: " For the Son of man also came not to be served but to serve and to give his life as a ransom for many " (Mk 10:45; cp Mt 20:28). Acceptance of this ideal means that the life of grace flowing from the Spirit is not impeded. It means that the sacred is fully fruitful and not invaded by the secular. Those in authority are custodians of the sacred. They can pervert it or they can respect, that is, serve it. They cannot serve it without help from the Spirit, for he is its source as the one who gives life and energy to the Church; the Church is the ultimate foundation of the sacred.

When we speak of the Church in this way we look to its essential nature, as the Mystical Body of Christ. We seem to idealize it, for the human condition is constantly apparent in its life. But it is the ideal Church that God desires to exist, and he has assured the existence of those necessary elements in its life by the ordinance to dissociate certain of its ministerial acts from the human weakness of the ministers who represent it and him. A sinful priest says Mass validly; a schismatic bishop consecrates, ordains, as we now say, other bishops validly. The absolution given by a sinful priest effects the forgiveness of sin.

Authority exercised in the Church unworthily by worldly people may serve the interests of the Body; the imperfect superior's defect may be effaced by heroic obedience on the subject's part. This, however, is not general practice, for heroism is not the stuff of everyday life. What happens is spiritual atrophy in the part of the Body concerned; a further phase may lead to spiritual death. Thus the Church has died in places where it once existed and even flourished. It may revive through an extraordinary divine intervention, that is, a singular action by the Spirit with the required response.

All authority carries responsibility and this responsibility through hidden springs in the human psyche may transform a man or woman—as it may break him or her. The responsibility assumed by a man or woman imbued with the Spirit may appear to have similar effects. But the similarity is superficial. For if his government is in the Spirit it is privileged to help a mystery unfold. This mystery worked out in human beings, transcends their immediate circumstances, joins a vast hidden pattern referrable to the Spirit, who gives life to the Church, who directs angels (qv) and men, who relates every detail of his supernatural action to the whole cosmic design which is his creation and his glory. Nothing done in the Spirit is lost. Being entirely his it cannot escape from his concern or his control. So it has often been seen that superiors apparently failing in authority in one sector of the Church were, when transferred elsewhere, prodigiously successful.

For authority may be impeded not only by failure from within the one exercising it but in those who owe him obedience. They may falsely claim a higher light; they may rebel; they may deliberately harm him. The Church has been

through it all. But as the human body carries within it forces which resist disease, so the Church, precisely because within it the Spirit dwells continuously, always attentive to its aspirations, its failure, its weakness, retains its capacity to surprise by swift recovery and startling, unexpected progress. The Spirit is the God of surprises. He surprises in the total transformation he can effect in the great converts, and he confounds the pessimists in guiding his Church through mountainous stormy seas, despite the presence on board of a panic-stricken crew, demoralized passengers and dangerous cargo. Such it appeared towards the end of the tenth century.

Life in the Church is destined to be passed within the person or social group context. Person and community must match their intentions and thrust, an apparently impossible task at times: impossible without the Spirit who speaks to the heart of each person, who masters the collective movement of the group to which each belongs, whose infinite resource in the bestowal of charisms meets every conceivable human need. The guidance of the Spirit does not dispense from the full confident use of the science of Human Relations, of all that the most advanced psychology tells us about personal interaction, group dynamics and social pathology.

To ignore such scientifically established findings and principles in the hope that the Spirit will provide would be like dispensing with tried and tested medicine and hoping for a miracle of healing. It is part of the Spirit's guidance and influence to help people to discover the natural means which may be made to serve supernatural ends. Those in authority have to know themselves and without the help of the Spirit full self-knowledge is impossible; they likewise need his assistance to discern the psychological make-up of those subject to them, to know how to combine the respect which is due to every person with the firmness which law exacts and the compassion due to the weak.

There are those with the gift of leadership, motivation as we say nowadays. They are expert in timing, in judging the pace of progress of each individual under their authority: for no two advance at the same speed. They know what to say and what not to say, how effective silence can be in certain moments. They judge people at their best and thus bring out the best in them. All this must be lifted to the supernatural level with the Gifts of the Spirit, here in particular the Gift of Counsel. Blunders in dealing with persons can scarcely be excused on the grounds of "It will hurt but do good."

----

[1] Cf. article "Law of the Spirit" with bibl.; S.E.Donlon,

Authority (ecclesiastical) NCE I, 1115; F.X. Lawlor, *Society (in theology)*, NCE XIII, 394, 95; J.M. Tillard, O.P., *Obéissance*, DSp XI, 535-563; id., *Koinonia*, DSp VII, 1762-1765.

B

BAPTISM IN THE SPIRIT[1]

The name used in the charismatic movement (qv) for the special outpouring of the Spirit which initiates a new phase of human life for the Christian committed to this movement, or similarly oriented. It is a reality of the existential order, a subject of experience. Yet it is profound in its effects. Consciousness of the Holy Spirit and of his dynamic immediate effect on the person involved forms part of the experience.

There has been understandable criticism of the term, apart from the kind of criticism which springs from hostility to all aspects of the charismatic movement. Obviously there is a danger among those insufficiently instructed, of confusion with the Sacrament of Baptism, first of the seven sacred in the Church and referred to Christ for their warrant; Baptism more clearly than some of the others. The answer in practice to this objection is education.

The side-effect of the objection when it is strongly urged may be to devalue the sacrament of Baptism, to give the idea or impression that the validly baptized still lack something essential to Christian life, an outpouring of the Spirit.

Much study of the beginning of Christianity, as narrated in Acts, is here called for. Case histories are available for study and this may be undertaken with respect and with obvious gain. One approach is to be discouraged as it is to be discountenanced in all collective movements: prying into people's private lives with the sole objective of finding something wrong or open to criticism.

But those baptized in the Spirit cannot object to the test, respectfully applied, 'by their fruits you shall know them.' Charisms sometimes accompany the experience which gives this undeniably new consciousness of God's presence and action; but this is not an essential feature. Nor is laying on of hands, though it is sometimes done. Baptism in the Spirit may be a wholly private experience, with no obligation to reveal it to others.

One particular theory of Baptism in the Spirit, that of J.D.G. Dunn, is dealt with in the article on that biblical scholar. A question debated among the highly competent Catholic theologians who have been interested in the subject is the precise relation of the experience to the Sacraments of initiation. What may broadly be called the non-sacramental view, one that is tenable, is held by F.A. Sullivan. He invokes the authority of St. Thomas Aquinas on the invisible mission of a divine Person: it may be seen in a special increase of grace whereby the recipient moves forward to some new act or some new state of grace; instances given are capacity to work miracles, to prophesy, to face martyrdom, renounce all one's possessions or perform any other similarly heroic deed. Sullivan sees such a moment as enclosing a new relationship with the indwelling Spirit, causing a more intimate experiential knowledge of God's presence, stirring fresh love.[2]

This opinion is not to be lightly dismissed. A number of Catholic theologians do hold what may be broadly called a "sacramental" theory. This is notable since the Malines Document (see art. Charismatic Movement) and the impetus given to thinking on these lines by the influential Cardinal Suenens; among supporters of the view are H. Muhlen, (qv) R. Laurentin, especially K. McDonnell. The latter sums up the position thus: "Baptism in this view is a bringing of the graces of initiation already received to awareness and a new actuality.'[3] K. and D. Ranaghan put their opinion thus: "'Baptism in the Holy Spirit' is not something replacing baptism and confirmation. Rather it may be seen as an adult re-affirmation and renewal of these sacraments, an opening of ourselves to all their sacramental graces."[4] R. Laurentin's opinion is thus framed: 'We may say, therefore, with greater accuracy, that the function and purpose of baptism in the Spirit is the effective accomplishment in a Christian's life of what baptism called for but to some extent did not accomplish."[5]

The important link between Baptism and the Holy Spirit is patent in the New Testament. The

Synoptics affirm that the Baptist (see art. John the Baptist) asserted that the one coming after him would baptize in the Spirit (Mt 3:11; Mk 1:8; Lk 3:16) —Mt and Lk add "and with fire." The Johannine text, 3:5, is well-known "Unless one is born of water and the Spirit, he cannot enter the kindom of God." The word of Peter to would-be converts reported in Acts is "Repent and be baptized every one of you in the name of Jesus Christ for the forgiveness of your sins; and you shall receive the Holy Spirit" (2:38). St. Paul abounds in the subject: "But you were washed, you were sanctified, you were justified in the name of the Lord Jesus Christ and the Spirit of God" (1 Cor 6:11); "For by one Spirit we were all baptized into one body" (1 Cor 12:13). "But it is God who establishes us with you in Christ, and has commissioned (anointed) us; he has put his seal upon us and given us his Spirit in our hearts as a guarantee" (2 Cor 1:21, 22). "He saved us, not because of deeds done by us in righteousness, but in virtue of his own mercy, by the washing of regeneration and renewal in the Holy Spirit, which he poured out upon us richly through Jesus Christ our Saviour, so that we might be justified by his grace and become heirs in the hope of eternal life" (Tit 3:5).

It is a sovereign benefit to help Christians make the truth so fully expressed creative in their lives.

Catholic theologians divide on the question of a sacramental aspect of Baptism in the Spirit. F.A. Sullivan thinks there is no relationship; there is just a new grace imparted by the Holy Spirit. With variations Cardinal Suenens, H. Mühlen (qv), R. Laurentin, K. and D. Ranaghan, S. Tugwell, D. Gelpi, K. McDonnell see a link. As the last-named says it would be "a bringing of the graces of initiation[6] already received to awareness and a new actuality."

For bibl., cf. R. Laurentin, *Catholic Pentecostalism*, London, 1977, 212, 213, *ibid.*, 26-47; S. Tugwell, *Did You Receive the Spirit?*, London, 1972; G.T. Montague, *Baptism in the Spirit and Speaking in Tongues: A Biblical Appraisal,* Paper read at the Catholic Biblical Association, 1 August, 1973, repr., *Theology Digest,* 21 (1973), 342-360, repr. in author's *The Spirit and his Gifts,* New York, 1974, 3-29; K. McDonnell, O.S.B., *Baptism in the Spirit as an Ecumenical Problem,* Notre Dame, 1972; id., esp., *Communion Ecclesiology and Baptism in the Holy Spirit: Tertullian and the Early Church,* ThSt 49 (1988), 671-693; repr. with study of Hilary of Poitiers and Cyril of Jerusalem (qqv) as introduction to *Open the Windows: The Popes and Charismatic Renewal,* South Bend, 1989; F.A. Sullivan, "'Baptism in the Spirit': A Catholic Interpretation of the Pentecostal Experience," Greg. 55 (1974), 49-66; id., *Charisms and Charismatic Renewal,* Ann Arbor, 1982, 59-75; H. Lederle, *Treasures Old and New,* Hendrickson, 1987, 64, [2]*Op. cit.,* Greg., 66, *Summa Théologiae,* I, q. 43, aa. 5, 6; 6 ad 2; [3]*Op. cit.* ThSt, 672; [4]*Catholic Pentecostals,* New York, 1969, 20: [5]*Catholic Pentecostalism,* 47. [6]*Op. cit.,* 671f.

BAPTISM OF JESUS CHRIST, THE[1]

The event is narrated by the four evangelists as follows:

"Then Jesus came from Galilee to the Jordan to John, to be baptized by him. John would have prevented him, saying, 'I need to be baptized by you, and do you come to me?' But Jesus answsered him, 'Let it be so now; for thus it is fitting for us to fulfil all righteousness.' Then he consented. And when Jesus was baptized, he went up immediately from the water, and behold the heavens were opened and he saw the Spirit of God descending like a dove, and alighting on him; and lo, a voice from heaven, saying, 'This is my beloved Son, with whom I am well pleased'" (Mt 3:13-17).

"In those days Jesus came from Nazareth of Galilee and was baptized by John in the Jordan. And when he came up out of the water, immediately he saw the heavens opened, and the Spirit descending upon him like a dove; and a voice came from heaven, 'Thou art my beloved Son; with thee I am well pleased'" (Mk 1:9-11).

"Now when all the people were baptized, and when Jesus also had been baptized and was praying, the heaven was opened, and the Holy Spirit descended upon him in bodily form, as a dove, and a voice came from heaven, 'Thou art my beloved Son; with thee I am well pleased'" (Lk 3:21, 22).

"And John bore witness, 'I saw the Spirit descend as a dove from heaven, and it remained on him. I myself did not know him; but he who sent me to baptize with water said to me, 'He on whom you see the Spirit descend and remain, this is he who baptizes with the Holy Spirit.' And I have seen and have borne witness that this is the Son of God'" (Jn 1:32-34).

This is a notable theophany of the Holy Spirit. Those interventions previously recorded were in private as at the Annunciation, or communicated interiorly as in the other events of the infancy Gospels. Now, in the river Jordan, there is a witness to what happens in the open. Matthew gives the impression of a public event.

Secondly, this is a descent of the Spirit on the Messiah, a fulfilment of the prophecy of Is 2: "And the Spirit of the Lord shall rest upon him, the spirit of wisdom and understanding, the spirit of counsel and might, the spirit of knowledge and the fear of the Lord." We are, therefore, at a pivotal moment in salvation history, one rightly ranked by Vatican II with the Annunciation and Pentecost, each a prime moment of the Spirit.[2]

Exegetes seek to discern the slight divergences in the three synoptic texts and explain them: the hesitancy of John in Matthew's account, the terse narrative of Mark, the detail "he was praying" in Luke. Was there an embarrassing problem in the baptism of Jesus by John, the preacher of repentance? Much is sometimes made of this problem. It is surely dwarfed by the unique feature, the descent of the Spirit.

The symbolism of the dove in its origins is discussed by biblical scholars. The unique aspect again is that each evangelist uses the symbol and makes it explicit: no doubt at all remains. Beneath this symbol takes place a great encounter and a poignant parting: the encounter between the Spirit and the Messiah in the domain and function of Messiah, by the one who, eternally united with him in the Holy Trinity, had "emptied himself," and to undertake the great mission of his life must needs receive him thus in this simple ceremony presided over by his creature; a parting between the Messiah and the precursor, who summed up their relationship thus, "He must increase and I must decrease," (3:30), who defined his baptizing mission thus, "'but for this I came baptizing with water, that he might be revealed to Israel'" (Jn 1:31).

---

[1]Cf. biblical commentaries to passages quoted, dictionary articles s.v., G.M. Montague, *The Holy Spirit*, 239ff, 340ff; [2]*Ad Gentes*, art. 4.

BARTH, KARL (1886-1968)

B. had a distinctive way of expressing the doctrine of the Holy Trinity, rooting it in the Bible, drawing it out of his rich theology of divine revelation. On the Holy Spirit he writes: "The one God reveals himself according to Scripture as the Redeemer, that is, as the Lord who sets us free. As such he is the Holy Spirit by receiving whom we become the children of God, because as the Spirit of the love of God the Father and God the Son he is so previously in himself."[1] In the exposition of his doctrine on the Holy Spirit in the *Church Dogmatics*, B. considers the *Filioque* (qv) at length. On his own general principles of God, the event of revelation, he defends it powerfully.[2] Taking account of the recognition that the Holy

Spirit may proceed from the Father and the Son in our lives he writes: "If the Spirit is also the Spirit of the Son only in revelation and for faith, if in eternity which means his proper and original reality he is only the Spirit of the Father, then the communion of the Spirit between God and man lacks objective content and ground.... Would that not mean an emptying of revelation."[3] The *Filioque* he thought immanent.

B. in dealing with the doctrine of reconciliation in the *Church Dogmatics*, IV, 1 considers at length the Holy Spirit and the gathering of the Christian community;[4] the Spirit's awakening power is the presupposition of the community; the role of faith, the being of the community, the time dimension engage his deep attention, with illuminating insights. Then he deals with the Holy Spirit and Christian faith, faith and its object, the act of faith. In *Church Dogmatics* IV, 4, B. surveys the Christian life in its vast ethical aspect; fundamental in the Christian life is Baptism with the Holy Spirit.[5]

---

[1]*Church Dogmatics*, I, 1, tr. G.J. Thomson, Edinburgh, 513; [2]On the Holy Spirit, 513-560; on the *Filioque* 541-554; [3]*Ibid.*, 550; [4]*Op.cit.*, IV, 1, 643-739; [5]*Op.cit.*, IV, 4, 3-40; bibl. on Barth, *Oxford Dictionary of the Christian Church*, 137; *Trinitas*, 49; cf. E. Busch, *Karl Barth, His Life from Letters and Autobiographical Texts,* London, 1976; C. O'Grady, *The Church in Catholic Theology: Dialogue with Karl Barth;* London, 1969, ch. xii; *The Mission of the Holy Spirit*, 123-142; J.-L. Witte, *DSp*, IV, 1, 1330. P. Rosato, *The Spirit as Lord. The Pneumatology of Karl Barth,* Edinburgh, 1981; K. McDonnell, O.S.B., *A Trinitarian Theology of the Holy Spirit*, ThSt 46 (1985) 191-227, with further references to the works of B.

BASIL 'THE GREAT', ST., DOCTOR OF THE CHURCH (c. 330-379)[1]

Remarkable in the theological group to which he belonged, the Cappadocians, and the age when he had a prominent teaching role in the Church, B. still stirs questioning if not controversy in regard to the theology of the Holy Spirit. Living through the post-Nicene Trinitarian debates, at one with Athanasius (qv), resisting a wide spectrum of heresies, most of them in some way arising from Arian roots, he fully embraced the Cappadocian distinction between *ousia* and *hypostasis*: "If you ask me to state shortly my own view, I shall state that *ousia* has the same relation to *hypostasis*, as the common has to the particular. Every one of us both shares in existence by the common term of essence (*ousia*), and by his own properties is such a one and such a one. In the same manner, in the matter in question, the term *ousia* is common, like goodness, or godhead, or any similar attribute; while *hypostasis* is contemplated in fatherhood, sonship or the power to sanctify. If then they describe the Persons as being without *hypostasis*, the statement is *per se* absurd; but if they concede that the Persons exist in real *hypostasis*, as they acknowledge, let them so reckon them that the principle of the *homoousion* may be preserved in the unity of the Godhead, and that the doctrine preached may be the recognition of true religion, of Father, Son and Holy Ghost in the perfect and complete hypostasis of each of the Persons named."[2]

Problems had arisen concerning B.'s use of a doxology which clearly implied equality of the Father, Son and Holy Spirit. He received a visit from Amphilochius, Bishop of Iconium (first cousin of his friend Gregory of Nazianzus, qv) who urged him to write a treatise on the Holy Spirit and clear up all doubts. This he did, sketching the situation which prompted the discussion: "Lately when praying with the people, and using the full doxology to God the Father in both forms, at one time '*with* the Son *together with* the Holy Ghost,' and at another '*through* the Son, *in* the Holy Ghost,' I was attacked by some of those present on the ground that I was introducing novel and, at the same time, mutually contradictory terms."[3]

B., though polemical in spirit and approach, ranges over many aspects of the subject, but he is all the time alert to the formulation of the doxology; this is his starting point. He does not compose a treatise in a manner that would be possible later. He is especially attentive to Sacred Scripture, which he quotes constantly. We shall build up an idea of the Spirit from what he rejects as improper in theorizing about him, and especially from the effects of his presence and action.

Thus B. writes: "It is not permissible they (the opponents) assert, for the Holy Spirit to be ranked with the Father and the Son, on account of the difference of his nature and the inferiority of his dignity. Against them it is right to reply in the words of the Apostles, 'We ought to obey God rather than men.' For if our Lord, when enjoining the baptism of salvation, charged his disciples to baptize all nations in the name 'of the Father and of the Son and of the Holy Spirit,' not disdaining fellowship with him, and these men allege that we must not rank him with the Father and the Son, is it not clear they they openly withstand the commandment of God."[4]

Again, on the operations of the three divine Persons B. writes: "Moreover, from the things created at the beginning may be learnt the fellowship of the Spirit with the Father and the Son.... But do thou, who hast power from the things that are seen to form an analogy of the unseen, glorify the Maker by whom all things were made, visible and invisible, principalities and powers, authorities, thrones, and dominions, and all other reasonable natures whom we cannot name. And in the creation think first, I pray thee, of the original cause of all things that are made, the Father; of the creative cause, the Son; of the perfecting cause, the Spirit; so that the ministering spirits subsist by the will of the Father, are brought into being by the operation of the Son, and perfected by the presence of the Spirit.... The Word then is not a mere significant impression on the air, borne by the organs of speech; nor is the Spirit of his mouth a vapour, emitted by the organs of respiration; but the Word is he who 'was with God in the beginning' and 'was God,' and the Spirit of the mouth of God is 'the Spirit of truth who proceeds from the Father.' You are, therefore, to perceive three, the Lord who gives the order, the Word who creates, and the Spirit who confirms."[5]

B. comes to the core of the question at times: "One, moreover, is the Holy Spirit, and we speak of him singly, conjoined as he is to the one Father through the one Son, and through himself completing the adorable and blessed Trinity. Of him the intimate relationship to the Father and the Son is sufficiently declared by the fact of his not being ranked in the plurality of the creation, but being spoken of singly; for he is not one of many, but One. For as there is one Father and one Son, so is there one Holy Spirit. He is consequently as far removed from created nature as reason requires the singular to be removed from compound and plural bodies; and he is in such wise united to the Father and to the Son as unit has affinity with unit. And it is not from this source alone that our proofs of the natural communion are derived, but from the fact that he is, moreover, said to be 'of God'; not indeed in the sense in which 'all things are of God,' but in the sense of proceeding out of God, not by generation, like the Son, but as Breath of his mouth. But in no way is the 'mouth' a member, nor the Spirit breath that is dissolved; but the word 'mouth' is used so far as it can be appropriate to God, and the Spirit is a Substance having life, gifted with supreme power of sanctification. Thus the close relation is made plain, while the mode of the ineffable existence is safe-guarded."[6]

Defending the thesis that the Spirit ought to be glorified, first listing the different names of the Spirit, B. soars to the heights: "And his operations, what are they? For majesty ineffable, and for numbers innumerable. How shall we form a conception of what extends beyond the ages? What were his operations before that creation whereof we can conceive? How great the grace which he conferred on creation? What the power exercised by him over the ages to come? He existed; he pre-existed. He co-existed with the Father and the Son before the ages. It follows that, even if you can conceive of anything beyond the ages, you will find the Spirit yet further above and beyond. And if you think of creation, the powers of the heavens were established by the Spirit, the establishment being understood to refer to disability to fall away from good." Thereon B. maintains all the spiritual good things we must attribute to the Spirit's power. He deals with an objection against his equality with the deity since "he intercedes" (Rom 8:26, 27). "Have you never heard concerning the Only-begotten that he 'is at the right hand of God who indeed intercedes for us?'" (Rom 8:34)

B. turns to what he considers "more lofty considerations": He selects a number of scriptural texts which, in his reading of them, show that the Spirit is called 'Lord'. "We have learnt from the Apostle, 'the Lord direct your hearts into the love of God and into the patient waiting for Christ' (2 Thess 3:5—recent tr. 'steadfastness of Christ'), *for our tribulations*. Who is the Lord that directs into the love of God and into the patient waiting for Christ for tribulations? Let those men answer us who are making a slave of the Holy Spirit. For if the argument had been about God the Father, it would certainly have said, 'the Lord direct you into his own love,' or if about the Son, it would have added 'into his own patience.' Let them then seek what other Person there is who is worthy to be honoured with the title of Lord."[7] B. quotes a parallel passage from 1 Thess 3:12, 13 and he draws fully on 2 Cor 3:14-18, especially vv 17, 18: "Now the Lord is the Spirit, and where the Spirit of the Lord is, there is freedom.And we all, with unveiled face, beholding the glory of the Lord, are being changed into his likeness from one degree of glory to another; for this comes from the Lord who is the Spirit."

B. deals at length with the glorification of the Spirit, having stated a fundamental truth in these words: "Moreover the surpassing excellence of the nature of the Spirit is to be learned not only from his having the same title as the Father and the Son, and sharing in their operations, but also from his being, like the Father and the Son, unapproachable in thought."[8] He devotes much space to the problem of how this glorification may be expressed, how he was justified in the formula he used, how it could be supported from previous writings.

B. never once said that the Holy Spirit is God. But the cumulative effect of the passages quoted is in that sense. He comes nearer the affirmation in his letters. "As then baptism has been given us by the Saviour, in the name of the Father and of the Son and of the Holy Spirit, so in accordance with our baptism, we make confession of the creed, and our doxology in accordance with our creed. We glorify the Holy Spirit together with the Father and the Son, from the conviction that he is not separated from the divine nature; for that which is foreign by nature does not share in the same honours. All who call the Holy Spirit a creature we pity, on the ground that, by this utterance, they are falling into the unpardonable sin of blasphemy against him."[9]

We get an idea of how he views the reality from the critique he makes of erroneous positions: "Now Sabellius did not even deprecate the formation of the Persons without hypostasis, saying as he did that the same God, being one in matter (*to hypokeimeno*) was metamorphosed as the need of the moment required, and spoken of now as Father, now as Son, and now as Holy Spirit."[10] Here it is clear that he considers the heresy equally offensive to the Spirit as to the Father and Son. In another passage he does come near an assertion of the divinity: "Wherefore, in the case of the Godhead, we confess one essence or substance so as not to give a variant definition of existence, but we confess a particular hypostasis, in order that our conception of Father, Son and Holy Spirit may be without confusion and clear. If we have no distinct perception of the separate characteristics, namely fatherhood, sonship and sanctification, but form our conception of God from the general idea of existence, we cannot possibly give a sound account of our faith. We must, therefore, confess the faith by adding the particular to the common. The Godhead is common; the fatherhood particular. We must, therefore, combine the two and say, 'I believe in God the Father.' The like course must be pursued in the confession of the

Son; we must combine the particular with the common and say, 'I believe in God the Son,' so in the case of the Holy Spirit we must make our utterance conform to the appellation and say 'in God the Holy Spirit.' Hence it results that there is a satisfactory preservation of the unity by the confession of the one Godhead, while in the distinction of the individual properties regarded in each there is the confession of the peculiar properties of the Persons."[11] There is a manuscript problem in regard to the phrase 'in God the Holy Spirit.' But the whole passage speaks of three Persons, apparently equal.

Why then the debate about B.'s orthodoxy? The charge is that B. never explicitly said in the treatise that the Holy Spirit is God and never applied the *homoousion* to him. He had taken time to consider the theology of the Spirit, since he first broached it in the *Contra Eunomium*.[12] His friend Gregory of Nazianzus (qv) is brought into the debate, for Gregory wrote to him giving him evidence that criticism of him had been voiced on this point— he had, it was said, at the feast of St. Eupsychius "spoken most beautifully and perfectly on the Godhead of the Father and the Son, as hardly anyone else could speak; but had blurred over the Spirit." Gregory related how he had tried, unsuccessfully, to defend B. He concluded: "But do you, O divine and sacred head, instruct me how far I ought to go in setting forth the divinity of the Spirit; and what words I ought to use, and how far to use reserve; that I may be furnished against opponents. For if I, who more than any one else know both you and your opinions, and have often given and received assurance on this point, still need to be taught the truth of this matter, I shall be of all men the most ignorant and miserable."[13] Basil was hurt by the letter as his reply showed clearly; he did not alter his procedure.[14]

As to the *homoousion* he had an opportunity to use it in this passage: "Ever be spoken among us with boldness that famous dogma of the Fathers, which destroys the ill-fated heresy of Arius, and builds up the churches in the sound doctrine wherein the Son is confessed to be of one substance with the Father, and the Holy Spirit is ranked and worshipped as of equal honour, to the end that through your prayers and cooperation the Lord may grant to us that same boldness for the truth and glorying in the confession of the divine and saving Trinity which he has given you."[15] Here the Spirit is "ranked and worshipped as of equal honour." Why did B. not continue the phrase "of one substance" in his regard? There are still those who think him defective in his theology, though outstanding patristic scholars like J.N.D. Kelly, B. Pruche, P. Piuslampe find him completely orthodox. A. Meredith is critical of him. He does admit that B. in *In Hex 2:6* attributes a role in creation to the Spirit: "Such is, as nearly as possible, the meaning of these words—the Spirit was borne: Let us understand, that is, prepared the nature of the water to produce living beings: a sufficient proof for those who ask if the Holy Spirit took an active part in the creation of the world." A. Meredith finds the other reference to creative power possibly restricted to recreation through the descent of the Spirit.[16]

It is important to note that the Creed of Constantinople (qv) does not use the word God or consubstantial of the Spirit; these truths are fully indicated, but not by explicit phrasing. We do well also to heed the word of Athanasius (qv) and the final judgment of Gregory. The former thought that B. practised economy so that "to the weak he might become weak to gain the weak."[17] Gregory, in the magnificent, very lengthy panegyric on his friend deals thus with the problem. His solution is acceptable: "That he, no less than any other, acknowledged that the Spirit is God, is plain from his having often preached this truth, whenever opportunity offered, and eagerly confessed it when questioned in private.

"But he made it more clear in his conversations with me from whom he concealed nothing during our conferences upon this subject. Not content with simply asserting it, he proceeded, as he had but very seldom done before, to call upon himself that most terrible fate of separation from the Spirit, if he did not adore the Spirit as consubstantial and coequal with the Father and the Son." "The enemy" Gregory had said earlier "were on the watch for the unqualified statement 'the Spirit is God'; which, although it is true, they and the wicked patron of their impiety imagined to be impious; so that they might banish him and his power of theological instruction from the city, and themselves be able to seize upon the church; and make it the starting-point and citadel from which they could overrun with the evil doctrine the rest of the world. Accordingly, by the use of other terms, and by statements which unmistakably had the same meaning, and by arguments necessarily leading to this conclusion, he so overpowered his antagonists, that they were left without reply, and involved in their own admissions,—the greatest proof possible of dialectical power and skill. His treatise on the subject makes it further manifest, being evidently written by a pen borrowed from the Spirit's store. He postponed for a time the use of the exact term, begging as a favour from the Spirit himself and his earnest champions, that they would not be annoyed at his economy, nor by clinging to a single expression, ruin the whole cause, from an uncompromising temper, at a crisis when religion was in peril."[18] B. Pruche's explanation of the difference between kerygma and dogma as then understood, complements this highly credible apologia.[19]

---

[1]Texts of the main work, *De Spiritu Sancto* ed. B. Pruche, O.P., *SC* 17, 1947, entirely new ed., *SC* 17bis, 1968; crit. ed., C.F. Johnson, Oxford, 1892; English tr., *LNPF*, VIII, 2-50; Cf. T. Schermann, *Die Gottheit des Heiligen Geistes nach den griech. Vätern des vierten Jahr.*, Freiburg i. Br., 1901, ch. IV, 89-145; F. Nager, *Die Trinitätslehre des hl. Basilius des Grossen*, Paderborn, 1912; H. Dorries, *De Spiritu Sancto, Der Beitrag des Basilius zum Abschluss des trinitärischen Dogmas*, Göttingen, 1956; B. Pruche, *L'Originalité du Traité de St. Basile sur le St. Esprit, RSPT* 32 (1948) 207-224; id., *Autour du Traité sur le St. Esprit de Basile de Césarée, RSR* 52 (1964) 204-232; articles in *Verbum Caro* 89 (1968): B. Bobrinskoy, *Liturgie et ecclésiologie trinitaire de St. Basile*, 1-32; J.-M. Hornus, *La divinité du St. Esprit comme condition de salut personnel selon Basile*, 33-62; T.F. Torrance, *Spiritus Creator*, 63-85; P.C. Christou, *L'Enseignement de St. Basile sur le Saint Esprit*, 86-99; J. Gribomont, O.S.B., *Intransigence and Irenicism, Word and Spirit*, 1979, reprint from *Estudios Trinitarios*, 9 (1975); R. Staats, *Die Basilianische Verherrlichung des Heiligen Geistes auf dem Konzil zu Konstantinopel 381, Ein Beitrag zum Ursprung der Formel 'Kerygma und Dogma'*, in *Kerygma und Dogma*, 25 (1979), 232-253; B. Schultze, S.J., *Die Pneumatologie des Symbols von Konstantinopel als abschliessende Formulierung der griechischen Theologie (381-1981) OCP*, 47 (1981), 5-54; H. Denard, *Das Problem der Abhaengigkeit des Basilius von Plotin*, Berlin, 1964; P. Piuslampe, *Spiritus Vivificans: Grundzuege einer Theologie des Heiligen Geistes nach Basilius von Caeserea*, Münster, 1981; A. Meredith, *The Pneumatology of the Cappadocian Fathers, ITQ*, 48 (1981), *Basil the Great*, 198-205; J. Wolinski, *La pneumatologie des Pères grecs avant le Concile de Constantinople I*, in *Atti del Congresso*, I, *Basile de Césarée et le 'Traité du Saint Esprit'*, 154-161; Kelly, *Doctrines*, 263-269; J. Quasten III, 228-33; *Handbuch der Dogmengeschichte*, 165-173; H. Dorries, "Basilius und das dogma von Heiligen Geist," *Lutherische Rundschau* 6 (1956/57), 247-262; repr. in *Wort und Stunde*, I, Göttingen, 1966, 118-144; *BT*, I, 271-278; *Basil of Caesarea. Christian, Humanist, Ascetic, A Sixteen Hundredth Anniversary Symposium*, ed. P.J. Fedwick, Toronto, Pontifical Institute for Medieval Studies, 1981. [2]Ep. 214, 4, *LNPF* 254; [3]*De Spiritu Sancto*, I, 3, *LNPF*, 3; [4]*Op. cit.*, X, 24, 16; [5]XVI, 38, 23, 24; [6]XVIII, 45, 46, 28, 29; [7]XIX, 49, 30, 31; XXI, 52, 33; [8]XXII, 53, 24; [9]Ep. 159, 2, 212; [10]Ep. 210, 5, 251; [11]Ep. 236, 6, 278; [12]Cf. A. Meredith, *op. cit.*, 200; [13]St. Greg. Nazianz., *Ep. 58, LNPF*, VII, 454, 5; [14]Cf. Ep. 121, 167; [15]Ep. 90, 2, 176; [16]*Op. cit.*, 200; [17]Ep. 63, *LNPF* IV, 580; [18]*In Laudem Basilii Magni, Or.*. 43, 68, PG 36, 587A, *LNPF*, VII, 418; [19]*Op. cit.* Add to bibl. *Basil of Caesarea. Christian, Humanist, Ascetic. A Sixteen Hundredth Anniversary Symposium*, ed. P.J.Fedwick, Toronto, Pontifical Institute for Medieval Studies, 1981. Add. to bibl. J. Vorhees, *Pneuma. Erfahrung und Erleuchtung in der Theologie des Basilius des Grossen*. Ostkirchliche Studien 25, 1976.

BEAUTY OF THE HOLY SPIRIT, THE

Beauty is an emanation of splendour perceived by the aesthetic sense with an immediate accompaniment of satisfaction, of pleasure, that is enjoyment proportionate to the beautiful perceived. We enter the domain of analogy when we transfer these ideas to God. He is the supreme truth, goodness and beauty. But in each of these transcendental values everything that we can know from created things is but a suggestion, a stimulus to thought, on the sublime ultimate reality of the deity as this is realised. Beauty in creatures is ephemeral, often superficial. In God beauty is total, profound, mysterious. When we speak of the beauty of the Holy Spirit we must bear in mind the immeasurable distance that separates from any merely human manifestation of this reality, the overwhelming, dazzling, existentially self-revealing beauty of the Godhead. His beauty is entirely spiritual; it is not perceptible to those devoid of spiritual power; it cannot be perceived fully without the direct vision of God, which is the state of the blessed in heaven. That gift, called by theologians the light of glory, equips the soul with power wholly new, opening the intellect to the divine vision, releasing it from danger of collapse in this awesome presence, sustaining it through all eternity. Rarely is the gratuitous gift related to God's beauty. This too is open to the soul's gaze. In such a blissful state it comprehends all that is God. Comprehension of his beauty is not possible in man's earthly state. But it is incumbent on him to prepare for such fulfillment, while in the divine paradox inherent in his condition, knowing that of himself he cannot ever reach it.

In such a piecemeal, inadequate approach we may reflect on the Spirit's beauty that is to be revealed to us. It is foreshadowed in great or less degree in all divine revelation: in the world, which has beauty in degrees ascending from inanimate things through the forms of life, to the immortal spirit, immaterial in the angelic world, yoked with matter in humankind; this human beauty is immeasurably exalted with the treasures of grace. These are the direct gift of the Spirit, who in his bestowal manifests who he is, how wonderful, splendid he is.

His sublime masterpiece totally resplendent is the sacred humanity of Jesus Christ (qv.). St. Thomas saw the constituents of beauty as integrity, proportion and clarity. In a world wherein, through the deviation from God's original design of harmony, weak or wicked men strove to deflect Christ from his mission to restore and consolidate this design his consistency was unfailing and total. Not a word or deed of Jesus Christ but breathes the essential splendour: missed alas by those who have not the golden key of faith. For this is the challenge of spiritual beauty. It is superior to all other forms, but is not discernible to all.

This is seen too in the life and personality of Mary. Paul VI once urged theologians to enter the *via pulchritudinis* in studying the mystery of Mary. It is a fruitful approach scarcely attempted as yet, though as with her divine Son one has the incalculable treasures of artistic beauty which she has inspired: not the theological appraisement, but at times pointing clearly in that direction; witness Fra Angelico, the Pietà of Michelangelo, Notre Dame de la Belle Verrière in Chartres and the world of Icons, one of which, Our Lady of Novgorod inspired Bulgakov's theology of Our Lady another, most beautiful of all, Our Lady of Vladimir, awaiting in the Tretiakov Museum the moment of destiny. So much beauty is but a pale reflection of the person. And that is the Spirit's masterpiece. As to a very much lesser extent is every soul brought to entire salvation. All of which points to his own indescribable beauty.

J.C. Roten has a succinct passage on Mary's beauty: "According to the theological aesthetics of Hans Urs von Balthasar, Mary is the highest paradigm of what is meant by the 'art of God.' She is the splendour and glory of humanity, because all of her different roles and attitudes are but a kaleidoscope of her transparency to Christ as *immaculata, virgo, mater, assumpta.* This is typically Marian beauty: irreducible transparence and accomplished parsonality—the second in no way obstructing or obscuring the first. Beauty wants to be *splendor veri,* to reveal in its limited meaningfulness, the fullness of meaning. Similarly Mary was made baeutiful, and at the same time radiates her beauty. She is the expression of God's *charis,* radiating and manifesting it. In Mary Trinitarian love becomes visible and is experienced; likewise, she expresses the very essence of the

Church as archetype and model, the true configuration of *anima ecclesiastica,* the highest realization of human holiness.[1]

---

[1] The Marian Library Newsletter, Summer, 1989, p. 6.

BIBLIOGRAPHY

Bibliographies are added to the articles. Some general indications are given here. Two of the French encyclopaedic works provide good bibliographies: *DTC, Esprit Saint*, V.A. Palmieri, 676-829, bibl., 819-829; *DSp, Esprit Saint* IV, J. Gribomont, O.S.B., P. Smulders, J. Guillet, F. Vandenbroucke, S. Tromp, S.J., J.L. Witte, 1246-1334; cf. also *Discernement des esprits*, III, J. Guillet, G. Bardy, F. Vandenbroucke, J. Pegon, H. Martin, 1222-1291; *Docilité au Saint Esprit*, III, J. Lecuyer, C.S.Sp., 1471-1497. The Proceedings of the International Symposium held in Rome for the 16th centenary of the Council of Constantinople, *Atti del Congresso* (qv) assemble practically all the important names in contemporary literature with much bibliographical information in notes to many articles. The *Handbuch der Dogmengeschichte* being edited by M. Schmaus, A. Grillmeier, L. Scheffczyk, M. Seybold, (Herder) has in the Faszikel 1a and Faszikel 1b of Band II, *Trinität in der Schrift und Patristik* and *Trinität in der Scholastik*, both by F. Courth, valuable bibliographies with different chapters.

Most important is the *Bibliotheca Trinitariorum* (*BT*), vols I and II. This is the most comprehensive catalogue of writings on the Holy Trinity ever made. It was produced by D. Edwin Schadel of Bamberg University, with the collaboration of Dieter Brunn and Peter Müller. Dr. Schadel is a faculty member in the School of Philosophy and enjoyed the academic support of the Professor, Dr. Heinrich Beck. The collaborators mentioned worked on the production of the book, typing especially. The author's research was based on the National Union Catalogue, Washington, on the Catalogue of the British Museum and the Catalogue Général, Paris; he also drew on the resources of his own university library, plus interlibrary loans, and personally visited ten of the largest libraries in Germany. Volume I (1984) gives, in alphabetical order by authors, the title of every relevant composition, book, review article, contribution to a collective work, and pamphlet published from the second century to the present decade of the twentieth. This gives over 4,700 items on 622 pages. After some entries there are useful notes on content, viewpoint and even some sectional titles. Modern critical editions are used. The author gives the reasons for his huge endeavour in an introduction, 17 pp., in German, English, French, Italian, Latin, Spanish.

Volume II (1988) gives a supplementary list of authors bringing the total to 5,679; this includes every title appearing since the first volume. Very useful to the student is the provision of analytical indices of volume I: a list of names of writers occurring within the entries in volume I, a list of special forms of representation, an analytical list of persons and one on regions and religions, especially a systematic list of themes or subjects. Here a number of sections like Indwelling, Mission, Person interest the present work, above all does *Pneumatologie* pp. 131-168, per page 3-column entries.

Good bibliographies are found in works cited here: Fr. Congar's (qv) three volumes, *The Holy Spirit*; R. Laurentin, *Catholic Pentecostalism*, London, 1977, pp. 204-222, 230 titles; J.D.G. Dunn (qv), *Jesus and the Spirit*, London, 1975, pp. 457-475, 500 titles, omitting commentaries and dictionary articles; R.P.C. Hanson, *The Search for the Christian God*, Edinburgh, 1988.

Noteworthy also is B. Sesboué, *Bulletin de Pneumatologie,* RSR 76 (1988) 115-128.

BOLOTOV, BASIL (1855-1900)

After a conference in Bonn in 1875 which brought together Orthodox, Angicans and Old Catholics the Russian Holy Synod named a commission to continue the work and to strengthen the links with the Old Catholics.[1] A report from historians was thought necessary; B. with A.L. Kalansky was asked to report on the *Filioque* (qv) in Russian Orthodox history. The final draft was published in the Old Catholic review, *Revue Internationale de Théologie Russe* in 1898, a full French translation was published in the ecumenical review *Istina* in 1973.

B. distinguished three levels of theological affirmation: the level of dogma in the creeds and ecumenical councils, that of individual theologies, and that of the theologoumena, expressions of faith framed by one or more Fathers when the Church was still undivided, and accepted by that undivided Church. B. appended to his thorough

study twenty-seven theses, of which the following are particularly relevant:

"The Russian Orthodox Church regards as a dogma that has to be believed only the following truth: the Holy Spirit proceeds from the Father and is consubstantial with the Father and the Son. The other aspects, insofar as they do not have the same meaning, should be regarded as theologoumena.

"The fact that the idea that the Holy Spirit proceeds, comes or shines from (*ekporeutai, proeisi, eklampei*) the Father through the Son is frequently found in patristic texts, its occurrence in the treatise on the *Orthodox Faith* by John of Damascus, above all its introduction into the synodicon of Tarasius of Constantinople, the orthodoxy of which has been confirmed not only by the East, but also by the orthodox West in the person of the Roman Pontiff Hadrian (or Adrian) and even by the SeventhEcumenical Council, gives to this idea of procession such importance that theologians cannot simply regard it as the private opinion of a Father of the Church, but are bound to accord it the value of an ecumenical theologoumenon, so to speak, with authority everywhere in the orthodox East.

"The opinion that the expression *dia tou Huiou* implies nothing but a temporal mission of the Holy Spirit in the world leans to violent distortions of some patristic texts.

"At least we cannot find fault with the interpretation, according to which the expressions frequently found in the teaching of the Fathers of the Church of the Holy Spirit's coming through the Son and his shining or manifestation from the Father through the Son contain an indication of a mysterious aspect in the activity, the life and the eternal relationships of the Holy Spirit with the Father and the Son, an aspect that is also known as the Holy Spirit's dwelling and remaining in the Son (*meson, anapauomenon*).

"This aspect is the imaginative expression of the identity of nature (*sumphues*) between the Spirit and the other two Persons, and of that incomprehensible truth revealed in the gospel, that the Holy Spirit is the third and the Son is the second Person of the Holy Trinity.

"This doctrine is not identical in meaning with that which is revealed in the words *ek tou Patros ekporeutai*, if these words are interpreted in the strict sense of the technical terms *ekporeutos* and *ekporeutai*.

As a result of this, the Holy Spirit proceeds

from the Father alone in the strict sense of the word *ekporeutos*. This thesis, however, is not a dogma but only a theologoumenon.

"The formula *ex Patre et Filio*, as found in the writings of St. Augustine (qv) is not identical in its terminology, not even in its meaning, with the teaching of the Eastern Fathers.

"The difference in opinions between western and eastern Christians is not so much in the words *ex Patre Filioque* as in the Augustinian idea that is connected with it, namely of a single spiration by the Father and the Son, according to which both form the single principle of the Holy Spirit. This idea is unknown to the Eastern Fathers; as we know none of them ever said that the Son was *spirans* or *sumproboleus*.

"Even as a private opinion we cannot recognize the western *Filioque* as equivalent to the eastern *di'Huiou*.

"Within God's unfathomable plan, however, no protest was made by the Eastern Church at the time of St. Augustine against the view suggested by him.

"Many western Christians who preached the *Filioque* to their flocks lived and died in communion with the eastern Church, and no objection was raised on either side.

"The eastern Church honours the Fathers of the early western Church as it honours its own Fathers. It is therefore quite natural that the West should regard the individual opinions of those Fathers as holy.

"Photius (qv) and those who followed him remained in communion with the western Church without obtaining from that Church an explicit and conciliar denial of the *Filioque* even, as far as we know, without asking for it.

"It was therefore not the question of the *Filioque* which caused the division in the Church.

"The *Filioque*, as an individual theological opinion, ought therefore not to constitute an *impedimentum dirimens* for the re-establishment of communion between the Eastern Orthodox and the Old Catholic Churches."

S. Bulgakov (qv) and P. Evdokimov (qv) accepted B.'s theses. V. Lossky (qv) rejected them outright.[3]

[1]See articles on *Filioque* and *Orthodox, The*; for bibl. in Russian cf. S. Virgulin, *Il Filioque nel Pensiero del Teologo Russo, V.B. Bolotov, Atti del Congresso*, I, 355-362, p. 356 n. 4; M. Jugie, A. A., *Theologia dogmatica Christianorum Orient. ab Eccl. cath. diss.*, II, Paris, 1933, 467-478; id., *Bolotov* in *Catholicisme*, II, Paris, 1949, 116f; S. Salaville, *Bolotov, DHGE* IX, 1937, 669-676; A. Palmieri, DTC, V, 2331-2342; Y.M.J. Congar, O.P., *The Holy Spirit*, III, 193f; *Trinitas*, 55-57; [2]681-712; [3]S.Bulgakov, *Le Paraclet*, Paris, 1944, 99f; P. Evdokimov, *L'Esprit Saint dans la tradition orthodoxe, Paris, 1969, 74f; V. Lossky, In the Image and Likeness of God*, London, 1975, 72.

BONAVENTURE, ST. DOCTOR OF THE CHURCH (c. 1217-1274)[1]

The great Franciscan doctor, the Prince of Mystics, represents the Augustinian tradition still strong despite St. Thomas Aquinas, his contemporary, who had rallied to Aritsotle. B.'s thinking on the Holy Spirit is contained in his commentaries on the *Liber Sententiarum* of Peter Lombard, (qv) *Distinctiones* II, X and XVIII of Bk I and for the Gifts *Dist.* XXXIV, XXXV of Bk III; in the *Collationes de Donis Spiritus Sancti*, the *Collationes in Hexaemeron* and in the *Breviloquium* and the *Itinerarium mentis in Deum*. The treatment of the Gifts must be seen in the general context of the great Doctor's theory and practice of contemplation, as in the whole background of the thirteenth century, an age when the European spirit, led and sustained by the Spirit of God, rose to astonishing heights of holiness.

B.'s theory of the Trinity must be recalled. He sums it up thus: "If you can, then, with the eyes of your spirit grasp the purity of the goodness which is the pure act of the principle of charity that loves with a gratuitous love and a due love that is a mixture of the two, making for perfect diffusion by way of nature and of will—a diffusion in the mode of the Word, in whom all things are said, and in the mode of Gift in whom all things are given—then you will see that from the sovereign communicability of the good there must be a Trinity of the Father, the Son and the Holy Spirit. In them, by reason of the supreme goodness, there must be supreme communicability and, by reason of that supreme communicability, there must also be a sovereign consubstantiality, and by virtue of that sovereign consubstantiality, there must also be a sovereign configurability and, because of (all) that, a sovereign co-equality and, for that reason, a sovereign eternity, and, as a result of that, a sovereign co-intimacy, by virtue of which the one is necessarily in the other through a sovereign circumincession, the one functions with the other through the totally undivided substance, virtue and functioning of the blessed Trinity itself."[2]

Two ideas dominate the Bonaventure doctrine:

the supreme good is self-diffusive, which is a legacy of Pseudo-Dionysius, and love is applied to the intra-divine life, in its perfect form of altruism or friendship. B. had from Richard of St. Victor the idea of *dilectus condignus* and *condilectus*, the distinction between gratuitous love, due or received love and the mixture of the two. He completed his synthesis by the idea of communication or emanation, by mode of nature and by mode of will and liberality. This theme led him to a justification of the existence of the third Person of the Trinity as necessary. This means that he considers the third Person as Love and Gift. He amplifies his explanation of this notion of love. Love can be attributed to all three Persons. How then can it be personal to one Person, the Holy Spirit? Love, he replies, exists in God in the essential and in the notional sense, namely as the personal name of the Holy Spirit. It is in the second sense that the Spirit is the mutual love of the Father and the Son.

B. insists on the theme of love: "we have either not to speak of a person in God who proceeds by mode of love or, if there is such a procession, it must be by mode of perfect reciprocal charity."[3] "The love that the Holy Spirit is does not proceed from the Father insofar as he loves himself, but he proceeds insofar as the one loves the other, because he is a bond."[4] "In divine reality the third Person proceeds by mode of generosity (*liberalitatis*) and is called Gift." The reason for this is the perfection of love, the perfection of the emanation and the perfection of will, and where this exists most generously, it cannot fail to produce a person; and this is the specific reason for this emanation. The Holy Spirit proceeds by the mode of will and of generosity. The third Person proceeds by mode of mutual charity.... Charity taken in a personal sense is the property of the Holy Spirit, essentially it means benevolence, notionally it refers to agreement in spiration."[5]

B. sees the Spirit proceeding from the Father and the Son in a very special manner. "The Spirit is properly called the link or unity of the Father and the Son. Spirit as taken in relation to spirituality is common to the whole Trinity, as it is said in regard to spiration it is proper to the Holy Spirit.... The Holy Spirit proceeds from the Father and the Son, not insofar as they are distinct Persons, but insofar as there is in them one fruitfulness of the will, or one active spiration." "The Holy Spirit proceeds from the Father before the Son in regard to authority, but not in regard to duration or causality or origin ... to be first in causality would be contrary to the unity of essence."[6]

B. explains the subtleties involved in the prior procession of the Son from the Father. The Spirit does not proceed more fully or more perfectly from the Father. He proceeds immediately and through the mediation of the Son. All the time the mystery remains.

As to the role of the Spirit in sanctification, B. is impelled by the very logic of his thought to consider the indwelling and the gift of grace: "The Holy Spirit is given both in his own Person and in the created gift which is grace." He gives a wonderful explanation of different names of the Spirit stressing that the very same Holy Spirit (from the Latin *spiritus*, breath) signifies love as the breath does coming from our lungs, from the very depths of our being, a vital act which does not cease; from love is given the very wrarmth of the soul, as breath gives that of the body. For B. the idea of Gift is of prime importance and he would probably have developed it more fully did the plan of the *Liber Sententiarum* (of Peter Lombard) not limit him.

B. had the advantage of knowing that the distinction between the virtues and the gifts was theologically established: it had been done by Philip the Chancellor in 1235. He built on this foundation a most impressive synthesis, relating the Gifts to the faculties, to the vices to which they are opposed, to the beatitudes towards which they lead. He analyses each Gift in particular with a wealth of spiritual knowledge. In particular he lifts the Gift of fear from the indifferent level at which some writers tend to leave it. It is based on an awareness of God's majesty. The general distinction between indispensable virtues, Gifts, and Beatitudes is that the virtues have a rectifying effect, the Gifts promote spiritual skill or agility, and the Beatitudes give perfection: three words summarize the difference, sufficiency, excellence, superabundance. The virtues deal with works that are of precept, the Gifts with counsels of perfection, the Beatitudes with the perfection of both. The first two are in the domain of merit, the last in that of reward. The virtues become beginners, are attuned to the active life, come within the first phase of the spiritual life, the purgative way; the Gifts are suited to contemplation, befit those making progress in the illuminative way. The Beatitudes belong to the state of perfection, the perfection of the active and contemplative life, the unitive way.[7]

B. not only accomplishes a magnificent theological synthesis; he stands as a faithful interpreter of his age, one resplendent with light, divine illumination and thrust totally directed by the Spirit.

---

[1] *Works,* Quaracchi, ed.; cf. J.G. Bougerol, *Introudction à l'étude de S. Bonaventure*, Paris, 1961; R. Guardini, *Systembildene Elemente in der Theologie Bonaventuras*, 1963, Leiden; De Régnon, II, 549ff; J.F. Bonnefoy, O.F.M., *Le Saint Esprit et ses dons selon St. Bonaventure*, Paris, 1929; E. Longpré, O.F.M., *DHGE* IX, 741-788; id. *DSp* I, (1937), 1768-1843, esp. 1783; Y.-M.J. Congar, O.P., *The Holy Spirit*, III, 109-115; *Trinitas*, 57-58; *Handbuch der Dogmengeschichte*, II, 1b, 126-136, bibl., esp. *Der Hl. Geist als Erlösungsgabe*, 134f; *BT* I, 490-96; II, 220-222; [2] *Itinerarium mentis ad Deum*, VI, 2, Quaracchi ed., V, 311; [3] *In I Sent.* d. X, a. 1, q. 3. p. 199; [4] *In I Sent.* d. XIII, unique art., q. 1, No. 4, p. 231; d. X a. 2. q. 2., p. 202; [5] *In I Sent.* d. X, a. 1. q. 1, 195, 199; [6] *In I Sent.* d., 2020, 204; d. XI, 215; [7] Diagrams to represent the theory, Bonnefoy, *op. cit.*, 216, 217, 220, 221.

BULGAKOV, SERGIUS (1871-1944)[1]

The great Russian Orthodox theologian, a singular proponent of sophiological theology, published one of the few substantial works on the Holy Spirit to appear in the thirties of the present century. He anticipated a whole movement of thought on the Spirit which would follow Vatican II; he also had intuitions on Mary's relationship with the Spirit which are in tune with contemporary thinking. He was a dedicated ecumenist, a member of *Faith and Order*, insistent on the need to present doctrine in its entirety, without theological compromise.

B.'s principal work, *Le Paraclet*, was part of a trilogy not all available in translation. The whole work was planned as an exposition of his sophiological theory. This he derived from Soloviev, but contended that it was patristic; divine wisdom is the explanation of God's relations with his creation. The section of *The Wisdom of God* published in London dealing with *Pentecost* and *Godmanhood* is also relevant to B.'s doctrine of the Spirit.[2] For reasons presently stated B. was opposed by V. Lossky, who worked to have his sophiological doctrine condemned by the Moscow patriarchate in 1935.

B.'s methodology was ahead of his time, the much vaunted "return to the sources" of the Catholic "New Theology" of the forties, which, it is maintained, came into its own in Vatican II: study of Sacred Scripture and the Fathers, with no presuppositions. He has lengthy chapters on the witness of Sacred Scripture, and his book opens with a lengthy introduction on the Holy Spirit in patristic literature; through primitive Christianity, the post-apostolic age, The Apologists, Tertullian, Origen, Athanasius, the Cappadocians, St. Augustine and St. John of Damascus. Even when he is attempting his own synthesis, in which Trinitarian love is central, he returns to St. Basil.

It is on the question of the procession of the Holy Spirit that B. took a highly original line for an Orthodox theologian, the opposite to that of V. Lossky. (qv) Having gone through patristic teaching in the East, with special attention to St. Epiphanius, St. Cyril of Alexandria and St. John of Damascus (qqv), he then surveyed the history of the Filioque controversy, with particular attention to Photius, the Council of Lyons and the Council of Florence. (qqv) He found the controversy sterile and concluded that no dogmatic question was at issue.

B. sought to integrate his sophiological theory with Trinitarian theology, and went on to deal with what he called the kenosis of the Holy Spirit in creation, asserting nonetheless the ubiquity of the Spirit's power. He discusses inspiration in the Old Testament, has significant things to say about Pentecost (qv), and with his deep insights into Marian theology, expounds the Annunciation powerfully: "The Annunciation was a complete and therefore hypostatic descent of the Holy Spirit with his entry to the Virgin Mary ... by his coming into the Virgin Mary he identifies himself in a way with her through her God-motherhood ... he does not at all leave her after the birth of Christ, but remains forever with her in the full force of the Annunciation."[2]

It is useful to supplement this opinion from two other works of the author. It was not an incarnation of the Spirit which took place. "He abides, however, in the ever-Virgin Mary as in a holy temple, while her human personality seems to become transparent to him and to provide him with a human countenance."[3] "If there were not an eternal motherless generation from the Father, there would not be a manless generation from the Mother. In this the one who joins both 'generations' is the Holy Spirit, in his relation to the Son, whom he eternally bears as the Only-begotten of the Father and, in the strength of this communicates the power of generation to his Mother. Therefore the seedless conception is accomplished by the presence of the Holy Spirit."[4]

B. analyses the gifts of Pentecost in different aspects of life, providing a spirituality, even morality, directly related to the Spirit's action. He deals with questions of sex and marriage, not overlooking the valuable, largely ignored concept of sublimation. At times his thinking has a cosmic sweep, but love he interprets most sensitively. His passages on kenosis and accomplishment, and on the eschatological aspect leave one with the certainty that here was a noble, powerful human spirit transcribing his own saintly experience of the divine Spirit in a language universally valid.

[1]Available works with bibl., M. O'Carroll, C.S.Sp., *Theotokos*, 90-92, 332 (art. Holy Spirit); add "The Work of the Holy Spirit in Worship," in *The Christian East* 13 (1932) 30-42; cf. esp., C.L. Graves, *The Holy Spirit in the Theology of Sergius Bulgakov*, Doctoral Dissertation, Basle University, World Council of Churches Geneva, 1972; also *Ephemerides Mariologicae* 3 (1953) 393-446; in *Maria*, ed. H. du Manoir, S.J., A. Wenger, A.A., V, 974-979; VI, B. Schultze, S.J., 229-235; A. Wenger, *Expérience et theologie dans la doctrine de Serge Bulgakov, NRT* 77 (1955) 939-962; *BT*, I, 630-636; II, 222; [2]*Le Paraclet*, Paris, 1946, 238, 39; [3]*The Wisdom of God*, London, 1937, 176; [4]C.L. Graves, *op. cit.*, from Kupina Neopalimaja, p. 158.

C

CALVIN, JOHN (1509-1564)[1]

C. sees an important role for the Church in the salvation of humankind, but the action of the Holy Spirit is for him primarily on the individual; the *testimonium Spiritus Sancti* is thus oriented. This *testimonium* certifies the truth of Scripture, and gives to the soul a perfect interior, personal certainty of the divine promise. This *testimonium* is the means by which the Spirit seals the promise in the heart of the chosen one. The Spirit is the bond by which the soul is united with Christ. But true to his whole theory of justification C. admits no ontological change by the gift. It is by virtue of the promise that one achieves union, and the promise, therefore also the *testimonium*, is rooted in predestination of the individual. The whole doctrine is worked out with that tight logic which characterizes the thinking of C. The Spirit is supremely free and without him means of salvation are null, just as he can deprive of their efficacity means prescribed by God, leading to the damnation of the one who thinks himself saved, but whose damnation may have been decreed. The Spirit is independent of the means he uses. C. was totally convinced of the corruption of humanity and yet imbued with unshakable confidence in the promise received in faith and sealed by the Spirit in man's heart.

In regard to the Spirit's role in the Church certain ideas of C.'s must be remembered. The Spirit is sent by the glorified Christ to apply to the predestined, and to them only, the fruits of Christ's mediation: Christ is the only Mediator. He remains in heaven, with no link between him and the Church, visible and invisible, but sinful on earth. His presence is realised, the force of his glorified body is made effective, by the force of the Spirit. Until the second coming the presence of Christ on earth is excluded. An ontological link between the glorified body of the Lord and the elect, who are the Church, does not exist. In regard to the Eucharist C. speaks of a presence *gratia Spiritus Sancti* or *virtute et gratia Spiritus Sancti*. He thinks of no other kind of presence. Between the Ascension and the parousia there can only be a *repraesentatio Christi* which is effected by the Spirit.

But C. is opposed to an exclusive activity of the Spirit. The Church, for him as for Luther, is the "Mother of Believers." But the Church, visible and invisible, is not mother save to the extent that the Spirit exercises in her his proper activity. For C. the Spirit's action is linked, in the first place, with the Word of the Scripture, and secondly, with the divine Word preached by the Church. Against extremists of his time he defends the link between the Spirit and the Sacraments; but the link is arbitrary and extrinsic; where the gospel is preached in its purity and the Sacraments rightly administered, there is the action of the Spirit, there is the true Church. But it is the Spirit who is dominant, granting to the Church representatives the needed charisms. C. seeks to allow due importance to the Church while recognising its shortcomings: he does not admit immediate, infallible direction of the community leaders by the Spirit. He thought that church councils could be, had been, mistaken. The presumption is in favour, he thinks, of church interpretation of Scripture; thus he can ask for respect for church teaching. But he wishes to retain the role of the individual *testimonium Spiritus Sancti*, to allow for a decision of the believer, who in prayer judges according to this *testimonium*. His eschatology foresees the ending of Christ's mediation at the final judgement but the activity of the Spirit remains in us. In the whole synthesis of Calvin this 'supremacy of the Spirit' is his original contribution to theology; Calvinistic spirituality has been marked by this doctrine of listening to the Spirit and Scripture. But enlarging the function of the Spirit in the work of redemption has been at the expense of the humanity of Christ and of the Scripture. "The same Spirit," he says in a characteristic passage, "who has spoken through the mouths of the prophets must penetrate into our hearts to persuade us that they faithfully proclaimed what had been divinely commanded.... It remains therefore for us to understand that the way to the Kingdom of God is open only to him whose mind has been made new by the illumination of the Holy Spirit."[2]

---

[1]Cf. T.F. Torrance, *A Calvin Treasury, The Heart of the New Translation of the Institutes of the Christian Religion*, Edinburgh, 1963; an anthology, 56-60; for C. bibl., W. Niesel, *Calvin-Bibliographie*, 1901-1959, Munich, 1961; C. Lelievre," *La maîtrise de l'Esprit". Essai critique sur le principe fondamental de la théologie de Calvin*, Cahors, 1901; Th. Preiss, *Le témoignage intérieur du Saint-Esprit*, Neuchâtel-Paris, 1946; E. Grin, "Quelques aspects de la pensée de Calvin sur le Saint-Esprit et leurs enseignements pour nous," *Theologische Zeitschrift*, 3 1947; W. Krusche, *Das Wirken des Heiligen Geistes bei Calvin*, Göettingen, 1957; L. Schummer, *L'Ecclésiologie de Calvin à la lumière de l'Ecclesia Mater*, Dissert. Protestant Faculty of Brussels, 1978, "Du lien du Saint-Esprit et de l'Eglise-Mère," pp. 47-51; [2]*Institutes*, I, (vii), 4, apud T.F. Torrance, p. 57f.

CHARISM[1]

A charism is a free gift of God the Holy Spirit, bestowed on an individual for the good of the Church. The word is used sixteen times by St. Paul (qv), occurs once elsewhere in NT (1 Pet 4:10). The meaning varies, but with time it has been taken in the sense here given, referring therefore to gifts which theologians call *gratiae gratis datae*; their gratuitous quality is distinctive, allows of

them being received by sinners or non-believers (Mt 7:22f; 1 Cor 13:1-3 and cf. Num 22-24; Jn 11:49-52).

The extraordinary gifts were foretold by the Prophet Joel (2:28; cp. Acts 2:16-21). They were promised by Christ to his followers: "'And these signs will accompany those who believe: in my name they will cast out demons; they will speak in new tongues; they will pick up serpents, and if they drink any deadly thing, it will not hurt them; they will lay their hands on the sick and they will recover'" (Mk 16:17f; cp. Mt 10:1, 8 and par; Jn 14:12).

The starting-point and first instance of the gifts was Pentecost (Acts 2:4-13). Mention of them recurs in the narrative fabric of Acts (10:44-46; 19:6). But it is Paul who has left us the fullest account of charisms. Along with one passage from Peter we have from him detailed empirical surveys of an important spiritual phenomenon made in the first age of the Spirit's working in the Church. His words must be studied:

"Having gifts that differ according to the grace given to us let us use them; if prophecy, in proportion to our faith; if service, in our serving; he who teaches, in his teaching; he who exhorts, in his exhortation; he who contributes, in liberality; he who gives aid, with zeal; he who does acts of mercy, with cheerfulness" (Rom 12:6-8).

"Now concerning spiritual gifts, brethren, I do not wish you to be uninformed. You know that when you were heathens, you were led astray by dumb idols, however you may have been moved. Therefore I want you to understand that no one speaking by the Spirit of God ever says 'Jesus be cursed!' and no one can say 'Jesus is Lord' except by the Holy Spirit. Now there are varieties of gifts, but the same Spirit; and there are varieties of service, but the same Lord; and there are varieties of working, but it is the same God who inspires them all in every one. To each is given the manifestation of the Spirit for the common good. To one is given through the Spirit the utterance of wisdom, and to another the utterance of knowledge according to the same Spirit, to another faith by the same Spirit, to another gifts of healing by the one Spirit, to another the working of miracles, to another prophecy, to another the ability to distinguish between spirits, to another various kinds of tongues, to another the interpretation of tongues. All these are inspired by one and the same Spirit, who apportions to each one individually as he wills" (1 Cor 12:1, 4-11).

"Now you are the body of Christ and individually members of it. And God has appointed in the Church first apostles, second prophets, third teachers, then workers of miracles, then healers, helpers, administrators, speakers in various kinds of tongues. Are all apostles? Are all prophets? Are all teachers? Do all work miracles? Do all possess gifts of healing? Do all speak with tongues? Do all interpret? But earnestly desire the higher gifts. And I will show you a more excellent way" (*Ibid.*, 27-31).

Then follows immediately the Pauline hymn to charity, some of which is relevant to what he has just said: "If I speak in the tongues of men and of angels, but have not love, I am a noisy gong or a clanging cymbal. And if I have prophetic powers, and understand all mysteries and all knowledge, and if I have all faith, so as to remove mountains, but have not love, I am nothing.... Love never ends; as for prophecies, they will pass away; as for tongues they will cease; as for knowledge it will pass away. For our knowledge is imperfect and our prophecy is imperfect, but when the perfect comes, the imperfect will pass away.... Make love your aim and earnestly desire the spiritual gifts, especially that you may prophesy" (1 Cor 13:1-2, 8-9; 14:1).

"In the law it is written, 'By men of strange tongues and by the lips of foreigners will I speak to this people, and even then they will not listen to me, says the Lord.' Thus tongues are a sign not for believers, but for unbelievers, while prophecy is not for unbelievers but for believers. If, therefore, the whole church assembles and all speak in tongues, and outsiders or unbelievers enter, will they not say that you are mad? But if all prophesy, and an unbeliever or outsider enters, he is convicted by all, he is called to account by all, the secrets of his heart are disclosed; and so falling on his face, he will worship God and declare that God is really among you. What then, brethren? When you come together, each one has a hymn, a lesson, a revelation, a tongue, or an interpretation. Let all things be done for edification" (*Ibid.*, 21-26).

"There is one body and one Spirit, just as you were called to the one hope that belongs to your call, one Lord, one faith, one Baptism, one God and Father of us all, who is above all and through all and in all. But grace was given to each of us according to the measure of Christ's gift. Therefore it is said, 'When he ascended on high, he led a host of captives, and he gave gifts to men'.... And his gifts were that some should be apostles, some prophets, some evangelists, some pastors and teachers, to equip the saints for the work of ministry, for building up the body of Christ, until we all attain to the unity of the faith and of the knowledge of the Son of God, to mature manhood, to the measure of the stature of the fullness of Christ" (Eph 4:4-8, 11-13).

St. Peter's words may be added: "As each has received a gift, employ it for one another, as good stewards of God's varied grace; whoever speaks, as one who utters oracles of God; whoever renders service, as one who renders it by the strength which God supplies; in order that in everything God may be glorified through Jesus Christ" (1 Pet 4:10-11).

An acceptable classification has been suggested for the Pauline charisms: gifts to teach, to exhort, to confirm and to perform special service.

To teach: the apostles, and their word of wisdom taking this word in a broad sense to include the associates of the twelve and missionaries and preachers of the gospel (1 Cor 12:28; Eph 4:11; Rom 16:7;—for the word of wisdom 1 Cor 12:8); evangelists (Eph 4:11); teachers or doctors (Eph 4:11) and their word of knowledge (1 Cor 12:8).

To exhort: prophecy (1 Cor 12:10; Rom 12:6) and prophets (1 Cor 12:28; Eph 4:11; Acts 13:1); discernment of spirits (1 Cor 12:10); exhortation (Rom 12:8); use of psalms (1 Cor 14:26); gift of tongues (1 Cor 12:10, 28, 30; 13:1; 14:2); gift of the interpretation of tongues (1 Cor 12:10, 30; 14:5, 13, 27f).

To confirm: faith (1 Cor 12:9), not the virtue of faith but an intuition of God's miraculous intervention; healing (1 Cor 12:9, 28, 30); miracles of other kinds (1 Cor 12:10, 28, 30).

To perform special service: assisting or help (1 Cor 12:28), to the poor, the sick, the destitute, almsgivers, performers of *works of mercy*; governing or power of administration (1 Cor 12:28).

There has been a certain difficulty in recent times in developing a theology of the charisms; they were, if not suspect, kept on the periphery. In an important doctrinal Encyclical, *Mystici Corporis Christi* (qv) Pius XII (qv) took account of them: "But it must not be supposed that this co-ordinated or organic structure of the Church is confined exclusively to the grades of the hierarchy or, as a contrary opinion holds, that it consists only of charismatics or persons endowed with miraculous powers, though these, be it said, will never be lacking in the Church."[2]

It was Vatican II (qv), however, after the

Council Fathers had heard interventions on the subject, notably by Cardinal Suenens, which restored the ancient idea, convinced of its validity: "The Holy Spirit sanctifies the People of God through the ministry and the Sacraments. However, for the exercise of the apostolate he gives the faithful special gifts besides (cf. 1 Cor 12:7) 'allotting them to each as he wills' (1 Cor 12:11) so that each and all, putting at the service of others the grace received may be 'as good stewards of God's varied gifts' (1 Pet 4:10), for the building of the whole body in charity (cf. Eph 4:16). From the reception of these charisms, even the most ordinary ones, there arises for each of the faithful the right and duty of exercising them in the Church and in the world for the good of men and the development of the Church, of exercising them in the freedom of the Holy Spirit, who 'breathes where he wills' (Jn 3:8), and at the same time in communion with his brothers in Christ, and with his pastors especially. It is for the pastors to pass judgment on the authenticity and good use of these gifts, not certainly with a view to quenching the Spirit but to testing everything and keeping what is good (cf. 1 Thess 5:12, 19, 21)."[3]

Thus the Council in the Decree on the Lay Apostolate. The basic text, the Constitution on the Church, speaks with equal lucidity: "It is not only through the Sacraments and the ministrations of the Church that the Holy Spirit makes holy the People of God, leads them and enriches them with his virtues. Allotting his gifts according as he wills (1 Cor 12:11), he also distributes special graces among the faithful of every rank. By these gifts he makes them fit and ready to undertake various tasks and offices for the renewal and building up of the Church, as it is written, 'the manifestation of the Spirit is given to everyone for profit' (1 Cor 12:7). Whether these charisms be very remarkable or more simple and widely diffused, they are received with thanksgiving and consolation since they are fitting and useful for the needs of the Church. Extraordinary gifts are not to be rashly desired, nor is it from them that the fruits of apostolic labours are to be presumptuously expected. Those who have charge over the Church should judge the genuineness and proper use of these gifts, through their office, not indeed to extinguish the Spirit, but to test all things and hold fast to what is good (cf. 1 Thess 5:12, 19-21)."[4]

Pope Paul VI (qv) gave advice to members of the charismatic movement during their world congress in Rome in 1975. He asked them to re-member fidelity to the authentic teaching of the Church, that all gifts from God should be received gratefully and that only love makes a perfect Christian.[5] One may add that the Pauline passages on charisms are too often isolated from their general context, thereby permitting lack of proportion in the Christian outlook. In practice this may happen when a personal conversion is directly linked with some charismatic happening (see especially article John Paul II).

Fr Y.-M.J.Congar, who himself would be an instructive case history in the action of the Spirit, so vast and enlightened is his theological corpus, thinks that the theology of charisms has been marred by two "serious defects." "On the one hand there is a false contrast in many of these publications which is elevated to a false problem, between 'charism' and 'institution' or institutional functions. This goes back to Harnack, Sohm and Troeltsch. Theological problems of pneumatology and ecclesiology are reduced to the level of the sociology of religion. On the other hand, 'charism' is often regarded as a particular gift of the Spirit representing a special register of activities. (These two defects are, of course, closely linked)."[6]

The immediate, determining source of the charisms is the Holy Spirit. The Spirit is, as Hans Urs von Balthasar taught, to us the most mysterious of the divine Persons. In the charisms he reveals himself in flashes of illumination. Here everything is personal, in, through, from him. He is the God of surprises because the charisms are surprising, surprising by their number in some cases, as St. Vincent Ferrer or St. John Bosco, or by the depth and power of one particular charism, as in St. Catherine of Siena, St. Teresa. His charismatic action is personal; it enlarges, strengthens the human personality he chooses.

The dynamic element in the Church is circumscribed by personal dimensions, human and divine. Charisms are given with the sovereign freedom of the Spirit. They are given by him for the good of the body, but he chooses the individual recipient, the kind of charism, the degree of spiritual intensity, the frequency, the moment and situation within which he acts. He knows with total certainty the capacity for reception by the subject on whom he acts; he judges the power of possible fidelity; he measures the level of response that may be evoked from the surrounding milieu. He provides for abuse of free will in the subject of the charism or in those who should benefit thereby.

The history of charisms in the entire past of the

Church from Pentecost to the present time has yet to be written: an arduous task. The notion that they were a feature of Church life restricted to the first phase of Christianity is now abandoned. We need also to nuance the idea that they are essentially extraordinary, fleeting, rarely experienced, elitist, constituting a privileged class. We need to examine how their exercise may be bound to a permanent ministry, of the kind that maintains the existence and unity of the Church, the fruitful celebration of the Eucharist, the creative, Christ-like exercise of authority (qv).

[1]General surveys with bibl. references: Y.-M.J. Congar, *The Holy Spirit*, I, 35-37, 42; R. Laurentin, *Catholic Pentecostalism*, New York, London, 1977; L. Cerfaux, *The Christian in the Theology of St. Paul*, London, 1967, 242-261; cf. J.A. Engelmann, *Von den Charismen im allgemeinen und den Sprachengaben im besonderen*, Ratisbon, 1848: H. Weinel, *Die Wirkungen des Geistes und der Geister im nachapostolischen Zeitalter bis auf Irenäus*, Tübingen, 1898; H. Gunkel, *Die Wirkungen des heiligen Geistes nach der populären Anschauung der apostolischen Zeit und der Lehre des Apostels Paulus*, 3 Göttingen, 1909; G.P. Wetter, *Charis, Ein Beitrag z. Geschichte d. ältesten Christentums* (Untersuch. zum Neuen Testament, 5) Leipzig, 1913, 168-187; T. Weatherspoon, *The Ministry in the Church in Relation to Prophecy and Spiritual Gifts (Charismata)*, London, 1916; W. Reinhardt, *Das Wirken des heiligen Geistes im Menschen nach den Briefen des Apostels Paulus* (Freiburger theol. Studien, 22, Heft), Freiburg i. B., 1918; K.L. Schmidt, *Die Pfingsterzählung und d. Pfingstereignis* (Arbeiten z. Religionsgeschichte d. Urchristentums, Bd. 1, H. 2), Leipzig, 1919; B. Maréchaux *Les charismes du Saint Esprit*, Paris, 1921; F. Buchsel, *Der Geist Gottes im N.T.*., Gütersloh, 1926; J. Brosch, *Charismen und Ämter in der Urkirche*, Bonn, 1951; L. Buonaiuti, *"I Carismi"*, *Ricerche religiose*, 4 (1928), 1928, 259-261; I. Goma Civit, *Ubi Spiritus Dei, illic Ecclesia et omnis gratia*, Barcelona 1954; H. Schlier, *Die Zeit der Kirche. Exegetische Aufsätze und Vorträge*, Freiburg i. B., 1956; D. Iturrioz, "Carismas. De la Encicla 'Mystici Corporis' al Concilio Vaticano," *EstEcl*, 30 (1956), 481-494; *id.*, "Los carismas en la Iglesia. La doctrina carismal en la Const. 'Lumen Gentium,'" *ibid.*, 43 (1968), 181-233; A. Dietzel, "Beten im Geist. Eine religionsgeschichtliche Parallele aus dem Hodayot zum Paulinischen Beten im Geist," *Theol. Zeitschr.*, 13 (1957), 12-32; Garcia Extremeno, "Iglesia, Jerarquia y Carisma," *La Ciencia Tomista*, 89 (1959), 3-64; H. Greeven, "Die Geistesgaben bei Paulus," *Wort und Dienst*, 7 (1959), 111-120; K. Wennemer, "Die charismatische Begabung der Kirche nach dem hl. Paulus," *Scholastik*, 34 (1959), 503-525; S. Tromp, S.J., *Corpus Christi quod est Ecclesia*, III, *De Spiritu Corporis Christi anima*, Rome 1960, 295-326; K. Stadler, *Das Werk des Geistes in her Heiligung bei Paulus*, Zurich, 1962; P. Rodriguez, "Carisma e institucion en la Iglesia," *Studium* 1966, 489ff; H. Schürmann, *Les carismes spirituels, L'Eglise de Vatican II* (Unam Sanctam 51b), ed. Y.-M.J. Congar, O.P., 1966, 541-573; H. Küng, *The Church*, London, 1967, 105-203, esp. 179-191; M.A. Chevalier, *Esprit de Dieu, paroles d'hommes. Le rôle de l'Esprit dans les ministères de la parole selon l'apôtre Paul*, (Bibl. theol.), Neuchâtel, 1966, bibl., K. Rahner, *The dynamic element in the Church*, London, 1964; G. Hasenhuttl, *Charisma, Ordnungsprinzip der Kirche*, (Ökumenische Forschungen 1/5; Freiburg i. B., 1970 with review Y.-M.J. Congar, *RSPT* 55 (1971), 341-42; U. Brockhaus, *Charisma und Amt. Die paulinische Charismenlehre auf dem Hintergrund der frühchristlichen Gemeindefunktionen*, Wuppertal, 1972; J. Hainz, *Ekklesia. Strukturen paulinischer Gemeinde-Theologie und Gemeinde-Ordnung*, Regensburg, 1972, 333-35, 338; G. Rombaldi, "Uso e significato di 'Carisma' nel Vaticano II," *Greg.*, 55 (1974), 141-62; B.N. Wambacq, "le mot 'charisme,'" *NRT* 97 (1975), 345-355; A.-M. Monléon, "L'expérience des charismes, manifestations de l'Esprit en vue du bien commun," *Istina*, 21 (1976) 340-373; *Catholic Biblical Encyclopaedia*, J.E. Steinmueller and K. Sullivan, NT, 1949, 100-104; H. Conzelmann, *TDNT*, IX, 402-406; J. Brosch, *LTK* I, 455-57; J. and K. Rahner, *LTK* II, 1025-30; H. Leclercq, *DACL* I, 1233-44; C. Boyer, *EC* III, 793-951; A. Lemmonyer *DBS* I, 1233-44; X. Duclos, *DSp* II, 1 503-567; *BT* II, 65; [2]17, *AAS* 35 (1943), 200; cf. 47, *ibid.*, 215; [3]*Decree on the Lay Apostolate*, 3; [4]*Constitution on the Church*, 12; [5]Address quoted E.D. O'Connor, C.S.C., *Pope Paul VI and the Holy Spirit*, Notre Dame, 1978, 228f; [6]*The Holy Spirit*, I. 35.

CHARISMATIC MOVEMENT[1]

The Catholic Charismatic Movement is twenty years old. It originated in an experience of the Spirit in Duquesne University, Pittsburgh, in 1967 and its growth and expansion in the intervening period has been phenomenal. René Laurentin calculates that in 1975 there were throughout the world between two and four million members; the number, he thought, may have been doubling annually. The movement has its characteristic features, prayer meetings, talking in tongues, periodical publications, congresses, national, regional, international and world. A very significant moment in the history of the movement was the international congress in Rome in 1975. It brought a direct encounter with the Pope, Paul VI, (qv) who had followed vigilantly the development thus far, and was changing his opinion on the basis of such practical knowledge, and as the members proved responsive to remarks which might denote reservation on his part.

The Rome congress also removed misunderstanding about the relationship between the charismatic movement and Marian outlook and piety. There was not, as some had insinuated, any reason whatever for conflict, competition or suspicion. As the charismatic congress was taking place in the Eternal City, Marian theologians were also holding an international congress and this was followed by an international Marian Congress, a gathering oriented towards pastoral and devotional concerns. The theme that year was Mary and the Holy Spirit. The two international assemblies exchanged lecturers. The Legate to the Marian Congress was Cardinal J.L. Suenens, who had in the preceding years played a notable part in the charismatic movement. He had a lifelong commitment to Marian idealism, apostolate and devotion in his association with the Legion of Mary, for which he became a theological apologist. His well-known work, *A New Pentecost*, highly relevant to the charismatic movement, had a chapter on Mary and the Spirit. His interventions in the course of discussion in Vatican II on charisms and on Our Lady had shown that he saw the profound theological validity for this idea.

Theologians sympathetic to all this growth do nonetheless raise certain questions. Fr. Yves-M.J. Congar, O.P., from such people deserves respectful consideration.[2] In his monumental work on the Holy Spirit he submits some points for consideration—having first acknowledged fully the positive achievement of the Charismatical Renewal. Use of the word "charismatic" can cause difficulties. It could create the impression that those who benefit by the charisms of the Spirit are a recognisable, exclusive number; are others then to go without the charisms which are so much spoken of? Are the charisms sought by the members extraordinary phenomena? Are speaking in tongues, "prophecy," healing, of this kind and does it mean that apart from such extraordinary, almost exceptional, happenings, there is place for nothing else that could be given the name?

Fr. Congar pushes his analysis further, though with respect and an obvious desire to help. Is there a danger of exaggerating the direct link with God, of omitting in the Christian life what can and should be thought out, planned and done by reason illumined by faith? God gives guidance and help, but he respects his own creation and its resources. The saints trusted God absolutely and left nothing at all to chance.

The reading of Scripture is, the same writer would contend, too closely related to personal experience. The great Doctors of the Church who brought holiness as well as knowledge to their interpretation of Scripture, did not minimize the role of the intellect. Sacred Scripture must be understood spiritually, but this very intellectual effort is needed to be spiritual.

Group experience, which is part of the life of the movement is, at times, as easily psychic in its origin as spiritual. The possibility is there. True,

this may be said about all human experience, all human striving; all is vulnerable to self-deceit, to confusion between natural and supernatural phenomena. Vigilance is clearly needed to avoid this confusion.

What is pointed out in these critical remarks is not essential to the movement, not such as to call in question its entire meaning and validity. It is rather to show the dangers which surround a high experience of its kind. The higher the Christian level on which souls live and move the greater is the risk that human frailty will manifest itself. The Charismatic Movement is a lived experience of the Spirit, in which fellowship, which is the essence of Christian life, operates without hindrance or inhibition. This transcends any risk and has the resource to avert it.

To ensure full use of this resource sound theological advice is indispensable. The Catholic Charismatic Movement has been fortunate in this regard. Theologians of stature have studied it in theory and practice, generally with balanced procedures and favourable findings. In Germany Heribert Mühlen (qv) has brought his special expertise in the theology of the Spirit to bear on the movement. In France the veteran Yves-M.J. Congar (qv) has done likewise, devoting a large section of his three-volume work, *I believe in the Holy Spirit* (II, pp. 145-228) to his analysis and assessment, from which we have already drawn; in France too René Laurentin has devoted an informative monograph to the subject, as he has been available for lectures to meetings and congresses. His work is a mine of bibliographical information.

The United States and Canada have made a notable contribution to the doctrinal foundation of the movement, appropriate in view of the fact that in that area what is called "Classic Pentecostalism" (qv) arose. Francis Sullivan of the Gregorian University has scrutinized theologically the principles and practices of the worldwide phenomenon. E.D. O'Connor, C.S.C., who has rendered enormous service already to Marian theology, author of the invaluable study of Paul VI and the Holy Spirit, published a basic work which helped many, in 1971, *The Pentecostal Movement in the Catholic Church*. Killian McDonnell, O.S.B., also experienced in scientific theological research, author of an important monograph on Calvin, a noted ecumenist, has notably added to the relevant literature. He was the principal redactor of the Statement of the *Theological Principles of the Catholic Charismatic Movement,* issued in 1973; he did have the collaboration of seven theologians and pastors, Heribert Mühlen among them. His published work covers essential doctrinal themes on the Holy Spirit, the theology of Baptism in the Spirit (qv), the repercussions of the movement on ecumenism, and collation for public readership of the church pronouncements at different levels of authority, papal and episcopal.

A landmark in theological thinking on the movement was the "Malines Document." This was drawn up at a conference held there, sponsored by Cardinal Suenens. It appeared as "*Le Renouveau charismatique. Orientations théologiques et pastorales*" in *Lumen Vitae* (Brussels) 29 (1974), 367-404. It was issued in Notre Dame, Indiana, 1974 as *Theological and Pastoral Orientations* on the Catholic Charismatic Renewal; it gives a theological basis for the whole movement, refers in an enlightened way to the New Testament, offers advice on discernment. Similar trends were noted in the statements by Paul VI (qv) and John Paul II (qv) and the episcopal statements, Canadian, American, West Indian and Belgian. (see art. Baptism in the Spirit).

---

[1]For bibl. cf. R. Laurentin, *Catholic Pentecostalism,* London, 1977, 204-222; cf. also for bibl. E.D. O'Connor, *The Pentecostal Movement in the Catholic Church,* Notre Dame, 1971, pp. 295-301; id., NCE XVII, 104-106; F.A. Sullivan, *Charisms and Charismatic Renewal,* Ann Arbor, 1982; id., DS XII 1036-1052; K. and D. Ranaghan, *Catholic Pentecostals,* Paramus, 1969; esp., K. McDonnell, O.S.B., *Charismatic Renewal and the Churches,* New York, 1976; *The Charismatic Renewal and Ecumenism,* Paramus, 1978, id., *Presence, Power and Praise, Documents on the Charismatic Movement,* 3 vols., Collegeville, 1980; id., *Open the Windows: the Pope and the Charismatic Renewal,* South Bend, 1986, also distributed by the international office in Rome: for doctrinal background cf. K. McDonnell, *A Trinitarian Theology of the Holy Spirit,* ThSt 46 (1985), 191-227; *id., The Determinative Doctrine of the Holy Spirit, Theology Today,* 39 (1982) 145-149; *id., Catholic Pentecostalism, Problems in Evaluation,* Dialog, 9 Winter 1970; [2]Y.-M.J. Congar, *The Holy Spirit,* II, 202-212.

CHRIST THE LORD[1]

Christology, it is nowadays maintained, gains by interpretation in the light of the Spirit. The role of the Spirit in the life, mission and achievement of Christ is so important, and so explicitly stated in the NT that this approach is warranted. One theme, the Christ event, and the other, the Spirit, Gift of God, origin of every gift, are, with profound reflection, mutually enriching. This is a change in methodology which should be welcomed.

The biblical evidence is strong. The Incarnation is revealed to us as a direct effect of the Spirit's action. The words of the angel in Lk 1:35 show a necessary relationship between Christ and the Spirit. Mary's consent followed the promise that the Son of God would become her Son through the action of the Spirit.

This role of the Spirit in the physical and psychic nature of Christ marked his entire human existence, still does so. It explains not only the virginal conception, but the virgin birth. It did not lessen, it enhanced his autonomy, his freedom, his independence of mind. These were expressed within a human endowment fashioned from the Virgin Mary by the Spirit.

A new dimension was added to Christ's activity after the Baptism (qv) when, as all four evangelists narrate, the Spirit descended on him. The parallel with Mary is instructive. Whereas St. Luke deems it necessary to state explicitly that Zechariah and Elizabeth and Simeon were "filled with the Spirit" or "led" by the Spirit, he does not preface his account of any action or saying of Mary by any such phrase: for example, before she pronounced her Fiat, before her departure to visit Elizabeth, or before she pronounced the Magnificat, or gave birth miraculously to the child, or "kept all these things in her heart, pondering them" (Lk 2:19, 51); or presented Jesus in the Temple or, after the three days' loss, addressed him with her anxious query. Clearly St. Luke assumed that since the descent of the Spirit on Mary at the Annunciation he remained with her as an active power.

It is likewise with Jesus. After the descent of the Spirit on him in the Jordan the evangelists, all four this time, appear to assume that he was constantly under the influence of the Spirit. St. Luke does make this assumption explicit at certain moments. "And Jesus, full of the Holy Spirit, returned from the Jordan, and was led by the Spirit for forty days in the wilderness, tempted by the devil" (4:1, 2). Luke reports Jesus as promising the Holy Spirit: "'If you then, who are evil know how to give good gifts to your children, how much more will the heavenly Father give the Holy Spirit to those who ask him'" (11:13). "'And when they bring you before the synagogues and the rulers and the authorities, do not be anxious how you are to answer or what you are to say; for the Holy Spirit will teach you in that very hour what you ought to say'" (12:12).

Jesus is represented as referring to the Spirit's

presence in him and power through him. "'And if I cast out demons by the Beelzebul, by whom do your sons cast them out? Therefore they shall be your judges. But if it is by the Spirit of God that I cast out demons, then the Spirit of God has come among you.'" (Mt 12:27, 28). On that occasion too Jesus refers to the "blasphemy against the Spirit" (31).

Again St. Luke reports the incident of Jesus' entry to the synagogue of Nazareth. "He opened the book and found the place where it was written: 'The Spirit of the Lord is upon me, because he has anointed me to preach the good news to the poor. He has sent me to proclaim release to the captives and recovering of sight to the blind, to set at liberty those who are oppressed, and to proclaim the acceptable year of the Lord.' And he closed the book and gave it back to the attendant and sat down and the eyes of all in the synagogue were fixed upon him. And he began to say to them, 'Today this scripture has been fulfilled in your hearing'" (Lk 4:17-21).

When, therefore, Jesus, in the last discourse reported by St. John (qv), the most important gospel statement on the Spirit, instructed the Apostles, he was drawing on his own experience. His words could be taken as a summary of his own experience as a man, with due allowance for the difference between his all-perfect human nature and the frailty of the Apostles: "But the Counsellor, the Holy Spirit, whom the Father will send in my name, he will teach you all things and bring to your remembrance all that I have said to you'" (Jn 14:26). "'When the Spirit of truth comes, he will guide you into all the truth; for he will not speak on his own authority, but whatever he hears he will speak, and he will declare to you the things that are to come. He will glorify me, for he will take what is mine and declare it to you. All that the Father has is mine; therefore I said that he will take what is mine and declare it to you'" (Jn 16:13-15).

Jesus had been taught "all things" by the Spirit, as Isaiah foretold in the prophecy which Jesus took to himself at Nazareth. The problem for the theologian is then to pursue the analysis of his knowledge as it unfolds and show how this came to his mind from the Spirit, one with his divine personality in the godhead: how the human nature existing in and through the Word, the sacred humanity of Jesus, was open to the Spirit, receptive of his continuous varied influence: taking the great lines of illumination which would be his

revelation to the world, his statement of Trinitarian existence, of his own saving mission, the high moral code of the Sermon on the Mount, his idea of the Church with its authority and Sacraments, especially his Eucharistic message in word and reality.

Through the Spirit Jesus became the great communicator of all time, using and perfecting a unique homiletic device, the parable, and enlightening us, as Vatican II says, "by the total fact of his presence and self-manifestation—by words and works, signs and miracles, but above all by his death and glorious resurrection from the dead, and finally by sending the Spirit of truth." The miracles open up a vast perspective of the Spirit's action. So does the death (qv) of Christ and of those who die in and with him.

It is in the communication of the Spirit's power to Jesus that we shall find the ultimate answer, which does not remove the mystery, to the problem of Jesus' self-knowledge. The action of the Spirit on his soul disposed it to the communion with the godhead of the second divine Person with which it was united substantially, a communion through which the soul would know the Word in an utterly unique way. He received everything that was not excluded by the lifelong programme of kenosis, or self-emptying, which he had deliberately embraced (Phil 2:7).

The Gifts of the Spirit attaining their fullness in Jesus gave a unique perfection to his prayer (qv). This prayer, we know, was constantly addressed to the Father so that there was a wondrous interplay of Trinitarian life in the soul of the Lord.

Death for Jesus was entirely unique, a moment of time capable of expansion beyond every physical limit, the beginning of his total mastery over time. This mastery would be formally marked by the Spirit. "When Jesus had received the vinegar, he said, 'It is finished'; and he bowed his head and gave up (handed over) the Spirit" (Jn 19:30). The Spirit raised him from the dead: "If the Spirit of him who raised Jesus from the dead dwells in you, he who raised Christ Jesus from the dead will give life to your mortal bodies also through the Spirit who dwells in you" (cp. Rom 1:3; 8:11). "He was manifested in the flesh, vindicated in the Spirit, seen by angels, preached among the nations, believed on in the world, raised up to glory" (1 Tim 3:16). "For Christ also died for sins once for all, the righteous for the unrighteous, that he might bring us to God, being put to death in the flesh, but made alive in the Spirit" (1 Pet 3:18).

The great Gift of the risen Jesus to the Apostles was the Spirit, given for the forgiveness of sins. In this Johannine "Pentecost," the Apostles are fully commissioned for their essential task: "Jesus said to them again, 'Peace be with you. As the Father has sent me, even so, I send you.' And when he had said this he breathed on them, and said to them, 'Receive the Holy Spirit. If you forgive the sins of any, they are forgiven; if you retain the sins of any, they are retained'" (Jn 20:21-23).

Throughout the whole lifework of Jesus, as John narrates it, the Spirit works in and through him. Like Paul (qv) the evangelist sees a close partnership between them. With so much evidence pointing the way, it is surprising that some recent Christologies scarcely advert to the plenary role of the Spirit.

_____

[1]Cf. Y.-M.J. Congar, O.P. *The Holy Spirit*, III, 1965-173; H. Mühlen, *Una mystica persona. Eine Person in vielen Personen*, Paderborn, 1964; J.D.G. Dunn, "Rediscovering the Spirit," *Expository Times*, 84 (1972-1973), 9-12; W. Kasper, *Jesus the Christ*, London, 1976; *id., Esprit-Christ-Eglise, L'expérience de l'Esprit. Mélanges E. Schillebeeckx*, Paris, 1976, 47-69; *id., Die Kirche als Sakrament des Geistes*, Freiburg, 1975, 14-55; P.J. Rosato, "Spirit Christology. Ambiguity and Promise," *TheolSt* 38 (1977), 423-449; P.J.A.M. Schoonenberg, "Spirit Christology and Logos Christology," *Bijdragen*, 38 (1977), 350-375; H. Urs von Balthasar, *Spiritus Creator*, Einsiedeln, 1968; *BT* II, 99.

CHURCH, THE

The Church took its origin in the immediate aftermath of the descent of the Spirit at Pentecost (qv). There is then a close relationship between them.[1] We should recall first the relationship between the Holy Trinity and the Church. This is a theme revived by Vatican II, which treated of the role of the Father, the Son and the Holy Spirit in three successive articles in the dogmatic Constitution on the Church, to conclude by adopting the words of St. Cyprian (qv): "Hence the universal Church is seen to be 'a people brought into unity from the unity of the Father, the Son and the Holy Spirit.'"[2] The annotation refers to two other Fathers of the Church, St. Augustine[3] and St. John of Damascus.[4] It is clear from the article on St. Ambrose that he also thought on these lines.

The Council speaks thus of the Spirit and the Church: "When the work which the Father gave the Son to do on earth (cf. Jn 17:4) was accomplished, the Holy Spirit was sent on the day of Pentecost in order that he might continually sanctify the Church, and that, consequently, those who believe might have access through Christ in one Spirit to the Father (cf. Eph 2:18). He is the Spirit of life, the fountain of water springing up to eternal life (cf. Jn 4:47; 7:38, 39). To men, dead in sin, the Father gives life through him, until the day when, in Christ, he raises to life Father their mortal bodies (cf. Rom 8:10-11). The Spirit dwells in the Church and in the hearts of the faithful, as in a temple (cf. 1 Cor 3:16; 6:19). In them he prays and bears witness to their adoptive sonship (cf. Gal 4:6; Rom 8:15-16 and 26). Guiding the Church in the way of all truth (cf. Jn 16:13) and unifying her in communion and in the works of ministry, he bestows upon her varied hierarchic and charismatic gifts, and in this way directs her; and he adorns her with his fruits (cf. Eph 4:11-12; 1 Cor 12:4; Gal 5:22). By the power of the Gospel he permits the Church to keep the freshness of youth. Constantly he renews her and leads her to perfect union with her Spouse. For the Spirit and the Bride both say to Jesus, the Lord: 'Come' (cf. Apoc 22:17)." (Constitution on the Church, 4).

Again in the Decree on the Church's Missionary Activity we read: "Now, what was once preached by the Lord, or fulfilled in him for the salvation of mankind, must be proclaimed and spread to the ends of the earth (Acts 1:8), starting from Jerusalem (cf. Lk 24:27), so that what was accomplished for the salvation of all men may, in the course of time, achieve its universal effect. To do this, Christ sent the Holy Spirit from the Father to exercise inwardly his saving influence and to promote the spread of the Church. Without doubt the Holy Spirit was at work in the world before Christ was glorified. On the day of Pentecost, however, he came down on the disciples that he might remain with them forever (cf. Jn 14:16); on that day the Church was openly displayed to the crowds, and the spread of the Gospel among the nations, through preaching, was begun. Finally, on that day was foreshadowed the union of all peoples in the catholicity of the faith by means of the Church of the new alliance, a Church which speaks every language, understands and embraces all tongues in charity, and thus overcomes the dispersion of Babel. The 'Acts of the Apostles' began with Pentecost, just as Christ was conceived in the Virgin Mary with the coming of the Holy Spirit and was moved to begin his ministry by the descent of the same Holy Spirit, who came down upon him while he was praying. Before freely laying down his life for the world, the Lord Jesus organized the apostolic ministry and promised to send the Holy Spirit in such a way that both would be always and everywhere associated in the fulfilment of the work of salvation. Throughout the ages the Holy Spirit makes the entire Church 'one in communion and ministry, and provides her with different hierarchical and charismatic gifts', giving life to ecclesiastical structures, being, as it were their soul, and inspiring in the hearts of the faithful that same sense of mission which impelled Christ himself. He even at times visibly anticipates apostolic action, just as in various ways he unceasingly accompanies and directs it" (art. 3, 4).

The Council repeats the doctrine taught by Leo XIII (qv) in *Divinum Illud* (qv) and by Pius XII (qv) in *Mystici Corporis Christi* (qv): the Spirit is the soul of the Church. It does so with perhaps less emphasis than that placed on the truth by the Popes: "In order that we might be unceasingly renewed in him (Eph 4:23) (Christ) has shared with us his Spirit who, being one and the same in head and members, gives life to, unifies and moves the whole body. Consequently his work could be compared by the Fathers to the function that the principle of life, the soul, fulfils in the human body." (Constitution on the Church, 7). "Being, as it were their soul" and "could be compared" are not as explicit, perhaps, as these words of Pius XII, quoting his predecessors: "This presence and operation of the Spirit of Christ (in the Church) has been vigorously and compendiously described by our wise predecessor of immortal memory, Leo XIII, in the following words: 'It is enough to state that, since Christ is the Head of the Church, the Holy Spirit is her soul.'"[5] One reason for the variation in the affirmation is to be sought in the ecclesiology of Vatican II. Whereas Pius XII thought of the Church essentially as the Mystical Body, with which he identified the Catholic Church, Vatican II took the concept of the People of God as the key to its synthesis. The Council certainly taught the doctrine of the Mystical Body: "For by communicating his Spirit, Christ mystically constitutes as his body those brothers of his who are called together from every nation." The principle thus enunciated is developed through several paragraphs of the same article 7 of the Constitution of the Church. But in the Council's over-all view the idea is somewhat displaced by that of the People of God, which was taken in chapter 2, just after the Mystery of the Church, basic therefore to the whole treatise. This too explains why the Council did not say that the Catholic Church is the one true Church. It chose rather to say: the true Church 'subsists' in the Catholic Church.

Pius XII, however, merits fuller consideration. He went back to the mysteries of Christ's redemptive action: "If it was by his death that our Saviour became, in the full and complete sense of the word, the Head of the Church, it was also through his blood that the Church became enriched with that most abundant communication of the Spirit which has divinely distinguished her since the 'Son of man' was raised up and glorified on his cross of pain. Formerly, as St. Augustine observes, the dew of the gifts of the Paraclete had descended only on Gideon's fleece, that is upon the people of Israel; but the fleece was now dried up and abandoned, and with the rending of the veil of the temple that dew spread out in abundance to bathe the whole earth, that is, the Catholic Church, which was to know no boundaries of race or territory. In the first moment of the Incarnation the Son of the Eternal Father had adorned with the fullness of the Holy Spirit the human nature which was substantially united with himself that it might be an appropriate instrument of the divinity in the bloody work of the Redemption. In like manner now, in the hour of his precious death, he willed his Church to be enriched with the most copious gifts of the Paraclete, so that in distributing the divine fruits of the Redemption it might be an effective and never-failing instrument of the Incarnate Word."[6]

The Pope goes on to relate Pentecost (qv) to the Church: "Having established the Church in his blood, he fortified it on the day of Pentecost with special power from on high. After solemnly installing in his exalted function him whom he had previously appointed to be his Vicar, he had ascended into heaven; and there, sitting at the right hand of the Father, he willed now to make known and promulgate his Bride by means of the visible descent of the Holy Spirit, coming with the sound of a mighty wind and with tongues of fire. When he himself was beginning his work of preaching he had been manifested by the Eternal Father, through the Holy Spirit under the form of a dove descending and remaining on him. So now in like manner, when the Apostles were about to begin their sacred work of preaching, Christ our Lord sent his Spirit from heaven to touch them with tongues of fire and, like a divine finger, to indicate the supernatural mission and function of the Church."[7]

The Pope was not satisfied with this treatment,

which located the moments of the Spirit in salvation history. He made a deeper analysis of the Spirit's role: how the Church draws life from him. "If now, we carefully consider this divine principle of life and power given by Christ inasmuch as it constitutes the very well-spring of every created gift and grace, we shall easily understand that it is none other than the Paraclete, the Spirit who proceeds from the Father and the Son, and who in a special manner is called 'the Spirit of Christ' or the 'Spirit of the Son' (Rom 8:9; 2 Cor 3:17; Gal 4:6). For it was with this Spirit of grace and truth that the Son of God adorned his soul in the Virgin's immaculate womb; he is the Spirit who delights to dwell in the Redeemer's pure soul as in his favourite temple; he is the Spirit whom Christ merited for us on the Cross with the shedding of his own blood; the Spirit whom he bestowed upon the Church for the remission of sins, breathing him upon the Apostles (cf. Jn 20:22). And while Christ alone received this Spirit without measure, (cf. Jn 3:14), it is only according to the measure of the giving of Christ and from the fullness of Christ himself that he is bestowed upon the members of the mystical Body. And since Christ has been glorified on the Cross his Spirit is communicated to the Church in abundant outpouring, in order that she and each of her members may grow daily in likeness to our Saviour. It is the Spirit of Christ who has made us the adopted sons of God, so that one day 'we all beholding the glory of the Lord with open face, may be transformed into the same image from glory to glory.'"[8]

The Pope attributes the unity of the Body through the diverse activities of its members to the Spirit: "This Spirit of Christ is the invisible principle to which we must also attribute the union of all the parts of the Body with one another and with their exalted Head, dwelling as he does whole in the Head, whole in the Body, and whole in each of its members, and assisting these with his presence in diverse manners according to their various functions and duties and their higher or lower degree of spiritual perfection. He, with his heavenly breath of life, is the source from which proceeds every single vital and effectively salutary action in all parts of the Body. It is he himself who is present in all the members and divinely acts in each, though he also acts in the lower members through the ministry of the higher. And, finally, it is he who, while by the inspiration of his grace giving ever new increase to the Church, refuses to dwell by sanctifying grace in members which are completely severed from the Body."[9]

Pius XII then quotes Leo XIII, as we have seen, and continues thus: "If, however, this vital force and power, through which the whole community of Christians is upheld by its Founder, is viewed not in itself but in the created effects which proceed from it, then it consists in those heavenly gifts which our Redeemer together with his Spirit bestows upon the Church, and of which he, giver of supernatural light and cause of sanctity, together with his Spirit, is the author. Thus the Church, as well as all her holy members, may make their own the eloquent words of the Apostle: 'I live, now not I; but Christ liveth in me' (Gal 2:20)."[10]

These words do not exhaust the Pope's thought on the theme we are studying. He rejects the erroneous distinction between the "Church shaped by charity" and "another society called juridical." For Christ willed his Church to perpetuate the work of the Redemption and to this end made it a perfect society as well as enriching it "by the Holy Spirit with heavenly gifts and powers." "Hence there can be no real opposition or incompatibility between the invisible mission of the Holy Spirit and the juridical office which Pastors and Teachers have received from Christ. Like body and soul in us, the two realities are complementary and perfect each other, both having their origin in our one and the same Saviour who not only said, as he breathed the divine Spirit upon the Apostles: 'Receive ye the Holy Spirit,' (Jn 20:22) but also enjoined aloud: 'As the Father hath sent me, I also send you' (Jn 20:21); and again: 'He that heareth you heareth me' (Lk 10:16)."[11]

Pius XII returns to the unifying role of the Spirit: "And the source (of unity) is most divine; it is not only the decree of the Eternal Father and the earnest desire of our Saviour, but also the interior inspiration and impulse of the Holy Spirit in our minds and hearts. For if even the least action conducive to salvation cannot be produced without the Holy Spirit, how can numberless multitudes of every nation and every race conspire with one intent to the glory of the Triune God, save by the power of him who is breathed by the Father and the Son with one eternal love?"[12] The Pope points to the union between the invisible guidance of the Church by the Spirit, and the mandate to Peter and his successors "to conduct the visible government of the Christian commonwealth."

Christ's presence in us is through his Spirit.

"Christ, as we have already said, is in us through his Spirit, whom he imparts to us and through whom he so acts within us that any divine effect operated in our souls by the Holy Spirit must be said to be operated in us also by Christ (cf. St. Thomas, *Comm. in Eph.*, II, 5). 'If any man hath not the Spirit of Christ' says the Apostle, 'he is none of his; but if Christ be in you . . . the spirit liveth, because of justification' (Rom 8:9-10)."[13] Pius returns to the theme of the Spirit briefly when he deals with the divine indwelling and again in the epilogue on invocation of the Mother of God" "She too it was who by her most powerful intercession obtained for the new-born Church the prodigious Pentecostal outpouring of that Spirit of the divine Redeemer who had already been given on the Cross."[14]

The biblical basis for the idea that the Spirit is the soul of the Church is to be sought in two Pauline texts: 1 Cor 12:13, "For by one Spirit we were all baptized into one body—Jews or Greeks, slaves or free—and all were made to drink of one Spirit," and Eph 4:4, "There is one body and one Spirit, just as you were called to the one hope, that belongs to your call."

Two patristic texts are quoted: St. Augustine, a sermon on Pentecost: "But what the soul is to the body of a man, this the Holy Spirit is to the Body of Christ which is his Church. The Holy Spirit does in the whole Church what the soul does in all the members of one body."[15] The great Latin Doctor says practically the same thing in a second sermon on Pentecost.[16] Among the Greeks St. John Chrysostom is fairly explicit. Commenting on Eph 4:3, "the unity of the Spirit," he writes: "What is the unity of the Spirit. As in the (human) body there is one spirit which contains everything, it is here likewise. Accordingly the Spirit was given that he might unite things divided in kind and in customs."[17]

What does the thought of the ages tell us? The Spirit from the first moment assures the existence of the Church; he maintains this existence, giving vitality; he especially assures the unity of the Church constantly threatened by disruptive forces; he enriches the life of the Church by the gifts or charisms (qv) bestowed on individual members for the building up of the Body. He is the soul of the whole Body, but this truth must be understood analogically. He is not dependent on the Body for completion, as the human soul depends on its body. He transcends the Body, the Church, is not bound by it or limited by it in his origin, operation,

sovereign freedom. He is, moreover, intimately related to the Church in his eternal indissoluble union with the Father and the Son in his Trinitarian life, enjoying in this community of Persons independence in being and relationships which have nothing to do with the Church, the creature of all the Blessed Three. A too tight understanding of the phrase "soul of the Church" would compromise the divine mystery in its essence and in its operation. The whole world of personal processions, properties, circumincession must be borne in mind.

----

[1]Cf. A. Vonier, O.S.B., *The Spirit and the Bride*, London, 1936; E. Bardy, *Le Saint-Esprit en nous et dans l'Eglise d'après le Nouveau Testament*, Albi, 1950; P. Bonnard, "L'Esprit Saint et l'Eglise selon le Nouveau Testament," *RHPR*, 37 (1957), 81-90; C. Journet, *L'Eglise e Verbe Incarné*, II, Paris, 1951, 522-580; N.J. Jaschke, "Die Entdeckung der pneumatologischen Dimension der Kirche durch das Konzil und ihre Bedeutung," in *Sapienter Ordinare*, (Festgabe E. Kleineidem Erf. Th. St. 24), 1969, 392-403; Symposium, *Lo Spirito Santo e la Chiesa*, AVE, Rome, 1970; J.D. Zizioulas, "La dimensione pneumatologica della Chiesa," *Communio* (8 (1973) 10-17; K. Rahner, S.J., "The Church as the Subject of the Sending of the Spirit," *Theol. Investig.*, VII (1971), 186-192; N. Afanassief, *L'Eglise du Saint Esprit*, Paris, 1975; L. Sartori, "Lo Spirito Santo e la vita della Chiesa," in '*Ut unum sint*,' 19 (1969), 5-18; S. Tromp, *De Spiritu Christi anima Corporis Christi quod est ecclesia*, Rome, 1960; *id.*, *De Spiritu Sancto anima*, I, *Testimonia e Patribus Graecis*, 2nd ed., Rome, 1948; II, *Testimonia e Patribus Latinis*, Rome, 2nd ed., 1952; *id.*, *Litterae encyclicae de Mystico Jesu Christi Corpore*, Rome, 3rd ed., 1958; P. de Letter, "The Soul of the Mystical Body," *ScEccl*, 14 (1962) 213-14; C. Lialine, "The Holy Spirit and the Mystical Body of Christ," *ECO*, 7 (1947/48), 69-94; see articles on Y.-M.J. Congar, O.P. and H. Mühlen; J. Moltmann, *L'Eglise dans la force de l'Esprit. Une contribution à l'ecclésiologie messianique*, tr. R. Givord, Paris, 1980; articles in *Atti del Congresso*, I. de la Potterie, S.J., "L'Esprit Saint et L'Eglise dans le Nouveau Testament, II, 791-808; R. Faricy, S.J., "The Spirit—Ecclesiology of 1 Cor, Rom and Eph," II 839-846; Joseph de Sainte-Marie, "Le role de Marie dans le don de l'Esprit du Christ à l'Eglise," II, 972-992; *NCE, XIII, "Soul of the Church,"* F.X. Lawlor, 473-474; *DSp*, "L'Esprit Saint, âme de l'Eglise,: IV, 2, 1295-1302, S. Tromp, S.J., *BT* II, 73-74; [2]*De Orat. Dom.*, 23, *PL* 4, 553; [3]*Serm.* 71, 20, 33, *PL* 38, 463; [4]*Adv. Iconocl.* 12, *PG* 96, 1358D; [5]CTS tr., 55; [6]*Ibid.*, 30; [7]*Ibid.*, 32; [8]*Ibid.*, 54; [9]*Ibid.*, 55; [10]*Ibid.*, 56; [11]*Ibid.*, 63; [12]*Ibid.*, 68; [13]*Ibid.*, 76; [14]*Ibid.*, 110; further references to the Spirit, 82, 86, 87, 91; [15]*Serm.* 267, 4, *PL* 38, 1231; [16]*Serm.* 268, 2, *ibid.*, 1232; [17] *In Eph.*, IV, 3, *PG* 62, 73.

CLEMENT OF ROME, POPE (fl. c. 96)

Clement, one of the earliest Popes, has left a remarkable document in his *Epistle to the Corinthians*, known as *First Clement*, for a second, spurious, has also been ascribed to him.[1] Early in this work is he conscious of the action of the Spirit: "Thus a profound and rich peace was given to all, you had an insatiable desire to do good, and the Holy Spirit was poured out in abundance on you all."[2] Overall C. sees the Spirit as the author of Sacred Scripture: "You have studied the Holy Scriptures, which are true, and given by the Holy Spirit."[3] Logically with this view he can introduce a quotation from Scripture thus: "For the Holy Spirit says, 'let not the wise man boast himself in his wisdom....'"[4] C. thought that he himself was inspired by the Spirit in what he wrote: "For you will give us joy and gladness, if you are obedient to the things which we have written through the Holy Spirit, and root out the wicked passion of your jealousy according to the entreaty for peace and concord which we have made in this letter."[5]

C. is conscious of the intimate association between Christ and the Spirit: "The sceptre of the greatness of God, the Lord Jesus Christ, came not with the pomp of pride or of arrogance, for all his power, but was humble-minded, as the Holy Spirit spoke concerning him:"[6]—there follows a long quotation from Is 53. Again: "Now the faith which is in Christ confirms all these things, for he himself through his Holy Spirit calls us thus: 'Come, children, hearken to me, I will teach you the fear of the Lord.'"[7]

C. had a sense of the Spirit at work in the Church: "The Christ therefore is from God and the Apostles from the Christ. In both ways, then, they were in accordance with the appointed order of God's will. Having therefore received their commands, and being fully assured by the resurrection of our Lord Jesus Christ, and with faith confirmed by the word of God, they went forth in the assurance of the Holy Spirit preaching the good news that the Kingdom of God is coming. They preached from district to district, and from city to city, and they appointed their first converts, testing them by the Spirit, to be bishops and deacons of the future believers."[8]

The Spirit was seen by C. to work within the soul: "Take heed, beloved, lest his many good works towards us become a judgment on us all, if we do not do good and virtuous deeds before him in concord, and be citizens worthy of him. For he says in one place: 'The Spirit of the Lord is a lamp searching the inward parts.' Let us observe how near he is, and that nothing escapes him of our thoughts or of the devices which we make."[9] And again: "Cast me not away from thy presence, and take not thy Holy Spirit from me."[10]

Is there any Trinitarian formula in *First Clement*? Answer is given in these texts: "Why are there strife and passion and divisions and schisms and war among you? Have we not one God, and one Christ and one Spirit of grace poured out upon us? And is there not one calling in Christ?"[11] "Receive our counsel and there shall be nothing for you to regret, for as God lives and as the Lord Jesus Christ lives, and the Holy Spirit, the faith and hope of the elect, he who with lowliness of mind and eager gentleness has without backsliding performed the decrees and commandments given by God shall be enrolled and chosen in the number of those who are saved through Jesus Christ, through whom is to him the glory for ever and ever."[12] Here we have the seeds not only of Trinitarian theology, but of Soteriology; the elaborate doctrine will come later.

---

[1]Text with tr. K. Lake, *The Apostolic Fathers*, I, London, 1914; also C. Richardson, *Library of Christian Classics*, vol. I, pp. 33-73; cf. F. Cavaera, *DSp*, II, 1, 962-63; H. Dressler, NCE, III, 926-29; [2]2, 2, Lake, p. 11; [3]45, 2, p. 85; [4]13, 1, p. 29; [5]63, 2, p. 119; [6]16, 2, p. 35; [7]22, 1, p. 49; [8]42, 2-4, p. 81; [9]21, 2-3, p. 47; cp. 8, 1, p. 21; [10]18, 11, p. 41; [11]46, 6, p. 89; [12]58, 2, p. 109.

COMMUNION OF SAINTS, THE

"Our union with the Church in heaven is put into effect in its noblest manner when with common rejoicing we celebrate together the praise of the divine majesty. Then all those from every tribe and tongue and people and nation (cf. Rev 5:9) who have been redeemed by the blood of Christ and gathered together into one Church, with one song of praise magnify the one and triune God. Such is especially the case in the sacred Liturgy, where the power of the Holy Spirit acts upon us through sacramental signs. Celebrating the Eucharistic sacrifice, therefore, we are most closely united to the worshipping Church in heaven as we join with and venerate the memory first of all of the glorious every-virgin Mary, of Blessed Joseph and the blessed Apostles and martyrs, and of all the saints. The most sacred synod accepts with great devotion the venerable faith of our ancestors regarding this vital fellowship with our brethren who are in heavenly glory or who are being purified after death."[1] Earlier the Council whose text is here chosen, had spoken of "the union of the whole Church" hoping that "it may be strengthened in the Spirit by the practice of fraternal charity (cf. Eph 4:1-6). For just as Christian communion among wayfarers brings us closer to Christ, so our community with the saints joins us to Christ, from whom, as from their fountain and head issue every grace and the life of God's People itself."

The Communion of Saints is an article of the Apostle's Creed. It has been understood in different ways, as a relationship based in grace between persons, and as a sharing in sacred things. It is the first meaning that is here considered: obviously there is no sharp partition. There is a "participation in the good things of the community of salvation together with the other members of the community." Charity is the principle of this participation, the charity, the love with which God loves himself: "God's love has been poured into our hearts through the Holy Spirit which has been given to us" (Rom 5:5).

What makes the truth so relevant to Christian living is that through the communion, organically instituted as a body around Christ, there is a transfer of merit. We are members of him and of one another and exchange of grace is constant, through the vital energising Spirit of the body. The Spirit is at the very origin of the Church, in the moment of Pentecost (qv) and, for each individual in the moment of entry to the Church, "For by one Spirit we were all baptized into one body—Jews or Greeks, slaves or free—and all were made to drink of one Spirit" (1 Cor 12:13). "There is one body and one Spirit, just as you were called to the one hope that belongs to your call, one Lord, one faith, one baptism, one God and Father of us all, who is above all and through all and in all" (Eph 4:4).

The Spirit creates the Communion of Saints, he maintains it in existence and he constantly, in great ways and small, directs its activity. Here we touch mystery upon mystery, the natural mystery of the human person, the interaction between persons, the supernatural mystery whereby this interaction transcends time and space, has eternal effects, may set in train incalculable repercussions. How does the Spirit secure the transfer of merit from a contemplative like Teresa of Avila or her French namesake, Thérèse of Lisieux, to a missionary needing special divine help, or to a sinner who stands in need of repentance and the will to amend his life? What determines the relationship and how is the choice made? Why one missionary rather than another? Why one sinner rather than another?

Similar questions arise in regard to the effects of prayer of petition. We pray for others on the belief that God, that is the Spirit, will as a result of our prayer intervene in their lives. The mass of evidence from the lives of the saints is overwhelming. Especially the apostolate (qv) of suffering relies on the fact of communion, sharing, mutual enrichment. But this enrichment may not follow identifiable lines. Suffering may be offered for one person and benefit another. It is handed over and thereafter is used at the will of the Spirit who gives. St. Paul said that he filled up "in his body those things wanting...." Martyrdom is the supreme instance of suffering in and with Christ, plenary in doctrine, witness and compassion with Christ in one moment. Hence its immense fruitfulness in the Body of Christ.

Pope St. Martin I emphasizes the intrinsic link with the Spirit in his letter to the Church in Carthage: "Whatever is ours is yours according to one undivided sharing in the Spirit."[2] So does St. Thomas: "the operation of the Holy Spirit unites the Church and communicates the goods of one to another."[3] "The good that Christ communicates is chiefly the Holy Spirit, who through the unity of love communicates the blessings of Christ's members one with another."[4]

[1]Cf. LG, 50; J.H. Newman, *The Communion of Saints, Parochial and Plain Sermons*, IV, 168-184; H.B. Swete, *The Holy Catholic Church, The Communion of Saints: A Study in the Apostles' Creed*, London, 1915; G. Morin, O.S.B., "Sanctorum Communionem, *Rev. d'Histoire et de Littérature Religieuses* 9 (1904) 209-36; J.P. Kirsch, *Die Lehre von der Gemeinschaft der Heiligen im christlichen Altertum*, 1900, English tr., 1910; W. Elert, "Die Herkunft der Formel 'Sanctorum communio,'" *Theologische Literaturzeitung* 74 (1949), 577-586; S. Tromp, S.J., *Corpus Christi quod est ecclesia*, I, Rome, 2nd ed., 152ff; A. Michel, "La Communion des Saints," Rome, *Doctor Communis* IX, (1956); A. Piolanti, *Il mistero della Communione dei Santi nella Rivelazione e nella teologia*, Rome, 1957; C. Journet, *L'Eglise du Verbe incarné*, II, Paris, 1951, 554ff, 659ff; J.N.D. Kelly, *Early Christian Creeds*, London, 1958 and later, 388-397; P.-Y. Emery, "L'unité des croyants au ciel et sur la terre. La communion des saints et son expression dans la prière de l'Eglise," *Verbum Caro* 63 (1962); S. Benko, *The Meaning of Sanctorum Communio*, Studies in Historical Theology, 3, London, 1964; J.M.R. Tillard, O.P., "La Communion des Saints," VS 113 (1965), 249-274; Y.-M.T. Congar, O.P., *Faith and the Spiritual Life*, London, 1969, 122-131; L.S. Thornton, *The Common Life in the Body of Christ*, London, 1950; L. Hertling, *Communione, Chiesa e Papato nell'antichità cristiana*, Rome, 1961; S. Muñoz Iglesias, "Communion with God in the New Testament," *XIII Semana Biblica Española*, 1952, Madrid, 1953, 195-224; E. Lamirande, *La Communion des Saints*, (Je sais, je crois), Paris, 1965. *DTC* III (1908), 429-54, P. Bernard, *Communion des saints, son aspect dogmatique et historique*; bibl. R.S. Bour, 454-480, *Communion des saints d'après les monuments de l'antiquité*

chrétienne, bibl.; H. Leclercq, O.S.B., *DACL* III, 2 (1914), 2447-2454; F. Baudurco, *EC* III (1950), 119-2; F.X. Lawlor, *NCE*, IV, 41-43; *BT* II, 163f; J.Y. Campbell, "Koinonia and its Cognates in the New Testament," in *Three New Testament Studies*, Leiden 1965, 1-28; [2]Epist. 4, PL 87, 147; [3]ST IIIa q. 68, a. 9, ad 2; [4]ST IIIa q. 82, a. 6 ad 3; *Communio*, XIII, 1, 1988, several authors.

CONFIRMATION, THE SACRAMENT

A succinct statement on Confirmation is contained in the Constitution on the Church issued by Vatican II: "By the Sacrament of Confirmation (the faithful) are more perfectly bound to the Church and are endowed with the special strength of the Holy Spirit. Hence they are, as true witnesses of Christ, more strictly obliged to spread the faith by word and deed."[1] The sentence emphasizing the role of the Spirit is reproduced in the Catechetical Directory.

The Constitution on the Liturgy has given this directive: "The rite of Confirmation is to be revised also so that the intimate connection of the Sacrament with the whole of the Christian initiation may more clearly appear. For this reason the renewal of baptismal promises should fittingly precede the reception of this Sacrament. Confirmation may be conferred within Mass when convenient. For conferring outside Mass, a formula introducing the rite should be drawn up."[2]

The Apostolic Constitution *Divinae Consortes Naturae* (qv) of Paul VI decreed the reform or revision called for by the Council. Theological research has been engaged on the significance of the Sacrament; it is relevant to much in Catholic life: the need for fuller awareness of the Holy Spirit and fuller, more explicit personal commitment to his sanctifying presence and activity, (see article, "Neglect of the Spirit"), the role of Confirmation in the Christian vocation; the special significance of the Sacrament in the apostolate (qv), in particular the lay apostolate; the meaning of witness; the relevance of the Sacrament to the universal priesthood of the laity.

Many of these aspects are touched on in Paul VI's Apostolic Constitution. A patristic scholar lends his authority to the unanimity of the Fathers on one point: the Sacrament gives the Holy Spirit.[3] If therefore there is neglect of the Sacrament, if it is accepted not only by the individual recipient but by the supporting community as a mere ceremony, as marking a stage in life, maturity, and no more, there is loss. For it has been well pointed out that the Sacrament must have an individual as well as a communitarian aspect, as it must be seen in true relationship to Baptism and to the Eucharist, while possessing its own finality. Within the entire ambit of the Christian life at its highest level this Sacrament will also have an eschatological dimension.

Theologians have to seek answers to questions on the relationship between Baptism and Confirmation. Does the latter add something to the former in the order of grace? The Holy Spirit is received in Baptism (Mk 1:8; Jn 1:33; 1 Cor 6:11; 12:13; Tit 3:5). Why is he received again and what does he then accomplish? The new rite of Baptism leaves no doubt about the Spirit's presence in the Sacrament. The prayer of exorcism and anointing before the ceremony has these words: "We pray for these children; set them free from original sin, make them temples of your glory, and send your Holy Spirit to dwell within them." To the parents and godparents the celebrant addresses these words: "You have come here to present these children for Baptism. By water and the Holy Spirit they are to receive the gift of new life from God, who is love." At the anointing with chrism the celebrant says: "God the Father of our Lord Jesus Christ has freed you from sin, given you a new birth by water and the Holy Spirit, and welcomed you into his holy people."[4]

In the words of introduction to the Lord's prayer in the concluding phase of the rite the celebrant says: "Dearly beloved, these children have been reborn in Baptism. They are now called children of God, for so indeed they are. In Confirmation they will receive the fullness of God's Spirit." This raises the question nicely: What is the fullness they will receive?

Theologians look for an analogy between the Paschal Mystery and Baptism on the one hand, and Pentecost and Confirmation on the other: Pentecost, moveover, is the preordained fulfilment of the Paschal Mystery. A further analogy is helpful: between Christ's conception by the Spirit through Mary's fiat—which, with sufficient reservation, evokes our Baptism—and his anointing by the Spirit at the Jordan for his mission, this, again with the necessary allowance for his infinite perfection, the type of our Confirmation.

The essential concept is reinforced by this deeply theological context: witness. It is not used in the merely technical legal sense of attestation of fact or truth, but in the plenary sense, which though including this transcends it. The Apostles are witnesses of Jesus (Lk 24:47; Acts 1:8, 22; 5:32; 2:32; 3:15; 10:39-43; 13:31). They attest the great events of his life, especially his death and resurrection, and this will be the criterion of selecting the successor to Judas. But their essential witness was to the true significance of these events, their import for those prepared to confess Christ. Eventually the witness would cost their lives and thus the word takes on its traditional sense of martyr.

It is clear that there are degrees in the mode of practising or giving witness. To confess Christ as Lord and Saviour is one form of witness, and even that, in certain circumstances, may mean committing one's entire being, life, future, career. The one word "yes" in answer to a crucial question put by a persecutor may lead at once to death with torture.

Since the Spirit plunges to the depths of the human person, witness inspired and fortified by him may be the total expression of a human life, values, options, bearing, conduct. A life that is through and through Christlike, that is lived to the full, constitutes unique witness. When it is found simultaneously in a community, there is a unique mode of evangelization, or, in post-Christian communities, reevangelization.

This witness is at times disastrously absent among Christians living in the secular city. They suffer from the divided Christian mind; there is in their lives a cleavage firmly drawn and maintained between their Christian faith and their professional, civic, political, social, economic activities. The disease is not restricted to the laity—far from it. Clerics who get immersed in financial, even political, affairs, can resolutely, even with a certain brazen style, adopt the values and tactics of a decadent, corrupt secular society. Religious values, Christian principles are despised as worthless piety, if not pietism—the world wins.

If it be true that one great evil of our times is secularism, the remedy for it, in Christian lives, lies in the grace received in Confirmation. It is an example of the working of the Spirit where one can perceive the fruits of the Spirit, as well as the Gifts which must operate. For often the Christian bearing witness in what he thinks an indifferent or even hostile milieu, proposing the Christian solution to a vexed problem, meets a welcoming response which may surprise him. For Christianity works. Honest men and women, agnostic perhaps in regard to religion, want the best solution to their problems. They have sometimes to search vainly for it, because of the timid, even cowardly silence of their Christian colleagues. When these speak, they rejoice. Thus the agnostic Secretary

General of the International Labour Office, Albert Thomas, was open to accept the papal social policy submitted by a Catholic colleague, E.J. Phelan. Thus is explained the continuous papal interest in this great organisation.

Akin to creative witness of this kind is the exercise of the apostolate by the laity. Vatican II linked this apostolate with the Sacrament: "The laity derive the right and duty with respect to the apostolate from their union with Christ their Head. Incorporated into Christ's Mystical Body through Baptism and strengthened by the power of the Holy Spirit through Confirmation, they are assigned to the Apostolate by the Lord himself. They are consecrated into a royal priesthood and a holy people (cf. 1 Pet 2:4-10) in order that they may offer spiritual sacrifices through everything they do, and may witness to Christ throughout the world. For their part the Sacraments, especially the most holy Eucharist communicate and nourish that charity which is the soul of the entire apostolate."[5]

To appreciate the relationship between Confirmation and the universal priesthood, we must recall the doctrine of the sacramental character (see article Sacraments). Each "character" Sacrament confers a certain configuration to the priesthood of Christ; each is linked with the Spirit, who acts through it. Priesthood is oriented to others.

Words are sometimes incorrectly used in regard to this Sacrament. Strength should not be confused with aggressive militancy, for strength in the true Christian sense includes resignation or endurance as well as audacity or boldness. Keeping the parallel with Pentecost in mind we should possibly think more of "power," which Christ promised to his Apostles in the farewell address before the Ascension.

Along with all that the Sacrament implies in regard to the Church and the world, to the building up of the Church and the triumph over the world, there must be recognition of the interior effect of the Sacrament on the individual. It is the divinely ordained means towards personal maturity in the Christian life. Here is where personal endowment and mission meet and complement each other, where within the mysterious communion and exchange made possible by the Mystical Body, the cloistered contemplative has a partnership mutually enriching with the fully committed apostle, where all witness is seen as a compelling manifestation of Christ in his members.[6]

Those who search for means of enhancing the

value of the Sacrament, of giving it relevance to life should take seriously the proposals of a committed lay apostle: a) that, in the model of Mary and the Apostles at Pentecost the confirmand should be directly oriented to apostolic action; b) that, he or she should be immediately, with the sense of obligation, enrolled in some form of the lay apostolate, and instructed on the link between its work and his newly acquired sacramental status.[7]

---

[1]Thomas Aquinas, *Summa Theologiae*, III, q. 72; Art. 11; cf. L. Cardinal Billot, S.J., *De Ecclesiae Sacramentis*, Rome, 1915, 290-309; F. Cuttaz, *Notre Pentecôte, ou la grâce du Chrétien militant*, Paris, 1936; E. Sauras, "Fundamento sacramental de la Accion catolica," *Revista española de Teologia* 3 (1943), 129-258; D. Winzen, "Anointed with the Spirit," *Orate Fratres*, 20 (1945-46), 337-343; 389-397; J.R. Gillis, "The Case for Confirmation," *The Thomist*, 10 (1947) 159-184; M.D. Koster, *Die Firmung im Glaubensinn der Kirche*, Regensburg and Münster, 1948; G.W.H. Lampe, *The Seal of the Spirit*, London, 1951; A.-G. Martimort, "La Confirmation," *Communion solennelle et Profession de foi*, (Lex Orandi), Paris, 1952, 159-201; D.L. Greenstock, "El Problema de la Confirmacion, *La Ciencia Tomista*, 80 (1953), 175-228, 539-590, 81 (1954), 201-240; P.T. Camelot, "Sur la Théologie de la Confirmation," *RSPT* 38 (1954), 637-657; L. Bouyer, C. Orat., "La signification de la Confirmation," *VS* (*Suppl.*) 29 (15 May 1954), 162-179; P. Ramwez, "La Confirmation constitutive d'une personnalité au service du Corps Mystique du Christ," *Lumen Vitae*, 9 (1954) 17-36; K.F. Lynch, *The Sacrament of Confirmation in the Early-Middle Scholastic Period*, London, 1957; Max Thurian, *La Confirmation, Consécration des Laics*, Paris, 1957; L.S. Thornton, *Confirmation. Its Place in the Baptismal Mystery*, Westminster, 1954; J. Lécuyer, C.S.S.p., "La Confirmation chez les Pères," *M.D.*, 54 (1958) 23-52; E. Llopart, "Las formulas de la confirmación en el Pontifical Romano," *Liturgica*, 2 (Montserrat) 1958, 121-180; P.M. Gy, "Histoire liturgique du sacrament de confirmation," *M.D.*, 58 (1959), 135-145; Adolf Adam, *Firmung und Seelsorge*, Düsseldorf, 1959; R. Bernier, "Le sacrament de Confirmation dans la théologie de S. Thomas," *Lumière et Vie* 51 (1961), 59-72; B. Neunheuser, *Baptism and Confirmation*, Herder History of Dogma, London, 1964; J.P. Bouhot, *La confirmation, sacrament de la communion ecclésiale*, Lyons, 1968; G. Austin, "The Essential Rite of Confirmation and Liturgical Tradition," *EL* 86 (1972), 214-224; *id.*, "What has Happened to Confirmation?," *Worship* 50 (1976), 42-46; *Anointing with the Spirit. The Rite of Confirmation. The Use of Oil and Chrism; Studies in the Reformed Rite of the Catholic Church*, New York, Pueblo, 1985; Ligier, *La confirmation. Sens et conjuncture oecuménique hier et aujourdhui* (Theol. historique, 23), Paris, 1973; S. Amougou-Atangana, *Ein Sakrament des Geistenempfangs? Zum Verhältnis von Taufe und Firmung*, Freiburg, 1974; H. Küng, "La confirmation comme parachèvement du baptême," *L'Experience de l'Esprit, Melanges E. Schillebeeckx*, Paris, 1976, 115-150; C. O'Donnell, O.Carm., *The Ecclesial Dimension of Confirmation. A Study in St. Thomas and the Reformed Rite*, Rome, Gregorian University, 1987, bibl.; [2]Art. 71; [3]J. Lécuyer, *op. cit*; [4]*The Rites*, Pueblo, 1976, 202, 205, 210; [5]*Decree on the Lay Apostolate*, art. 3; [6]*The Rites*, 306, 313; [7]K. Kennedy, *op. cit*; T.Marsh, *The Meaning of Confirmation ITQ* 21 1964; 47-70;id. *ITQ* 36 (1979), 151-170; K. Kennedy, "Confirmation and the Lay Apostolate," *The Furrow*, 1986, 151-171.

CONFIRMATION—DIVINAE CONSORTES NATURAE, 15 AUGUST 1971

Text of the Apostolic Constitution of Paul VI (qv) on the Sacrament of Confirmation.

"The sharing in the divine nature which is granted to men through the grace of Christ has a certain likeness to the origin, development, and nourishing of natural life. The faithful are born anew by baptism, strengthened by the Sacrament of Confirmation and finally are sustained by the food of eternal life in the Eucharist. By means of these Sacraments of Christian initiation they thus receive in increasing measure the treasures of divine life and advance toward the perfection of charity. It has rightly been written: 'The body is washed, that the soul may be cleansed; the body is anointed, that the soul may be consecrated; the body is signed, that the soul may be fortified; the body is overshadowed by the laying on of hands, that the soul too may be enlightened by the Spirit; the body is fed on the body and blood of Christ, that the soul too may be nourished by God.'[1]

"Conscious of its pastoral purpose, the Second Ecumenical Vatican Council devoted special attention to these Sacraments of initiation. It prescribed that the rites should be suitably revised in order to make them more suited to the understanding of the faithful. Since the Rite for the Baptism of Children, revised at the mandate of that General Council and published at our command, is already in use, it is now fitting to publish the rite of Confirmation, in order to show the unity of Christian initiation in its true light.

"In fact, careful attention and application have been devoted in these last years to the task of revising the manner of celebrating this Sacrament. The aim of this work has been that 'the intimate connection which this Sacrament has with the whole of Christian initiation should be more lucidly set forth.'[2] The link between Confirmation and the other Sacraments of initiation is shown more clearly not only by closer association of these Sacraments but also by the rite and words by which Confirmation is conferred. This is done so that the rite and words of this Sacrament may 'express more clearly the holy things which they signify. The Christian people, so far as possible, should be able to understand them with ease and take full and active part in the celebration as a community.'3

"For that purpose, it has been our wish also to include in this revision what concerns the very essence of the rite of Confirmation through which the faithful receive the Holy Spirit as a Gift.

"The New Testament shows how the Holy Spirit assisted Christ in fulfilling his messianic mission. On receiving the Baptism of John, Jesus saw the Spirit descending on him (see Mark 1:10) and remaining with him (see Jn 1:32). He was impelled by the Spirit to undertake his public ministry as the Messiah, relying on the Spirit's presence and assistance. Teaching the people of Nazareth, he shows by what he said that the words of Isaiah, 'The Spirit of the Lord is upon me' referred to himself (see Lk 4:17-21).

"He later promised his disciples that the Holy Spirit would help them also to bear fearless witness to their faith even before persecutors (see Lk 12:12). The day before he suffered he assured his Apostles that he would send the Spirit of truth from his Father (see Jn 15:26) to stay with them 'for ever' (Jn 14:16) and help them to be his witnesses (see Jn 15:26). Finally, after his resurrection, Christ promised the coming descent of the Holy Spirit: 'You will receive power when the Holy Spirit comes down on you; then you are to be my witnesses' (Acts 1:8; see Lk 24:49).

"And in fact, on the day of the feast of Pentecost, the Holy Spirit came down in an extraordinary way on the Apostles as they were gathered together with Mary the Mother of Jesus and the group of disciples. They were so 'filled with' the Holy Spirit (Acts 2:4) that by divine inspiration they began to proclaim 'the mighty works of God.' Peter regarded the Spirit who had thus come down upon the Apostles as the gift of the messianic age (see Acts 2:17-18). Those who believed the Apostles' preaching were then baptized and they too received the 'gift of the Holy Spirit' (Acts 2:38). From that time on the Apostles in fulfilment of Christ's wish, imparted the gift of the Spirit to the newly baptized by the laying on of hands to complete the grace of Baptism. Hence it is that the Letter to the Hebrews lists among the first elements of Christian instruction the teaching about Baptism and the laying on of hands (Heb 6:2). This laying on of hands is rightly recognized by Catholic tradition as the beginning of the Sacrament of Confirmation, which in a certain way perpetuates the grace of Pentecost in the Church.

"This makes clear the specific importance of Confirmation for sacramental initiation by which the faithful 'as members of the living Christ are incorporated into him and made like him through Baptism and through Confirmation and the Eucharist.'4 In Baptism, the newly baptized receive forgiveness of sins, adoption as sons of God, and the character of Christ, by which they are made members of the Church and for the first time become sharers in the priesthood of their Saviour (see 1 Pet 2:5, 9). Through the Sacrament of Confirmation, those who have been born anew in Baptism receive the inexpressible Gift, the Holy Spirit himself, by which they are endowed ... with special strength.'5 Moreover, having received the character of this Sacrament, they are 'bound more intimately to the Church'6 and 'they are more strictly obliged to spread and defend the faith both by word and by deed as true witnesses of Christ.'7 Finally, Confirmation is so closely linked with the holy Eucharist8 that the faithful, after being signed by holy Baptism and Confirmation, are incorporated fully into the Body of Christ by participation in the Eucharist.9

"From ancient times the conferring of the Gift of the Holy Spirit has been carried out in the Church with various rites. These rites underwent many changes in the East and the West, while always keeping the significance of a conferring of the Holy Spirit.10

"In many eastern rites, it seems that from early times a rite of anointing, not then clearly distinguished from Baptism, prevailed for the conferring of the Holy Spirit. That rite continues in use today in the greater part of the churches of the East.

"In the West there are very ancient witnesses concerning the part of Christian initiation which was later distinctly recognized as the Sacrament of Confirmation. After the baptismal washing and before the eucharistic meal, the performance of many rites is indicated, such as anointing, the laying on of hands and consignation.11 These are contained both in liturgical documents12 and in many testimonies of the Fathers. In the course of the centuries, problems and doubts arose as to what belonged with certainty to the essence of the rite of Confirmation. It is fitting to mention at least some of the elements which, from the thirteenth century onwards, in the ecumenical councils and in the documents of the popes, cast light on the importance of anointing while at the same time not allowing the laying on of hands to be obscured.

"Our predecessor Innocent III wrote: 'By the

anointing of the forehead the laying on of the hand is designated, which is otherwise called Confirmation, since through it the Holy Spirit is given for growth and strength.'[13] Another of our predecessors, Innocent IV, recalls that the Apostles conferred the Holy Spirit 'through the laying on of the hand, which Confirmation or the anointing of the forehead represents.'[14] In the profession of faith of Emperor Michael Palaeologus, which was read at the Second Council of Lyons, mention is made of the Sacrament of Confirmation, which 'bishops confer by the laying on of the hands, anointing with chrism those who have been baptized.'[15] The Decree for the Armenians, issued by the Council of Florence, declares that the 'matter' of the Sacrament of Confirmation, which 'bishops confer' is 'chrism made of olive oil ... and balsam,'[16] and, quoting the words of the Acts of Apostles concerning Peter and John, who gave the Holy Spirit through the laying on of hands (see Acts 8:17), it adds: 'in place of that laying on of the hand, in the Church Confirmation is given.'[17] The Council of Trent, though it had no intention of defining the essential rite of Confirmation, only designated it with the name of the holy chrism of Confirmation.[18] Benedict XIV made this declaration: 'therefore let this be said which is beyond dispute: in the Latin Church the Sacrament of Confirmation is conferred by using sacred chrism of olive oil, mixed with balsam and blessed by the bishop, and by tracing the sign of the cross by the minister of the Sacrament on the forehead of the recipient, while the same minister pronounces the words of the form.'[19]

Many theologians, taking account of these declarations and traditions, maintained that for valid administration of Confirmation there was required only anointing with chrism, done by placing the hand on the forehead. In spite of this, however, in the rites of the Latin Church a laying of hands upon those to be confirmed was always prescribed before the anointing.

With regard to the words of the rite by which the Holy Spirit is given, it should be noted that, already in the primitive Church, Peter and John, in order to complete the initiation of those baptized in Samaria, prayed for them to receive the Holy Spirit and then laid hands on them (see Acts 8:15-17). In the East, in the fourth and fifth centuries there appear in the rite of anointing the first indications of the words *'signaculum doni Spiritus Sancti.*'[20] These words were quickly accepted by the Church of Constantinople and are still used by the Churches of the Byzantine rite.

"In the West, however, the words of this rite, which completed Baptism, were not defined until the twelfth and thirteenth centuries. But in the twelfth-century Roman Pontifical the formula which later became the common one first occurs: 'I sign you with the sign of the cross and confirm you with the chrism of salvation. In the name of the Father and of the Son and of the Holy Spirit.'[21]

"From what we have recalled, it is clear that in the administration of Confirmation in the East and the West, though in different ways, the most important place was occupied by the anointing, which in a certain way represents the apostolic laying on of hands. Since this anointing with chrism well represents the spiritual anointing of the Holy Spirit, who is given to the faithful, we intend to confirm its existence and importance.

"As regards the words which are pronounced in Confirmation we have examined with due consideration the dignity of the venerable formula used in the Latin Church, but we judge preferable the very ancient formula belonging to the Byzantine rite, by which the Gift of the Holy Spirit himself is expressed and the outpouring of the Spirit which took place on the day of Pentecost is recalled (see Acts 2:1-4). We therefore adopt this formula, rendering it almost word for word.

"Therefore, in order that the revision of the rite of Confirmation may fittingly embrace also the essence of the sacramental rite, by our supreme authority we decree and lay down that in the Latin Church the following should be observed for the future:

"The Sacrament of Confirmation is conferred through the anointing with Chrism on the forehead, which is done by the laying on of the hand, and through the words: '*Accipe Signaculum Doni Spiritus Sancti.*'

"Although the laying of hands on the candidates, which is done with the prescribed prayer before the anointing, does not belong to the essence of the sacramental rite, it is nevertheless to be held in high esteem, in that it contributes to the integral perfection of that rite and to a clearer understanding of the Sacrament. It is evident that this preceding laying on of hands differs from the laying on of the hand by which the anointing is done on the forehead.

"Having established and declared all these elements concerning the essential rite of the Sacrament of Confirmation, we also approve by our apostolic authority the order for the same Sacrament, which has been revised by the Congregation for Divine Worship, after consultation with the Congregations for the Doctrine of the Faith, for the Discipline of the Sacraments, and for the Evangelization of Peoples as regards the matters which are within their competence. The Latin edition of the order containing the new form will come into force as soon as it is published; the editions of the vernacular languages, prepared by the episcopal conferences and confirmed by the Apostolic See, will come into force on the dates to be laid down by the individual conferences. The old order may be used until the end of the year 1972. From 1 January 1973, however, only the new order is to be used by those concerned.

"We intend that everything that we have laid down and prescribed should be firm and effective in the Latin Church, notwithstanding, where relevant, the apostolic constitutions and ordinances issued by our predecessors, and other prescriptions, even if worthy of special mention."

---

[1]Tertullian, *De resurrectione mortuorum*, VII, 3, *CCL* 2, 931; [2]Vatican II, *Sacrosanctum Concilium*, 71, *AAS* 56 (1964), 118; [3]*Ibid.*, 21, p. 106; [4]Vatican II, *Ad Gentes*, 36, *AAS* 58 (1966) 963; [5]Vatican II, *Lumen Gentium* 11, *AAS* 57 (1965) 15; [6]*Ibid.*; [7]*Ibid.*, see *Ad Gentes* 11, *AAS* 58 (1966) 959-962; [8]Vatican II, *Presbyterorum Ordinis* 5, *AAS* 58 (1966) 987; [9]*Ibid.*, 997, 998; [10]See Origen, *De Principiis*, I, 3, 2: *GCS* 22, 49f; *Comm in Ep ad Rom.*, V, 8: *PG* 14, 1038; Cyril of Jerusalem, *Catech* XVI, 26; XXI, 1-7; *PG* 33, 956; 1088-1093; [11]See Tertullian, *De Baptismo*, VII-VIII, *CCL* 1, 282f; B. Botte, *La tradition apostolique de Saint Hippolyte: Liturgiewissenschaftliche Quellen und Forschungen*, 39 (Münster in W., 1963) 52-54; Ambrose, *De Sacramentis*, II 24; III, 2, 8; VI, 2, 9; *CSEL* 73, pp. 36, 42, 74-75; *De Mysteriis*, VII, 42, *ibid.*, p. 106; [12]*Liber Sacramentorum Romanae Ecclesiae Ordinis Anni circuli*, ed. L.C. Mohlberg: *Rerum Ecclesiasticarum Documenta, Fontes*, IV, (Rome, 1960) 75; *Das Sacramentarium Gregorianum nach dem Achener Urexemplar*, ed. H. Lietzmann: *Liturgiegeschichtliche Quellen*, 3 (Münster in W., 1921) 50f; *Liber Ordinum*, ed. M. Ferotin, *Monumenta Ecclesiae Liturgica*, V (Paris, 1904) 33f; *Missale Gallicanum Vetus*, ed. L.C. Mohlberg: *Rerum Ecclesiasticarum Documenta, Fontes*, III (Rome, 1958) 42; *Missale Gothicum.*, ed. L.C. Mohlberg, *Rerum Ecclesiasticarum Documenta* V (Rome, 1961) 67; C. Vogel -R. Elze, *Le Pontifical Romano-Germanique du XIIe siècle, Le Texte*, II, *Studi e Testi* 227 (Vatican City, 1963) 109; M. Andrieu, *Le Pontifical Romain au Moyen-Age*; t. 1, *Le Pontifical Romain du XIIe siècle: Studi e Testi* 86 (Vatican City, 1938) 247f., 289; t. 2, *Le Pontifical de la Curie Romaine au XIIIe siècle, Studi e Testi*, 87 (Vatican City, 1940) 452f; [13]Ep. *Cum venisset* PL 215, 285. The profession of faith which the same Pope prescribed for the Waldensians includes the following: *Confirmationem ab episcopo factam, id est impositionem manuum, sanctam et venerande accipiendam esse censemus*: *PL* 215, 1511; [14]Ep. *Sub Catholicae professione*: Mansi, *Conc. Coll.*, t. 23, 579; [15]Mansi, *Conc. Coll.* t. 24, 71; [16]*Epistolae*

Pontificiae ad Concilium Florentinum spectantes, ed. G. Hofmann: *Concilium Florentinum*, vol I, ser. A. part II (Rome, 1944) 128: [17]*Ibid.*, 129; [18]Concilii Tridentini Actorum pars altera, Ed. S. Ehses: *Concilium Tridentinum*, V. Act II (Freiburg i. Br., 1911) 996; [19]*Ep Ex quo primum tempore*, 52: Benedict XIV ... *Bullarium*, t. III (Prato, 1847) 320; [20]See Cyril of Jerusalem, *Catech XVIII*, PG 33 1056; Asterius, Bishop of Amasea, *In parabolam de filio prodigo*, in "Photii Bibliotheca" Cod. 271: *PG* 104, 213. See also *Epistola cujusdam Patriarchae Constantinopolitani ad Martyrium Episcopum Antiochenum*: PG 119, 900; [21]M. Andrieu, *Le Pontifical Romain au Moyen-Age*, t. 1. *Le Pontifical Romain du XIIe siècle: Studi e Testi*, 86 (Vatican City, 1938), 247.

CONGAR, YVES – M.J. (1905-)

C. has fulfilled a mighty theological career, marked by the cross in his early days; he was one of those under suspicion in the fifties, punished for a while, eventually vindicated, enjoying, in the post-conciliar age richly deserved renown.[1] His principal theological interests have been ecumenism and ecclesiology, but his work has covered many other sectors. Increasingly in recent years he has been led to research and reflection on the Holy Spirit. His main contribution here is in the three volumes; *Je crois en l'Esprit Saint*, 1970-80. Many other studies have come from his pen before and after these. His thinking is expressed in these studies: "L'Esprit Saint dans l'Eglise," *Lumière et Vie*, 10 (1953), 51-74 (=*Les Voies du Dieu Vivant*, Paris, 1962, 165-184), *La Pentecôte*, Paris, 1956; "La pneumatologie dans la théologie catholique," *RSPT* 51 (1967), 250-258 (=*Vocabulaire oecuménique*, Paris 1970, 197-210); "Pneumatologie et Christomonisme dans la tradition latine?," *ETL* 45 (1969), 394-416 (=*Ecclesia a Spiritu Sancto edocta*, *Mélanges G. Philips*, Gembloux, 1970) "Actualité renouvelée du Saint Esprit," *Lumen Vitae*, 4 (1972), 543-560; "Actualité d'une pneumatologie," *Rev. du Proche Orient Chrétien*, 23 (1973), 121-132; "La Tri-unité de Dieu et l'Eglise," *VS* 604 (1974), 687-703 =*Essais oecuméniques*, Paris, 1984, 297-312; "Le Saint Esprit dans la consécration et la communion selon la tradition occidentale," *Nicolaus = Rivista di Teologia Ecumenica-Patristica* 2 (1981), 383-86; *Pneumatologie dogmatique* in L.B. Refoulé, ed., *Initiation à la pratique de la théologie*, II, Paris, 1982, 483-514; *Esprit de l'homme, Esprit de Dieu*, Paris, 1983; "Actualité de la pneumatologie," *Atti del Congresso*, I, 15-28; *BT*, I, 835-847; *La Parole et le Souffle*, Paris, 1983, English tr. *The Word and the Spirit*, London, 1986; For bibl. cf. *Bibliographie du P.Y.-M.J. Congar, O.P.*, Paris, Cerf, 1987.

[1]Studies on C.'s work are: J.P. Jossua, *Le P. Congar. La théologie au service du peuple de Dieu*, Paris, 1967, bibl to that date; H. Janin, *Il Cristo e lo Spirito Santo come principi dell'unità della Chiesa. Studio sull'ecclesiologia di Y.-M.J. Congar*, St. Thomas de Urbe, Pars Dissertationis ad Lauream, Fac. Theol., 1972; M. Meini, *Lo Spirito Santo nell'ecclesiologia di Y. Congar*, Dissert. Doct. Gregorian University, 1979; *Studio comparativo sulla pneumatologia di Paul Evdokimov (Ortodosso) e Yves Congar* (cattolico). Excerptum e Dissert. ad Lauream, PUS, Rome, 1980; Pawel Czyz, *Excerpta. Il Rapporto tra la dimensione cristologica e pneumatologica dell'Ecclesiologia nel pensiero di Y. Congar*, Gregorian University 1986; *BT* I, 835-847; II, 331.

CONGRESS, COMMEMORATION OF CONSTANTINOPLE I

Besides a special double liturgical celebration on Pentecost Sunday, 1981, marking the sixteen hundredth anniversary of the Council of Constantinople (qv) and the fifteen hundred and fiftieth anniversary of the Council of Ephesus, Pope John Paul II (qv) wished to have a theological congress where the theme of Constantinople and its continuing relevance to the Church would be examined and discussed by acknowledged experts.[1] In the event his wish was amply fulfilled. He entrusted organisation to the committee of rectors of Roman universities and higher institutes; the venue was the Hall of the Episcopal Synod, in the Vatican. There the sessions of the congress took place from 22 to 26 March 1982. Participants, i.e., readers of either *Relazioni* or *Comunicazioni*, numbered more than a hundred; they came from 50 countries from the five continents. Besides Roman Catholics, they included Orthodox, Lutheran, Reformed, Anglican and Methodist theologians—this ecumenical presence was noted with joy by the Pope in his address on the final day.

The proceedings as published run to over 1500 pages and the contents are in five main sections: the theology and background, historical, cultural, patristic, credal of the First Council of Constantinople; the doctrine of the Holy Spirit of the churches of the east and west, with attention to Christian spirituality and liturgy; the Holy Spirit in the Bible; the Holy Spirit in the experience of the Churches today; the Holy Spirit as the principle of Christian unity.

We have then in this publication a collective monumental work on the Holy Spirit, an enrichment of Catholic theology, a quarry for all future research.

[1]*Credo in Spiritum Sanctum, Atti del Congresso Teologico Internationale di Pneumatologia*, Rome, 22-26 March 1982, Libreria Editrice Vaticana, ed. José Saraiva Martin, 1983.

CONSCIENCE

The inspiration of the Spirit may transcend the dictates of conscience acting in the light of reason; it thereby imposes a dictate more binding. The reward of obedience is an enlargement of personality, a fulfilment (qv) impossible without the Spirit. The clear case is martyrdom, in which the fulfilment and eternal reward are simultaneous. Some instances of martyrdom, that of St. Thomas More and St. Maximilian Kolbe (qv), afford scope for full analysis. Some crucial decisions may call for the help of spiritual direction (qv). As with its exercise in the natural order, conscience, under the guidance of the Spirit develops, attains greater clarity with experience, learning beneficially from those qualified to teach the things of the Spirit. For this activity of the faculty in the supernatural order is not free from difficulty. Where self-deceit may enter in the natural order, spirits not to be trusted exist in the supernatural life. Hence the need for true discernment (qv). There can be no conflict ultimately between mature conscience acting with its own natural resources and rightly discerned inspiration of the Holy Spirit. But such harmony is not attained overnight, if we are to accept the judgement of those with expertise. It is a question on the one side of moral compulsion coming from a grasp of the personal and circumstantial elements within which a moral principle binds, on the other of seeking an intuition on the direction along which Another wills to lead the person involved; certainly not to overlook the concrete elements, but to focus principally on the comprehensive divine plan. Harmony is attainable, as is all human perfection, with the assistance of the Spirit who decides.

CONSTANTINOPOLITAN CREED, THEOLOGY[1]

The Council was a landmark in theological statement. It proclaimed the divinity of the Holy Spirit in face of different heresies. It is noteworthy that the language used in this affirmation does not include the word 'God' or *homoousios*. What St. Basil (qv) is known to have done the Council chose to do. But the language chosen is mostly Scriptural and conveys the meaning intended: the Spirit is called 'Lord' (*Kyrion*), which is derived from 2 Cor 3:17—"Now the Lord is the Spirit and where the Spirit of the Lord is, there is freedom"; he is also called 'Life-giver' (*Zoopoion*), which is taken from Jn 6:63—"It is the spirit that gives life, the flesh is of no avail; the words that I have spoken to you are spirit and life"; he is said to 'have spoken through the prophets,' from 2 Pet 1:21—"no prophecy ever came by the impulse of man, but men moved by the Holy Spirit spoke from God."

Hypostasis is not used, significantly, though it was in current theological language already. The approach is not speculative or metaphysical, but existential, in the context of the economy, soteriological. There is some non-Scriptural language: "Worshipped and glorified together with the Father and the Son." Here worship, liturgical practice, is treated as a touchstone of revealed truth. The Council does not make worship solely its measure; the Scriptural language it chose has its own weight. Of two doxologies current, one stressed worship "with" the Father and the Son and this was favoured; by which it is not meant that the other is excluded. The important point is that the formulation of the credal dogma is in the context of the oikonomia.

The creed states that the Holy Spirit proceeds from the Father. First, seen in the light of Cappadocian theology, this ensures the relationship to the Person; the Spirit does not merely emanate from the divine substance. He comes from love and freedom and not of substantial necessity. In the limited sense which equality of the persons imposes, the Father is the "cause" of the Spirit. The *Filioque* (qv) is not in the credal text. To what extent it was, at least in mitigated terms, part of the thinking which preceded the Council, is a matter for very specialized, expert research. St. Cyril of Alexandria (qv) saw that the Son had a role of some kind in the procession of the Spirit. St. Gregory of Nyssa (qv) also saw some kind of mediating position for the Son. But Gregory would fix certain reservations: the notion of "cause" (*aition*) is restricted to the Father, with the Son and Spirit equally related to him in this respect; the substantial, relationship of the Spirit to God is primarily to the Father. To what extent the Council was influenced by such thinking is to be explored. The relevant passage is: "And (we believe) in the Holy Spirit, the Lord, the Giver of life; he proceeds from the Father, is adored and glorified together with the Father and the Son; he spoke through the prophets."[2]

---

[1]For historical background cf. *Trinitas*, 73-75, bibl; add R.P.C. Hanson, *The Search for the Christian God*, Edinburgh, 1988, 791-823; A.M. Ritter, *Das Konzil von Konstantinopel. Studien zur Geschichte und Theologie des II Ökumenischen,* Gottingen, 1965. *Handbuch der Dogmengeschichte*, II, 1a 119-126; [2]*DS*, 150.

CREEDS

Reference to the Holy Spirit in the creeds of the Church can be studied in certain documents which stand out by reason of the historic circumstances in which they appeared or the enduring impact which they had in Christian life: the Apostles' Creed, the Nicene Creed, the Creed of Constantinople, the Athanasian Creed, the Profession of Faith of the Council of Trent and the Credo of the People of God of Paul VI (qv).[1] Account has to be taken of other formularies emerging out of the same situation especially in the early centuries when Christological and Trinitarian debates claimed so much attention. Many such formularies were drawn up between the Council of Nicaea, 325, and the Council of Constantinople, 381, due to the Arian controversy.

The Apostles' Creed (known as T) grew out of the old Roman Creed (R) and it was to take a fixed and important place in Christian life, used universally in the West for baptismal services, surviving the Reformation in all communions (save that Luther substituted "Christian" for "Catholic"), an agreed statement for Christian unity in the present age. Both T and R have just "I believe in the Holy Spirit"; the "I believe" is inclusive from the first article in R. There is no affirmation of the divinity of the Holy Spirit or in his function, whereas such belief is explicit in regard to the Father and Son: "I believe in God, the Father Almighty, creator of heaven and earth. And in Jesus Christ, his only Son, our Lord. . . ." There are disparate elements mentioned along with the article on the Holy Spirit; little difference here from R.

A factor in the history of T is the interrogatory creed which is textually found—as a work of restoration—in the *Apostolic Tradition* of St. Hippolytus: "Do you believe in the Holy Spirit and the holy Church, and the resurrection of the flesh? And he who is being baptized shall say: I do."

Marcellus of Ancyra delivered to Pope Julius I in Rome in 340 a creed which, as reproduced by Epiphanius, closely resembles R. The article which concerns us says: "And in the Holy Spirit."[2] True,

Marcellus prefixes his whole creed by an anathema against any one who said that the Son or the Spirit was part of the Father.

The Nicene creed has this simple article: "And in the Holy Spirit." The creed read by Eusebius of Caesarea (d.c. 340) at the Council of Nicaea (A.D. 325), was well received, especially by the emperor[3]— at least, so the bishop informed his flock. It ends thus: "And we believe also in one Holy Spirit."

Between Nicaea and Constantinople I (qv) a number of creeds were published: the recourse to such a form of expression was a phenomenon of the age, a concomitant if not simultaneously cause and effect of another marked feature of the time, the frequent journeying of bishops to councils, at the expense of the emperor, for Church and State were one.

To be noted among this series of formularies is first the first creed of the Council of Antioch, 341, which merely says: "And we believe also in the Holy Spirit." The second ("Dedication") creed of the same council is one of the first which elaborates the Spirit's function: "And in the Holy Spirit, who is given to those who believe for comfort, and sanctification, and consummation, as also our Lord Jesus Christ enjoined his disciples saying, 'Go, teach all nations, baptizing them in the name of the Father, and of the Son, and of the Holy Spirit' (Mt 28:19); namely of a Father who is truly Father, and a Son who is truly Son, and of the Holy Spirit, who is truly Holy Spirit, the names not being given without meaning or effect, but denoting accurately the peculiar subsistence, rank, and glory of each that is named, so that they are three in subsistence, and in agreement one."[4]

At the time Theophronius of Tyana drew up a creed which resembled the third and fourth creeds of the Council of Antioch. On our subject it reads thus: "And in the Holy Spirit, the Paraclete, the Spirit of truth (Jn 15:28), which also God promised by his prophet to pour out (Joel 2:28) upon his servants, and the Lord promised to send to his disciples; which also he sent, as the Acts of the Apostles witness."[5]

After some months, a formulary was drafted for presentation to the Emperor Constans. The relevant section is: "And in the Holy Spirit, that is the Paraclete; which, having promised to the Apostles, he sent forth after his ascension into heaven, to teach and remind them of all things; through whom also he sanctified the souls of those who believe in him."[6] A similar statement was made in the creed of the 344 Antiochene Council, known as the Macrostich.

A first creed of Sirmium, 355, does not alter this formulary. The second creed there drawn up in 357, the "Blasphemy" in St. Hilary's word, had this sentence: "And entire and perfect is the number of the Trinity; but the Paraclete, the Holy Spirit, sent forth through the Son, came according to the promise, that he might teach and sanctify the Apostles and all believers."[7] The Dated Creed, 359, uses much the same language: "And in the Holy Spirit, whom the Only-begotten of God himself, Jesus Christ, had promised to send to the race of men, the Paraclete...."[8] The words are borrowed by the Creed of Nice in 359, or 360, and by that of Constantinople, 360.

The Tome of Damasus and the Council of Constantinople are treated separately; as is the Athanasian Creed. Moving forward to Trent, we find that its Profession of Faith repeats the words of the Creed of Constantinople. Paul VI is dealt with separately.

---

[1]Cf. articles, "Apostles' Creed," "Athanasian Creed," "Constantinopolitan Creed" and "Nicene Creed" in *Trinitas*, ample bibl.; R.P.C. Hanson, *The Holy Spirit in Creeds and Confessions of Faith in the Early Church*, in *Atti del Congresso*, I, 291-302; A. Hahn, *Bibliothek der Symbole und Glaubensregeln der alten Kirche* (revised and enlarged G.L. Hahn), Breslau, 1897; [2]Tr. Bettenson, *Documents of the Christian Church*, Oxford, 1943, 33; [3]Repr. by St. Athanasius, *LNPF*, IV, 75; [4]Athanasius, *De synodis*, 23, *LNPF*, IV, 461; Hahn, *op. cit.*, 185, 86; [5]*De synodis*, 24; Hahn, 187, 88; *LNPF*, IV, 462; [6]*De synodis*, *LNPF*, IV, 462; Hahn, *ibid.*; [7]*De synodis*, 28, *LNPF*, IV, 466; [8]*De synodis*, 8, *LNPF*, IV, 454.

CYPRIAN, ST. (d. 258)

A rhetorician converted, with remarkable immediate effects, to Christianity, C. was named bishop of Carthage two years later, lived through persecutions, was finally martyred.[1] He became famous for debates on how the "lapsed," those who had given way under persecution, should be received back into full ecclesial communion, and on those who could minister the sacrament of Baptism. An interesting passage on this Sacrament is found in his Letter 63 which has the Eucharist as its theme. "And he (Christ), indeed, reminding us again of what was predicted beforehand by the prophet, cries out and says: 'If anyone thirst, let him come and drink. He who believes in me, as the Scripture says, from within him there shall flow rivers of living water' (Jn 7:37-38). And that it might be the more apparent that the Lord is speaking there not of the cup, but of Baptism, Scripture adds, saying: 'He said this, however, of the Spirit whom they who believed in him were to receive' (Jn 7:39). But through Baptism the Holy Spirit is received and thus do those who have been baptized and have received the Holy Spirit come to drink the cup of the Lord.'[2]

C. had studied Tertullian (qv), but not slavishly. But he believed that he should spell out the role of the Holy Spirit institutionally, not as Tertullian had understood it. Christ, he thought, the Holy Spirit, the Church and Baptism could not be separated. He was dealing with bishops who thought that the name of Jesus was adequate for Baptism even outside the Church: "Or if they assign the efficacy of Baptism to the majesty of the name so that they who are baptized in the name of Jesus Christ, anywhere and in any way it may be, are considered renewed and sanctified, why in the name of the same Christ, are not hands imposed upon the baptized there for him to receive the Holy Spirit? Why does not the same majesty of the same name which they contend was valid for the sanctification of Baptism prevail for the imposition of hands? For, if he who was born outside the Church can be made a temple of God, why cannot the Holy Spirit also be infused into the temple? For whoever, after his sins have been made manifest, has been sanctified in Baptism and reformed spiritually to the new person has become fit to receive the Holy Spirit since the Apostle says, 'As many soever of you as have been baptized into Christ, have put on Christ' (Gal 3:27). But he who, baptized among the heretics can put on Christ, can much more receive the Holy Spirit whom Christ sent. Otherwise, he who has been sent will be greater than he who sends, that the one baptized outside should, indeed, begin to have put on Christ, but should not have been able to receive the Holy Spirit, as if either Christ could be put on without the Spirit or the Spirit separated from Christ."[3]

C. believed that the Holy Spirit was especially with the martyrs, inspiring them what to speak;[4] and he also believed that he personally received communication from the Spirit on an impending trial for the Church.[5]

---

[1] Works, critical ed. *CSEL*, 3 vols III, 1-3; English tr. *Letters*, R.B. Donna, *FC* 51; cf. A. Harnack, *Cyprian als Enthusiast, ZNW* 3 (1902) 171-191; A. d'Alès, *La théologie de saint Cyprien*, Paris, 1922; H. Koch, *Cyprianische Untersuchungen*, Bonn, 1926; E.W. Benson, *Cyprian, His Life, His Times, His Works*, London, 1897; J. Ludwig, *Der heilige Märtyrerbischof, Cyprian von Karthage*, Munich, 1951; C. Bardy, DSp, II, 2, 2661-2669; The Message, 79-87. [2] *Epistle* 63, *CSEL* III, 2, 707; [3] *Epistle* 74, 5, *FC* 51, 288; [4] *Epistle* 10, *FC* 51, 26; [5] *Epistle* 57, 5, *FC* 161.

CYRIL OF ALEXANDRIA, ST., DOCTOR OF THE CHURCH (d. 444)

The great doctor of Theotokos, specialist among the Fathers in patristic science, wrote frequently, in brief passages, of the Holy Spirit, at some length in his defence of the ninth Anathema against Nestorius, in the Commentary on St. John and in the two works on the Trinity, *Thesaurus de sancta et consubstantiali Trinitate, De sancta et consubstantiali Trinitate dialogi.*[1] The ninth Anathema reads: "If anyone says that the one Lord Jesus Christ was glorified by the Spirit, as it were using through him a power belonging to another, and that he received from him the power to work against unclean spirits, and to perform miracles for men, and does not say rather that the Spirit through whom he worked the miracles was his own; let him be anathema."[2]

C. lived in an age when the heretical challenge about the divinity of the Spirit could be taken as much abated, if not past; we are, as he wrote his principal relevant works, almost three decades after the Council of Constantinople (qv). He still found it necessary to insist on the divinity of the third Person of the Trinity. Since he was, in the Alexandrian tradition, much interested in the reality of divinization, he intertwines the two concepts. "If, sealed by the Holy Spirit, we are given again the divine form, how shall the one be created through whom the image of the divine substance is impressed on us, and the signs of uncreated nature inhere in us. For he does not, as if he were a painter, depict the divine substance in us, as if he were foreign to it; nor does he lead us to the likeness with God in this way; but he, who is God and proceeds from God, is invisibly impressed in the manner of a seal in the hearts of those who receive him, as in wax, refashioning nature to the beauty of its model, by his own communication and likeness, restoring man to the image of God."[3]

He likes to dwell on the idea: "I would like to question those who, through their ignorance of many things, have chosen to adopt other views and have armed their tongues to attack the glory of the Holy Spirit. What would they reply when we say, 'If the Spirit is created and foreign to the divine substance, as you say, then how could God dwell in us through him? Or how does a person share in the divine by receiving the Holy Spirit? If we could share in that divine and ineffable nature through some created substance, then what would prevent God from setting aside the Spirit and dwelling in us, sanctifying us through any other creature he might choose? This, however, is impossible. A person can share in the divine nature only through the Spirit. The Spirit is therefore God and of God; he is not one of the creatures, as some suppose.... Since we are both created and made, the Spirit in whom we participate is of a nature different from ours. The Spirit, therefore, is not created. If this is true, and it certainly is, then the Spirit is God and of God, as we have said. Nothing can be considered uncreated except he who is by nature God, from whom the Holy Spirit ineffably proceeds so that the one from whom he comes may dwell in us. He belongs to his substance, like a property of his holiness."[4]

The relationship between the Spirit's presence to Christ and to others was thus expressed by C.: "John the Baptist witnessed this, 'I saw the Spirit descend from heaven and rest upon him' (Jn 1:32). How was it that he received? We must explain what we have said. Did he receive what he did not have? In no way! The Spirit belongs to the Son. He is not sent into him from outside, as God bestows him on us. The Spirit is naturally in him just as he is in the Father. The Spirit proceeds through him to the saints as the Father bestows him on each one in the appropriate way. We say that the Son received the Spirit insofar as he had become human, and it was appropriate for him to receive him as human.... The Only-begotten became human like us so that the good things which were returned and the grace of the Spirit might first be grounded in him, and thereby firmly preserved for the whole nature."[5]

C. was very conscious of the way in which the Spirit and Christ worked together in souls: "Christ is formed in us in virtue of a divine form which the Holy Spirit infuses into us by sanctification and justice."[6] The Spirit makes us conform to Christ by a certain quality which is in santification. Christ is engraved in us.

C. elaborates the doctrine of the image in relation to Christ and the Spirit: "He is called 'the Holy Spirit' by the voice of the Saviour, which in truth introduces the Spirit into the souls of believers and has him dwell therein; by this Spirit and in him, he (the Saviour) remoulds them in their original form, that is according to himself, or again to a likeness with himself by sanctification; thus he restores us to the first form of the image, that is the impress of the Father. This true impress, of total precision in point of likeness, is himself, the Son; the flawless resemblance in reality of the Son is the Spirit, to whom we are made conformed by sanctification and this shapes us to the very form of God. A word of the Apostle will convince us of it: 'My little children, with whom I am again in travail until Christ be formed in you' (Gal 4:19). But he is formed by the Spirit who restores us to our relationship with God through him. Thus then we are formed according to Christ, from him we receive the impress and figure of the Spirit, as of someone like him in nature; which means that the Spirit is God, he who makes us conform to God not at all by grace of which he would be minister, but in so far as he makes to those worthy of it a present of participation in the divine nature. As for the true resemblance of the Spirit to the Son, you have but to hear what Paul writes of it." C. then quotes Rom 8:29, 30. He continues: "We are remodeled to an effigy which is that of the Holy Spirit, in other words of God, by faith, sanctification and a relation with him—evidently a relation of participation super-added, even if, as to us, one speaks of communication of the divine nature."[7]

Cyril believes that the Spirit divinises us. But he saw the Trinity as the ultimate source: "What happens to us and generally what is done among creatures, may very well appear allocated to each Person; we believe nonetheless that everything is from the Father, through the Son in the Spirit."[8]

What of the *Filioque*? C. is generally taken as the chief eastern Father to have taught it. This text reads very much in that sense: "Since the Holy Spirit is sent into us that he should make us like God, and since he proceeds from the Father and the Son, it is clear that he is of the divine substance, is substantially in it and proceeding from it."[9] C. also taught that the Spirit proceeded from the Father through the Son.[10] Theodoret of Cyrrhus contended that C. changed his opinion on the procession, as a result of his own criticism. The opinion is not justified. C. remained consistent.

---

[1]Principal works required, *PG* 70, 72, 73, 75, *SC* 246; cf. H. du Manoir, S.J., *Dogme et Spiritualité chez St. Cyrille d'Alexandrie*, Paris 1944; id., *DSp* II, 2, 2672-2683, esp., "Pneumatologie," 2680-2681; N. Charlier, C.SS.R., "Le Thesaurus de Trinitate de St. Cyrille d'Alexandrie. *RHE* 14 (1950), 25-81; J. Saques, *El Espiritu Santo en la sanctificación del Hombre segun la doctrina de S. Cirillo Alejandrino*, Madrid, 1947; J. Mahe, *DTC* III (1908) 2476-2527, esp. 2505,

2506; *The Message*, 160-165; [2] *DS* 260; [3] *Thesaurus*, 34, *PG* 75, 609; [4] *In Joann.*, X, *PG* 74, 291; [5] *op. cit.*, V, 2, (Jn 7:39), *PG* 73, 755; [6] *In Is.* IV, 2, *PG* 70, 936; [7] *Dialogi*, VII, *SC* 246, 164-166; [8] *PG* 74, 336B; [9] *Thesaurus*, 34, *PG* 75, 585; further texts *DTC* 2505; [10] *Ibid.*, Theodoret, *PG* 83, 1484.

CYRIL OF JERUSALEM, ST., DOCTOR OF THE CHURCH (c. 315-386)

Enigma surrounded the name of the great catechetical doctor through his well known refusal to use the word *homoousios*, the watchword of Nicene orthodoxy.[1] The enigma has been practically dispelled by Newman in the nineteenth century and the Louvain patrologist, Joseph Lebon, in the present age.[2] C. also suffered vicissitudes in his office as Bishop of Jerusalem, through his proximity to a troublemaker, Acacius of Caesarea (d. 366). He lived to attend the Council of Constantinople (qv) where he may have played a key role: he may have recited the Creed (qv) of Jerusalem, possibly revised by himself in a Nicene sense, thus providing the text of the Creed of Constantinople (qv). Some conjecture here undoubtedly.

Lecture XVI of C.'s Catecheses is devoted to the article, 'And in one Holy Ghost, the Comforter, who spoke through the prophets.' He opens thus: "Spiritual in truth is the grace we need, in order to discourse concerning the Holy Spirit; not that we may speak what is worthy of him, for this is impossible, but that by speaking the words of the divine Scriptures, we may run our course without danger." C. has a methodology in the matter. "It must therefore belong to Jesus Christ's grace itself to grant both to us to speak without deficiency, and to you to hear with discretion.... Let us then speak concerning the Holy Ghost nothing but what is written; and whatsoever is not written let us not busy ourselves about it. The Holy Ghost himself spoke the Scriptures; he has also spoken concerning himself as much as he pleased, or as much as we could receive. Let us therefore speak those things which he has said; for whatsoever he has not said, we dare not say."[3]

If we go back momentarily to C.'s initial outline of the faith we get something more positive: "Believe thou also in the Holy Ghost and hold the same opinion concerning him, which thou hast received to hold concerning the Father and the Son, and follow not those who teach blasphemous things of him. But learn thou that this Holy Spirit is one, indivisible, of manifold power; having many

operations, yet not himself divided; who knoweth the mysteries, who searcheth all things, even the deep things of God; who descended upon the Lord Jesus Christ in form of a dove; who wrought in the law and the prophets; who now also at the season of Baptism sealeth thy soul; of whose holiness also every intellectual nature has need; against whom if any dare to blaspheme he has no forgiveness, neither in this world, nor in that which is to come: 'Who with the Father and the Son together' is honoured with the glory of the godhead: of whom also thrones, and dominions, principalities and powers have need.' For there is one God, the Father of Christ; and one Lord Jesus Christ, the Only-begotten Son of the only God; and one Holy Ghost, the Sanctifier and Deifier of all, who spoke in the Law and the Prophets, in the Old and in the New Testament."[4]

Before listing the heresies against which he warns his readers C. in Chapter XVI asserts the unity of the Trinity: "We neither separate the Holy Trinity, like some; nor do we as Sabellius, work confusion. But we know according to godliness One Father, who sent his Son to be our Saviour; we know one Son who promised that he would send the Comforter from the Father; we know the Holy Ghost who spoke in the prophets, and who, on the day of Pentecost, descended on the Apostles in the form of fiery tongues, here, in Jerusalem, in the Upper Church of the Apostles; for in all things the choicest privileges are with us. Here Christ came down from heaven; here the Holy Ghost came down from heaven. And in truth it were most fitting, that we discourse concerning Christ and Golgotha here in Golgotha, so also we should speak concerning the Holy Ghost in the Upper Church; yet since he who descended there jointly partakes of the glory of him who was crucified here, we here speak concerning him also who descended there; for their worship is indivisible."[5]

C. likes the existential, the factual in this doctrinal area. Having expounded the image or water for the grace of the Holy Spirit he turns to the works of the Spirit: "And though he is one in nature, yet many are the virtues which by the will of God and in the name of Christ he works. For he employs the tongue of one man for wisdom; the soul of another he enlightens by prophecy; to another he gives power to drive away devils; to another he gives to interpret the divine Scriptures. He strengthens one man's self-command; he teaches another the way to give alms; another he teaches to fast and discipline himself; another he teaches to despise the things of the body; another he trains for martyrdom: diverse in different men, yet not diverse from himself, as it is written:"[6] then follows the Pauline text, 1 Cor 12:7-11.

Or again: "First, his coming is gentle; the perception of him is fragrant; his burden most light; beams of light and knowledge gleam forth before his coming. He comes with the bowels of a true guardian; for he comes to save, and to heal, to teach, to admonish, to strengthen, to exhort, to enlighten the mind, first of him who receives him, and afterwards of others also, through him."[7]

C. delays lovingly on the help the Spirit gives the martyrs; he calls up examples of the divine action through Sacred Scripture. He warns the reader again what not to expect: "And it is enough for us to know these things; but inquire not curiously into his nature or substance; for had it been written, we would have spoken of it; for what is not written, let us not venture on; it is sufficient for our salvation to know, that there is Father, Son and Holy Ghost."[8]

In chapter XVII C. picks up many NT incidents where the Holy Spirit is active. On the Annunciation for example he says: "It is Gabriel who says to her, I am the herald of what shall be done, but have no part in the work. Though an Archangel, I know my place; and though I joyfully bid thee 'All hail,' yet how thou as shalt bring forth is not of any grace of mine."[9] Then follows Lk 1:35. Again on the Baptism of the Saviour: "For it was fit, as some have interpreted, that the primacy and first-fruits of the Holy Spirit promised to the baptized should be conferred upon the manhood of the Saviour, who is the giver of such grace."[10]

The Johannine 'Pentecost' (Jn 20:22) is dealt with as is the Lucan: "On the day of Pentecost they were sitting, and the Comforter came down from heaven, the Guardian and Sanctifier of the Church, the Ruler of souls, the Pilot of the tempest-tossed, who leads the wanderers to the light, and presides over the combatants and crowns the victors."[11] Thereafter follows much commentary on the Lucan narrative, and these words: "For many passages are still to come from the Acts of the Apostles (qv) in which the grace of the Holy Ghost wrought mightily in Peter and in all the Apostles together; many also from the Catholic epistles and the fourteen epistles of Paul; out of all which we will now endeavour to gather a few, like flowers from a large meadow, merely by way of remembrance."[12] C. warns the soul that the Spirit tests, but he holds out promise of things "beyond man's power." In Mystagogic Sermon III (XXI) he adds reflections on the Spirit in Baptism.

----

[1]Works *PG* 33, 33-1180; critical ed., W.K. Rieschl and J. Rupp, 2 vols 1848, 1860, repr. Hildesheim 1967; English tr. E. Telfer, *Cyril of Jerusalem and Nemesius of Emesa*, London, 1955; L. McCauley and A.A. Stephenson, *The Works of St. Cyril of Jerusalem*, 2 vols, Washington, 1969, 1970; E.H. Gifford, *LNPF* VII, 1-183, here used; T. Schermann, *Die Gottheit des Heiligen Geistes nach den griechischen Vätern des vierten Jahrhunderts*, Freiburg i. B., 1901, 17-47; P. Galtier, O.P., *Le Saint Esprit en nous d'après les Pères grecs*, Rome, 1946, 105-115; H. Leclercq, O.S.B., *DACL* VII, 2, 2374-2392; X. Le Bachelet, *DTC* III (1908) 2527-2577; M. Jugie, A.A., *EC* III (1950), 1725-28; G. Bardy in *DSp* II, 2. 2683-87; *Trinitas.*, 81-82; *The Message*, 92-97; [2]Newman, Preface to the Lectures of C. in the *Library of theFathers*, apud *LNPF* VII, xlviif; J.Lebon, *RHE* 20 (1924), 181-210, 357-386, *La position de St.Cyrille de Jérusalem dans les luttes provoquées par l'Arianisme*; [3]XVI, 2, p. 115; [4]IV, 16, p. 23; [5]XVI, 4, p. 116; [6]*Ibid.*, 12, p. 118; [7]*Ibid.*, 16, p. 119; [8]*Ibid.*, 24, p. 121; [9]XVII, 6, p. 125; [10]*Ibid.*, 9, p. 126; [11]*Ibid.*, 13, p. 127; [12]*Ibid.*, 20, p. 129.

D

DAMASUS, TOME OF

This set of twenty-four canons was approved by a council held in Rome, sometime between 377 and 382 A.D. Recent scholars, G.L. Dossetti, C. Pietri, bring conclusive arguments in favour of 377. St. Ambrose (qv) had sent a letter to Pope Damasus, denouncing heretics;the council preferred to draw up a summary of Christological and Trinitarian doctrine, with particular emphasis on the Holy Spirit—the divinity of the third divine Person was still denied in places. The introductory passage reads: "(After this Council, which was assembled in the city of Rome by the Catholic bishops, they made additions concerning the Holy Spirit). And because afterwards this error became so fixed that they even dared to say with sacrilegious words that the Holy Spirit was made by the Son:

(1) We anathematize those who proclaim quite freely that he is not of one power and substance with the Father and the Son."

The other canons relevant are:

"(3) We anathematize Arius and Eunomius who with equal impiety, though in different terms, declare that the Son and the Holy Spirit are creatures.

(4) We anathematize the Macedonians who, springing from the root of Arius, have changed not the perfidy, but the name.

(10) If anyone does not say that the Father does always exist, the Son does always exist, and the Holy Spirit does always exist, he is a heretic.

(16) If anyone does not say that the Holy Spirit, just as the Son, is truly and properly of the Father, of divine substance, and is not true God, he is a heretic.

(17) If anyone does not say that the Holy Spirit can do all things and knows all things and is everywhere just as the Son and the Father, he is a heretic.

(18) If anyone says that the Holy Spirit is a creature, or was made by the Son, he is a heretic.

(19) If anyone does not say that the Father made all things through the Son and his Holy Spirit, that is the visible and the invisible; he is a heretic.

(20) If anyone does not say that there is one divinity of Father and Son, and Holy Spirit, one sovereignty, one majesty, one power, one glory, one dominion, one kingdom, and one will and truth, he is a heretic.

(21) If anyone does not say that there are three true persons of Father, and of Son and of Holy Spirit, equal, immortal, containing all things visible and invisible, ruling all things, judging all things, vivifying all things, creating all things, saving all things, he is a heretic.

(22) If anyone does not say that the Holy Spirit ought to be adored by every creature just as the Son and the Father, he is a heretic.

(23) If anyone thinks well of the Father and the Son, but does not rightly esteem the Holy Spirit, he is a heretic, because all heretics who think erroneously about the Son (of God) and the (Holy) Spirit are found in the perfidy of the Jews and the pagans.

(24) But if anyone divides, saying that God (Christ's) Father, and God his Son, and God the Holy Spirit are gods, and does not thus say God on account of the one divinity and power which we believe and know (to be) the Father's, and the Son's, and the Holy Spirit's, but taking away the Son or the Holy Spirit, thus believes that the Father alone is called God, or in this manner believes God one, he is a heretic in every respect, nay rather a Jew, because the name of gods was attached and given both to angels and to all saints from God, but of the Father and of the Son and of the Holy Spirit because of their one and equal divinity, not the name of gods but of God is declared and revealed to us, in order that we may believe, because we are baptized only in the Father, and the Son, and the Holy Spirit and not in the names of archangels or angels, as heretics, or Jews, or even demented pagans. This then is the salvation of Christians, that believing in the Trinity, that is, in the Father, and in the Son, and in the Holy Spirit (and) baptized in this, we believe without doubt that there is only one true divinity and power, majesty, and substance of the same."[1]

---

[1]Text *DS* 152-180; C.H. Turner, *Eccl.Occ. Monumenta Juris antiq.*, I, II, part 1,Oxford, 1913, 281-296; cf. P. Galtier, "Le 'Tome de Damase'", *date et origine, RSR* 26 (1936), 385-418; G.L. Dossetti, *Il simbolo di Nicea e di Constantinopoli*, Rome, 1967; C. Pietri, in *Atti del Congresso*, I, 80-81; R.P.C. Hanson, *ibid.*, 299, 300.

DEATH[1]

It is possible to read extended essays on the theology of death without meeting the name of the Holy Spirit even once. How does one explain this? In the case of one who is in the state of grace, the Spirit is the Sweet Guest of the soul (see Indwelling) attentive to all the needs, all the aspirations, all the spiritual efforts and acts of this person. Charisms flowing directly from the Spirit have perhaps marked this life, as possibly prayer to the Spirit, certainly prayer in the Spirit.

Now the moment of dissolution has come, the final determining phase in this life. The soul will shortly be released to enter eternal life, while the body will be subject to decay; urgency is now the mark of a failing existence, urgency to ensure the proper and happy end. Who can best evaluate this urgency? Who can penetrate through all the depths of this mystery which we call the human person except the Spirit of God?

Death is the decisive moment of encounter between the person and God, and to ensure the encounter the body must be stripped away. Finality is then assured. Finality which must have one of two only outcomes, eternal bliss or damnation. Bliss may be delayed, but if decreed it cannot fail. Here is truly effective the word of Paul: "But as it is written, 'What no eye has seen, nor ear heard, nor the heart of man conceived, what God has prepared for those who love him,' God has revealed to us through the Spirit. For the Spirit searches everything even the depths of God. For what person knows a man's thoughts except the spirit of the man which is in him? So also no one comprehends the thoughts of God except the Spirit of God. Now we have received not the spirit of the world, but the Spirit which is from God, that we might understand the gifts bestowed on us by God. And we impart this in words not taught by human wisdom but taught by the Spirit, interpreting spiritual truths to those who possess the Spirit" (1 Cor 2:9-13).

Existentially death is universal and, save for those who inflict death on themselves, uncertain. Ironically the uncertainty increases as humankind achieves increasing control of the material world. Humans are killed by manmade machines. Humans are killed in vast numbers by weapons of destruction. Death millionfold occurs in the womb. Death millionfold takes place through diversion of scientific expertise from relief to arms production. The era which is either ending or moving to an unimaginable culmination has made death its idol.

Only a massive conversion of humankind to the creative Spirit of God can achieve the desirable ending to this era of frightfulness. "Send forth your Spirit and they shall be created and you shall renew the face of the earth" (Ps 104:30). This conversion must be enlightened by the Spirit on the horror of death. It is the wages of sin and the first stage of illumination is to see clearly this link between sin and death. An age which has lost the sense of sin is not patently equipped for that task.

Why God should decree universal death because of sin is mysterious (Rom 5:12; 1 Cor 15:21-23; Jas 1:15). But the mystery has its solution in redemption and life through Christ. Death is now a prelude to life. It is still existentially unknowable. Not even Christ who triumphed over death has communicated to us what it is experientially: each one must learn that personally. But each now entering into the death and resurrection of Christ, growing in the Spirit which is an intrinsic concomitant of the following of Christ, can forestall death's assault and absorb it into growing life. This happens especially in the case of martyrdom, and may be instantaneous.

Life is lived at many levels. The Christian cooperating with the indwelling Spirit becomes increasingly immune to the fear which death causes; he is rising to a level where this fear has no meaning. He knows that what is being created within him by the Spirit is a work calling for a necessary completion, which only his abuse of his free will can thwart. To acquire this knowledge takes more or less time, according to the work of the Spirit, his choice of the moments for his action. But sooner or later the conviction must take root that what he does, by its very meaning, is oriented, through phases of change, through vicissitudes, to a future reality which will be everlasting. This is where the Spirit unites the thought of death and destiny (see Personality Fulfilment). The growing conviction of his power and especially his concern removes the sense of guilt which death sometimes creates.

The Spirit operates on still another level, that of the communion of saints (qv), he is the living source of this communion. Here we touch the social dimension of death, which seems so intensely private. History abounds in success obtained by the death of a man to whom it was denied in life. "The blood of martyrs is the seed of Christians." No analysis has been made of the means, the communicating channel, by which the effect is produced. In fact little analysis is available of how example works. Why is one person motivated by what another does? Any why simultaneously does the same example fail with another?

Can we, with due regard to the immense difference, derive knowledge from the death of Christ. He "handed over the Spirit" (Jn 20:30). Does the Spirit, possessed by a believing, devout Christian, pass from him, in the moment of death, in imitation, distant though it be, of the death of Christ? And is it received by one properly receptive? Is this what death means in the Communion of Saints? To take an instance from our time, does the Spirit, so active in the life of Hans Urs von Balthasar, pass from him to others?

Death as the moment of transition from one mode of existence to another is entirely in the hands of the Spirit. "Do you not know that your body is a temple of the Holy Spirit within you, which you have from God? You are not your own; you were bought with a great price. So glorify

God in your body" (1 Cor 6:19). "But you are not in the flesh, you are in the Spirit, if in fact the Spirit of God dwells in you. Anyone who does not have the Spirit of Christ does not belong to him. But if Christ is in you, although your bodies are dead because of sin, your spirits are alive because of righteousness. If the Spirit of him who raised Jesus from the dead dwells in you, he who raised Christ Jesus from the dead, will give life to your mortal bodies also through his Spirit which dwells in you" (Rom 8:9-11).

With the Spirit as with all the divine Persons everything is planned in its totality and to the minutest detail; all is foreseen, all assumes, by reason of the divine intention and attention, a majestic quality. We can then speak of the majesty of Christian death. Thus is justified the respect bestowed on the body after death, respect enhanced by noble liturgical service. Through the close-knit composition of body and soul this dead body was once participant in a life instilled and nourished by the Spirit. The departed soul carries with it countless signs of this partnership. Each has been imprinted by the Spirit; each is retained in his enduring treasury of discernment, recognition, conservation.

In physical terms a constructed duplicate of the human brain would occupy more than the surface of the whole earth. What are we to think of the innumerable threads of spiritual thought and volition accumulated during one life, all within the intimate dominion of the Spirit of God? In the reading of general history we often see how death explains and establishes life, as it sometimes remarkably completes it: even to the point of atoning dramatically for its failures. Life before and after death is at every moment related, referable to the Spirit who has, in the case of the faithful Christian, become its dominant centre. He it is then who explains, establishes, completes the life of the Christian.

Through total fidelity to the Spirit's impulse the soul, in the final moment, enters into the highest state of freedom possible. The faithful Christian lives death as a sublime manifestation of freedom. He realizes the truth of St. Paul's words: "If the Spirit of him who raised Jesus from the dead dwells in you, he who raised Christ Jesus from the dead will gife life to your mortal bodies also through the Spirit who dwells in you" (Rom 8:11). This will be more fully developed in the article on Eschatology in the present author's forthcoming work, *Christus Pantocrator,* Christ, ruler, first cause, consummation of all, Lord of history, Master of each individual life and death.

---

[1]Cf. esp. two works often quoted K. Rahner, *On the Theology of Death, Quaestiones Disputatae,* 2, London, 1961; L. Boros, *The Moment of Truth, Mysterium Mortis,* London, 1965 and following editions; for bibl., A. Michel, *DTC* X, 2, 2489-2500; J.A. Wright, *NCE* IV, 687-695; *DSp* X, 1747-1777; "La Bible," P. Grelot; "Réflexion philosophique," E. Borne; "La Liturgie," P. Adnes.

DIDYMUS THE BLIND (c. 313-398)

Blind from the age of five D. had a great career as head of the Catechetical School of Alexandria and writer. Of his writings the *De Spiritu Sancto* and *De Trinitate* interest us, as does the fifth book *Contra Eunomium* attributed to St. Basil (qv), as it treats of the Holy Spirit. The first book, of some importance for us, exists only in a Latin translation by St. Jerome, one of D.'s pupils. The *De Trinitate* contains his remarkable teaching on the outpouring of the Spirit. Both treatises contain valuable information on the heresy of the time, that propagated by the *Pneumatomachi* (qv). Relevant passages on the Holy Spirit are found in *Trinitas, S.V.*[1]

---

[1]*Op. cit.,* 86-88; add *BT* 1, 996-999; G. Bentivegna, "L'effusione dello Spirito Santo nel pensiero di Didimo il cieco," in *Atti del Congresso,* I, 209-218.

DIRECTION, SPIRITUAL[1]

Spiritual direction has been for centuries, practically from earliest times, a means used by those striving to make progress towards Christian perfection. It has taken different forms, as church life was organised in successive generations, varying for those living the eremitical life or those who chose membership of monastic orders, or religious congregations. Fixed tradition, if not formal prescriptions, sometimes made choice of a director obligatory. The scope of his decision, the degree of obedience demanded also varied, as did the range of choice allowed in regard to his person.

Scientific hagiography abounds with instances of beneficial direction and also offers evidence of faulty, defective, even damaging direction. Certain people have the gift of discernment (qv), a spiritually intuitive sense. Some provide adequate advice for the ordinary problems of life, temptations, prayer, apostolic activity, but fail when there is a question of unusual kind to be solved, choice of a state in life, change of religion, launching of a wholly new apostolic initiative, such as the foundation of a lay association, a secular institute or a religious congregation. How many founders have been understood?

The ideal director has the ability to guide in the solution of practical problems, and also to impart instruction where this is wanting; he also conveys a certain conviction that what he advises is not only feasible but preferable. He can encourage by his words and by his presence. Such people are rare. Rarer still are those who in direction exercise genuine charismatic power, as Adrienne von Speyr did for Hans Urs von Balthasar (qv), as Sister Briege McKenna (qv) has done for countless priests, for the distinguished Belgian artist, Leopold Baijot.

Holiness is not a necessary guarantee of excellence here, as a well-known incident in the life of St. Teresa of Avila reminds us. There has to be clear understanding of the meaning of direction, counselling if this word is preferred. What is the aim of the one discharging this function? It is not to satisfy his sense of power, to impose his ego, to put on an air of omniscience, of a direct line to God, to ask for a vow of obedience which in many cases may occasion scrupulosity. It is not to form the soul of the disciple, to plan his life to a fixed programme, to prescribe rules, prohibit certain things. Misunderstanding of this kind creates the many pitfalls which the story of ascetical practice reveals.

The aim of the director should be to help the disciple see clearly the will of God. To that end every modern skill may be used, but in its rightful place, everything that sound psychology teaches. The objective is paramount. That everything must serve. That too must influence the disciple in the difficult task of choosing a director. Here too mistakes are so often made. Something akin to fashion dictates the choice made of a spiritual guide, with possible painful consequences. A director need not be clerical or male. He or she must have some affinity with the disciple, some knowledge, preferably doubled with experience, of the milieu and vocation.

In all this most important work—*ars artium regimen animarum* advertence and prayer to the Holy Spirit are vitally necessary. He is the master of the interior life, for through him the Holy Trinity dwells in the soul; he is the author of holiness through the Gifts which are brought into play essentially in the enterprise of Christian perfection. Through the gift of wisdom he imparts to the director a sense of divine things, of realities intangible but accessible through his intervention; he implants and nourishes a truly spiritual, disinterested outlook. Through the gift of understanding he enables the guide to penetrate the sense of revealed things; through the gift of counsel he helps in the discernment of right solutions to pressing problems.

On the disciple's side the Spirit gives his assistance, again through counsel, in making the right choice of director; through wisdom he lifts the mind of the aspirant to perfection on to the level of the divine things which abide, which outlast all vicissitudes. Through piety and fear of the Lord he helps the soul to overcome and eliminate the deep-seated enemies of holiness, all that stems from the unbridled ego, not least self-deceit.

Above all it is in a shared consciousness of the Spirit's presence, power, immediate relevance that master and disciple truly cooperate in the accomplishment of a truly divine reality in the midst of human frailty.

---

[1]For detailed treatment of the history and theory of spiritual direction, with bibl., cf. DSp, II, 1002-1214, E. des Places, I. Hausherr, F. Vanderbroucke, A. Rayez, G. Bardy, M. Olphe-Galliard, J. McAvoy, G. de Sainte Marie Madeleine, A. Delchard, R. Rouquette, O. Lacombe.

DISCERNMENT OF SPIRITS

The discernment of spirits is the recognition of the Spirit of God at work, in situations where error is possible; this implies the power to identify what is spurious and misguided.[1] It is an area of considerable complexity, where the resources of advanced psychology may be used but fail beyond a particular point. There the charism (qv) which St. Paul speaks of is truly needed. The OT and NT show us discernment in operation; in the OT it was the role of the prophets to enable the children of Israel, God's people, to discern his design for them, to enable them to hearken to his call, to give an attentive response to what be intended. This they could easily miss in the medley of events, crises, conflicts through which they passed.

The monks of Qumran (qv) have left some interesting directives in regard to the question, highly relevant to them with their belief in the duality of spirits: "The Master shall instruct all the sons of light and shall teach them the nature of all the children of men according to the kind of spirit which they possess, the signs identifying their works during their lifetime, their visitation for chastisement, and the time of their reward."[2] "But when a man enters the Covenant to walk according to all these precepts that he may join the holy congregation, they shall examine his spirit in community with respect to his understanding and practice of the law...."[3]

Throughout the whole of the New Testament the question of recognition of the good source of influence in Christian life is never altogether absent; especially in the gospels and Acts there is much evidence to show this need for discrimination. St. Paul makes explicit mention of "discernment of spirits" (1 Cor 12:10). It is associated with prophecy and in 1 Cor 14:24, 25 Paul insinuates the effect of prophecy as discernment. He points to the criteria by which discernment of the Spirit works: judgement by the fruits, (Gal 5:19-23); the effect in building up the Church (1 Cor 14:4, 12, 26; cp. 12:7); signs of power such as miracles, firmness in asserting the word of God, in facing persecution (1 Thess 1:4, 5; 2 Cor 12:12); divine communication by revelation, as Paul knew by experience (Rom 1:1; Gal 1:16, 16; Phil 3:12; Gal 2:9); peace (1 Cor 14:32, 33; Rom 8:6; 14:17); fraternal charity (2 Cor 6:4-7; Phil 1:9; Eph 4:14, 15); finally, the attitude towards Jesus Christ (1 Cor 12:3 and cp. 2:8-10).

Through the experience of subsequent ages the inherent drama of the Christian life, carrying the possibility of error, the possibility of failure in recognising and following the Spirit, remains open to our scrutiny, though this scrutiny does not always master the mystery: the twofold mystery, human in the personality of man, divine in the Spirit of God.

---

[1]Cf. DSp II, 1222-1291, bibl., J. Guillet, G. Bardy, F. Vandenbroucke, J. Pegon, H. Martin; [2]*The Community Rule*, III, in the Dead Sea Scrolls in English, G. Vermes, Pelican Book, 1962, p. 75; [3]*Ibid.*, V, op. cit., p. 80.

DIVINUM ILLUD MUNUS, 9 MAY 1897[1]

Leo XIII's (qv) Encyclical on the Holy Spirit. It was published, therefore, by the Pope who had made the genre of Encyclical famous with *Rerum Novarum* and other examples; and it appeared in his eighty-eighth year, within five years of his death. It is not a lengthy document, but it is admirably planned and composed. The Pope sets the theme in a Trinitarian setting. His ultimate goal is "that faith in the mystery of the august Trinity may be awakened and grow strong in souls. Whoever, therefore writes or speaks of the Trinity,

must keep before his eyes the prudent advice of St. Thomas Aquinas: 'When we speak of the Trinity, we must do so with carefulness and moderation, because as Augustine says, nowhere else is error more dangerous, nor research more laborious, nor discovery more fruitful.' The danger arises from this, that, either in faith or worship, the divine Persons may be confused with one another, or that their one nature may be separated. 'The Catholic faith is that we adore one God in Trinity and Trinity in unity.' That was why Innocent XII, our predecessor, absolutely refused to grant any feast in honour of the Father only. Although individual mysteries of the Incarnate Word are honoured on fixed feastdays, the Word is not honoured by any separate feast, according to his divine nature alone. The feast of Pentecost itself was instituted in ancient times, not merely to honour the Holy Spirit in himself, but rather to commemorate his coming or his external mission. All these things were wisely decreed, lest anyone, in separating the divine Persons, might, perhaps, be led into separating the divine essence too. In fact, in order to preserve her children in the integrity of the faith, the Church instituted the feast of the Most Holy Trinity. Pope John XXII ordered that this feast should be celebrated everywhere. He permitted altars and churches to be dedicated to the Most Holy Trinity. He also, and not without the guidance of heaven, approved of the Religious Order for the Ransom of Captives, which is entirely devoted to the Trinity and rejoices in his name."

The Pope then—to "properly guard the religious devotion owed to the whole Most Blessed Trinity"—expounds the prayer "From him, through him and to him, are all things," in the light of appropriation. Next the role of the Spirit in the Incarnation and in the sanctification of Christ is developed. The role of the Spirit in the origin of the Church as a public entity and then in the life of the Church, of which he is the soul, is considered, as is his work in the spiritual endowment of the soul, in making us sons of God. "Now these great blessings are rightly attributed to the Holy Spirit, as properly belonging to him."

Likewise in regard to the divine indwelling. "God, by grace, resides in the just soul, as in a temple, in a way completely intimate and special...." "Although (this indwelling) is most certainly brought about by the presence of the whole Blessed Trinity in the soul—'We will come to him and make our home with him'—yet it is to be attributed to the Holy Spirit (see article Indwelling), as being specially his."

There is a brief mention of the Gifts (qv): "By the action of these Gifts, the soul is equipped and strengthened so that it more easily and more promptly obeys his voice and impulse. These Gifts, moreover, are so effective that they lead the just soul to the highest point of sanctity, and they are of such excellence that they continue to exist in heaven, though in a more perfect way." There are references also to the fruits (qv). The Pope, at some length urges devotion to the Holy Spirit, warns against the "sin against the Spirit of truth," explains the need of the Holy Spirit, and himself proclaims an annual Novena in preparation for the feast of Pentecost. He ends with a passage on Mary: "At your exhortation let all Christian peoples join their prayers also, invoking the powerful and ever acceptable intercession of the Most Blessed Virgin. You well know the intimate and admirable relations existing between her and the Holy Spirit, so that she is deservedly called his Immaculate Spouse. The prayer of the Virgin herself was of great avail, both for the mystery of the Incarnation and for the coming of the same Paraclete upon the Apostles."

As to sources the Encyclical relies mostly on Johannine and Pauline texts—there are others—from Scripture and on St. Augustine (qv) among the Fathers, eight references, with some other Patristic texts. There are likewise eight quotations from St. Thomas (qv).

----

[1]Text *ASS* 29 (1897), 644-658 and *Leonis XIII, Acta*, XVII, Rome, Tipographia Vaticana, 1898, 125-148; English tr. Holy Spirit Publications, Dublin; cf. A. Huerga, O.P., "La Enciclica de Leon XIII sobre el Espiritu Santo," in *Atti del Congresso* I, 507-516; C. Boyer, S.J., *Introductio brevis a: Leo Papa XIII, De Spiritu Santo*, Rome, Gregorian University, 1952.

DOMINUM ET VIVIFICANTEM, 18 MAY 1986

This Encyclical, to which some previous pronouncements of John Paul II (qv) were by way of prelude almost, constitutes the most substantial essay on the Holy Spirit from the Magisterium in modern times:[1] Leo XIII's Encyclical, *Divinum illud munus* (qv), is slight by comparison; the section in Pius XII's Encyclical, *Mystici Corporis*, important but still slight in scope.

The Encyclical is in three parts: 1. The Spirit of the Father and of the Son given to the Church; 2. The Spirit who convinces the world concerning sin; 3. The Spirit who gives life. There is a certain amount of patristic material, reference that is. The striking thing, however, is the rich biblical content of the text: of 297 footnotes, over 240 are references to scriptural texts. The Pope makes it clear in the introduction that he fully appreciates the contribution of the Orient to this theology: "In our own age, then, we are called anew by the ever ancient and ever new faith of the Church, to draw near to the Holy Spirit as the giver of life. In this we are helped and stimulated also by the heritage we share with the Oriental Churches, which have jealously guarded the extraordinary riches of the teachings of the Fathers on the Holy Spirit." In this context John Paul evokes the Sixteenth Centenary of the First Council of Constantinople, "one of the most important ecclesial events of recent years," celebrated simultaneously in Constantinople and Rome on the Solemnity of Pentecost, 1981. The Holy Spirit was then seen as the "supreme source of unity."

The Encyclical is a response from the Church, as we approach the end of the second Millennium after Christ, to a universal quest for God, a hope for a new creation.

With a wealth of scriptural texts the first sections of the Encyclical unfold the phases and modes of the gift to church and humanity of the Spirit who gives life. The starting point of all is the mystery of the Trinity. Thus we are told that "in the farewell discourse at the Last Supper the highest point of the revelation of the Trinity is reached" (n. 9). Noteworthy is the fact that the new salvific "self-giving of God, in the Holy Spirit" is "a new beginning in relation to the first, original beginning of God's salvific self-giving, which is identified with the mystery of creation itself" (n. 12). The first self-giving was thwarted by sin in its purpose. Now the Spirit comes after the Cross of Christ. But this time the promises are becoming certainties. He comes at the price of Christ's departure. "At the price of the Cross which brings about the Redemption, in the power of the whole Paschal Mystery of Jesus Christ, the Holy Spirit comes in order to remain from the day of Pentecost onwards with the Apostles, to remain with the Church and in the Church, and through her in the world" (n. 14).

The Encyclical reproduces the OT texts when it comes to dealing with the anointing of the Messiah by the Spirit, the prophetic words of Isaiah. But there is a reservation: "The prophetic texts quoted are to be read in the light of the Gospel—just as, in its turn the New Testament draws a particular clarification from the marvellous light contained in these Old Testament texts" (n. 16). There is no suggestion in the Old Testament context of a distinction of subjects or of the divine Persons as they subsist in the mystery of the Trinity, and as they are later revealed in the New Testament. Both in Isaiah and in the whole of the Old Testament the personality of the Holy Spirit is completely hidden: in the revelation of the one God, as also in the foretelling of the future Messiah.

There are enlightening passages on the theophany of the Jordan, which is rightly characterised as 'Trinitarian,' and analyses of the post-Resurrection giving of the Spirit, and especially of the Pentecostal outpouring, which abound in stimulating insights. "We find ourselves on the threshold of the Paschal events. The new, definitive revelation of the Holy Spirit as a Person who is the gift is accomplished at the precise moment. The *Paschal events*—the Passion, Death and Resurrection of Christ—are also the *time of the new coming* of the Holy Spirit, as the Paraclete and the Spirit of truth. They are the time of the 'new beginning,' of the self-communication of the Triune God to humanity in the Holy Spirit through the work of Christ the Redeemer" (n. 23).

The Encyclical emphasizes the era of the Church. Thus we read: "The era of the Church began with the 'coming', that is to say, with the descent of the Holy Spirit on the Apostles, gathered in the Upper Room in Jerusalem, together with Mary, the Lord's Mother. The time of the Church began at the moment when the promises and predictions that so explicitly referred to the Counsellor, the Spirit of truth, began to be fulfilled in complete power and clarity upon the Apostles, thus determining the birth of the Church. The Acts of the Apostles (qv) speak of this at length and in many passages, which state that in the mind of the first community, whose convictions Luke expresses, the *Holy Spirit* assumed the invisible—but in a certain way 'perceptible'—guidance of those who after the departure of the Lord Jesus felt profoundly that they had been left orphans. With the coming of the Spirit they felt capable of fulfilling the mission entrusted to them" (n. 25).

Part two of the Encyclical is quite unusual in its elaborate treatment of the theme of sin as the object of the Spirit's action. There is a close-knit interpretation of the word of the Master: "And when he (the Counsellor) comes, he will convince the world concerning sin and righteousness and judgement: concerning sin, because they do not believe in me; concerning righteousness, because I go to the Father, and you will see me no more; concerning judgment, because the ruler of this world is judged'" (Jn 16:8-11). An interesting comment in passing is that Christ's saving mission— "he did not come into the world only to judge and condemn it; *he came to save it* (Jn 3:17; 12:47)—is emphasized by "the assertion that 'judgement' concerns only the 'prince of this world,' Satan, the one who from the beginning has been exploiting the work of creation against salvation, against the covenant and the union of man with God" (n. 27).

It is the Spirit who reveals to humankind the meaning of sin—something that is rarely thought of: "Convincing concerning sin means showing the evil that sin contains and this is equivalent to revealing the *mystery of iniquity*" (n. 39). It is made clear that "it is not possible to grasp the evil of sin in all its sad reality without searching the depths of God" (*ibid.*). This is applied forcefully to the original sin. But the 'convincing,' which comprehends the reality of the Cross invites conversion or conversion requires it. This conversion "includes the interior judgement of the conscience, and this, being a proof of the action of the Spirit of Truth in man's inmost being, becomes, at the same time, a new beginning of the bestowal of grace and love: 'Receive the Holy Spirit' (Jn 20:22). Thus in this 'convincing concerning sin' we discover *a double gift*: the gift of the truth of conscience and the gift of the certainty of redemption. The Spirit of Truth is the Counsellor" (n. 31).

This theology of sin is developed to comprehend all sin, especially the original sinful act. The meaning of human disobedience and the role of Satan are clarified: "Man's disobedience, nevertheless, always means a *turning away from God*, and in a certain sense the closing up of human freedom in his regard. It also means a certain opening of this freedom—of the human mind and will—to the one who is the "father of lies." This act of conscious choice is not only "disobedience," but also involves a *certain consent to the motivation* which was contained in the first temptation to sin and which is unceasingly renewed during the whole history of man on earth.... Here we find ourselves at the very centre of what could be called the 'anti-Word,' that is to say the 'anti-truth.' For the truth about man becomes falsified; who man is and what are the insuperable limits of his being and freedom. This 'anti-truth' is possible because at the same time there is a complete falsification of the truth about who God is. God the Creator is placed in a state of suspicion, indeed of accusation, in the mind of the creature" (n. 37). It is in this context, which is more fully explained, that the Pope can write: "Who can completely 'convince concerning sin,' or concerning the motivation of man's original independence, except the one who alone is the gift and the source of all giving of gifts, except the Spirit, who 'searches the depths of God' and is the love of the Father and the Son?" (*ibid.*). The Pope also deals with suffering and has enlightening things to say on the sin against the Holy Spirit. A pithy quotation from Pius XII: "the sin of the century is the loss of the sense of sin."

The third part of the Encyclical is presented in the context of the third millennium, which may surprise. But the basis of reference is Christological. We commemorate the birth of Christ, "who was conceived by the Holy Spirit." "The Incarnation of God the Son signifies the taking up into unity with God not only of human nature, but in this human nature in a sense, of everything that is 'flesh'; the whole of humanity, the entire visible and material world. The Incarnation, then, also has a cosmic significance, a cosmic dimension. The 'first-born of all creation,' (Col 1:15) becoming incarnate in the individual humanity of Christ, unites himself in some way with the entire reality of man, which is also 'flesh,' and in this reality with all 'flesh,' (cf. Gen 9:11; Deut 5:26; Job 34:15; Is 40:10; Ps 145, 144:21; Lk 3:6; 1 Pet 1:24) with the whole of creation" (n. 50).

This third part of the papal document treats of the Holy Spirit in humankind's inner conflict, of the inner strength which the Holy Spirit gives the 'inner person,' the Church as the sacrament of intimate union with God; there are reflections on prayer in the section entitled "The Spirit and the Bride say 'Come.'" In the conclusion the Trinitarian idea which recurs is made explicit: "He is the Spirit of the Father and of the Son; like the Father and the Son he is uncreated, without limit, eternal, omnipotent, God, Lord (creed *Quicunque, DS* 75). . . . Before him I kneel at the end of these considerations, and implore him, as the Spirit of the Father and the Son, to grant to all of us *the blessing and grace*, which I desire to pass on, in the name of the Most Holy Trinity, to the sons and daughters of the Church and to the whole human family" (67).

The Encyclical is a worthy contribution from

the Teaching Authority to the varied literature on the Holy Spirit in our age.

---

[1]Text *AAS* 78 (1986), 809-900; English tr. Vatican Polyglot Press, Catholic Truth Society, London: *L'Osservatore Romano*, English ed. 9 June 1986, 1-16; cf. Cardinal Hamer's statement presenting the Encyclical to the Press, 30 May, *ibid.*, 16, 17.

DOXOLOGY

A formula intended to give glory to God by its terms and the recitation of it.[1] The greater Doxology is the *Gloria in excelsis*; the lesser Doxology is the *Gloria Patri*. Doxology was integral to Jewish prayer and the practice recurs in NT, exemplified in hymns or formulas of praise directed to God as Father and to Christ as God. In the NT there is no Doxology directed to the Holy Spirit. As is stated in the article on Glory, there are but few references to his glory; one may possibly add the oblique allusion in 2 Cor 3:18, which follows a much disputed text, "Now the Lord is the Spirit. . . ." (Ibid., 17)[2]

The writings of the Apostolic Fathers have Doxologies to the Father and the Son. *The Martyrdom of Polycarp* contains a Trinitarian Doxology: "For this reason I also praise thee for all things. I bless thee, I glorify thee through the everlasting and heavenly High Priest, Jesus Christ, thy beloved Child, through whom be glory to thee with him and the Holy Spirit, both now and for ages that are to come. Amen."[3]

As the Doxology took the Trinitarian form, assuming a large place in the Church's worship, it became, in the manner of formulation, the test case of orthodoxy: it was an age in which the divinity of the Holy Spirit was challenged. In Antioch the Catholic bishop Eustathius was banished in 330. The Arians, to signify their triumph, imposed the Doxology "Glory to the Father *through* the Son *in* the Holy Spirit": the Catholics used "Glory to the Father and to the Son and to the Holy Spirit." The two formulas were the passwords of the two parties. Bishop Leontius (344-358) sympathetic to the Arians, but not willing to rouse the Catholics, would not recite the Doxology aloud; not even those standing near him knew which he spoke.[4]

In Caesarea the provocative incident involved St. Basil the Great (qv). He was heard one day reciting "to the God and Father *with* the Son *together with* the Holy Spirit," alongside "*through* the Son *in* the Holy Spirit." To the storm that arose we owe Basil's work *De Spiritu Sancto*, a milestone on the way to Constantinople, 381. The tradition of equal glory to the Three Persons had already taken root; the formula is found in the writings of St. Clement of Alexandria[5] (qv), Origen,[6] St. Cyril of Jerusalem[7] and St. Athanasius[8] (qqv).

The *Gloria Patri* is henceforth part of the Church's prayer, ending psalms, the decades of the Rosary, joined with the *Our Father* and *Hail Mary* in intercessory prayers. A notable Trinitarian Doxology ends the Eucharistic Prayer during Mass. The Byzantine liturgy, as other oriental liturgies, has a striking Doxology. "For thou art a kind and loving God and we offer up praise to thee, the Father, the Son and the Holy Spirit, now and always and unto all eternity."[9]

It is part of the mystery of the Holy Spirit, "the Unknown One beyond the Word" as Hans Urs von Balthasar spoke of him, that it should have taken so long in the first centuries to recognize and in practice vindicate his claim to glory. Depth upon death of mystery.

[1]Cf. article Doxology in *Trinitas*, 90-92, bibl.; cf. J.A. Jungmann, S.J. *The Mass of the Roman Rite*, London, 1959, 455-461; id., *The Place of Christ in Liturgical Prayer*, London, 1965, 172-190; id., *Doxologie*, LTK III (1959), 534-36; H. Leclercq, O.S.B., DACL IV, 2 2525-1536; H.R.E.Masterson, NCE IV, 1029-30; E.J. Gratsch, *ibid.*, 1030; J.V.Taylor, *The Go-between God, the Holy Spirit and the Christian Mission,* Philadelphia, 1973 [2]For a discussion of the text cf.A.Feuillet, *Christologie paulinienne et tradition biblique*, Paris, 1965, 23-33; [3]J.A.Jungmann, *op. cit.*, 475; for St. Basil, 176f; [4]XX,2, K.Lake, *The Apostolic Fathers*, II,339; [5]*Paedogogus*, III,c.12 GCS *Clem.Al.* I, 291; 1-12, Stahlin; [6]St. Jerome's tr., PG13, 1896; [7]Cat 7, ed. Reischl and J. Rupp, I,226; [8]LNPF IV, 172; [9]Apud Jungmann, op. cit., 457.

DUFF, FRANK (1889-1980)

On 7 September 1921 Frank Duff, a Dublin layman, member of the St. Vincent de Paul Society, founded an association, the Legion of Mary, which was destined to achieve a vast membership throughout the Church, especially in missionary lands.[1] The founder, like his contemporary, Desiré-Joseph Cardinal Mercier, had been captivated by the classic of Marian spirituality, St. (still at the time Blessed) Louis Marie Grignion de Montfort's treatise on *True Devotion to the Blessed Virgin Mary*. He accepted, as did Mercier, the saint's thesis on Mary's universal mediation of grace. He infused into his association a special Marian idealism, on which it certainly thrived.

It would then be normal to expect that the central point of personal dedication proposed to Legion members would be Our Lady. Or, following the precise example of St. Louis Marie, possibly Incarnate Wisdom might have been chosen. But the legionary promise, the act of definite commitment, essentially a declaration of apostolic faith, was, from the outset, addressed to the Holy Spirit. Thus the splendid formula opens: "Most Holy Spirit, I (name of the candidate), desiring to be enrolled this day as a Legionary of Mary, yet knowing that of myself I cannot render worthy service, do ask of thee to come upon me and fill me with thyself, so that my poor acts may be sustained by thy power and become an instrument of thy mighty purposes. But I know that thou, who hast come to regenerate the world in Jesus Christ, hast not willed to do so except through Mary; that without her we cannot know or love thee; that it is by her, and to whom she pleases, when she pleases, and in the quantity and manner she pleases, that all thy gifts and virtues and graces are administered; and I realize that the secret of a perfect Legionary service consists in a complete union with her who is so completely united to thee."

The promise ends thus: "Confident that thou wilt so receive me—and use me—and turn my weakness into strength this day, I take my place in the ranks of the Legion, and I venture to promise a faithful service. I will submit fully to its discipline, which binds me to my comrades, and shapes us to an army, and keeps our line as on we march with Mary, to work thy will, to operate thy miracles of grace, which will renew the face of the earth, and establish thy reign, Most Holy Spirit, over all. In the name of the Father and of the Son and of the Holy Ghost. Amen."[2]

This formula was drawn up and universally adopted in the twenties, which emphasizes its singularity, uniqueness as an act of dedication in associations of the lay apostolate. It was thus explained by the founder: "It was pointed out that the Legionary Promise was addressed to the Holy Ghost, who received far too little devotion from the general body of Catholics, and for whom Legionaries must needs have special love. Their work, which is the sanctification of themselves, and of the other members of the Mystical Body of Christ, is dependent on the power and operation of the Holy Ghost, and hence calls for a very close union with him. Two things are essential to this: deliberate attention to him, and devotion to the

Blessed Virgin, with whom he works in inseparable union."[3]

The iconography of the Legion teaches the same lesson. The vexillum, or standard, modelled on that of the Roman Legion, has replaced the eagle by the Dove, symbol of the Holy Spirit; the colour is red, symbolic also. The tessera or official prayer leaflet, has a similar design. Readers who need reassurance on the status of Our Lady as a creature will have it in these words also found in the Handbook: "The Legion is built in the first place upon a profound faith in God and in the love he bears his children.... Under God, the Legion is built upon devotion to Mary, 'that ineffable miracle of the Most High' (Pius IX). But what is the place of Mary herself in relation to God? It is that he brought her, as he brought all the other children of earth, out of nothing; and though he has since then exalted her to 'a point of grace immense and inconceivable,' nevertheless, in comparison to her Maker, she still remains as nothing. Indeed, she is—far more than any other—his creature, because he has wrought more in her than in any other of his creatures. The greater the things he does to her, the more she becomes the work of his hands."[4]

F.D. returned to the subject in addresses or occasional papers, to be found among the collections made from these compositions. He had derived some of these ideas from St. Louis Marie, and like the saint he liked to speak of Mary as Spouse of the Holy Spirit. Yet the idea of direct dedication to the Holy Spirit did not come from St. Louis Marie. F.D. thought that it had come as a result of guidance from on high.

As a revelation of the working in practice of F.D.'s ideas his vast correspondence awaits full study, a herculean task. Since at his death the association existed in 1,300 dioceses across the world, especially in Africa, Latin America and the Far East, and maintained a vast variety of works, including annual team visits to eastern Europe, Russia and Africa, and since over the long years of the founder's service he had a vast number of friends and acquaintances, with constant visits from overseas to Dublin, the demands on him as a letter writer were enormous and incessant. The total output may be well in excess of a quarter of a million items—a fund of spiritual advice, testimony to a case history of the Spirit's action in one remarkable life. Among the many envoys directed by correspondence from this source, two like F.D. himself, are proposed for beatification: Edel-Mary Quinn (Kenya and other areas in East Africa,

Mauritius), Alfie Lambe (Brazil). F.D. is the first Lay Auditor of Vatican II in this noble category.

---

[1]While awaiting the definitive biography, cf. T. O'Floinn, C.M., *Frank Duff as I Knew Him*, Dublin, 1981; L. O'Broin, *Frank Duff, A Biography*, Dublin 1982; H. Firtel, *Conquest for Mary*, Dublin, 1962; *id.*, *A Man for Our Time: Frank Duff and the Legion of Mary*, Cork, 1985; R. Bradshaw, *Frank Duff, Founder of the Legion of Mary*, Bay Shore, New York, 1985; on the Legion cf. Fr. J. Ripley and F.S. Mitchell (pen-name for Frank Duff), *Souls at Stake*, Dublin, 1948; C. Hallack, *The Legion of Mary*, 5th ed., with additional ch. by M. O'Carroll, C.S.Sp., London, 1950; L.C. Morand, *The Character of the Legion of Mary in the Law of the Church*, London, 1955; L.J. (Cardinal) Suenens "Spiritualité et rayonnement de la Légion de Marie" in *Maria*, ed. H. Du Manoir, S.J., III, 1954, 637-658; *id.*, *Une heroine de l'apostolat*, Edel-Mary Quinn, Bruges, 1953 and subsequent ed., many tr.; writings of F.D., *The Official Handbook of the Legion of Mary*, many editions, 1964 here used; translations in all European languages and others including Russian, Chinese, Korean; *The De Montfort Way*, London, 1950; *Walk with Mary, Virgo Praedicanda*, Dublin, 1967; *The Woman of Genesis*, Dublin, 1976; *Victory Through Mary*, Dublin, 1981; cf. S. Grace, *Frank Duff, Exemplar of Spirituality*, paper given to International Conference of the Ecumenical Society of the Blessed Virgin Mary, Easter Week, 1989, communicated to the author; esp., F. Flanagan, *John Henry Newman and Frank Duff*, Dublin, 1982; [2]*Handbook*, p. 50, 51, for the theology of the promise cf. L.J. (Cardinal) Suenens, *The Theology of the Apostolate*, Cork, 1954, reissue, *La promesse légionnaire*, Paris, 1982; [3]*Ibid.*; [4]*Handbook*, p. 10, 11.

DUNN, JAMES D.G. (1939–)

At the age of thirty this distinguished biblical scholar, Methodist, published the most significant work in English on the Holy Spirit since Henry Barclay Swete (qv); his total corpus to date eclipses that of Swete, is unique in the English language, though Swete did have the double interest, biblical and patristic.[1] The main thesis of D.'s first work, *Baptism in the Holy Spirit* (1970) challenged traditional Catholic teaching and a basic assumption of the Pentecostals; the author was prompted to investigate the subject by the presence and size of the Pentecostal movement. Catholics, D. thinks, emphasizing water-baptism reduced the Spirit to the Church, "until in all but name 'the Church' stood above the Spirit."[2] On the other hand, "In scholastic Protestantism the Spirit became in effect subordinate to the Bible and the latter replaced the sacraments as the principal means of grace and salvation."[3] Pentecostals reacting against extremes in one communion and the other insisted on *experience* of the Spirit, but D. thinks, with two unfortunate defects: "First the Pentecostal has followed the Catholic in his separation of Spirit-baptism from the event of conversion-initiation (represented in water-baptism), and has made the gift of the Spirit an experience which follows after conversion.... The second mistake of the Pentecostal is that he has followed the Protestant in his separation of faith from water-baptism. Conversion is for him Spirit-engendered faith reaching out to 'receive or accept Jesus,' so that a person is a Christian before his water-baptism and the latter is little more than a confession of a past commitment.... The NT writers would to a man reject any separation of the decisive movement of faith (*pisteusai*) from baptism, either by way of putting the act of faith prior to baptism, thereby reducing baptism to a mere symbol, or by way of putting it after baptism, thereby exalting baptism to an instrument of divine power which operates on a person without his knowledge or consent."[4]

D. sums up his own theory thus: "I hope to show that for the writers of the NT the baptism in or gift of the Spirit was part of the event (or process) of becoming a Christian, together with the effective proclamation of the Gospel, belief in (*eis*) Jesus as Lord, and water-baptism in the name of the Lord Jesus; that it was the chief element in conversion-initiation so that only those who had thus received the Spirit could be called Christians; that the reception of the Spirit was a very definite and often dramatic *experience*, the decisive and climactic experience in conversion-initiation, to which the Christian was usually recalled when reminded of the beginning of his Christian faith and experience.... The high point in conversion-initiation is the gift of the Spirit, and the beginning of the Christian life is to be reckoned from the experience of Spirit-baptism."[5]

D., never losing sight of the Pentecostals, analyses the important events in the Gospels or Acts which would yield material for the fabric of his thinking, expecially Acts, for on this, as he contends, "Pentecostalism is built four-square." He deals with incidents of importance, beginning with the Baptist and Jesus at Jordan, giving special attention to Pentecost and "the riddle of Samaria." He then devotes a number of chapters to Pauline doctrine, John's Gospel and Letters, Hebrews and Peter's Letters. Always his erudition is plenary and well controlled, his exposition clear. He notes that for the Pentecostals "Paul is more an embarrassment than an asset."

Those who disagree with the main contention may still learn very much from the painstaking research. R. Laurentin sums up the Catholic response: "Catholic scholars writing more recently have generally accepted D.'s first conclusion, that the reception of the Spirit is part of Christian initiation, as may be seen, for example, from Paul's reaction to those 'disciples' who had not received the Holy Spirit (Acts 19:1-7). These scholars, however, reject D.'s second conclusion in which he dissociates sacramental water baptism and Baptism in the Spirit. Their position is that water baptism is a complete initiation and bestows the Spirit, and that, in accordance with established teaching we must not confuse the basic rite of water baptism with the secondary and specialized phenomenon of Baptism in the Spirit. All these writers link Baptism in the Spirit with water baptism, although their descriptions of the relationship vary slightly."[6]

Fr. Y.-M.T. Congar writes: "D. regards the sacrament of Baptism simply as a rite. In reality, however, Baptism is a reality which includes conversion, the Church, an action carried out by God (by Christ through his Spirit) and a rite which refers back to the Baptism of Jesus himself, all in one organic whole."[7]

D. does maintain that "If the NT is to be our rule, therefore, the rite of water-baptism may not be given the central role in conversion-initiation. It symbolizes the spiritual cleansing which the Spirit brings and the finality of the break with the old life; it is a stimulus to faith and enables commitment to come to necessary expression; it is the rite of acceptance by the local Christians or congregation as representative of the world-wide Church; but otherwise it is not a channel of grace, and neither the gift of the Spirit nor any of the spiritual blessings which he brings may be inferred from or ascribed to it."[8] Can D.'s thesis be reconciled with the Catholic position stated by Fr. Congar? The incompatibility would certainly be less marked if the Church were taken in its plenary sense as the Body of Christ, not considered institutionally, if the faith which D. sees as the condition of the gift of the Spirit may be linked with aspiration to life in the Church, given an ecclesial dimension, seen as passing through stages to reach its perfect expression with actual awareness of the Spirit. Vast problems.

D.'s second work, *Jesus and the Spirit*, is the most detailed scholarly examination that has been made of the experience factor in the revelation of the Spirit as recorded in NT. He concludes his massive exercise in erudition thus: "We began by asserting the primacy of experience in shaping the course and character of first-generation Christianity. The validity of this assertion has been repeatedly demonstrated in the intervening pages. It is clearly evident that at every stage we have been dealing with a theology and theologizing that is certainly rational, but which is not mere thinking or talking about God, far less a rationalizing of him. The theological thinking of Jesus, of the first Christians, of Paul and John, has been at all times something dynamic, something rooted in their experience of God, something lived and growing out of their religious experience. In particular, we have seen how the distinctive notes of Jesus' preaching sprang at once from his own experience—of God who is near (Father), of God's eschatological power already in operation (Spirit). So too it has been very noticeable how much of Paul's theology we have in fact covered in our study of his understanding of religious experience—how much of his theology, in other words, is experience based—not merely his soteriology, but also his theology (in the narrower sense), his Christology, ecclesiology and ethics, and even in no small measure his eschatology. As for John, we need merely remind ourselves of the extent to which his gospel is the product of his experience of the other Paraclete."[9] Not everyone will agree with this summary judgement. Everyone will be grateful for the immense documentation, the careful annotation, the comprehensive bibliography.

---

[1] *Baptism in the Holy Spirit*, SCM Press, London, 1970; *Jesus and the Spirit*, SCM Press, London, 1975; among D.'s publications the following are relevant to the present work: "2 Corinthians 3:17—'The Lord is the Spirit'", *JTS*, NS 21 (1970) 309-20; "Spirit-baptism and Pentecostalism," *Scottish Journal of Theology* 23 (1970) 397-407; "Spirit and Kingdom," *Expository Times*, 82 (1970-71) 36-40; "'Jesus—Flesh and Spirit': An Exposition of Romans 1:3-4," *JTS* NS 24 (1973) 40-68; "1 Corinthians 15:45—'Last Adam, Life-giving Spirit'" *CSNT* 127-41; "Romans 7:14-25 in the Theology of St. Paul," *TheolZeits* 31 (1975) 257-283; "Prophetic 'I'—sayings in the Jesus Tradition: the Importance of Testing Prophetic Utterances within Early Christianity," *NTS* 24 (1977-78) 175-198; "According to the Spirit of Jesus," *Theological Renewal*, No. 5 (1977), 16-22; "The Birth of a Metaphor—Baptized in the Spirits," *Expository Times* 89 (1977-78), 134-138, 173-175; "Spirit, Holy Spirit," in *The New International Dictionary of New Testament Theology*, III (Paternoster 1978) 689-709; "Discernment of Spirit—A Neglected Gift" in *Witness to the Spirit*, W. Harrington, ed., Irish Biblical Association/Koinonia; Dublin, Manchester, 1979, 79-96; *Christology in the Making: An Inquiry into the Origins of the Doctrine of the Incarnation*, London, SCM Press, Philadelphia, Westminster Press, 1980; "Rediscovering the Spirit (2)," *Expository Times* 94 (1982-83), 9-18; "Fruit of the Spirit," "Gifts of the Spirit," "Experience of Jesus," "Pauline Spirituality," "Peace," "Holy Spirit," in *A Dictionary of Christian Spirituality*, G.S. Wakefield, ed. SCM Press 1983, 166-167; 173-4; 221-2; 289-90; 290-92; 357-8; "Enthusiasm" in *The Encyclopaedia of Religion*, M. Eliade ed., New York, 1987, V, 118-124 (double c); "Ministry and the Ministry: The Charismatic Renewal's Challenge to Traditional Ecclesiology," in *Charismatic Experiences in History*, C.M. Robeck ed., with Hendrickson,, Peabody, Massachusetts, 1987, 81-101; [2] *Baptism in the Holy Spirit*, 224; [3] *Op.cit.*, 225; [4] *Op.cit.*, 226f; [5] *Op.cit.*, 4; [6] *Catholic Pentecostalism*, 1977, 37f; [7] *The Holy Spirit*, II, 194; [8] *Op.cit.*, 228; [9] *Jesus and the Spirit*, 360f.

E

ECUMENISM[1]

The Decree on Ecumenism issued by Vatican II (qv) speaks of the ecumenical movement as born under the action of the Holy Spirit (art. 1). Expounding its doctrine on ecumenism the Council speaks thus: "Raised on the cross and then entering on glory, the Lord Jesus sent the Spirit whom he had promised. Through him he called and united the people of the new covenant, which is the Church, in the unity of faith, hope and charity, as the Apostle teaches: "There is one body and one Spirit, just as you were called to the one hope that belongs to your call, one Lord, one faith, one baptism, one God and Father of us all." (Eph 4:4-5) "For as many of you as were baptized into Christ have put on Christ ... you are all one in Christ Jesus." (Gal 3:27,28) The Holy Spirit who dwells in the faithful, who fills and rules the whole Church (qv) achieves this admirable communion of the faithful, and unites them so intimately in

Christ that he is the principle of unity of the Church. It is he who achieves the diversity of graces and ministries (cf 1 Cor 12:4-11), enriching the different offices of the Church of Jesus Christ, "for the equipment of the saints, for the work of ministry, for building up the body of Christ" (Eph 4:12) (art. 2). Later the Decree speaks of the "love and veneration—the cult almost—that the separated brethren of the western communities have for the Sacred Scripture, going on to say: "Invoking the Holy Spirit it is in the Scriptures themselves that they seek God as the one who speaks to them through Christ whom the prophets had announced and who is the Word of God incarnate for us." (art. 21). There is unfortunately no reference in the part of the Decree dealing with the Orthodox to the sense of the Spirit in their theology and liturgy. The problem of the *Filioque* which concerns the very doctrine of the Spirit is dealt with in a separate article.

---

[1]See articles with bibl., Barth, K., Bolotov, B. Bulgakov, S., Calvin, J., Dunn, J.G.D. Evdokimov, P., Lossky, V., Luther, M., Orthodox, The, Quakers, The, Swete, H.B., Wesley, J., cf., *L'Esprit Saint et l'Eglise. L'Avenir de l'Eglise et de l'oecumenisme*, Fayard, Paris, 1969, Proceedings of the Monaco Symposium; 1966. J. Thompson, *The Holy Spirit and the Trinity in Ecumenical Perspective*, ITQ 47 (1980).

EPHRAEM OF SYRIA, ST., DOCTOR OF THE CHURCH (c. 306-373)

Trained by Bishop James of Nisibis (303-338), who had been at the Council of Nicaea (qv) and by his second successor, Vologesus (343-361) E., ordained deacon by James, taught first in Nisibis, but, after the advent of the Persians, went to live at Edessa in the Roman Empire.[1]

Though called "the lyre of the Holy Spirit" because of his inspired writings, E. said little about the subject in his early works, *De Paradiso* and the *Sermones de Fide*. His doctrine is found in the hymns *De Fide*, especially in hymn 77. In one respect he recalls St. Basil (qv).

Those, in the same age as E., involved in the defence of Nicaea (qv) and resistance to residual Arianism (qv) were logically led to consider the person of the Spirit, as they were engaged in vindicating the person of the Son. This was the case with Athanasius and the Cappadocians, as it was with E.

Orthodox doctrine drew on the baptismal formula, rooted as it was in Scripture. The way the three names were placed side by side pointed to the divinity of the Holy Spirit: "The names of the Father and Son and Holy Spirit are equal and agreeing in the invocation of Baptism. With the names agreeing, there is an equal effect of one will. And as they are equal in the invocation of Baptism, they are so also in (essential) agreement."[2]

E. considered the Baptism of Christ (qv) as a concrete example; he thought it was performed through the three divine Persons: "Who can declare the three names false, when their invocation had conferred (Christ's Baptism) in the Jordan? There is truth in the names in which your body is baptized. For bodies are baptized and although there are many names for the Lord of the universe, we baptize (with the names of) the Father and the Son and the Holy Spirit separately."[3] E. is at pains to show that though what is mingled sometimes loses its value, but it is not so in the Holy Trinity.

Here was where E. founded his faith: "I brought my faith to the Father and he signed his fatherhood in it; I brought it to the Son and he mingled with it his generation and the Holy Spirit his holiness. And I concluded in that faith a creed sanctifying all things."[4] But this was not his innovation; it was handed down by the Apostles: "Baptism is attached to these three names; in these three mysteries our faith shines forth; Our Lord gave these three names to the Apostles, to whom we turn."[5] E.'s great commentator and textual critical editor, Dom Edmond Beck, maintains that when he uses the word "name" he wishes to convey what we express by "person."[6]

In hymn 77[7] E. uses a symbol or metaphor to express his idea of the Trinity: the sun, God the Father, the light or beam God the Son, the heat, God the Holy Spirit. The symbol is of unity as of Trinity: "The heat is not cut off from the beam with which it is mingled, nor from the sun with which it is united." "Heat has power in all things, wholly in all, wholly in each. When it is poured out over creatures, each takes as much as he can."

Continuing the metaphor E. enlightens us on the operations of the Spirit, equipping humans, especially the Apostles for their tasks. As heat matures things, the Spirit sanctifies. Cold is overcome in the body by heat; uncleanliness (of soul) by the Spirit. As heat stirs the earth in its depths, the Spirit stirs the Church.

There are hints, more than hints of the divinity of the Spirit in the hymn—reference to "infinite treasure," to the diminitive nature of all things beside him—and also a reminder of the manifold power symbolized in the tongues of fire. Yet we meet the same problem as with St. Basil: Why, even in hymn 59 where he combats the Pneumatochians (qv) and defends the divinity of the Spirit, does he not call him God? Why does he not speak directly of the Godhead, the divinity, of the Spirit? He was faced with a similar situation to St. Basil and had to practise economy. There is no doubt at all that he believed in the divinity of the Spirit: not only from his opposition to the Pneumatochians, but from such affirmations as that he is equal to the Father and the Son, as has been seen, that he is not a creature, nor a work, that he is exalted above creation.

E. has a rich Eucharistic doctrine, wherein he holds that the Holy Spirit is especially present in the Eucharist.

---

[1]Cf. esp. E. Beck, O.S.B., *DSp*, IV, 788-800, esp. 799; id., *Die Theologie des Hl. Ephrem in seinen Hymnen, über den Glauben, Studia Anselmiana*, 21, Rome, 1949, p. 81-86; P. Yousif, "St. Ephrem on Symbols in Nature, Faith, the Trinity and the Cross," in *Eastern Churches Review*, 10 (1978), 52-60; [2]Hymn 77, 2, apud Beck, 81; [3]Humn 51, 7, *op.cit.*, 81; [4]Hymn 13, 2, *op. cit.*, 82; [5]Hymn 13, 5, *ibid.*; [6]*Op. cit.*, 81; [7]E. Beck, ed., *Des Heiligen Ephraem des Syrers, Hymnen De Fide, herausg. von E. Beck, O.S.B., übersetzt von E. Beck, CSCO* 155, Louvain, 1955, Hymn 74, p. 194-196.

EPICLESIS, THE

This is the invocation made to God to send the Holy Spirit during the celebration of the Eucharist. It can, in a wide sense, refer to any invoking of a divine name, such as is made in the Sacraments of Baptism, Confirmation and Ordination, even at the blessing of a font. There has been a difference of opinion between east and west on the meaning and importance of the Epiclesis. The subject is dealt with, with bibl., in the author's work, *Trinitas*, s.v.,[1] in the articles on the Holy Spirit and the Eucharistic Prayers in *Corpus Christi*.[2]

---

[1]*Op. cit.*, 98-100; [2]s.v.

EUCHARIST, THE

It is noteworthy that Acts (qv) speaks of the apostles and the others gathered around Mary as "with one accord devoting themselves to prayer" (1:14), but makes no mention ot the "breaking of bread" until after the descent of the Spirit. "And they devoted themselves to the apostles' teaching and fellowship, to the breaking of bread and the prayers." (Acts 2:42). In the next reference there is a hint of the separation from worship in the temple and the "breaking of bread": "And day by day,

attending the temple together and breaking bread in their homes, they partook of food with glad and generous hearts, praising God and having favour with the people." (*Ibid.*, 46,47).[1] "Breaking bread was the Eucharist.

There has been an increasing interest in the relationship between the Spirit and the Eucharist. The ecumenical movement has stimulated research in the Epiclesis as practised and understood in the East. One mighty figure, Nicholas Cabasilas (14th century) was polemical on the subject, accusing the Latins of misunderstanding and some confusion: he thought they denied the necessity of the Epiclesis and yet used it in a veiled way. Cabasilas linked the promise of the Saviour "you shall receive power "(Lk 24:49; Acts 1:8) with his injunction "Do this in memory of me" (Lk 22:19; 1 Cor 11:24). "But he would not have ordered them to do it, if he were not about to give them the power, by which they could do so. And what was the power? The Holy Spirit, the power which descending from on high equipped the Apostles in accordance with the word spoken to them by the Lord: *Remain in the city of Jerusalem ___ you shall receive power*."[2]

There is a difference between the eastern and western approach to the mystery of consecration. The western tradition for centuries has emphasized *in persona Christi*. A modern Orthodox theologian, Paul Evdokimov (qv) is critical of the tradition: "For the Latins, the *verba substantialia* of the consecration, the institutional words of Christ are pronounced by the priest *in persona Christi*, which bestows on them a value which is immediately consecratory. For the Greeks, however, a similar definition of the priestly action—*in persona Christi*—which identifies the priest with Christ is absolutely unknown. Indeed it is unthinkable. For them the priest invokes the Spirit precisely in order that the words of Christ, reproduced and cited by the priest, acquire all the effectiveness of the speech-act of God."[3] Yet Fr. Congar, (qv) who quotes these words, has aligned a number of quotations from St. John Chrysostom and Severus of Antioch to recent eastern authorities accepting or affirming the idea of *in persona Christi*.

It is well known that the Eucharistic Prayers introduced in the Latin church since the Council have the epiclesis, in its twofold significance, prior to the consecration on that act, after distribution of the fruits among the faithful. There is clearly need for deeper reflection on the twofold aspect of the problem of the Spirit and the Eucharist: the relationship between the Spirit and Christ present in the Eucharist and the relationship between the Spirit and the grace which comes to the individual through the Eucharist, sacrament and sacrifice.

The great Syrian Doctor of the Church, St. Ephraem, was particularly sensitive to this reality of Christ and the Spirit in the Eucharist. This was vital for him, for his theory of spiritualization through the Spirit and Christ. "Spirit in your bread. Fire in your wine, a sublime wonder, which our lips receive." "Here is the power hidden in the veil of your Holy Spirit, power which no thought has ever grasped. His love was lowered, descended and hovered over the altar of reconciliation."[4] "Fire and Spirit in the womb of your Mother; Fire and Spirit in the river wherein you were baptized; Fire and Spirit in our baptism (Lk 3:16); in the Bread and in the Cup, Fire and Holy Spirit."[5]

It is well known that the Latin and eastern traditions vary with an emphasis on the Trinity by the easterns and a Christological approach by the Latins. The ideal of *in persona Ecclesiae* as well as *in persona Christi* favours, in practice, a harmonious synthesis which helps the individual participant and communicant in the Eucharist to enliven his sense of the Spirit and of Christ together. For the Church is the Body of Christ and the Spirit it is who gives it life, unity and growth. Towards this ideal consciously or unconsciously have been moving those who promote enlightened participation by all in the Eucharist as sacrament and sacrifice. (See art. Scheeben, M.J.)

[1]Cf. author's *Trinitas*, art. Epiclesis with bibl. 98-100; in author's *Corpus Christi* art. Cabasilas, 43-45; cf. J.H. McKenna, *Eucharist and Holy Spirit, The Eucharistic Epiclesis in 20th Century Theology*, London, 1976; Y.M. Congar O.P. (qv), *The Holy Spirit* III, 228-274; P. McGoldrick, *The Holy Spirit and the Eucharist*, ITQ 50 (1983) 48-66; Theresa F. Koernko, *The Pneumatological Dimension of the Eucharist; The Contribution of Modern Catholic Theology to the Relationship between Office, Eucharist and Holy Spirit*, Diss. Notre Dame, 1983; E.J. Kilmartin, *The Active Role of Christ and the Spirit in the Sanctification of the Eucharistic Elements*, ThSt 45 (1984), 225-253; J.M. Tillard, L'*Eucharistic* Pâque de l'Eglise, Paris, 1944; [2]*The Exposition of the Divine Liturgy*. PG 150,425; [3]L'*Orthodoxie*, Paris, 1959, 250; [4]Op. cit., 237; [5]Reference to Hymn De Fide, X, apud M.O'Carroll, *Corpus Christi*, 79,80.

EVDOKIMOV, PAUL (1901-1970)

E., an expatriate Russian, was influenced by the thinking of Vladimir Solovieff, but especially by S. Bulgakov (qv) of the Serge Institute in Paris, of which institution he was to become an ornament

himself.[1] He wrote considerably, especially on the spirituality of marriage, on the significance of icons and on woman's role in the Church. In his last years he was led to deal with Orthodox theology of the Holy Spirit; in these years the ecumenical outlook he inherited from Bulgakov was also especially alert. Not surprisingly his last public lecture was an address, *Pangion et Panagia*, on Mary and the Holy Spirit, given to the French Society of Marian Studies meeting in Fribourg in 1970.[2]

E.'s contribution to the theology of the Holy Spirit is in these works: *L'Orthodoxie*, Paris, 1959; *L'Esprit Saint dans la tradition orthodoxe*, Paris, 1969, reissued 1977 as *Présence de l'Esprit Saint dans la tradition orthodoxe*, 1977; *L'Esprit Saint pensé par les Pères et vécu par la Liturgie*, in *Le Mystère de l'Esprit Saint* with H. Cazelles and A. Grenier, Paris, 1968;[3] "L'Esprit Saint et l'Eglise d'apre1²s la tradition liturgique," in *L'Esprit Saint et l'Eglise. L'avenir de l'Eglise et l'Oecuménisme*. Two collections of articles published posthumously are relevant, *La sainteté dans la tradition de l'Eglise orthodoxe*, 1971; and especially *La Nouveauté de l'Esprit; Etudes de spiritualité*, 1977.

The repetition of the word tradition in the titles of E.'s works says something about his deep faith in the Orthodox church. He was also convinced of the omnipresent Spirit, whom he thought relevant to every aspect of Christian thought and practice. The author of the first monograph on his teaching on the Spirit has been able to follow him in this thinking and writing through the central themes of theology, revelation, Trinitarian life, humanity and Christ, the saving economy, the Church, Mary, the epiclesis and ecumenism, the cosmos, beauty, history, the final age.

E. had some finely balanced, searching things to say about innovation in theology: "Today in addition to the opposition of different confessions, there is an inner division centred on secularized Christianity, on Christ in a world without God, and even Christ without God. What strikes one about the leaders of this 'new theology' is the absence of Trinitarian theology and all reference to the Fathers of the Church. They follow the world in secularizing the Bible and Tradition."[4] How different is his own attitude, in the Orthodox tradition, "Orthodoxy is attentive to the 'unspeakable sighs of the Spirit' and places theology under the sign of the epiclesis." The Spirit inspires faith in the mysteries.

E. was much preoccupied by the controversy

on the procession of the Holy Spirit. "In the last thousand years," he wrote, "pneumatology has been reduced completely to controversy about the procession of the Holy Spirit. The unilateral way in which the problem has been posed makes it a false problem centred on a sterile discussion between monopatrism and filioquism. The formula of Photius (qv)—*ek monou tou Patros*—from the Father alone—is a polemical formula set against the *Filioque*. The patristic viewpoint is neither one nor the other, but a third position which is immeasurably more refined, though not entirely explicit."[5]

E. thinks that the Eastern and Western positions are *theologoumena*. He was one of those who accepted B. Bolotov's opinion that the Filioque is not an *impedimentum dirimens* to re-union between East and West. But he would require an important change; the *Filioque* should not be imposed as a dogma.

E. discusses without sympathy the Western philosophic structure invoked in Trinitarian theology, on the origin of the Persons. He seeks to justify the doctrine of St. Gregory Palamas (qv) on the divine energies, intent on the Eastern attachment to the idea of deification. He elaborates the doctrine of the Spirit's mission and relates it to the Eucharist. A dedicated ecumenist, he gave very great importance to the question of the epiclesis (qv), which he thought as relevant to progress as the *Filioque*. Thus he saw the contrast between East and West: "For the Greeks, however, a similar definition of the priestly action—*in persona Christi*—which identifies the priest with Christ is absolutely unknown. Indeed it is quite unthinkable. For them the priest invokes the Holy Spirit precisely in order that the words of Christ, *reproduced and cited* by the priest, acquire all the effectiveness of the speech-act of God."[6]

E. was not at all prevented by the view of such differences between the confessions from preserving intellectual serenity, true charity and an unshakable conviction of the Spirit's universal presence, power and fruitfulness.

---

[1]Cf. esp. P.G. Gianazza, *Paolo Evdokimov, Cantore dello Spirito Santo,* Rome 1983, bibl. 170-180; P. Corcoran, S.M., "Some Recent Writing on the Holy Spirit, Evdokimov," *ITQ* 39 (1972), 278-284; see article "Orthodox, The [2]*Etudes Mariales,* Bulletin de la Société francaise d'E.M., 1970; [3]*Académie Internationale de Sciences Religieuses,* 1969, 85-111; [4]*L'Esprit Saint dans la tradition orthodoxe,* 12-13, apud P. Corcoran, *op. cit.,* 278; [5]*Op. cit.,* 69, P. Corcoran, 279; [6]*Op. cit.,* 101.

EXPERIENCE OF THE SPIRIT

With experience we enter the domain of the personal and existential, that is the world of endless variety, of human mystery. If we seek a completely satisfactory account of the subject we must survey the history of the Church, of the Jewish people, eventually of the true elements which Vatican II recognises in the world religions. Two great contemporary theologians have dealt with the problem, Karl Rahner (qv) and Y.-M.J. Congar, (qv), the former analytically with reference to Christian living, at many levels, the latter in the perspective of history.[1]

There is a vague idea that the Spirit was especially active in the early days of the Church, with an abundance of charisms (qv) to manifest his active presence, but that this has changed, and in some way the Church and her members must not now count on such things. Mention of charisms was considered something of an innovation during the proceedings of the Second Vatican Council. But eventually the Council included the subject in its teaching, the first Council to do so. (See article on Neglect of the Spirit)

It is believable that the Spirit does not lend himself to the same kind of experience in our time as in the springtime of the Church. But he remains; his role does not change; our need is basically identical with that of the early Christians, though the circumstances may alter the mode which gives this need expression.

"Our time" is an ambiguous phrase in regard to religion, as to so many other areas of life. There are vast populations which await evangelization; there are countries which need reevangelization; there are regions where the faith is strong and practice not negligible. If the Spirit is experienced in our time, as he certainly is, it will be in different ways in these widely differing situations, while along with the difference there will quite possibly be similar effects due to the cohesion of the Mystical Body. That organic cohesion transcends and triumphs over all divisive or differentiating elements.

There have been many attempts to achieve accurate transcription of the itinerary marked out for souls by the Spirit. Not all match the mystical graces received by Sister Julitta Ritz (qv) or Sister Briege McKenna (qv). But the literature of the charismatic movement (qv) abounds in records reliable and valuable as evidence of the Spirit's intimate concern for the members of Christ's Body.

The literature of experience through the ages is vast with the testimonies from the exceptionally privileged—St. Paul and others less so, but still remarkable, like St. Patrick (qv) and Newman (qv). It is a field awaiting detailed study, exploration which will surely yield surprising results.

We must finally allow for the experience which, as Karl Rahner suggests, may be authentic but anonymous: "Within our existence, which always thrusts us beyond particular data into the seeming emptiness of absolute mystery, we experience God through grace and God's Spirit. More often than not this experience is anonymous, and is not reflected on or put into words. We usually suppress it in our preoccupation with the objects and tasks of everyday life. But it is still there, and at certain times we become aware of it, even within everyday existence. It presses forward and offers itself to reflection and to human freedom. There is no lack of examples of such experience of the Spirit and of God in the Spirit."[2] The author fills in details of this generalization elsewhere in his writings.[3]

---

[1]Volume I of Fr. Congar's work, *The Holy Spirit*, is entitled *The Experience of the Spirit*, tracing the theme through OT, NT, history and theological writers; on religious experience cf. W.J. Hill, *NCE*, V, 751-53 and *ibid.,* on experience theology, M.B. Schepers, 753f; [2]*Karl Rahner in Dialogue*, Conversations and Interviews, 1965-1982 ed. P. Imhof and H. Biallowons, tr. H.D. Egan, New York, 1986, 141; [3]"Experience of the Spirit and Existential Commitment," in *Theological Investigations* XVI, 1979, 24-34; "Das Charismatische im der Kirche," in *Stimmen der Zeit*, 160, (1956), 57, 181-186 and see article, "Rahner, Karl."

F

FILIOQUE[1]

Three aspects of this question merit attention: the theological validity of the word, the appearance and development of controversy on the subject between East and West through the ages, the possibility in our time of resolving the difficulty in a new spirit of ecumenical dialogue.

Procession within the Trinity poses the problem how one Person proceeds from another. Theologians agree that the Son and the Spirit proceed; the Father does not. The Son proceeds from the Father in generation, as his Only-begotten; the Spirit also proceeds from the Father, Only-begotten from the Father or conjointly from the Father and the Son.

The biblical evidence is slight, mostly from St. John. "But when the Counsellor comes, whom I shall send to you from the Father, even the Spirit of truth, who proceeds from the Father, he will bear witness to me'" (15:26). "He (the Spirit of truth) will glorify me, for he will take what is mine and declare it to you'" (16:14). In the first of these texts it is clear that the Spirit proceeds from the Father, as it is clear that he is sent by the Son. In the second text a very close relationship between the Spirit and the Son is described. It is not stated explicitly that he proceeds from the Father and the Son, but what is said is in harmony with this truth.

"'I and the Father are one,'" said Jesus (Jn 10:30). If to this is added the word in Jn 20:22, the *Filioque* may seem to be implied: "And when he had said this, he breathed on them, and said to them: 'Receive the Holy Spirit.'" The Spirit is named third, equal to the others in the baptismal formula in Mt 28:19, but there is no hint there of procession. Some other texts are mentioned as possibly suggesting the double procession: "And because you are sons, God has sent the Spirit of his Son into our hearts crying, 'Abba, Father!'" (Gal 4:6). "But you are not in the flesh, you are in the Spirit, if in fact the Spirit of God dwells in you. And any one who does not have the Spirit of Christ does not belong to him" (Rom 8:9). Since in the second text God probably means Father, the conjunction of "Spirit of God" and "Spirit of Christ" is important. There is reference to the "Spirit of Jesus Christ" in Phil 1:19.

The doctrine of the *Filioque* was to become a distinctive element of western Trinitarian theology. Texts are reproduced from Tertullian, Marius Victorinus, St. Hilary and, with much less confidence, St. Ambrose, to show that thought was moving that way.[2] St. Augustine (qv) brought complete clarity: "And we cannot say that the Holy Spirit does not also proceed from the Son; for it is not in vain that the same Spirit is called the Spirit of the Father and the Spirit of the Son. Nor do I see what else he wished to express when breathing on the face of the disciples he said, 'Receive the Holy Spirit' (Jn 20:22). Nor was that physical breath proceeding from the body with the meaning of bodily contact the substance of the Holy Spirit, but the proof by appropriate expression that the Holy Spirit proceeds not only from the Father but from the Son."[3] And among other texts this also: "It must be confessed that the Father and the Son are one principle, not two, of the Holy Spirit; but as the Father and Son are one God, and in regard to the creature, one Creator and one Lord, thus in regard to the Holy Spirit they are one principle."[4] Several western Fathers repeated the opinion.

The opinion nearest to the Latin which is found in the East is procession through the Son. One Greek Father, St. Cyril of Alexandria (qv) is quoted as supporting the *Filioque* and one, St. Epiphanius, may have countenanced the idea. St. John of Damascus summing up here as in so many questions the eastern tradition writes: "The Holy Spirit is the power of the Father, making the secrets of the deity known and proceeding from the Father through the Son in a way that he knows, but which is not begetting."[4] With Photius (qv) the eastern tradition was hardened; he would think of procession only from the Father alone, *ek monou tou Patros*.

At the level of church authority the Papacy was slow to pronounce on the matter. Spain was the home of early credal assertions. At Toledo in 589 King Recarred, a convert from Arianism, gave publicity to the *Filioque* and a century later, in 680 the synod of Hatfield did likewise. After a council at Gentilly had affirmed the doctrine, St. Paulinus of Aquileia, ecclesiastical supporter of Charlemagne, secured further conciliar agreement, going so far himself as to brand opponents "heretics." Charlemagne himself, desirous to influence matters liturgical and doctrinal, sought to influence Pope Leo III to take a public stand in the question: he failed, though the Pope accepted the doctrine privately. He had the original creed without the addition inscribed on two silver tablets placed at the tomb of St. Peter.

The practice of including *Filioque* was, however, gaining ground. St. Anselm (qv) who was present at the Council of Bari in October 1098, there defended the doctrine against the Greek monks; he further developed and expressed his thought in his work *De processione Spiritus Sancti;* he was critical of *a Patre per Filium*. St. Thomas Aquinas expounded both the *Filioque* and *per Filium*. In the year of his death, 1274, the doctrine of the *Filioque* was defined at the Council of Lyons, which was attended by delegates of Michael Palaeologus. The clergy and people of Constantinople would not agree, despite severe pressure from the emperor.

The next attempt to secure agreement was at the Council of Florence. After much discussion of patristic, scriptural and biblical texts, and many vicissitudes, agreement was reached and expressed in the Bull *Laetentur coeli*, 6 July 1439. It was a document not so much of compromise but of accommodation, for both formulae, *Filioque* and *per Filium* were admitted. The relevant passage reads thus: "In the name of the Holy Trinity, of the Father, and of the Son, and of the Holy Spirit, with the approbation of this holy general Council of Florence we define that this truth of faith be believed and accepted by all Christians, and that all likewise profess that the Holy Spirit is eternally from the Father and the Son, and has his essence and his subsistent being both from the Father and the Son, and proceeds from both eternally as from one principle and one spiration; we declare that what the holy Doctors and Fathers say, namely that the Holy Spirit proceeds from the Father through the Son, tends to this meaning, that by this it is signified that the Son also is the cause, according to the Greeks, and according to the Latins, the principle, of the subsistence of the Holy Spirit, as is the Father also. And that all things, which are the Father's, the Father himself has given in begetting his only-begotten Son; without being Father, the Son himself possesses this from the Father, that the Holy Spirit proceeds from the Son; this the Son has eternally from the Father, from whom he was moreover eternally begotten. We define, in addition that the explanation of the word *Filioque*, for the sake of declaring the truth and also because of imminent necessity, has been lawfully and reasonably added to the Creed."[5] The Council did not have lasting success.

Attempts have been made in modern times to heal the divisions caused by the *Filioque*. A conference was held in Bonn in 1875 attended by bishops and priests of the Orthodox Church, by

American and English representatives of the Anglican Church, by a number of Old Catholics, and by Döllinger. They agreed that "the addition of the *Filioque* was not made in a way that was in conformity with the rules of the Church." They also stated: "We reject every representation or mode of expression containing any acceptance of the idea of two principles, *archai* or *aitiai*, in the Trinity." They accepted theses taken from the writings of St. John of Damascus (qv); included therein is the statement that the Holy Spirit does not come from the Son, but that he does come from the Father through the Son.

The Russian Holy Synod appointed a commission to continue the work begun at Bonn and two historians were named to prepare a report. Basil Bolotov (1855-1900) went into the patristic history at some length and while clarifying the differences ended his report thus: "Many western Christians who preached the *Filioque* to their flocks lived and died in communion with the eastern Church and no objection was raised on either side. The eastern Church honours the Fathers of the early western Church as it honours its own Fathers. It is therefore quite natural that the West should regard the individual opinions of those Fathers as holy. Photius (qv) and those who followed him remained in communion with the western Church without obtaining from that Church an explicit and conciliar denial of the *Filioque* even, as far as we know, without asking for it. It was therefore not the question of the *Filioque* which caused the division in the Church. The *Filioque* as an individual theological opinion, ought therefore not to constitute an *impedimentum dirimens* for the re-establishment of communion between the Eastern Orthodox and the Old Catholic Churches."[6]

Bolotov's theses caused controversy during his life. In the present century they were found acceptable by Sergius Bulgakov (qv) and Paul Evdokimov. But Vladimir Lossky (1903-1958) rejected them. He clung rigidly to the opposition to the Latin *Filioque*, expressing himself in such terms as these: "By the dogma of the *Filioque* the God of the philosophers and savants is introduced into the heart of the living God, taking the place of the *Deus absconditus, qui posuit tenebras latibulum suum*. The unknowable essence of the Father, Son and Holy Spirit receives proper qualifications. It becomes the object of natural theology; we get 'God in general,' who could be the god of Descartes or the god of Leibnitz, or

even perhaps, to some extent, the god of Voltaire and of the dechristianized Deists of the eighteenth century."[7] Lossky hoped for better things, for a day when "together we shall confess our catholic faith in the Holy Trinity, who lives and reigns in the eternal light of his glory."[8]

Much intellectual activity has been expended on the problem in recent times, in a spirit of ecumenical dialogue. The French language ecumenical reviews, *Istina* and *Irenikon* have published special studies. *Faith and Order* of the World Council of Churches has done likewise. The great ecumenist, specialist in the theology of the Church, Fr. Y.-M.J. Congar, has written at length on the problem, with historical and theological analyses. He thinks that the *Filioque* could be omitted from the Creed on two conditions: 1. "Together with recognized and authoritative representatives of the Orthodox Churches, the non-heretical character of the *Filioque* properly understood should be made clear and recognized, as should the equivalence and complementarity of the two dogmatic expressions, 'from the Father as the absolute Source and from the Son' and 'from the Father through the Son'.... 2. "The Christian people on both sides should be prepared for this so that it may be done in the light, in patience, with respect for each other's legitimate sensibilities, and in love. We should 'love one another' so that we are able to profess with a single heart our faith in the Father, the Son and the Holy Spirit, the one consubstantial and indivisible Trinity."[9] Explaining the first condition he points out that it was the path followed at Florence, but today it would be in a more propitious climate: there is better understanding of and respect for the Orthodox tradition. He would ask the Orthodox not "to go beyond the implications in the 'from the Father alone' of the monarchy of the Father, and the demands made by the New Testament texts."

Since Benedict XIV, 1742, Greeks are not obliged to recite the *Filioque*. A number of Catholic theologians agree with Fr. Congar. Catholics participated at the meetings organised by Faith and Order at Klingethal, 25-29 October 1978 and 24-27 May 1979 to discuss possible change. This resolution was voted unanimously: "The original form of the Niceno-Constantinopolitan creed on the Holy Spirit ... (the text of that article follows) ... should be recognised by all as the normative form of the creed and re-introduced into the liturgy." On 31 May 1973 the Greek Catholic hierarchy decided to suppress the formula in the Greek text of the creed. At the commemorative congress (qv) held in Rome for the sixteenth centenary of the First Council of Constantinople, 381-1981, the question of change was not on the public agenda.

---

[1] Cf. article "Filioque" with bibl., *Trinitas*, 108-111: article "Photius" in present work with bibl., add "Exkurs: Das Filioque" in *Handbuch der Dogmengeschichte*, II, 1a, 126-137; J.S. Rhodes, *Christ and the Spirit: 'Filioque Reconsidered.'* BTB, 18 (1988), 91-93; [2] *Trinitas, art. cit.*, 109; [3] *De Trin.* IV, 20, 29, *PL* 42, 908; [4] *De Trin.* V, 14, 15, *PL* 42, 921; [5] *De Fide Orthod.*, I, 12 *PG* 94, 849; [6] *DS* 1300-1302; [7] For delay in full publicity for the text cf. article "Bolotov," *Trinitas*, 55-57; for text, *Istina* 17 (1973) 261-289; English tr. ibid., *Trinitas*; Y.-M.J. Congar, *op. cit.*, 194, 95; [8] *In the Image and Likeness of God*, English tr., 1974, 88, 96; for Bulgakov's reaction, *Le Paraclet*, Paris, 1946, 99f, 116, 137; for Evdokimov's view, *L'Esprit Saint dans la tradition orthodoxe*, Paris, 1969, 74-75; [9] *The Holy Spirit*, III, 206.

FLORENCE, COUNCIL OF (1439)

The reunion Council dealt with questions dividing east and west. The most important text for our subject is contained in the Bull "Laetentur coeli," 6 July 1439; it deals with the *Filioque* (qv) as follows: "In the name of the Holy Trinity, of the Father, and of the Son, and of the Holy Spirit, with the approbation of this holy general Council of Florence we define that this truth of faith be believed and accepted by all Christians, and that all likewise profess that the Holy Spirit is eternally from the Father and the Son, and has his essence and his subsistent being both from the Father and the Son, and proceeds from both eternally as from one principle and one spiration; we declare that what the holy Doctors and Fathers say, namely that the Holy Spirit proceeds from the Father through the Son, tends to this meaning, that by this it is signified that the Son also is the cause, according to the Greeks, and according to the Latins, the principle of the subsistence of the Holy Spirit, as is the Father also. And that all things, which are the Father's the Father himself has given in begetting his only-begotten Son; without being Father the Son himself possesses this from the Father, that the Holy Spirit proceeds from the Son; this the Son has eternally from the Father, from whom he was moreover eternally begotten. We define, in addition, that the explanation of the words 'Filioque,' for the sake of declaring the truth and also because of imminent necessity, has been lawfully and reasonably added to the Creed."[1]

The text was accepted after much debate and the presentation of many arguments from one side and the other. The Greek delegation was strong in number and ecclesiastical dignity. The emperor was not without hope that he would gain help from the western powers against the Turks seriously threatening his realm. The Pope of the day, Eugenius IV, had strongly supported the Council in its work.

---

[1] *Trinitas*, s.v., bibl. 112-113.

FREEDOM[1]

Freedom is the power to choose means with an end in view. Choice is the essential element. Immediately the limitations of freedom in the general human capacity and actual condition, and in each individual case are easily discernible. Humans are not free to choose what the powers of human nature cannot accomplish, mentally or physically—the limitation of capacity. They are not free to choose what is rendered impossible by their circumstances, for example food in an area of starvation, tranquil behaviour in a war zone—the limitation of the human condition. A man or woman may no longer be free to choose what former ill-conduct has placed beyond the range of their deliberate action, for example a victim of sexual, gambling, alcoholic or drug addiction has in effect narrowed, if not destroyed the act of choice as a meaningful exercise in part of his life; he has personally undermined his freedom—the limitation of the individual case.

These are broad sketches and each sector would call for much detailed analysis. Biological and psychological factors bring endless variation to what may appear static, unchangeable situations; heredity, nurture, environment, education, the unforseen, incalculable effects of human encounters, the impact of charismatic leaders, the final inexplicable mystery of the human person form the total picture, make the agenda unpredictable. Human ciphers suddenly erupt into responsible persons.

How much more so when to the human free will there is intrinsically joined another Personality of unlimited power. The process of self-mastery entails a programme of maintaining the full flexibility of personal freedom, and widening its sphere of action. Eventually this means deepening of the spiritual, interior area of choice, for with the passage of time external, physical elements shrink in importance. The mature, which does not necessarily mean the elderly, need and find more time for what is spiritual in the broadest sense of the word, see physical, especially material things increasingly as symbolic.

Jesus promised freedom to his followers: "'If you continue in my word, you are truly my disciples, and you will know the truth and the truth will make you free'" (Jn 31-32). Through his apostle Paul he enlarged this revelation and pointed to its source. Paul spoke of the "glorious liberty of the children of God" (Rom 8:21), of the "freedom which we have in Christ Jesus" (Gal 2:4), said, "For freedom Christ has set us free" (Gal 5:1), and "For you were called to freedom, brethren" (Gal 5:13). Paul associated his freedom with the Spirit: "For the law of the Spirit of life in Christ Jesus has set me free from the law of sin and death" (Rom 8:2). "Now the Lord is the Spirit and where the Spirit of the Lord is, there is freedom" (2 Cor 3:17). "And do not make God's Holy Spirit sad; for the Spirit is God's mark of ownership on you, a guarantee that the Day will come when God will set you free" (Eph 4:30). "But now we are discharged from the law, dead to that which held us captive, so that we serve not under the old written code but in the new life of the Spirit" (Rom 7:6).

The experience of life tells us painfully that humans can be deprived of their political, social and economic freedom. Since the guarantee of the Spirit is infallible, it must principally relate to interior, spiritual freedom, freedom from sin and sinfulness with which the word "bondage" is traditionally linked, freedom from the influence or power of the evil one. This is freedom in its most precious meaning; it is wide-ranging, bears directly on the multiple attachments which fetter the human spirit, goes deep into the layers of the subconscious mind where motivation is so often powerfully determined. No person is free who has not mastery of the dynamic impulses of his/her subconscious. One of the poignant sights in life is an individual asserting with vigour, every kind of emphasis, his autonomy, but remaining a prisoner to the mean and base instincts of fallen nature.

Is the spiritual freedom spoken of in the gospel and by St. Paul totally different from two themes around the concept given much airing in the Catholic Church in recent times: religious liberty discussed and finally officially stated in the Council, and "liberation" brought to the forefront of theological thinking in Latin America? Each subject can be fully integrated with New Testament

teaching. The primacy of the Spirit and the universal law of love must be respected.

---

[1]Cf. article "Law"; *In libertatem vocati estis. Miscellanea Bernhard Häring* (Studia Moralia XV), Rome, 1977; R. Parent, *L'Esprit Saint et la liberté chrétienne*, Paris, 1976; Y.-M.J. Congar, O.P., *The Holy Spirit*, II, 124-133; L. Cerfaux, *The Christian in the Theology of St. Paul*, London, 1967, 452-460; S. Lyonnet, S.J., "Liberté chrétienne et loi de l'Esprit selon St. Paul," in *La vie selon l'Esprit*, (Unam Sanctam 55), Paris, 1965; articles in dictionaries covering many aspects of the subject: H. Schlier, "eleutheros, eleutheria," *TDNT*, II, 487-502; J. Kosnetter, in *Encyclopaedia of Biblical Theology*, ed. J.B. Bauer, 280; J. Baucher, *DTC* IX, 660-703; K. Rahner and others, LTK IV, 325-337; *DSp* IX "Libération (approche anthropologique), E. Pousset, 780-793; "L'Ecriture" J. Guillet, 793-809; "Pères de l'Eglise," A. Solignac, 809-824; "Expérience des mystiques," P. Agaesse, 824-838; K. Rahner, *Grace in Freedom,* New York, 1969, esp. ch. VIII, *True Freedom,* 203-264; S. Lyonnet, *Christian Freedom and the Law of the Spirit* in I. de la Potterie, S.J., and S. Lyonnet, S.J. The Christian Lives by the Spirit, New York, 1970, 145-174.

FRUITS OF THE SPIRIT, THE

"But I say, walk by the Spirit, and do not gratify the desires of the flesh. For the desires of the flesh are against the Spirit, and the desires of the Spirit are against the flesh; for these are opposed to each other, to prevent you from doing what you would. But if you are led by the Spirit you are not under the law. Now the works of the flesh are plain: fornication, impurity, licentiousness, idolatry, sorcery, enmity, strife, jealousy, anger, selfishness, dissension, party spirit, envy, drunkenness, carousing, and the like. I warn you, as I warned you before, that those who do such things shall not inherit the kingdom of God. But the fruit of the Spirit is love, joy, peace, patience, kindness, goodness, faithfulness, gentleness, self-control; against such there is no law. And those who belong to Christ Jesus have crucified the flesh with its passions and desires" (Gal 5:16-24).[1]

Speculation on the Fruits of the Holy Spirit begins with this Pauline text. Lines of thought to enable understanding of them are study of the idea of "fruit" in the Bible, appreciation of the contrast between the "works of the flesh" and the fruit of the Spirit, and inquiry into the relationshp between the Virtues and Gifts and the fruits as enumerated.

Fruit in the NT is more explicitly spiritual than in the OT (Mt 3:3; Jn 4:36-38; 15:5, 8). The tree judged by its fruit (Mt 7:16-18) is an image of the authenticity or the opposite of virtue. Paul (Rom

6:22; Phil 1:10-11) relates the word to immediate holiness; peace manifests the change effected now, whose ultimate outcome will be eternal.

There are problems about translation of the Pauline text. All the Greek MSS, the oldest MSS of the Vulgate, the Greek Fathers and other ancient versions have nine fruits, as in the RSV tr. here given; the Clementine Vulgate lists twelve, *charitas, gaudium, pax, patientia, benignitas, bonitas, longanimitas, mansuetudo, fides, modestia, continentia, castitas.* Certain Greek words have given rise to different translations. The number need not then enter into interpretation: St. Ambrose thought of ten fruits and related them to the decalogue;[2] St. Thomas (qv) relates the twelve fruits to the twelve fruits of the Tree of Life in the Book of Revelation.[3] Yet these considerations must remain arbitrary.

Likewise, whereas "works" of the flesh is in the plural, the "fruit" of the Spirit is in the singular. Commentators have from early times studied the plural. But some commentators saw a point in the contrast. Fruitfulness is natural and springs from one source; works, and here all are not enumerated, are unnatural.

The classification of the fruits has been differently explained, though in the case of St. Thomas and the biblical scholar H.B. Swete (qv) there is a remarkable concurrence of opinion. St. Thomas working with twelve fruits considers them in groups: a) as they affect the individual in himself/herself, charity, joy, peace, patience and longanimity; b) as they affect what is near one, one's neighbour, goodness, kindness, mildness, faithfulness; c) as they affect things beneath one, modesty, continence, chastity.

Swete's classification is as follows: a) fruits concerning intimate life with God, charity, joy, peace; b) fruits affecting our relations with our fellows, patience, kindness, goodness; c) fruits which regulate external acts, words, bearing, faithfulness, modesty, self-control. There is speculation on the coincidence between the two lists.

The meaning of the word "spirit" used by St. Paul is likewise a matter of discussion. Even if it be taken as the human spirit there will be an implied action by the Divine Spirit as the indispensable author of these benefits. The list need not be taken as exhaustive and it may be viewed existentially, as conveying a total picture of the new creature, which is the work of the Spirit, emphasis varying from one individual and situation to another.

We enter indeed into the whole world of Christian perfection and spirituality through this recognition of the Spirit. If we use our freedom rightly, do not hinder the Spirit nor sink lower even than the "Law" into a new slavery, doing the works of the flesh, we shall enjoy the effects of the Spirit's action. "The impetus of the Spirit corresponds with the constant affirmation of St. Paul's thesis: we are holy, sons of God, temples of the Spirit. According to this doctrine, our Christian life develops in a climate of privileged optimism, divinely guaranteed by hope. The inspiration of the Spirit which we can experience for ourselves, the Christian privileges confirmed by our faith, are true realities which are the very root of our new nature; in other words the 'fruit' of the Spirit is sure; love flowers naturally in our hearts by its own intrinsic strength and produces the Christian virtues."[4]

[1]Cf. commentaries on Gal at relevant passage; H.B. Swete, *The Holy Spirit in the New Testament*, London, 1909; B. Froget, *De l'habitation du Saint Esprit dans les âmes justes*, Paris, 1900; Abbé de Bellevue, *L'Oeuvre du Saint Esprit*, Paris, 1901; F. Buckle, *Die Idee der Fruchtbarkeit in den Paulusbriefen*, Fribourg (S.), 1953; A. Viard, "Le fruit de l'Esprit, *VS*, 88 (1953), 451-470; E. Underhill, *Fruits of the Spirit, Abba, Light of Christus*, London, 1956; T. Renata, *Sehet und kostet die Früchte des Heiligen Geistes*, Freiburg i.B., 1932; B. Jimenez Duque, "Los frutos del Espiritu Santo," *La ciencia tomista* 72 (1947), 334-354; M. Ledrus, "Fruit du Saint Esprit" *VS* 76 (1947) 714-733; A. Lozeron, *La notion de fruit dans le Nouveau Testament*, Lausanne, 1957; W. Barclay, *Flesh and Spirit*, London, 1962; Louis M. Martinez, *The Sanctifier*, Paterson, New Jersey, 1957, 199-258; A. Gardeil, "Fruits de Saint-Esprit," *DTC* VI, 1914, 944-49; C.A. Bernard, *DSp* V, 1964, 1569-75; [2]*In Epist ad Gal.*, PL 17, 368; [3]Ia IIae q. 70, art 3; [4]L. Cerfaux, *The Christian in the Theology of St. Paul*, London, 1967, 464, 5.

FULGENTIUS OF RUSPE (468-533 or c. 462-527)

F. left the Roman civil service to become a monk, was named Bishop of Ruspe, which appointment brought him into conflict with the Arian king Thrasamund, to whom he addressed one of his works, who exiled him twice, once with sixty other bishops.[1] In theology he was a strictly faithful disciple of St. Augustine (qv) with an incessant reflection on Sacred Scirpture; his interpretation cannot always win assent. F. writes of the Holy Spirit in a recently discovered tract, *Commonitorium de Spiritu Sancto*, in the *De Trinitate, De Fide ad Petrum*, in occasional passages elsewhere, but especially in *Contra*

Fabianum, substantial 'fragments' of which have survived. He has original insights in this area, and especially in regard to the epiclesis advances on his own. To him belongs too the honour of clarifying that the sacrifice of the Mass is offered to the Holy Trinity, not merely to the Father.

F. states the essential dogma of the Holy Trinity thus: "There is not a different essence of the Father, the Son and the Holy Spirit. For if there were, the Son would not be truly begotten from the Father, nor would the Holy Spirit proceed from the Father and the Son. But since he is true Son, that is begotten from the essence of the Father, the Holy Spirit is true proceeding from the Father and the Son. But if the Son or the Holy Spirit is of a different kind to the Father, the Son is not truly of the Father for the different essence makes him a stranger, nor likewise could the Holy Spirit proceed from the Father and the Son.... There are therefore three coeternal, consubstantial, coessential ... (the Fathers) spoke of three Persons, one essence, as one essence would declare God to be one, three Persons would show the Trinity."[2]

F., as the excerpt shows, is firm on the *Filioque*. "When it is asked what Holy Spirit the angel announced to the Virgin, we say that it was he who is of the Father and the Son without whom not only could the flesh of Christ not be formed or baptized, nor could it be raised from the dead."[3] "He is not only the Spirit of the Father, but at the same time of the Father and the Son." "He is wholly the Spirit of the Father and wholly of the Son because he is naturally the Spirit of the Father and the Son, he remains wholly in the Father and the Son, because he so remains that he may proceed, so proceeds that he may remain." "Hold most firmly and in no way doubt that the same Holy Spirit who is one Spirit of the Father and the Son proceeds from the Father and the Son. For the Son says, 'When the Spirit of truth comes who proceeds from the Father,' where he taught that the Spirit is his, for he himself is the truth. That the Holy Spirit proceeds from the Son also, prophetic and apostolic teaching confirms for us."[4]

F. adds to this doctrine some complicated exegesis of texts in 2 Thess, Jn 20:22 and on the symbolic two-edged sword from Rev 1:16. He is at great pains to clarify the theological nomenclature, to show when Spirit, which may have different uses, refers only to the Holy Spirit and must so be taken. He returns to the affirmation of the divinity of the Spirit to whom he likes to apply the word Immense. "In this the natural immensity of the Holy Spirit is recognized that as men are baptized in the name of the Father and the Son, so are they in the name of the Holy Spirit. And lest anyone should think that the name of the Holy Spirit is pronounced everywhere but that his presence is not everywhere, the Apostle says to the faithful: "Do not grieve the Holy Spirit of God, in whom you were sealed for the day of redemption" (Eph 4:30). F. then adds other Pauline texts, on the Spirit given by God "in our hearts as a guarantee" (2 Cor 1:21; cf. 2 Cor 5:5, Eph 1:13, 14).

Indulging thus his love for Sacred Scripture he continues: "By these words he shows that the Holy Spirit is not only naturally immense, but also true God, for he has declared him the pledge of our inheritance."[5] F. then draws on the Vulgate "Dominus pars hereditatis meae et calicis mei" (Ps 16:5) to reinforce his argument.

Later in the same chapter he argues thus on the divinity of the Spirit: "Who does not see that the works of the Holy Spirit are suited to the supreme Godhead? *Verbo enim Domini coeli firmati sunt et Spiritu oris ejus omnis virtus eorum* (Ps 33:6, Vulgate rendering)." In the Spirit's power, says F., the Lord Jesus claimed to cast out devils and St. Paul links the "signs and wonders" wrought through him by Christ with the Holy Spirit (Rom 15:18, 19).

The Spirit is sent by the Father and the Son, for he proceeds from the Father and the Son. F. begins a lengthy, intricate explanation of the unity of nature in the Trinity with the words—referring to the Spirit in the Baptism of Christ—"Do you not see that this is the Spirit of God whom you irreverently blaspheme and seek to lessen?" He concludes: "Accordingly, recognize the majesty of the Holy Spirit, Fabianus, and cease from blaspheming him; for he is begged to come and bless the (baptismal) font, so that having bestowed the remission of sins, he may grant the gift of adoption as children. He comes in the generosity of his gifts, since he does not cease to fill the whole world. The Father sends him, for he proceeds from the Father; he sends him with an origin of majesty, not an imperative command. But thus the Holy Spirit, who is wholly everywhere, comes, as the Son was accustomed to come from God the Father. The mission of the Spirit, therefore, is the conferring of an invisible gift, not a personal apparition; because that mission is not to be taken in a local sense where the one sent has natural immensity."[6] F. felt obliged because of the strange views he was resisting to show the distinction between the mission of the Spirit and angelic missions; interestingly in another context, he writes of the angels thus: "By the same Spirit charity is spread in the hearts of men, as it is in the minds of angels. The Holy Spirit is then immense, for it is he, one and the same, who fills the world, who also fills the spirits of the heavenly angels."[7] There is scarcely an OT or NT word or phrase on the Spirit to which he does not refer.

He thought much on the Spirit and the Eucharist, achieving insights possibly through his great personal holiness; he is an authority in the West on the epiclesis (qv). After expounding the importance of the soul's attitude to the Spirit in prayer, F. writes: "Acknowledge then what is at issue in offering sacrifices, that from this you may understand why therein the advent of the Holy Spirit is besought." That is fulfilled in offering sacrifices which, as the blessed Apostle tells us, our Saviour himself commanded." Then follows the institution narrative as in 1 Cor 11:23ff, after which F. continues: "Sacrifice then is offered in order to proclaim the death of our Lord and honour the memory of the one who laid down his life for us. For he said himself: 'Greater love has no man than this, that a man lay down his life for his friends' (Jn 15:15). Since Christ then died for love, when we commemorate his death at the time of sacrifice, we are asking to be filled with love by the coming of the Holy Spirit."[8]

F. elaborates his thought elsewhere: "Since then, as we have said, the whole Trinity, by the unity of the divinity, remains naturally immense and infinite and is not locally anywhere, being nevertheless nowhere absent, and is so wholly everywhere that it can neither be divided by the particular parts of all creation, nor confined by the whole created universe, as often as the Holy Spirit is asked of the Father to consecrate sacrifice, the first dictate of the faith and the first saving solicitude that all Christians must assume is the realization that in no way can the coming of the Holy Spirit be thought of or judged in a local sense. For the Apostle tells the faithful, 'Do you not know that you are God's temple and the Spirit of God dwells in you?' (1 Cor 3:16). Therefore we must consider that sometimes by the name of the Spirit gifts of spiritual grace are designated. When, therefore, the coming of the Holy Spirit is begged to sanctify the sacrifice of the whole Church, it seems to me that nothing else is being begged but that through spiritual grace the unity of charity

should be continuously kept unbroken in the Body of Christ (which is the Church). For this is the principal gift of the Holy Spirit, without which anyone who speaks in the tongues of men and of angels, like a noisy gong or a clanging cymbal can make sound but cannot have life (1 Cor 13:1). When, therefore the Church begs that the Holy Spirit be sent to her from heaven, she begs for herself bestowal from God of the gift of charity and a united spirit. But when more fittingly may holy Church (which is the Body of Christ) plead for the coming of the Holy Spirit than for the consecration of the body of Christ—it knows that its very Head was born in the flesh from the Holy Spirit. For this was done through divine charity that the Body of that Head should be reborn from the Spirit from which the Head himself was born. We needed things thus that as Christ was born of the Holy Spirit when God only-begotten united with men in the womb of the Virgin *came forth like a bridegroom leaving his chamber* (Ps 19:5), so the Church by the gift of the Holy Spirit should cleave to Christ, as a woman to her husband and as the body to its Head."[9]

Has the meeting-point of Spirit, Church and Eucharist ever been so finely shown? F. also destroyed the lingering remnants of heresy on the divinity of the Spirit as these had been condemned a century and a half before his death at Constantinople. And almost with greater clarity than his master Augustine he taught the *Filioque* (qv) thereby bringing consolation. He was not inattentive to the inner sanctifying role of the Spirit, nor to the "variety of gifts."

---

[1]Texts *PL* 65, *CCSL* 91, 91A, J. Fraimont, O.S.B., and J. Solano, S.J., *Textos Eucaristicos Primitivos*, Madrid, 1954, repr., 1979, II, 571-603; cf. G.G. Lapeyre, *St. Fulgence de Ruspe. Un évêque africain sous la domination vandale*, Paris, 1929; A. d'Alès, S.J., "St. Fulgence de Ruspe. Commonitorium de Spiritu Sancto," *RSR* 22 (1932) 304-316; on which C. Lambot, O.S.B. *Bull. d'ancien. litt. chrét. latine*, II, 511; A. Souter, "The Commonitorium of Fulgentius of Ruspe on the Holy Spirit, *JTS* 14 (1913) 481-488; M. Schmaus, "Die Trinitätslehre des Fulgentius von Ruspe" in *Charisteria, Festschrift Al. Ruach*, Reichenberg, 1930, 165-175; M. Jugie, A.A., "Considérations générales sur la question de l'épiclèse. A propos de certains textes de Saint Fulgence de Ruspe, *Echos d'Orient*, 35 (1936) 324-330; S. Salaville, A.A., "L'Epiclèse africaine," *Echos d'Orient*, 39 (1941-1942), 268-282; id., "Epiclèse" in *DTC* V, 244-45, 289; H. Diener, *Fulgentius von Ruspe, als Theologe und Kirchenpolitiker*, Stuttgart, 1966; P. Godet in *DTC* s.v. "Fulgence de Ruspe," VI, 968-972; M. Pellegrino, *DTC* V, 1802-1805; M. Jourjon, *DSp*, V, 1612-1615; [2]*De Trinitate ad Felicem*, II; [3]*CCSL* 91A, 635; [3]A fragment, *ibid.*, 869; [4]*De Fide ad Petrum*, 53,

CCSL 746; *Ad Ferrand.* XIV, 28, *CCSL* 91 420; *De Fide ad Petrum*, 54, 747; ⁵*Contra Fabianum*, XXVIII, 809; ⁶*Op. cit.*, XXIX, 818f; ⁷*Op. cit.*, XXVIII, 810; ⁸*Ibid.*, 813; ⁹*Ad Monimum*, 7, *PL* 65, 180.

G

GELASIAN DECREE, THE[1]

"It has been said: We must first treat of the sevenfold Spirit, which reposes in Christ, the Spirit of wisdom: *Christ, the power and the wisdom of God* (1 Cor 1:24). The Spirit of understanding: *I will give thee understanding, and I will instruct thee in this way, in which thou shalt go* (Ps 31:8). The Spirit of Counsel: *And his name shall be called angel of great counsel* (Is 9:6 LXX). The Spirit of power (as above): *The power of God and the wisdom of God* (1 Cor 1:24). The Spirit of knowledge: *on account of the excellence of the knowledge of Christ Jesus the apostle* (Eph 3:19). The Spirit of truth: *I am the way and the truth and the life* (Jn 14:6). The Spirit of fear (of God): *The fear of the Lord is the beginning of wisdom* (Ps 111:10) . . . (*there follows an explanation of the various names of Christ*: Lord, Word, Flesh, Shepherd, etc.). . . . For the Holy Spirit is not only the Spirit of the Father or not only the Spirit of the Son, but the Spirit of the Father and of the Son. For it is written: *If anyone loves the world, the Spirit of the Father is not in him* (1 Jn 2:15; Rom 8:9). Likewise it is written: *Now if any man have not the Spirit of Christ, he is none of his* (Rom 8:9). When the Father and the Son are mentioned in this way, the Holy Spirit is understood, of whom the Son himself says in the Gospel, that the Holy Spirit *proceeds from the Father* (Jn 15:26) and *he shall receive of mine and announce it to you* (Jn 16:14)."

This is the section of the G.D. which deals with the Holy Spirit. The document has been variously attributed to St. Damasus (Pope 366-384), Gelasius (Pope 492-496) and Hormisdas (Pope 514-523). The recent critical editor thinks it non-papal, a work from Italy, not Rome, sixth century.

---

[1]*DS* 179.

GIFTS, THE[1]

"There shall come forth a shoot from the stump of Jesse, and a branch shall grow out of his roots. And the Spirit of the Lord shall rest upon him, the spirit of wisdom and understanding, the spirit of counsel and might, the spirit of knowledge and the fear of the Lord. And his delight shall be in the fear of the Lord" (Is 11:1-3). This description of the spiritual endowment of the Messiah is at the origin of thinking on the Gifts of the Holy Spirit through the ages. At once the problem arises: Why was a seventh Gift added to the enumeration, or the names given in Isaiah? It was the Greek translation, LXX which added *eusebia* and this was rendered *pietas* by the Vulgate. Attempts have been made to show that the repetition of "fear of the Lord" would be compatible with an interpretation of "piety" in the second place.

Another text may compare with the Isaiah list. In Ex 35:31 we read, "And Moses said to the people of Israel, 'See the Lord has called by name Bezalel the son of Uri, son of Hur, of the tribe of Judah; and he has filled him with the Spirit of God, with ability, with intelligence, with knowledge and with all craftsmanship.'" These somewhat detailed descriptions tally with a recurring idea in OT on the Spirit's action illuminating people and helping them in different problems of life. It is generally wisdom, accompanied at times by another attribute, which is the effect of the Spirit's action. "And Joshua, the son of Nun, was full of the Spirit of wisdom, for Moses had laid his hands upon him" (Deut 34:9); "therefore I prayed, and understanding was given me; I called upon God and the spirit of wisdom came to me" (Wis 7:7); "For wisdom, the fashioner of all things, taught me. For in her there is a spirit that is intelligent, holy . . . " (*ibid.*, 22); "Who hath learned thy counsel, unless thou hast given wisdom and sent thy holy Spirit from on high" (Wis 9:17).

The idea of the Spirit acting in the soul in this way was accepted in the Jewish world of the last generation before Christ: *The Testament of the Twelve Patriarchs* and *The Psalms of Solomon* are cited in evidence. *The Book of Enoch* has striking similarities with Is 11:2, but the date of the work is disputed. Thus in Levi's messianic hymn we read: "The heavens shall be opened, and from the temple of glory shall come upon him sanctification, with the Father's voice as from Abraham to Isaac. And the glory of the Most High shall be uttered over him, and the Spirit of understanding and sanctification shall rest upon him (in the water).... And he shall give to the saints to eat from the tree of life, and the Spirit of holiness shall be on them."[2]

The Psalms of Solomon portray the national Messiah fulfilling the religious and moral ideal. "His piety is shown in what was the heart of Jewish religion from the time of Isaiah onwards: that in the fear of God, and trusting in him, he never falls into the sin of pride, which is characteristic of heathen powers, who trust in human might and understanding."[3] "(He will be) mighty in his works, and strong in the fear of God, (he will be) shepherding the flock of the Lord faithfully and righteously."[4] "Under the rod of chastening of the Lord's Anointed in the fear of the Lord, in the spirit of wisdom and righteousness and strength; that he may direct (every) man in the works of righteousness by the fear of God, that he may establish them all before the Lord, a good generation (living) in the fear of God in the days of mercy."[5]

The Book of Enoch has a passage which reflects the messianic tradition, enlightening too on the Son of Man theme: "For wisdom is poured out like water, and glory faileth not before him for evermore. For he is mighty in all the secrets of righteousness, and unrighteousness shall disappear as a shadow, and have no continuance; because the Elect One standeth before the Lord of Spirits, and his glory is forever and ever, and his might unto all generations. And in him dwells the spirit of wisdom, and the spirit which gives insight, and the spirit of understanding and of might, and the spirit of those who have fallen asleep in righteousness. And he shall judge the secret things, and none shall be able to utter a lying word before him; for he is the Elect One before the Lord of Spirits according to his good pleasure."[6]

All the time through these passages we are faced with a concept of the Spirit as the OT saw him, the dynamic force of God, varied in action, but not as yet seen as a separate divine Person. What interests is to discern the stages by which with increasing clarity on the Person the schema of the Gifts should still continue.

Here, as in so many other sectors of theology, the Fathers helped the transition, but gradually. St. Clement (qv) speaks briefly in II, 2 as follows: "Thus a profound and rich peace was given to all, you had an insatiable desire to do good, and the Holy Spirit was poured out in abundance on you all."[7] When we come to St. Justin (qv) we get more precision: "Just therefore as God did not at that time bring his wrath upon them, for the sake of those seven thousand (who had not bowed the knee to Baal), so now also he has not yet brought the judgement, nor has begun to bring it, because he knows that every day some are becoming disciples unto the name of his Christ, and are leaving the way of error, who also receive gifts, each as they are worthy of them, being enlightened by the name of this Christ. For one receives the spirit of understanding, another of counsel, another of might, another of healing, another of foreknowledge, another of teaching, another of the fear of the Lord."[8] This is not the list given by Isaiah; the number seven is accepted.

It would be consecrated by the other passage in which Justin deals with the subject: "At this point in my discourse Trypho said: 'Do not suppose hereafter that I am trying to upset your arguments, when I make any fresh inquiry, for I desire to learn about the very questions that I put to you. Tell me then about the word said by Isaiah: A rod shall come forth from the root of Jesse, and a flower shall arise from the root of Jesse, and the Spirit of God shall rest upon him, the spirit of wisdom, and understanding, the spirit of counsel and might, the spirit of knowledge and piety, and shall fill him with the spirit of the fear of God.'" He said that although he granted me that this was spoken with reference to Christ, I say that he already existed as God, and that he was incarnate according to the will of God, and became man by the virgin. How then, he asked, can he be proved to have already existed, seeing that he is filled by the powers of the Holy Spirit which the word enumerates by Isaiah, as though he lacked them?"

Justin's answer was categorical: "These powers of the Spirit thus enumerated are said by the word to have come upon him, not as though he lacked them, but as being about to take their rest permanently upon him, that is, to come to an end with him, that there should be no longer prophets in your nation after the old manner, as you also can plainly see, for after him there has been no prophet at all among you." Justin then explains how the Spirit's gifts were distributed in OT times. "For Solomon had the spirit of wisdom, Daniel that of understanding and counsel, Moses of might and piety, Elijah of fear, and Isaiah of knowledge; and the others also in the same way either had one each, or alternately one power and another, as had Jeremiah, and the Twelve, and David, and in fact all the other prophets who have been among you."[9]

Are there then no gifts of the Spirit after Christ had received the plenitude of them? "But after him, as this dispensation among men began in his time, it was necessary that those gifts should cease being among you, and yet, when they had taken their rest in Christ, should again, as was prophesied, be given by the grace of the power of that Spirit to them that believe in him, according to his knowledge of the deserts of each." With Justin then we have the number seven fixed and we have the explanation that henceforth the Gifts come to us through Christ. This is a notable advance on thinking about this theme.

The *Shepherd of Hermas* has little explicit information on the Gifts. A passage in *Mandate V* seems to refer more to discernment (qv) of spirits: "Be, said he, long-suffering and prudent and you shall have power over evil deeds and shall do all righteousness. For if you are courageous the Holy Spirit which dwells in you will be pure, not obscured by another evil spirit, but will dwell at large and rejoice and be glad with the body in which it dwells, and will serve God with great cheerfulness, having well-being in itself. But if any ill temper enter, at once the Holy Spirit, which is delicate, is oppressed, finding the place impure, and seeks to depart out of the place, for it is choked by the evil spirit, having no room to serve the Lord as it will, but is contaminated by the bitterness. For the Lord dwells in long-suffering and the devil dwells in ill-temper."[10]

St. Irenaeus (qv), in line with Justin, offers another important contribution. He thus describes the descent of the Spirit on Jesus: "The Apostles could have said that 'Christ descended on Jesus' or 'the Saviour from on high on him who is involved in the economy (i.e., the dispensation of salvation), or (Christ) from invisible regions on the (son) of the Demiurgus.' But they did not know or speak of anything of the kind. They told

of what happened, that the Spirit of God descended on him like a dove, the Spirit of whom it was spoken by Isaiah, 'and the Spirit of God will rest upon him,' (Is 11:2) as we have already explained. And again, 'The Spirit of the Lord (God) is upon me, because he has anointed me' (Is 61:1). The Lord declares of this Spirit, 'It is not you who will speak, but the Spirit of your Father who will speak in you' (Mt 10:20). Similarly in giving the disciples the power of rebirth into God, he said to them, 'Go and teach all nations, baptizing them in the name of the Father and of the Son and of the Holy Spirit' (Mt 28:19). God promised through the prophets that in the last days he would pour out this Spirit on his servants and handmaids, so that they would prophesy (Jl 2:28, 29). For this reason, he also descended upon the Son of God, made Son of Man, and thus in union with him became accustomed to dwell in the human race, to rest with human beings and to dwell in the works formed by God. He accomplished the Father's will in them and renewed them from their old habits into the newness of Christ."[11]

The two texts from Isaiah quoted briefly here are more fully reproduced in an earlier chapter of the same book, III, of the *Adversus Haereses*: "The Word of God, Saviour of all and Lord of heaven and earth, that is Jesus (as we have already shown), who took flesh and received the anointing of the Spirit, became Jesus Christ."[12] Irenaeus then quotes Is 11:1-4. He continues: "Elsewhere Isaiah foretold his anointing and the reason for this anointing saying ..." Then follows a quotation from Is 61:1-2.

In chapter XVII Irenaeus returns to the subject of the Gifts: "God chose Gideon to save Israel from the power of the foreign nations. Gideon foresaw this gracious gift and changed his request. At first the dew was only on the fleece of wool which represented the people. By his request he prophesied that it would be dry, indicating that they would no longer have the Holy Spirit of God (Jg 6:36-40). As Isaiah says, 'I will also command the clouds not to rain upon it' (Is 5:6). The dew which represented the Spirit of God who descended upon the Lord, would be spread throughout all the earth, 'the spirit of wisdom and understanding, the spirit of counsel and might, the spirit of knowledge and piety, the spirit of the fear of God' (Is 11:2). Further he conferred the Spirit upon the church and sent the Comforter from heaven throughout all the world. The Lord tells us that the devil was cast down from the heavens like lightning" (Lk 10:18).[13]

The great genius of Alexandria Origen (qv) was constantly interested in the Gifts. The passages where he makes an enumeration are most studied by historians of theology.[14] In one he adds to the seven now accepted three others, energy, love and prudence. Like Justin Origen was convinced that only in Christ was the plenitude of the Gifts realized. The Fathers in the East and West continue to evoke the Is 11:1-3 text, but without any systematic result. St. Augustine and St. Gregory the Great (qqv) are more elaborate than the others.

The reflection continued through the Middle Ages, but only after the renaissance of the twelfth century. Between the Fathers and the eleventh century little progress was made. From the twelfth century the principal point studied in the research of historians is the distinction between the Gifts and the virtues. The distinction was not fully grasped until the thirteenth century, for though there was growing awareness of it, the system to justify and explain it was lacking. In the Dominican and Franciscan milieux of the thirteenth century the Gifts were seen to be different from the virtues and superior to them. Classifications emerged; the role of the Gifts in spiritual progress was studied.

Then came St. Thomas Aquinas (qv). His theory of the Gifts was elaborated in the light of scholasticism, as he had perfected it. They inhere in the soul which has been justified, endowed with grace, permanently, to supplement where necessary the Christian virtues which are also given to the soul with grace. All are in the category that St. Thomas calls *habitus*, fixed qualities or properties attached to the powers of the soul, enabling them to perform their characteristic, required acts. The Gifts are therefore directly oriented to humankind's supernatural end. They are dispositions of the soul which facilitate the immediate action of the Spirit, which, in certain moments, is needed. Thus the Gifts are necessary for salvation.

As to the interrelation of the Gifts and virtues St. Thomas displays remarkable subtlety. This is especially true of the theological virtues. For these are substantially superior to the Gifts, being intrinsically supernatural. For humans to receive the inspiration of the Spirit, they must be united to God. It is by the theological virtues, faith, hope and charity that this union is effected. "Hence," says St. Thomas, "these three virtues are presupposed for the Gifts, as the roots, so to speak of the Gifts. Therefore all the Gifts are related to these virtues as derived from them."[15]

Yet, though derived from them, the Gifts bring to the theological virtues a new perfection. This seems at first sight self-contradictory. For though reason, in St. Thomas' thinking, is what rules ordinary virtue and the Gifts are superior to reason, this is not the rule of virtues intrinsically supernatural, as faith, hope and charity. These require no measure, no middle course between excess and defect, but of their essence tend to the maximum. But they are exercised in the human condition. "The theological virtues are in us proper energies of this (divine) nature; they are certainly divine, a participation in the life of God; but they are realised in us with imperfections which are characteristic, especially in the time of trial, when our participation in God's self-knowledge is still but faith. Thereon one can see where help from the Gifts will bear. Neither faith, hope or charity, through them, reach their object more immediately or fully; they can nevertheless, through the effect of interior inspiration, be freed from certain conditions in their exercise. This is due to their human mode, springing from the rational and discursive character which marks our spiritual activities until we have the beatific vision."[16] St. Thomas suggests different ways of grouping or classifying the Gifts; the best is probably that developed in the IIa IIae, where they are related to the theological virtues.

The saint's contemporaries, Philip the Chancellor, St. Albert the Great and St. Bonaventure (qqv) dealt also with the Gifts, though not with the elaborate, systematic approach of the Angelic Doctor. His influence was to last, prompting one remarkable treatise, deemed worthy of translation in the present century, by John of St. Thomas (qv) and commentary by Fr. Garrigou-Lagrange, O.P.

As to the general history of the doctrine, in the fourteenth and fifteenth centuries certain names, John Ruysbroeck and Denis the Carthusian (qqv), stand out, not always those one expects to meet. Important contributions later are noteworthy: St. Francis de Sales, Louis Lallemant, S.J., John Baptist Saint Jure and St. John Baptist de la Salle.

The existence of the Gifts is established, though recent biblical scholarship will nuance the value of Is 11:2 as an adequate scriptural basis for the systematic presentation of St. Thomas; what he really erected into a system was an intuition and perception of truth, initially prompted by Is 11:2, but gathering its value from the collective reflection of teachers and theologians through the ages.

---

[1]See article "John of St. Thomas"; cf. Denis the Carthusian, *Opera omnia* Montreuil Tournai, vol XXXV, 137-262; J.B. Belot, *Les sept dons du Saint Esprit. Traité ascétique d'après les saints docteurs*, Clermont Ferrand, 1864; Mgr. Landriot, *L'Esprit Saint. Dons et symboles*, Paris, 1879; M.J. Friaque, O.P., *Le Saint Esprit. Sa grâce, ses figures, ses dons, ses fruits, ses béatitudes*, Paris, 1886; M. Meschler, *Die Gabe des heilige Pfingstfestes*, Freiburg in Breisgau, 1892; J. de Blic, "Pour l'histoire de la théologie des dons," *RAM* 22 (117-179), 117-79; B. Lavaud, O.P., "Les dons de St.Esprit d'après Albert le Grand, *RT* 36 (1931) 386-407; *Le royaume des amants de Dieu et Ruusbroeck Genootschap*, I, Malines, 1932; K. Boeckh, *Die sieben Gaben des Heiligen Geistes in ihrer Bedeutung für die Mystik nach des 13 und 14 Jahrhunderts*, Freiburg im Brisgau, 1931; O. Lottin, *Psychologie et Morale aux XIIe et XIIIe siècles*, III, Louvain, 1949, IV 1954; A. Gardeil, *DTC* IV, 1, 1911, 1754-1779; Luiz (Mgr) Martinez, *The Sanctifier*, 119-195, Paterson, New Jersey, 1957; B. Kelly, C.S.Sp., *The Seven Gifts of the Holy Ghost*, Dublin, 1940; *DSp*, III, 1579-1641, G. Bardy, F. Vandenbroucke, H. Rayez, M-Michel Labourdette, C. Bernard; M.A. Philipon, O.P., *Les Dons du Saint Esprit*, Paris, 1963; [2]*Testament of the XII Patriarchs*, R.H. Charles, London, 1917, 47; [3]Apud S. Mowinckel, *He That Cometh*, Oxford, 1956, 310; [4]XVII, 37, 44, ibid.; [5]Ibid., XVII, 8-10 (7-9); [6]*Book of Enoch* 49, 1-4, tr. R.H. Charles, 1921, London, p. 87f; Mowinckel, 375f; [7]*The Apostolic Fathers*, tr. K. Lake, 1912, p. 11; [8]*The Dialogue with Trypho*, 39, tr. A. Lukyn Williams, 1930, 77; [9]Ibid., 87, 185f; [10]K. Lake, II,87f; [11]St. Irenaeus, *Adversus Haerses.*, III, 17, 1, *SC*, M. Sagnard, 302, 3; [12]Ibid., 9, 3, 158, 9; [13]Ibid., 17, 3, 306, 7; [14]E.g., *In Numeros hom*, 6, 3, *GCS* VII, 33, Cf. G. Bardy, *DSp* III, 1583; [15]Ia IIae, q. 68, art 4, ad 3; [16]M.-Michel Labourdette, *DSp* III, 1627.

GLORY OF THE HOLY SPIRIT, THE

We pray constantly to the glory of the Father and the Son and the Holy Spirit. Yet the concept of glory, which is so fundamental to divine revelation is relevant, in a plenary sense, to consideration of the Holy Spirit. Sacred Scripture is apparently silent on the subject. Jesus, in Jn 16:14 says, "He (the Spirit) will glorify me, for he will take what is mine and declare it to you." The other NT writers, with one exception, do not speak of glory in connection with the Spirit. Peter is the exception. In his first letter he is conscious of the Holy Spirit, speaking of "The good news preached through the Holy Spirit sent from heaven, things into which angels long to look." (1:12). He also speaks of God who raised Christ "from the dead and gave him glory, so that your faith and hope are in God" (1:21). In the light of those ideas then he is of interest when he writes: "If you are reproached for the name of Christ, you are blessed,

because the Spirit of glory and of God rests upon you" (4:14). But what is this glory so often mentioned in Sacred Scripture, so rarely by theologians—with the glorious exception of Hans Urs von Balthasar (qv) who made of it, with the concept of beauty, the centerpiece of his immense, enlightening synthesis. What we have to consider is the meaning of glory and the mode of its manifestation. The meaning, as so many biblical instances reveal, is complex, rather it is mysterious. Since the usage begins with the OT we recall that the word signifies weight; it refers to inner value, which commands respect. Applied to Yahweh it means instant total recognition of who he is, of his power, his majesty, his transcendence. On the one side there is a wholly acceptable proclamation of this; on the other immediate unquestioning acceptance of it. Divine glory is the Godhead dominant over all in the very moment of his appearance; the assertion, wholly unchallengeable, of his being and his power. And yet there remains an element of mystery; how could it be otherwise. How to apply all this to the Holy Spirit? It is, modesty apart, the burden of this whole work to seek to expound the why and the how of the Spirit's glory. One ends with the feeling, with the conviction rather, that all of us, individuals like the present writer, the whole Church of Christ, are groping our way to a mystery yet to be unfolded fully, the activity of the Spirit in and about us, in which his glory will be more and more clearly revealed. Glory in its plenitude belongs solely to God; glory to the Father as he has deigned to reveal himself, glory to the Son so often recalled in the sacred word, and like, full glory to the Spirit. But for this the Spirit must be recognised in all his essential meaning, role, power, majesty; above all in his essential love, his will to enter into intimacy with each one of us, the meaning of "Sweet Guest of the soul".

Cf. Hans Urs von Balthasar, *La Croix et la Gloire*, III, *La Nouvelle Alliance*, Part II, 6, L'Esprit me glorifiera. 215-217.

GREGORY THE GREAT, ST., DOCTOR (c. 540, Pope 590-604)

The great controversies about the Trinity and the Holy Spirit had been settled long before G.'s pontificate began; there had been a Latin theologian of the Holy Spirit in the person of St. Ambrose (qv) and three Latin theologians of the Trinity, Novatian, Hilary and Augustine (qqv).[1]

94

G.'s contribution was to be on the action of the Spirit in the souls of the just, particularly notable in his treatment of the Gifts of the Holy Spirit; to such an approach his experience of the contemplative life oriented him. That the Spirit was often in his thought is illustrated by the references tabulated in the *Thesaurus Sancti Gregorii Magni*, compiled by Cétédoc, Louvain la Neuve, under the direction of Professor Tombeur; most of these references would be to the Holy Spirit. Those involved in detailed research must also consult the microfiches. In passing, the debate opened again by F. Clark on the authenticity of the *Dialogues* may be recalled, as may the informed reply from R. Gooding.[2]

References in the Cétédoc compilation are as follows: *Spiritu*, 321; *Spiritui*, 31; *Spiritum*, 333; *Spiritus*, 1327 (503 in the *Moralia super Job*). The references to Gift and Gifts are: *Dona*, 248 (*Moralia super Job, 99*), *Donis*, 53; *Dono*, 64; *Donorum*, 31; *Donum*, 99.

G. had a strong sense of the oneness of Jesus and the Spirit. In his commentary on the Song he writes: "The perfumes of the anointing of the Lord are the virtues; the perfume of the anointing of the Lord was the Holy Spirit. On this subject he is told by the mouth of the prophet: 'God your God has anointed you with oil beyond all your companions.' He was anointed with this oil in the moment of his Incarnation, for he did not become man first only to receive the Holy Spirit afterwards; but since he was incarnate through the mediation of the Holy Spirit, he was anointed with this same oil from the moment when, as man, he was created. The odour of the anointing perfume is then the aroma of the Holy Spirit, who proceeding from him, remained in him.[3]

G. comments with relish on the metaphor of water for the grace of the Spirit and when it is used in the plural he is reminded of the seven Gifts (qv): "And not to speak of water, but of waters in the plural means returning to the sevenfold grace of spiritual gifts, for it is as if we are filled with as many gifts as water is poured upon us."[4]

G. sees the Gifts of the Spirit as armour against manifold evil: wisdom against folly, intelligence against stupidity, counsel against rashness, courage against fear, knowledge against ignorance, piety against hardness, fear (of the Lord) against pride.[5]

In the commentaries on Ezekiel G. has a lengthy passage on the Gifts taken in ascending or descending order: "By seven steps ascent is made to the door, because by the sevenfold grace of the Holy Spirit the way into heavenly life is opened to us. Isaiah listing the sevenfold grace, in our Head himself and in his Body which we are, says: 'The spirit of wisdom and understanding shall rest upon him, the spirit of counsel and might, the spirit of knowledge and piety, and the spirit of the fear of the Lord shall fill him' (11:2). He listed these steps in descending rather than ascending order, namely wisdom, understanding, counsel, might, knowledge, piety, fear of the Lord, as he was speaking of heavenly things. And since it is written, 'The fear of the Lord is the beginning of wisdom,' it is clear beyond doubt that the ascent is made from fear to wisdom, but there is no return from wisdom to fear, for in truth wisdom holds perfect charity. And it is written, 'Perfect love casts out fear' (1 Jn 4:18). The prophet, therefore, since he was speaking of heavenly things, began rather with wisdom and moved down to fear. But we, who strive towards heavenly things from what is of the earth, list the same steps in ascending order, so that we should be able to reach wisdom from fear. In our mind the first step in the ascension is fear of the Lord; the second, piety; the third, knowledge; the fourth, might; the fifth, counsel; the sixth, understanding; the seventh, wisdom."[6]

G. analysing the difficulties of a kind of isolation among the Gifts reaches a theory of their interrelation: "Since therefore through fear we rise towards piety, through piety we are led to knowledge, by knowledge we are strengthened to might, by might we move towards counsel, through counsel we advance to understanding, through understanding we reach the fullness of wisdom; we ascend by seven steps to the door through which entry to the spiritual life is opened to us."[7]

Understandably G. urging the disciple to rise above "the weight of earthly desires" goes on: "But we could not act thus, if we were not flooded with the grace of the Holy Spirit ..." With G. the theology of the Gifts had passed a clear point of development. There will be refinements. But the main point is gained. This is interior spiritual equipment for the soul striving towards Christian perfection.

---

[1]Works here needed, *PL* 75 ff; *CCSL* 142, 144, SC 212, 314; cf. R. Gillet, O.S.B., *DSp*, VI, 1967, 872-910; id., *DHGE*, 21 (1987), 1387-1419; G. Bardy, *DSp* III, 1587; C. Butler, O.S.B., *Western Monasticism*, London, 1922, 91-133; F. Lieblang, *Grundfragen der mystichen Theologie nach Gregor des Grossen, Moralia und Ezechielhomilien*, Freiburg i. Breisgau, 1934; 82-99; F. Westhoff, *Die Lehre Gregors des Grossen über die Gaben des Heiligen Geistes*, Hiltrup, 1940; L.M.

Weber, *Hauptfragen der Moraltheologie Gregors des Grossen*, Lucerne, 1941; G. Farkas, *Typische Formen der Kontemplation bei Gregor dem Grossen*, Dissert. Gregorian University, 1948; G.C. Carluccio, *The Steps to Spiritual Perfection according to St. Gregory the Great*, Ottawa, 1947; M. Frickel, *Deus totus ubique simul. Untersuchungen zur allgemeinen Gottesgegenwart im Rahmen der Gotteslehre Gregors des Grossen*, Freiburg in Breisgau, 1956; Esp. J. Leclercq in *A History of Christian Spirituality*, J. Leclercq, Francois Vandenbroucke, Louis Bouyer, Vo. II, London, 1968, "The Teaching of St. Gregory, 3-30; Cétédoc, 1986; [2]F. Clark, *The Pseudo-Gregorian Dialogues*, 2 vols., Leyde, 1987; R. Gooding, "Les Dialogues de Gregoire le Grand," *AB* 106 (1988), 201-29; [3]*In Cant. Cant.*, 14, *CCSL* 144, 16; [4]*Moralia in Job*, XI, 14, *SC* 212, A. Bocognano, 62; cp. on the Gifts XI, 8, *ibid.*, 52, 54; XV, 19, 20, *SC* 221, A. Bocognano, 38, 40; [5]*Moralia in Job*, II, 49, 77, *SC* 32 (R. Gillet, O.S.B.), 370-72; *PL* 75, 592, 93; [6]*In Hiezech.*, II, Hom vii, 7, *CCSL* 142, 320; [7]*Ibid.*, 321, 22.

GREGORY OF NAZIANZUS, ST., DOCTOR OF THE CHURCH (329-389)

Known, because of his "Five Theological Orations" on the Trinity, as "The Theologian" or "The Divine," G., fully involved in the doctrinal conflicts of his time, had a sure source of inner fortitude;[1] a mystical experience of the Trinity which he has thus described—he was "blinded by the light of the Trinity whose brightness surpasses all that the mind can conceive for from a throne high exalted the Trinity pours upon all, the ineffable radiance common to all three."[2] Known too as "the minstrel of the Trinity" G. could certainly be given the title "minstrel of the Holy Spirit." The Spirit is a presence felt throughout his work. He had consecrated himself to the Spirit: "I opened my mouth, and drew in the Spirit, and I give myself and my all to the Spirit, my action and speech, my inaction and silence, only let him hold me and guide me, and move both hand and mind and tongue whither it is right, and he wills: and restrain them as it is right and expedient. I am an instrument of God, a rational instrument, an instrument tuned and struck by that skilful artist, the Spirit."[2]

G. deals with the Holy Spirit in his correspondence with St. Basil (qv) and in his panegyric on this saint with whom he was so closely linked in friendship, whom he resembled in family background and in lofty culture. The subject at issue in letters was the divinity of the Holy Spirit. G. reported to B. critical remarks made at a gathering which included "many distinguished friends" of theirs. "I have just come" said a critic "from the festival of the martyr Eupsychius (and so it really was) and there I heard the great Basil speak most beautifully and perfectly upon the godhead of the Father and the Son, as hardly anyone else could speak; but he slurred over the Spirit ..." "As for you" said the same speaker to G. "you do now express yourself openly on the Godhead of the Spirit": and, adds G., he referred to some remarks of mine in speaking of God at a largely attended Synod, as having added in respect of the Spirit that expression which has made a noise (how long shall we hide the candle under the bushel?) "But the other man hints obscurely, and as it were, merely suggests the doctrine, but does not openly speak out the truth; flooding people's ears with more policy than piety, and hiding his duplicity by the power of his eloquence."[3]

Basil was pained and spoke of the "slanderer," whom, he felt he would not satisfy: "I have never yet given this man's brethren any evidence of my sentiments about God, and I have no answer to make now. Men who are not convinced by long experience are not likely to be convinced by a short letter. If the former is enough let the charge of the slanderers be counted as idle tales."[4] If G. had kept closer contact with him, for their own sakes and the sake of the churches, "there would have been no opening for these calumniators. Pray have nothing to do with them. Let me persuade you to come here and assist me in my labours, particularly in my contest with the individual who is now assailing me."[5]

G. replied, regretting the hurt, protesting his good intentions and offering to come to B. "For who would flinch, who would not rather take courage in speaking and contending for truth by your side." But he did say: "But it would have been better to have set this matter straight, rather than be angry with those who offer you counsel."[6] G. was to return to the subject in his defence of B.'s attitude in the course of his great panegyric on his friend. Though without ecclesiastical ambition B. had to be on his guard against those who "might banish him and his power of theological instruction from the city, and themselves be able to seize upon the church, and make it the starting-point and citadel, from which they could overrun with their doctrine the rest of the world." G. thought that for B. to say "the Spirit is God" would play into the hands of the enemy. "He postponed for a time the use of the exact term, begging as a favour from the Spirit himself and his earnest champions, that they would not be annoyed at his economy, nor by clinging to a single expression, ruin the whole cause, from an uncompromising temper, at a crisis when religion was in peril." G. was certain that B. "no less than any other, acknowledged that the Spirit is God," that he "publicly preached it," "eagerly confessed it when questioned in private," and "he proceeded to imprecate upon himself that most terrible fate of separation from the Spirit, if he did not adore the Spirit as consubstantial and coequal with the Father and the Son."[7]

G.'s formal teaching on the Holy Spirit is contained in the fifth Theological Oration and in the Sermon on Pentecost. He was attentive to the notion of doctrinal development. He expressed thus the work of the Spirit in OT: "This was proclaimed by the Prophets in such passages as the following: 'The Spirit of the Lord is upon me (Is 61:1)'; and, 'There shall rest upon him seven spirits'; and 'the Spirit of the Lord descended and led them' (Is 11:1; 63:14); and the Spirit of Knowledge filling Bezaleel (Ex 26:3), the master-builder of the Tabernacle; and the Spirit provoking to anger; and the Spirit carrying away Elias in a chariot, and sought in double measure by Eliseus; and David led and strengthened by the good and princely Spirit. And He was promised by the mouth of Joel first, who said, 'And it shall be in the last days that I will pour out my Spirit upon all flesh'. . . ."[8]

G. explains the development thus: "The Old Testament proclaimed the Father openly, and the Son more obscurely. The New manifested the Son and suggested the Deity of the Spirit. Now the Spirit himself dwells among us, and supplies us with a clearer demonstration of himself. For it was not safe, when the Godhead of the Father was not yet acknowledged, plainly to proclaim the Son; nor when that of the Son was not yet received, to burden us further (if I may use so bold an expression) with the Holy Ghost. . . . For this reason it was, I think, that he gradually came to dwell in the Disciples measuring himself out to them according to their capacity to receive him, at the beginning of the Gospel, after the Passion, after the Ascension, making perfect their powers, being breathed upon them, and appearing in fiery tongues. And indeed it is by little and little that he is declared by Jesus, as you will learn for yourself if you will read more carefully. I will ask the Father, he says, that he will send you another Comforter, even the Spirit of Truth. This he said that he might not seem to be a rival God, or to make his discourses to them by another authority.

Again he shall send him, but it is in my name. He leaves out the 'I will ask' but he keeps the 'shall send,' then again, 'I will send,'—his own dignity. Then shall come the authority of the Spirit."[9]

On the divinity of the Spirit G. is firm: "This, then, is my position with regard to these things, and I hope it may be always my position, and that of whosoever is dear to me; to worship God the Father, God the Son and God the Holy Ghost, three Persons, one Godhead, undivided in honour and glory and substance and kingdom, as one of our own inspired philosophers not long departed showed."[10]

In the Oration on Holy Baptism he is equally explicit: "This (confession of the Father and the Son and the Holy Spirit) I commit unto you today; with this I will baptize you and make you grow. This I give you to share, and to defend all your life, the one Godhead and Power, found in the Three in unity, and comprising the Three separately, not unequal in substances or natures, neither increased nor diminished by superiorities or inferiorities; in every respect equal, in every respect the same; just as the beauty and the greatness of the heavens are one; the infinite conjunction of three infinite ones. Each God when considered in himself; as the Father so the Son, as the Son so the Holy Ghost; the Three one God when contemplated together. Each God because consubstantial; one God because of the Monarchia. No sooner do I conceive of the one than I am illumined by the splendour of the Three; no sooner do I distinguish them than I am carried back to the one."[11]

Still more firmly elsewhere: "What then? Is the Spirit God? Most certainly. Well then is he consubstantial? Yes, if he is God."[12] G. was on the path of the great doctrine of the relations as the basis of Trinitarian distinction: "But the difference of manifestation, if I may so express myself, or rather of their mutual relations one to another, has caused the difference of their names."[13] "Father is not the name either of an essence or an action. . . . But it is the name of the relation in which the Father stands to the Son, and the Son to the Father."[14]

G. set down two marvellous litanies of the Spirit. He begins the first with the "swarm of testimonies . . . from which the deity of the Holy Spirit shall be shown to all who are not excessively stupid, or else altogether enemies to the Spirit to be most clearly recognized in Scripture. Look at these facts: Christ is born; the Spirit is his forerunner. He is baptized; the Spirit bears witness. He is tempted; the Spirit leads him up. He works miracles; the Spirit accompanies him. He ascends; the Spirit takes his place. What great things are there in the idea of God which are not in his power? What titles which belong to God are not applied to him, except only Unbegotten and Begotten?"[15]

G. introduces his litany thus: "Indeed I tremble when I think of the abundance of titles, and how many names they outrage who fall foul of the Spirit. He is called the Spirit of God, the Spirit of Christ, the Mind of Christ, the Spirit of the Lord, and himself the Lord, the Spirit of adoption, of truth, of liberty; the Spirit of Wisdom, of Understanding, of Counsel, of Might, of Knowledge, of Godliness, of Fear of God. For he is the maker of all these, filling all with his essence, containing all things, filling the world in his essence, yet incapable of being comprehended in his power by the world; good, upright, princely, by nature not by adoption; sanctifying not sanctified; measuring not measured; shared, not sharing; filling not filled; containing not contained; inherited, glorified, reckoned with the Father and the Son; held out as a threat; the Finger of God, fire like God; to manifest, as I take it, his consubstantiality; the Creator Spirit, who by Baptism and by Resurrection creates anew; the Spirit that knows all things, that teaches, that blows where and to what extent he lists; that guides, talks, sends forth, separates, is angry, or tempted; that reveals, illumines, quickens, or rather is the very Light and Life; that makes temples; that deifies; that perfects so as even to anticipate Baptism, yet after Baptism to be sought as a separate gift; that does all things that God does; divided into fiery tongues; dividing gifts; making Apostles, Prophets, Evangelists, Pastors, and Teachers; understanding manifold, clear, piercing, undefiled, unhindered, which is the same thing as most wise and varied in his actions; and making all things clear and plain; and of independent power, unchangeable, almighty, all-seeing, penetrating all spirits that are intelligent, pure, most subtle (the Angel Hosts I think); and also all prophetic spirits and apostolic in the same manner and not in the same places; for they lived in difference places; thus showing that he is uncircumscribed."[16]

There is another similar hymn of litanic praise in the *Sermon on Pentecost*.[17] In other of his works, as especially in the *Farewell Discourse*[18] at Constantinople and in the *Oration on the Holy Lights*,[19] G. returns to thought on the Spirit. One could venture the suggestion, surely supported by his diverse, profound writing on the subject, unequalled for many centuries that he enjoyed a mystical union with the Spirit, rarely granted in the history of the Church, or, if frequently enjoyed, rarely manifest or described.

---

[1]Cf. H.L. Bouquet, *Théologie de la Trinité d'après Grégoire de Naziance*, Paris, 1876; J. Hergenrother, *Die Lehre von der göttlichen Dreieinigkeit nach dem hl. Gregor von Nazianz, dem Theologen*, Regensburg 1850; Tschermann, *Die Gottheit des Heiligen Geistes nach den griechischen Vëtern des veirten Jahrhunderts*, Freiburg i. B., 1901, 143-167; J. Dräseke, "Neoplatonisches in des Gregorios von Nazianz Trinität-slehre," *Byzantinische Zeitschrift*, 15 (1906), 141-160; P. Galtier, *Le Saint Esprit en nous d'après les Pères Grecs*, Rome, 1946, 175-180; B. Wyss, "Gregor von Nazianz. Ein griechischchristlicher Denker des IV Jahrhunderts," *Museum Helveticum* 6 (1949) 177-210—separate issue, Darmstadt; J. Plagnieux, *St. Grégoire de Nazianze, théologien*, Paris, 1952; B. Otis, "Cappadocian Theology as a Coherent System," *Dumbarton Oaks Papers*, 12 (1955) 29-57; Ph. Rouillard, "La révélation de la Trinité d'après St. Grégoire de Nysse, Fête de la Sainte Trinité," *Assemblees du Seigneur*, 53, Bruges-Paris, 1964, 49-58; J.M. Seymusiak, *Gregor teologen*, voznan, 1965, bibl; *DTC* VI, P. Godet, 1839-44; *DSp* VI, J. Rousse, 932-71; *Trinitas*, 117-18; *BT* I, 1509, 1511; *Handbuch der Dogmengeschichte*, II, 1a, 173-181; R.P.C. Hanson, *The Search*, 772-790; 669-714; [2]*Oration to his Father, XII*, 1, *LNPF* VII 245; [3]*Letter 58*, ibid., 455; [4]*Letter 71, LNPF* VIII 167; [5]*Ibid.*; [6]*Letter 59, LNPF* VII, 456; [7]*Orat.* 43, Panegyric on St. Basil, 68, 69, p. 418; [8]*On Pentecost*, 13, 383; [9]*Theol. Orat.* V, 26, p. 326; [10]*Ibid.*, 28, 326, 7; [11]*Orat. 40, On Holy Baptism*, 41, p. 375; [12]*On the Holy Spirit*, 10, p. 321; [13]*Ibid.*, 9, p. 320, cf. J. Chevalier, O.P., *St. Augustin la pehsée grecque, et les relations trinitaires*, Fribourg, 1940; [14]*Orat. 29, Third Theological Oration*, on the Son, 16, p. 307; [15]*Oration V*, 29, ibid., 327; [16]*Ibid.*; [17]IX, 382; [18]15-18, 390f; [19]XII, 356.

GREGORY OF NYSSA, ST., (c. 335 - c. 395)[1]

The mystical theologian among the Cappadocians with a sure speculative bent G., younger brother of St. Basil (qv), a monk then a bishop, highly educated, found himself inevitably at grips with the theological questions about the Holy Spirit: it was an age of heretical challenge from Eunomius and the Macedonians (qqv), would call for conciliar intervention from the Council of Constantinople (qv). G.'s firm basic position was the doctrine of Nicaea (qv); he suffered ejection from his see by the Arians, returned, went on to champion Nicaea at Constantinople.

G.'s doctrine of the Holy Spirit is contained in the 'Catechetical Oration,' in the treatises against Eunomius, the sermon on the Holy Spirit against the followers of Macedonius, the treatise on the Holy Trinity, much of which is attributed to St.

Basil (Letter 189), the *Quod non sunt tres dii* and the third sermon on the "Our Father." G., a true mystic, had a sense of the Spirit as guiding and helping him.

We have an idea of what G. faced; he thus states the position of Eunomius, quoting him 'word for word': "The whole account of our doctrines is summed up thus; there is the Supreme and Absolute Being, and another Being existing by reason of the first, but after it, though before all others; and a third Being not ranking with either of these, but inferior to the one as to its cause, to the other, as to the energy which produced it: there must, of course, be included in this account the energies that follow each Being and the names germane to these energies. Again, as each Being is absolutely single, and is in fact thought one, and its energies are bounded by its works, and its works commensurate with its energies, necessarily, of course, the energies which follow these Beings are relatively greater and less, some being of a higher, some of a lower order; in a word their difference amounts to that existing between their works; it would in fact not be lawful to say that the same energy produced the angels or stars, and the heavens or man..."[2]

G. had to cope also with the errors of the followers of Macedonius: "What then is the charge they bring against us? They accuse us of profanity for entertaining lofty conceptions about the Holy Spirit. All that we, in following the teachings of the Fathers, confess as to the Spirit, they take in a sense of their own, and make it a handle against us, to denounce us for profanity. We, for instance, confess that the Holy Spirit is of the same rank as the Father and the Son, so that there is no difference between them in anything, to be thought or named, that devotion can ascribe to a divine nature. We confess that, save his being contemplated as with peculiar attributes in regard of Person, the Holy Spirit is indeed from God and of the Christ, according to Scripture, but that, while not to be confounded with the Father in being never originated, nor with the Son in being the Only-begotten, and while to be regarded separately in certain distinctive properties, he has in all else, as I have just said, an exact identity with them. But our opponents aver that he is a stranger to any vital communion with the Father and the Son; that by reason of an essential variation he is inferior to, and less than they in every point; in power, in glory, in dignity, in fine in everything that in word or thought we ascribe to deity: that in

consequence, in their glory he has no share, to equal honour with them he has no claim; and that, as for power he possesses only so much of it as is sufficient for the partial activities assigned to him; that with the creative force he is quite disconnected."[3]

"He is divine," G. insists, "and absolutely good, and omnipotent, and wise, and glorious, and eternal; he is everything of this kind that can be named to raise our thoughts to the grandeur of his being." In many different ways, picking up the weak points in his opponents' case, not always in a perceptibly logical sequence, but firmly, explicitly, making his own main point. "The Holy Spirit is, to begin with, because of qualities that are essentially holy, that which the Father, essentially holy, is; and such as the only-begotten is, such is the Holy Spirit, then again, he is so by virtue of life-giving, of imperishability, of unvariableness, of everlastingness, of justice, of wisdom, of rectitude, of sovereignty, of goodness, of power, of capacity to give all good things, and above them all life itself, and by being everywhere, by being present in each, filling the earth, residing in the heavens, shed abroad upon supernatural powers, filling all things according to the deserts of each, himself remaining full, being with all who are worthy, and yet not parted from the Holy Trinity. He ever 'searches the deep things of God,' ever 'receives' from the Son, ever is being 'sent' and yet not separated, and being 'glorified' and yet he has always had glory."[4]

Accordingly our worship falls far short of what is due to the Spirit: "But with regard to service and worship, and the other things which they so nicely calculate about, and bring into prominence, we say this: that the Holy Spirit is exalted above all that we can do for him with our merely human purpose; our worship is far beneath the honour due; and anything else that in human customs is held as honourable is somewhere below the dignity of the Spirit; for that which in its essence is measureless surpasses those who offer their all with so slight and circumscribed and paltry a power of giving."[5]

G. was not happy with his attempt to apply theses of neoplatonism to the Trinity, though he remains totally convinced of the reality of the Blessed Trinity. "For, in personality, the Spirit is one thing and the Word another, and yet again, that from which the Word and Spirit is, another. But when you have gained the conception of what the distinction is in these, the oneness, again, of the nature admits not division, so that the supremacy of the one First Cause is not split and cut up into differing Godships, neither does the statement harmonize with the Jewish dogma, but the truth passes in the mean between these two conceptions, destroying each heresy, and yet accepting what is useful to it from each. The Jewish dogma is destroyed by the acceptance of the Word, and by the belief in the Spirit; while the polytheistic error of the Greek school is made to vanish by the unity of the nature abrogating this imagination of plurality."[6]

The unity of operation in the Trinity is central to G.'s thought. From it he deduces the unity of nature: "Since among men the action of each in the same pursuits is discriminated, they are properly called many, since each of them is separated from the others within his own environment, according to the special character of his operation. But in the case of the divine nature we do not similarly learn that the Father does anything in himself in which the Son does not work conjointly, or again that the Son has any special operation apart from the Holy Spirit; but every operation extends from God to the creation, and is named accordingly to our variable conceptions of it, has its origin from the Father, and proceeds through the Son and is perfected in the Holy Spirit. Since then the holy Trinity fulfils every operation in a manner similar to that of which I have spoken not by separate actions according to the number of the persons, but so that there is one motion and disposition of the good will, which is communicated from the Father through the Son to the Spirit, so neither can we call those who exercise this divine and superintending power and operation towards ourselves and all creation, conjointly and inseparably, by their mutual action three gods."[7]

Likewise in the text of doubtful authenticity, on the Holy Trinity: it is almost certainly his not Basil's: "For since it is said 'the angels do always behold the face of my Father who is in heaven,' and it is not possible to behold the person of the Father otherwise than in fixing the sight upon it through his image; and the image of the person of the Father is the Only-begotten, and to him again no man can draw near whose mind has not been illumined by the Holy Spirit, what else is shown from this but that the Holy Spirit is not separated from any operation which is wrought by the Father and the Son."[8]

Did G. teach the *Filioque* (qv)? It is compatible

with his general teaching. "For as the Son is bound to the Father, and, while deriving existence from him is not substantially after him, so again the Holy Spirit is in touch with the Only-begotten, who is conceived of as before the Spirit's subsistence only in the theoretical light of a cause."[9]

G. was clear on the consubstantiality: "Thus the identity of operation in Father, Son and Holy Spirit shows plainly the undistinguishable character of their substance. So that even if the name of godhead does indicate nature, the community of substance shows that this appellation is properly applied also to the Holy Spirit."[10]

The Great Catechetical Oration contains a succinct summary of G.'s thought: "The like doctrine have we received as to God's Spirit; we regard it as that which goes with the Word and manifests its energy, and not as a mere effluence of the breath; for by such a conception the grandeur of the divine power would be reduced and humiliated, that is if the Spirit that is in it were supposed to resemble ours. But we conceive of it as an essential power, regarded as self-centred inits own proper Person, yet equally incapable of being separated from God in whom it is, or from the Word of God whom it accompanies, as from melting into nothingness; but, as being, after the likeness of God's Word, existing as a Person, able to will, self-moved, efficient, ever choosing the good, and for its every purpose having its power concurrent with its will."[11]

[1]Full bibliographies: Bibliographie zu Gregor von Nyssa, M. Altenburger, F. Mann, Leiden, 1988; *DSp,* VI, 971-1011; cf. V. Koperski, *Doctrina S. Gregorii Nysseni de processione Filii Dei,* Rome, 1936; P. Galtier, *Le Saint Esprit en nous d'après les Pères grecs,* Rome, 1946; 180-197; G. Isaye; "L'unité de l'opération divine dans les écrits trinitaires de S. Gregoire de Nysse," *RSR* 27 (1937) 429-39; S. Gonzalez, "La identidad de operación en las obras exteriores y la unidad de la naturaleza divina en la teologia trinitaria de S. Gregorio de Nisa, *Greg* 19 (1938), 280-301; M. Gomez de Castro, *Die Trinitätslehre des hl. Gregor von Nyssa,* Freiburg i. B., 1938; esp., W. Jaeger, *Gregor von Nyssa's Lehre von Heiligen Geist,* Leyte, 1966; *The Message,* 138-142; J. Quasten, III, 285-87; *DTC* VI 1675-77, J. Godet; *Trinitas,* 119-120; [2]*Against Eunomius* I, 13, *LNPF* V, 50; [3]*Against Macedonius, ibid.,* 315, 6; [4]*Ibid.,* 316; 323; [5]*Ibid.,* 320; [6]*The Great Catechetical Oration* III, 477; [7]*Quod non sint tres dii,* 334; [8]329; [9]*Against Eunomius*I, 42, 100; cp., *Quod non sint tres dii,* 336; [10]*On the Holy Trinity,* 329; [11]II, 477; cp. *Third Sermon on the Lord's Prayer, ACW* 18, 54-55.

GUERRA, ELENA, BLESSED (1835-1914)
The significance of this Italian Beata is that she

may have influenced Leo XIII (qv) in the publication of important papal documents on the Holy Spirit, the Encyclical *Divinum illud munus* and the letters *Provida Matris Caritate*, and *Ad fovendum in Christiano populo* (qqv), as we know the same Pope was influenced in writing his Encyclical *Annum Sacrum* on the Sacred Heart, by another nun, Sister Droste-Vischering of the Good Shepherd Sisters. Blessed Elena was of a noble Italian family, and privately educated.[1] With other members of a group whom she motivated towards charitable works, she founded a Pious Union of Spiritual Friendship in 1872, taking as patroness a thirteenth-century Italian saint, St. Zita (d. 1278), a working class girl, patroness of servant girls. The Society was approved in 1911 as the Oblate Sisters of the Holy Spirit, with the objective of spreading devotion to the third Person of the Holy Trinity; they are mostly known as Sisters of St. Zita. Blessed Elena wrote several times to the Pope and it is thought that to her were due the important papal documents. She was beatified in 1959; she left devotional writings.

---

[1]P. Scavizzi, *Elena Guerra, apostola dello Spirito Santo*, Lucca, 1939; L. Cristani, *Apôtre du Saint Esprit*, Paris, 1964; F.C. Sottocornola, *NCE* VI, 832-33; *AAS* 51 (1959), 337-342.

H

HEART OF MARY, THE

If we look for a scriptural basis of the very special, intimate relationship between the Spirit of God and the Heart of Mary, we must advert to the one explicit NT text, one repeated in the Lucan infancy narrative: "But Mary kept all these things pondering them in her heart" (2:19); "and his Mother kept all these things in her heart" (2:51).[1] A question arises at once: why does the evangelist not indicate that this was under the influence of the Spirit, as he does when introducing words or acts of Zechariah (1:67), Elizabeth (1:41) or Simeon (2:26, 27)? The explanation may be given by the great Orthodox theologian, Sergius Bulgakov (qv): "The Virgin Mary remained, even after the birth of Christ, in the force of the Annunciation, that is of the Holy Spirit's presence."[2] Paul VI (qv) in his Letter *E con sentimenti* to Cardinal Suenens for th Marian Congress in 1975 wrote thus explicitly: "It was the Holy Spirit who proffered to the Virgin the good advice to keep faithfully in her heart the memory of the words and deeds related to the birth and infancy of her only Son, in which[3] she had participated so intimately and with such great love (Lk 2:19, 33, 51)." The Spirit being one with Mary is assumed to act constantly in and through her. Emergence of the idea of centering piety in a special way on the Heart of Mary would come when the patristic doctrine of a close partnership between Jesus and Mary had developed and when his Heart had come into a dynamic place in Christian consciousness. With time too the Spirit's action in Mary's life and the theme of Mary and the Spirit would assume importance. Moments of some sequence may be noted. The first prayer addressed to the Heart of Mary was composed by Ekbert of Schonau (d.1184). One line is of relevance to our theme: "Hail, unique sanctuary, which God sanctified to himself in the Holy Spirit"—Ekbert is addressing the Heart of Mary directly.[4]

In the same century Hugh of St. Victor (d.1143) saw the mystery of the Spirit and the Heart especially in the moment of the Annunciation: "Mary therefore conceived of the Holy Spirit, not that she had received the seed of her offspring from the substance of the Holy Spirit, but because through love and the operation of the Holy Spirit, nature from the flesh of the Virgin supplied (human) substance to the divine offspring. For since in her heart love of the Holy Spirit was singularly ardent, in her flesh the power of the Holy Spirit worked wonders. And since the love for him in her heart was shared with none, his operation in her flesh was unexampled."[5]

It is well known that the theology of the Hearts

was grasped and lived by the monastery of Helfta in its great moment, during the thirteenth century. It is in a passage where St. Gertrude the Great relates the Heart of Mary to the Persons of the Holy Trinity that we shall see a reflection on the Holy Spirit and the Heart of Mary: "During Matins, as the *Ave Maria* was sung she saw three forceful streams proceed from the Father and the Son and the Holy Spirit; they entered, with the gentlest approach the heart of the Virgin Mary, and from this heart, bounded back to their source with the liveliest movement. From this influx of the Holy Trinity it was given to the Blessed Virgin to be the most powerful after the Father, the wisest after the Son, and the kindest after the Holy Spirit." [6] A suggestion, but how significant.

In the same century Richard of St. Laurent (d. after 1245) described the Heart of Mary as the resting-place of the whole Trinity. The elaboration of this idea will be the work of the seventeenth-century French spiritual writer and religious founder, St. John Eudes (d. 1680). The saint distinguished three meanings of the word heart: corporeal, the heart of flesh; the spiritual heart which comprises the intellect, will and memory, as well as "the point of the spirit," the soul, the psyche; the divine heart, which is really God himself, in the case of Mary uniquely communicating his love to her. He then treats of each Person as a "foundation" of devotion to the Heart of Mary. On the third Person he writes thus: "The Holy Spirit is the consummation and accomplishment of the adorable mystery of the most Holy Trinity. The Heart of the Mother of God is the consummation, the summary and the perfection of all the works of the most Holy Trinity in purely created reality, since it contains preeminently all that is great, all that is rare in all creatures. For this reason we can say with Hesychius, Bishop of Jerusalem, that it is *complementum Trinitatis* (*Sermo de Laudibus B. Mariae*), the accomplishment of the most Holy Trinity, and as we have already seen, it contributed with the Father, the Son and the Holy Spirit to produce the Godman by the mystery of the Incarnation. In this work all the power, wisdom, goodness and all the other perfections of the Deity must have been used, and, as it were, exhausted, since God can do nothing greater."

"The Holy Spirit has been sent into the world to light the darkness, to kindle the fire of divine love in hearts, to accomplish what is lacking in the works, the sufferings and the Passion of the Son of God and in all his mysteries. What is waiting?

That the fruit be applied to souls. But the Heart of the Mother of God is a sun which sheds its light and its fire on all the world. And the very ardent desire it has that the Son of God should not be denied the effect of his designs, and all that he did and suffered in this world for the salvation of men should not be in vain and useless, compels this Heart to busy itself incessantly so as to procure, in every possible manner, that the fruit should be applied to their souls." [7]

This is the Trinitarian perspective opened by St. John Eudes. It was also developed by another seventeenth-century spiritual writer, the Italian Fr. Pinamonti, S.J. (1632-1703). It is found too in a remarkable sermon on the Heart of Mary by the nineteenth-century Jesuit, Irish-born, who lived in France, Nicolas Tuite de McCarthy (1769-1833). His sermon was preached at a time when Marian doctrine and piety were coming slowly out of the pitiful decline which marked the end of the eighteenth century. He introduces reflections on Mary and the three divine Persons thus: "The Lord has decreed in his eternal counsels that the world would be saved by the incarnation of his Word, and that this ineffable mystery would be accomplished in the womb of a Virgin, by the operation of the Holy Spirit. There upon it was to the glory of the whole adorable Trinity that nothing would be lacking in the perfection of a creature called to so sublime a destiny. The Father adopted in a very special manner the one who was to be the Spouse of his Spirit and the Mother of his only Son." Fr. de McCarthy concludes his Trinitarian considerations with these words: "Finally to say everything briefly, what must have been the Heart whose sentiments matched the sublimity of these incomprehensible relations with the three divine Persons, being worthy in every way of the Daughter, the Spouse and the Mother of God." [8]

This approach, thoroughly doctrinal, has in it something schematic, none the less valid for that. The nineteenth-century Jewish convert, Francis Libermann (1802-1852) moved in an existential spiritual world. His ideas on the Heart of Mary and the Holy Spirit were an intuitive reading of his own profound and exceptional experience—he once said that he had never, in the life of any saint, met the equivalent of his own experience of divine action in his soul.

Libermann with others, still seminarists like himself, founded in 1841 a Society of the Holy Heart of Mary, for the conversion of the black race. Events dictated the choice of patronage and thus he expressed it. The congregation consecrated each of its members, their works and enterprises "to the Most Holy Heart of Mary, this Heart eminently apostolic, all inflamed with desires for the glory of God and the salvation of souls. We shall consider it as a perfect model of the apostolic zeal by which we should be consumed and as an abundant and ever open source, from which we must draw."[9]

Meanwhile in the Congregation with which Libermann's would one day be united, the early eighteenth-century foundation, the Congregation of the Holy Ghost, a decision had been taken in 1847 which is described as follows: "Consecration of the Congregation of the Holy Spirit to the Holy Spirit and to the Immaculate Heart of Mary: On the Sunday within the octave of the feast of Mary's Immaculate Conception, after Compline, the members of the Congregation of the Holy Spirit, with the novices, meeting in the Mother House, will renew their consecration to the Holy Spirit and to the Immaculate Heart of Mary."[10] At this time there was no question of union with Libermann's younger society: the terms of the consecration are intriguing in the light of the eventual fusion.

When it had taken place Libermann had to rewrite the relevant section of rule which he did as follows: "To introduce its members to a devotion fundamental and full of holiness, and to secure for them a source and a powerful means of sanctification, in the accomplishment of the duties of their personal, community and apostolic life, the Congregation consecrates them specially to the Holy Spirit, the Author and perfector of all holiness, and the inspirer of the apostolic spirit, and to the Immaculate Heart of Mary, who was abundantly filled by the divine Spirit, with the fullness of holiness and of the apostolate, who shares most perfectly in the life and sacrifice of Jesus Christ, her Son, for the redemption of the world.

This double devotion is special and distinctive to the Congregation. They (the members) will find in the Holy Spirit, living in their souls, a source of the interior life and an all-powerful principle of that perfect charity which is the soul of zeal and of all the other apostolic virtues. They will consider the Immaculate Heart of Mary a perfect model of fidelity to all the holy inspirations of the divine Spirit and of the interior practice of the virtues of the religious and apostolic life. They will find there a refuge to which they will have recourse in their works and in their sufferings, and will open their hearts to her, with childlike confidence in their weaknesses and their temptations."[11]

Libermann reassured his subjects belonging to the Society of the Holy Heart of Mary who feared a certain deprivation of their idealism by their joining with the older institute—one of those lacking enthusiasm for the merger was Blessed James Laval, Apotle of Mauritius, though his fear was grounded in the known lack of fervour in that body. Nothing had really changed, Libermann asserted. "We have always placed our repose and our happiness in the Heart of Mary, filled with eminent superabundance of the Holy Spirit, and if we have not given expression to that thought of the fullness of the Holy Spirit in the Heart of Mary, it nonetheless forms the essence of our devotion to that most Holy Heart. Well then, we do not change; only what was understood, what we supposed formerly, we express now ... God has united all of us in the Holy Heart of Mary. We remain there, united by the power and graces of the Holy Spirit."[12]

It was under this double sign of the Spirit and the Heart that Libermann pioneered the modern African missionary movement. Many others would later enter the field. In numbers and discernible fruits, the evangelisation of this continent eclipses any undertaken by the Church in a thousand years; the unique achievement has taken less than a century and a half. The exemplar at the outset was that which opened the initial evangelisation by the Church of Christ, the union of the Spirit and the Heart of Mary in the event of Pentecost.

The urgent lesson from the teaching and experience of the past is that this idealism must be assimilated into the entire personality of the believing Christian. It has possibly suffered from superficial, naturalistic, even superstitious interpretations. A theology of the Heart directly associated with the Holy Spirit should be preserved from such distortion. The Heart of Mary speaks of her entire personality, of depths unequalled of power and compassion; her Heart realizes all that the Old and New Testament express by use of this term, vitality, ardour of spirit, the very centre of the human person, a concept which comprises fully the sum-total of human powers, but gives them a dynamic existential unity.

It is here whence all thought and resolve radiates that the Spirit of God is united with Mary Mother of God; nothing extraneous or inferior lessens his presence, weakens his impulse, frustrates her response to his creative guidance. Both unite most perfectly in attention to the Christian who is a member of Christ, for both brought him into the world. Both wish him to govern by his wisdom and strength the whole universe.

[1]For bibl. cf. M. O'Carroll, *Theotokos*, article "Heart of Mary," 166-168 and article, "Spirit, the Holy," 329-332; cf. *Spiritan Papers*, Autumn 1988, Congregation of the Holy Spirit, Rome; M. O'Carroll, C.S.Sp. "La dévotion au Coeur de Marie dans l'histoire de la Congrégation du Saint Esprit et du Coeur Immaculé de Marie," *Marianum* 46 (1984), 247-260; [2]*Le Paraclet*, Paris, 1946, 238, 239; [3]Apud E.D. O'Connor, C.S.C., *Pope Paul and the Spirit*, Notre Dame, 1972, 220f; [4]Text ad. critically H. Barré, C.S.Sp., "Une prière d'Ekbert de Schonau au Saint Coeur de Marie," *Ephemerides Mariologicae* 2 (1952), 412; [5]*De Beatae Mariae Virginitate*, 2 PL 176, 871C-872A; [6]*Legatus divinae pietatis, SC* 139, 334-35; [7]*Le Coeur admirable de la très sacrée Mère de Dieu*, Caen, 1681, Bk V, ch. 12' [8]*Sermons de R.P. McCarthy*, vol. II, Paris, Lyon, 1840, 101, 108; [9]*Règle provisoire de la Société du Saint Coeur de Marie*, ch. II, art. 3, *Notas et Documents relatifs à la vie et á l'oeuvre du Ven F.M.P. Libermann*, Paris, 1929 ... vol. II, 238; [10]*Regulae et Constitutiones Sodalitii et Seminarii Sancti Spiritus sub Immaculatae Virginis Tutela*, Paris, 1848, p. 68; [11]*Notes et Documents,* X, 567; [12]*Lettres Spirituelles*, IV, p. 598.

HEBREWS, LETTER TO THE

This great vindication of the high priesthood of Jesus Christ written by an Alexandrian Jew of great culture—so it is surmised—had some dependence on St. Paul (qv); no one now of substance maintains that Paul himself wrote the document.[1] Thus the first explicit reference to the Holy Spirit seems to echo Paul: "It was declared at first by the Lord, and it was attested to us by those who heard him, while God also bore witness by signs and wonders and various miracles and by gifts of the Holy Spirit distributed according to his own will" (2:3). The resemblance with 1 Cor 12:4, 11, is patent.

An important text occurs in chapter VI on the need to persevere in face of temptations to apostasy: "For it is impossible to restore again to repentance those who have once been enlightened, who have tasted the heavenly gift, and have become partakers of the Holy Spirit, and have tasted the goodness of the word of God and the powers of the age to come, if they then commit apostasy, since they crucify the Son of God on their own account and hold him up to contempt" (6:4-6). This is an important instance of the experiential dimension which Christian thinking sees in the Holy Spirit. He lives and acts in the Church, is tasted, to use the strong metaphor.

[1]G.T. Montague, *The Holy Spirit*, 316-320.

HILARY OF POITIERS, ST., DOCTOR OF THE CHURCH (c. 315-367)

The great defender of orthodoxy in the West, author of the first substantial treatise on the Trinity as the Church emerged from the Arian crisis—he was of course preceded by Novatian (qv) in subject matter, but not in formidable opposition—H. developed his doctrine on the Incarnation at length but did not give the same attention to the personality, properties and dignity of the Holy Spirit.[1] It may have been the wish to avoid too many enemies at once; it does not appear to stem from any doubt on essentials. Account must be taken of discussion on the very core of H.'s Trinitarian teaching, on his understanding of the *homoousion*.

It has been said that there are two sets of statements by H. on the Holy Spirit: those in which he shows a certain doctrinal vagueness and those where he is more explicit. What he thought is contained in passages in the *De Trinitate* and *De Synodis*, briefly elsewhere. In the latter work in his explanation of the anathemas of the Synod of Sirmium, 351, he has this comment on anathema XX: "We remember that the Paraclete was sent by the Son, and at the beginning of the creed explained this. But since through the virtue of his nature, which is exactly similar, the Son has frequently called his own works the works of the Father, saying, *I do the works of my Father* (Jn 10:37): so, when he intended to send the Paraclete, as he often promised, he said sometimes that he was to be sent from the Father, in that he was piously wont to refer all that he did to the Father. And from this the heretics often seize an opportunity of saying that the Son himself is the Paraclete: while by the fact that he promised to pray that another Comforter should be sent from the Father he shows the difference between him who is sent and him who is asked."[2] Commenting on Anathema XX which condemned those who asserted that the Holy Spirit was "a part of the Father or the Son," H. wrote: "Since the name of Holy Spirit has its own signification, and the Holy Spirit the Paraclete has the office and rank peculiar to his Person, and since the Father and the Son are everywhere declared to be immutable, how could the Holy Spirit be asserted to be a part either of the Father or of the Son?"[3]

H., as is well known, does not call the Spirit consubstantial, nor does he give him the name God, even, some urge, in passages where it would be expected. He has a revealing passage at the very end of *De Trinitate*: "Again, Paul recounts all things as created in him (Christ), in heaven and on earth, visible and invisible. And while he declared that everything was created in Christ and through Christ, he thought, with respect to the Holy Spirit, that the description was sufficient when he called him thy Spirit. With these men, peculiarly thine elect, I will think in these matters; just as, after their example, I will say nothing beyond my comprehension, about thy Only-begotten, but simply declare that he was born, so also after their example I will not trespass beyond that which human intellect can know about thy Holy Spirit, but simply declare that he is thy Spirit. May my lot be no useless strife of words, but the unwavering confession of an unhesitating faith."[4] A few lines on, practically at the end of the book we read: "Let me, in short, adore thee our Father, and thy Son together with thee; let me win the favour of thy Holy Spirit, who is from thee, through thy Only-begotten."[5]

These views throw light then on such a passage as this: "But, for my part, I cannot be content by the service of my faith and voice, to deny that my Lord and my God, thy Only-begotten Jesus Christ, is a creature; I must also deny that this name of 'creature' belongs to thy Holy Spirit, seeing that he proceeds from thee and is sent through him, so great is my reverence for everything that is thine. Nor, because I know that thou alone are unborn and that the Only-begotten is born of thee, will I refuse to say that the Holy Spirit was begotten or assert that he was ever created."[6]

This may appear ambiguous, but H. seems to aim at something more explicit in the lines that follow: "I fear the blasphemies which would be insinuated against thee by such use of the title 'creature,' which I share with the other beings brought into being by thee. Thy Holy Spirit, as the Apostle says, searches and knows thy deep things, and as intercessor for me speaks to thee words I could not utter; and shall I express or rather dishonour, by the title 'creature,' the power of his nature which subsists eternally, derived from thee, through thine Only-begotten?"[7]

Some may not find this quite satisfactory so we should reproduce the passage often quoted: "There is no need to speak, because we are bound to confess him, proceeding as he does from the Father and the Son. For my own part I think it wrong to discuss the question of his existence. He does exist, inasmuch as he is given, received, retained. He is joined with Father and Son in our confession of the faith, and cannot be excluded from a true confession of Father and Son; take away a part and the whole faith is marred. If any man demand what meaning we attach to this conclusion, he, as well as we, has read the words of the Apostle ... "[8] There then follow a number of Pauline texts, Gal 4:6, 1 Cor 2:12, Rom 8:9.

H. recognized the confusion some may feel that the word "Holy Spirit" is used to signify the Father or the Son. H. contends that "the words *God is Spirit*, do not alter the fact that the Holy Spirit has a name of his own, and that he is the Gift to us."[9]

In the passage quoted the words "proceeding as he does from the Father and the Son" seem to express the *Filioque* (qv). The Latin words used '*qui Patre et Filio auctoribus confitendus est*' are susceptible of another rendering "confess him on the evidence of the Father and the Son."[10] Another passage reads: "For referring to his words that the Holy Spirit should take of his, he says, *All things whatsoever the Father hath are mine, therefore said I, he shall take of mine*; that is, the Holy Spirit takes of his, but takes also of the Father's; and if he receives of the Father's he receives also of his. The Holy Spirit is the Spirit of God, and does not receive of a creature, but teaches us that he receives all these gifts, because they are all God's. All things that belong to the Father are the Spirit's; but we must not think that whatever he received of the Son, he did not receive of the Father also; for all that the Father hath belongs equally to the Son."[11] Is the context here solely one of the economy?

[1]Works *PL* 9, 10; *CSEL* 22, 65; English tr. of *De Trinitate, LNPF* IX, used here; S. McKenna, Fathers of the Church, Washington, 1954; cf. J.P. Balzer *Die Theologie des hl. Hilarius vonPoitiers*, Rottwell, 1879; Th. Froster "Zur theologie des Hilarius," *Theologische Studien und Kritiken*, vol 61, (1888) 645-686; A. Beck, *Die Trinitätslehre des hl. Hilarius*, Mainz, 1903; S. Palumbo, *Unità e distinzione in Dio secondo S. Hilario*, Capua, 1940; esp. P. Smulders, *La doctrine trinitaire de St. Hilaire de Poitiers*, Rome, 1944; cf. esp. review of this book by J. Lebon, *RSR* 33 (1946) 484-89; M. Simonetti, "La processione dello Spirito Santo nei Padri Latini," *Maia* 7 (1955) 308-24; J. Moingt, "La théologie trinitaire de St. Hilaire" in *St. Hilaire et son temps. Actes du*

Colloque de Poitiers, 1968, *Etudes Augustiniennes*, Paris, 1968; C. Kannengieser, *DSp*, VII, 466-499, exhaustive bibl.; *The Message*, 110-14; *Trinitas*, 123-26; Introduction to *LNPF*, 83-84; [2]*LNPF* IX, 19; [3]*Ibid.*; [4]Bk XII, 56, p. 233; [5]57, *ibid.*; [6]Bk XII, 55, p. 233; [7]*Ibid.*; [8]Bk II, 29, p. 60; [9]Bk II, 30, p. 60; [10]Cf. *LNPF*, p. 60, n. 8; [11]Bk IX, 73; p.180.

HISTORY[1]

If we succeed in constructing a theology of history, it must be Trinitarian. God who exists and acts in history is Trinity. The problems to be solved in the search for a Trinitarian sense, even pattern, in the life of humankind, start from one factual acquisition: the irruption of the divine into history clearly affirmed in the event of Pentecost. This is true in whatever sense we take history. It may be the sum-total of all that has happened to the human race, taken in the individual human lives which have composed it, or in the collective experience and achievements of all together.

That dichotomy is severely limited, for communal forces are frequently released by one individual with a gift which is diversely named but may be expressed by the conventional word leadership. But not in the narrow sense in which it is generally used, action by figures in public life on their contemporaries to secure political ends. Leadership can be taken in as wide a sense as influence by one human being on others may extend, in the world of ideas, values, aesthetic taste, artistic creation, sentiment, behavioural attitudes, modes of relaxation and recreation, communication, dress.

How can we succeed in tracing the divine in all that? We can refer it all generally to divine Providence, which is not a solution to our immediate problem. Did we not have the incident of Pentecost we should at this stage perhaps abandon the enquiry. For those who have faith in the divine revelation of Christ, Pentecost forms part of a divine sequence, in which the Incarnation is totally central and fundamental. Eventually a Christian theology of history must find its full explanation therein. But we have to proceed in stages, even if the first seems to hold us at the periphery.

It may appear beyond our intellectual power with the data made available to us in divine revelation to attain complete, satisfying knowledge, to reach a final stage. To hope for this may appear to forestall the final eschatological summary, statement, explanation of the fortunes of humankind. Yet tentative groping is at times a substitute for successful research, which is not only permissible, but imperative on those with a sense of the divine in human affairs.

In such painstaking progress we have to see not only the pivotal point of Pentecost, but the initiation of all by the act of creation, work of the Father in the Son through the Holy Spirit. All that was thereby imprinted on the created universe by divine action is given a new reading for us through the entry into creation of a divine Person, who, by an act of self-emptying, of kenosis, accepted the total reality of our world, without sin.

The Spirit participated in this entire human experience, this abbreviation, chronologically speaking, of the whole divine action on humankind. As the human life of Jesus throws out illuminating shafts of light on the vast panorama of history, the Spirit is the ultimate source to which this light is traceable.

We have to seek his help to know history. So much falsehood has been published about past events, so many strange forces work to deprive us of the truth. At times it is done crudely, at other times subtly. Where history has become official, a regime maintains it in a version deemed acceptable. To dismantle a whole apparatus of selected textual material, to fill spaces kept deliberately blank or vague with the hard truth, to undermine a whole thought system composed of narrative mixed with ideology and cut to serve it, is so daunting a task that the Spirit alone can ensure success.

We need the Spirit to understand history. What is this flow of ideas, events, personalties which coalesce to give at times an impression of continuity, even to a discernible sequence of cause and effect, at other times appear disrupted, sporadic? Is there an over-all discoverable grand design, or, as a well-known English historian contended, is it folly to seek such comprehension? Is history what historians write and talk about? Or are they conditioned to select what is palatable, as newspapers choose the sensational, the fashionable, going even to the limit that only bad news is news?

The Spirit is himself at the heart of history as it really happened; he holds the key to humankind's march through time; he sees human persons individually and collectively, their thoughts, acts, products at their true value, relating all infallibly to the initial design which he shared with the Father and the Son, to the final outcome wherein all, that is each single man and woman, will stand fully revealed and judged in the light of that design.

The hidden years of Christ, totally unnoticed by those attentive to the public events of the time, is a most precious part of history; it is also a lesson in the understanding of all history: what is passed over in silence may have prodigious importance and effects. It is at times death (qv) which reveals these things. Down to 1897 those knowing of Lisieux saw no importance to one sister living in the Carmel, Thérèse de l'Enfant Jésus et de la Sainte Face. Death intervened in that year and almost immediately a worldwide spiritual movement was born. This, we know, was possible because another worldwide movement followed the death and resurrection of Jesus. As we understand his hidden life in the light of this happening, we understand the hidden years in Lisieux in the light of the "miracle of virtues and the prodigy of virtues," as Pius XI called Ste. Thérèse.

The saint also reminds us that it is in the history of the Church that we have the full manifestation of the Spirit. Not all those active at points of importance in the Church in past times were attentive to the Spirit. He was at all times attentive to all within the Church. The forces of evil, human malice and weakness have their momentary triumphs. But with infinite resource the Spirit also sustains within the Body of Christ, at times hidden in multiple mystery, the vital pulse, dramatically forestalls total collapse and initiates recovery in splendour.

In the Church the Spirit is truly the God of surprises. The lessons of its history are a revelation, an intimation of his astonishing personality, his designs which infinitely surpass our most arduously elaborate schemes. He sees to the growth of the Church, acting as he did at the outset. Not as we should plan or expect: who would have forecast the growth of the Body in western Europe, while its presence remains minimal in the nation, the race and the continent of Jesus Christ: he was a Jew, a Semite and an Asiatic. When we think thus we forget that the Spirit is the Lord of what we call time. Time is his creature, is subject to him; he is outside time, not locked within it, as we are, free to telescope or stretch it as he pleases, free above all to accomplish in one momentary contact with it all that we should need, years, perhaps centuries, to achieve.

This too is why history has its full meaning only in reference to him, for time is the fabric on which history is embroidered, in patterns woven into it. From him we must strive to learn the inner meaning, conscious that it must to some extent remain elusive, in final analysis mysterious. Through his light we shall penetrate to the real lessons of history. The old dictum, "History repeats itself," needs qualification, notably "not to order."

The role of the Spirit in history has been very clearly shown by Hans Urs von Balthasar (qv): "First then, we must show the point of departure from which the individual historical existence of Christ can be so universalized as to become the immediate norm of every individual existence. This universalizing is in a special way an action of the Holy Spirit. It is the Spirit who will 'guide you into all truth; for he will not speak on his own authority, but whatever he hears he will speak ... he will take what is mine and declare it to you' (Jn 16:13-14). It is he who sets his stamp upon the Church and on the individual believer, and on the history of both, by interpreting the life of Jesus (which is itself an interpretation of the Father), giving it the form and force of an unfailingly valid norm. In doing so, he does not issue a further, new revelation; he only exposes the full depth of what has been completed, giving it a dimension which is new for the world: a total relevance to every moment of history."[2] The author develops his thought by pointing to factors "all interconnected in their dependence upon the Holy Spirit, but nevertheless distinguishable: the working of the Holy Spirit on the incarnate Son himself, archetypally in the forty days after the Resurrection, the working of the Spirit as he relates to Christ, thus transformed to the historical Church of every age, (expressed typically in the Sacraments and most fully in the Eucharist), the creating by the Spirit of the missions of Church and individual as applications of the life of Christ to every Christian life and the whole life of the Church."

[1]For bibl., G. Thils, "Bibliographie sur la théologie de l'histoire, *ETL* 26 (1950) 87-95; for books dealing with the theology of history, to which the reader must in most cases supply the missing doctrine of the Spirit, cf. H. Butterfield, *Christianity and History*, London, 1949; N. Berdiaeff, *The Meaning of History*, London, 1936; *id.*, *Freedom and the Spirit*, London, 1935; *id.*, *The Destiny of Man*, London, 1960; O. Cullmann, *Christ and Time*, London, 1951; *id.*, *Salvation in History*, 1967; J. Frisque, *Oscar Cullmann, Une théologie de l'histoire du salut*, Paris, 1960; J. McIntyre, *The Christian Doctrine of History*, London, 1957; M.C. D'Arcy, S.J., *The Sense of History, Secular and Sacred*, London, 1959; J. Maritain, *On the Philosophy of History*, esp. ch. IV, *God and the Mystery of the World*, London, 1959; H. (Cardinal) Urs von Balthasar, *A Theology of History*, esp. The Role of the Holy Spirit, 78-81; London, 1964; *id.*, *Man in History; A Theological Study*, London, 1968; A. Richard-

son, *History Sacred and Profane*, London, 1964; J.V. Langmead Casserly, *Towards a Theology of History*, London, 1965; H. Berkhof, *Christ the Meaning of History*, London, 1966; J. (Cardinal) Daniélou, *The Lord of History*, London, 1960; *id.*, *Essai sur le mystère de l'histoire*, Paris, 1982; K. Rahner, S.J., "Questions on the Theology of History," in *Theological Investigations*, V 1966, 97-153; R.P. Mohan, "The Philosophy of History," *NCE* VII, 22-26; P.L. Hug, "The Theology of History," *ibid.*, 26-31, both with bibl. O. Lewry, O.P., *The Theology of History*, (Cork, 1969, esp., G. Bof, "Per una comprensione della presenza dello Spirito Santo nella storia," in *Atti del Congresso*, II, 1473-1483; [2]*Op.cit.*, 79-80.

HUMOUR

Humour is a part of life. As such it clearly may come under the influence of the Spirit, who governs all life. But to that rather simplified summary one must add certain deeper considerations. Is humour susceptible of perfection as a human attribute, this improvement being seen as the work of the Holy Spirit? Is humour an effect of certain Fruits (qv) of the Spirit? How can humour be used for advancement in holiness, which means advancement in docility to the Spirit? Is humour dependent on humankind's social nature, or may it exist in the solitary individual existence?

It is assumed that humour is not an imperfection, that it is not something which lowers the soul, or impairs the personality. It is natural, that is not intrinsically linked with a source outside the range of human power and activity. As a faculty to perceive and present appropriately what within a particular culture or sub-culture, passes for comical, provocative of immediate relaxation, generally expressed in laughter, humour seems to have little to do with the supernatural.

But for those with faith, there is a further stock of ideas which may facilitate the discovery of those elements which, because they are incongruous or apparently contradictory, produce a humorous effect, even a heightened one. The lives of St. Philip Neri and especially of St. Don Bosco and of St. Thomas More, the writings of Chaucer and Chesterton afford many examples of a supernatural sense of humour. At its best this truly marks the action of the Spirit.

Chesterton said that after the grace of God the best gift in life was a sense of humour: he could have said that one of grace's benefits was a sense of humour. It is a blessing when it is auto-critical. Taking oneself seriously is baneful in the spiritual life; it means substituting egocentrism for Christocentrism, which is the desirable goal. How to eradicate it is not always evident. Those with an autocritical sense of humour have one efficacious means of doing this.

The spiritual life is a constant struggle for personal fulfilment, which means personal simplicity, the removal of all that impedes total expression of the self, in the two ultimately essential activities, love of God and love of our neighbour. Complications prevent the full yield, halt the thrust of the soul towards God, interfere with the self-donation which true service of the neighbour calls for. There is a constant in gospel teaching and in church history: a gift to a fellow-Christian solely and totally for Jesus Christ is received by Jesus Christ personally. But how many acts of charity have this unblemished purity?

As there are many on their way to Christ who do not yet realize that it is he who will be the final encounter on their pilgrimage, so there are many who, discovering the value of humour, may thus be working their passage to the same happy ending. Pagans, non-Christians with a growing sense of humour are, in fact, shedding things which blind them to the vision of the meek and humble Saviour: bitterness, harshness, hardness, arrogance, self-sufficiency. Many heretics would have been saved if they had a sense of humour.

It is an effect of grace, then the work of the Spirit, a spiritual mechanism which he uses to keep us in a state of joy. It means a deep reversal of trends within us caused by sin, the original or personal additions. It means the gradual readiness to take God and others seriously and ourselves solely in regard to them. Here is where a higher Gift has its importance, Wisdom.

To assert so much is to place humour on a very high level, to give it very great importance. This it deserves. As an effect of wisdom it helps rid the soul of much that impedes spiritual progress, so much lumber, some trivial, some decaying and poisonous. Universally prevalent, thorough, genuine and not spurious, not borrowed and artifical, it would remove from our midst the sad spectacle of Christians fettered by memories of past wrongs, refusing to expose to the sunlight of God's love wounds which will go on festering in the dark. Yes, humour is a subject to be taken seriously.

I

INDWELLING OF THE HOLY SPIRIT, THE

There has been a welcome renewal of the personalist aspect of divine grace, matched fortunately with a revival of the doctrine of the divine image.[1] On the latter theme Hans (Cardinal) Urs von Balthasar (qv) in one of his principal works aligns important testimonies from modern thinkers on the crucial significance it has for Christian anthropology.[2] In regard to the indwelling the traditional teaching has been that the Holy Trinity takes up their abode in the soul with divine grace, and that this inhabitation is appropriated to the Holy Spirit.

K. Rahner (qv) has rightly pointed out that Sacred Scripture speaks of the indwelling as personal: "'If a man loves me, he will keep my word, and my Father will love him, and we will come to him and make our abode with him'" (Jn 14:23). More pertinently still to our subject is the word of St. Paul" "And because you are sons, God has sent the Spirit of his Son into our hearts crying, 'Abba! Father!'" (Gal 4:6). Fr. Rahner's opinion is highly relevant: "It would have to be proved in the strictest possible way that it was impossible for there to be this kind of communication of the divine Persons each in his own particularity, and hence a non-appropriated relation to the three Persons. There is no way of producing such a proof. Consequently there can be absolutely no objection to maintaining on the basis of the positive data of revelation that the attribution of determinate relations of the recipient of grace to the three divine Persons is not merely a matter of appropriation, but is intended to give expression to a proper relationship in each case. In Scripture it is the Father in the Trinity who is our Father, and not the threefold God. The Spirit dwells in us in a particular and proper way."[3] This passage may be compared with what M.J. Scheeben wrote on Uncreated and created grace, ending, or helping to end a formalist treatment of the subject of grace: "Thus according to the Latins the Holy Spirit produces fellowship with the Son especially as efficient and exemplary principle of charity; according to the Greeks he produces this fellowship especially in so far as he descends or as the Son of God makes him descend in the adoptive creature as substantial image of the divinity.... The substantial indwelling of the Holy Spirit in the creature as Uncreated Grace joined to created grace is to seal the relations of friendship of the children of God with their Father or to establish this very sonship as fellowship with God resting on substantial and merciful generation. The Holy Spirit is the substantial complement of accidental sanctifying grace and of grace *gratum faciens*.[4]

---

[1]Cf. *Trinitas*, s.v. bibl., 133-135; also Image of God, 131-133; [2]*La dramatique divine*, II, Paris, 1976, p. 275; [3]*Theological Investigations* I, 345, cf. footnote quoted, *Trinitas*, 134. [4]*Dogmatique,* French tr., III, Paris, 1881.

INFALLIBILITY

The First Vatican Council defined the infallibility of the Pope in these words: "the Roman Pontiff, when he speaks *ex cathedra*, that is, when carrying out the duty of the pastor and teacher of all Christians in accord with his supreme apostolic authority he explains a doctrine of faith or morals to be held by the universal Church, through the divine assistance promised him in blessed Peter, operates with that infallibility with which the divine Redeemer wished that his Church be instructed in defining doctrine on faith and morals; and so such definitions of the Roman Pontiff from himself, but not from the consensus of the Church, are unalterable."[1]

There is no reference ot the Holy Spirit in this statement but in the explanatory part of the Dogmatic Constitution shortly before it, occur these words: "For, the Holy Spirit was not promised to the successors of Peter that by his revelation they might disclose new doctrine, but that by his help they might guard sacredly the revelation transmitted through the Apostles and the deposit of faith, and might faithfully set it forth."[2]

Vatican II is more explicit on the role of the Holy Spirit: "The infallibility with which the divine Redeemer willed his Church to be endowed in defining a doctrine of faith and morals extends as far as extends the deposit of divine revelation, which must be religiously guarded and faithfully expounded. This is the infallibility which the Roman Pontiff, the head of the college of bishops, enjoys in virtue of his office, when, as the supreme shepherd and teacher of all the faithful, who confirms their brethren in their faith (cf. Lk 22:32), he proclaims by a definitive act some doctrine of faith or morals. Therefore his definitions, of themselves, and not from the consent of the Church, are justly styled irreformable, for they are pronounced with the assistance of the Holy Spirit, an assistance promised to him in blessed Peter. Therefore they need no approval of others, nor do they allow an appeal to any other judgement. For then the Roman Pontiff is not pronouncing judgement as a private person. Rather, as the supreme teacher of the universal Church, as one in whom the charism of the infallibility of the Church herself is individually present, he is expounding or defending a doctrine of the Catholic faith."[3]

Occasionally the difficulty is proposed: Suppose the bishops and the faithful disagree with the Pope on what he wishes to declare infallibly? The answer of the Council: "The infallibility promised to the Church resides also in the body of bishops when that body exercises supreme teaching authority with the successor of Peter. To the resultant definitions the assent of the Church can never be wanting, on account of the activity of that same Holy Spirit, whereby the whole flock of Christ is preserved and progresses in unity of faith."[4] Referring earlier to the "body of the faithful anointed as they are by the Holy One (cf. 1 Jn 2:20, 27)," which "cannot err in matters of belief" the Council gives this explanation: "For, by this sense of faith which is aroused and sustained by the Spirit of truth, God's people accepts not the word of men, but the very Word of God (cf. 1 Thess 2:13)."[5]

The Spirit then is the source of infallibility. How it derives from him in the life of the Church is

most instructive. There is here a vast programme of research to be undertaken. It will investigate the notable instances of conciliar and papal infallibility; the great conciliar and Marian dogmas. The preparatory process for these latter should prove instructive. For the dogma of the Immaculate Conception Newman studied the preliminaries in Rome. He was impressed by the consultation of the entire episcopate, especially by the fact that, in the Encyclical issued by Pius IX to this end, *Ubi Primum*, (2 February 1849) the bishops were asked to inform the Pope "concerning the devotion which animates your clergy and your people regarding the Immaculate Conception of the Blessed Virgin and how ardently glows the desire that this doctrine be defined by the Apostolic See."

Less than a hundred years later, (1 May 1946) Pius XII made a similar consultation as a preliminary to the dogma of the Assumption; he inquired "about the devotion of your clergy and people (taking into account their faith and piety)" toward the Assumption, and whether "in addition to your own wishes (on the dogmatic definition) this is desired by your clergy and people."

Of 603 bishops consulted by Pius IX 546 favoured definition; four opposed the definability; the remainder were undecided either as to its opportuneness or the manner of presenting the doctrine. Of 1181 residential bishops consulted by Pius XII 22 dissented. But only six doubted that the Assumption was revealed truth—the others questioned the opportuneness of the dogmatic definition.

Each Pope sought theological advice. In different committees on which leading theologians, some of them specialists in the doctrine, like Fr. Giovanni Perrone, S.J., Dom Gueranger, O.S.B., and Carlo Passaglia served, eight separate drafts were prepared for the final official text of the Bull *Ineffabilis Deus*, 8 December 1854. Pius XII named a preparatory committee for the Apostolic Constitution on the Assumption—it would be named *Munificentissimus Deus*—which included scholars of repute and two authors of very substantial monographs on the history of the doctrine, Fr. C. Balic, O.F.M. and M. Jugie, A.A. This had not been at all so controversial as that on the Immaculate Conception—as late as the seventeenth century the prolific Marian theologian, Ippolyto Marracci (1604-1675), was placed under some kind of "house arrest," for publishing books defending the doctrine. But the research was not omitted, and it could draw on a great scientific literature quite recent. Interestingly the Pope took the advice of one of his experts, Fr. Jugie, on an important point, that he should not include a statement on Our Lady's death in the dogmatic definition. This he did by using the non-committal words "when the course of her earthly life was completed."

Each Pope published a lengthy statement giving the theological reasons which supported the dogma, showing why it must, in each case, belong to the body of revealed truth; and each used the formula "We declare, pronounce and define" to specify the dogma. More relevant is the fact that each invoked the Holy Spirit formally and explicitly. But this invocation had not precluded the fullest use of every possible means and resource to avoid error and attain the exact truth. Pius IX's words were: "Wherefore, in humility and fasting, we unceasingly offered our private prayers as well as the public prayers of the Church to God the Father through his Son, that he would deign to direct and strengthen our mind by the power of the Holy Spirit. In like manner did we implore the help of the entire heavenly host as we ardently invoked the Paraclete." The Pope then used the words "Accordingly by the inspiration of the Holy Spirit" as he stated the motives for his defining the dogma.

Pius XII's words were: "For which reason, after We have poured forth prayers of supplication again and again to God, and have invoked the light of the Spirit of Truth. . . ." After these comes the statement of the Pope's motives.

Analysts of the Spirit's action in these dogmatic formulas may compare them with a similar statement made by an eminent theologian, by a Doctor of the Church, to discover the mode of the Spirit's influence. There is combined or concerted intellectual activity, all of it related to the life of the Church; there is a union of two diverse elements in the Church, authority and personal intelligence, each contributed by different individuals; there is acceptance by those who may be equipped with the highest knowledge and intelligence of the right of someone less well equipped to direct, control, judge and finally take or reject the fruits of their research.

All this is not found in the writing of a theologian. There is less scope for the Spirit's action in his case, less evidence of the varied impulse of the Spirit, on the diverse participants in the process which is under his control, wherein each acts freely under the prompting of his grace. The Church, in the holders of different ministries, in different elements of its spiritual fabric, in a disposition of time sequence for the testing of ideas and the discovery of the required formulas, is all under the control of the Spirit. Every relevant person, in varying phases of psychological development and reaction is subject to the same comprehensive rule. It is our faith that when human factors have accomplished everything, there is the moment when God acts, either by averting error or by ratifying truth: the Spirit of God, totally master of his own handiwork.

There is a welcome emphasis on the role of the Spirit in the life of the Church and its exercise of the teaching office, in the Declaration issued in 1973 by the Congregation for the Doctrine of the Faith, *Mysterium Ecclesiae*.[6]

---

[1]For bibl. cf. G. Thils, "L'Infaillibilitè de l'Eglise 'in credendo' et 'in docendo,'" *Salesianum* 24 (1962), 98-336; *id.*, *L'Infaillibilité du peuple chrétien 'in credendo'*, Louvain, 1963; *id.*, *L'Infaillibilité pontificale* Gembloux, 1969; O. Rousseau and others, *L'Infaillibilite de l'Eglise* (representatives of the different communions, theological and historical aspects), Gembloux, Chevetogne, 1963; E. Castelli, ed., *L'Infaillibilité. Son aspect philosophique et théologique*, (philosophical-theological, historical aspects, ecumenical contributions); P. Chirico, S.S., *Infallibility, The Crossroads of Doctrine*, Wilmington, Dublin, 1982; A. Dulles, S.J., "Papal Authority in Roman Catholicism" in P.J. McCord, ed., *A Pope for All Christians*, London, 1978, 48-70; L. Orsy, S.J., *The Church Learning and Teaching*, Dublin, Leominster, 1987, esp. "Teaching Authority," 45-78; DS 3073, 4; [2]DS 3069, 70; [3]*Constitution on the Church*, 25; [4]*Ibid.*, [5]*Constitution on the Church*, 12; [6]English tr. P.F. Swarbrick, Ribbleton, Preston, England. cf. esp. II, *The Infallibility of the Universal Church*, and III, *The Infallibility of the Church's Magisterium*.

INSPIRATION, BIBLICAL

Christ, who is "the mediator and fullness of all revelation" (Vatican II) accomplished, as part of his redemptive work, the permanent presence of his essential saving message to those who were to benefit by it through all ages. This would demand written work.[1] He, who did not himself leave writings, had chosen and trained associates who would do so. In that he was keeping continuity with an important custom of his people. Their sacred books, thought to be of divine origin by the community in which they were composed, were so regarded by him and his associates—as some 350 NT references testify. The Church which he founded would in time have its sacred books also and one God would be the author of all the books of the Old and New Testaments.[2]

Out of this statement, however, arise many problems as to the content and reliability of the collective writings. All these problems are not considered here; only such as are directly related to the theme of the work, the Holy Spirit. Since we receive our sacred books from the Church, we should first listen to the Church in what she says about them.

As a result of theorizing in the nineteenth century, the First Vatican Council declared as follows: "But the Church holds these books as sacred and canonical, not because, having been put together by human industry alone, they were then approved by its authority; not because they contain revelation without error; but because, having been written by the inspiration of the Holy Spirit, they have God as their author and, as such, they have been handed down to the Church itself."[3] The phrase "inspiration of the Holy Spirit" was already used by the Council of Florence.[4]

The precise subject of inspiration now became a matter of speculative inquiry by a prominent Roman theologian, J.B. Franzelin, S.J. He distinguished two elements in Sacred Scripture, formal and material, held that the first, the thought content, was essentially inspired, the second, composition and language used, was the work of the human authors—God would prevent them from erroneous exposition of the ideas. The dichotomy was for different reasons not acceptable and the necessary correction was made by Leo XIII.

The Pope, in his encyclical *Providentissimus Deus*, gave a definition of inspiration since considered classic: "Therefore it matters not at all that the Holy Spirit took men as instruments for the writing, as if anything false might have slipped, not indeed from the first Author, but from the inspired writers. For, by supernatural power, he so roused and moved them to write, he stood so near them, that they rightly grasped in mind all those things, and those only, which he himself ordered, and willed faithfully to write them down, and expressed them properly with infallible truth, otherwise he himself would not be the author of all Sacred Scripture."[5] God the Holy Spirit, therefore was the principal author, the writer being instrumental.

The papal condemnation of Modernism touched on errors related to the theory of inspiration. But the subject was not dealt with at length. Pius XII, in his epoch-making encyclical on the Bible, *Divino afflante Spiritu*, 1943, gave more attention to the problem and showed his awareness of the

complexity it has in the light of modern scholarship: "For if our age accumulates new problems and new difficulties it also supplies, by God's bounty, new aids and helps to exegesis. Especially noteworthy among these is the fact that Catholic theologians, following the teaching of the holy Fathers and especially of the Angelic and Common Doctor, have investigated and explained the nature and effects of divine inspiration better and more fully than was the custom in past centuries. Starting from the principle that the sacred writer in composing the sacred book is the *organon* or instrument of the Holy Spirit, and a living and rational instrument, they rightly observe that under the influence of the divine motion he uses his own faculties and powers in such a way that from the book which is the fruit of his labour all may easily learn, the distinctive genius and the individual characteristics and features of each author." The Pope went on to draw this conclusion: "Let the interpreter therefore use every care, and take advantage of every indication provided by the most recent research, in an endeavour to discern the distinctive genius of the sacred writer, his condition in life, the age in which he lived, the written or oral sources he may have used, and the literary forms he employed. He will thus be able better to discover who the sacred writer was and what he meant by what he wrote. For it is evident that the chief law of interpretation is that which enables us to discover and determine what the writer meant to say, as St. Athanasius tells us: 'Here, as in all other passages of the divine Scripture, we must observe the occasion of the Apostle's utterance, and note accurately and carefully the person and the subject which were the cause of his writing, lest ignorance or error concerning these points lead us to misconceive the meaning of the author.'"

The Pope then exhorts scholars to study literary forms with all the available resources: "It is absolutely necessary for the interpreter to go back to those remote centuries of the East, and to make proper use of the aids afforded by history, archaeology, ethnology, and other sciences, in order to discover what literary forms the writers of that early age intended to use and did, in fact employ."[6]

It is clear that Pius XII pays more attention, in his pronouncement, to the human author than did Leo XIII; with the latter the human author did not disappear under the weight of inspiration, but the Pope issued a caveat against the "many who examine and publish the monuments of antiquity, the customs and institutions of peoples, and evidence of similar things, but more often with this purpose, that they may detect lapses of error in the sacred books, as a result of which their authority may even be shaken and totter."[7]

The next important intervention of the Teaching Authority is from Vatican II (qv). Its teaching was drawn up with some dependence on Pius XII, with awareness of the revolution in biblical studies which followed the use of Form-Criticism. The opening sentence is tightly phrased: "The divinely revealed realities, which are contained and presented in the text of sacred Scripture, have been written down under the inspiration of the Holy Spirit." The text continues: "For Holy Mother Church relying on the faith of the apostolic age, accepts as sacred and canonical the books of the Old and New Testaments, whole and entire, with all their parts, on the grounds that, written under the inspiration of the Holy Spirit (cf. Jn 20:31; 2 Tim 3:16; 2 Pet 1:19-21; 3:15-16) they have God as their author and have been handed on as such to the Church itself."[8] The Council then explains that though God "acted in them and by them, it was as true authors that they consigned to writing whatever he wanted written and no more."

Much of the debate on inspiration has been on how to explain the kind or degree of inerrancy it guarantees. Here the Council nuances its position: "Since, therefore, all that the inspired authors, or sacred writers, affirm should be regarded as affirmed by the Holy Spirit, we must acknowledge that the books of Scripture firmly, faithfully and without error, teach that truth which God, for the sake of our salvation, wished to see confided to the sacred Scriptures."

The chief relevance of the subject to the theme of the present work is the light it sheds on the presence and mode of action of the Holy Spirit in a specific sector of the Church's life. If, as J.L. McKenzie says, theologians "generally agree that the theory of inspiration is incomplete in many respects," this may be due to the fact that our theology of the Third Divine Person has been undeveloped.

All the official texts quoted refer inspiration directly to the Holy Spirit. We have then to see his action here as a charismatic activity on individuals, but we must not forget that he is living and active in the whole community. But first arises the question of appropriation: In what sense is the divine action on the writer and on the community which speaks, to some extent, through him, directly from the third Divine Person or from all three Persons but attributed to him by appropriation? If it is directly from him can we seek some parallel with the dominant interventions by him at turning-points in the history of salvation, the Incarnation, the Baptism, Pentecost? If it is a question of charisms are these charisms utterly unique, restricted in effect to just this area? We can distinguish varied action by the Spirit, but the Spirit himself is indivisible.

With the need arising from understanding of the complexity of biblical authorship for deeper reflection on the nature of inspiration, much rethinking has been done on the precise meaning of principal and instrumental causality which can be supported by a text from St. Thomas. Analysis has been made of the mental powers involved, the speculative and practical intellect, the will. Fr. Lagrange thought of a special illumination possible to the whole person since instrumental causality means the effect is the result of the principal and instrumental causes. Fr. Benoit thought of the illumination as touching the writer in the operative or active area, guiding him in choice of form and style.

Benoit distinguished two charisms, one of revelation in the speculative intellect, the other, inspiration, in the practical. His suggestion has not been universally accepted. It has one advantage: it can extend inspiration to all those involved in the composition of the biblical text. Henceforward, unquestionably there must be an ecclesial dimension to theories of inspiration, the church in firm outline and hope in the OT, fully realized in the New, bought by the Lord with his blood (cf. Acts 20:28), filled with his Spirit, and provided with those means which befit it as a visible and social unity. One of those means is sacred books, wherein the revealed treasure is preserved free of the contamination of error.

Just as we do not hear of the disciples coming together for the "breaking of bread" until the Spirit has been sent and descended, so this mighty event must also precede the writing of the sacred books. And the new community of the Spirit would confer special value on the pre-existing sacred books of Israel by acceptance and docility to their content. Jesus related all such things to the personal mission of the Spirit, "'the Advocate, the Holy Spirit, whom the Father will send in my name, he will teach you everything and will remind you of all that I have told you'" (Jn 14:26).

A wholly new era of divine action on the human

mind, personal and collective, began with Pentecost. Its focus was unmistakable, the encounter between the creative and the created spirits, where the divine entered the responsive human soul to give it light and strength. Whatever was necessary to that end was guaranteed by the Spirit. Those who were chosen to transmit the message in the early days before it was written down, the different "sources" within the community, were selected and protected; those who, in the course of time, would commit the necessary things to writing, were under the same influence of the Spirit, an influence which extended through the entire range of time, through every moment of each life which would be in any way involved in the preparation or composition of the sacred texts.

When that has been said we are still lacking in knowledge about the meaning of authorship and of book in the world in which the Bible was created. That names were affixed to separate works has not the same meaning as it would have in our age and in our western culture. Communal factors were much more important then and in that particular milieu than we think of nowadays. In all this world the Spirit, who never changes, was active. Why should we hesitate to see his inspiration active on the community from which the book originated as well as on the one who finally composed the text which we now have?

As to the inerrancy we must abide by the teaching of Vatican II already quoted: "that truth which God, for the sake of our salvation, wished to see confided to the Sacred Scriptures" is guaranteed free of error. This was taught or emerged to consciousness within the salvation community, where the Spirit's action was prime, at a time when the whole Christian community was sensitive and responsive to his inspiration and impulse. Did the overwhelming inspiration which gave us our sacred texts cease with the passing of the first generation, the witnesses or their close associates, as Karl Rahner contends? Were the writers of the final text conscious of direct inspiration by the Spirit? Did they fully know? Or did everyone then think of himself as inspired by the Spirit? So many unanswered questions.

One is not unanswered. This was not a descent of the Spirit in the mode of the Annunciation, the Baptism and Pentecost. It was a charism whereby he achieved a specific result. For this reason it is also unwise to invoke the doctrine of appropriation. It is not action by all three Persons appropriated to the Spirit because of his personal property. It is he acting charismatically in continuation of his descent at Pentecost, when he began this manner of action on human affairs. Here is the great unsolved problem: how are charisms, and the charism of inspiration in particular, a precise effect of the descent on Pentecost? An immense field here opens for research, for a true union of forces between divine revelation and existentialism.

We must not forget that inspiration is, in God's eternal design, a subordinate element in his self-communication as Father to men and women whom he wishes to make his children. There is the whole process of what we call revelation, God's self-disclosure to man. What is revelation? At how many levels is it operative? How is humankind prepared to receive it? How is it communicated? What is the difference between revelation conceived in propositional terms and revelation in the personalist manner which is central to the New Testament, "'I am the Light of the world'"; "'I am the way and the truth and the life'" (Jn 14:6)? Inspiration of any written work serving this purpose, of revealing God to us personally in Christ, must bear a relation to this vital reality.

[1]For bibl., L. Swain, *A New Catholic Commentary on Holy Scripture*, London, 1969, "The Inspiration of Scripture," 53-60, R.F. Smith, S.J., *Jerome Biblical Commentary*, Vol II, "Inspiration," 499-514; D.M. Stanley, "The Concept of Biblical Inspiration" in *The Apostolic Church in the New Testament*, Westminster, 1965, 67-89, notes with bibl., 408-414; Pontifical Biblical Commission, *Instruction on the Historical Nature of the Gospels*; repr. with English tr., *CBQ* 26 (1964), 299-312; B. Vawter, *Biblical Inspiration* (Theological Resources) London, 1972; J.A. Sanders, *Canon and Community. A Guide to Canonical Criticism*, Philadelphia, 1972; M. McNamara, M.S.C., in *The New Dictionary of Theology*, 1987, Michael Glazier, Wilmington, 522-526; R.F. Collins in *The New Jerome Biblical Commentary,* 1023-1033. [2]Cf. *Constitution on Divine Revelation,* 16; [3]DS 3006; [4]DS 1335; [5]DS 3293; [6]CTS tr.; [7]*Ibid.,* [8]*Constitution on Divine Revelation,* 11.

IRENAEUS, ŞT. (c. 130-c. 200)

The "father of Christian theology," author of the first great scheme incorporating the elements in the mystery of salvation wrought by Christ, the "recapitulation," most enlightened exponent of the doctrine of Mary as the "New Eve," notably furthered thinking on the personal identity and manifold functions of the Holy Spirit.[1] I. gives the Spirit many names—the divine seal, the unction with which Christ was anointed, Paraclete, Gift, living Water, dew of God, pledge of our incorruption, especially and often like St. Theophilus of Antioch, Wisdom.

The Trinitarian ground-plan is clearly stated by I. At the beginning of his great apologetic work, the *Adversus Haereses* he thus enunciates it: "The Church ... has received from the apostles and their disciples faith in one only God, the Father almighty who made heaven and earth and the seas, and all that they contain; and in one Christ Jesus the Son of God, incarnate for our salvation; and in the Holy Spirit who announced by the prophets the 'economies.'"[2] Matching this is a succinct statement at the end of the work, which speaks of "a firm tradition which comes from the Apostles, which fixes our minds on one only faith, all confessing one only same Father, all believing in the same economy of the incarnation of the Son of God, all recognising the same gift of the Spirit."[3] In the striking catechetical work, *The Proof of the Apostolic Preaching* I. after stating the first article about God the Father and the second about the Word, through whom all things were made and who became man for the recapitulation of all things "so as to abolish death and bring to light life, and bring about the communion of God and man," goes on thus to the Holy Spirit: "And the third article is the Holy Spirit, through whom the prophets prophesied and the patriarchs were taught about God and the just were led in the path of justice, and who in the end of time has been poured forth in a new manner upon humanity over all the earth, renewing men to God."[4]

Vatican II (qv) laid down that the structure of divine revelation is Trinitarian. Here is how I. states the same truth seventeen centuries earlier: "Therefore the baptism of our rebirth comes through these three articles, granting us rebirth unto God the Father, through his Son, by the Holy Spirit. For those who are bearers of the Spirit of God are led to the Word, that is, to the Son; but the Son takes them and presents them to the Father; and the Father confers incorruptibility. So without the Spirit there is no seeing the Word of God, and without the Son there is no approaching the Father; for the Son is knowledge of the Father, and knowledge of the Son is through the Holy Spirit. But the Son, according to the Father's good-pleasure, administers the Spirit charismatically as the Father will, to those to whom he will."[5]

Elsewhere I., again with a perspicacity wonderful in his time, says: "Hence too his Apostle Paul well says: *one God, the Father*, who is above all, and with all and in us all; for 'above all' is the Father, but 'with all' is the Word, since it is through him that everything was made by the Father, and 'in us all' is the Spirit, *who cries: Abba, Father*, and has formed man in the likeness of God. So the Spirit manifests the Word, and therefore the prophets announced the Son of God, but the Word articulates the Spirit, and therefore it is himself who gives their message to the prophets, and takes up man and brings him to the Father."[6]

I. taught formally that it was after the descent of the Spirit at Pentecost that the Apostles were filled with all the gifts of Spirit; "they had perfect knowledge."[7] "What would we do if the Apostles had left no scriptures? In that instance would it not be necessary to follow the tradition which they handed down to those they gave charge of the churches? Many barbarian peoples who have come to believe in Christ assent to this tradition. They have salvation written in their hearts, without paper or ink (2 Cor 3:3)."[8] Here there is a clear intimation of the role of the Spirit in preserving tradition.

In one of the great passages of *Adversus Haereses*, III, I. develops the theme of water and the Spirit. This has been studied in a remarkable doctorate thesis at the Gregorian University on immortality and incorruptibility according to I.[9] "The whole question of incorruptibility is one of the relation between the divine *pneuma* and the human *sarx*. If the flesh or the work fashioned by God, has lost, through sin, the immortality and incorruptibility of paradise, it is, on the contrary, by the outpouring of the Pneuma of the glorious Christ that corruption will be destroyed in it, and that it will receive already here below, the pledge of incorruptibility. But the flesh of Christ itself had to be anointed by the Spirit and made spiritual through the passion-resurrection-ascension before it could pour out the Spirit. The *Pneuma-sarx* relation passes through the flesh of Christ, for it is through his incorruptible flesh that Christ pours his Spirit on men, as pledge of incorruptibility, at Pentecost, before he communicates him through his flesh, real food in the Eucharist."[10]

After recalling the promises of the OT (Is 11:2; Is 61:1 and Joel 2:28, 29) and the Lord's reassurance (Mt 10:20) I. writes: "David asked this Spirit for the human race, 'Establish me with your all-governing Spirit' (Ps 51:12). As Luke says he descended upon the disciples on the day of Pentecost after the Lord's ascension. He had power over all nations to lead them into the way of life and to open the new Covenant to all. By his power the disciples were of one accord and sang praises to God in all different languages. The Spirit joined distant tribes into unity and offered to the Father the first-fruits of all nations (Acts 2). Thus the Lord promised to send the Comforter, who would join us to God. Just as dry wheat cannot be shaped into a cohesive lump of dough or a loaf held together without moisture, so in the same way, we many could not become one in Christ Jesus without the water which comes from heaven. As dry earth bears no fruit unless it receives moisture, so we also were originally dry wood and could never have borne the fruit of life without the rain freely given from above. Our bodies have been joined into the unity which leads to incorruption through the washing, our souls have received it through the Spirit. Both are necessary, since both contribute to the divine life. Our Lord had compassion on that erring Samaritan woman who committed fornication by contracting many marriages rather than remaining with one husband. He pointed out and promised living water to her so that by having living water springing up to eternal life within her, she would no longer thirst or have to seek out and work to acquire refreshing water (Jn 4:7-26). The Lord received this living water as a gift from his Father and himself confers it on those who share in him by sending the Holy Spirit over the earth."[11]

The Spirit and the Church is a theme much studied since the Encyclical, *Mystici Corporis Christi* of Pius XII (qv). It was a theme dear to I., who could write thus: "Further, he conferred this Spirit upon the Church and sent the Comforter from heaven throughout the world."[12]

Elsewhere he is more elaborate: "We have received this faith from the Church and carefully preserve it. By the Spirit of God it continually renews its youth. Like a precious treasure in an excellent container, it causes the containing vessel to renew its youth as well. This gift of God has been entrusted to the Church just as breath was given to the work God formed so that all the members may be vivified by receiving it. The Holy Spirit has been distributed through the Church as the means of communion with Christ and of confirming our faith, as the pledge of incorruption and the ladder of ascent to God. 'For in the Church' it is said 'God has established Apostles, prophets, teachers' (1 Cor 12:28) and all the other

ways in which the Spirit works. Those who do not join themselves to the Church do not share in him. Instead they deprive themselves of life by their perverse opinions and scandalous behaviour. Where the Church is, there is the Spirit of God; where the Spirit of God is, there is the Church and every grace. The Spirit is truth. Therefore those who do not share in the Spirit are neither nourished to life from the mother's breast nor do they enjoy that most clear fountain which springs from the body of Christ. Instead they dig themselves broken cisterns, made from ditches of dirt, and drink putrid water from the mud. They flee the faith of the Church to avoid being proven wrong and reject the Spirit so that they will not be taught."[13]

I. saw the Spirit as preparing humankind for the coming of the God incarnate, as he attributed to him a role in creation and in revelation. He also showed how through the Spirit the resurrection of the flesh would take place. "The flesh taken as an inheritance by the Spirit forgets what it is and takes on the character of the Spirit and is conformed to the Word of God. Thus the Apostle says, 'As we have borne the image of the earthly, so also shall we bear the image of the heavenly' (1 Cor 15:49). What is the earthly? What was fashioned. What is the heavenly? The Spirit. He asserts that when we were deprived of the heavenly Spirit, we lived according to the oldness of the flesh in disobedience to God. So, now that we have received the Spirit, 'let us walk in the newness of life,' in obedience to God (Rom 6:4). Since, therefore, we cannot be saved without the Spirit of God, the Apostle urges us to guard the Spirit of God by faith and a pure life. For if we do not share in this divine Spirit, we will lose the Kingdom of Heaven. This is the reason why he proclaims that flesh and blood alone cannot inherit the kingdom of God."[14]

I. then, it is clear, opened many areas of speculation on the Holy Spirit of God. Some of his intuitions appear singularly relevant to our modern thinking. It is possible that his contribution to the development of doctrine on the Holy Spirit has not been fully appreciated for the simple reason that we had not awareness of the very problems he faced; this awareness has now come to us.

---

[1]For bibl., cf. *Trinitas*, 137; *Handbuch der Dogmengeschichte* II, 1a, 67; Y. de Andia, *Homo Vivens, Incorruptiblité et divinisation de l'homme selon*, 190 *Irénée de Lyon*, Paris, 1986, 206; critical ed. of works, *SC* 151, 153, 210, 211, 213,

214; *The Proof of the Apostolic Preaching*, English tr. J.P. Smith, *ACW*; French tr., L.M. Froideveaux, *SC* 62; Quasten I, 287-313; F. Vernet, *DTC* VII, (1923) 2394-2533; L. Doutreleau, S.J., L. Regnault, O.S.B., *DSp* VII, 1923-1969; *The Message*, 31-42; A. d'Ales, S.J., "La doctrine de l'Esprit en St. Irénée, *RSR 6 (1916) 185-211; G. Kretschmar, "Le développement de la doctrine du Saint Esprit du NT à Nicée",* *Verbum Caro*, 22 (1968) 4-55; H.J. Jaschke, "Pneuma und Moral. Der Grund chrislicher Sittlichkeit aus der Sicht des Irenäus von Lyons, *SM* 14 (1976) 144-186; *BT* I, 1931-32; [2]*Adv. Haer*, I, 10, 1; [3]*Op. cit.*, V, 20, 1; [4]*ACW*, 7, 52; [5]*Ibid.*' [6]*ACW* 5, 50; [7]*Adv. Haer*, I, 1; [8]*Adv. Haer*, III, 4, 1; [9]Y. de Andia, *op, cit.*; [10]*Op.cit.*, 205f; [11]*Adv. Haer*, III, 17, 2; [12]*Adv. Haer*, III, 17, 3; [13]*Ibid.*, 24, 1; [14]*Adv. Haer.*, V, 9, 3.

J

JEWISH-CHRISTIAN THEOLOGY

In Jewish-Christian writings, that is the expression of religious thought of those who, within a Semitic structure, developed a theology which preceded the Hellenistic Christian reflection of the Apologists, some interesting points emerge concerning the Holy Spirit.[1] Inevitably affinities with Qumran (qv) are noted. Trinitarian doctrine and angelology converge and intertwine. There is then a preference for the archangels, in particular Michael and Gabriel. But when the Jewish-Christian texts speak of Michael it is the Word of God they have in mind. So the commentators explain a passage from the Shepherd of Hermas: "And the great and glorious angel is Michael, who has power over this people and governs them; for this is he who put the law into the hearts of those who believe."[2]

Likewise for St. Gabriel. He is called the angel of the Holy Spirit and as one editor of the text of the *Ascension of Isaiah* wrote, it is not clear whether he is speaking of the third divine Person or an angel; the possibility exists.[3]

Jewish Christian literature also ex-pounds the theme of the two spirits, found in the Qumran (qv) texts. In particular the *Shepherd of Hermas* favours the idea with striking insights on the Holy Spirit.

---

[1]Cf. J. (Cardinal) Daniélou, S.J., *Théologie du Judeo¹-Christianisme*, Paris, *L'Espirt Saint et Gabriel*, 177-180; [2]*The Shepherd of Hermas*, The Apostolic Fathers, ed. K. Lake, II, *Similitudes*, VIII, 3, 3, p. 197; [3]E. (Cardinal) Tisserant, *Ascension d'Isaie*, Paris, 1909, 156.

JOACHIM OF FIORE (c. 1132-1202)

One of the figures in church history who stirs interest, controversy, a kind of magic. J. had a career with many vicissitudes. His interest to the subject of the present work is in three works: *Concordia novi et veteris Testamenti, Expositio in Apocalypsim* and *Psalterium decem chordarum*. He wrote a number of other works and there is much apocryphalliterature. The essence of his thought is a reading of history in strict correlation with the three Persons of the Trinity. There are three stages (*status*) or phases in history, each with a beginning (*initiatio, exordium*), a period of growth to a peak (*fructificatio, claritas*), then decadence (*defectio*), towards an end (*consummatio, finis*). The first phase was of God the Father, from Adam, through a peak in Abraham, to Christ; the second is of the Son, corresponding broadly to the New Testament. The first phase was represented by marriage or the lay state, *ordo conjugatorum seu laicorum*; the second is represented by the *ordo clericorum*.

The third phase belongs to the Holy Spirit; it may be called the age of the *ordo monachorum* or *contemplantium*. It began with St. Benedict and began to bear fruit from the twentieth generation after him; it will have its consummation at the end of the world. Whereas the first age was marked by servile subjection, and humans lived according to the flesh, and the second age marked by filial obedience, and humans lived between the spirit and the flesh, the third will be the age of liberty and they will live "*sub spirituali intellectu.*" The sequence is of fear, faith and charity, of old people, young people and children.

J. has been reproached with tritheistic views, with endangering equality between the divine Persons; some of his later followers moved towards a form of Millenarianism. There is no theological basis for his theory.[1]

[1] *Trinitas*,138f, bibl.; cf. esp. C. Barant, *DSp* VIII, 1179-1291, ample bibl.

JOHN THE BAPTIST

"And you, child, shall be called the prophet of the Most High" (Lk 1:76). "Why then did you go out? To see a prophet? Yes, I tell you and more than a prophet" (Mt 11:9; cp. Lk 7:26). John the Baptist had a mighty role, the last prophet of the OT, the first martyr of the NT—his martyrdom, if not directly related to Christ, arose from his prominence, which was linked with his role as the Lord's precursor (see art. Prophecy).[1] The evangelists emphasize the Spirit's presence in great moments of his career. He would be "filled with the Holy Spirit even from his mother's womb" (Lk 1:15). Tradition has located the event in the moment of the Visitation, when, the mother also experienced the Spirit, "And when Elizabeth heard the greeting of Mary, the babe leaped in her womb; and Elizabeth was filled with the Holy Spirit and she exclaimed with a loud cry, 'Blessed are you among women, and blessed is the fruit of your womb'" (Lk 1:41, 42). Soon after, Luke narrates the Baptist's birth, and his naming. Again the Spirit's intervention is explicitly declared, "And his father Zechariah was filled with the Holy Spirit, and prophesied, saying, 'Blessed be the Lord, the God of Israel ... '" (Lk 1:67, 68).

Luke tells us that "the child grew and became strong in spirit, and he was in the wilderness till the day of his manifestation to Israel" (Lk 1:80). He also tells us that "a message came from God to John, the son of Zechariah in the desert" (Lk 3:2). Is the explanation of these succinct statements to be found in a stay by John in the Qumran community at some time in his life? J. Steinmann, emphasizing the spirituality of the desert, thought that he belonged to Qumran. P. Benoit, O.P., the eminent exegete, author of a monograph on John's infancy as portrayed in Lk 1, thought the evidence linking them could be explained by the general eschatological thinking in the desert at the time.

What is the evidence? We note it, for the whole question is not unrelated to a doctrine of the Spirit current at the time. If the geographical tradition on the rite of John's baptizing is right, he could not miss knowing the monastic settlement; for he could see it from the spot. There is affinity in teaching, in the use of Is 40:3, "In the wilderness prepare the way of the Lord, make straight in the desert a highway for our God" (1 QS 4:20-22: Lk 3:4). John, as related by all four evangelists, announces one who will baptize "with the Holy Spirit" (Jn 1:33; two synoptics add "with fire," Mt 3:11; Lk 3:16; Mk 1:8 without "with fire"). The parallel Qumran text is "God will purge by his truth all the deeds of man refining for himself some of mankind in order to abolish every evil spirit from the midst of his flesh, and to cleanse him through a holy Spirit from all wicked practices, sprinkling upon him a Spirit of truth as purifying water" (1 QS 4:20f).

On the basis of such evidence John A.T. Robinson proposed a thesis on the possible connection between the baptism of John and the Qumran community.[2] He saw the possibility of adoption, recalling what Josephus said of the Essenes: "They neglect wedlock, but choose out other persons' children, while they are pliable, and fit for learning; and esteem them to be of their kindred, and form them according to their own manners."[3] The Qumran monks had a preference for priestly families, despite their opposition to some of their priestly contemporaries. Robinson was supported by an expert in Qumran studies, J. Fitzmyer, S.J., who has made much use of Qumran documents in his commentary on St. Luke's gospel.[4] Research and evaluation by scholars is continuous. One summary of such research is thus expressed: "Nowhere (in the Qumran texts) is there question of an initiation bath. Repetition rules out the unique character which the NT and Josephus attribute to the baptism of John. Nonetheless different aspects may be taken as partially parallel, such as the Baptist's teaching, eschatology, the Messiah, the nearness of the end, as ascetical practice. These similarities and differences should not be related to John's baptism, but to the common source, the OT."[5]

The texts in the Manual of Discipline to be taken with that already quoted in order to assess this judgement are especially III: 1-12 and V: 13, to be read preferably with Dupont-Sommer's commentary.[6] The over-ruling contrast between John and Qumran, at the moment when John walks onto the stage of salvation history is between a closed group, and a charismatic figure who preached to everyone and attracted a large following. They intended continuity; he withdrew when his mission was accomplished. Among his baptizands there was only one accompanied by an anointing of the Spirit. We may enter the field of conjecture: John could have spent some time, formative, as far as it went, in the Qumran community. He may have benefitted by their insistence on the Holy Spirit—the name occurs frequently in the passages cited or mentioned; he would then have disengaged his thought from the dualism in their thinking of spirits. The day came when John, the new Elijah, received his vocation as a prophet.

We are now dealing with a towering spiritual figure, marking an epoch of cosmic significance, and such people break the mould. If we apply the test "by their fruits you shall know them," we are led to think of a unique interior illumination, an experience of the kind that we acknowledge in the OT prophets—with this difference, that they were seized by the Spirit in some phase of their lives, whereas he was moulded by the Spirit, unique author of prophecy, from his mother's womb. We are reminded of the spiritual lineage, surpassed in fact, by the striking parallel, "This is my beloved Son, with whom I am well pleased" (Mt 3:17; cp. Mk 1:11; Lk 3:22) in the synoptic accounts and Is 42:1, "Behold my servant, whom I uphold, my chosen, in whom my soul delights; I have put my Spirit upon him, he will bring forth justice to the nations."

John made the same kind of bold claim an OT prophet would make: "I myself did not know him; but he who sent me to baptize with water said to me, 'He on whom you see the Spirit descend and remain, this is he who baptizes with the Holy Spirit.' And I have seen and have borne witness that this is the Son of God" (Jn 1:33, 34). This language is an echo of "Thus says Yahweh," the prophetic signal in the OT; thus spoke John "the burning and the shining light" (Jn 5:35).

John is the first human being in the NT to give a specific revelation about the Holy Spirit, and as the precursor of Christ, he linked the Saviour's mission to the Holy Spirit; all four evangelists, as just stated, record the Baptist's promise the Christ will "baptize with the Holy Spirit" (Mt 3:11; Mk 1:8; Lk 3:16, Jn 1:33). When we say the first human being we advert to the fact that it was Gabriel who made the revelation to Zechariah and to Mary. Besides Jesus himself no other speaks of the Spirit until after Pentecost. The privileged utterance of John in regard to baptism with the Holy Spirit is possibly among those sayings in Holy Writ which has been allowed to go dead. It must be replete

with meaning, with force and with ultimate, eventually eschatological impact on the course of salvation history. John, as a figure of the Spirit, is not yet fully appreciated. To him alone, after Jesus, it was given to recognize the Spirit in the moment of the baptism: "I saw the Spirit descend as a dove from heaven, and it remained on him" (Jn 1:32).

---

[1]Cf. C.H. Kraeling, *John the Baptist*, New York, 1951; P. Benoit, O.P., *L'enfance de Jean Baptiste selon Luc I*, NTS 3 (1956-1957), 169-194; id., *Qumran et le Nouveau Testament*, NTS 7 (1960-1961), 276-296; A. Feuillet, P.S.S., *Saint Jean Baptiste et les hommes du désert, Cahiers Evangeliques* 27 (1957) 33-38; R.H. Brownlee, *John the Baptist in the New Light of the Ancient Scrolls*, in *The Scrolls and the New Testament*, ed. K. Stendhal, New York, 1957; J.A.T. Robinson, *The Baptism of John and the Qumran Community*, HTR 50 (1957) 263-281; id., *Elijah, John and Jesus. An Essay in Detection.* NTS 4 (1957-1958) 263-281; H.H. Rowley, *The Baptism of John and the Qumran Sect*, Manchester University Press, repr. *New Testament Essays*, ed. H.J.B. Higgins, 1959; J. Steinmann, *John the Baptist*, New York, 1958; J. Pryke, *John the Baptist and the Qumran Community, Revue de Qumran*, IV, 16 (1964) 483-496; A. Dupont-Sommer, *Les Ecrits Esséniens découverts près de la Mer Morte*, 3rd ed., Paris, 1968, p. 384; F. Leitzen-Deiz, *Die Taufe Jesu nach den Synoptiken, Literarkritische und gattungsgeschichte Untersuchungen*, Frankfort on Main, 1970, esp. with review by M. Carrez, *Revue de Qumran*, VIII, 29 (1972) 128-130; J. Fitzmyer, S.J., St. Luke, Anchor Bible, I, 1981, 453, 54; id., *The Qumran Scrolls and the New Testament Forty Years after*, in *Revue de Qumran*, Mémorial Jean Carmignac, 1989, p. 611; [2]*Op. cit.*, NTR; [3]*De Bello Judaico*, II, 120; [4]Anchor Bible, 28, II, 453; [5]M. Carrez in *Revue de Qumran*, op. cit., 130; [6]*Op. cit.*, 384.

JOHN OF DAMASCUS, ST., DOCTOR OF THE CHURCH (c. 675—between 749-753)[1]

J. is important because he sums up in his work, especially in the *De fide orthodoxa*, the teaching of the previous centuries in the East. In his doctrine there is no separation between economy and theology; they are part of a single vision. He expounds the inter-relation of the three divine Persons without becoming either filioquist or monopatrist. The Spirit reveals the Word and the Word reveals the Father. The Spirit rests in the Word and accompanies him, that is, he participates indissolubly in his activity by making him manifest. He is the revelation and image of the Son. The procession of the Spirit goes back to the begetting of the Son; at the level of the perichoresis, the Spirit comes from the Father through the Son and is poured out in him. In the divine activity the Son provides the basis of the work that is wanted by the Father and the Spirit perfects it.

At an international conference held in Cologne and Bonn in 1874-1875 at which Orthodox, Anglicans—from America and England—and some Old Catholics met, in the context of the *Filioque* (qv) controversy, a summary of the teaching of J. was accepted as follows:

"1. The Holy Spirit comes from the Father (*ek tou Patrou*) as from the principle (*arche*), the cause (*aitia*) and the source (*pege*) of divinity (*De rect. sent.* I; *Contra Man* 4); 2. The Holy Spirit does not come from the Son (*ek tou Huiou*), because there is only one principle (*arche*) and one cause (*aitia*) in the divinity through which everything that is in that divinity is produced (see *De Fide orthod.: ek tou Huiou de to Pneuma ou Legomen, Pneuma di Huiou onomazomen*); 3. The Holy Spirit comes from the Father through the Son (*De Fide orthod.*, I 12; *Contra Man* 5; *De hymno Trisag.* 28; *Hom. in Sabb. S.* 4; 4. The Holy Spirit is the image of the Son, who is himself the image of the Father (*De Fide orthod.* I, 13) proceeding from the Father and dwelling in the Son as his radiating power (*De Fide orthod.* I, 7, I, 12); 5. The Holy Spirit is the personal procession coming from the Father, who is of the Son, but not coming from the Son, because he is the Spirit from the mouth of the divinity, expressing the Word (*De hymno Trisag.* 28); 6. The Holy Spirit is the medium between the Father and the Son and he is connected to the Father through the Son (*De Fide orthod.* I, 13). In the summary a number of textual quotations are added, only one of which, in no. 2, is reproduced here.[2] J. was translated into Latin in the twelfth century, had considerable influence in the west. As to the treatise *De Sanctissima Trinitate* from an author who was J.'s contemporary, the reader is referred to a specialist study.[3]

[1]Works *PG* 94-96; bibl. *Trinitas*, 140; cf. esp., J. Bilz, *Die Trinitätslehre des Johannes von Damaskus*, Paderborn, 1909; J. Grégoire, "La relation éternelle de l'Esprit au Fils d'après les écrits de Jean de Damas", *RHE* 64 (1969) 713-755; Y.-M.J. Congar, O.P., *The Holy Spirit*, III, 36-48; *Trinitas*, 139, 40; [2]Apud Y.-M.J. Congar, *op. cit.*, 192, 93; [3]B. Fraigneau-Julien, "Un Traite anonyme de la Sainte Trinité attribué à St. Cyrille d'Alexandrie," *RSR* 49 (1961), 188-211, 386-405.

JOHN THE EVANGELIST, ST.[1]

St. John's contribution to the theology of the Spirit is distinctive, with significant passages in 1 Jn and in the gospel. Beginning with the gospel we take at once the Johannine account of the encounter between Jesus and John the Baptist at the Jordan. The fourth evangelist does not mention the baptism explicitly, one way of meeting the problem implicit in the whole episode: Did the baptism make Jesus dependent on John, making Jesus' reception of the Spirit dependent on his baptism by John? John safeguards the primacy of Jesus in other ways:

"And this is the testimony of John, when the Jews sent priests and Levites from Jerusalem to ask him, 'Who are you?' He confessed he did not deny, but confessed, 'I am not the Christ.' And they asked him, 'What then? Are you Elijah?' He said 'I am not.' 'Are you the prophet?' And he answered, 'No.' They said to him then, 'Who are you? Let us have an answer for those who sent us. What do you say about yourself?' He said, 'I am the voice of one crying in the wilderness, "Make straight the way of the Lord," as the prophet Isaiah said.' Now they had been sent from the Pharisees. They asked him, 'Then why are you baptizing, if you are neither the Christ, nor Elijah, nor the prophet?' John answered them, 'I baptize with water; but among you stands one whom you do not know, even he who comes after me, the thong of whose sandal I am not worthy to untie.' This took place in Bethany beyond the Jordan, where John was baptizing. The next day he saw Jesus coming toward him and said, 'Behold, the Lamb of God, who takes away the sin of the world! This is he of whom I said, "After me comes a man who ranks before me, for he was before me." I myself did not know him; but for this I came baptizing with water, that he might be revealed to Israel.' And John bore witness, 'I saw the Spirit descend as a dove from heaven, and it remained on him. I myself did not know him; but he who sent me to baptize with water said to me, "He on whom you see the Spirit descend and remain, this is he who baptizes with the Holy Spirit." And I have seen and borne witness that this is the Son of God'" (1:19-34).

Jesus is here presented as redeemer in his title as Lamb of God, the one who removes sin. The title also has a fiery eschatological sense. There is no mention of the voice from heaven, as in the synoptic narratives. But John had received assurance that he would recognize and identify the one who would baptize with the Holy Spirit. In the divine message given him one idea was evocative of a past oracle and pointed to the future with a sense of limitless potential: "'He on whom you see the Spirit descend and remain.'" The oracle is Is 11:2, "And the Spirit of the Lord shall rest upon him, the spirit of wisdom and understanding, the spirit of counsel and might, the spirit of knowledge and the fear of the Lord." The future fulfilment is related by Jn (3:5, 35; 7:38, 39; 14:15-18, 26; 15:26; 16:7-16; 20:22). Hence the central importance of the theophany at the Jordan, with the moment of the Incarnation an event of cosmic eternal significance, the irruption into salvation history, into the ongoing 'economy,' of the Trinity, the Son eternally immanent in the Father's bosom and giving with him the Spirit, entering the human story at the Incarnation, the Spirit, already involved in this prodigious innovation, now assuming a role in the flow of Christ events. Spirit and Saviour will be henceforth inseparable in the divine work to be accomplished by human means, human means at the level of instruments in God's hand.

Next John gives us Jesus' own first words about the Spirit: "Jesus answered (Nicodemus), 'Truly, truly I say to you, unless one is born of water and the Spirit, he cannot enter the kingdom of God. That which is born of the flesh is flesh, and that which is born of the Spirit is spirit. Do not marvel that I said to you, "You must be born anew." The wind blows where it will, and you hear the sound of it, but you do not know whence it comes or whither it goes; so it is with everyone who is born of the Spirit'" (3:5-8).

The parallel between this revelation to a representative of the human race and the impact of the Spirit on Jesus himself is an arresting one. In one case it was his baptism, the coming of the Spirit on him; in the other the universal need for baptism, the rebirth "of water and the Spirit." Commentators point to the many levels on which the passage, the words of Christ have meaning. Later, towards the end of the chapter occur the words, "'For he whom God has sent utters the words of God, for it is not by measure that he gives the Spirit; the Father loves the Son and has given all things into his hands'" (3:34). This statement may complete the two previous references to the Spirit.

John has important texts in chapters four and seven, in his account of the conversation with the Samaritan woman and of the words spoken "on the last and greatest day of the festival" on the symbolism of living water and the Spirit, symbolism found also in Qumran texts (4:10-14; 23, 24; 7:37-39).

It is, however, in the part of the farewell discourse where Jesus speaks of the Paraclete that we get the fullest Johannine theology of the Spirit (14:15-18, 25, 26; 15:26-27; 16:4-15). The word Paraclete conveys many meanings: defender, helper, comforter, assistant, advocate, solicitor, counsellor, mediator, one who exhorts and makes urgent appeals. The Johannine texts have been analysed and appraised incessantly, especially in recent times; the bibliography grows continuously. The Paraclete has been studied in his relationship with the Father, with the Son, with the disciples and with the world. The Paraclete has been studied in his relationships with the *Pneuma* (the Spirit), in the actions of which he is subject and those of which he is object. And there is the most suggestive parallel between the Paraclete and Jesus himself.

Certain ideas dominate the lengthy portrait, either by the force of repetition or by the total novelty of their meaning and implication. The Paraclete, we are told three times, is the "Spirit of truth" (14:17; 15:26; 16:13). What does this mean? Especially since "'he will guide (the apostles) into all truth.'" It is not philosophical or abstract truth which is in question; it is something very much more than personal veracity. Some clue may be available in the use of the word in Qumran literature, where alone it is found proper to the NT.

It is therefore the whole triumphant way of life revealed and supported by God that we are by these parallel passages prompted to think of. But there is more in John.[4] We recall the word of Jesus: "'I am the way, the truth and the life; no one comes to the Father but by me'"—words spoken during this same farewell discourse. Earlier Jesus had spoken thus: "'If you continue in my word, you are truly my disciples, and you will know the truth and the truth will make you free'" (Jn 8:31, 32). Thus to believers; to the non-believers these were his words: "'Why do you not understand what I say? It is because you cannot bear to hear my word. You are of your father, the devil, and your will is to do your father's desires. He was a murderer from the beginning, and has nothing to do with the truth, because there is no truth in him. When he lies, he speaks according to his own nature, for he is a liar and the father of lies. But because I tell you the truth, you do not believe me. Which of you convicts me of sin? If I tell the truth, why do you not believe me? He who is of God hears the words of God; the reason why you do not hear them is that you are not of God'" (Jn 8:43-47).

Truth is therefore the essential touchstone of

the whole way of life centred on Christ, coming from him, dependent on him, theocentric because christocentric. It is a meeting-point of the highest philosophy—*Omne ens est verum, bonum, pulchrum*, all reality is true, good, beautiful—with a key point in God's revelation. In so far as life enters into reality, in the fullest sense of the word, it is one with the Spirit of truth.

Another idea strikes by its innovative character: the Spirit identified with the Paraclete is "given," "sent" (Jn 14:16; 15:26; 16:7). We must remember here that there is question, in the words of Jesus, of "another Paraclete" (Jn 14:16). He will take the place of Jesus, who himself was a Paraclete. But it is the idea of being given, being sent that is, in biblical history, a development of OT recorded interventions of the *Ruah*; then he came on judge, king or prophet. An added personal dimension is conveyed by the word "given," as by "sent." Hence we have the theology of processions, of mission in outline.

The manifold action of the Paraclete will, on close scrutiny, appear to match the varied needs of the follower of Christ, of the member of his Church. It is a vast, varied programme of spiritual initiation, encouragement, consolidation.

One passage in the discourse was singled out especially by John Paul II (qv) in his Encyclical *Dominum et Vivificantem* (qv), "'And when he comes he will convince the world concerning sin and righteousness and jugement: concerning sin, because they do not believe in me; concerning righteousness, because I go to the Father, and you will see me no more, concerning judgement, because the ruler of this world is judged'" (Jn 16:8-11). It provides a suitable prelude to the final passage on the Spirit in Jn. "Then the disciples were glad when they saw the Lord. Jesus said to them again, 'Peace be with you. As the Father has sent me, even so I send you.' And when he had said this, he breathed on them, and said to them. 'Receive the Holy Spirit. If you forgive the sins of any, they are forgiven; if you retain the sins of any, they are retained'" (Jn 20:20-23). The mystery of sin is disclosed by the Spirit and it takes the special power of the Spirit to erase sin from the soul. A twofold action is foreseen: forgiveness and retention, due account being taken of the sinner's disposition. Here too the Spirit is seen to be in his action intertwined with the official, or institutional Church. It was to the first priests of Christ that he was given as a source of divine pardon through their words.

In 1 Jn there are five passages of interest to a theology of the Spirit: the "anointing that comes from the Holy one," (2:20) not an explicit reference but with the scriptural association of anointing and the Spirit (1 Sam 10:1ff; Lk 4:18; 2 Cor 1:21) open to that interpretation; testing the spirits (4:1-6); the Spirit and the divine indwelling (4:13); the Spirit, the water and the blood (5:6-10). Again there is in some of these verses emphasis on truth and on the gift of the Spirit.

---

[1]Bibliographies to the relevant passages in the commentaries on Jn: Cf. H.B. Swete, *The Holy Spirit in the New Testament*, London, 1909, 129-168; F. Büchsel, *Der Geist Gottes in Neuen Testament*, Gutersloh, 1926, 485-511; P. van Imschoott, "Baptême d'eau et baptême d'Esprit," *ETL*, 13 (1936), 653-664; Mgr. C. Besobrasoff, *La Pentecôte johannique* (*Jn 20:19-23*), Valence, 1939; K. Rahner, S.J., "Flumina de ventre Jesu, Die patristische Auslegung von Joh 7:37-39," *BB* 22 (1941), 269-302, 307-403; F.M. Braun, O.P., "Le baptême d'après le 4e évangile," *RT*, 48 (1948), 358-368; *id.*, "L'eau et l'Esprit," *RT* 49 (1949), 5-30; C.K. Barrett, *The Holy Spirit and the Gospel Tradition*, London, 1947; *id.*, "The Holy Spirit in the Fourth Gospel," *JTS*, N.S. 1, (1950), 1-15; M.F. Berrouard, "Le Paraclet, défenseur du Christ devant la conscience du croyant (Jn 16:8-11)," *RSPT*, 33 (1949), 361-389; J.G. Davies, "The Primary Meaning of parakletos, *JTS*, N.S. 4 (1953), 35-38; J. Guillet, "La révélation progressive du Saint Esprit dans l'Ecriture," *LumV*, 8 (1953),18-32; id., "Baptême et Esprit," *LumV* 26, (1956), 85-104; J.-E. Menard, "L'interprétation patristique de Jean 7:38," *Revue de l'Université d'Ottawa, Section spéciale*, 25 (955) 5*-25*; F.J. Crump, *Pneuma in the Gospels*, Washington, 1954; Pietro della Madre di Dio, "Lo Spirito Santo nel IV Vangelo," *Eph. Carmelit.*, 7 (1956), 401-527; J. Daniélou, S.J., "Le symbolisme de l'eau vive," *RSR* 32 (1958), 335-346; M.-E. Boismard, O.P., "De son ventre couleront des fleuves d'eau vive," *RB*, 65 (1958), 523-546; P. Grelot, same title, *RB* 66 (1959), 369-374; id., "Jean 7:38: Eau du Rocher ou Source du Temple," *RB* 70 (1963), 43-51; J. Isaac, *La révélation progressive des Personnes divines*, Paris, 1960; F. Mussner, "Die johanneischen Parakletsprüche und die apostolische Tradition," *BZ* 5 (1961), 56-70; A. Feuillet, P.S.S., "Les fleuves d'eau vive de Jn 7:38," *Parole de Dieu et sacerdoce. Etudes présentees à Mgr. Weber*, Tournai and Paris, 1962, 107-120; I. de la Potterie, S.J., *La vie selon l'Esprit, Condition du chrétien*, (Unam Sanctam 55) Paris 1965, esp. "L'onction du chrétien par la foi," 107-167, Naître de l'eau et naître de l'Esprit. Le texte baptismal de Jn 3:5," 31-63; D. Betz, *Der Paraklet*, Leiden and Cologne, 1963; H.-M. Drion, "L'origine du titre de 'Paraclet': à propos d'un livre récent, *SE*, 17 (1965), 143-149; R.E. Brown, P.S.S., "The Paraclete in the Fourth Gospel," *NTS* 13 (1967), 113-132; id., *The Gospel according to John*, II, Garden City, NY, 1970, Appendix V; G. Bornkmann, "Der Paraklet im Johannes-Evangelium," *Geschichte und Glaube. Erster Teil. Gesammelte Aufsätze*, III, Munich 1968, 68-89; G. Richter, "Blut und Wasser aus der durchbohrten Seite Jesu," *Münchener Theologische Zeitschrift*, 21 (1970), 1-21; G. Johnston, *The Spirit-Paraclete in the Gospel of John*, Cambridge, 1970 with review by E. Malatesta, BB 54 (1973),

539-550; esp. F. Porsch, *Pneuma und Wort*, Stuttgart, 1974, with bibl. 700 titles; J. Behm, *Parakletos* in *TDNT*, 5, 800-814; E. Schweizer, *Pneuma* in *TDNT*, 6, 437-444, 448-449, 449-451; G.T. Montague, *The Holy Spirit*, 333-365.

JOHN PAUL II (1920, POPE 1978 -)

The Pope's teaching on the Holy Spirit is contained primarily in his Encyclical Letter, *Dominum et Vivificantem* (qv). The full corpus, however, comprises a number of other papal pronouncements.[1] The sixteen hundredth anniversary of the Council of Constantinople (qv), 1981 stirred him to different initiatives. On 25 March 1981, he sent a letter to the bishops of the Catholic Church, *A Concilio Constantinopolitano I*, recalling the great themes of the Council's creed and announcing the ceremonies to be held in commemoration of it; twinned with these would be ceremonies to celebrate the fifteen hundred and fiftieth anniversary of the Council of Ephesus, where Mary's divine motherhood was proclaimed. On Pentecost Sunday, 7 June the morning ceremony in St. Peter's would recall Constantinople; the late evening gathering in St. Mary Major would evoke Ephesus. Between the publication of the letter and the ceremonies planned an attempt was made on the life of the Pope, 13 May 1981.

"In this anniversary," wrote the Pope, "we not only call to mind a formula of faith that has been in force for sixteen centuries in the Church; at the same time we make ever more present to our spirit, in reflexion, in prayer, in the contribution of spirituality and theology, that personal divine which gives life, that hypostatic Gift—*Dominum et vivificantem*—that Third Person of the most Holy Trinity who in this faith is shared in by each individual soul and by the whole Church. The Holy Spirit continues to vivify the Church and to guide her along the paths to holiness and love."[2]

Dealing with the Council of Ephesus the Pope says: "These two anniversaries, though for different reasons and with differing historical relevance, redound to the honour of the Holy Spirit. All was accomplished *by the the power of the Holy Spirit*.... The two phrases in the Niceno-Constantinopolitan Creed, 'Et *incarnatus est* de Spiritu Sancto' and 'Credo in Spiritum Sanctum Dominum *et vivificantem*', remind us that the greatest *work* of the Holy Spirit, one to which all the others unceasingly refer as a source from which they draw, is that of *the incarnation of the Eternal Word* by the power of the Spirit from the Virgin Mary."[3] The Pope develops these ideas, showing how Mary's maternal link with the Church is part of the whole plan.

The Pope has occasionally spoken of the Spirit in the Wednesday audiences to which he willingly gives a catechetical orientation. On 3 August 1983 his theme was the Holy Spirit as the law of humankind redeemed. "What," he asks, "is the meaning of 'the law of man redeemed is the Holy Spirit'? It means that in the 'new creature,' the fruit of Redemption, the Spirit has taken up his abode, realizing a presence of God much more intimate than that following upon the act of creation." There follows a searching analysis of human personality under the influence of the Spirit which the Pope concludes thus: "This then is the definition of the ethos of the Redemption and of liberty; it is the ethos which has its origin in the gift of the Spirit who dwells in us; it is the liberty of him who does what he *likes* by doing what he *ought*."[4] In the Wednesday of Whit week that year the Pope had also spoken of the great work of reconciliation with Christ and with God, of which Pentecost was the prototype.[5]

In the autumn of 1985 John Paul II devoted the Wednesday audiences to a catechesis on the articles of the Creed. On 13 and 20 November he commented on the articles which profess faith in the Holy Spirit. He delayed particularly on the *Filioque* (qv). Recalling the Scripture texts which call the Spirit of the Father, Spirit of the Son and Spirit of Jesus he went on: "Therefore the Latin Church professes that the Holy Spirit proceeds from the Father and the Son (*qui a Patre Filioque procedit*) while the Orthodox Churches profess that the Holy Spirit proceeds from the Father through the Son. He proceeds 'by way of will,' 'in the manner of love' (*per modum amoris*). This is a *sententia certa*, that is, a theological doctrine commonly accepted in the Church's teaching and therefore sure and binding." The Pope then gives a lengthy explanation of the spiration, origin of the Holy Spirit. He quotes from the Athanasian Creed, recalls the names the Fathers gave to the third Person. "It can be said that God in his innermost life is 'love' which is personalized in the Holy Spirit, the Spirit of the Father and the Son. The Spirit is also called *Gift*. In the Spirit in fact who is Love there is the source of every gift having its origin in God in regard to creatures: the gift of existence by means of creation, the gift of grace through the economy of salvation."[6]

The *Atti del Congresso* reproduce the text of John Paul's address to the members, 26 March

1982 (see article Congress, Commemoration). He rejoiced in the ecumenical character of the gathering and hoped for much from the combined work of the experts: "For our Church is the Church of the Spirit. And faith in the Holy Spirit is at the heart of our Christian faith, as the creed of the holy Councils professes. It is the Holy Spirit who is at the heart of the sanctification of Christ's disciples. It is he who gives life to their missionary zeal and to their ecumenical prayer. The Spirit it is who is the source and moving power of the renewal of the Church of Christ."[7] The Pope lauded the work of the theologians, pointing to the need there was for genuine theology to counteract "too many popular works, superficial, insufficiently based, of a kind that could disturb the faith of the Christian people, the faith of the holy Councils."[8] Interspersed with such practical remarks are briefly phrased insights: "the Holy Spirit is mysteriously present in the non-Christian religions and cultures. And that also you have sought to articulate.... Of the Holy Spirit it can also be said: each one has part of him and all have him wholly, so inexhaustible is his generosity. In the experience of the Churches he is the invisible ferment, recognisable in his fruits as St. Paul helps us to discern them in the spiritual life of Christians: in their prayer which regains its sense of praise and gratitude, as well as its confident boldness; in the living communities full of joy and charity, which the Holy Spirit raises up and transfigures; in the spirit of sacrifice; in courageous apostolate and fraternal action in the service of justice and peace. In all the Holy Spirit stimulates the quest for the meaning of life, the obstinate pursuit of beauty, of the good beyond evil.... The Holy Spirit acts in persons, in the simplest as in those highly placed—and in communities, beginning with the little domestic churches, families."[9]

The Pope took note of the reawakening of devotion to the Holy Spirit, which called for sound theology; he spoke with great confidence and insistence of the "special grace which we hope for from the Holy Spirit," the realization of Christian unity; and he spoke with feeling of his own personal devotion to the Holy Spirit.

Pope John Paul has had other occasions to express his thoughts on the Holy Spirit, in an address to young people whom he had confirmed on 9 June 1985, in a message for World Mission Day, on 20 October 1985. Noteworthy is the passage on Charisms (qv) in the Apostolic Exhortation, *Christifideles Laici*, 30 December 1988:

"The Holy Spirit, while bestowing diverse ministries in Church communion, enriches it still further with particular gifts or promptings of grace called *charisms*. These can take a great variety of forms, both as a manifestation of the absolute freedom of the Spirit who abundantly supplies them, and as a response to the varied needs of the Church in history. The description and the classification given to these gifts in the New Testament are an indication of their rich variety."

The Pope then quotes 1 Cor 12:7-10 and refers to 1 Cor 12:4-6, 28-31; Rom 12:6-8; 1 Pt 4:10-11. He continues: "Whether they be exceptional and great or simple and ordinary, the charisms are graces of the Holy Spirit that have, directly or indirectly, a usefulness for the ecclesial community, ordered as they are to the building up of the Church, to the well-being of humanity and to the needs of the world.

Even in our own time there is no lack of a fruitful manifestation of various charisms among the faithful, women and men. These charisms are given to individual persons, and can even be shared by others in such ways as to continue in time a precious and effective heritage, serving as a source of a particular spiritual affinity among persons. In referring to the apostolate of the lay faithful the Second Vatican Council writes ..." (here follows the passage from the Decree on the Lay Apostolate, art. 3).

"By a logic which looks to the divine source of this giving, as the Council recalls,[10] the gifts of the Spirit demand that those who have received them exercise them for the growth of the whole Church.

"The charisms are received in gratitude both on the part of the one who receives them, and also on the part of the entire Church. They are in fact a singularly rich source of grace for the vitality of the apostolate and for the holiness of the whole Body of Christ provided that they be gifts that come truly from the Spirit and are exercised in full conformity with the authentic promptings of the Spirit. In this sense the discernment of charisms is always necessary. Indeed the Synod Fathers have stated: 'The action of the Holy Spirit, who breathes where he will, is not always easily recognized and received. We know that God acts in all Christians, and we are aware of the benefits which flow from charisms both for individuals and for the whole Christian community. Nevertheless, at the same time we are also aware of the power of sin and how it can disturb and confuse the life of the faithful and of the community.'

"For this reason no charism dispenses a person from reference and submission to the Pastors of the Church." There follows a quotation from the Constitution on the Church, art. 12.[11]

[1]While awaiting a monograph, recourse must be had to individual texts in *AAS, OR, Insegnamenti*; [2]Full text *A Concilio Constantinopolitano I, AAS* 73 (1981), 513-537; passage quoted, 514; [3]*Ibid.*, 518, 522; [4]*OR* 4 August 1983; [5]*OR* 26 May 1983; [6]*OR* 21 November 1985; [7]*Atti del Congresso*, II, 1515; [8]*Ibid.*, 1518; [9]*Ibid.*, 1519, 1520; [10]Footnote quotes the same article of the Decree on the Lay Apostolate; [11]*Christifideles Laici*, 25, tr. Veritas, Dublin, p. 64-67.

JOHN OF ST. THOMAS (1589-1644)

Born in Lisbon of an Austrian father and Portuguese mother J. studied in Coimbra and Louvain, after his entry to the Dominican Order taught in Alcala.[1] His lifework was a commentary on St. Thomas Aquinas (qv). Of the *Cursus Theologicus* one disputation, dealing with St. Thomas' treatment of the Gifts in Ia IIae, q. 68, is very well known, *The Gifts of the Holy Ghost*. It was translated into French by Raissa Maritain in 1930, into English in 1951 by Fr. Dominic Hughes, O.P.—evidence of its important place in the literature. To have J.'s complete thought his treatment of the Gift of fear in the commentary IIa IIae, q. 19 must also be considered.

J. deals first with the scriptural basis for the doctrine of the Gifts, then considers them generally, after which he treats of them separately. Throughout he is a disciple of St. Thomas Aquinas (qv), though his work is enriched with thoughts from other writers; it is, at times, polemical, in view of opinions expressed by other theologians after St. Thomas, particularly Scotus and Suarez. J. often has to cope with objections against the Thomistic teaching. The mental categories of scholasticism are assumed.

J. defends the Thomistic view that the Gifts differ from the virtues. Both are habits, that is permanent qualities of the soul. "The Gifts and virtues do not merely differ accidentally. The Gifts differ from the virtues both from the point of view of the mover or efficient cause, and from the point of view of the regulative principle and measure. In distinguishing the Gifts from the virtues by means of their definition, St. Thomas affirms that in the definition of virtue the words 'a quality by which a man lives rightly' mean a right living according to the limitation of reason. By this phrase he distinguished the definition of virtue from the definition of the Gifts. In the latter definition the notion of right living should be understood as right living according to a divine measure which is above human capacity ... the Gifts are habits or dispositions of the intellect and the will. They dispose these faculties to follow the impulse of the Holy Spirit, who regulates and delimits the object of the Gifts."[2]

Another succinct passage merits quotation: "According to the testimony of St. Thomas the Gifts of the Holy Spirit are given as habits not as an impulse moving the soul but for a special obedience by which the soul is subject to the motion of the Holy Spirit. This obedience and disposition which is a preparation for habitual subjection to the Holy Spirit should remain constant in the faithful. However its exercise depends on a motion and actual impulse which is not within the power of man. It is in his power, however, to be always prepared to obey, to be docile to the Holy Spirit."[3]

J. in dealing with the Gifts separately has also illuminating things to say: "The Gifts of wisdom and knowledge judge of supernatural things in an analytic manner: wisdom judges through the supreme causes, through an intimate union with God. Knowledge judges through lesser causes or effects, since it is concerned with creatures. Faith judges or is moved to effective assent, through neither causes nor effects, but through the naked testimony of God revealing. The Gift of understanding does not judge analytically, nor does it reason about supernatural truths through their causes. From an interior impulse of the Holy Spirit and from an affection toward spiritual things, it discerns spiritual realities from corporeal, and separates the things to be believed from those which are not to be believed, or errors. The evidence of a reasoning process is not required for this type of judgement. It does not proceed from cause or from effect, nor does it resolve the conclusion to its principles, since the Gift of understanding, like the habit of first principles, is concerned with principles. Rather this judgement is formed from a better and keener penetration of the terms in these truths, their congruity, and the incongruity of the opposing errors."[4]

J. devotes more space to the Gift of understanding than to any of the others. "The Gift of understanding," he writes, "does not sharpen and perfect the mind through study and metaphysical inquiry, but by mystical connaturality and union with divine truths." The author shows how the

Gift differs "from every other type of knowledge and habit."[5]

In regard to faith for instance J. has this to say: "There is a difference between assent by belief and assent by penetration and experience. One who believes adheres to the testimony which has been offered, and his action is restricted to assent, for he neither seeks nor probes further. Understanding, however, penetrates to the core, investigates the hidden reaches of the thing, extending even to its antecedents. It strives to lift the veil and to illuminate the darkness. Through the Gift of understanding God dispels the mists."[6]

On wisdom J. writes: "The formal nature by which wisdom knows the highest causes is an internal experience of God and divine things. It is a taste, love, delight, or internal contact, of the will with spiritual things. By reason of its union with spiritual truths the soul is, as it were, made connatural to things divine. Through this tasting wisdom discerns spiritual truths from the sensible and created. In this life wisdom acts only imperfectly by means of negation, but in heaven it acts quite perfectly, through positive evidence."[7]

In regard to wisdom J. is involved with problems raised by Suarez, as he is when dealing with the Gift of knowledge. He keeps constantly comparing the three gifts, wisdom, understanding, and knowledge as he does each with faith. In dealing with knowledge he helps the reader to grasp its meaning by an existential consideration: "Love forms a correct judgement concerning creatures, both to despise them, lest the soul should be distracted by them, and to love them moderately, ordaining them to God. In the words of the Apostle, *Do you seek a proof of the Christ who speaks in me? For this I have suffered the loss of all things, and I count them as garbage, that I may gain Christ* (Phil 3:8). Flight from creatures and a knowledge of their limitations, bitterness, and nothingness are very conducive to the perfect union with God and an experience of his immense goodness."[8]

Such knowledge helps the soul to know God more perfectly for he is known "by stripping away the imperfections of creatures." The "right judgement from the motion of the Holy Spirit with an ordered love of God and creatures" is the science of the saints.

J. distinguishes counsel, "the prudence of the Spirit," from the infused virtue of prudence, for the latter is limited in scope; there are areas in which a direct divine impulse is needed.

Piety, fortitude and fear of the Lord. J. shows how piety differs from the exercise of the virtue of religion. Whereas religion is related to a sense of obligation or debt towards God because of his gifts "piety honours and magnifies God for his own sake, regardless of whether he bestows good or evil."[9] This piety will logically extend to people as children of God for the greatness of God's glory "is considered both in his infinity itself and in the participating of it found in those who are the sons of God and consorts of the divine nature." [10]

J. develops his idea, the one generally held, that the Gift of fortitude "depends solely upon divine power; it is, as it were, clothed with strength from on high."[11] The impulse of the Holy Spirit does not consist "in a new precept or a new relation, light or knowledge. It is rather a new constancy and firmness of soul infused by the ministration of the Holy Spirit strengthening human powers and preparing human infirmity to conquer all difficulties."[12]

On the Gift of fear J. is most expansive. It has the widest scope among all the Gifts. J. quotes St. Thomas: "Fear of God is compared to the whole human life regulated by the wisdom of God as the root to a tree; the root of wisdom is to fear the Lord."[13] J. enunciated his opinion thus: "The principal act of fear as a Gift is not flight and an outlook upon evil but a reverential act toward good, that is toward the divine eminence, which is a provocative cause of evil."[14] Following St. Thomas he asserts that filial fear has two acts, to have reverence for God and to fear evil. [15] He deals with all the consequences of this position, answers objections with the same confidence as throughout the work. It remains one of the basic works on this important subject, one somewhat obscured latterly through insistence on the charisms, but durable, as all that was touched by the mighty genius of St. Thomas Aquinas.

---

[1]Cf. Introduction to English tr., D. Hughes, O.P., M. Egan, O.P. 1-23; Preface W. Farrell, O.P., bibl. to 1931 ed. Solesmes, 1931; M. Cuervo, *La inhabitación de la Trinidad in toda alma en gracia segun Juan de Santo Tomas,* Salamanca, 1946; D.G. Maguire, *The Gifts of the Holy Spirit in John of St. Thomas,* Diss. Gregorian, Rome, 1969; J.H. Ramirez, O.P., *DTC* VIII, 1924, 803-808; M. Duquesne, *Catholicisme,* VI, 1964, 622-25; H. Hoffmann, *LTK* V, 1078-79; *DSp* VIII, V. Rodriguez, 710-714; [2]II, 42, 43, *op. cit.,* p. 62; [3]II, 61, p. 71; [4]III, 18, 19, p. 84; [5]III, 46, p. 98; [6]*Ibid.,* 51, p. 101; [7]IV, 6, p. 125; [8]*Ibid.,* 57, p. 151; [9]VI, 11, p. 179; [10]*Ibid.,* 20, p. 185; [11]*Ibid.,* 29, p. 189; [12]*Ibid.,* 39, p. 194; [13]*Appendix,* II, 1, p. 222; [14]*Ibid.,* 2, p. 222; [15]*Ibid.,* p. 223.

JOSEPH, ST.

Reflection on the presence of the Spirit in the life of St. Joseph must take account of many factors.[1] The saint grew up in the age of the "Quenched Spirit" (qv). "The idea of the quenching of the Spirit is an expression of the consciousness that the present time is alienated from God. Time without the Spirit is time under judgement. God is silent. Only in the last days will the disastrous epoch of the absence of the Spirit come to an end and the Spirit return again. There is abundant evidence of the degree to which the people longed for the coming of the Spirit."[2]

Things changed dramatically in the lifetime of the saint. The first public sign of the "Return of the Quenched Spirit" was the promise to Zechariah, "'he (John the Baptist) will be filled with the Holy Spirit, even from his mother's womb'" (Lk 1:15). The capital moment was the Annunciation (qv). St. Joseph's role therein is given in the annunciation which he received. To relate this, St. Matthew uses the dream motif. But first occurs the sentence which reveals the great change: "When his mother Mary had been betrothed to Joseph, before they came together, she was found to be with child of the Holy Spirit" (Mt 1:18).

This was the presence of the Spirit, his action, in a way unknown to prophets, high priests, judges and kings of the OT: direct intervention in the conception of a child by a virgin. How was the intervention identified? By whom was she found to be with child of the Holy Spirit? Did Mary herself reveal the fact to Joseph? Why should she tell it to anyone else? Hoping that this would be an intermediary? She had already shown her greatness of heart in rising to cooperate with the Spirit by her free consent to the conception. Would she not do her duty, a rather obvious one, to her betrothed?

These questions are not asked by those who debate the "doubt" or hesitation of Joseph, the problem raised by the words which come immediately after those quoted, "and her husband Joseph, being a just man and unwilling to put her to shame, resolved to divorce her quietly" (*Ibid*).It is well known to commentators of the NT that three explanations have been given of the doubt: Joseph suspected Mary of adultery (St. Justin Martyr, St. John Chrysostom, St. Ambrose and St. Augustine, and first, the *Protoevangelium* of James—"If I hide her sin, I am fighting the law of the Lord"); he was in a state of perplexity, in which certain things, above all Mary's innocence, were clear to him and others unknown or uncertain (St. Jerome, Suarez, many Catholic writers); he thought she had become pregnant by a divine intervention (Eusebius, St. Basil, St. Ephraem, St. Romanos the Singer, Ps-Origen in Paul the Deacon's *Homilarium*, esp. St. Bernard followed by St. Antoninus of Florence).

In Matthew's narrative two key words are singled out, "just" (*dikaios*) and "son of David" (1:20). The word *dikaios* presents difficulty for each of the first two theories on the doubt. It undermines the suggestion that Joseph suspected Mary for, as an upright or law-abiding man, he must in that case denounce her. If, as the second theory maintains, he was in a state of perplexity, his action in sending Mary away quietly would appear irresponsible, for he would be making a positive decision which must have immense effects on her life, without knowledge of the facts.

If Joseph knew that the Child was of divine origin and feared with a holy fear, he would logically conclude that God would provide for the future of his own work. He was, moreover, a descendant of David, and could not claim a child in the Davidic line if he did not know the purpose of God's miraculous action. The point of the angelic message then would be reassurance on the future of the Child and on the purpose of the miraculous conception: Joseph himself would, in the divine plan, be the guarantor needed. A number of modern biblical scholars contend that this interpretation is the valid one of the angel's message: "Joseph, son of David, do not fear to take Mary, your wife; *true* (suggested tr. for *gar*, generally tr. "for") that which is conceived in her is of the Holy Spirit; she will bear a son, and you shall call his name Jesus, for he will save his people from their sins" (Mt 1:20-21). This case has been very strongly made by Fr. X. Léon-Dufour, S.J.

Whatever view is taken about Joseph's previous knowledge, he started his virginal married life with Mary, his parenthood of the Child Jesus with the certain knowledge that the Holy Spirit was the guiding force in their lives. Through the marriage, the reality of which was vindicated by St. Augustine (qv) he was made participant in Mary's spiritual endowment: the marriage was the basis of sharing and communion in everything that was not a purely personal privilege enjoyed by Mary.

To avoid becoming schematic and abstract in such a reflection we should study such biblical data as may be relevant. Joseph was heir to the

Davidic inheritance, the last before the Messiah, who fulfilled the divine promise. David at the origin of the line, had had a plenary gift of the Spirit: "Then Samuel, with the horn of oil in hand, anointed him in the midst of his brothers; and from that day on, the Spirit of the Lord (rushed) came mightily upon David" (1 Sam 16:13). As Joseph, who had often heard the reading, knew, this was a foreshadowing of the overwhelming effusion of the Spirit that was to come on the Messiah: "And the Spirit of the Lord shall rest upon him, the spirit of wisdom and understanding, the spirit of counsel and might, the spirit of knowledge and the fear of the Lord. And his delight shall be in the fear of the Lord" (Is 11:2). "The Spirit of the Lord God is upon me, because the Lord has anointed me to bring good tidings to the afflicted" (Is 61:1; cp. Lk 4:18). Joseph in the Davidic line was in the mainstream of the Spirit's influence in Israel; it would reach its highest level in the Annunciation. It was supported by other forces emanating from him, more general, such as the Torah. "The expression 'Holy Spirit' which we occasionally encountered in the Old Testament, becomes a commonplace among the rabbis to express the divine revelation which is found in the words of the Torah or on the lips of the prophets. A word of the Torah is a word of the Holy Spirit, since every word of Scripture is divinely inspired. The Holy Spirit not only inspired the prophets; even the acts of the righteous recorded in the Bible, are 'done in the Holy Spirit' (Gen R. 97 on 49:27). This does not mean the Holy Spirit inspired their ethical life but that their actions were indeed prophecies of what was to come."[3]

Joseph received direct divine intimations as to his conduct. Mt. conveys these through the dream motif (2:13, 20). Any such intervention Joseph would attribute ultimately to the Holy Spirit. As he would be the guidance he and Mary received on their conduct as Lk narrates the happenings of the infancy. Lk states that the secondary characters were "filled" or "inspired" by the Spirit, John the Baptist (1:15), Elizabeth (1:41), Zechariah (1:67), Simeon (2:26, 27). The evangelist did not feel the need to state this about Mary, for she was one with the Spirit; nor, because of Joseph's closeness to her, about him (2:4, 22, 23).

The magnitude of Joseph's role in salvation history is not as fully grasped by all as it was by Karl Barth—"he protected the Child, he will protect the Church." There is a vast field of research on Old and New Testament typology awaiting study. While awaiting further reflection we may apply to him the words of St. Thomas: "It is clear that the righteous have, through the spirit of prophecy, a certain familiarity with the interior instinct of the Holy Spirit and are wont to be taught thereby, without the guidance of sensible signs."[4]

[1]Bibl., M. O'Carroll, C.S.Sp., *Theotokos*, Wilmington, 1982; 206-209 esp. "Bibliografia fundamental josefina" in *Estudios Josefinos*, Valladolid, 20 (1966), 41-139; A. Trottier, *Essai de bibliographie sur St. Joseph*, 4th ed., Montreal, 1968; *Saint Joseph durant les quinze premiers siecles de l'Eglise*, several authors, Montreal, 1971; *DSp* VIII, 1289-1323; F.L. Filas, S.J., several works, esp. *The Man Closest to Jesus*, Boston, 1962; B. Llamera, O.P., *St. Joseph*, St. Louis, 1962; M. O'Carroll, C.S.Sp., *Joseph, Son of David*, Dublin, 1963; on Joseph's "doubt" cf. article s.v. in *Theotokos*, 123-124, bibl., esp. X. Léon-Duford, S.J., "L'Annonce à Joseph," in *Etudes d'Evangile*, Paris, 1965, 65-81, K. Rahner, S.J. (qv), "Nimm das Kind und seine Mutter," in *Geist und Leben*, 30 (1957), 14-22; esp., A.B. Calkins, *The Justice of Joseph Revisited*, in *Homiletic and Pastoral Review*, 88 (1988), 8-19; [2]J. Jeremias, *New Testament Theology,* I, London, 1971, 82; [3]C.T. Montague, S.M., *The Holy Spirit*, 113; [4]*Summa theol.*, IIIa, q. 36, a. 5, c. and ad 2um. For Karl Barth, cf. *Theotokos*, s.v. 69, 70; reference for quotation *Una Sancta* 18 (1963), 308; cf. F. Filas, S.J., *St. Joseph after Vatican II*, Chicago, 1966, 97-99.

JUSTIN MARTYR, ST. (d. c. 165)

Trained in philosophy J., a remarkable convert to Christianity, pondered God's action as revealed in the Old Testament, giving us the results in his *Dialogue with Trypho*, a Jew.[1] He is a landmark in the biblical theology of the Holy Spirit, the first to study the content of the Is 11, 2-3 text. In ch. 39 he speaks of those "becoming disciples unto the name of his Christ, and are leaving the way of error, who also receive gifts, each as they are worthy of them, being enlightened by the name of this Christ. For one receives the spirit of understanding, another of counsel, another of might, another of healing, another of foreknowledge, another of teaching, another of the fear of the Lord."[2] Clearly this enumeration is not identical with that of Isaiah, but it is inspired by it. There is a fleeting allusion to Is 11:1 in ch. 86, "That the Christ would come as a rod from the root of Jesse did Isaiah prophesy."[3]

It is in ch. 87 that J. really comes to grips with the problem of the text, composing a lengthy passage thereon: "At this point in my discourse Trypho said: Do not suppose hereafter that I am trying to upset your arguments, when I make any fresh inquiry, for I desire to learn about the very questions that I put to you. Tell me then about the word said by Isaiah: *A shoot shall come forth from the stump of Jesse, and a branch shall grow out of his roots. And the Spirit of the Lord shall rest upon him, the spirit of wisdom and understanding, the spirit of counsel and might, the spirit of knowledge and the fear of the Lord. And his delight shall be in the fear of the Lord.* He said that although he granted me that this was spoken with reference to Christ, I say that he already existed as God, and that he was incarnate according to the will of God, and became man by the virgin. How then he asked, can he be proved to have already existed, seeing that he is filled by the powers of the Holy Spirit, which the word enumerates by Isaiah, as though he lacked them?

"I answered: you have asked a most sensible and intelligent question; for indeed it does seem to be a puzzle. But listen to what I say, that you may see the reason even of this. These powers of the Spirit thus enumerated are said by the word to have come upon him, not as though he lacked them, but as being about to make their rest permanently upon him, that is, to come to an end with him, that there should be no longer prophets in your nation after the old manner, as you also can plainly see, for after him there has been no prophet at all among you. And further (that you may understand) that the prophets you have had, receiving each perhaps one or two powers from God, did and spoke these things which we have learned from the Scriptures, consider what I say. For Solomon had the spirit of wisdom, Daniel that of understanding and counsel, Moses of might and piety, Elijah of fear, and Isaiah of knowledge; and others also in the same way either had one each, or alternately one power and another, as had Jeremiah and the Twelve, (i.e., Prophets) and David and in fact all the other prophets who have been among you. The Spirit rested therefore, ceased, in other words, when Christ came. But after him, as this dispensation among men began in his time, it was necessary that those gifts should cease being among you, and yet, when they had taken their rest in Christ, should again, as was prophesied, be given by the grace of the power of that Spirit to them that believe on him, according to his knowledge of the deserts of each. And that it was prophesied that this would be done by him after his ascent to heaven, I have already said and now repeat. It said therefore: *He ascended on high; he led captivity captive; he gave gifts to the sons of men* (Ps 68:18, AV used by tr.). And again it is said in another prophecy: *And it shall be after these things that I will pour out my Spirit upon all flesh, and upon my men-servants and upon my maid-servants, and they shall prophesy* (Joel 2:28, 29 AV)."[4]

J. does not enter into an elaborate theology of the Trinity in the light of his philosophical attainments. He concentrates clearly on what emerges from reflection on Sacred Scripture, on the economy. But he is attentive to the teaching of Scripture and one may venture to say that he has a certain experiential knowledge to prompt his reflection and the formulation of his opinions.

Besides an initial intuition, inevitably incomplete, of the gifts of the Spirit, J. exemplifies also the missionary appeal that can be made on the basis of the Spirit's presence in OT—in the case of the Jews evidently. He is thus led to develop his Christology. Some examples: "And further, with a view to persuade you that you have no understanding of the Scriptures, I will mention also another Psalm spoken to David by the Holy Spirit, which you say is spoken with reference to Solomon who also himself became king. But it too has been spoken with reference to our Christ." J. quotes the Psalm, 72, at length, to support his assertion, "For Christ is proclaimed as King and Priest and God and Lord and Angel and Man and Chief Captain and Stone and Child born, and liable to suffering at first, then as going up to heaven and coming again with glory and having his kingdom forever, as I prove from all the Scriptures."[5] Again, "Christ is called in parable by the Holy Spirit both God and Lord of Hosts and Jacob."[6] "Give me an answer therefore whether you say that the Holy Spirit speaks of another as God and as Lord, besides the Father of the universe and his Christ."[7] "Yet another testimony from the Scriptures will I give you, my Friends, I said, namely that God has begotten as a Beginning before all his creatures a kind of Reasonable Power from himself, which is also called by the Holy Spirit the Glory of the Lord, and sometimes Son, and sometimes Wisdom, and sometimes Angel, and sometimes God, and sometimes Lord and Word."[8]

Referring, for the second time, to the Baptism (qv) at the Jordan, J. writes, "the Holy Spirit fluttered down on him in the form of a dove, for men's sake, as I said before, and a voice came at the same time out of the heavens. This also had been spoken by David, who, as in his own person, spoke what was hereafter to be said to him by the

Father: *Thou art my Son, today I have begotten thee*, meaning that his birth began for men, when they first knew that it was he."[9] How J. viewed the Spirit in OT is seen in such a passage as this: "For sometimes the Holy Spirit caused what was to be a type of the future to be performed openly, and sometimes he also uttered sayings about things that were to happen in the future, as though they were then taking place, or had already taken place."[10]

J. advanced thinking about the Spirit on the level he knew, the experience of salvation history. It would be for later times to carry the analysis into realization of the Logos as related to the Father and the Spirit substantially, with all traces of subordinationism removed.

[1]Text *PG* 6; English tr. ANCL; A.L. Williams, Translations of Christian Literature, *The Dialogue with Trypho*, (here used) 1930; T.B. Falls, *Dialogue with Trypho*, Fathers of the Church, Washington, 1965; J.C.M. van Winden, *An Early Christian Philosopher, Justin Martyr, Dialogue with Trypho*, ed., commentary, Leyden, 1971; cf. J. Lebreton, S.J., *Histoire du dogme de la Trinité*, II, 1948, 405-84; J. Daniélou, S.J., *Nouvelle Histoire de l'Eglise*, Paris, I, 1958, 87-127; G. Aeby, *Les missions divines de S. Justin à Origène*, Fribourg, Switzerland, 1958, 6-15; E. Bellini, "Dio nel pensiero di San Giustino," *La Scuola Cattolica*, 9 (1962), 387-406; J.P. Martin, *El Espiritu Santo en les origenes del Christianismo, Estudios sobre ... Justino*, Zurich, 1971; A. Gardeil, O.P., "Les dons," *DTC*, IV, 1911, 1754ff; G. Bardy, *DSp*, III, 1959, 1580; J.N.D. Kelly, *Doctrines*, 70-76; J. Wolinski, *Atti del Congresso*, I, 132-33; other references in the same collection; cf. index; *Trinitas*, 143, 4; *The Message*, 26-28; [2]A.L. Williams, 77; [3]183; [4]185-86; part of biblical tr. *Common Bible*; [5]Ch. 34, 1, A.L. Williams, 65, 66; [6]Ch. 36, 2, 71; [7]Ch. 56, 14, 115; [8]Ch. 61, 1, 126; [9]Ch. 88, 8, 190; [10]Ch. 114, 235; cp. ch. 113, 4, 233.

K

KENOSIS[1]

"Have this mind among yourselves which was in Christ Jesus, who though he was in the form of God, did not count equality with God a thing to be grasped, but emptied himself taking the form of a servant (or slave), being born in the likeness of men. And being found in human form he humbled himself and became obedient unto death, even death on a cross" (Phil 2:5-8). "The gospel concerning his Son, who was descended from David according to the flesh and designated Son of God in power according to the Spirit of holiness by his resurrection from the dead, Jesus Christ our Lord ..." (Rom 1:3, 4). Thus read St. Paul's closely packed summaries of the mystery of the Incarnation. The first text states the kenosis, the self-emptying of Jesus, a manifold mystery which must increasingly challenge reflection. An aspect of this kenosis, rarely dwelt on is the acceptance by the Incarnate Word of fragile, human persons as his messengers to mankind; this fragility is apparent even in the composition of the written records which he must deem necessary to perpetuate his message. Whence there is no reason for panic in face of the labours of modern biblical scholars; unwittingly they are disclosing an aspect of the kenosis.

Here too there arises the question of a possible kenosis of the Holy Spirit. It is a vast area scarcely imagined, without speaking of detailed exploration. Since, in the moment of the Incarnation, the Spirit was the principal agent, he it was who effected the kenosis as an inherent element in the structure of the Incarnate Word. The decision to embrace this condition involved the Holy Trinity, and St. Paul speaks of God as highly exalting Christ: the action of the Father at the term of the mystery in its earthly phase. At its inception and all through the phases which preceded the exaltation, the Spirit was Jesus' close partner, ensuring total fidelity to the initial resolve, "ruling" his life, as Hans Urs von Balthasar taught. Did this imply, does it still, in the mystical life of Christ in his Church, imply a kenosis of the Spirit himself? A question which goes to the roots of our knowledge of all being, Creator and creation.

We should begin with patient analysis of the moments in which the Spirit has a dominant role. He is dominant as to his action, yet he is veiled as to his person. He does not manifest himself as one who holds the initiative, who directs, speaks, announces. It is not he who appears to Mary, but an angel; it is not he who announces his coming but when he has come. Our Lady is told that he will descend on her (Lk 1:35) but he does not have a moment of revealing self-expression. It had been likewise with John the Baptist (Lk 1:15). At the baptism of Christ (qv) the Spirit is hidden in a symbol. He is spoken of (Mt 3:16; Mk 1:10; Lk 3:22; Jn 1:32, 33) but it is the Father who speaks.

In Acts things change. To the study of Acts elsewhere undertaken we must add an analysis of the moments where he appears to take the initiative—we may overlook the scriptural passages where his action is described (Acts 2:17, 18, 33, 38; 5:32; 8:15, 17, 19; 10:45, 47; 15:8; 19:2). More relevant are the occasions where he speaks, 1:16; 8:29; 10:19; 11:12; 13:2; 19:1; 21:11; 28:25, where he witnesses 5:32; 20:23, where he seizes, 8:39, where he sends, 13:4, establishes, 20:28, impedes, 16:6, comforts, 9:31. In all these instances there is no personal direct revelation of the Spirit's nature, of his distinctive personal constituents within the Holy Trinity. It is likewise when we turn to the gifts linked with him: wisdom, 6:3, 10, faith, 6:5; 11:24; joy, 13:52, consolation and fear of the Lord, 8:31, power, 1:8 and Lk 24:49; 10:38. Always the Spirit's intervention is seen as overwhelmingly important. Always the Spirit himself is mysteriously in the background. "The Spirit is supremely active, he is in fact the essential agent in the entire history recounted in Acts. But, at the same time, he comes from elsewhere, he is sent, he is given, he is promised. And he never acts save through men to whom he manifests himself in different ways, though all are related to the mind and heart. He is, if one dare say so, himself only in coming from Another and in acting through others."[2]

Care has clearly to be taken in applying the concept of kenosis to the Spirit. We have here a deep, deep reality and as we ponder its solution we may have enlightenment on the presence and activity of the Spirit in the Church during the early ages and ever since. Vatican II tells us that the Church "as ages pass, moves towards the fullness of divine truth, until the words of God receive their consummation in her." (Constitution on Divine Revelation).

---

[1]Cf. esp. P. Henry, *Kénose*, DBS V, 7-161; H. Urs von Balthasar, *Mysterium Salutis* XII FRench ed. 15-177; id., *The Glory of the Cross*, III, 2, 196-217; *Kénose* (de l'Eglise) *DSp*, IV, 183-191; B. Sesboué, *RSR* 59 (1971), 83-89; A. Feuillet, *Christologie paulinienne et tradition biblique*, Paris, 1971, 85-161; Hans Urs von Balthasar (qv), *Der unbekannte jennseits des Worts*, in *Spiritus Creator*, Einsiedeln, 1967, 95-105; [2]DBS XI, 183, J. Guillet, S.J.

L

LALLEMANT, LOUIS, S.J. (1588-1635)[1]

An unusual instance of posthumous literary and spiritual influence, L., associate of a heroic generation in his institute, experienced in the guidance of souls, is known through a work which appeared almost sixty years after his death, edited by one member of the Society, Pierre Champion, from notes taken during the lifetime of L. by another, Jean Rigoleuc. The title: *La vie et la doctrine spirituelle du Père Louis Lallemant de la Compagnie de Jesus*, Paris, 1694. The relevance of this work to our subject is that a large part of it, almost a hundred pages in a recent edition, Paris, 1924 (pp 175-283) deals with docility (qv) to the Holy Spirit and the Gifts (qv)—pp 108-179 in the English edition here used.

The work, which has had considerable influence falls into seven sections, dealing with: the end of life; the idea of perfection; purity of heart; docility to the guidance of the Holy Spirit; recollection and the interior life; union with Our Lord; and the order and degrees of the spiritual life.

The author deals with docility under the following headings: the nature of docility to the guidance of the Holy Spirit; the motives which lead to the practice of this docility; of the Gifts of the

Holy Spirit in general; of the Gifts of the Holy Spirit in detail, of the Fruits of the Holy Spirit; the obstacles which the devil puts in our way in the practice of docility to the guidance of the Holy Spirit.

He thus introduces his thought on the nature of docility: "When a soul has given itself up to the leading of the Holy Spirit, he raises it little by little, and directs it. At the first it knows not whither it is going; but gradually the interior light illuminates it, and enables it to behold all its own actions, and the governance of God therein, so that it has scarcely aught else to do than to let God work in it and by it whatever he pleases; thus it makes wonderful progress."[2]

As a figure of this guidance L. takes the pillar of cloud and the pillar of fire by which God guided the Israelites of old. "They followed the movements of this pillar, and halted when it halted; they did not go before it, they only followed it and never wandered from it. It is thus we ought to act with respect to the Holy Spirit."[3]

L. then turns to the means by which this docility can be attained: to obey faithfully God's will so far as we know it. "We are often ignorant of God's will, but we must be faithful to the knowledge that we have; let us fulfil his designs so far as he has made them known to us, and he will manifest them to us more fully ; to renew often the good resolution of following in all things the will of God, and strengthen ourselves in this determination as much as possible; to ask continually of the Holy Spirit this light and this strength to do the will of God ... above all in every important change of circumstances, to pray God to grant us the illumination of the Holy Spirit, and sincerely protest that we desire nothing else, but only to do his will ; let us watch with great care the different movements of our soul."

L. then considers the objections which are occasionally made against the practice of docility, such as that it smacks of the Calvinist "inner light," that it clashes with the proper obligation of obedience, that it renders all deliberation and counsel useless, and there are people who know nothing of it. The author can deal with these points satisfactorily. Docility to the Spirit aids and facilitates true obedience, to which it will be subordinate, but L. has some sharp things to say about superiors who do not support the Spirit's action in souls. Deliberation and counselling are means used by the Spirit to guide souls.

For L. perfection and even salvation depend on docility to grace; there are few perfect souls because there are few who follow the guidance of the Holy Spirit; there is a certain injustice in offering opposition to it. But L. holds out the prospect of consolation. The Holy Spirit exercises the office of Comforter. This, we are told, he does in three ways. In the uncertainty of our salvation with which we must live, a thing which has caused saints to tremble, he comforts us being the *Spirit of adoption of sons* (Rom 8:15): he is the pledge and assurance of the heavenly inheritance. "The Holy Spirit bears inward witness to fervent and faithful souls, of what they are to God and what God is to them; and this witness banishes their fear and forms their consolation."[4]

"Secondly," says L., "the Holy Spirit comforts us in the temptations of the devil, and in the contradictions and distresses of life." Here the author uses the words "unction" and "sweetness." Thirdly, the Spirit comforts us as we feel deep within us the absence of God, the "infinite void" which holy souls feel, a kind of martyrdom which would be intolerable "without the consolations which the Holy Spirit gives them from time to time."[5]

L. then turns to consideration of the Gifts of the Spirit in general and in detail. He outlines the whole supernatural organism which is fitted to the soul, first the theological virtues which unite the soul immediately to God, then the Gifts of the Holy Spirit; they come next after the theological virtues, because they are, as it were, their fulfilment, and serve to make them operate in a more excellent manner. Then in descending order come the supernatural moral virtues, the fruits of the Holy Spirit, which are "nothing else than infused virtues, when we arrive at exercising them not only without pain or repugnance, but with joy and pleasure. When these same virtues are fully developed, and have become perfect acts, they are called beatitudes."[6] Last come the natural moral virtues, which perfect the soul only according to reason and not according to faith ; they are separable from sanctifying grace.

In dealing with the Gifts L. follows St. Thomas fairly closely; he does now and then add a suggestive detail. For example he contrasts wisdom and knowledge thus: "There is this difference between wisdom and knowledge, that the latter does not ordinarily produce that spiritual taste which the former communicates to the soul."[7] Likewise in dealing with the Gift of Understanding he pleads for more reading of Sacred Scripture. "All other spiritual books speak the language partly of grace and partly of nature. The frequent reading of Holy Scripture is a means of receiving the Holy Spirit and of being guided by his direction. It is a great mistake to read spiritual books so much and Sacred Scripture so little."[8]

L. speaks of the Gift of Counsel making the soul certain that it is walking in the way of God and his divine Providence, never going astray. "The Gift of piety," he says, "is an habitual disposition which the Holy Spirit communicates to the soul to excite it to a filial perfection for God."[9] Fortitude is an habitual disposition which the Holy Spirit communicates to the soul and to the body both to do and to suffer extraordinary things, undertake the most arduous actions; to expose ourselves to most formidable dangers, to undergo the most toilsome labours, to endure the most grievous pains and that with constancy and heroism."[10] "Fear is an habitual disposition which the Holy Spirit communicates to the soul to maintain it in a state of reverence before the majesty of God, of dependence upon and submission to his will, causing it to fly from everything that can displease him."[11]

There is a notable difference in mode of presentation here from the work of John of St. Thomas, each valuable in its own special context, in the audience foreseen. The same quality marks the presentation of the Fruits of the Spirit (qv) by the gifted Jesuit spiritual writer.[12] He has the existential touch too when warning against the obstacles put up by the devil, where, for instance, he talks of the "secret illusions" which do so much spiritual damage.[13]

---

[1]Cf. A. Hamon, "Qui a écrit la Doctrine Spirituelle du P. Lallemant" *RAM* 5 (1924), 233-68; H. Brémond, *Histoire littéraire du sentiment religieux en France*, V (3), 3-65; A. Pottier, *Essai de théologie mystique comparée, Le P. Lallemant et les grands spirituels de son temps*, 3 vols., Paris, 1927, 29; J. Jimenez, S.J., "En torno de la formación de la 'Doctrine Spirituelle' del P. Lallemant," *AHSI* 32 (1963) 225-292; *id.*, "Précisions biographiques sur la vie du P. Lallemant," *AHSI* 33 (1964), 269-303; J. Weissmayer, *Theologie und Spiritualität*, Ein Beitrag zur theologischen Interpretation der Doctrine Spirituelle der Lallemant, Mem. MS, Vienna, 1974; *Catholicisme*, VI, 1676-78, F. Courel; *DTC* VIII, 2439-64, P. Bouvier; esp., G. Bottereau, *DSp* X, 125-135; [2]*The Spiritual Teaching of Father Louis Lallemant*, ed. A.G. McDougall, tr. inspired by Fr. Faber, author unknown, London 1928, *Fourth Principle, Of the Guidance of the Holy Spirit and Docility thereto*, Ch I, Art 1, (i), p. 108; [3]*Ibid.*, (ii); [4]*Ibid.*, art 2, p. 109; [5]Ch. II, (iv), p. 120; [6]*Ibid.*; [7]Ch. II, art 1, (i), p. 121; [8]Ch. IV, art 2, p. 137; [9]*Ibid.*, art 5, p. 153; [10]*Ibid.*, art 6, p. 156; [11]*Ibid.*, art 7, p. 161; [12]Pp. 166-172; [13]P. 176.

LAW[1]

The *Torah* was a great uplifting force for the people brought into one by Moses, as God's instrument. It meant more than mere legal prescription bringing with it some knowledge of divine reality, even if this was not universally received (Hos 4:2). The promise was made that it would be superseded, when the old covenant, with which it was linked, was replaced. Let us not forget that Christ did not come to abolish the law, but to fulfil it (Mt 5:17f). His fulfilment was thus foreshadowed: "'Behold, the days are coming, says the Lord, when I will make a new covenant with the house of Israel and the house of Judah, not like the covenant which I made with their fathers when I took them by the hand to bring them out of the land of Egypt, my covenant which they broke, though I was their husband, says the Lord. But this is the covenant which I will make with the house of Israel after those days, says the Lord: I will put my law within them, and I will write it upon their hearts; and I will be their God, and they shall be my people'" (Jer 31:31-33). "'A new heart I will give you, and a new spirit I will put within you; and I will take out of your flesh the heart of stone and give you a heart of flesh. And I will put my spirit within you and cause you to walk in my statutes and be careful to observe my ordinances'" (Ez 36:26-27).

The very first years of the Church manifest the tension caused by the changes: Jewish Christians wished to keep the Torah in force for the newly converted pagans. Peter made the first break in practice when he baptized Cornelius and those received with him: "While Peter was still saying this, the Holy Spirit fell on all who heard this word. And the believers from among the circumcised who came with Peter were amazed, because the gift of the Holy Spirit had been poured out even on the Gentiles. For they heard them speaking in tongues and extolling God. Then Peter declared, 'Can anyone forbid water for baptizing these people who have received the Holy Spirit just as we have?' And he commanded them to be baptized in the name of Jesus Christ" (Acts 10:44-48). The question was, as a matter of general import, brought to a head at the Council of Jerusalem, where Peter and James publicly accepted Paul's thesis (Acts 15:7-19).

Paul builds up the theory which will be more fully developed later: "God's love has been poured into our hearts through the Holy Spirit who has been given to us" (Rom 5:5). "For the law of the

Spirit of life in Christ Jesus has set me free from the law of sin and death. For God has done what the law, weakened by the flesh, could not do; sending his own Son in the likeness of sinful flesh and for sin, he condemned sin in the flesh, in order that the just requirement of the law might be fulfilled in us, who walk not according to the flesh, but according to the Spirit.... For all who are led by the Spirit are sons of God" (Rom 8:3-4, 14).

St. Leo the Great (qv) following other Fathers, established a contrast between the old law and the gift of the Spirit at Pentecost. "A first point," writes J. Lécuyer, "to which Tradition abundantly testifies, following the double testimony of the Letter to the Hebrews, about which we have spoken already (Heb 8:8-12 and 10:16-18) is that the new Law is an interior law, written in hearts and not imposed from without, as the old law written on stone tablets. But then, what will this new reality be which takes its place in the hearts of Christians and serves them as law? From the opposition which Paul constantly establishes between the old law and grace (cf. Rom 6:14-15) it is clear that it is the latter which constitutes the New Law; nor is it advisable to distinguish very precisely what later theology will call 'created gift' from the 'uncreated Gift,' who is the Holy Spirit: we can then say that the new Law is the 'very presence of the Holy Spirit' in our hearts, or the Holy Spirit himself, or, as St. Thomas says, 'the very proper effect of the Holy Spirit' *scilicet fides per dilectionem operans.* This last formula can be summarized in one word: charity. All the commandments formerly written on the tablets of the law *'may be summarized in this word: You shall love ... therefore love is the fulfilling of the law'* (Rom 13:9-10). This is not written on tablets of stone, but is poured into our hearts by the Holy Spirit who has been given to us (Rom 5:5). The law of God then is charity. The Holy Spirit, grace, charity—it is this inseparable ensemble which the concept of the 'New Law' expresses, the ensemble which we still call 'the state of grace.'[2]

Newman (qv) seized on this truth and expounded it thus: "We Christians are indeed under the law as other men, but, as I have already said, it is the new law, the Law of the Spirit of Christ. We are under grace. That law, which to nature is a grievous bondage, is to those who live under the power of God's presence, what it was meant to be, a rejoicing. When we feel reluctant to serve God, when thoughts rise within us as if he were a hard Master, and that his promises are not attractive enough to balance the strictness of his commandments, let us recollect that we, as being Christians, are not in the flesh, but in the Spirit, and let us act upon the conviction of it. Let us go to him for grace. Let us seek his face. Let us come where he gives grace. Let us come to the ordinances of grace, in which Christ gives his Holy Spirit, to enable us to do that which by nature we cannot do and to be the 'servants of righteousness.'"[3]

The first instance of the operation of the new law of grace occurred in the moment of the Annunciation (qv). Mary's fiat was an act totally beyond the content of the Torah; it was in direct obedience to the new law of grace. Its mainspring was the Holy Spirit. Her conscience was informed by the Spirit and she was empowered to identify him and act with him. So far from lessening the role of her personality this was raised to the level of the divine. This is the highest single instance of fully Christian morality outside the life of the God-man, an imperative coming directly from the Spirit and plenary response on the human side. It was an act which called into being a new life with unique responsibility on the agent herself. It was an act which created for her a whole new set of duties. It was an act which opened the way to another person's vocation, creating obligations for him. Mary's independence was absolute in dependence on God. She did not consult her parents, or her betrothed.

Mary's fiat in the moment of the Annunciation is the paradigm, irreplaceable, inspiring but inimitable, of every truly authentic act of obedience to the New Law. Since the intrinsic meaning of it was cosmic and its effects universal it may rightly be said to encompass, to give validity to, every other human decision and act which are totally rooted in the divine.

---

[1]Cf. J.H. Newman, *The Strictness of the Law of Christ* in *Parochial and Plain Sermons*, IV, 1-17, 1877 ed. here used; J. Lécuyer, C.S.Sp., "Pentecôte et loi nouvelle," *Vie Spirituelle*, May 1953, 471-490; Y.-M.J. Congar, O.P., "Variations sur le thème, 'Loi Grâce'", *RT* 71 (1972) 420-438; *id.*, "Le Saint Esprit dans la théologie thomiste de l'agir moral," in *Atti del Congresso Internazionale 1974*, Naples, 1976, 9-19, bibl.; R. Yates, *St. Paul and the Law in Galatians*, ITQ, 51 (1985) 105-124; [2]*Op. cit.*, [3]*Op. cit.*, 16f.

LEEN, EDWARD (1885-1944)[1]

Irish missionary, educationalist, director of retreats L. exercised very wide influence in the English-speaking world by his spiritual writings in the thirties. He had, after brilliant studies in Dublin and Rome, helped to plan catechetics for the great missionary Bishop Joseph Shanahan in Southern Nigeria, then at the incipient stage of its phenomenal Catholic expansion; he later cooperated closely in the foundation and first years of the new society launched by the Bishop, *The Holy Rosary Sisters.* He worked as Prefect of Studies and president of Blackrock College, facing the problems of secondary education in Ireland now independent. Spiritual retreats and counselling claimed much of his time though he taught philosophy in the seminary of his Congregation. In his last years, 1941 to 1944, he was deeply involved in a remarkable ecumenical movement, *The Mercier Society.*

L. was Christocentric in his spiritual outlook. This is evident in all his writings, especially in *In the Likeness of Christ,* 1939, *Why the Cross,* 1938, *The True Vine and its Branches, The Church Before Pilate,* 1939. His work on Christian education *What is Education?* gives to this question the answer of Christian humanism. Very concerned about ignorance among the faithful of the riches of divine grace, the gifted author brought out in 1936 the one substantial work in English in those decades and for some time after on the Holy Spirit, *The Holy Ghost.*

The chapter, *The Sending of the Spirit of Jesus* in *In the Likeness of Christ* presents succinctly leading ideas on the Holy Spirit, notably the relationship between Jesus and the Spirit: "The Incarnate God *reconciled* fallen man to his Maker by the destruction in his flesh of the enmities which kept them apart. . . . The Holy Ghost *transformed* that *reconciliation* into profound mutual sympathy and a strong deep love. Christ merited grace; the Holy Spirit moulds souls to the graces thus merited. Christ revealed God to his creatures from without; God the Holy Ghost reveals the same God to his creatures by inward communications. God the Son made man wrought our salvation by meriting it; God the Holy Ghost wrought our salvation by accomplishing it. God the Son saved us; God the Holy Ghost sanctifies us."[2] Again he returns to the theme: "Christ is the Word of God. He is the Godhead expressed divinely and humanly. Christ is the *Book of God*—in itself perfectly revealing God, but hard to be deciphered by human souls. The Holy Ghost is the great Teacher who by his secret and inward il-

luminations takes up this book and expounds it to us. It is only by him that we can grasp the meaning and the significance of Christ and his life. 'Without me' says Jesus, 'you can do nothing.' 'Without me' the Holy Ghost might say, 'you can understand nothing. Christ the Word of God, would be without me, a hidden word, a sealed Book to you.'"[3]

L. wrote in the Introduction to *The Holy Ghost*: "An interest in the process of sanctification naturally directs attention to the Person of the Blessed Trinity, to whom, by the law of appropriation, are attributed all the operations of sanctification in the Church itself and in individual members of it. With the widespread interest in things of the spiritual life, there has grown up an eagerness to have a deeper and more accurate knowledge of the Holy Spirit. There are many indications that the years that are at hand will witness a great development of Devotion to the Third Person of the Most Blessed Trinity. It is certain that an understanding of the role that the Holy Ghost plays in the supernatural formation of the soul would inspire the sincere Christian with a desire to address his prayers more frequently and more fervently to that Person, who, as it were, holds the keys to the treasures of divine grace."[4]

The first eight chapters of the book deal with the Person of the Holy Spirit; the remaining five with his operation in the human soul. For the Spirit's work in the Church the author referred the reader to Dom Anscar Vonier's work *The Spirit and the Bride.* L. believed that "an analysis of the names which are ascribed to the Third Divine Person in the Liturgy and in theology discloses to us his distinctive personal characteristics."[5] L. is sparing in references to authors, save St. Thomas and a few times Terrien's *La grâce et la gloire,* which had much influenced his thinking, the writings of Libermann (qv) and Froget's *De l'Habitation du St. Esprit dans les âmes justes;* he constantly quotes Sacred Scripture. The work expounds the great themes about the Spirit, with an occasional flash of insight which reveals personal experience—L. had passed through ordeals of the spirit, taken heroic spiritual options. The book was translated into French, *La Pentecôte continue,* Paris-Montreal, 1952, and into Spanish, *El Espiritu Santo, Las ventajas de una Amistad,* Madrid, 1960.

---

[1]Cf. M. O'Carroll, C.S.Sp., *Edward Leen, C.S.Sp.,* Dun Laoghaire, 1952; id., *DSp* IX, 514; B.J. Kelly, C.S.Sp., *The*

Voice of a Priest, ed. posthumously with introduction; Dublin; [2]*Op. cit.*, 317f; [3]*Ibid.*, 320; [4]*Op. cit.*, 19; [5]*Ibid.*, v.

LEO THE GREAT, ST. DOCTOR OF THE CHURCH (Pope from 400, d. 461)[1]

Taken up with an immense government and administrative programme, at times the defender of Rome against the Barbarians, L. did not deal at length with theological problems;[1] he had his great moment in the Council of Chalcedon, 451, which accepted his *Letter to Flavian*, the Tome, as the proper formulation of Christological dogma.

L's sermons and letters contain his theology. Three on Pentecost give us his ideas about the Holy Spirit, with which we also receive his Trinitarian theology. Dealing with the "majesty" of the Spirit he writes: "Invisible by nature, and common to the Father and the Son he showed the quality of his gift and his work in the way he wished but kept the property of his essence in his Godhead: for human gaze cannot reach the holy Spirit, as it cannot reach the Father or the Son. For in the divine Trinity nothing is dissimilar, nothing unequal; and nothing that can be thought of that substance can be discerned by its power or glory or eternity. Though as to the properties the Father is one and the Son another, and the Holy Spirit another, yet there is not another deity or different nature. Indeed since the Son is the only-begotten from the Father, and the Holy Spirit is the spirit of the Father and the Son, he is not so as any creature who is of the Father and the Son, but as one living and powerful with each, and eternally subsistent by that through which the Father and the Son are.... Some things are not of the Father and others of the Son and others again of the Holy Spirit, but everything the Father has the Son has and so has the Holy Spirit; nor was there a time when this communion did not exist in the Trinity, for there to have everything is to exist forever. Let no times, no degrees, no differences be thought of and if no one can explain what God is, let him not assert that he is not. It is more excusable not to speak things worthy of the ineffable nature than to proclaim things opposed to it. Whatever therefore devout spirits can conceive of the eternal and incommunicable glory of the Father let them also think of the Son and of Holy Spirit without separation or difference between them. For thus we confess this Blessed Trinity as one God, as in these three persons there is no difference of substance or of power or of will or of operation."[2]

L. then condemns the Macedonians as the Arians, using the strong Latin word *detestamur*: "for though they attribute equality to the Father and Son, they nonetheless think that the Holy Spirit is of an inferior nature." He applies to them the threat of punishment in Mt 12:32. Having quoted 1 Cor 12:4-6, L. goes on: "By these dearly beloved, and other texts in which the authority of divine oracles shines countless times, we are urged together to veneration of Pentecost, rejoicing in honour of the holy Spirit, through whom the whole Catholic Church is sanctified, every rational soul is trained; who is the inspirer of faith, the doctor of knowledge, the fount of love, the seal of chastity, and the cause of all virtue. Let the minds of the faithful rejoice that one God, Father, Son and Holy Spirit is praised by a confession of all tongues, and that the meaning shown in the appearance of fire continues in work and gift. For the Spirit of truth himself causes the house of his glory to shine with the effulgence of his light; in his temple he wishes nothing dark or lukewarm."[3]

L., in his second sermon, still has much to say of the Trinity. Again he insists that the Spirit is of the Father and the Son; as on the eternity and equality: "The unchangeable deity of the Blessed Trinity is one in substance, undivided in work, agreeing in will, the same in power, equal in glory." This is newly elaborated soon after, as if L. wished to start from certainty on the Trinity as he treated of the Holy Spirit: "Having, dearly beloved, firmly grasped this faith, we do not err if we think that when the Spirit filled the disciples of the Lord on the day of Pentecost, it was not the beginning of his gift, but extra generosity; since the patriarchs and prophets and priests and all the saints who existed in ancient times were nourished by the same sanctifying Spirit. And without this grace no Sacraments have ever been instituted, no mysteries celebrated, so that it was the same power in the charisms, though not the same measure in the gifts."[4]

The Apostles did not lack the Spirit, L. thinks, before the Passion. They had his indispensable power to forgive sins. He here refers to and quotes Jn 20:22. But something greater would come on Pentecost, "a greater grace and more abundant inspiration so that they would take what they had not yet received or be able to possess more excellently what they had already taken." Hence the words of the Lord in Jn 16:12-14. He touches on the heresy of Manicheism, thinks that fasting

136

which comes from apostolic tradition is to be counted among "the great gifts of the Holy Spirit".

A similar idea is expressed by L. in his third homily. "He increased not began his gifts; he was not new in operation, but richer in bounty. For the majesty of the Holy Spirit is never separate from the omnipotence of the Father and the Son, and whatever the divine government accomplishes in the ordering of all things proceeds from the providence of the whole Trinity. Among them are unity of mercy and loving-kindness, unity of judgement and justice, nor is there any division in action where there is no divergence of will. What therefore the Father enlightens, the Son enlightens, and the Holy Spirit enlightens. While there is one Person of the Sent, another of the Sender and still another of the Promiser, both the unity and the Trinity are at the same time revealed to us."[5]

L. then goes on to consider the "economy." Here the distinction of persons enters. "The fact, therefore, that with the cooperation of the inseparable Godhead still intact, certain things are performed individually by the Father, certain by the Son, and certain by the Holy Spirit, in particular belongs to the ordering of our redemption and the plan of our salvation. For if humanity, made after the image and likeness of God, had retained the dignity of its own nature, and had not been deceived by the devil's tricks into transgressing through lust the law laid down for him, the Creator of the world would not have become a creature, the eternal would not have entered the sphere of time, nor would God the Son, who is equal with God the Father, have assumed the form of a slave and the likeness of sinful flesh ... the mercy of the Trinity divided for itself the work of our restoration in such a way that the Father should be propitiated, the Son should propitiate, and the Holy Spirit enkindle."[6] L. points out that this scheme allowed for "those who are to be saved to do something on their part." It will need the guidance of grace to "faithfully and wisely understand what is particular to the Father, to the Son and to the Holy Spirit, and what is common to the three in our restoration."[7] Again L. does not use the concept of appropriation.

[1]Works, *PL* 54; *SC* 74; [2]*Sermo* 75, *De Pentecoste*, I, 3, 401f; [3]*Ibid.*, 5, 403; [4]*Sermo* 76, *De Pentecoste* II, 3 405; [5]*Sermo* 77, 1, 411f; [6]2, 412; 3. 413, tr. *Sermo* 77; [7]C. L. Feltoe, *LNPF*, ser. 2, XII, 191-92.

LEO XIII (1810-1903), POPE (1878)

Automatically called to mind for his social teaching, author of the most remarkable papal document in this area, *Rerum Novarum*, 15 May, 1891, Leo's many contributions to the spiritual life of the Church were of very high value, in regard to the Sacred Heart, the Eucharist, Our Lady and St. Joseph, without being exhaustive. Three important documents are relevant to doctrine and devotion centered on the Holy Spirit: the Apostolic Letter, *Provida Matris Caritate*, the Encyclical, *Divinum Illud Munus* and the Letter to the Bishops, *Ad fovendum in Christiano Populo* (qqv).

A religious foundress, Blessed Elena Guerra (qv) had influence, which was possibly decisive, on the Pope in each instance. Her religious institute, The Sisters of St. Zita, later known as the Oblates of the Holy Spirit, expressed a conviction that there was need for a whole ecclesial and personal renewal of attitude towards the third divine Person. She took the initiative of writing to the Pope to convince him of this great need and was successful: she wrote to Leo ten times in all. It is known that before he decided on the public consecration of the human race to the Sacred Heart of Jesus in 1900, he had received a communication from a religious of the Good Shepherd, Sister Mary von Droste-Vichering, assuring him that this was the will of God. In neither case did the Pope refer publicly to the messages he had received from these individuals. The ensuing documents are composed without any such link.

The fact remains: this was the most significant papal teaching on the Holy Spirit for centuries and there was no immediate sequel, not before Pius XII (qv).

LIBERMANN, FRANCIS (1802-1852)[1]

The convert Jew, missionary founder, pioneer in the modern evangelization of Africa, was a highly valued spiritual director. His thinking on the Holy Spirit took on an existential dimension from his experience in this ministry; it developed too in his work as a founder, especially when it came to the fusion of his institute, the Society of the Holy Heart of Mary (qv) with the older Congregation of the Holy Spirit (qv). But we have evidence, independent of these apostolic works, of his profound interest in a vital, mystical theology of the Spirit.

Libermann lived through years of apparent futility. Barred from the priesthood by epilepsy, he led a nondescript existence as a seminarist with no hope of advancement. He was, for a while,

Novice Master to the Eudists. All the time his powers of discernment and counselling were active and highly valued. The decision to leave the Eudists and, with two other seminarists from the colonies, to found a missionary society, brought him to Rome, and frustration. Though this was lifted dramatically, he had lived for some time in penury in the Eternal City. The time of waiting was spent in writing the rule for his future institute, and in composing a commentary of St. John's Gospel.

On Jn 3:5 L. writes: "But, after our Baptism, the Holy Spirit dwells in us in a living, vivifying manner, he is with us to become the principle of all the movements of our soul, he becomes as the soul of our soul. It depends on us to allow ourselves to be moulded and influenced by him, to follow more or less his holy impulses, as there is more or less grace in us, according to the degree of our good dispositions. The more the Holy Spirit becomes the principle of the movements of our soul, the more he influences its sentiments and dispositions, and the more he is followed, the more perfect will his life be in us, the holier we shall be. But, if after Baptism we depart from the influence of the Holy Spirit through the state of mortal sin, then our soul is dead because its soul, who is the Holy Spirit, is no longer in it, no longer communicates his life to it. That is why damnation is called eternal death, because souls in this unfortunate state, have no longer the divine soul which was meant to animate them in such admirable manner, and thus things will be eternally. What misfortune!"[2]

The author states the essential teaching on the Persons of the Holy Trinity and goes on to consider each in turn. On the Holy Spirit he writes first as to the origin in the Trinity. He continues: "He proceeds then from the Father and the Son. But, as these relations and this procession are essential, eternal, substantial, it results from this that the Holy Spirit is the very substance of the Father and the Son, as much as they are so themselves, and that the Father and the Son are in the Holy Spirit as much as they are in themselves, and as much as they are one in the other, since the Holy Spirit proceeds essentially and substantially from this being, substantial and essential of the Father in the Son and of the Son in the Father. In the same way the Holy Spirit is in the Father and the Son as much as he is in himself. Hence the perfect unity of nature and the perfect Trinity of Persons, mystery adorable and forever incomprehensible to any creature, on this earth of ignorance and of sin."[3]

L's doctrine of the indwelling Spirit is conceived in the existential terms of spiritual direction. "The Holy Spirit must be your guide," he writes to one who was to fulfil a great hope—he would be the founder of the French Seminary in Rome, entrusted to L's congregation, Fr. Lannurien. "It is not necessary for you to see your progress, for it is not you who ensures your progress but the Holy Spirit, who must be your guide, and not your own personal spirit. It must suffice for you that he knows how he is guiding you, and you have nothing else to do but to follow always his divine impulse.... Entrust yourself to the guidance of the Holy Spirit, and do not seek to know what you are to do. You must go to God more by the heart than by the mind. If you go to him with a will determined and full of love, your mind will know sufficient for your guidance."[4]

It is the duty of the director to study the action of the Holy Spirit in the soul of the disciple: "Direction has then to do two things: to aim ceaselessly at favouring the movement of this sanctifying grace so as to see that it rules the soul, to follow step by step the interior guidance of the divine Spirit who alone can guide towards this movement of sanctifying grace, and increase and extend its power in the soul. He must in all circumstances favour this guidance of the Holy Spirit and the expansion of sanctifying grace."[5] Speaking of general pastoral action: "If a pastor wishes to speak to souls and render them docile to grace, let him be filled with the Spirit of Our Lord, and let him talk thus in this divine Spirit of his Master; and good souls will hear this voice which is so well known to them, will yield at once and allow themselves to be ruled and led very easily."[6]

The director's role is very subordinate: "He is an echo; he is then not much and his word is not of itself a living, vivifying word. He is an echo of the Holy Spirit; it is then the interior word of the divine Spirit which he transmits, which is life and vivifies."[7] On the disciple's side the great rule is to do nothing save by the movement of the Holy Spirit, the Spirit of holiness, the Spirit of the holiness of Jesus, who effects in us the holiness he effected in Jesus. "He is the sole agent of sanctification, the principle of sacrifice and of immolation, the unique driving-power and the unique life of souls, who does everything in us. "If Fr. Libermann seems to speak indifferently of the presence and action of Jesus or of the Holy Spirit in our souls, in countless letters he clarifies, with the rigour of theological formulas, the nature of the relations between these two Persons and their particular causality in our sanctification. "The Holy Spirit residing personally, in the depth of your soul, by the power of Our Lord." "The Word of life only lives in us by the Holy Spirit who dwells in us."[8] L. emphasizes the continuity, consistency, uniformity, of the Spirit's action in each individual soul. "I believe that the Holy Spirit breathes constantly in the same way in the same soul."[9]

On the effects of the Spirit's action L. wrote convincingly: "The Holy Spirit while acting powerfully, fills your soul with sweetness and with peace. He establishes in you the life of Jesus, the affections, desires and loves of Jesus.... When the divine Spirit acts in us, our soul is burning and in the midst of this fire, it is borne as it were, united to God, without confusion, without agitation, without irritation, without movement of self-love, and, on the contrary, with a movement of self-abasement, not only before God, but within ourselves and before all creatures. My dear, how lucky we are when we are under the power of the divine Spirit, completely under the influence of the Spirit of love of Jesus. All in us becomes love."[10]

Or again: "May the Spirit of Jesus animate all your actions, may he form all the sentiments of your soul, may he deaden and restrain all vivacious sallies of the mind, all hard and harsh sentiments of the heart, in a word all that is passionate and disordered in the soul; may he rule all your impulses, direct and lead all the movements of your soul, may he communicate to your heart the meekness and humility of which the divine Master has given us example ... the Spirit of Jesus cannot animate those who have not these two sanctifying virtues, this divine Spirit is more often replaced by a personal spirit and sometimes by the spirit of darkness."[11]

We may conclude with L's beautiful prayer: "O must holy and adorable Spirit of my Jesus, let me hear your sweet and adorable voice. Refresh me by your delightful breath. I wish to be before you as a light feather, that your breath may bear me off where it will; that I may never offer it the slightest resistance."[12]

[1]Writings, *Lettres spirituelles*, 4 vols., Paris, 30 Rue Lhomond, 1874; *Ecrits Spirituels*, Paris, 1891; *Notes et Documents relatifs à la vie et à l'oeuvre du Ven F.M.P. Libermann*, 13 vols, ed. A. Cabon, C.S.Sp., Paris, 1929-1941; bibl., XIII, 1-15; *Commentaire de l'Evangile selon St. Jean*, Paris, Poussielgue, 1874; select passages ed. L. Vogel, C.S.Sp., 1957, here used; cf. M. Briault, C.S.Sp., *Le Vénérable P. F.M.P. Libermann*, Paris, 1946; V. Lithard, C.S.Sp., *Spiritualité spiritaine*, Paris, 1938; L. Liagre, C.S.Sp. *Le Vénérable Pere Libermann, L'homme, la doctrine*, Paris, 1948; B.J. Kelly, C.S.Sp., *The Spiritual Teaching of Venerable Francis Libermann*, Dublin, 1955; J. Gay, C.S.Sp., *Libermann, Juif selon L'Evangile* (Préface André Frossard), Paris, 1977; H. Koren, *The Spiritans*, Pittsburgh, 1983; B.J. Kelly, C.S.Sp., *Life Began at Forty, The Second Conversion of Francis Libermann*, Dublin, 1983; esp. P. Blanchard, *Vénérable Libermann*, Etudes Carmelitaines, 2 vols; Paris, 1958; esp. P. Coulon, P. Brasseur, ed., *Libermann*, Paris, 1988, Préface Léon Senghor; P. Sigrist, *DSp*, IX, 763-779, bibl.; [2]*Commentaire de l"Evangile selon St. Jean, op.cit.*, 133; [3]*Ibid.*, 252f; [4]*Lettres Spirituelles* II, 588f; *Notes et Documents*, III, 73-74; [5]*Ecrits Spirituels*, I, 360' [6]*Commentaire de l'Evangile selon St. Jean*, [7]*Ecrits*, I, 361; [8]*Lettres spirituelles, II, 407, 410; P. Blanchard, op. cit.*, I, 200, with many references; [9]*Lettres Spirituelles*, II, 313; [10]*Notes et Documents*, III, 87, 88; [11]*Notes et Documents*, XIII, 144; [12]*Commentaire de l'Evangile selon St. Jean*, 2nd ed., 86.

LOMBARD, PETER (c. 1100-1160)

The importance of P.'s Trinitarian teaching is principally that it afforded the groundplan on which the great medieval thinkers, notably the great Scholastic Doctors, would work to develop their thinking.[1] Here as throughout his work he is the great compiler, putting down passage after passage from the Fathers and other writers. His theology of the Spirit is contained in Dist. X through XVIII of Bk. I.[2] The compilation is almost exclusively from St. Augustine (qv) who dominates, by large excerpts from his *De Trinitate*, page after page. P. is more concerned with settling points of terminology, what words may or may not be used of the Holy Spirit than with any original speculation. Thus he begins by a discussion on the use of Love as a name for the Spirit, when God himself, that is the Trinity is called love, is said to be love. St. Augustine solves it for him, saying that we sometimes think of the substance, sometimes of the Persons—with wisdom likewise for the Son.

P. is firm on the *Filioque*, though not adept at handling the evidence. He thinks that "from the Doctors of the Greeks we have open testimonies whereby it is shown that the Holy Spirit proceeds from the Father and the Son. *Let every tongue then confess* that the Holy Spirit proceeds from the Father and the Son."[3] But some of his testimonies are alas spurious, quoting the Athanasian Creed for instance as by St. Athanasius. His favourite Greek, St. John of Damascus, (qv) is absent from these pages. Thereafter, there is question of nomenclature, such as whether *genitus*, begotten or *ingenitus*, unbegotten can be used about the Spirit, or why we can speak of the Son as proceeding when this is specially used of the Spirit.[4]

In the same way P. does a work of clearing the ground terminologically when it comes to the mission of the Spirit, the different senses, and to consideration of the Spirit as Gift. He is ever solicitous to insist on the equality of the Persons in dealing with concepts which, accepted in a merely human sense, might seem to imply more or less, before or after.[5] He maintains Augustine's key concept, *caritas*.

But it has been agreed from early on, that he drew a wrong conclusion, identifying the Holy Spirit and the virtue of charity, denying that this is a created *habitus*. "From what has been said it is clear that the Holy Spirit is charity, whereby we love God and our neighbour; whence it is easier to show us how the Holy Spirit is sent and is given to us."[6] He wrestles with other linguistic difficulties, always looking for rescue to Augustine. To say this is not to lack respect and gratitude for one of the great intellectual pathfinders of the Christian ages. Many of the hundreds who used his textbooks, the basis for extended reflections, travelled farther on the way; the greatest, one feels, would acknowledge their debt to his pioneering labours.

[1]Works, *PL* 190, 191; Sentences ed. here used, Quaracchi, 1916; cf. O. Baltner, *Die Sentenzen des Petrus Lombardus* (Studien zur Geschichte und der Kirche, viii, Hft 3, 1902); F. Stegmuller, ed., *Repertorium Commentarum in Sententias Petri Lombardi*, 2 vols., Würzburg, 1947; J. de Ghellinck, S.J., *Le mouvement théologique au XIIe siècle*, 1914, 73-244; 2nd ed, Musseum Lessianum, x, 1948, 113-373; id. *DTC* XII, 2 (1935), 1941-2019; A. Piolanti, *EC* IX (1952), 1438-1440; A. Emmen, *NCE* XI, 221-22, I. Brady; *LTK* VIII, 367-369, I. Brady, A. Emmen; *DSp* XII, 1604-1612; [2]*Op.cit.*,pp. 73-124 [3]Dist. 11, ch. 2, p.81; [4]Dist 13, ch, 1,4, p. 85f, 87f; [5]Dist. 12, ch 1, Dist. 15, ch 10, pp. 81 f, 101f; [6]Dist 15, ch 1-6, quotation ch 3, p. 109.

LOSSKY, VLADIMIR (1903-1958)[1]

A Russian expatriate theologian, one of the distinguished group centred in Paris, L. had varied education, in Russia, Prague and Paris, with some experience of life in the U.S. He opposed Bulgakov's (qv) sophiological doctrine. Central to his thinking was the idea of the Trinity. He was attracted to Eckhart in his last years, St. Gregory of Palamas (qv) influenced him and he helped promote knowledge of the Doctor of Hesychasm:

he thought that when St. Gregory spoke of God he always had the Trinity in mind.

What L. has to say about the Holy Spirit is contained mostly in his collected theological essays, *The Image and Likeness of God*, and in his great work, *The Mystical Theology of the Eastern Church*. He was an inflexible opponent of the *Filioque* (qv) and rejected the theses of Basil Bolotov (qv).

On our knowledge of the Spirit L. writes as follows: "Now we cannot know God outside of the economy in which he reveals himself. The Father reveals himself through the Son in the Holy Spirit, and this revelation of the Trinity always remains 'economic' inasmuch as, outside the grace received in the Holy Spirit, no one can recognise in Christ the Son of God and in this way be elevated to knowledge of the Father."[2]

L. thought, however, that the theologian must rise above the knowledge conditioned by the economy to the "notion of absolute hypostatic difference and the equally absolute essential identity of the Father, the Son and the Holy Spirit."[3] He thought that it was essential to safeguard the position of the Father as the principle of unity in the Trinity, the 'cause' but cause of the equality of the other Persons with himself.

L. thought that "all triadology depends on the question of the procession of the Holy Spirit." In his rejection of the *Filioque* he went to extremes. He thought that the two processions *per modum intellectus* and *per modum voluntatis* were, from the point of view of Orthodox theology "an inadmissible error." He went much further. "By the dogma of the *Filioque* the God of the philosophers and savants is introduced into the heart of the living God, taking the palce of the *Deus absconditus, qui posuit tenebras latibulum suum*. The unknowable essence of the Father, Son and Holy Spirit receives positive qualifications. It becomes the object of natural theology; we get 'God in general' who could be the God of Descartes, or the God of Leibnitz, or even perhaps, to some extent, the God of Voltaire and of the dechristianized Deists of the eighteenth century."[4] Difficult to understand how such an intelligent man could write thus of the theology of St. Thomas Aquinas, Newman, Scheeben, Hans Urs von Balthasar, (qqv) to mention but a few luminaries of the Latin Church.

But L. remained optimistic. He does not think that the *Filioque* is the greatest obstacle to reunion. He was convinced that modern Byzantine theologians preserve the theology of the Fathers of the first five centuries. "The Greeks have ceased to be Greeks in becoming sons of the Church. That is why they have been able to give to the Christian faith its imperishable theological armory. May the Latins in their turn cease to be solely Latins in their theology! Then together we shall confess our catholic faith in the Holy Trinity, who lives and reigns in the eternal light of his glory."[5] L. was above all Trinitarian in his theological outlook: "The Trinity is for the Orthodox Church the unshakeable foundation of all religious thought, of all piety, of all spiritual life, of all experience. It is the Trinity that we seek in seeking after God, when we search for the fullness of being, for the end and meaning of existence."[6]

---

[1]Cf. O. Clement, "Vladimir Lossky, un théologien de la personne et du Saint Esprit" in *Messager de l'Exarchat du Patriarche russe en Europe occidentale*, 30-31, (1959), 137-206; B. Schultze, S.J., *DSp* IX, 1018-1019; *id., NCE*, XII, 760; B. Dupuy, in *Catholicisme*, VII, 1091-92; *Trinitas*, 155f; [2]*In the Image and Likeness of God*, 1974, 15f; [3]*Ibid.*, [4]*The Procession of the Holy Spirit*, repr., in *In the Image and Likeness of God.*, 82; [5]*Ibid.*, 96; [6]*The Mystical Theology of the Eastern Church*, 1957, 65.

LOUIS-MARIE GRIGNION DE MONTFORT, ST. (1673-1716)

There is occasional misunderstanding about the doctrine of St. Louis Marie; briefly that he exaggerates the role of Mary in the Christian and religious life.[1] A complete reading of his works would remove this misunderstanding. The doctor of Mary's universal mediation has a clear grasp of the central truths of the Christian religion. The consecration which he suggests is to Jesus Christ, the incarnate wisdom, by the hands of Mary. He states explicitly: "Jesus Christ, our Saviour, true God and true man, must be the ultimate end of all our other devotions; otherwise they would be false and misleading. Jesus Christ is the *alpha* and *omega*, the beginning and end of all things. We labour not, as the Apostle says, except to make all men perfect in Jesus Christ, because in him alone dwells the entire plenitude of the divinity, and all other plenitudes of graces, of virtues and of perfections; because in him alone we have been blessed with every spiritual blessing." There follow a series of titles of Jesus with their justification, Master, Lord, Head, Model, Physician, Shepherd, Way, Truth, Life, and "our All in all things, who must satisfy us." "There is no other name under heaven, but the name of Jesus by which we must be saved."[2] "If then", the saint insists, "we are establishing solid devotion to Our Blessed Lady, it is only to establish more perfectly devotion to Jesus Christ, to provide an easy and sure means of finding Jesus Christ."

Another striking feature of the saint's doctrine is the clear exposition of the Holy Spirit's role in salvation and sanctification: Mary is seen in close relationship to him. In one passage St. Louis seems to exceed theological limits: "God the Holy Spirit being barren in God, that is producing no other divine Person, became fruitful by Mary, whom he espoused. It is with her and in her and of her that he produced his masterpiece, God made man, and with her and in her daily to the end of time he produces the predestined and the members of the Body of this adorable Head. It is for this reason that the more he finds Mary, his dear and inseparable Spouse in a soul, the more active and powerful he becomes to produce Jesus Christ in that soul, and that soul in Jesus Christ."[3]

The passage is quoted out of context for the following lines in the work redress the balance. It must be admitted that the opinion is not found in any other important work on Our Lady. The following lines read: "This does not mean that the Blessed Virgin gives fruitfulness to the Holy Spirit, as if he did not possess it; for being God, he has like the Father and the Son, fruitfulness or the capacity to produce, although he does not put it into act, since he produces no other divine Person. But it means that through the Blessed Virgin whom he deigns to use, without absolutely needing her, the Holy Spirit puts into act his fruitfulness, producing in her and by her Jesus Christ and his members: a mystery of grace unknown even to the most learned and spiritual of Christians."[4]

St. Louis then outlines the Trinitarian plan for the sanctification of souls. He briefly considers each Person. On the Holy Spirit he writes thus: "God the Holy Spirit has communicated his gifts which are too great for words, to Mary, his faithful Spouse, and he chose her as the dispensatrix of all he possesses; so that she distributes all his gifts and graces to whom she wills, in the measure she wills, how she wills and when she wills, nor does he give any heavenly gift to man which does not pass through her hands. For such is the will of God who has decreed that we should have all things through Mary; thus she will be enriched, exalted and honoured by the Most High who, during the whole of her life made herself poor, humiliated and hidden in an abyss of nothingness, by her profound humility."[5]

The words "to whom she wills, in the measure she wills, how she wills and when she wills" have been criticised. They would not be acceptable were the preceding assertion not made: "God the Holy Spirit has communicated his gifts.... and he chose her his faithful Spouse, as the dispensatrix of all he possesses" and the important link words "so that she distributes" not inserted. The opinion is borrowed textually from St. Bernardine of Siena.[6] The words "For such is the will of God who has decreed that we should have all things through Mary" are from St. Bernard.[7] The great Marian doctor's dictum is quoted by Pius IX, Leo XIII, St. Pius X, Pius XII, John XXIII.[8]

The primacy of the Holy Spirit is also clearly affirmed in this passage: "God the Holy Spirit wishes to raise up for himself elect in her and by her, and he says to her, *In electis meis mitte radices*: My well-beloved, my Spouse, place the roots of all your virtues in my elect, that they may grow from virtue to virtue and from grace to grace. I was so pleased with you when you were living on earth in the practice of the most sublime virtues, that I still wish to find you on earth, without your ceasing to be in heaven. Reproduce yourself, then, in my elect so that with delight I may see in them the roots of your invincible faith, profound humility, universal mortification, sublime prayer, ardent charity, firm hope, all your virtues. You are my Spouse, as faithful, pure and fruitful as ever. Let your faith give me faithful, your purity virgins, your fruitfulness elect and temples."

The saint's thought moves to a climax: "With the Holy Spirit Mary produced the greatest thing that ever was or ever will be: a God-man; she will produce, consequently, the greatest things that will come to be in the latter times. The formation and education of the great saints who will live at the end of the world is reserved to her, for only this singular and miraculous Virgin can produce, in union with the Holy Spirit, singular and extraordinary things. When the Holy Ghost, her Spouse, finds Mary in a soul, he flies there and enters fully; he communicates himself to that soul in abundance and to the extent that it makes room for his Spouse. One of the chief reasons why the Holy Spirit does not work striking wonders in souls is that he fails to find in them a sufficiently close union with his faithful and inseparable Spouse. I say 'inseparable Spouse' for from the moment the substantial Love of the Father and the Son espoused Mary to form Jesus Christ, the Head of the elect, and Jesus Christ in the elect, he had never repudiated her, for at all times she has been faithful and fruitful."[9]

The spousal relation between Mary and the divine Persons is a complicated problem. The Fathers sometimes spoke of her as Spouse of the Father, Scheeben (qv), as is well known, proposed a theory of the bridal motherhood. St. Louis departs from the view generally expressed by the French school that Mary was the Spouse of the Father. His opinion is sometimes found with medieval writers, and has been expressed by Popes Leo XIII, Pius XII and John Paul II, by St. Maximilian Kolbe and Frank Duff. (qqv)

The saint's Christocentrism is especially seen in his work entitled *The Love of the Eternal Wisdom*. Here too he has occasion to speak of the Spirit. "The Eternal Wisdom communicates to the soul that possesses him his all-enlightening Spirit: *Optavi et datus est mihi sensus; et invocavi et venit in me Spiritus sapientiae* (Wis 7:7) "Therefore I prayed, and understanding was given me: I called (upon God) and the Spirit of wisdom came to me. "This subtle and penetrating Spirit causes men, after the example of Solomon, to judge of all things with great discernment and a keen intelligence."[10] St. Louis speaks briefly of the Gifts (qv). "When the Eternal Wisdom communicates himself to a soul he confers on it the Gifts of the Holy Spirit and all the great virtues in an eminent degree."[11] Elsewhere he speaks of the Holy Spirit who, by the cross, "cuts and polishes all the living stones of the heavenly Jerusalem."[12] In this work too he repeats the opinion he had taken from St. Bernardine, this time including the Gifts of the Holy Spirit with the good things Mary freely bestows. There are frequent references to the Spirit in the saint's *The admirable Secret of the most holy Rosary*; in *The Secret of Mary* there is an abbreviated version of the doctrine elaborated in the *True Devotion*.

St. Louis was bound by close friendship with Claude-Francois Poullart des Places (qv), a fellow student at Rennes. When Claude-Francois founded the Community and Seminary of the Holy Spirit in Paris in 1703,[13] St. Louis requested that the members of his institute be trained there. This service continued after the death of the two founders. It has occasionally been suggested that the idea of a Community dedicated to the Holy Spirit came from St. Louis. There is no evidence for this.

But both shared a common ideal of devotion to the Third Person of the most Holy Trinity.

---

[1]*Oeuvres complètes*, Paris, Editions du Seuil, 1966; English tr. *True Devotion* and *The Love of Eternal Wisdom* by the De Montfort Fathers, here used, references to numbers, slight changes on French text; cf. S.de Fiores, S.M.M., *Itinerario spirituale di S. Luigi M. di Montfort nel peiodo fino al sacerdozio*, Rome, 1974; L. Perouas, *DSp* IX, 1073-1081; *id., Ce que Grignion de Montfort croyait et comment il a vécu sa foi*, Paris, 1973; [2]*True Devotion*, 61; [3]*Ibid.*, 20; [4]*Ibid.*, 21; [5]*Ibid.*, 25; [6]*Sermo de 12 Priv.*, I, 2,c.8, *Opera Omnia*, Quarrachi, II, 378; [7]*Sermo de Aqued.*, 7, *Opera Omnia* ed. J. Leclercq, O.S.B., and H. Rochais, V, 279; [8]References in *Theotokos*, 245; [9]True Devotion, 34,35,36; [10]*The Love of Eternal Wisdom*, 92 [11]*Ibid.*, 99; [12]*Ibid.*, 176; [13]Cf. H. Le Floch, C. S. Sp *Claude-Francois Poullart des Places, fondateur du Séminaire et de la Congrégation de Saint Esprit (1679-1709)*; H. J. Koren, C. S. Sp., *The Spiritual Writings of Father Claude Francis Poullart des Places, Founder of the Congregation of the Holy Ghost*, Duquesne Studies, Spiritan Series 3, Pittsburgh, 1959; esp., J. Michel, *Claude Francois Poullart des Places, fondateur de la Congrégation du Saint Esprit*, Paris, 1962; *Claude Francis Poullart des Places*, Writings, Rome, Spiritan Centre, 1988.

LUKE, ST.[1]

St. Luke is par excellence the evangelist of the Holy Spirit. As the author of a gospel and of the Acts of the Apostles (qv), he has given us the largest corpus of writing in the NT, more even than Paul. The word "spirit" occurs four times in Mk and five times in Mt; Lk uses the expression "Holy Spirit" thirteen times in the gospel and forty-one times in Acts. The continuity in the theme is important because Lk viewed the two works as one composition.

Lk is, moreover, the narrator of the three capital moments in which the Spirit intervened in salvation history, the Annunciation (qv), the Baptism of Jesus (qv) and Pentecost (qv). Of the three only the Baptism is narrated by other NT writers. By reason of his privileged role as historian of these events, Lk, we may assume, was especially attuned to the inspiration of the Spirit; his close spiritual association with St. Paul, (qv) the theologian of the Holy Spirit, would sharpen his response.

The Spirit is active in the great moments of the life, activity and teaching of Jesus. In the infancy narrative he is promised to the Lord's precursor (1:15), who is sanctified in his mother's womb, as she is filled with the Spirit (1:41); Zechariah also is filled with the Holy Spirit (1:67) before prophesying and speaking the Benedictus; to the aged Simeon it had been revealed by the Spirit that "he should not die before he had seen the Lord's Christ" (2:26), and "inspired by the Spirit he came into the temple" (*Ibid.*, 27).

After the Baptism Jesus faced the ordeal of temptation. Mk says: "The Spirit immediately drove him out into the wilderness" (1:12) and Mt that he was "led up by the Spirit into the wilderness" (4:1). Lk has more detail. He opens the narrative thus: "And Jesus, full of the Holy Spirit, returned from the Jordan and was led by the Spirit for forty days in the wilderness, tempted by the devil" (4:1-2). When the story ends with the departure of the devil Lk adds: "And Jesus returned in the power of the Spirit into Galilee, and a report concerning him went out through all the surrounding country" (4:14).

Then occurred the incident in the synagogue at Nazareth. Jesus read the passage from Is 61:1-2, beginning, "The Spirit of the Lord is upon me . . ." (4:17, 18). Lk's narrative continues: "And he closed the book, and gave it back to the attendant, and sat down; and the eyes of all in the synagogue were fixed on him. And he began to say to them, 'Today this scripture has been fulfilled in your hearing'" (4:20, 21).

Lk is the only evangelist who says that Jesus, after the baptism, received the Spirit while he was praying (3:21, 22). He has a revealing variant on Mt's text on the answer to prayer, changing "good things" to "the Holy Spirit": "'If you, then, who are evil, know how to give good gifts to your children, how much more will the heavenly Father give the Holy Spirit to those who ask him'" (11:13). Lk here is telling us that the Holy Spirit is the summum bonum of prayer, that which includes all other things we may wish to ask for.

Not only petition, but praise. In this the evangelist is highly distinctive. Praise is for him Spirit-inspired: "At that moment Jesus rejoiced in the Holy Spirit and said: 'I praise you, O Father, Lord of heaven and earth, for you have hidden these things from the wise and understanding and revealed them to babes; yes, Father, for such was your gracious will'" (10:21). Lk is one with Mt on the response of the Lord to those who accused him of casting out demons "by Beelzebul"—for "Spirit of God" he uses a phrase with that meaning: "'But if it is by the finger of God that I cast out demons, then the kindgom of God has come upon you'" (11:20).

On public witness Lk reports, as do the other synoptics, the Master's severe warning about a particular sin against the Holy Ghost: "'And every one who speaks a word against the Son of Man will be forgiven; but he who blasphemes against the Holy Spirit will not be forgiven'" (12:10; Mt 12:31-32; Mk 3:28-29). But Lk has this very consoling addition, so appropriate from one who lived with the thought of the Spirit: "'And when they bring you before the synagogues and the rulers and the authorities, do not be anxious how or what you are to answer or what you are to say; for the Holy Spirit will teach you in that very hour what you are to say" (12:11, 12). An explanation proposed of the first text is that the warning about blasphemy applies to the post-pentecostal phase when the Spirit has been given and denial of Christ is rejection of the Spirit.

Lk's tendency to show the preponderant role of the Spirit, to interpret the kingdom in the light of the Spirit was recognised in early tradition. Some MSS show in the text of the Lord's prayer, as reproduced by the evangelist, the words "the Holy Spirit come upon us and cleanse us" instead of "thy kingdom come." St. Gregory of Nyssa in the fourth and St. Maximus of Turin in the fifth century knew the reading. Though it is highly doubtful that Lk's original gospel had it, "it was not completely out of line with Lk's theology, for he saw the Holy Spirit to be as important an object of petition as the kingdom."[2]

---

[1]Cf. Bibl. article *"Infancy Narratives"* in *Theotokos*, 184-185; commentaries, esp., J. Fitzmyer, *The Gospel According to Luke* (I-IX), Anchor Bible, Garden City, NY, 1981, 288-348; M.J. Lagrange, O.P., *Evangile selon St.Luc*, Paris, 1948, 1-98; R. Laurentin, *Les evangiles de l'enfance du Christ*, Paris, 1982, 80-135; R.E. Brown, *The Birth of the Messiah*, Garden City, NY, 1977, part II; C.K. Barrett, *The Holy Spirit and the Gospel Tradition*, London, 1947; H.B. Swete, (qv) *The Holy Spirit in the New Testament*, London, 1909; G.W.H. Lampe, "The Holy Spirit in the Writings of St. Luke," in *Studies in the Gospel. Essays in Memory of R.H. Lightfoot*, Oxford, 1955, 159-200; H. von Baer, *Der Heilige Geist in den Lukas schriften*, Stuttgart, 1926; J. Borremans, "L'Esprit Saint dans la catéchèse évangélique de Luc," *Lumen Vitae*, 25 (1970), 103-122; G.T. Montague, *The Holy Spirit*, 253-270; Y.-M.J. Congar, O.P., *The Holy Spirit*, I, 44-49; *DBS*, XI, 300-398; J.A. Fitzmyer, S.J., *Luke the Theologian: Aspects of his Teaching*, New York, 1989; [2]Montague, *op. cit.*, 260.

LUTHER, MARTIN (1483-1546)

L's fundamental view that justification was brought about by faith alone through the imputation of Christ's merits to the sinner colours strongly his doctrine of the Holy Spirit.[1] He maintains the orthodox doctrine of the Holy Spirit, believes that his personal being is founded on the infinite eternal being of God. He speaks of creation as a work of the Trinity, within which conservation of things created in love is attributed to the Spirit. We know of him through his role in Redemption. L. does not enter into deep discussion of Trinitarian problems.

L. expressed very strong views on the Spirit's activity in the individual soul; here he saw a greater importance and presence than in the Church as a whole. As in creation so in redemption the Spirit begins from nothing. The Spirit works with the instruments or signs, that is the word and sacraments, but not *ex opere operato;* he enjoys in regard to these signs absolute sovereignty. The Spirit makes Christ present in the sinner, by his creative activity, Christ, the *Deus absconditus in carne*. He impels the one justified to the love of God, and this is expressed by gratuitous love of the neighbor. The Spirit, for L. is also *Illuminator*. By his *testimonium internum* and only by this one understands the Sacred Scripture, discerning the letter from the liberating spirit. The way in which the Holy Spirit acted especially in the soul of the sinner at the Lord's Supper was elaborated by L. Through the Lord's Supper, as through the other forms of the proclamation, the Holy Spirit made the grace of God in the death of Christ contemporary. L. also developed a whole theory of thanksgiving. L. conceived a grace of new creation, which was especially the gift of the Holy Spirit, not a static gift, but dynamic; it effected a radical transformation in the recipient, and made him a new being. Thanksgiving for the gift of grace was, therefore, not simply gratitude for favours received but the expression of the transformation wrought by the Holy Spirit.

The Church's role is also restricted by L. The Church, "Mother of believers," announcing salvation is indissolubly one with the Spirit, but it is merely the place where the Spirit makes Christ's redemptive work present through preaching and the Sacraments. L. does not value the idea of the Mystical Body, still less that of the Church as the spouse of Christ. It is to the individual soul that he applies the spousal image. He views the Church eschatologically; it looks to the final resurrection of the dead and eternal life, remaining meantime sinful.

---

[1]Cf. K.D. Schmidt, *Luthers Lehre vom Heiligen Geist*, in *Schrift und Bekenntnis*, Festschrift S. Schoffel, Berlin, 1950, 145ff; R. Prenter, *Spiritus Creator*, Studien zur Luthers Theologie, Munich, 1954; J.L. Witte, *DSp*. IV, 1.

M

MANNING, HENRY EDWARD (1808-1892)[1]

A notable convert like Newman from the Oxford Movement, M. differed in his philosophical and theological outlook, as in his career, from the other great English Cardinal of that century. His life and his thinking have to be studied in their own right, not merely to illuminate Newman by way of contrast. His responsibility was in the area of government; he was a force at Vatican I; he had deep and sincere social concern. And he was a spiritual writer on themes like the Sacred Heart of Jesus, the Catholic priesthood, and especially the Holy Spirit.

M's two works on this subject are *The Temporal Mission of the Holy Ghost*, 1865 and *The Internal Mission of the Holy Ghost*, 1875. M defines the temporal mission as follows: "The sending, advent, and office of the Holy Ghost through the Incarnate Son, and after the day of Pentecost." He adds that "the eternal procession of the Holy Ghost completes the mystery of the Holy Trinity ad intra; the temporal mission of the Holy Ghost completes the revelation of the Holy Trinity ad extra."[2] A central idea in his synthesis is that "the Holy Ghost came at Pentecost to constitute a union between himself and the mystical Body that would be absolute and indissoluble." The Spirit is thus the guarantor of all in the Church that is important and distinctive.

In subsequent chapters M.'s thinking moves into areas which would be matter of apologetics; the relation to revelation of reason which is its servant and champion; the whole theory of inspiration (qv) and the controversies it has stirred—here he takes a rigid position; as he does in dealing with the interpretation of Scripture and with the importance of Tradition.

The starting-point to each of these themes is their relationship to the Holy Spirit, but M. takes up a number of points which were then controversial, so that at times his text reads like a defence of Catholic principles. As such the book would have been welcome to those of M.'s communion who felt themselves intellectually attacked.

The plan of the second book, on the internal mission, is very different. In the first chapters M. relates grace and salvation to the Holy Spirit. Then he devotes chapters successively to the virtues of faith, hope and charity, to the glory of filial adoption, after which he deals in a chapter with the Gifts taken generally and then devotes a chapter to each separately, ending with separate treatment of the Fruits and the Beatitudes. A final chapter discusses devotion to the Holy Spirit. His language is not difficult, he does not delve deep into theology, aiming rather at an audience that would be known to him pastorally.

M.'s classification of the gifts may not prove universally acceptable. Apart from the three which obviously are attached to the will, he speaks of four which enter the domain of the intellect, two that perfect the speculative intellect, understanding and wisdom, two which perfect the practical intellect, science (or knowledge) and counsel. M. speaks thus of the three Gifts perfecting the will, "Holy fear is the beginning of the obedience of the children of God, piety is the filial affection of the sons of God; and fortitude makes the good soldiers of Jesus Christ."[2] He gives further description. Filial fear is of losing God, it is a fear of sin, a fear of the occasions of losing God, because it is by sin and its occasions that we may fall away from God.[3]

Fortitude he likewise makes explicit: it is a Gift of the Holy Spirit strengthening the soul against pain and fear, and supporting the soul in fulfilling every duty, not according to the light of nature only nor only according to the Ten Commandments, but according to all the higher works of perfection which come from the Gift of Counsel. M. calls on the soul, in regard to devotion, to weigh what it owes (Rom 5:5) and he calls for adoration and reparation.[4] His own personal odyssey is of interest. While he was still Archdeacon of Chichester he was asked by a reader of his sermons why he said so little about the Holy Spirit:

"From that day I never passed a day without acts of reparation to the Holy Ghost. I bought every book I could find on the work of the Holy Ghost and studied them. After five or six years I reached the last step to which reason alone could lead me, namely that the unanimous witness of the universal Church is the maximum of historical evidence for the revelation of Christianity. But the historical evidence is only human and human evidence is fallible after all. Then, and not before, I saw that the perpetual presence and office of the Holy Ghost, etc., raises the witness of the Church from a human to a divine certainty. And to him I submitted in the unity of the One Faith and Fold. Since then the Holy Ghost has been the chief thought and devotion of my whole soul."[5]

---

[1]Lives: A. W. Hutton, *English Leaders of Religion*, 1984; J. Fitzsimons, *Manning: Anglican and Catholic*, 1951; V. A. McClelland, *Manning, His Public Life and Influence*, 1865-92, 1951; S. Leslie, 1921; Y.-M.J. Congar, O. P., *The Holy Spirit*, I, 154-159; A. Boland, *DSp* X, 222-227; [2]Ed. 1865, p.295; [3]*Ibid.*, p.263; [4]*Ibid.*, 267; [5]Apud E. S. *Purcell, Life of Cardinal Manning, Archbishop of Westminster*, 1986, vol. II, 795-96.

MARIALIS CULTUS, 2 FEBRUARY, 1974[1]

The most important document issued by Paul VI (qv) on theology and devotion centred on the Blessed Virgin Mary, one of the greatest papal statements on this subject.[1] Its relevance to the theology of the Holy Spirit is seen in the section dealing with the Trinitarian aspect of the Marian theme. The Pope in a particularly rich passage deals with the relationship between Mary and the Holy Spirit and urges pastors and theologians to pursue studies on the subject. "From this research the basis of the hidden relationship between the Spirit of God and the Virgin of Nazareth will stand out conspicuously as will their common action in the Church. From these truths of the faith more profoundly pondered will come a piety more intensely lived." (art 27).

---

[1]Text in *AAS*, 66 (1974), 113-168; presentation by J. Galot, S.J., Cath. 1974, 319-321; commentaries, A. Kniazeff (Orthodox), M. Thurian, (French Reformed Church at the time, now a Catholic priest), Y.-M. Congar, O.P. (qv), *La Maison Dieu* 121 (1975) 98-121; Saggi sulla Esortazione apostolica 'Marialis Cultus': 7 contributors in *Marianum*, 1977, I-II, 7-131.

MARK, ST.

St. Mark is conscious, from the beginning of his Gospel, of the Spirit.[1] He gives us John the Baptist's promise: "'After me comes he who is mightier than I, the thong of whose sandals I am not worthy to stoop down and untie. I have baptized you with water; but he will baptize you with the Holy Spirit.'" (1:7-8). Next comes the narrative of the Baptism of Jesus with the clear account of the descent of the Spirit: "In those days Jesus came from Nazareth of Galilee and was baptized by John in the Jordan. And when he came up out of the water, immediately he saw the heavens opened and the Spirit descending upon him like a dove: and a voice came from heaven, 'Thou art my beloved Son; with thee I am well pleased.'" (1:9-11). There are snatches of OT texts but the essential reality is new: "In this scene of Jesus' baptism we have a fusion of many scripture-based teachings about Jesus. At his appearance on the stage of history the New Age has begun. He is prophet, Messiah and Son of God. The Holy Spirit, manifested in the form of a dove, functions in relationship to each of these motifs. He who will baptize with the Holy Spirit is shown to be one on whom the Spirit rests. The age promised by the prophets has begun."[2]

Mk gives us then the story of Christ's temptation. "The Spirit immediately drove him out into the wilderness. And he was in the wilderness forty days, tempted by Satan; and he was with the wild beasts; and the angels ministered to him" (1:12-13). This completes the prologue to the public ministry of Jesus. In the exercise of the ministry occurs an episode, with the comment from Jesus, which has special significance. Accused by his enemies of casting out devils "by the prince of demons," he refutes their argument and ends with the words: "'Truly, I say to you, all sins will be forgiven the sons of men, and whatever blasphemies they utter; but whoever blasphemes against the Holy Spirit never has forgiveness, but is guilty of an eternal sin'—for they had said, 'He has an unclean spirit.'" (3:28-30). "To call the Spirit of Jesus unclean is to sin against the Holy Spirit. And this response could only come from a sin against the light, calling evil what is good, ugly what is beautiful, falsehood what is truth. Since this saying of Jesus must be balanced against his constant call and offer of repentance, it is understandable how Christian tradition interpreted the 'sin against the Holy Spirit' to be that of final impenitence."[3]

This is not an elaborate doctrine of the Holy Spirit; but taken with the rest of the NT witness it coheres theologically.

---

[1]Cf. standard commentaries on relevant passages; G.T. Montague, S.M., *The Holy Spirit*, 237-252; [2]*Op. cit.*, 242; [3]*Op. cit.*, 247.

MATTHEW, ST.[1]

Like St. Mark Matthew relates the testimony of the Baptist: "'I baptize you with water for repentance, but he who is coming after me is mightier than I, whose sandals I am not worthy to carry; he will baptize you with the Holy Spirit and with fire.'" (3:11). Two details are distinctive: "not worthy to carry" for "to untie" and the addition of "with fire." Matthew also records the theophany of the baptism: "And when Jesus was baptized he went up immediately from the water, and behold, the heavens were opened and he saw the Spirit of God descending like a dove, and alighting on him; and lo, a voice from heaven, saying, 'This is my beloved Son, with whom I am well pleased'" (3:16-17). It is noteworthy that where Mark has "the Spirit," Matthew has "the Spirit of God (*to pneuma tou Theou*)."

There are variations too in Matthew's version of the controversy about exorcism. According to him Jesus says explicitly: "'But if it is by the Spirit of God that I cast out demons, then the kingdom of God has come among you.'" (12:28). Besides the affirmation that "'blasphemy against the Spirit will not be forgiven'" (12:31), Jesus declares: "'And whoever says a word against the Son of Man will be forgiven; but whoever speaks against the Holy Spirit will not be forgiven either in this age or in the age to come.'" (12:32).

In the Synoptic gospels it is in the power of the Spirit that Jesus fulfils his mission (Mt 3:11,16; 4:1; 12:18,28; Lk 4:14,18; 10:21). Whereas blasphemy against the Spirit may be understood as in Mark, "to speak against the Spirit" seems to make another point; this would be total rejection of salvation as offered by Jesus.

Matthew has two distinctive passages when compared with Mark. He reports: "When his mother Mary had been betrothed to Joseph, before they came together she was found to be with child of the Holy Spirit ... " (1:18). There follow the verses about St. Joseph, which are so much debated. (see article on St. Joseph.) But the primordial role of the Spirit is clearly marked and

this, also emphasized by Lk, was to become basic in the Christology of the New Testament.

The second singular contribution of Matthew is in 12:15-21: "Jesus, aware of this, withdrew from there. And many followed him, and he healed them all and ordered them not to make him known. This was to fulfil what was spoken by the prophet Isaiah: 'Behold, my servant whom I have chosen, my beloved with whom my soul is well pleased. I will put my Spirit upon him, and he shall proclaim justice to the Gentiles. He will not wrangle or cry aloud, nor will anyone hear his voice in the streets; he will not break a bruised reed or quench a smouldering wick, till he brings justice to victory; and in his name will the Gentiles hope.'" The passage from Isaiah is freely translated, the thrust is to depict a gentle Messiah. The inclusion of the reference to the Holy Spirit does in fact prepare for the next passage, which has already been considered on the exorcism and the debate ensuing. Here Matthew provides more than Mk or Lk. In general "Matthew's central discerning sign is Jesus himself. It is upon him that the Spirit rests (3:16; 12:18). If the Church has the Spirit it is only because she has Jesus. Or to put it another way, it is not because of the Spirit that she has Jesus (Luke's view) but because of Jesus that she has the Spirit."[2]

---

[1]G. T. Montague, *The Holy Spirit*, 302-310; standard commentaries on the relevant passages; [2]G. T. Montague, op.cit., 308.

MAXIMILIAN KOLBE, ST. (1894-1941)[1]

The manner of St. Maximilian's death seems to embody perfectly the action of the Holy Spirit. To choose death so as to release another person from the sentence, to do so spontaneously and to adhere to one's choice to the point of consummation is explainable, as it is justifiable, only by belief in the Spirit's presence and power. The event sealed a life increasingly ruled by the Spirit. M. was an ardent apostle, missionary in Japan, founder of vast Christian communites, ready to mobilize modern means of evangelization, especially the media; and a very remarkable theologian in the Franciscan tradition. The idea of "the Immaculate one" was intrinsic to his outlook; belief in Mary's universal mediation a bedrock.

M. developed his thought on the Holy Spirit most originally. He was led into these hitherto unknown depths by his contemplation of the Immaculate one. He was captivated, as a result of a visit to Lourdes, by the words spoken to Bernadette: "I am the Immaculate Conception; he kept turning them over in his mind with the words of God to Moses, "'I am who am.'" Eventually he was led to a daring conclusion, an insight received in prayer, some say. In the Holy Trinity the Spirit is an Immaculate Conception, so called on the basis of analogy; thus there is added meaning to the title Immaculate Conception, created, given to our Lady. "Whereas the mission of the Son terminates in the hypostatic assumption of a human nature so as to be his proprium, to be his exclusive possession, to be a man who is a divine person, that of the Holy Spirit terminates in a sponsal union with a human person, not assumed hypostatically, but so perfectly appropriated as to share the Holy Spirit's name: Immaculate Conception. The naming of the Holy Spirit as the eternal Immaculate Conception deserves to be considered as a major contribution to the progress of theology and an accurate explicitation of one of the pillars of Franciscan theology, the Immaculate Conception of the Mother of God. As with the names of the other divine Persons, so too this one entails an analogy. Conception among creatures, in particular human, involves two elements: first being the fruit of the mutual love of parents, and second whose mutual love is the beginning of existence of the child conceived. In so far as conception is predicated properly and univocally of created persons, both elements must be present. Angels are not conceived. Neither were Adam and Eve. In his humanity our Lord is conceived as the fruit of the love of the Father and of the Virgin but is not a conception, because his conception is not the beginning of his origin as a Person. The Holy Spirit, however, in the proper, though analogical sense, is a conception, because the fruit of the mutual love of Father and Son, even if they are not thereby his parents. Secondly, that conception is his origin, even if being eternal, it is not the beginning of the existence of one who like Father and Son, being divine, has no beginning in existence, but is eternal. Further, that love of Father and Son being divine, therefore without defect, without any impurity, utterly generous or liberality itself, the conception of the Holy Spirit is immaculate and the person so conceived is the Immaculate Conception. Therein is the peculiar connection with the human person whose beginning of existence is a conception, but whose conception, unlike that of any other creature is im-

maculate, and she the Immaculate Conception because in her is the total love of Father and Son that is in the Holy Spirit, and makes his purity to be without defect or stain; in her by grace, in him by nature."[2]

M. outlines the Trinitarian background to the mystery of Mary. "The summit of the love of creation returning to God is the Immaculate one, the being without the stain of sin, wholly faithful, wholly of God. Not even for an instant did her will depart from the will of God. She belonged always and freely to God. And in her takes place the miracle of God's union with creation.... The Father, as he was her spouse, entrusted his Son to her; the Son descended into her virginal womb, becoming her Son, while the Holy Spirit formed the body of Jesus in her in a prodigious manner, and taking up his abode in her soul compenetrates it so ineffably that the title 'Spouse of the Holy Spirit' is a very remote image to express the life of the Holy Spirit in her, and through her. In Jesus there are two natures, the divine and human and one person, divine, while here there are two natures and there are also two persons, the Holy Spirit and the Immaculate one, yet the union of the divinity with the humanity is beyond all understanding."[3]

M. insists on the closeness of the bond between the Spirit and the Immaculate one: "The union of the Holy Spirit with the Immaculate Virgin is so close that the Holy Spirit, who has deeply compenetrated the soul of the Immaculate one, exerts no influence on souls save by means of her. Precisely because of this she became the Mediatress of all graces, for this reason precisely she is the Queen of angels and saints, and the Help of Christians and the Refuge of Sinners."[4]

Hans Urs von Balthasar (qv) thought that many theological questions in regard to the Trinity were avoided because of their challenge. M., through his contemplation of the Immaculate one, was led to explore problems about the Holy Spirit and propose solutions hitherto undreamt of. He was influenced by the great Franciscan Doctors, St. Bonaventure (qv) and John Duns Scotus, and by St. Louis Marie Grignion de Montfort (qv); but he broke out of the "classical" mould, and suggested new, daring ideas which will, when fully assimilated into Trinitarian theology, especially that which treats of the Holy Spirit, invigorate and revitalize the whole of our thinking. Stemming from his intuition of the Spirit as the Eternal Immaculate Conception, he related a fundamental concept in Christian thought, obedience, to the procession of the Spirit. Obedience here is total conformity with the divine will. Obedience is here understood in its plenary sense, which comprises the maximum of freedom and initiative. All through the intellectual analysis, so delicate, so easily misunderstood, the analogy intrinsic to our speculation must prevail.

"Obedience," says one of M.'s best commentators, "understood as conformity of will of a person conceived with the divine will, is the essence of love and entails a *'perfectio simpliciter simplex'* precisely in relation to the position of the Holy Spirit within the order of divine Persons. In the Holy Spirit this conformity is majestic in character, for the conformity of will is but the independence and unity of the divine nature. In the created person the conformity is humble and obedient in character, being rooted in the dependence of the creature and proportionate to the perfection of its humility. Where that conformity is perfect by grace, as in the conception of Mary, that person is the Immaculate Conception, because she enjoys as a person a position in relation to the Father and the Son parallel to that of the Holy Spirit; the fruit of their mutual love, and in whom their total love reposes, a 'part' of the Trinity."[5]

M. applied the concept of fecundity to the Holy Spirit; here he seems to echo St. Louis Marie de Montfort (qv). When he speaks of the Spirit's "infecundity" he has in mind the fact that no other Person comes from him. This casts a veil over the entire Godhead. The fecundity of the Holy Spirit removes this veil by the Immaculate Conception, which culminated in the Incarnation. Through the operation of this mystery, which was the work of the Holy Spirit the Trinity itself would be revealed.

Again M. applies to the Spirit the idea of mediation. This function too M. would see as rooted in the name of the Spirit, the eternal Immaculate Conception; it is exercised outside, not within the Trinity and when it is so exercised this is done through the instrumentality of the Immaculate. Thus it is a kind of fecundity, the spiritual maternity of the Mother of God. Through the fecundity of the Spirit the Word comes to us; through his mediation we come to the Word. To elaborate this idea and others expressed by this saint of our time will be the task of his true disciples. Thus the stress in the Franciscan school on the objective character of appropriation needs to be considered. "The merit of St. Maximilian rests in showing how the mission of the Holy Spirit, capable of multiple visible forms in contrast to the one visible form of the Son, centres in one person, the Immaculate, and the focus for all the rest; and that mission so centred is best formulated in terms of the doctrine of appropriation."[6]

M. showed admirably how theology of the Spirit is enriched, advanced, by reflection on the mystery of Mary. In that he joins many great thinkers of Vatican II, which he did not live to see on earth, for which he, in so many different ways, not least by the witness of his heroic death, helped to prepare. A Marian theologian of the Council, H. M. Manteau-Bonamy, who believed that its teaching on the Spirit and Mary marked a landmark in Latin theology, knows how to explain a controverted text in which M. spoke of Mary as "in a certain sense the incarnation of the Holy Spirit" (words spoken a fortnight before his arrest). H. M. Manteau-Bonamy thinks that as Vatican II was moving towards an explanation of Mary's mediation according to the Holy Spirit, a text by M. would admirably express such thinking, from which these extracts are taken: "To this day our relation, in the economy of the Redemption to Mary Co-Redemptress and Dispenser of graces, has not been perceived in its perfection.... The work of the Redemption depends immediately on the second divine Person, Jesus Christ, who reconciled us to the Father by his blood, atoned for the sin of Adam and merited for us sanctifying grace and different actual graces, not less than the right to enter the kingdom of heaven. Nevertheless the third divine Person of the most Holy Trinity participates also in this work. In fact by the power of the Redemption wrought by Christ, the Holy Spirit transforms the souls of men into temples of God; he secures for us adoption as sons of God and makes us heirs of the heavenly kingdom, according to St. Paul's word, 'you have been washed, you have been justified by the name of our Lord Jesus Christ and by the Spirit of our God' (1 Cor 6:11).

"Descending to the most intimate part of our souls the Holy Spirit, God Love, unites us with the two other divine Persons. That is why St. Paul in his letter to the Romans says: 'for we do not know how to pray as we ought, but the Spirit himself intercedes for us with sighs too deep for words.' (Rom 8:26). In the same way it is said in the Epistle to the Corinthians that the distribution of graces depends on the Holy Spirit's will—1 Cor 12:8-11 is quoted. In the same way as the Son, to manifest his immense love, became man, so the third Person, God Love, wished to show his mediation with the Father and the Son by a visible sign. This sign is the Heart of the Immaculate Virgin, as the saints tell us, especially those who consider Mary as Spouse of the Holy Spirit.... In the same way then as the second divine Person appears in his Incarnation as the 'fruit of the Woman' so does the Holy Spirit visibly manifest his participation in the work of Redemption through the Immaculate Virgin, who while being a person distinct from him, is so united to him that it surpasses our human manner of understanding. Then though the hypostatic union of the human and the divine in the unique Person of Christ is different, all the same nevertheless the action of Mary is the very action of the Holy Spirit. In fact Mary as Spouse of the Holy Spirit is so elevated above every created perfection that she accomplishes in everything the will of the Holy Spirit, who dwells in her since the first moment of her conception."[7]

Mary, M. concludes, was made Co-redemptress of the human race, as Mother of Jesus the Saviour; as Spouse of the Holy Spirit she participates in the distribution of all graces. He sees the doctrine of the New Eve as a way of speaking of true and strict mediation. "In these latter times especially we contemplate Mary in her role as our Mediatress."

---

[1]Bibl. E. Piacentini, *Miles Immaculatae* 7 (1971) 437-447; bibl. on M's Marian theology, *Theotokos*, 215; cf. esp., "La Mariologia di S. Massimiliano M. Kolbe," *Atti del Congresso Internazionale Roma*, 8-12 ottobre 1984; Rome Ed. Miscellanea Francescana, 751pp, 1985; in this collection cf. esp., E. Piacentini, OFMConv., "Analisi degli scritti di P. Kolbe e loro valorizzazione teologica," 327-381, esp., "Attualità e validità del linguaggio kolbiano oggi," 380f; P. Fehlner, OFMConv., "The Immaculate and the Mystery of the Trinity in the Thought of S. Maximilian Kolbe," 382-416, esp., "The Holy Spirit," 391-404; H. M. Manteau-Bonamy, O.P., "Saint Maximilien Marie Kolbe et la médiation de l'Immaculée," 508-530, esp. 518-530; D. Bertetto, S.D.B., "La maternità sprituale di Maria negli scritti di Kolbe e negli atti del Vaticano II," 531-563; esp., 558-563; E. Piacentini, *DSp* X, 860f; cf. F. Villepelée, *Le Bienheureux P. Kolbe. L'Immaculée révèle le Saint Esprit*, Paris, 1974; E. Piacentini, OFMConv., "Valutazione teologica e ripercussioni ecumeniche nella Mariologia del P. M. M. Kolbe," *Ephemerides Mariologicae* 21 (1971) 217-256; H. M. Manteau-Bonamy, O.P., *La doctrine mariale du P. Kolbe*, Paris, 1975; [2]P. Fehlner, *op. cit.*, 391f; 721, [3]*Scritti*, III, apud D. Bertetto, *op. cit.*, 560 [4]*Scritti*, III, 769, apud D. Bertetto, *op. cit.*, 538; [5]P. Fehlner, OFMConv., *op. cit.*, 394; [6]*Ibid.*, 400; [7]H. M. Manteau-Bonamy, O.P., *op. cit.*, 521, 527f; he is quoting from *Miles Immaculatae*, IV-VI, 1938.

MAXIMUS THE CONFESSOR, ST. (c. 580-662)

To the works in which M.'s Trinitarian theology was sought until recently we must now add a remarkable recent find.[1] In 1987 Michel van Esbroeck, S. J. published the long awaited Byzantine *Life of Mary*, from which extracts had been published by Martin Jugie, A. A., Antoine Wenger, A. A., and Jean Galot, S. J., in the belief that it was the work of John the Geometer. In his edition of a Georgian manuscript of the text M. van Esbroeck claimed that the real author was M. There are passages of interest to his theology of the Holy Spirit. Cardinal Hans Urs von Balthasar (qv) active in the first days of revival in studies on M. found the Marian text "recognisable" as from the great Byzantine.[2] The international congress held in Fribourg in 1982, itself an indication of the interest in his writings, could not take account of the discovery, scarcely less than sensational.[3]

M.'s whole cast of thought has been rightly called Trinitarian, and from Gregory of Nazianzus (qv) he took sound doctrine on the importance of relations in the distinction of Persons. "For relation has the capacity to show one in the other at the same time those of which it is and is said to be in relation not allowing them to be considered one after another."[4] He also had a finely argued theory of the Monad and the Triad, of the *ousia* (the nature) and the *hypostasis* (person) as this is found in all three.

M. has many references to the Spirit. His attitude to the *Filioque* (qv) has understandably provoked comment. The question has been exhaustively studied recently by P. Piret in his monograph on M.'s Christology and Trinitarian theology, and in a paper presented to *Studia Patristica*, the 1983 Patristic Congress, by G. C. Berthold.

M. had come under western influence, taken part in the Lateran Council, 649 which condemned the Monothelite heresy. He was viewed with suspicion in the eastern capital by theologians and officials and had to defend himself. His thought was subtle and resolutely objective. He held that the Spirit came from the Father through the Son: "Now just as the Holy Spirit is by nature and in essence the Spirit of God the Father so is he by nature and essence the Spirit of the Son, since he proceeds substantially and in an ineffable way from the Father through the begotten Son."[5] This formula had already a sacred history, in the east with Origen, Athanasius, Basil and Gregory of

Nyssa, in the west with Tertullian, Hilary and Marius Victorinus; it will be used later by St. John of Damascus and will be justified by St. Thomas Aquinas (qv).

M. sought to explain the Latin position: "(The Roman theologians) displayed the concordant usage of the Latin Fathers, and also of Cyril of Alexandria, taken from the sacred study which he accomplished on St. John the Evangelist. Starting from there they have shown that they themselves do not make the Son cause (*aitian*) of the Spirit. They have in effect seen that the Father is sole cause (*mian aitian*) of the Son and of the Spirit, of the former by begetting (*kata ten gennesin*), and of the latter by procession (*kata ten ekporeusin*). But they will show deliberately the fact of the Spirit's proceeding as through the Son. Thus they preserve communion in the *ousia* and its non-succession."[6]

The word "cause" used here does not imply inferiority. M. wishes to show that the Latins did not compromise the identity of the *ousia*: "In fact whoever recognises the simplicity of the *ousia* common to the three hypostases at the same time as the Trinitarian order of the Father and the Son and the Holy Spirit, will equally recognise that the divine *ousia* of the Spirit, who is caused by the Father, is the *ousia* of the Father who eternally begets the Son." How then came the confusion between Latins and Greeks in regard to faith which seems common to both? "From the fact, M. thinks, that the two languages are different and bear with unease their respective translations. In the relation of the Spirit to the Father and the Son, we can consider the *ekporeuesthai* of the Spirit from the Father, and his *proienai* from the Father through the Son. Thus Maximus proposes a distinction between the *ekporeuesthai*, which means the unique starting-point of the origin of the Spirit, that is the Father, and the *proienai*, which means the progression in the passage of the Spirit, namely the Father and the Son."[7] Thus M. thought to preserve the identity of the *ousia* and the right order of Persons.

In the *Life of Mary* M. writes thus of the Holy Spirit in the Annunciation: "Meanwhile your conception will not be of a kind to lose your virginity, but rather a seal and guarantee of the absence of all stain and a source of holiness. For the Holy Spirit will come upon you beforehand to adorn you as a betrothed of the Lord, to sanctify from the beginning, your soul which is holy and endowed with divine charm, and your body. And

immediately the immortal betrothed, your Son, who is the power of the Most High, will cover you, for Christ is the power of God and the wisdom of God; he it is who will cover you and build within you the temple most holy of his body."[8] This is an idea found among some of the early Fathers, that it is the Lord himself who fashions his body.

Later M. states that Mary was overjoyed and convinced that nothing was impossible with God by the archangel's announcement that the Holy Spirit would come upon her and the power of the Most High overshadow her; he assumes that she knew fully what the Spirit meant in the scheme of things. Before commenting on the Magnificat he tells us that Elizabeth, because she was filled with the Holy Spirit, knew from him of Mary's virginal conception. A little further on he thus introduces Mary's own words: "Then this blessed Mary, adorned with every grace, as she was a virgin and mother in a way surpassing nature, became here the cause of prophecy for others. Thus also she spoke words full of prophecies, full of graces, of prayer and prediction, for she was filled with the Holy Spirit, as the evangelist informs us."[9] This view is akin to that of Sergius Bulgakov (qv).

M.'s comment on the Baptism (qv) of Jesus is of interest: "Nevertheless it was not only then that the Holy Spirit stayed with him, or only at that moment that he came, for how could that be for one in whom dwelt from the beginning all the fullness of the godhead? but that he should be seen by all, he who is the true Son of God and the true God. And I think that, as he worked numerous other miracles as signs for us, thus there was a sign for us after the descent of the Holy Spirit at the Baptism. Thus the coming of the Holy Spirit took place, and with the coming the Father's voice was heard bearing witness to the Lord Jesus: 'this is my beloved Son in whom I am well pleased. And thus at the Jordan the unique Holy Trinity was manifested, united in essence and divided in three hypostases. A threefold hypostasis for to each came his own designation. The Son saw himself with the body in the Jordan, the Spirit descended on him as a dove, the Father from on high bore witness to his well-beloved Son."[10] M. explains why the voice was heard by all, but only John saw the descent—he recalls the episode of Moses (qv) on Sinai. Later M. shows Mary preparing the apostles by prayer and fasting for the coming of the Spirit.

Dealing with the Spirit as the author of grace,

M. shows how nature and the supernatural work together: "We cannot say that grace alone works knowledge of divine mysteries in the saints without the natural powers of intelligence. Otherwise we should imagine that the holy prophets were not capable of understanding the power of the illuminations which the Holy Spirit granted to them. The grace of the Holy Spirit does not, in the saints, work either wisdom without their reason which receives it, or gnosis without the understanding faculty, or faith in the certainty of mind and reason about things to come still hidden from all, or the gift of healing without natural love of men, or any other gift without the appropriate habit and power."[11] M. insists on the divine aid needed.

[1]Works *PG* 90, 91; bibliography: P. Sherwood, *An Annotated Date-List of the Works of Maximus the Confessor*, Rome, 1952; I. Dalmais, *DSp* X, 835-847; critical edition of *Quaestiones ad Thalassum*, CCSG, J. Declerck, 1982; cf. Hans Urs von Balthasar, *Kosmische Liturgie*, 2 ed., Einsiedeln, 1961, French tr., 1947; W. Volker, *Maximus Confessor als Meister des geistlichen Lebens*, Wiesbaden, 1965; Michel Garrigues, *La charité, avenir divin de l'homme, Maxime le Confesseur*, Paris, 1976; esp. P. Piret *Le Christ et la Trinité selon Maxime le Confesseur*, Paris 1983; esp. F. Heinzer and C. Schönborn (ed.), *Maximus Confessor*, Fribourg, 1982; G. C. Berthold, "Maximus the Confessor and the Filioque" *Studia Patristica*, 1983, 113-117; V. Grumel, *DTC* X, 1, 448-459; *Trinitas*, 160-61; [2]Communication from M. van Esbroeck to the author: [3]Cf. M. O'Carroll, C.S.Sp., "The Life of Mary", *ITQ* 53 (1987), 235.6; [4]*Pater, PG* 90, 884C; [5]*Quaestiones ad Thalassum*, 63, *PG* 90, 672C; [6]*Op.cit.*, 98-105; [7]*L.cit.*; [8]*Maxime le Confesseur, Vie de la Vierge*, tr. M-J. van *Esbroeck, S.J., CSCO* 479, Scriptores Iberici, 22, no. 23, p.18; [9]*Ibid.*, 26, p. 21; [10]*Ibid.*, 66, p. 56: [11]*Quaestiones ad Thalassum*, 59, *PG* 90, 606B.

McKENNA, SISTER BRIEGE (1946-)

One of the truly great charismatic figures of this, or perhaps any, century, this Poor Clare Sister from Newry, Northern Ireland, has exercised a remarkable dual ministry, on the one hand of healing and with it a spiritual therapy of the most profound kind for priests. No lay person has preached retreats to priests and bishops as widely and frequently as she has done. This ministry to the ordained ministers has taken her to places as far apart as Japan, Brazil, Korea, Australia, Chile, Peru, Venezuela, the Philippines, Central African states, Belgium, the United States, England and her native Ireland. She has helped priests remake their lives; she has prayed with and for people of any and every social class; she prayed with the president of Peru and was invited by the president of Brazil to speak with him and pray with him. Her personal messages from the Lord to priests have been restorative and invigorating.

The personality behind this varied, beneficial programme is of interest to the theologian of the Spirit. Briege McKenna was born on Pentecost Sunday, 1946 and has a sense of Pentecost as personally important to her. It is Jesus who speaks to her the very many internal locutions which have been meaningful for her and others, but it is the Spirit whom she sees as the light and force of all. Writing on "Baptism in the Holy Spirit" she says: We receive the gift of the Spirit at Baptism. We receive the Holy Spirit throughout our lives—at communion time and through all the Sacraments. It's like receiving a birthday gift. If I received a birthday gift and I got totally distracted by the petty wrappings and never opened the gift, I could never use the contents. The contents are valuable, not the wrappings, the externals. So it is with the release of the Holy Spirit. The Holy Spirit is given to us by Jesus himself. Jesus said: "I will send my Spirit and he will teach you all things and help you to understand.' Baptism in the Spirit is opening up the gifts we receive through Baptism and becoming open to the power of the Spirit to understand the Sacraments and the power of the Sacraments. Baptism in the Spirit enables us to understand all the gifts given to us to enable us to grow in holiness. Through this Baptism in the Spirit the Sacraments themselves take on greater meaning."[1]

Sister Briege has worked many miracles of healing. Her ministry began with her own miraculous recovery from rheumatoid arthritis, already incurable, and very painful: "The Lord, as though he had read my mind, said to me: 'Don't look at him, look at me.' I remember looking at the clock as I closed my eyes. It was 9:15 a.m., December 9, 1970. The only prayer I said was 'Jesus, please help me.' At that moment, I felt a hand touch my head and thought it was the priest who had come over to me. I opened my eyes and no one was there, but there was a power going through my body ... I looked down. My fingers had been stiff, but not deformed like my feet. There had been sores on my elbows. I looked at myself. My fingers were limber, the sores had gone, and I could see that my feet, in sandals, were no longer deformed. I jumped up screaming, 'Jesus, you're right here'"[2] Sister Briege received, with the Master's explicit assurance, the gift of healing. After initial hesitation she has used it.

All the time she is conscious of the Spirit's action: "I went from December of 1970 to June of 1971 having a marvellous experience of Pentecost."[3] Her personal sanctification and her efficacy in ministry spring from Jesus and are the work of the Spirit.

---

[1] *Miracles do Happen*, by Sister Briege McKenna, O. S. C., Ann Arbor, Michigan, Dublin, 1987; a personal record; p. 57; [2] *Op. cit.*, p. 4' [3] *Op. cir.*, p.5.

MISSION OF THE SPIRIT, THE

A mission of a divine Person is a projection outside the godhead of a procession (qv) which is immanent in the divine life: a prolongation at a moment in time which leads to the existence of the eternal divine Person in a new manner in a rational creature.[1] Theologians distinguish visible and invisible missions; the first has traditionally been affirmed of the Incarnation, the Baptism of Jesus, and Pentecost, of the Son in the Incarnation, the "mission of missions", and of the Holy Spirit in the Baptism and Pentecost. Recently Fr. H.M. Manteau-Bonamy, O.P., has contended that the mission of the Spirit at the Annunciation was also visible, the first time this has been taught by the Latin Church.

The mission of the Son is frequently affirmed in St. John's gospel: "For God sent the Son into the world, not to condemn the world, but that the world might be saved through him" (Jn 3:17; cp. 5;23; 6:38,39; 6:58; 12:44; 17:23; esp. 20:21). St. Paul is equally explicit: "But when the time had fully come, God sent forth his Son, born of a woman, born under the law, to redeem those who were under the law, so that we might receive adoption as sons" (Gal 4:4).

The mission of the Spirit at Pentecost was thus described in a promise: "'But the Counsellor, the Holy Spirit, whom the Father will send in my name, he will teach you all things, and bring to your remembrance all that I have said to you.'" (Jn 14:26; cp. Lk 24:29; Acts 1:4-5). For the visible mission of the Spirit at the Baptism the gospels use the word "descend" (Mt:3-17; Mk 1:9-11; Lk 3:21-22: Jn 1:31-34). It is traditionally spoken of as a mission.

St. Paul thus describes the invisible mission of the Spirit: "And because you are sons, God sent the Spirit of his Son into our hearts crying 'Abba! Father!'" (Gal 4:6). Hence arises the problem of the indwelling (qv).

---

[1] Cf. *Trinitas*, s.v., 161-162.

MISSIONARY ACTIVITY[1]

One of the important, most welcome fruits of the Second Vatican Council was the rightful prominence given to the Holy Spirit in the theology of the Missions. An indicator of the changed thinking would be the difference there is in teaching on this subject between the Encyclicals on the Missions published before the Council and the outstanding papal document which appeared after it, *Evangelii Nuntiandi* (qv), Paul VI's (qv) Apostolic Exhortation. This text reflects the thinking which had been stimulated by the Council. Benedict XV's *Maximum Illud*, 30 November, 1919, Pius XI's *Rerum Ecclesiae*, 28 February, 1926, Pius XII's *Evangelii Praecones*, 2 June, 1951 and *Fidei Donum*, 15 January, 1957 and John XXIII's *Princeps Pastorum*, 28 November, 1959, all had a deep effect on the life and missionary programme of the Church. *Rerum Ecclesiae* and *Fidei Donum* had probably the greatest impact due to a combination of favourable circumstances in each case. *Rerum Ecclesiae* was supported by an immense tide of missionary zeal, manifest in new institutes and new upsurge in older ones, as it was a charter for the neophytes flocking into the Church in certain areas of the world. *Fidei Donum* appeared at a time when it was becoming clear that the Missions were not the concern merely of missionaries: the whole Church was conscious of its duty in this task. Hence the large numbers of priests released from their own dioceses to labour directly in the field. All the time the great central agencies directed from Rome were increasing organisational and recruitment skills.

What then needed to be done by the Council? The story of the schema on the Church's missionary activity tells the answer: a faltering one strangely but in the end satisfactory. After some early drafts, the Missions suffered the same fate as other themes, reduction of the text to a skeleton composed of propositions, which of their nature could be read as platitudes. The text was presented to the third session of the Council and severely criticised, notably by a missionary bishop, Donal Lamont, O. Carm., of Umtali; it was sent back for redrafting. This time, with the help of theologians versed in ecclesiology, among them, Fr. Y.-M.J. Congar, O. P. (qv), a succinct theology of the missions was stated, Trinitarian in its general reference as the Church itself: "The Church on earth is by its very nature missionary since, according to the plan of the Father, it has its origin in the mission of the Son and the Holy Spirit. This plan flows from 'fountain-like love,' the love of God the Father. As the principle without principle from whom the Son is generated and from whom the Holy Spirit proceeds through the Son, God in his great and merciful kindness freely creates us and moreover, graciously calls us to share in his life and glory."[2] After outlining the plan of salvation and the sending of the Son as the "true Mediator", the text returns to the theme of the Spirit: "Christ, whom the Father sanctified and sent into the world (cf. Jn 10:36), said of himself: 'The Spirit of the Lord is upon me, because he anointed me; to bring good news to the poor he sent me, to heal the broken-hearted, to proclaim to the captives release, and sight to the blind' (Lk 4:18)."[3]

The Council text gives a more explicit teaching on the role of the Holy Spirit. "Now what was once preached by the Lord, or fulfilled in him for the salvation of mankind, must be proclaimed and spread to the ends of the earth (Acts 1:8), starting from Jerusalem (cf. Lk 24:27), so that what was accomplished for the salvation of all men may, in the course of time, achieve its universal effect. To do this Christ sent the Holy Spirit from the Father to achieve inwardly his saving influence, and to promote the spread of the Church. Without doubt, the Holy Spirit was at work in the world before Christ was glorified. On the day of Pentecost, however, he came down on the disciples that he might remain with them forever (cf. Jn 14:16); on that day the Church was openly displayed to the crowd and the spread of the Gospel among the nations, through preaching, was begun. Finally, on that day was foreshadowed the union of all peoples in the Catholicity of the faith by means of the Church of the New Alliance, a Church which speaks every language, understands and embraces all tongues in charity, and thus overcomes the dispersion of Babel. The 'acts of the Apostles' began with Pentecost, just as Christ was conceived in the Virgin Mary with the coming of the Holy Spirit and was moved to begin his ministry by the descent of the same Holy Spirit, who came down upon him while he was praying. Before freely laying down his life for the world, the Lord Jesus organized the apostolic ministry and promised to sent the Holy Spirit, in such a way that both would be always and everywhere associated in the fulfilment of the work of salvation. Throughout the ages the Holy Spirit makes the entire Church 'one in communion and ministry; and provides her with different hierarchical and charismatic gifts', giving life to ecclesiastical structures, being as it were their soul, and inspiring in the hearts of the faithful that same spirit of mission which impelled Christ himself. He even at times visibly anticipates apostolic action, just as in various ways he unceasingly accompanies and directs it."[4]

Later the conciliar text reads: "The mission of the Church is carried out by means of that activity through which, in obedience to Christ's command and moved by the grace and love of the Holy Spirit, the Church makes itself fully present to all men and peoples in order to lead them to the faith, freedom and peace of Christ by the example of its life and teaching, by the Sacraments and other means of grace."[5]

This thinking was to influence the deliberations of the episcopal synod of 1974 and therefore of Paul VI's (qv) Apostolic Exhortation *Evangelii Nuntiandi* which was based on this synod's findings. The Council helped to clarify and give emphasis to two ideas which are complementary and effectively focussed attention on the Holy Spirit: Missions are the concern of the whole Church; to understand what Missions mean we must go right to the pure initial source, biblical that is. There the central essential role belongs to the Holy Spirit, and it is he who confers the note of universality on the Church's missionary vocation.

Such a conception simplifies much that has been noted in discourse, discussion and debate on the theology of Mission. With the central thesis in place, it is easy to fit all the subordinate ideas into their logically suitable place. Full allowance can be made for the charismatic personalities who have always and will always be used by God for the expansion and development of the Christian missions. Allowance can be made also for the hidden preparation effected by God in the peoples whom he calls, at the moment decreed by his divine Providence, to the Faith.

The effect of the existing active community on non-Christian lands is now given importance. So as a matter of Christian common-sense is witness, especially witness of a heroic kind, in works of charity, exceptionally powerful in martyrdom which marks the growth of Church through the centuries. Through all the diverse factors and forces which combine to foster missionary beginnings and growth the Spirit is dominant.

[1]For general bibl. cf. L. Vriens et al., *Critical Bibliography of Missiology*, tr. Nymegen, 1960; A. Retif, *Foi au Christ et Mission d'après les Actes des Apôtres*, Paris, 1953; Y. Goudreault. *L'Eglise missionaire et ses fondements bibliques: L'Eglise dans la Bible* (Studia 13) Montreal 1962; F. Hahn, *Das Verständnis der Mission im Neuen Testament*, Neukirchen-Vluyn, 1963; J. Dupont, "Le Salut des Gentils et la signification théologique du livre des Actes." *Etudes ser les Actes des Apôtres* (Lectio divina 45), Paris, 1967, 93-119, English tr., New York, 1979; M. Hengel, "Die Ursprunge der Christlichen Mission" *NTS* 18 (1971,72) 15-38; J. Legrand, J. Pathrapankal, M. Vellanickel, *Good News and Witness. The New Testament Understanding of Evangelization*, Bangalore, 1973; Q. G. Wilson, *The Gentiles and the Gentile Mission in Luke-Acts*, Cambridge, 1973; *L'oeuvre de Luc, Actes et Evangile. Le ministères selon le Nouveau Testament*, Paris, 1974, 207-240; G. Haya Prats, *L'Esprit force de l'Eglise*, Paris, 1975; E. Cothenet, "Les prophètes chrétiens comme exégètes charismatiques de l'Ecriture" in *Prophetic Vocation in New Testament Times and Today*, J. Panagopoulos, Leyden, 1977, 77-107; A. Trites, *The New Testament Concept of Witness*, Cambridge, 1977; F. Bovon, *Luc le théologien*, Paris, 1978, 342-361; *DSp*, XIII, "Mission et Missions", esp "Mission et Missions dans la Bible", E. Cothenet, 1361-73; for the Council teaching cf. J. Schotte, ed., *Mission nach den Konzil*, 1967, Y.-M.J. Congar, O.P., "Theologische Grundlegung", 134-172; *Commentary on the Documents of Vatican II*, ed. H. Vorgrimler, London, 1969, IV, Suso Brechter, 87-181, esp. 96-100; Unam Sanctam series of commentaries, *L'activité missionaire de l'Eglise*, Paris, 1967. D. Senior, c.p. and C. Stuhlmueller, C.P. *The Biblical Foundations of Mission*, New York, 1983; [2]Decree, 2, Flannery I, 814; [3]*Op.cit.*, 3, 815; [4]*Ibid.*, 814,5; [5]*Ibid.*, 5.

MOSES[1]

There may appear to be slight evidence of the presence of the Spirit in the life of Moses, or of his consciousness of the Spirit. It may appear necessary to impose a schema on the varied materials presented to us in the sacred text: an exercise which may seem arbitrary. Such an interpretation has not so far been attempted.

And yet the invitation to do so is clear. Twice in Acts we are reminded of the word of Moses: "'The Lord your God will raise up for you a prophet like me from among you, from your brethren—him you shall heed—just as you desired of the Lord your God at Horeb on the day of the assembly, when you said, "Let me not hear again the voice of the Lord my God, or see this great fire any more, lest I die." And the Lord said to me, 'They have rightly said all that they have spoken. I will raise up for them a prophet like you from among their brethren; and I will put my words in his mouth, and he shall speak to them all that I command him. And whoever will not give heed to my words which he shall speak in my name, I

myself will require it of him.'" (Deut 18:15-19). At Solomon's portico in the temple after the healing of the lame man, when Peter addressed those drawn by the miracle, he applied these words to Christ. (Acts 2:22). So did St. Stephen in his apologia before the council before his death (Acts 7:37).

Though Moses "is not precisely conceived as a prophet" (J. McKenzie) the words of Deut must have a meaning: "And there has not arisen a prophet since in Israel like Moses, whom the Lord knew face to face, none like him for all the signs and wonders which the Lord sent him to do in the land of Egypt, to Pharaoh and to all his servants and to all his land, and for all the mighty power and all the great and terrible deeds which Moses wrought in the sight of all Israel." (Deut 34:9-12). This reads like a summary of the life of one led by the Spirit, enjoying to the full the Gifts (qv) and the Fruits (qv).

We are encouraged to take some such view, rather to seek to penetrate its sense by another passage, this time in Num: "And the Lord said to Moses, 'Gather for me seventy men of the elders of Israel, whom you know to be the elders of the people and officers over them; and bring them to the tent of meeting, and let them take their stand there with you. And I will come down and talk with you there; and I will take some of the spirit which is upon you and put it upon them; and they shall bear the burden of the people with you, that you may not bear it yourself alone.... 'Then the Lord came down in the cloud and spoke to him, and took some of the spirit that was upon him and put it upon the seventy elders; and when the spirit rested upon them, they prophesied. But they did so no more." (Num 11:16-17, 25).

Can we maintain then that the mighty career of Moses, servant and friend of God, to whom God revealed his name, to whom he gave a mission to liberate his people, which also would make him in a human sense the creator of Israel, is to be attributed directly to the Spirit of God? Was his role as mediator of the covenant fulfilled with the special help of the Spirit? Was he in a manner quite singular, endowed by the Spirit to receive the law? Was he inspired by the Spirit in his successful intercession on behalf of the people of Israel, that they should triumph over their foes and receive pardon for their sins? So many vast chapters to explore.

A distinction is important. One may hold that the Spirit had this preponderating influence on the mind and conduct of Moses without asserting that this truth is explicitly taught in the Old Testament. The reality, one may contend, was there but not the explicit formulation. Since we know from the doctrine of divine grace (qv) as it has been developed from the revelation of the New Testament, that it is Trinitarian in origin and is by appropriation seen as especially the work of the Holy Spirit, we are not only entitled, but obliged to believe, and seek to discern that God is at work as Trinity in the great moments of Old Testament salvation history. That he did not fully reveal himself as Trinity in that phase does not mean that he did not exist and operate as Trinity. (See article on Art)

[1]Cf. J. Blenkinsopp, The Structure of P, *CBQ* 38 (1976), 275-292; repr. in J. Blenkinsopp, *The Priestly Work (P): The Second Stage*, Prophecy and Canon, University of Notre Dame, 1977, 54-79.

MÜHLEN, HERIBERT (1927-)[1]

M. has devoted study and reflection to a renewal of the theology of the Holy Spirit and sought over thirty years to give a vital orientation to the subject. His first major work to this end was *Der Heilige Geist als Person. Beitrag zur Frage nach dem Hl. Geist eigentumliche Funktion in der Trinität bei der Inkarnation und im Gnadenbund. Ich-Du-Wir, Munster, 3rd ed. by 1969.* In this as in his subsequent principal work M. has a distinctive methodology: the use of dialogical categories, derived from the comparative linguistics of Von Humbolt, the philosophies of Ebner and Buber and especially from Dietrich Von Hildebrand; the assimilation of biblical themes like corporate personality; and a central determining role in his synthesis to the anointing of Jesus at his Baptism.

Interestingly M.'s starting-point was the Marian theology of M. J. Scheeben (qv). His aim is to manifest with entire lucidity the personal identity of the Holy Spirit—he thinks that the very name Holy Spirit brings together two words which are equally applicable to all three Persons. M. would thus free the thinking about the Spirit from the constricting influence of "appropriation." The Spirit would be seen to have a *proprium*. Difficulties have been raised about the validity of "the We in Person" concept of the Spirit. Could it mean that he is "said" as is the Son? Is he then totally distinct from the Son in his mode of origin? M. seeks support in Scripture. "It is easy enough

to find 'I-Thou' sayings, as between the Son and the Father and the 'We-sayings' apart from the final chapters of St. John are less frequent. As tradition has found out over centuries, the more significant meaning is not just in the 'I-Thou' form, but in the use of terms like Father, Son (Word), Spirit to indicate the different Persons."[2]

Relying on a certain interpretation of 'mission' in Scripture and on a post-biblical theological interpretation of the anointing of Jesus as a mission of the Holy Spirit, as a proper function of the Holy Spirit over against the humanity of Jesus, M. thinks the way is clear to affirm a proper function of the Spirit in the economy of salvation. These suggestions have aroused much debate, inevitable in an important pioneering essay. For M. is concerned with the Spirit's role in the Trinity, in the Incarnation (see article Jesus Christ) and in the covenant of grace. His work has rendered very great service to theology.

With the thesis of the first work he associates that of the second, which deals with the Spirit in the Church: "*Una mystica Persona. Die Kirche als das Mysterium der heilsgeschichtlichen Identität des Heiligen Geistes in Christus und den Christen*, Paderborn, 2nd ed. by 1967; French translation as *L'Esprit dans l'Eglise*, 1969, 2 vols. The key phrase here is "one Person in many persons"; it is almost M.'s definition of the Church that it is "only One Person, the Holy Spirit, in several persons, Christ and the believers." The Church is the continuation in the economy of salvation of the anointing of Jesus with the Holy Spirit in his baptism. "The anointing of Jesus by the Holy Spirit and its consequences intended by Jesus himself become the central theme of ecclesiology. For this reason we do not interpret the formula 'One Person in many persons' to mean, imply, that the Spirit is the mediator between the glorified Jesus and us. By virtue of his mission the Spirit of Christ links us also to the historical Christ, and does this through succession in the ministry, and the tradition of the word. One can truly say that the Spirit is one Person in Christ and in us, and that he transcends the time-gap which separates us from the historical Jesus. The doctrine of the anointing of Jesus avoids two ecclesiological errors mentioned above: it avoids mysticism by underlining the distinction (and non-separation) of the Incarnation and the Anointing; it also avoids naturalism in underlining the non-separation (and the distinction) of the Pneuma and his function."[3]

M. has been accused of establishing a monopoly

of the Spirit. The criticism is unjustified and may indeed spring from a mentality which was quite comfortable with a minimum somewhat lifeless reference to the third person of the Holy Trinity. The author of the Acts of the Apostles (qv) would on this kind of reasoning, be accused of setting up a total monopoly of the Spirit. M.'s entry to the charismatic movement was an event of significance, given his giant stature. His decision was taken after reflection lasting eight months. His explanation: "I would like simply to say that for 15 years I have known the Holy Spirit with my head, but now I also know him with my heart, and wish the same joy for you. For 15 years people said to me: 'What you are writing is speculation, not real.' But now I am seeing it come to reality all over the world. The Holy Spirit is real, and is being sent by the Father and the Son to bring the human race to a knowledge of them. I longed for this, but it was in my head, and an unfulfilled longing. Now it is in my heart, changing my life."[4]

---

[1]Cf. works of M., *Sein und Person nach Johannes Duns Scotus. Beitrag zur Grundlegung einer Metaphysik der Person*, Werl 1954 (Franziskan. Forschungen. H. 11)—on the concepts of substance, person, relation; "Person und Appropriation. Zum Verständnis des Axioms: In Deo omnia sunt unum, ubi non obviat relationis oppositio," *Münchener theolog. Zeitschr.*, 16 (1961) 37-57; *Das Vorverständnis von Person und die evangelisch-katholische Differenz. Zum Problem der theolog. Denkform*, Münster, 1965; "El concepto de Dios. Nuestra epoca necessita un punto de partida pneumatologico-trinitario, *Estudios Trinitarios* 6 (1972) 535-59; "Die epochale Notwendigkeit eines pneumatologischen Ansatzes der Gotteslehre," *Wort und Wahrheit* 28 (1973) 275-287; "Mysterium—Mystik—Charismatik," *Geist und Leben* 46 (1973) 247-256; *Die Erneurung des christlichen Glaubens. Charisma-Geist-Befreiung*, Munich, 1974; *Morgen wird Einheit sein. Das kommende Konzil aller Christen. Ziel der getrennten Kirchen*, Paderborn, 1974; "Die Geisterfahrung als Erneurung der Kirche," in ed. Otto A. Dilschneider, "*Theologie des Geistes*," Gutersloh, 1980, 69-94; *Entsakralisisierung*, (on the sacred in view of his doctrine of the Spirit), Paderborn, 1971; cf. on Muhlen's works, A. Hayen, S.J., "L'être de la personne selon le B. Jean Duns Scot," *Rev. philosophique de Louvain*, 53 (1955) 525-41; J. Kuhlmann, *Der dreieinige Gott*, Nurnberg, 1968; B. Langemeyer, "Die Kirche als Mysterium des Hl. Geistes. Zu dem Buch von Heribert Mühlen: Una Mystica Persona," *Franziskan. Studien* 48 (1966), 161-66; N. Silanes, "El Espiritu Santo en la Iglesia", *Estudios Trinitarios* 6 (1972), 561-64; Y.-M.J. Congar, O.P., *The Holy Spirit*, I, 22-25, II, 203; *id.*, review of M's book, *Morgen wird Einheit sein, RSPT*, 59 (1975), 517-519; R. Laurentin, *Catholic Pentecostalism*, London, 1977, 185f, 328f; esp. P. Corcoran, "Some Recent Writing on the Holy Spirit, H. Mühlen," *ITQ*, 40 (1973) 55-61; *BT*, 2756-2764; R. T. Sears, *Spirit, Divine and Human Relevance of the Theology of the Holy Spirit of H. M. for Evaluating the Data of Psychotherapy*, Ph.D. Dissertation, Fordham, 1974; [2]P. Corcoran, *op. cit.*, 57; [3]*L'Esprit dans l'Eglise*, I, 246; [4]R. Martin, "An Interview with Fr. Heribert Mühlen, Theologian of the Holy Spirit," *New Covenant*, July 1974, p. 6.

N

NEGLECT OF THE SPIRIT[1]

This neglect has taken different forms and may be considered doctrinally or in the sphere of devotion, as well as in iconography. Neglect of the Spirit in the Church's teaching is evident in the absence, over lengthy periods, of any official teaching, that is formal teaching, on the Holy Spirit. Including the Council of Trent and from then no significant contribution was made to a theology of the Holy Spirit by either Popes or Councils until *Divinum illud munus* (qv) by Leo XIII (qv). Again there is comparative silence until *Mystici Corporis Christi* (qv) by Pius XII (qv).

Pontificates much admired, for one reason or another, such as those of St. Pius X and Pius XI, show nothing in the area of this theology. Vatican II is considered separately. Its earlier sessions followed the same trend which could not be characterized as indifference; the matter just did not appear urgent or sufficiently important for renewed teaching. Why this should be so is certainly a subject for investigation.

There has been a notable change since Vatican II. Paul VI (qv) and John Paul II (qv) have made valuable contributions to the growing theology. It must be added that when Trent is spoken of as lacking a theology of the Spirit, or a plenary exposition of such a theology, the Council Fathers are not accused of ignorance. "At the Council of Trent, the legate Cervini, the Fathers and the theologians justified, by appealing to the constant activity of the Spirit, the faithful handing down of the apostolic traditions and the trust that should be placed in those traditions as in the canonical Scriptures. The Council spoke only of apostolic traditions but in line with what had been taught by the Fathers, the other councils and the theologians of the Middle Ages, the activity of the Spirit was extended to doctrinal and ethical pronouncements made by the 'Church'..... Insofar as Christians were at that time aware of development of dogma, they tended to attribute this too to the help of the Holy Spirit."[1]

Since the Reformation, theologians also have been reluctant to deal extensively with the Holy Spirit. Petavius (d.1952) expounded a theory of grace which emphasized the presence of the Holy Spirit in the soul. In the nineteenth century M. J. Scheeben (qv) wrote considerably on the Spirit. Cardinal Manning (qv) published two works that are relevant: *The Temporal Mission of the Holy Ghost* and *The Internal Mission of the Holy Ghost*. Newman (qv) as an Anglican and Catholic wrote powerfully on the subject.

The Holy Spirit figures little in Catholic literature during the first half of the present century. A work of some substance came from the pen of the Irish spiritual writer, Edward Leen, C. S. Sp. (qv); occasional papers or lectures appeared. But to some extent these were the years of *The Forgotten Paraclete (Le divin Méconnu)* of Mgr. Landrieux, the years when Dom Columba Marmion would introduce a lecture on the Holy Spirit by a reference to Acts 19:2, "'No, we have never even heard that there is a Holy Ghost.'"

The revival did not come from where it might be expected. Few of the European theologians brought to prominence before and during the Council were drawn to write extensively on the Holy Spirit. Hans Urs von Balthasar (qv) returned to the subject frequently; his writings have prompted a substantial study. Fr. Congar (qv) published the results of his lifelong research, but as late as 1979, *I Believe in the Holy Spirit*.

Long before that, Orthodox and Anglican theologians had made a contribution to the literature: Sergey Bulgakov (qv) H. B. Swete (qv) and C. K. Barrett notably. Nikos Nissiotis was, during the Council sessions, to act as a stimulus.

Devotion is more difficult to assess at different times in recent history. The official impulse to such devotion has varied. We touch here a point of inter-action between church authority and the body of the faithful. In recent times the Charismatic or Renewal Movement (qv) has exemplified this interaction. Apart from such general statements we must allow for the action of the Spirit in individual cases. These may be hidden, but immensely effective through the whole scale of the institutional Church. Popes who have not issued formal teaching on the Holy Spirit, thinking that no controversy called for such an intervention, may have been, in their private lives, intensely devoted to him.

One reason why attention and intentions have not been focussed on the Spirit may be the heavy coat of abstraction which surrounds the theology of the Holy Trinity. It makes the divine Persons remote. It is to be feared henceforth that the use of the word Pneumatology, which comes with the best intentions from respected writers, may substitute an ideology for the living Person. Christology is of course a valid term, but excessive use of it may obscure the Person and vital teaching of Jesus Christ the Word; Mariology may have a similar effect.

---

[1]Y.-M. Congar, The Holy Spirit, I, 152. C. J. Sirks, *The Cinderella of Theology. The Doctrine of the Holy Spirit*, HTR, 50 (1957), 80-89; K. McDonnell, O.S.B., "*A Trinitarian Theology of the Holy Spirit,*" ThSt 46 (1985), 191-227.

NEWMAN, JOHN HENRY (1801-1890)

N. had a powerfully sure sense of the revelation of the most Holy Trinity from his profound knowledge of Sacred Scripture, which was nourished by prolonged study of the Fathers.[1] His Anglican sermons are replete with biblical quotations. His work for LNPF which demanded lengthy translations of the Fathers and carefully composed notes gave him immense learning, while his elaborate theory of development enabled him to distinguish and clarify essential truths. N. did not compose a formal treatise on the Holy Spirit. But in his doctrinal, historical and homiletic work from early in his Anglican days the subject attracted him and prompted him to compositions which assembled would make an interesting anthology.

In an early sermon on *The Mystery of the Holy Trinity*, N. after listing the scriptural phrases showing the unique personality of the Son goes on: "And again, what is true of the Son is true of the Holy Ghost; for he is 'the Spirit of God'. He proceeds from the Father; he is in God as 'the spirit of a man' that is in him; he 'searches all things, even the deep things of God;' he is 'the Spirit of Truth;' the 'Holy Spirit' at the creation, he 'moved upon the face of the waters;' 'Whither shall I go' says the psalmist 'from thy Spirit?' He is the giver of all gifts, 'dividing to every man severally as he will;' we are born again 'of the Spirit.' To resist divine grace is to grieve, to tempt, to quench, to do despite to the Spirit. He is the Comforter, Ruler and Guide of the Church; he reveals things to come; and blasphemy against him has never forgiveness. In all such passages, it is surely implied both that the Holy Ghost has a Personality of his own, and that he is God."[2]

N. composed contemplative prayers, not unlike those of St. Anselm (qv). Four to the Paraclete summarize his doctrine. The first is addressed to the Paraclete, the Life of all things: "I adore thee as the Life of all that lives. Through thee the whole material universe hangs together and consists, remains in its place and moves internally in the order and reciprocity of its several parts. Through thee the earth was brought into its present state, and was matured through its six days to be a habitation for man." Then the author mentions various parts of the material world. He continues: "Thou art the Life of the whole creation, O eternal Paraclete—and if of this animal and material framework, how much more of the world of spirits! Through thee, Almighty Lord, the angels and saints sing thee praises in heaven. Through thee our own dead souls are quickened to serve thee. From thee is every good thought and desire, every good purpose, every good effort, every good success. It is by thee that sinners are turned into saints. It is by thee the Church is refreshed and strengthened, and champions start forth, and martyrs are carried on to their crown. Through thee new religious orders, new devotions in the Church come into being; new countries are added to the faith, new manifestations and illustrations are given of the ancient Apostolic creed."

N. adds a personal note: "I acknowledge and feel, not only as a matter of faith but of experience, that I cannot have one good thought or one good act without thee.... When I was young, thou didst put into my heart a special devotion to thee. Thou hast taken me up in my youth, thou wilt not forsake me."[3]

The second prayer is to the Paraclete, the Life

of the Church. "Thou hast founded the Church, thou hast established and maintained it. Thou fillest it continually with thy gifts, that men may see, and draw near, and take, and live. Thou hast in this way brought down heaven upon earth. For thou hast set up a great company which Angels visit by that ladder which the patriarch saw in vision. Thou hast by thy presence restored the communion between God above and man below. Thou hast given him that light of grace which is one with and the commencement of the light of glory. I adore thee and praise thee for thy infinite mercy towards us, O my Lord and God."[4]

N. then once again speaks in a personal vein, with moving thankfulness for all the Spirit's favours to him, up to and including the entry "to thy Church." His third prayer is to the Paraclete, the "Life of my Soul". "Thou hast taken on thyself the office of a minister, and that for those who did not ask for it.... Thou dwellest in me by thy grace in an ineffable way, uniting me to thyself and the whole company of angels and saints. Nay, as some have held, thou art present in me, not only by thy grace, but by thy eternal substance, as if though I did not lose my own individuality, yet in some sense I was even here absorbed in God. Nay—as though thou hadst taken possession of my very body, this earthly, fleshly wretched tabernacle—even my body is thy Temple. O astonishing, awful truth! I believe it, I know it, O my God."[5]

Lastly N. addresses a prayer to the "Paraclete, the Fount of Love." "Thou art that living Love, wherewith the Father and the Son love each other. And thou art the Author of supernatural love in our hearts—'*Fons vivus, ignis, charitas*' (N.'s spelling). As a fire thou didst come down from heaven on the day of Pentecost; and as a fire thou burnest away the dross of sin and vanity in the heart and dost light up the pure flame of devotion and affection.... My God, the Paraclete, I acknowledge thee as the Giver of that great gift, by which alone we are saved, supernatural love. Man is by nature blind, hard-hearted in all spiritual matters; how is he to reach heaven? It is by the flame of thy grace, which consumes him in order to new-make him, and so to fit him to enjoy what without thee he would have no taste for." N. ends: "Increase in me this grace of love, in spite of all my unworthiness. It is more precious than anything else in the world. I accept it in place of all the world can give me. O give it to me. It is my life."[6]

Already in 1838 as an Anglican in the *Lectures*

on Justification N. had written pages which not only anticipate much of very recent theology on the Resurrection as a mystery of salvation, but on the Spirit as uncreated grace. "Christ's work of mercy has two chief parts; what he did for all men, what he does for each ... that is his Atonement and the application of his Atonement, or his Atonement and our justification; he atones by the offering of himself on the Cross; and as certainly (which is the point before us) he justifies by the mission of his Spirit."[7]

N. elaborates thus: "His Atonement is his putting away the wrath of God for our sins. In order to do this he took flesh; he accomplished it in his own Person, by his crucifixion and death. Justification is the application of this precious Atonement to this person or that person, and this he accomplishes by his Spirit. For he ceased, I say, to act towards us by his own hand from the day of his ascension; he sent his Spirit to take his place,—'I will not leave you orphans' he says, 'I will come to you.'—'I will pray the Father, and he will give you another Comforter, that he may abide with you for ever.' (Jn 14:16-18). Whatever then is done in the Christian Church is done by the Spirit; Christ's mission ended when he left the world; he was to come again, but by his Spirit. The Holy Spirit realizes and completes the redemption which Christ has wrought in essence and virtue. If the justification, then, of a sinner be a continual work, a work under the New Covenant, it *must* be the Spirit's work and not simply Christ's. The Atonement for sin took place during his own mission, and he was the chief Agent; the application of that Atonement takes place during the mission of his Spirit, who accordingly is the chief Agent in it."[8]

N. turns about this theme viewing it from every aspect. "Further, it would appear as if his going to the Father was, in fact, the same thing as his coming to us spiritually. I mean there is some mysterious unknown connection between his departing in his own Person, and his returning in the Person of the Spirit. He said that unless he went, his Spirit would not come to us; as though his ascending and the Spirit's descending, if not the same act, yet were very closely connected, and admitted of being spoken of as the same. And thus his rising again was the necessary antecedent of his applying to his elect the virtue of the Atonement which his dying wrought for all men.... Thus he died to purchase what he rose again to apply. 'He died for our sins; he rose again for our justification;' he died in the flesh; he rose again

'according to the Spirit of holiness', which, when risen, he also sent forth from him, dispensing to others that life whereby he rose himself. He atoned, I repeat, in his own Person; he justifies through his Spirit."[9] N. adds; "For he himself was raised again and 'justified' by the Spirit; and what was wrought in him is repeated in us who are his brethren, and the complement and ratification of his work." He also says that God the Son and the Holy Ghost have "so acted together in their separate Persons, as to make it difficult for us creatures always to discriminate what belongs to each respectively. Christ rises by his own prayer, yet the Holy Ghost is said to raise him; hence the expression in St. Paul, 'according to the Spirit of holiness', as applied to his resurrection, may be taken to stand either for his divine nature or for the third Person in the Blessed Trinity."[10]

N.'s doctrine of the Resurrection in the plan of salvation is singularly attuned to modern thinking, to the whole doctrine of the Paschal Mystery as we now see it. On the very essence of justification he will be found most acceptable by modern theologians of Uncreated Grace. "If it (an inward divine presence) be vouchsafed to us, neither Protestant nor Romanist ought to refuse to admit, and in admitting to agree with each other, that the presence of the Holy Ghost shed abroad in our hearts, the Author both of faith and of renewal, this is really that which makes us righteous, and that our righteousness is the possession of that presence." N. notes that "justification actually *is* ascribed in Scripture to the presence of the Holy Spirit," and that immediately, neither faith nor renewal intervening. He quotes biblical texts which appear to him to favour this view; Pauline texts among them: "For the law of the Spirit of life in Christ Jesus has set me free from the law of sin and death." (Rom 8:2); "For you did not receive the spirit of slavery to fall back into fear, but you have received the Spirit of sonship, whereby we cry 'Abba! Father!'" (ibid. 8:15—RSV); "When we cry 'Abba! Father!' it is the Spirit himself bearing witness with our spirit that we are children of God" (cf. 8:16). N. presses on: "Scripture expressly declares that righteousness is a definite inward gift, while at the same time it teaches that it is not any mere quality of mind, whether faith or holiness." After an analysis of the many biblical references to gift and gifts he continues: "Now, turning to the Gospel we shall find that a gift is actually promised to us by our Lord; a gift which must of necessity be at once our justification and our sanctification, for it is nothing short of the indwelling (qv) in us of God the Father and the Word Incarnate through the Holy Ghost. If this be so, we have found what we sought: This is to be justified, to receive the divine Presence within us, and be made a Temple of the Holy Ghost."[11]

Newman elaborates this point very cogently in a sermon on *Righteousness not of us but in us*, for the feast of the Epiphany: "When he ascended, he did not leave us to ourselves; so far the work was not done. He sent his Spirit. Were all finished as regards individuals, why should the Holy Ghost have condescended to come? But the Spirit came to finish in us what Christ had finished in himself, but left unfinished as regards us. To him it is committed to apply to us severally all that Christ had done for us. As then his mission proves on the one hand that salvation is not from ourselves, so does it on the other that it must be wrought in us. For if all gifts of grace are with the Spirit, and the presence of the Spirit is within us, it follows that these gifts are to be manifest and wrought in us. If Christ is our sole hope, and Christ is given to us by the Spirit, and the Spirit be an inward presence, our sole hope is an inward change. As a light placed in a room pours out its rays on all sides, so the presence of the Holy Spirit Ghost imbues us with life, strength, holiness, love, acceptableness, righteousness. God looks on us in mercy, because he sees in us 'the mind of the Spirit', for whoso has this mind has holiness and righteousness within him. Henceforth all his thoughts, words, and works, as done in the Spirit, are acceptable, pleasing, just before God; and whatever remaining infirmity there be in him, that the presence of the Spirit hides...."

N. then shows how what was actually done in Christ in the flesh "is in type and resemblance really wrought in us one by one even to the end of time." "He was born of the Spirit, and we too are born of the Spirit. He was justified by the Spirit and so are we. He was pronounced the well-beloved Son, when the Holy Ghost descended on him; and we too cry Abba, Father, through the Spirit sent into our hearts. He was led into the wilderness by the Spirit; he did great works by the Spirit; he offered himself to death by the eternal Spirit; he was raised from the dead by the Spirit; he was declared to be the Son of God by the Spirit of holiness on his resurrection: we too are led by the same Spirit into and through this world's temptations; we, too, do our works of obedience by the Spirit; we die from sin, we rise again unto righteousness through the Spirit; and we are declared to be God's sons,—declared, pronounced, dealt with as righteous,—through our resurrection unto holiness in the Spirit."[11a]

The great Tractarian, as he then was, preached another sermon on the feast of the Epiphany, on *The Law of the Spirit*, in which he expresses similar ideas, referring to "a number of passages (in St. Paul's writings) concerning the office of the Holy Spirit which are equally opposite to show that he it is who vouchsafes to give us inward righteousness under the Gospel, or to justify, to make us acceptable to God." (texts quoted, 1 Cor 6:11; 2 Cor 3:8,9; Gal 4:5,6; Rom 8:26,27; 5:18-21). He pursues the thought and sums up thus: "But when I speak of righteousness I speak of the work of the Spirit, and this work, though imperfect considered as ours, is perfect as far as it comes from him. Our works, done in the Spirit of Christ, have a justifying *principle* in them, and that is the presence of the all-holy Spirit. His influences are infinitely pleasing to God, and able to overcome in his sight all our own infirmities and demerits. This we are expressly told by St. Paul, in reference to one work of the Holy Ghost, the exercise of prayer, as I just now quoted his words. 'He who searches the hearts of men knows what is the mind of the Spirit, because the Spirit intercedes for the saints according to the mind of God.'" (Rom 8:27).[11b]

N. preached two remarkable sermons on the divine inhabitation. "Such", he says, "is the inhabitation of the Holy Ghost. Such is the great doctrine which we hold as a matter of faith and without actual experience to verify it in us. Next I must speak briefly concerning the manner in which the Gift of grace manifests itself in the regenerate soul; a subject which I do not willingly take up and which no Christian perhaps is ever able to consider without some effort, feeling that he thereby endangers either his reverence towards God, or his humility, but which the errors of this day, and the confident tone of their advocates oblige us to dwell on, lest truth should suffer by silence. The heavenly gift of the Spirit fixes the eyes of our mind upon the Divine Author of our salvation, within us, applying to us individually the precious cleansing of Christ's blood, in all its manifold benefits."[12]

N. speaks of an occasional experience of the Spirit "amid trial or affliction, special visitations and comfortings from the Spirit, 'plaints unutterable' and passing gleams of God's eternal election, and deep stirrings of wonder and thankfulness thence following."[13] Was this a veiled transcription of his own experience?

N. deals with the special case of divine action on the authors of the biblical works: "(The Spirit) inspired the Holy Evangelists to record the life of Christ, and directed them which of his words and works to select, which to omit; next he commented, (as it were) upon these, and unfolded their meaning in the Apostolic Epistles. The birth, the life, the death and resurrection of Christ, has been the text which he has illuminated. He has made history to be doctrine; telling us plainly, whether by St. John or St. Paul, that Christ's conception and birth was the real Incarnation of the Eternal Word,—his life, 'God made manifest in the Flesh'—his death and resurrection the atonement for sin, and the justification of all believers."[14]

In the second sermon, entitled *The Gift of the Spirit* Newman takes up the idea of glory in the context of the indwelling: "Next, if we consider the variety and dignity of the gifts ministered by the Spirit, we shall, perhaps, discern in a measure, why our state under the Gospel is called a state of glory. It is not uncommon, in the present day, to divide the works of the Holy Ghost in the Church into two kinds, miraculous and moral." The first, as N. explains them, are "marvels out of the course of nature." "On the other hand by moral operations or influences are meant such as act upon our minds, and enable us to be what we otherwise could not be, holy and accepted in all branches of the Christian character; in a word, all such as issue in Sanctification, as it is called. These distinct works of the Holy Spirit, viewed in their effects, are commonly called extraordinary and ordinary, or *gifts* and *graces*."[15]

N. discusses the different aspects of this problem, bringing forward many texts and he concludes: "By this new birth (of water and of the Spirit) the Divine Shechinah is set up within him, pervading soul and body, separating him really, not only in name, from those who are not Christians, raising him in the scale of being, drawing and fostering into life whatever remains in him of a higher nature, and imparting to him, in due season and measure, his own surpassing and heavenly virtue. Thus, while he carefully cherishes the Gift, he is, in the words of the text, 'changed from glory to glory, even as by the Spirit of the Lord.'"[16]

The action of the Spirit in the Church is implicit in much that N. wrote on the subject. In a sermon on the Communion of Saints he is explicit: "Such is the difference between the Church before the Spirit of Christ came, and after. Before God's servants were as the dry bones of the Prophet's vision, connected by profession, not by inward principle; but since, they are all the organs as if of one invisible, governing Soul, the hands or the tongues, or the feet, or the eyes of one and the same directing Mind, the types, tokens, beginnings, and glimpses of the Eternal Son of God." He goes on to talk of the glory given by the saints, and continues: "Such is the Christian Church, a *living* body, and *one*; not a mere framework artificially arranged to *look* like one. Its being alive is what makes it one; were it dead it would consist of as many parts as it has members; but the living *Spirit* of God came down upon it at Pentecost, and made it *one*, by giving it *life*." The sermon was preached on Pentecost, when, as N. said, "we commemorate the quickening or vivifying of the Church, the birth of the spiritual and new creature out of an old world."[17]

"The Church is invisible, because the greater number of her children have been perfected and removed, and because those who are still on earth cannot be ascertained by mortal eye; and had God so willed, she might have had no visible tokens at all of her existence, and been as entirely and absolutely hidden from us as the Holy Ghost is, her Lord and Governor. But seeing that the Holy Ghost is our life, so that to gain life we must approach him, in mercy to us, his place of abode, the Church of the Living God, is not so utterly veiled from our eyes as he is; but he has given us certain outward signs, as tokens for knowing, and means for entering that living Shrine in which he dwells."[18]

N. then had a comprehensive theology of the Holy Spirit. His theology of Our Lady expressed in sermons and in the *Essay on Development*, was, at the time of writing, that is before his conversion, unequalled by any contemporary, Catholic or Protestant. The same may be said of his theology of the Holy Spirit. All the texts here quoted are from his writings while he was a Protestant. Some of his ideas are more attuned to contemporary thinking than to the doctrine circulating in his lifetime. But there is no one in any Christian communion to rival him at the time of composition. His admission of a personal call to devotion must be borne in mind: "When I was young thou didst put into my heart a special devotion to thee." But his doctrine has a hard core, is profoundly biblical, stands the test of searching reflection. The baffling thing is that it has been so neglected.

---

[1]Excellent bibl. as well as list of N's writings, P. Murray, O. S. B., *Newman the Oratorian*, Dublin, 1969, xix-xxv; cf. W. Ward, *The Life of John Henry Cardinal Newman*, 2 vols., London, 1912; M. Trevor, *Newman the Pillar of the Cloud*, London, 1962; id., *Newman Light in Winter*, London 1962; C.S. Dessain, *The Letters and Diaries of John Henry Newman*, XI, xi-xxiii; id., *John Henry Newman*, London, 1966; esp., id. "Cardinal Newman and the Doctrine of Uncreated Grace," *The Clergy Review*, 47 (1962), 207-225, 269-288; J.H. Walgrave, *Newman the Theologian*, London, 1960; H. Davies, *Worship and Theology in England from Newman to Martineau*, 1850-1900, London 1962; J. P. Whalen, *NCE* X, 412-419; T. Gornall, *DSp* XI, 163-181, bibl.; see article 'Law'; esp., J. Rickaby, S. J., *Index to the Works of John Henry Cardinal Newman*, London, 1914, s.v., Holy Ghost, 74-75; [2]*Parochial and Plain Sermons*, VI, 24, date unknown, p. 359; [3]*Meditations and Devotions*, London, 1894, 546,7,8; [4]*Ibid.*, 550; [5]*Ibid.*, 553,4,5; [6]Ibid., 556,7,8,9; [7]Ed. 1874, 203; [8]*Ibid.*, 204; [9]Ibid., 206; [10]Ibid., 207,8 [11]*Ibid.*, 137, 144; [11a]*Parochial and Plain Sermons*, V, 138f; [11b]*Ibid.*, 155, 157; [12]*The Divine Indwelling, Parochial and Plain Sermons*, II, 19, 1834, end of year, p. 224; cf. P. and P. Sermons, VI, 126f; [13]*Ibid.*, p.226 [14]*Ibid.*, p. 227 [15]*Parochial and Plain Sermons*, III, 18, 8 November, 1835, p. 258; [16]*Ibid.*, 266,7; [17]*Parochial and Plain Sermons*, IV, 11, p. 170f; 14 May 1837; [18]Ibid., p. 173.

NOVATIAN (Third century)

First Latin theologian, founder of a schismatic church, N. is not very well known; his works, listed, though not entirely by St. Jerome, have had a struggle for identified survival, some lost in the writings of St. Cyprian (qv).[1] On the one work which concerns us, *The Trinity*, there is textually no problem. But on the specific theme of the present work, the Holy Spirit, interpreters differ. The Italian patrologist, M. Simonetti, goes so far as to say that for N. the Holy Spirit is a creature, and that his idea of the deity was not really Trinitarian; the American patrologist, R. J. de Simone, excellent translator of N., with others thinks that N. held the Spirit to be a divine Person. Fortunately the evidence on which judgements seek to rely is open to study by all.

Writing of Christ's divinity N. has this to say about his relationship with the Paraclete: "If he received from Christ the things which he will make known, then surely Christ is greater than the Paraclete, since the Paraclete would not receive from Christ unless he were less than Christ. Now, the fact that the Paraclete is less than Christ proves that Christ is also God, from whom he receives what he makes known. This, then, is a great testimony to Christ's divinity, inasmuch as the Paraclete, having been found to be less than Christ, takes from him what he gives to others. If Christ were only man, Christ would receive from the Paraclete what he should say; the Paraclete would not receive from Christ what he should make known."[2]

On the relationship between the Spirit and the Father we have N.'s opinion as follows: "He instructed the prophets by his Spirit and through all of them promised his Son, Christ; and he sent him at the time he had solemnly promised to give him. He willed that through Christ we should come to a knowledge of him; he also lavished upon us the abundant treasures of his mercy by giving his Spirit to enrich the poor and the downtrodden."[3]

There is here not a reasoned analysis of the personal inter-relations. Nor shall we look for that in the treatment of the theme of the Spirit in chapter XXIX of the treatise. It opens thus: "Next, well-ordered reason and the authority of our faith bid us (in the words and writings of our Lord set down in orderly fashion) to believe, after these things, also in the Holy Spirit, who was in times past promised to the Church and duly bestowed at the appointed, favourable moment."[4]

He quickly proceeds to review the Spirit's action in the Old and New Testament, insisting that he is one: "Therefore it is one and the same Spirit who is in the prophets and in the Apostles. He was, however, in the former only for a while; whereas he abides in the latter forever. He has been apportioned to the former in moderation; to the latter, he has been wholly poured out. He was sparingly given to the one; upon the other lavishly bestowed."[5]

Making it clear then that the Spirit came on the promise of Jesus, N. describes his manifold beneficial action, through gifts and extraordinary signs; he concludes: "Thus, he makes the Church of the Lord perfect and complete in every respect and in every detail."[6]

Then the author turns to the Spirit's action on Christ, buttressing this statement with words from Isaiah, 11:2 and 61:1 "For the fountainhead of the entire Holy Spirit abides in Christ, that from him might be drawn streams of grace and wondrous deeds because the Holy Spirit dwells affluently in Christ."[7] N. then adds considerable concrete detail to show the activity of the Spirit: "It is he who checks insatiable desires, breaks unbridled lust, quenches illicit passions, overcomes fiery assaults, averts drunkenness, resists avarice, drives away wanton revelries, binds together noble loves, strengthens good affections, does away with factions, explains the rule of Truth, refutes heretics, banishes the impious and guards the Gospels."[8]

Each category of saint is the handiwork of the Spirit. N. concludes his account of the sanctifying role with the words: "He keeps the Church uncorrupted and inviolate in the holiness of perpetual virginity and truth."[9]

---

[1]Text of *De Trinitate PL* 3, 911-82; critical ed. G. F. Diercks, *CCSL* 4, 1-78; English tr., H. Moore, SPCK London, 1919; R. J. de Simone, Fathers of the Church, 67, used here; cf. A. d'Alès, *Novatien, Etude sur la théologie romaine au milieu du IIIe siècle*, Paris, 1925; M. Kriebel, *Studien zur älteren Entwicklund der abendländischen Trinitätslehre bei Tertullian und Novatian*, Dissert., Marburg, 1932; G. Abey, *Les missions divines de St. Justinà Origène*, Fribourg, Switzerland, 1958, 103-115; M. Simonetti, "Alcune osservazioni sul De Trinitate di Novaziano," *Studi in onore di Angelo Monteverdi*, 2, Modena, 1959, 771-83; R. De Simone, *The Treatise of Novatian the Roman Presbyter on the Trinity: A Study of the Text and the Doctrine*, Rome, (Eph. August. IV,) 1970; id., "The Holy Spirit according to Novatian's De Trinitate," *Augustinianum*, 10 (1970) 360-387; Quasten II, 217-19, 226-33; *EC*, E. Peterson, VIII, 1976-80; *DSp* R. De Simone, XI, 479-83; *NCE* X, P. H. Weyer, 534-35; *Trinitas*, 169; *The Message* 75-79; [2]*Op.cit.*, 8, p. 62; [3]8, p.39; [4]p.99; [5]p.100; [6]p.101; [7]p.102; [8]p.103; [9]p.104.

O

OLD TESTAMENT, THE[1]

The word *ruah* 'spirit' is used 378 times in OT; 277 times it is translated *pneuma* by LXX. This word *pneuma* is used in NT for the Spirit of God, or the Holy Spirit. We face, therefore, at once a question of terminology. There is at least verbal continuity between OT and NT. What underlying meaning, if any, persists throughout? Or is it a case of such enlargement of meaning that the core is transformed while the external fabric remains?

All biblical scholars are agreed that as the Spirit is spoken of in OT there is not a revelation of his personality. The origin of the word used for him relates it to breath or wind, natural phenomena. Raised to divine context the dominant note is of dynamic force. This force takes over individuals, acts on them and through them to achieve his designs on his people. Of Joseph for example we read: "And Pharaoh said to his servants, 'Can we find such a man as this, in whom is the Spirit of God' (Gen 41:38)? The Lord took "some of the spirit" that was upon Moses and put it upon the seventy elders "'and they shall bear the burden of the people with you, that you may not bear it yourself alone'" (Num 11:17). Moses to allay Joshua's anxiety said: "'Would that all the Lord's people were prophets, that the Lord would put his spirit upon them'" (11:29)! When Moses came to name his successor thus he spoke: "'Take Joshua, the son of Nun, a man in whom is the spirit, and lay your hand upon him'" (27:18).

Israel endured a number of crises during the 150 years which separate Joshua's conquest from the establishment of the kingship. Chieftains, charismatic warriors named Judges were then raised up by the Spirit of God. Simple sons of peasants apparently unprepared for such leadership, they cannot resist the divine seizure and under its influence they are transformed.

Othniel: "But when the people of Israel cried to the Lord, the Lord raised up a deliverer for the people of Israel who delivered them, Othniel the son of Kenaz, Caleb's younger brother. The Spirit of the Lord came upon him and he judged Israel; he went out to war, and the Lord gave Cushanrishathaim, king of Mesopotamia, into his hand; and his hand prevailed over Cushanrishathaim. So the land had rest forty years. Then Othniel the son of Kenaz died" (Judg 3:9-11).

Gideon: "But the Spirit of the Lord took possession of Gideon; and he sounded the trumpet, and the Abiezrites were called to follow him" (6:34).

Jephthah: "Then the Spirit of the Lord came upon Jephthah, and he passed through Gilead and Manasseh, and passed on to Mizpah of Gilead and from Mizpah of Gilead he passed on to the Ammonites" (11:29).

Samson: "And the Spirit of the Lord began to stir him in Mahanehdan, between Zorah and Eshtaol." ... "And behold a young lion roared against him; and the Spirit of the Lord came mightily upon him, and he tore the lion asunder as one tears a kid; and he had nothing in his hand." ... "And the Spirit of the Lord came mightily upon him, and he went down to Ashkelon and killed thirty men of the town, and took their spoil and gave the festal garments to those who had told the riddle" (13:25; 14:6,19).

With Saul we pass from the judges to the monarchy. Soon the Spirit will act not so much in sudden, unexpected manner as with the judges, but with a certain intrinsic continuity. This is more evident in the case of David: "Then Samuel took the horn of oil, and anointed him in the midst of his brothers; and the Spirit of the Lord came mightily upon David from that day forward" (1 Sam 16:13). With this assurance of stability in the presence of the Spirit there is a foreshadowing of the abiding wholly unique presence of the Spirit on the Messiah. The kings have a permanent office marked by special anointing. They are types of the One whose relationship with the Spirit is thus described by Is: "There shall come forth a shoot from the stump of Jesse, and a branch shall grow out of his roots. And the Spirit of the Lord shall rest upon him, the spirit of wisdom and understanding, the spirit of counsel and might, the spirit of knowledge and the fear of the Lord. And his delight shall be in the fear of the Lord" (Is 11:1-3). This reality is for the future, but the portrait was fixed in OT times and was intrinsic to the enduring treasury of hope. Is uses the word *Ruah* fifty times, Ezechiel forty-six times, showing thereby how deeply the idea had penetrated thinking during the Davidic kingship and the days of the fall of Jerusalem foretold and witnessed by Ez.

Third Is is notable for the universal extension of the choice made of Israel: "And nations shall come to your light, and kings to the brightness of your rising" (Is 60:3). "Foreigners shall build up your walls, and their kings shall minister to you" (60:10). This new departure is placed firmly under the sign of the Spirit: "The Spirit of the Lord God is upon me, because the Lord has anointed me to bring good tidings to the afflicted; he has sent me to bind up the brokenhearted, to proclaim liberty to the captives and the opening of the prison to those who are bound" (61:1).

Striking indeed are the memorable passages in Ez 36,37: "A new heart I will give you, and a new spirit I will put within you; and I will take out of your flesh the heart of stone and give you a heart of flesh. And I will put my spirit within you, and cause you to walk in my statutes and be careful to observe my ordinances" (36:26,27).

"The hand of the Lord was upon me, and he brought me out by the Spirit of the Lord, and set me down in the midst of the valley; it was full of bones. And he led me round among them; and behold, there were very many upon the valley; and lo, they were very dry. And he said to me, 'Son of man, can these bones live?' And I answered, 'O Lord God, thou knowest.' Again he said to me, 'Prophesy to these bones, and say to them, O dry bones, hear the word of the Lord'. ... So I prophesied as he commanded me, and the breath came into them, and they lived, and stood upon their feet, an exceedingly great host" (37:1-4,10).

"Then they shall know that I am the Lord their God because I sent them into exile among the nations, and then gathered them into their own land. I will leave none of them remaining among the nations any more; and I will not hide my face any more from them, when I pour out my Spirit upon the house of Israel, says the Lord God" (39:28,29).

A new note is struck in the exilic writings, interior renewal, holiness: "For I will pour water on the thirsty land, and streams on the dry ground; I will pour my Spirit upon your descendants, and my blessing on your offspring" (Is 44:3; cp. 63:11-14).

After the return from exile the theme continues, as in Hag 2:5, "My Spirit abides among you; fear not." Likewise Zech 4:6. "Then he said to me, 'This is the word of the Lord to Zerubbabel: Not by might, nor by power, but by my Spirit, says the Lord of hosts'" (cp. ibid. 12:10; Neh 9:20). With Joel this assumes an eschatological dimension: "And it shall come to pass afterward, that I will pour out my Spirit on all flesh; your sons and your daughters shall prophesy, your old men shall dream dreams, and your young men shall see visions. Even upon the menservants and maidservants in those days, I will pour out my Spirit" (2:28,29). To these words St. Peter appealed on the day of Pentecost. With the Wisdom literature of the last centuries before Christ new problems arise (see article Wisdom).

A recurring idea from as early as Elijah (1 K 19:12f) is the connection between the Spirit and the Word of God. The Spirit opens the prophets to the Word of God, even revealing to them the glory of God (Ez 3:12, 8:3: he makes them "stand on their feet" [Ez 2:1; 3:24] to speak to the people [Ez 11:5], thus making witnesses of them and as he does so, himself giving witness to God [Ne 9:30; cf. Ze 7:12]).

The Spirit is sanctifying, consecrates. He embodies immense promise of a new creation, to bring right and justice in a land renewed, to give fidelity to God's word (Is 59:21; Ps 143:10) and to his covenant (Ez 36:27), to foster supplication (Ze 12:10) and praise (Ps 51:17). The consummation will be Israel's regeneration in the Spirit; she will recognize her God and God will find again his people: "I will no longer hide my face from them because I shall have poured out my Spirit on the house of Israel" (Ez 39:29).

But this is promise and hope. The Spirit in the OT is "not yet given" (Jn 7:39). The people can "sadden the Spirit" (Is 63:10). They pray for someone who "will rend the heavens and descend" (Is 63:19).

The "Word" is the key to the whole content: "If the Servant is able to bring to the nations the Word of salvation it is because the Spirit rests upon him. If Israel one day is able to keep the Word in her heart it will be only in the Spirit."[2]

Yet the Word and the Spirit differ notably: "The Word penetrates from the outside, as a sword lays bare the flesh; the Spirit is fluid and infiltrates imperceptibly. The Word makes itself heard and known; the Spirit remains invisible. The Word is revelation; the Spirit an interior transformation. The Word stands erect, upright, holding forth; the Spirit falls, spreads itself, submerges."[3] This partnership of beings distinct, complementary and inseparable, is projected into the NT on a higher level. The Word is incarnate through the operation of the Spirit, lives and acts under his "rule", as Hans Urs von Balthasar has it, achieves the consummation of his lifework by the sending of the Spirit as an everlasting Gift.

[1]Cf. P. van Imschoot, "L'action de l'Esprit de Jahvé dans l'Ancien Testament," *RSPT* 23 (1934) 553-587; L'Espirít de Jahvé, source de víe dans l'Ancien Testament, RB 44 (1935) 481-501; *id.,* "L'Espirit de Jahvé et l'alliance nouvelle dans l'Ancien Testament," *ETL* 22 (1936); E. Schweizer *et al.,* "pneuma", *TDNT*, VI, 332-451, separate issue, *The Spirit of God* London, 1960; R. Koch, "Der Gottesgeist und der Messias," *BB* 27 (1946) 241-268; 276-403; *id.,* "La théologie de l'Esprit de Jahvé dans le livre d'Isaïe," *Sacra Pagina*, ed. J. Coppens *et al.,* Paris, Gembloux, 1959, I, 419-433; E. Haulotte, "L'Esprit de Jahvé dans l'Ancien Testament,"

L'homme devant Dieu. Mélanges H. de Lubac, I, Paris, 1963, 25-36; D. Lys, '*Ruach*': Le Souffle dans l'Ancien Testament, Paris, 1962; J. Guillet, *DSp* IV, 1, 1246-50; *id.,* "La révelation progressive du Saint Esprit dans l'Ecriture," *Lumen Vitae*, 8 (1953), 18-32; E. Jacob, *Théologie de l'Ancien Testament*, Neuchâtel, 1955, 98-102; Y.-M.J. Congar, O. P., *The Holy Spirit*, I, 3-14; G. T. Montague, *The Holy Spirit*, 3-115; [2]J. Guillet, in X. Léon-Dufour, *Dictionary of Biblical Theology*, London, 1967, 502; [3]*Ibid*; cf. DBS XI, pp. 127-156, H. Cazelles, R. Kuntzmann, M. Gilbert.

ORIGEN (c. 185-254)

The mighty genius of Alexandria furthered the development of theology in this subject, as well as in so many others.[1] Later controversies have clouded his valuable contribution. The greatest contemporary expert in the theology of O., Henri Crouzel, S.J., exonerates him from the charge of subordinationism, while admitting that vocabulary may not always have been precise, and distinguishing theological from dogmatic formulation. It has been thought better to follow this authority here. He sums up prolonged research into O.'s theology of the Trinity: "His conception of the Trinity aims at safeguarding the divine unity and the personality of the Persons, while insisting on the hierarchy of origin, which makes the Father the origin of the divinity which he communicates to the other two and the principle who sends the Son and the Spirit on mission." "That," the author adds, "is, allowing for certain clumsy texts, all that is to be said about the 'subordinationism' of O. The Holy Spirit comes from the Father through the Son, who communicates to him his *epinoiai*; he is the Sanctifier and constitutes the 'nature' or the 'matter' of the 'charisms' corresponding to our 'actual graces.'"[2] Elsewhere H. Crouzel says: "This subordinationism is nevertheless of a different kind from that of the Arians and when the word is used attention must be given to its clearly different meanings, otherwise one risks pushing into heterodoxy the whole Church of martyrs, for almost all the Fathers of this period can be accused of subordinationism."[3]

O.'s faith was based on the ecclesiastical tradition and is thus expressed on the Holy Spirit: "Finally apostolic tradition associates the Holy Spirit with the Father and the Son, in honour and in dignity. Is he begotten or not? Must he or must he not be considered the Son of God? This does not appear clearly; it is a question that must be settled by attentive study of Sacred Scripture, and by the effort of theological reasoning. What the Church teaches without the shadow of a doubt is that this same Spirit is the inspirer of all the hagiographers, before as after the coming of Christ."[4]

G. L. Prestige thought that O. was the first of the Fathers to use *hypostasis* in defining the Persons.[5] The relevant passage elaborates the theology of the Holy Spirit: "For us who are persuaded that there are three subsistent realities (*hypostases*), the Father, the Son and the Holy Spirit, and who believe that none other than the Father is without origin, we hold it as more conformed to piety, and as true that if all things were through the Word, the Holy Spirit has greater dignity than all else and that he is of a higher rank than all that is of the Father through Christ. That is possibly the reason why he does not have the title of Son of God, for the Son alone is, from the beginning, Son by nature, and it appears that the Holy Spirit needs his mediation, to subsist individually, and not only to exist, but to be wise, intelligent, just and all that we must think him to be, since he participates in the attributes of Christ which we have listed. I believe that the Holy Spirit provides the matter of the charisms (*charismaton*) of God, if one may put it that way, for those who, thanks to him and because they participate in him, are called saints: this matter of the charisms of which I have spoken, is produced by God, obtained by Christ and subsists according to the Holy Spirit. What leads me to believe that things are so is what Paul writes about the charisms: 'There is certainly a variety of charisms, but it is the same Spirit, a diversity of ministries but it is the same Lord, a diversity of operations but it is the same God who works all in all'" (1 Cor 12:4-6).[6]

In the interior life of the Christian O.'s thought is of a constant progress in perfection towards which the sanctity conferred by the Spirit in baptism gives a potential and orientation. The creature "perfects itself and ascends in its progress towards higher degrees."[7] The Father "gives himself to us through the Son and the Spirit in a new life which begun in baptism, opens to happiness endlessly growing." The more we shall feel beatitude, "the more our desire ought to develop or increase in us, while we grasp and hold, with ever more ardour and capacity, the Father, the Son and the Holy Spirit."[8] The gift of the Spirit is, by O., attached, as it bestows the new life, to the newness of the Resurrection. This is magnificently set forth:

"It is written in the Psalms: 'You will take away your Spirit and they will lose strength and return to their earth. You will send your Spirit and they will be created, and you will renew the face of the earth' (Ps 104:29f); that is clearly to be applied to the Holy Spirit, so that when sinners and the unworthy are removed and destroyed, he may create himself a new people and renew the face of the earth, when with the grace of the Holy Spirit they will have laid aside the old man with his works and will behave according to a new life. That is why it is right to say that the Holy Spirit dwells, not in those who are flesh, but in those of whom the earth has been renewed. The Holy Spirit was, for this reason, imparted by imposition of the Apostles' hands, after the grace and renewal brought by baptism. And the Saviour himself after the Resurrection, when former things had passed away and all was made new, since he was himself the new man and the first-born from the dead, said to his Apostles, similarly renewed by the evidence of his Resurrection: 'Receive the Holy Spirit' (Jn 20:22)."[9]

O. raises problems about OT and NT texts which he interprets in the context of the Spirit's relationship with Christ. Christ can be considered 'beneath' the Spirit, sent by him and by the Father, because of his humanity. O. continues with this fine passage: "But we must win over the one who takes exception to our saying that the Saviour was lowered beneath the Holy Spirit because he became man, by the words in the Epistle to the Hebrews, where Paul declares that because he suffered death, Jesus was lowered even beneath the angels. 'We see Jesus who for a little while was made lower than the angels, crowned with glory and honour because of the suffering of death' (Heb 2:9). Perhaps one may add this: creation begged to be delivered from the slavery of corruption, and the human race (asked) also that a blessed and divine power would become incarnate to restore equally all things on earth; in a certain way this action was incumbent on the Holy Spirit, but not being able to undertake it, he puts forward the Saviour as alone capable of sustaining such a combat; if then the Father, in so far as he has authority, sends the Son, the Holy Spirit sends with him and accompanies (the Son); for he promises to descend at the right time on the Son of God and collaborate with him in salvation of men.... He does that after the baptism, when, in corporeal form, he flies over him like a dove, remains and does not depart, as he does doubtless in the case of men, incapable of bearing his glory continually. That is why when the Christ was to be identified, John not only points to the descent of the Spirit on him, but to his remaining with him. According to Scripture John in fact declared, 'He who sent me to baptize said to me: "The one on whom you see the Spirit descend and remain this is he who baptizes in the Holy Spirit and in fire."' He did not only say, "'The one on whom you will see the Spirit descend'"—for he has descended perhaps on others—but "'descend and remain on him.'"[10]

O. thought it necessary to state explicitly that the Holy Spirit is eternal: "Some, I know, misunderstanding the newness of the Spirit have concluded that the Holy Spirit is new, in the sense of not having existed beforehand, and as if he had not been known to the ancients; and they are not aware that they commit a serious blasphemy. For the Holy Spirit is in the Law as he is in the Gospel. He is with the Father and the Son, he is, he has been and he will always be with the Father and the Son. He is not then new, but he renews all who are believers when he leads them from former evils to a new life and a new observance of the religion of Christ, and from being sensual makes them spiritual."[11]

There is a passage on the three divine Persons in O.'s greatest work, the *De Principiis (Peri Archon)* which seems to say that the three divine Persons are unequal. The validity of the interpretation rests on an accusation of mistranslation of Origen's text by Rufinus. This is the charge of St. Jerome, who had turned against O., and of Justinian: "*Propter hoc consequenter adest etiam gratia Sancti Spiritus ut ea quae substantialiter sancta non sunt, participatione ipsius sancta efficiantur. Cum ergo primo ut sint habeant ex Deo, Patre, secundo ut rationabilia sint habeant ex Verbo, tertio ut sancta sint habeant ex Spiritu Sancto.*" This is the doctrine of appropriation, not a statement of the relative power of the divine Persons. That it must be so read, that Rufinus did not mistranslate is very carefully argued, on the basis of evidence from the martyr St. Pamphilus (d. 309) and the Doctor of the Incarnation, St. Athanasius (qv), by H. Crouzel.[12] His conclusion: "Pamphilus and Athanasius confirm Rufinus then and contradict Jerome and Justinian."[13] O. was here as elsewhere chiefly interested in clearing away doubt that might arise from the Synoptics' account of the sin against the Spirit—the danger of an inverse hierarchy, the superiority of the Spirit over the Son and of the Son over the Father.

O. pondered an important question, the knowability of the Holy Spirit. "But as to the being of the Holy Spirit, no one could even imagine it at all, except those who have studied the law and the prophets, or those who profess their belief in Christ. For about God the Father, though no one can discourse worthily, nevertheless some understanding can be got from contact with visible creatures and from those things which the human mind perceives naturally: and in addition it is possible to have confirmation of this from the sacred scriptures. But about the Son of God, though 'no one has known the Son except the Father' nevertheless the human mind is instructed from the divine scriptures how it should also think, and this not only from the New, but also from the Old Testament by the deeds of the saints which refer to Christ in figure, from which there can be awareness of his divine nature and the human nature he assumed.

"Many texts of Scripture taught us that the Holy Spirit exists; David says in the fifty first psalm, 'Take not your holy Spirit from me' and Daniel, 'The Spirit of the holy God is in you.' In the NT we are instructed by many testimonies, when it is written that the Holy Spirit decended on Christ, and when Christ himself breathed on the Apostles after the resurrection, saying, 'Receive the Holy Spirit', and Mary is told by the angel, 'The Holy Spirit will come upon you.' But Paul teaches that 'no one can say, "Jesus is Lord" except by the Holy Spirit.' In Acts we read that 'The Holy Spirit was given in baptism by the imposition of the Apostles "hands"' (Acts 8:18). We have learned from all this that the subsistent being of the Holy Spirit is of such great authority and dignity that that saving baptism cannot be accomplished other than by the authority of the Trinity of all most excellent, that is by the naming of the Father and of the Son and of the Holy Spirit, that to the unbegotten Father and the only-begotten Son, the name of the Holy Spirit should also be joined. Who will not feel awe at the majesty of the Holy Spirit when he hears that he who has spoken a word against the Son of Man can hope for forgiveness, but that he who has blasphemed against the Holy Spirit, has forgiveness neither in this world nor in the next."[14]

As with the charge of Origenism in general, the corrective to what may be erroneously interpreted is found in O.'s own works. So, taking all that he wrote on the Holy Spirit, it is he himself who restores the balance where it may appear wanting. He had opened the way for a union of Hellenistic speculation with the truths of Christianity, with the Word whom he showed to be so magnificently the revealer, and the Spirit in the same role. To him we owe not only the meaningful term *hypostasis*, but other keywords in the fabric of Trinitarian thinking, *physis, ousia, theanthropos*, possibly even *homoousios*, apparently not *Theotokos*.

With such a debt in mind we can integrate the contents of this text into O.'s thought: "But we, persuaded by the Saviour who declares 'the Father who has sent me is greater than I' and who for this reason did not consent to receive even the name 'good', which was given him in its proper, true and plenary sense, but transferred it back to his Father with thanksgiving, while censuring the one who wished to glorify the Son excessively, do say that the Saviour as the Holy Spirit transcends all creatures not comparatively but with absolute transcendence, but is himself transcended by the Father, as much and even more than he and the Holy Spirit transcend other beings who are not however to be neglected."[15] "Transcend" clearly here refers, not to superiority in power but to primacy in origin. Thus the integration with O.'s total synthesis is possible.

---

[1]*Trinitas*, 170-172, bibl., add H. B. Swete, *The Holy Spirit in the Ancient Church*, 1912, 61-65; M. Simonetti, "Note sulla teologia trinitaria di Origene," *Vetera Christianorum*, 8 (1971), 273-307; *id.*, "Sull, interpretazione di un passo del 'De Principiis' di Origene" (1,3:5-8) *Rivista di cultura classica e medievale* 6 (1964), 15-32; H. Crouzel, S.J., esp. "Les personnes de la Trinité sont-elles de puissance inégale selon Origène, Peri Archon, I, 3,5-8?" *Gregorianum*, 57 (1976), 109-123; *id.*, *Origène*, Paris, 1985; A. Grillmeier, *Jesus der Christus*, Freiburg, 1979, 266-280; E. Schadel, "Zum Trinitätskonzept des Origenes," *Origeniana quarta*, hrsg., L. Lies, (Innsbrucker theol. Stud., 19), 1987, 203-214; *Handbuck der Dogmengeschichte*, II, 1a, 93-109; J. Wolinski, "La pneumatologie des Pères Grecs avant le Concile de Constantinople," in *Atti del Congresso*, 127-162, esp., 134-142; *BT* I, 2919-2927; [2]*Catholicisme*, X, 250; [3]*Origène* Paris, 264; [4]*De principiis*, I, praef., *GCS*, Origenes Werke, V. Koetschau, 11; [5]*God In Patristic Thought*, London, 1952, 2nd. ed., 179; [6]*In Joann*, II, 10, 75-77; *GCS*, IV, 65; *SC* 120, 256-258; [7]*De principiis*, I, 3,8, 57; *SC* 252, 162, 163; [8]*De principiis, ibid.*, [9]*De principiis*, I, 3,7, *SC* 252, 157-159; [10]*In Joann*, II, 10, 82-84, *SC* 120, 260-262; [11]*In Rom*. VI, 7, *PG* XIV, 1076; [12]Cf. H. Crouzel, in *Gregorianum*, l.cit.; [13]*Ibid.*, p.121; [14]*De principiis*, 13,1, Koetschau, 49. [15]*In Joann*, XIII,25, *PG* XIV, 411; *SC* 222, 112-114, C. Blanc.

ORTHODOX, THE

The Orthodox, who have always sought to maintain intellectual continuity with the great Fathers and Doctors of the East, have a strong tradition of doctrine about the Holy Spirit.[1] In recent times this thinking is found in the highly articulate group of expatriate Russian Orthodox centred in Paris, mostly associated with the St. Serge Institute. As elsewhere the Orthodox approach to the theology of the Trinity must be recalled: a beginning from the Persons, with consideration of the nature following, whereas the Latin tradition since St. Augustine (qv) begins with the nature and then studies the Persons. The Trinity in thought and church life, in Liturgy, holds high priority for the Orthodox.

Articles in this work deal with Orthodox writers, Basil Bolotov, Sergius Bulgakov, Paul Evdokimov, Vladimir Lossky. A number of Orthodox theologians contributed to the International Theological Congress (qv) held in Rome, 22-26 March, 1982 to mark the sixteenth centenary of the Council of Constantinople I. Contributors, in order of appearance, some of them well known in wider circles, were: Prof. Dr. J. D. Zizioulas of Glasgow University,[2] Archbishop Georges Khodr, from the Lebanon,[3] Dr. Dumitro Staniloae from Bucharest,[4] Bishop Demetrius Trakatellis from Athens.[5]

Noteworthy contributions have come from other Orthodox writers. John Meyendorff, specialist in the theology of St. Gregory Palamas (qv) and critical editor of some of his works, author of works on Orthodoxy, will figure in any list. So will Nicolas Afanasieff, whose work *L'Eglise du Saint Esprit* was published posthumously, 1975. So will Professor Nikos Nissiotis, of the University of Athens, at one time Editor of *The Ecumenical Review*, organ of the World Council.[6]

In this office N. Nissiotis published an article which had an impact.[7] He put cogently a criticism which, as Père Congar noted,[8] was occasionally voiced at the weekly meetings with Observers to Vatican II, organised by the Secretariat for Christian Unity: the conciliar texts lacked a pneumatology. According to the French Dominican the disappointment was expressed by Orthodox, Protestants and Anglicans. N. Nissiotis saw the defect especially in the Constitution on the Church and in that, already in draft form, on Divine Revelation. The stricture is one to be evaluated (see article Vatican II); it is mentioned to indicate the kind of reaction that came from the Orthodox who were interested in the Council's working and teaching.

As Moderator of the WCC Commission for Faith and Order, N. Nissiotis spoke with effect of the Holy Spirit in keynote addresses to the body;

on the occasion of the fiftieth anniversary of the First World Conference of Faith and Order, in Lausanne, May 1977,[9] he developed the theme, "The significance of the invocation of the Spirit for Church Unity."

Boris Bobrinskoy of the St. Serge Institute has been very observant of the trends of thought in the Orthodox world to which he belongs. He has described prayer in the Oriental Church for *DSp*,[10] clarifying the prominence there given to the Spirit and he wrote on *Le Filioque hier et aujourdhui* for Faith and Order Document 103, a collection of papers on the theology of the Holy Spirit, in dialogue between East and West, edited by Lukas Vischer:[11] His views are also found in other publications, with important insights on the Eucharist, the Spirit and Church.[12] Mention too must be made of another Orthodox writer, Olivier Clement, disciple of Vladmir Lossky (qv), particularly active in the world of communication.

Orthodox theologians have been much preoccupied in recent times with the *Filioque* controversy. This is understandable in the light of the ecumenical movement. There has been a certain flexibility in the thinking of some who were influenced by Basil Bolotov (qv), as Catholics like Yves-M.J. Congar and André de Halleux have sought a means by which there could be agreement with honour safeguarded on both sides.

One way in which unity may be hastened is the transfer of theological dialogue and exchange to another area. While it is clear that the inner life of the Trinity is the highest level conceivable and must therefore preempt all other options, the divine mystery is so profound and manifold that intellectual penetration may be assured by a change in approach. Hence the interest aroused by recent Orthodox thinking on the theme of the Spirit and the Church.

Memories are stirred of a Russian theologian who wrote over a century ago on the theology of the Church with such emphasis on the Spirit that the Christ event was minimised and the human aspect of the Church so overlooked that he seemed to think of the eschatological kingdom of God already achieved.

Two of the Orthodox theologians already mentioned, N. Nissiotis and B. Bobrinskoy, one from the Greek, the other from the Russian tradition, seek to fashion a theology of the Church free of any such defect, but with the fullest possible statement of the primary role of the Spirit, in the Church and ultimately in the cosmos. Here per-

haps is where the Latin and Orthodox traditions may join to discover many unsuspected facets in the personality and work of the Spirit, moving therefrom to a fuller intuition of the inner sublime mystery. In the economy the mystery is reflected.

[1] Bibliographical items of interest *Trinitas*, art. "Filiogue," 111f.; *EstTrin*. XI(1977), Numero estraordinario. Bibliografia trinitaria, Orthodox, 45-77; general introductions to Orthodox Church: S. Bulgakov (qv), *The Orthodox Church*, London, 1935; J. Meyendorff, *L'Eglise orthodoxe hier et aujourdhui*, 1960, English tr. *The Orthodox Church, its Past and its Role in the World Today*, New York, 1962; N. (M) Zernov, *Eastern Christendom. A Study of the Origin and Development of the Eastern Orthodox Church*, London, 1961; T. Ware, *The Orthodox Church*, Harmondsworth, 1963; P. Evodkimov (qv), *L'Orthodoxie*, Paris 1965; A. J. Philippou, ed., *The Orthodox Ethos*, Oxford, 1964; id. ed., *The Historical Appeal of Orthodoxy*, London, 1965; on our subject, esp. A. S. Khomiakov (Xomjakov), *L'Eglise latine et le protestantisme au point de vue de l'Eglise d'Orient*, Lausanne and Vevey, 1872; P. Corcoran, "Some Recent Writing on the Holy Spirit (Orthodox)", *ITQ* 39 (1972) 276-287; P. O.'Leary, O. P., "The Holy Spirit in the Church in Orthodox Theology," *ITQ* 46 (1979), 177-184; T. Spidlik, "Lo Spirito nell 'antropologia orientale," *Atti del Congresso*, 409-421; Maria Ryk, "L'Esprit Saint dans notre vie selon la théologie orientale, *Atti del Congresso*, 423-444; M. M. Garijo-Guembe, "La pneumatologia en la moderna teologia Ortodoxa," *EstTrin* 9 (1975) 359-382; [2] *The Teaching of the 2nd Ecumenical Council on the Holy Spirit in Historical and Ecumenical Perspective*, 29-54; [3] *L'Esprit Saint dans la tradition orientale*, 377-408; [4] *Le Saint Esprit dans la théologie byzantine et dans la réflexion orthodoxe contemporaine*, 661-679; [5] *The Holy Spirit and Mission: Basic Aspects in the New Testament*, 829-837; [6] Cf. *The Byzantine Legacy in the Orthodox Church*, 1982; id., "La procession du Saint Esprit chez les Pères orientaux," in *Russie et Chrétienté*, 1950, 158-178; id., "Unity of Church, Unity of Mankind," *St. Vlad. Theol. Quart.* 15 (1971), 167f; [7] "The Main Ecclesiological Problems in the Second Vatican Council and the Position of the Non-Roman Churches facing it", *The Ecumenical Review* 2 (1965) 31-62; further contributions from N. Nissiotis: "Pneumatological Christology as a Presupposition of Ecclesiology", in *Oecumenica, Jahrbuch für Okumenische Forschung*, Minneapolis, 1967; "Spirit, Church and Ministry", in *Theology Today* 19 (1963), 4, pp. 484-499; "Pneumatologie orthodoxe," in Le Saint Esprit, ed. F. J. Leenhardt et al., Geneva, 1963; "The Importance of the Doctrine of the Trinity for Church, Life and Theology, in *The Orthodox Ethos*, ed. A.J. Philippou; "La pneumatologie ecclésiologique au service de l'unité de l'Eglise", in *Istina* 12 (1967), 323f; *Die Theologie der Ostkirche im ökumenischen Dialog: Kirche und Welt in orthodoxer Sicht*, Stuttgart, 1968; [8] *Atti del Congresso*, "Actualité de la pneumatologie", 15; [9] Cf. W.H. Lazareth, in *Atti del Congresso*, 1320; [10] *DSp* IX, "Liturgies orientales", 914-923; [11] *La théologie du Saint Esprit* Presses de Taizé, 1981, pp. 148-164; further contributions by B. Bobrinskoy: "Le Saint Esprit dans la liturgie," *Studia Liturgica* 1 (1962) 47-60; "Presence réelle et communion, eucharistique," *RSPT* 53 (1969), 402-430; "The Holy Spirit, Life of the Church," *Diakonia* 6 (1971), 4, pp 303-320; "Quelques réflexions sur la

pneumatologie," in *Mélanges liturgiques* ... B. Botte, O. S. B., Louvain, 19-29; [12]On the relation of the Church to Spirit and Eucharist- cf. J. Zizioulas, "La communauté eucharistique et la catholicité de l'Eglise," *Istina* 14 (1969) 67-98; id., "The Local Church in a Eucharistic Perspective—Orthodox Contribution," in *In Each Place, towards a Fellowship of Local Churches truly United*, Geneva, 1977; id., "Christologie, Pneumatologie et institutions ecclésiales," in *Las Eglises après Vatican*; II, Paris, ed. G. Alberigo, 1981, 131-148 cf. also from the same author, *L'Etre ecclésial*, Geneva, 1981; *Implications ecclésiologiques de deux types de pneumatologie*, in Communio Sanctorum, Mélanges offerts à J.J. Von Allmen, Geneva, 1982, 141-154; *Die pneumatologische Dimension der Kirche*, IntKathZeitComm 2 (1973), 133-147.

P

PALAMAS, ST. GREGORY (1296-1359)[1]

An understanding of the doctrine of P. is important for two reasons principally. Western educated Christians, and not only theologians, need to know and value the treasures of eastern Christian literature, Liturgy, tradition and iconography in every sector of life. Hence the satisfaction of knowing that St. Maximus the Confessor (qv) attracts such scholarly and general interest. The second reason is ecumenical. There is need for knowledge of the whole Orthodox world, especially their leading thinkers and their distinctive religious practices, not forgetting their spirituality.

P. is the doctor of Hesychasm, and he is also the author of a developed theology of divinization, which, in some points, seriously challenges western thinking. In the extensive literature, which has grown up about him in recent times, Catholic opinion has been divided on the response to this challenge. V. Lossky did much to make him known. Previous indifference would be exemplified in the fact that T. de Régnon in his four-volume work on the Trinity (1892-98) did not mention him; or in the absence of any substantial writing on him in the first decades of the present century. His life exhibited qualities of deep contemplative ardour and spiritual courage; he is linked with the great monastic centre of Mount Athos.

The doctrine of P. which in its controversial theses is globally described as Palamism, touches a theology of the Holy Spirit in more ways than one. His Trinitarian orthodoxy is not in doubt: "God is the same in himself because the three hypostases possess each other naturally, totally, eternally and indivisibly, and also without mixture or confusion, and because they interpenetrate each other so as to possess one only energy."[2] "The divine energy is then one because every divine act *ad extra* is always a Trinitarian act; in fact the whole of creation was produced by the energy of God, one, uncreated, coeternal."[3] But P. has a qualifying notion: "Nonetheless there is, in addition, a personal mode according to which each divine hypostasis exercises the energy which is common, which allows us to speak of manifestation (or energies) of the Son and the Holy Spirit. The movement of the divine will is initiated by the primordial Principle, the Father, it proceeds through the Son and manifests itself in the Holy Spirit."[4]

On the Spirit P. has a passage that seems to evoke St. Augustine (qv): "This Spirit of the Word from on high is like a mysterious love of the Father for the Word mysteriously begotten; the Word, beloved Son of the Father, shows this love towards the one who has begotten him; he does so in so far as he comes from the Father conjointly with this Love and this Love rests on him."[5]

The hypostasis of the Father is for P. the active principle of unity. "God is one not only because he is one in his nature, but also because the persons who proceed go back to a unique Person."[6] To explain patristic texts, especially from St. Cyril of Alexandria, on the procession of the Spirit from the Father and the Son P. writes thus: "When you hear it said that the Holy Spirit proceeds from the two, because essentially he comes forth from the Father through the Son, you must understand his teaching in this way: what is poured out is the essential powers and energies of God, but not the divine hypostasis of the Spirit."[7] "The hypostasis of the Holy Spirit does not come from the Son; it is not given nor is it received by anyone, only divine grace and energy (are so received)." P. thinks that the patristic passages which appear to favour the Latin *Filioque* do not assert that the Spirit proceeds from the hypostasis of the Son, but from the nature of the Son. But what comes from the nature is the energy, not the hypostasis.

P. summarizes his thought thus: "The Holy Spirit belongs to Christ by essence and energy, because Christ is God; however, according to the essence and hypostasis, he belongs to him but does not proceed from him, while according to the energy he belongs to him and proceeds from him."[8] This distinction between essence and energy allows P. to adopt a more flexible attitude towards Latin thinking. He used such language as that the Spirit was poured out "from the Father through the Son, or if one wishes, from the Son" on all worthy of him. "Let us not lack propriety for quarrels over words." He would accept these formulas so long as the personalism dear to the Fathers and the traditional Byzantine theory of the "economic" procession of the Spirit from the Son were preserved.

P. spoke eloquently on the universal presence of the Spirit: "For he himself (the Lord) is with the Father and the Spirit, not as to his Person, but as to his divinity; and God is one in three, in one omnipotent divinity, abiding in three Persons; for the Holy Spirit always was and he was with the Son in the Father. For indeed how would the Father and the eternal mind have existed without the coeternal Son and Word? But how would the coeternal Word have existed without the coeternal Spirit? Accordingly the Holy Spirit always was, is and will be, creating with the Father and the Son things made in time, renewing what is decadent, preserving what is permanent, ubiquitous, filling all things, ruling and guarding all. For the psalmist says to God: 'Whither shall I go from thy Spirit? Or whither shall I flee from thy presence?' (Ps 139:7). Truly not merely everywhere, but above all things, and in every age and time, but before all ages and times; nor is the Holy Spirit only to be with us, as has been promised, until the end of the age, but much more will he remain with the saints in the age to come, and their bodies endowed with immortality he will also fill with eternal glory. Pointing out this the Lord said to his disciples: 'And I will pray the Father, and he will give you another Counselor, to be with you forever' (Jn 15:16)." P. goes on to show that it is the Spirit

which confers immortality on the human body; it will be "clothed with immortality, glory and incorruptibility by the power of the Spirit."[9]

P. insists that, as Paul teaches, it is in the Spirit that we have true discernment. He is not unfailingly easy to follow when he relates divinization to the Spirit as in this passage from the *Defence of the Hesychast Saints*: "Only the beings united to (the divinity) have been deified by the total presence of the one who anoints them; they have received an energy identical with that of the deifying essence, they possess it in its entire fullness, and reveal it through themselves. And in fact, according to the Apostle, in Christ the whole fullness of deity dwells bodily (Col 2:9). That is why some saints, after God came in the flesh, have seen this light like a limitless sea, pouring out extraordinarily from a unique sun, the adored body, in the same way as the Apostles saw it on the mountain. It was then in that way that the 'first fruits' of our human composite were deified. But the deification of angels and deified men is not the superessential essence of God; it is not manifested in these deified beings, as art is manifested in the object of art, for that is how productive power is manifested in the objects created by it, universally visible and even reflecting itself in them; deification is manifested in these beings, according to the great Basil (qv), '*as the art in him who has acquired it,*' (*De Spir. Sancto*, 26, *PG* 32, 180C). That is why the saints are instruments of the Holy Spirit, having received the same energy as him. As positive proof of what I say one can quote the charisms of healing, the performing of miracles, foresight, the unanswerable wisdom which the Lord called even *the Spirit of your Father* (Mt. 10:20), and also the sanctifying transmission of the Spirit, which those who are sanctified with them receive from them and through them. God said, in fact, to Moses (qv), 'I will take some of the Spirit which is upon you and put it upon them;' in the same way when Paul *had laid his hands* on the twelve Ephesians, *the Holy Spirit came upon them*, and at once *they spoke with tongues and prophesied* (Acts 19:6). Hence, when we consider the proper dignity of the Spirit, we see him equal to the Father and to the Son; but when we think of the grace which he works on those who participate in it, we say that the Spirit is in us, *that he is poured out on us, but is not created, that he is given to us, but is not drawn from nothingness, that he is granted to us, but is not produced.* (Ps. Basil, *Contra Eunomium*, V, *PG* 29, 772D). To speak again as the great Basil,

172

he is present in those who are imperfect, in such wise only that they can use him, for their judgement lacks stability; on the other hand, he is present in those who are more perfect, in virtue of the state which they have acquired, a state which is established, and even more than that. The energy of the Spirit is in the purified soul, as the visual faculty in a healthy eye," he says.[10]

P. has edifying things to say about the Spirit in his homily on the Annunciation. In the homily on Pentecost he points to a double role of the Spirit, "not only is he sent but he is also of the number of those sending and consenting.... Accordingly not only is the Holy Spirit sent, but he sends the Son who is sent by the Father, from which it is clear that he is of the same nature and dignity, of the same operation and honour as the Father and the Son."[11]

There are difficulties for Catholic theologians in some of the views related thus far, though they may not be insuperable. It is when P moves into the area of knowledge of the deity, especially the knowledge possessed by the blessed in heaven, that Palamism becomes really controversial. The Apostles and saints though divinized did not see the essence, but the energy of the Godhead. The Blessed in heaven will not see the essence of God but only the energy. This seems irreconcilable with the edict *Benedictus Deus* published by Benedict XII, 29 January, 1336. Therein the Pope repeatedly speaks of an "intuitive vision of the divine essence."[12]

The real stumbling-block for some Catholic theologians will be the uncreated energy distinct from the divine essence; it seems irreconcilable with the Thomistic concept of the divine simplicity. Possibly a closer analysis of P.'s doctrine of participation may help to solve the problem. Here, for example, is how he applies this doctrine to Mary: "Since it is the eternal law in heaven that the lesser should from the greater participate in the nature of him who is and who sits in heaven, and since the Virgin Mother is greater than all without exception, it is through her that those who participate in the nature of God receive this (gift); whoever knows God will possess her and they who celebrate God will celebrate her after God. She is the cause of those who have gone before her, the author of those who have followed her, she is the dispenser of eternal things."[13] Admittedly P.'s concept of participation has to be fully analysed and evaluated.

[1]For bibliography cf. D. Stiernon, A.A., *REB* 30 (1972), 231-341; Y.-M.J. Congar, O.P. *The Holy Spirit*, III, 67-71; *Trinitas*, 175; J. Meyendorff, *Introduction à l'étude de Grégoire Palams*, Paris, 1959, Appendix I, 331-399; id. *DSp*, XII,81-107; Works, *PG* 150, 151; for Catholic criticism of P. cf. M. Jugie, A.A., "Palamas et Palamite (Controverse), *DTC* XI (1932) 1735-1818; id., *Theologia dogmatica Christianorum Orient. ab Ecclesia cath. diss.*, II, Paris, 1933, 47-183; S. Guichardan, *Le problème de la simplicité divine en Orient et en Occident aux XIVe et XVe siècles, Grégoire Palamas, Duns Scot, Georges Scholarios*, Lyons, 1933; articles in *Istina*, 1974; Catholics favourable, in different degrees, A. de Halleux, "Palamisme et tradition, Irenikon, 48 (*1975*) 479-493; id., "Palamisme et Scolastique", *RTL* 4 (1973) 409-422; id., "Orthodoxie et Catholicisme; du personnalisme en pneumatologie," *RTL* 6 (1975) 3-30; esp. C. (Cardinal) Journet, "Palamisme et thomisme. A propos d'un livre récent, "RT 60 (1960) 429-452; J. Kuhlmann, "Die Taten des einfachen Gottes. Ein romisch-katholische Stellungnahme zum Palamismus" *Das östliche Christentum*, (New Series, 21) Wurzburg 1968, 294-99; G. Philips, "La grâce chez les Orientaux, *ETL* 48 (1972) 37-50, repr. in *L'union personnelle avec le Dieu vivant*, Gembloux, 1972, 241-260; [2]*Chapters* 112, *PG* 150, 1197B; [3]*Chapters* 140, 1220A; [4]112, 1197C; [5]*Chapters* 36, 114D; [6]J. Meyendorff, *Introduction*, 314; [7]*Apodictic Treatise*, apud [8]*Ibid.*, 315; [9]Hom. XXIV, *PG* 151, 316D, 317A; 621-23; [10]ed. J. Meyendorff, *Triade III*, 33, [11]Hom XXIV, *PG*, 151, 307C,D; [12]*DS*, 1000; [13]Hom XXXVII *in Dorm. PG* 151, 474; for a discussion of participation in regard to P. cf. Y.-M.J. Congar, O.P., *The Holy Spirit*, III, 65,66.

PAPACY, THE

Since the Holy Spirit enters into a special relationship with the Apostles and with all those who exercise authority within the Church, his action is plenary at the summit of Church authority, the Papacy.[1] The Papacy, in the person of Peter, was especially marked by the Spirit in its inception. Vatican II tells us that "The Apostles preaching everywhere the Gospel (Mk 16:20), received by their hearers under the action of the Holy Spirit, gather the universal Church, which the Lord founded on the Apostles and which he built on Blessed Peter, Christ Jesus himself being the corner-stone." "To fulfill such great duties, the Apostles were enriched by Christ with a special outpouring of the Spirit who came upon them (cf. Acts 1:8; 2:4; Jn 20:22-23), and they themselves, by the imposition of hands, pass on to their co-workers the gift of the Spirit (cf. 1 Tim 4:14; 2 Tim 1:6-7) which has been handed down to our times in episcopal consecration."

After the event of Pentecost, a change took place which, as the Council insinuates, was the immediate effect of the Spirit's descent: "And they were all filled with the Holy Spirit and began to speak in other tongues, as the Spirit gave them utterance" (2:4). The spokesman of the newly born Church to the waiting world was Peter: he made a first key pronouncement. He appealed as justification for what was being done to the prophet Joel: 'And in the last days it shall be, God declares, that I will pour out my Spirit upon all flesh, and your sons and daughters shall prophesy, and your young men shall see visions, and your old men shall dream dreams, yea and on my menservants and my maidservants in those days I will pour out my Spirit; and they shall prophesy'" (Act 2:17, 18).

Peter is the dominant figure in the first part of the Acts of the Apostles, before Paul's conversion and entry on the missionary scene. Before the full Jewish religious establishment, "their rulers and elders and scribes gathered together with Annas the high priest and Caiaphas and John and Alexander, and all who were of the priestly family," Peter proclaimed the message of Christ. We are told that he was "filled with the Holy Spirit" for this task (Acts 4:8). When a new missionary prospect opened up in Samaria the Apostles at Jerusalem "sent to them Peter and John, who came down and prayed for them that they might receive the Holy Spirit; for it had not yet fallen on any of them, but they had only been baptized in the name of the Lord Jesus. Then they laid their hands on them and they received the Holy Spirit" (Acts 8:15-17).

The conversion of Cornelius was eventful, epoch-making in the early Church: the first gentile. As the story is told the Spirit's action on Peter is emphasized. While Peter was pondering the vision he had had (Acts 10:11-16, 19), "the Spirit said to him, 'Behold, three men are looking for you. Rise and go down, and accompany them without hesitation; for I have sent them'" (10:19-20). When Peter had entered the house of Cornelius and heard of his mystical experience he preached the good news to those gathered with him; a key sentence included the words "how God anointed Jesus of Nazareth with the Holy Spirit and with power" (10:38).

The episode closes thus: "While Peter was still saying this, the Holy Spirit fell on all who heard the word. And the believers from among the circumcised who came with Peter were amazed, because the gift of the Holy Spirit had been poured out even on the Gentiles. For they heard them speaking in tongues and extolling God. Then Peter declared, 'Can any one forbid water for baptizing these people who have received the Holy Spirit just as we have?' And he commanded them to be baptized in the name of Jesus Christ" (10:44-48).

In the full perspective of church beginnings, Peter first faced a confrontation with the circumcision party, a kind of curtain raiser for the big moment in the unfolding Christian drama: the official opening to the pagan world. He reminded them of the Spirit's intervention: "'At that very moment three men arrived at the house in which we were, sent to me from Caesarea. And the Spirit told me to go with them, making no distinction'" (Acts 11:11,12). Telling of his encounter with Cornelius and his household Peter says: "'As I began to speak, the Holy Spirit fell on them just as on us at the beginning. And I remembered the word of the Lord, how he said, "John baptized with water, but you shall be baptized with the Holy Spirit." If then God gave the same gift to them as he gave to us when we believed in the Lord Jesus Christ, who was I that I could withstand God'" (11:15-17)?

The full decision was taken when the "apostles and elders" gathered at Jerusalem, prototype of an oecumenical council. The keynote speech was given by Peter: "After there had been much debate, Peter rose and said to them, 'Brethren, you know that in the early days God made choice among you, that by my mouth the Gentiles should hear the word of the gospel and believe. And God who knows the heart bore witness to them, giving them the Holy Spirit just as he did to us; and he made no distinction between us and them, but cleansed their hearts by faith'" (Acts 15:7-9).

After contributions by Barnabas and Paul and James the official letter expressing the consensus of the assembly was drawn up, the charter document of the conversion of the Gentiles. The essential words were: "'For it has seemed good to the Holy Spirit and to us to lay upon you no greater burden than these necessary things: that you abstain from what has been sacrificed to idols and from blood and from what has been strangled and from unchastity'" (15:28, 29).

The Church was then set on its expansion throughout the known world of the time, and ever after. The acceptance of a universal mission is basic to the dispersion of the Apostles and their association with such widely different churches. The central figure in the early days which were so critical, in the office of teaching and ruling, was

Peter: Peter, it is made clear, as an instrument of the Spirit.

If the imprint of the Spirit is so discernible in the beginnings of the Papacy as an office we should expect it to continue. Here we meet the question of continuity put by Protestants: Did the Petrine promise made by Christ include his successors? "'Thou art Peter and upon this rock I will build my Church'".... "'I have prayed for you Peter that your faith fail not and you being once converted, confirm thy brethren'". We can but appeal to the sense of the Church attested in many documents; we must also recall that Christ wished to establish a community which would endure and the same needs would exist within this community as time passed, until the end of time.

To elaborate these theses and deal with objections is the task of apologetics. We accept the fact of the Papacy's survival as a unique phenomenon in world history, despite weakness at times in the individuals who have held the office. Accompanying features of the office vary as different cultures, social patterns, concepts of authority succeed each other through the ages, as the ideal of personal holiness grows or wanes within the ecclesiastical establishment.

The question of the Spirit's action on the individual as a disciple of Christ, and on the same person as representing the teaching, ruling and priestly offices of the Saviour to the whole Church is one which demands a complex answer. The First Vatican Council chose to emphasize the infallibility and the primacy of the Petrine office. Explicit conditions are laid down to help identify infallible statements. Personal holiness is not one of these conditions; fortunately, as we should find it impossible to apply. Who can be certain of the holiness of his fellow Christian? Great saints have not been recognised as such. Some of them have been denounced and punished as evil-doers by their fellow Christians, witness St. John of the Cross, St. Joan of Arc, Blessed Anne Mary Javouhey.

A first notable effect of the Spirit's action is the perpetuity of the office. This is linked to the Spirit's presence to the Church as a guarantee of its survival, of its very life. His unfailing, manifold operation, nullifying decadence from within or assault from without, must focus on the centrepiece: "Where is Peter, there is the Church." The Spirit is particularly vigilant in times of crises. Which brings us back to the deeper question: How distinguish the Spirit's influence on the Pope as an individual from his guidance of one exercising teaching ruling authority which binds all the faithful? Personal holiness, obtainable only through the Spirit, will keep the Pope sensitive and attentive to the needs of the faithful. A holy Pope responsive to the Spirit's impulse will discern the moment when his intervention may be beneficial, in some ways necessary; he may do so with a sureness which a less holy Pope will lack.

But as to the essence of the pronouncement he makes or the authoritative decision he takes, the prime factor is not his holiness. The charism he exercises does not flow from this holiness but from the Spirit, who uses him for the good of the Church. The distinction is not too subtle or superfine. It is rooted in the very meaning of the Church. This is Christ's Mystical Body, and whereas each member enjoys the benefits of communion, action on the whole Body is directly from Christ through his instruments equipped by anointing for this work.

Modern communications expose the person of the Pope to almost continuous observation. When this occurs in areas where Catholics have lost their nerve, but remain curious and vocal, it is not surprising that there should be criticism of the Pope. It takes various forms, from the extreme conservative right to the liberal far left—allowing for some lack of precision in these hackneyed terms.

These critics rarely advert to principles deemed sacred in the conventional wisdom of our time—sacred does not mean always valid. It is assumed that people must submit to the dictate of their own conscience. This the Pope must do. It is assumed that those not experientially involved in human situations or relationships—marriage for instance—should refrain from teaching or judgement in regard to people so involved. Celibate priests should not teach or judge married people.

The principle is not valid. Whereas it is wise to seek adequate information at the experiential level, to exclude normative or judicial pronouncements solely on the grounds of defective experience would wreck the social order. Yet the very people who would uphold the principle against moral teaching about married life, overlook it in their criticism of the Pope. They have no experience of his office, his responsibility, his power. They go ahead regardless. They may do so with good intentions. The painful fact is sometimes observable that in areas within their own experience, they are not either enlightened or competent.

A Pope is chosen for qualities of mind and will,

seen within the Christian context. He has available sources of information not accessible to ordinary people. Critics claim that they think better and know more: a claim at times patently unwarranted.

It is, however, in the theology of the office that we can detect the critic's most serious handicap. The guidance and strength of the Spirit are given to the Pope, as person and as head of the Church. It is in no way arguable that the Spirit communicates to others indiscriminately, especially to those with manifest prejudice, the inspiration he gives to the Pope, that he inspires them about the very content of his special help to the Pope. If he does exceptionally give an individual a message for the Pope, he or she would be obliged to transmit this, with an appropriate warrant. St. Catherine of Siena did this. In modern times individuals have communicated directly with Popes, before the consecration of the world to the Sacred Heart of Jesus and to the Immaculate Heart of Mary, before the institution of the Feast of the Kingship of Christ, before the Encyclical *Humanae vitae*. The final judgement remains with the Pope himself.

There have been "bad" Popes. It was, in that case, the duty of those immediately sharing authority with them to take action. Popes have made mistakes, privately in the area of doctrine, in church government, in their dealings with secular goverments. Pius XII (qv) admitted in his tribute to Benedict XIV that this Pope's dealings with Frederick of Prussia were a subject of controversy. Pius himself was lauded immediately after the war for his immense humanitarian effort on behalf of the stricken Jews—in the opinion of one Jewish scholar he saved 860,000 Jewish lives, more than all governments and international agencies together; another claimed that by 1965, 360,000 Jews who owed their lives to Pius had gone to Israel from Roumania alone. Those who since the appearance of Rolf Hochhuth's play in 1963 have blamed Pius for not publishing an indictment of the Nazi death camps do not mention these facts. Nor the evidence that shows that such a public condemnation would have worsened the evil. They have no experience of the situation in which this Pope worked, they are ignorant of the information available to him then. They do not have the inspiration of the Spirit which he had. A flaming condemnation is now a subject of theoretical argument; then it had to be balanced in terms of life and death. That this man's priority was to save Jewish lives is utterly undeniable.

[1]Bibl. "Petrus" in bibl. of *Archivum Historiae Pontificiae*, Rome, Gregorian University, annually since 1963; P. Nober, "Petrus", *Elenchus Bibliographicus, Biblica*, Rome, Biblical Institute, annually since 1955; C. Ghidelli, "Bibliografia Biblica Petrina," *La Scuola Cattolica*, Supplemento Bibliografico 96 (1968), pp. 62-110; P. Gaechter, *Petrus und seine Zeit. Neutestamentliche Studien*, Innsbruck, 1958; A. Rimoldi, *L'Apostolo San Pietro, fondamento della Chiesa, principe degli apostoli ed ostiario celeste della Chiesa primitiva dalle origini al concilio di Calcedonia, Analecta Gregoriana, 96 Series Facultatis Historiae Ecclesiasticae*, sectio B (n. 18), Rome, 1958; P. Benoit, O.P., "La primauté de saint Pierre selon le Nouveau Testament", *Exégèse et Théologie*, II, Paris, 1961, 250-84; O. Cullmann, *Peter: Disciple, Apostle, Martyr. A Historical and Theological Essay*, London, 2nd ed. 1962; O. Karrer, *Peter and the Church: An Examination of Cullmann's Thesis, Quaestiones Disputatae*, 8, New York, London, 1963; A. Vogtle, *LTK*, 1964, VIII, 334-40; A. (Cardinal) Bea, S. J. and others, *San Pietro, Atti della Settimana Biblica. Associazione Biblica Italiana*, Brescia, 1967; B. Rigaux, O.F.M., "Saint Peter in Contemporary Exegesis," *Progress and Development in the History of Church Renewal*, ed. A. Aubert, New York, 1967; Porubcan, "The Consciousness of Peter's Primacy in the New Testament," *Archivum Historiae Pontificiae* 5 (1967) 9-39; R. Schnackenburg, "*Das Petrusamt.*" *Die Stellung des Petrus zu den anderen Aposteln, Wort und Warheit. Zeitschrift für Religion und Kultur* 26 (1971) 206-215; summary, "The Petrine Office. Peter's Relationship to the Other Apostles," *Theology Digest*, 20 (1972), 148-52; W. Trilling, "Zum Petrusamt im Neuen Testament. Traditiongeschichtliche Uberlegungen anhand von Matthaus, Petrus und Johannes, *Theologische Quartalschrift* 151 (1971), 110-133; R. E. Brown, K. P. Donfried, J. Reumann, *Peter in the New Testament*, London, 1974; P. J. McCord, ed., *A Pope for all Christians*, London, 1978; J. M. R. Tillard, *The Bishop of Rome*, London, 1980.

PATRICK, ST. (c. 390 - c. 460)

P.'s theology of the Holy Spirit is experiential, though his rule of faith (*mensura fidei*, cp. Rom 12:3) contains a doctrinal statement, which has led some to see in the whole creed a link between Nicaea and Constantinople I (qv); it would answer the question why apparently there is no use of the Constantinopolitan formulary before it was authorized by the Council of Chalcedon, 451.[1] The whole formulary set down by P. is traceable to Victorinus of Pettau, with some additions which reflect the Arian debate. The article on the Holy Spirit reads thus: "And he shed on us abundantly the Holy Spirit, the gift and pledge of immortality, who makes those who believe and obey to become children of God the Father, and joint heirs with Christ, whom we confess and adore as one God in the Trinity of the Holy Name."[2] This is then part of the rule of faith of the British church, from which Patrick came to Ireland.

176

P. justifies his decision to write his testimony by reliance on the Spirit, "for as the Spirit yearns, the human disposition displays the souls of men and their understandings.... And if perchance it seems to not a few that I am thrusting myself forward in this matter with my want of knowledge and my *slow tongue* (Ex 4:10), yet it is written, *The tongue of the stammerers will quickly learn to speak peace—will speak readily and distinctly*, (RSV, Is 32:4). How much rather should we earnestly desire to do who are, he says, *the epistle of Christ for salvation unto the ends of the earth*, although not a learned one, yet *ministered*, most powerfully, *written in your hearts, not with ink, but with the Spirit of the living God— You yourselves are our letter of recommendation, written on your hearts, to be known and read by all men; and you show that you are a letter of Christ delivered by us, written not with ink, but with the Spirit of the living God. (2 Cor 6:3)"*[3] And again the Spirit witnesses, *And husbandry was ordained by the Most High—farm work, created by the Most High*" (RSV, Sir 7:15).

P. tells of an ordeal to which Satan submitted him; he would remember it as long as he was in his body. "And he fell upon me as it were a huge rock, and I had no power over my limbs. But whence did it come to me—to my ignorant mind—to call upon Helias? And on this I saw the sun rise in the heaven, and while I was shouting 'Helias' with all my might, lo, the splendour of that sun fell upon me, and straightway shook all weight from off me. And I believe that I was helped by Christ my Lord, and that his Spirit was even then calling on my behalf. And I trust that it will be so in the day of my trouble, as he says in the Gospel, *In that hour*, the Lord testifies, *(for) it is not you who speak but the Spirit of your Father speaking through you*" (Mt 10:19,20)."[4]

P. had a singular experience of the Spirit praying within him: "And another time I saw him praying within me, and I was as it were within my body; and I heard (One praying) over me, that is, over the *inner man* (Eph 3:16); and there he was, praying mightily with groanings. And meanwhile I was astonished, and was marvelling and thinking who it could be that was praying within me; but at the end of the prayer he affirmed that he was the Spirit. And so I awoke, and I remembered how the Apostle says, *Likewise the Spirit helps us in our weakness; for we do not know how to pray as we ought, but the Spirit himself intercedes for us with sighs too deep for words* (Rom 8:26). And again, *The Lord our Advocate* (1 Jn 2:1) *intercedes for us*" (Rom 8:34).[5]

P. had a very strong sense of the indwelling Spirit: "I have said enough. Nevertheless I ought not to hide the gift of God which he bestowed upon us in the land of my captivity; because then I earnestly sought him, and there I found him, and he kept me from all iniquities—this is my belief—*because of his indwelling Spirit* (Rom 8:11) who has worked in me until this day."[6]

The great missionary recalls the precept of the Master to preach the gospel and baptize in the name of the Father and of the Son and of the Holy Spirit. He sets down the words of the prophet Joel (2:28-32) recalled by St. Peter (Acts 2:17,18). He would have liked to visit his homeland and even "to go as far as Gaul in order to visit the brethren and behold the face of the saints of my Lord—God knows that I used to desire it exceedingly." "Yet," he continues, "*I am bound in the Spirit*, who *testifies to me* (Acts 20:22) that if I should do this, he would note me as guilty."[7]

In the second authentic document from P., the Letter to Coroticus, he repeats the Pauline phrase: "Was it without God, or according to the flesh, that I came to Ireland? Who compelled me? *I am bound in the Spirit* not to see any one of my kinsfolk."[8]

P.'s intuition of the Spirit and his fidelity to the Spirit's inspiration throw light on the phenomenal success of his mission to the Irish, a mission which, apart from the immense flowering of Christianity in the island in the ensuing centuries, may be said to have influenced church history over whole continents down to the present time.

---

[1]Works ed. with French tr., R. P. C. Hanson and C. Blanc, *SC* 249; English tr., Newport J. D. White, *The Writings of St. Patrick*, London S.P.C.K., 1954; L. Bieler, *The Works of St. Patrick, ACW* 17; cf. R. P. C. Hanson, *St. Patrick His Origins and Career*, Oxford, 1968, bibl.; M. O'Carroll, C. S. Sp., *DSp*, XII 477-483, bibl.; L. Bieler, *The Life and Legends of St. Patrick*, Dublin, 1949; review of this T. O'Rahilly, *Irish Historical Studies*, 8 (No. 31, March 1953); D. Binchy, "St. Patrick and his Biographers", *Studia Hibernica*, 2 (1962), 7-173; R.P.C. Hanson, "The Rule of Faith of Patrick and of Victorinus," in Latin *Script and Letters*, (Festschrift Ludwig Bieler), ed. J. O'Meara and B. Neumann, 1976, 25-36; id., "Witness from St. Patrick to the Creed of 381," *AB* 101 (1983) 297-299; Y.-M.J. Congar, *The Holy Spirit*, I, 69f; *Trinitas*, 175f; [2]*Confession*, 4, tr. N. White, p. 8 [3]*Ibid.*, 11, p. 10; [4]*Ibid.*, 20, p. 13f; [5]*Ibid.*, 25, p.15; [6]*Ibid.*, 33, p. 17; [7]*Ibid.*, 43, p. 21; [8]*Letter*, 10, p. 30.

PAUL, ST.[1]

"For we know, brethren beloved by God, that he has chosen you; for our Gospel came to you not only in word, but also in power and in the Holy Spirit and with full conviction. You know what kind of men we proved to be among you for your sake. And you became imitators of us and of the Lord, for you received the word in much affliction, with joy inspired by the Holy Spirit" (1 Thess 1:4-6). These are the first words written in the NT on the Holy Spirit; the First Letter to the Thessalonians was written by Paul about 51 A.D., the first document of the collection of writings accepted in the Church's canon. Paul went on to mention the Spirit (*pneuma*) 146 times, 117 times in the great early epistles. His approach is in the context of the Risen Lord, the incarnate Son of God, through whose death by crucifixion we are saved. That this experience of the risen Lord should be his source of knowledge and experience of the Spirit, and not the event of Pentecost, which he never mentions, is striking and revealing. His doctrine of the Spirit is never far from the world of experience, an existential framework. Thanks to his prolonged contact with one early Christian community, that at Corinth, and his study of its inter-action with the Spirit, he was able to provide a case history which, for all future ages, serves as a paradigm.

In the Epistle to the Galatians, Paul identifies the gift of the Spirit as the culmination, the definitive fulfilment, of the deepest aspiration of God's people, nourished in faith from the days of Abraham. Through this gift those born children of Abraham would become the sons of God. "O foolish Galatians! Who has bewitched you, before whose eyes Jesus Christ was publicly portrayed as crucified? Let me ask you only this: Did you receive the Spirit by works of the law, or by hearing with faith? Are you so foolish? Having begun with the Spirit, are you now ending with the flesh? Did you experience so many things in vain?—If it really is in vain. Does he who supplies the Spirit to you and works miracles among you do so by works of the law, or by hearing with faith? Thus Abraham 'believed God, and it was reckoned to him as righteousness'.... Christ redeemed us from the curse of the law, having become a curse for us—for it is written, 'Cursed be every one who hangs on a tree'—that in Christ Jesus the blessing of Abraham might come upon the Gentiles, that we might receive the promise of the Spirit through faith" (Gal 3:1-6, 13-14).

Our real life for Paul is "in Christ" and he can sum up his own whole life in terms of his commitment to Christ, to an experience of Christ, "For me to live is Christ. It is no longer I who live, but Christ who lives in me; and the life I now live in the flesh I live by faith in the Son of God, who loved me and gave himself up for me" (Gal 2:20). Inextricably intertwined with this Christo-centrism is Paul's insistence on the Holy Spirit. The Spirit is at the very centre of things: "Do you not know that you are God's temple, and that God's Spirit dwells in you? If any one destroys God's temple God will destroy him. For God's temple is holy and that temple you are" (1Cor 3:16-17).

This assurance is given to the community. Paul made it strictly personal in a subsequent passage in the same letter: "Do you not know that your body is a temple of the Holy Spirit within you, which you have from God? You are not your own; you were bought with a price. So glorify God in your body" (6:19-20). Yet it is the Spirit who unites the Body: "For just as the body is one and has many members, and all the members of the body, though many are one body, so it is with Christ. For by one Spirit we were all baptized into one body—Jews or Greeks, slaves or free—and all were made to drink of one Spirit" (1 Cor 12:12,13). The metaphor of drinking evokes the image of water for the Spirit, also found in Jn (7:37-39).

The passages which indicate a similar, practically identical interest, activity, influence of Christ and the Spirit—called by Paul "the Spirit of Christ" (Rom 8:9; Phil 1:19), "the Spirit of the Lord" (2 Cor 3:17) and the "Spirit of his Son" (Gal 4:6)—are distinctive and complement the teaching of Jn on the Paraclete: "that in him (Christ) we might become the righteousness of God" (2 Cor 5:21)—"righteousness and peace and joy in the Holy Spirit" (Rom 14:17); "justified in Christ (Gal 2:17)—justified in the name of the Lord Jesus Christ and in the Spirit of our God" (1 Cor 6:11); "those who are in Christ Jesus" (Rom 8:1)— "But you are not in the flesh, you are in the Spirit, if the Spirit of God dwells in you" (Rom 8:9); "Rejoice in the Lord" (Phil 3:1)—"joy in the Holy Spirit" (Rom 14:17); "the love of God in Christ Jesus our Lord" (Rom 8:39)—"your love in the Spirit" (Col 1:8); "And the peace of God, which passes all understanding, will keep your hearts and your minds in Christ Jesus" (Phil 4:7)— "Righteousness and peace and joy in the Holy Spirit" (Rom 14:17); "sanctified in Christ Jesus"

(1 Cor 1:2)—"so that the offering of the Gentiles may be acceptable, sanctified by the Holy Spirit" (Rom 15:16); "as men of sincerity, as commissioned by God, in the sight of God we speak in Christ" (2 Cor 2:17)—"Therefore I want you to understand that no one speaking by the Spirit of God ever says 'Jesus be cursed' and no one can say 'Jesus is Lord' except by the Holy Spirit" (1 Cor 12:3); "one body in Christ" (Rom 12:5), "baptized into Christ" (Gal 3:27)—"For by one Spirit we were all baptized into one body" (1 Cor 12:13).

Paul often combines Christ and the Spirit in the same statement: "I am speaking the truth in Christ, I am not lying; my conscience bears me witness in the Holy Spirit" (Rom 9:1); "But you were washed, you were sanctified, you were justified in the name of the Lord Jesus Christ and in the Spirit of our God" (1 Cor 6:11). "The Gospel concerning his Son, who was descended from David according to the flesh and designated Son of God in power according to the Spirit of holiness by his resurrection from the dead, Jesus Christ our Lord (*Kyrios*)" (Romans 1:3-4); "If the Spirit of him who raised Jesus from the dead dwells in you, he who raised Christ Jesus from the dead will give life to your mortal bodies also through his Spirit which dwells in you" (Rom 8:11).

Here we see in the ultimate eschatological context how the Spirit of Jesus establishes him in his condition as 'Son of God in power' and *Kyrios*. From this mysterious, eternal partnership all that the Spirit and Jesus confer on us may be understood. Our adoptive sonship, a preparation for the final happy destiny, is assured by the Spirit: "For all who are led by the Spirit of God are sons of God. For you did not receive the spirit of slavery to fall back into fear, but you have received the spirit of sonship. When we cry, 'Abba! Father!' it is the Spirit himself bearing witness with our spirit that we are children of God . . . . "(Rom 8:15-16); "And because you are sons, God has sent the Spirit of his Son into our hearts, crying, 'Abba! Father!' So through God you are no longer a slave but a son, and if a son then an heir." (Gal 4:6-7).

It is the Spirit also who empowers the sons to enter into relationship with their heavenly Father in prayer (qv). "Pray at all times in the Spirit, with all prayer and supplication" (Eph 6:17); "Likewise the Spirit helps us in our weakness; for we do not know how to pray as we ought, but the Spirit himself intercedes for us with sighs too deep for words. And he who searches the hearts of men knows what is the mind of the Spirit, because the Spirit intercedes for the saints according to the will of God" (Rom 8:26-27).

Thus the soul is led to mysteries unfathomable: "But, as it is written, 'What no eye has seen, nor ear heard, nor the heart of man conceived, what God has prepared for those who love him', God has revealed to us through the Spirit. For the Spirit searches everything, even the depths of God. For what man knows a man's thoughts except the spirit of man which is in him? So also no one comprehends the thoughts of God except the Spirit of God. Now we have received not the spirit of the world, but the Spirit which is from God, that we might understand the gifts bestowed on us by God. And we impart this in words not taught by human wisdom but taught by the Spirit, interpreting spiritual truths to those who possess the Spirit" (1 Cor 2:9-13). That St. Paul was at all times conscious of the manifold influence of the Spirit in Christian theory and practice will be evident to the reader who, in the present work, consults the articles: Baptism in the Spirit; Charisms; Church; Communion of Saints; Death; Freedom; Fruits; Indwelling; Law; Paul VI; Personal Fulfilment Power; Prayer; Tongues; Vatican II.

---

[1]Cf. J. Gloel, *Der Heilige Geist in der Heilsverkündigung des Paulus*, Halle, 1888; E. Sokolowski, *Die Begriffe Geist und Leben bei Paulus*, Göttingen, 1903; H. B. Swete, *The Holy Spirit in the New Testament*, London, 1912, I, ch. IV-VI; K. Deissner, *Auferstehungshoffnung und Pneumagedanke bei Paulus*, Leipzig, 1912; H. Bertrams, *Das Wesen des Geistes nach der Anschauung des Apostels Paulus*, Münster 1913; E. Scott, *The Spirit in the New Testament*, London, 1923; F. Büchsel, *Das Geist Gottes im Neuen Testament*, Gutersloh, 1926, 267-451; P. Gächter, "Zum Pneumabegriff des hl. Paulua," *ZKT*, 53 (1929), 345-408; R. B. Hoyle, *The Holy Spirit in St. Paul*, London, 1926; E. Fuchs, *Christus und der Geist bei Paulus*, Leipzig, 1932; F. Prat, *The Theology of St. Paul*, London, 1945, II, 132-34, 142-46; 288-94, 395; K. Prümm, "Die katholische Auslegung von 2 Kor 3:17 in den letzen vier Jahrzehnten," *BB* 31 (1950) 316-45; 459-82; B. Schneider, *Dominus autem Spiritus est*, Rome, 1951; J. Schmid, "Geist und Leben bei Paulus," *GL24* (1951), 419-29; H. D. Wendland, "Das Wirken des Heiligen Geistes in den Glaübigen nach Paulus," *TLZ* 77 (1952), 457-70; B. Schnedier, "The Meaning of St. Paul's Antithesis of the Letter and the Spirit," *CBQ* 15 (1953), 163-207; E. Schweizer, "Rom 1:3f und der Gegensatz von Fleisch und Geist vor und bei Paulus," *ET* 15 (1955) 563-71; M. Dibelius, *Der Herr und der Geist bei Paulus*, Tübingen, 1956; L. Cerfaux, *Le Christ dans la théologie de St. Paul*, Paris, 1951, 216-222; id., *The Christian in the Theology of St. Paul*, London, 1967, 239-311; N.Q. Hamilton, "The Holy Spirit and Eschatology in Paul," *Scottish Journal of Theol* (occasional papers 6), 1957; G. Schneider, "Die Idee der Neuschöpfung beim Apostel Paulus

und ihr religionsgestchlicher Hintergrund," *Trierer Theol Zeitschr.*, 68 (1959), 257-270; R. T. Fortna, "Romans 8:10 and Paul's Doctrine of the Spirit," *ATR* 151 (1959), 77-84; P. Bläser, "Lebendigmachender Geist," *Sacra Pagina*, 2 (1959) 404-13; K. Stalder, *Das Werk des Geistes in der Heiligung bei Paulus*, Zurich, 1962; R. Koch, "L'aspect eschatologique de l'Esprit du Séigneur d'après Saint Paul," *Stud. Paulin. Congressus Internat. Cath.* I, Rome, 1963, 131-141; V. Warnach, "Das Wirken des Heiligen Geistes in den Gläubigen nach Paulus," *Pro Veritate. Festgabe L. Jaeger und W. Stählin*, ed. E. Schlink and H. Volk, Münster and Kassel, 1963, 156-202 (same title H.—D. Wendland, *op. cit.*; K. Niederwinner, "Das Gebet des Geistes. Rom 8:20f, "*TZ* 20 (1964), 252-65; P.—A. Harle, "Le Saint Esprit et l'Eglise chez St. Paul," *Verbum Caro*, 74 (1965) 13-29; A. Feuillet, P. S. S., *Le Christ, Sagesse de Dieu*, Paris, 1966, 121ff, *passim*; M.A. Chevallier, *Esprit de Dieu, paroles d'hommes. Le role de l'Esprit dans les ministères de la parole selon l'apôtre Paul*, Neuchâtel, 1966; J.D.G. Dunn, "2 Cor 3:17 The Lord is the Spirit", *JTS*, N. S., 21 (1970) 309-320; G. T. Montague, *The Holy Spirit*, 127-236; J. Guillet, *DSp*, IV, 1, 1253-56; Y.-M.J. Congar, *The Holy Spirit*, I, 29-43; R. Koch in Bauer, *Encyclopaedia of Biblical Theology*, III, 887f; DBS XI, 192-327, J.P. Lémonon.

PAUL VI (1897-1978; Pope from 1963)

Pope Paul on 6 June, 1973 made a statement which is taken as capital.[1] It is quoted by John Paul II (qv) in his Encyclical *Dominum et Vivificantem* (qv): "The Christology and particularly the ecclesiology of the Council must be followed by a new study of and devotion to the Holy Spirit."[2] In the previous year Paul had asked the question "What is the greatest need of the Church today?" and answered thus: "The Spirit, the Holy Spirit, who animates and sanctifies the Church, who is her divine breath, the wind in her sails, the principle of her unity, the inner source of her light and strength, her support and consoler, the source of her charisms and songs, her peace and joy, the pledge and prelude of her blessed and eternal life."[3]

There is much evidence to show how Pope Paul himself strove to fulfill the programme he outlined, prepare for the advent of the Spirit he awaited. He was a Father of Vatican II. After the death of John XXIII he became the Pope of the Council. He saw the emergence of the theme of the Holy Spirit as the Council moved towards its conclusion and he witnessed the different movements of thought and devotion centred on the Holy Spirit in the Council's aftermath. It has been said that if Vatican II had lasted longer it would have felt obliged to issue a conciliar document on the Holy Spirit. What the Council did teach in the 258 references to the Spirit is dealt with separately.

One phenomenon Paul VI had to cope with, the charismatic movement (qv), arose and spread within the Catholic Church at a time when the body was enduring singular stress and tension: the post-conciliar upheaval. He took time, for different reasons, to reach a confident judgement about it. His first reactions were not enthusiastic. "As a result of human frailty," he said in 1971, "charisms may be confused at times with one's own disordered ideas and inclinations. Hence it is necessary to judge and discern charisms in order to check their authenticity, and to correlate them with criteria derived from the teachings of Christ, and with the order which should be observed in the ecclesial community. Such an office pertains to the sacred hierarchy, which is itself established by a singular charism."[4]

In the following year the Pope, at the ordination of nineteen bishops, spoke of those who "have recently ventured to place the charismatic and hierarchical Church in opposition." While calling attention to the reality of charisms in the Church, he added a word of caution: "But as (St.) Paul also emphasizes, the charisms granted to the faithful are subject to discipline, which is ensured only by the charism of pastoral power, in charity."[5]

The year 1973 was marked by a certain rapprochement between the Pope and the charismatic movement. They had an intermediary in Cardinal Suenens who enjoyed the Pope's confidence and spoke for them. When the 'International Leaders' Conference of the Catholic Charismatic Renewal' brought 120 representatives from 34 countries, the Pope, at the Cardinal's request, gave an audience to 13 of them. His words were guarded, but the fact of the encounter was encouraging. Soon after on 19 May, 1975 Pope Paul met the members of the International Conference on the Charismatic Renewal in the Catholic Church, which was being held in Rome. Ten thousand people had taken part and when Cardinal Suenens with many bishops and several hundred priests concelebrated Mass in St. Peter's the Pope came in and addressed them in French; he added some remarks in Spanish, English and Italian.

Critics of the Charismatic movement have tried to minimize the importance of the Pope's words: they have been dismissed as in the routine style of greeting to the different groups who come to Rome and are admitted to a papal audience. The content of the papal address does not bear out this view. After his preliminary remarks the Pope addressed himself to the essential point in the movement: 'Alas! God has become a stranger in the lives of how many people, even of those who continue to profess his existence by tradition, and to pay him worship and duty!

"For such a world, more and more secularized, nothing is more necessary than the witness of this 'spiritual renewal', which we see the Holy Spirit stirring today, in such diverse regions and circles. Its manifestations are varied: deep communion of hearts and close contact with God in faithfulness to the commitments undertaken at Baptism, and in prayer that is often in groups, in which each one expresses himself freely, thus helping, supporting and nourishing the prayer of others. At the basis of everything, there is a personal conviction which has its source not only in instruction received by faith but also in a kind of personal experience of the fact that, without God, man can do nothing, whereas with him, everything becomes possible. Hence this need to praise him, thank him, celebrate the marvels that he works around us and in us everywhere. Human existence finds again its relationship with God, its so-called 'vertical dimension', without which man is irremediably mutilated."

"How then," the Pope said a little later, "could this 'spiritual renewal' be anything but beneficial for the church and for the world? And if this is the case, how could we fail to take all means in order that it may remain so?

"The Holy Spirit, dear sons and daughters, will in his graciousness show you these means, according to the wisdom of those whom he himself made 'guardians to feed the Church of God' (Acts 20:28). For it was the Holy Spirit that inspired St. Paul with certain very precise directives, which we will merely recall for you. Fidelity to them will be your best possible guarantee for the future.[6]

"You know how highly the Apostle esteemed 'spiritual gifts': 'Do not quench the Spirit', he wrote to the Thessalonians (1,5:19), adding immediately: 'Test everything. Hold fast what is good' (5:21). He deemed, therefore, that discernment was always necessary, and he entrusted responsibility for it to those he had put at the head of the community (5:12). With the Corinthians, some years later, he went into greater detail. In particular, he pointed out three principles, in the light of which they could more easily carry out this indispensable discernment.

"The first one, with which he began his exposition, is fidelity to the authentic teaching of the faith (1 Cor 12:1-3). Nothing that contradicts it could come from the Holy Spirit. The one who distributes his gifts is the same one who inspired

the Scriptures, and who assists the living Magisterium of the Church, to which Christ entrusted the authentic interpretation of Scripture, as Catholic faith holds. That is why you feel the need of a deeper and deeper doctrinal formation in Scripture, spirituality and theology. Only such a formation, the authenticity of which must be assured by the hierarchy, will preserve you from deviations, which are always possible, and will give you the certainty and the joy of having served the cause of the Gospel 'without beating the air' (1 Cor 9:26).

"The second principle. All the spiritual gifts are to be received gratefully; and you know that the list given is a long one and does not claim to be complete. But while the gifts are accorded 'for the common good' (1 Cor 12:7) they do not all procure it to the same degree. Hence the Corinthians must 'earnestly desire the higher gifts' (1 Cor 12:31), those most useful to the community (14:1-5).

"The third principle is, in St. Paul's mind, the most important. It has inspired what is surely one of the most beautiful pages in all literature, which a recent translator has piquantly entitled, 'Love soars above everything.'" The Pope then enlarged on this idea of charity, as the essence of Christian perfection, recalling how the Fathers vied with each other in expounding the truth: St. Fulgentius for example who wrote thus: "the Holy Spirit can confer all kinds of gifts without being present himself; it is when he grants love that he shows himself present through grace."[7] Paul finally urged his listeners to be faithful to the Apostle's directives and faithful also in celebrating the Eucharist, frequently and worthily, according to the teaching of the same Apostle (1 Cor 11:26-29). "This," he said succinctly, "is the way chosen by the Lord whereby we may have his life in us (Jn 6:53)."

The Pope met during the post-conciliar years of his pontificate another very vital current of idealism centred on the Holy Spirit: the inspiration coming from research and reflection on the link between Mary and the Spirit. Since the Spirit had been evoked very forcefully in the last session of the Council, Marian theologians disappointed in some of their aims and objectives in the first three sessions, seized on this avenue opened to their advance and progress. The great Societies for Marian Study, French notably and Spanish, devoted annual sessions to the theme of Mary and the Spirit, the French, in accordance with their custom, over three years, ending with a strong ecumenical set of lecturers. Henri Chavannes,

Swiss Calvinist, Paul Evdokimov, Orthodox, disciple of the great Sergius Bulgakov (qv), with pluridisciplinary Catholic participation including the noted Scripture scholar André Feuillet, P.S.S. and Mgr. Gerard Philips of Louvain, joint draftsman with Fr. Karl Balic of the Marian chapter in *Lumen Gentium*, textual coordinator and editor for the whole Constitution on the Church.[8] Some other collective labours on the theme were also noteworthy.[9]

The Pope's noted encounter with those influenced by this thinking coincided in time with the Rome Charismatic Congress in 1975. The International Mariological Congress was followed, at a venue in the Eternal City by the International Marian Congress, May 18-21, which had for its theme; "The Holy Spirit and Mary." Paul expressed his views on the subject in the official letter, *E con sentimenti* to the Papal Legate, Cardinal Léon-Joseph Suenens, a noted patron of two movements with an interest in the event, the Legion of Mary and the Charismatic Movement. Taking note of the advance in scientific Marian theology in recent times the Pope said: "The Holy Spirit intervenes personally, while in indivisible communion with the other Persons of the Holy Trinity, in the work of human salvation. But the Catholic Church has always believed that he has associated the humble Virgin of Nazareth with himself in this, and that he has done so in a way in keeping with his nature as Personal Love of the Father and the Son. That is to say, by an action at once very powerful and very sweet, he has adapted perfectly Mary's whole person, with all her faculties and energies physical as well as spiritual, to the tasks assigned to her on the plane of redemption. This belief springs from an understanding of the sacred texts that has grown deeper and clearer in the course of time. On this basis, Fathers and Doctors of the Church, in both east and west, have attributed Mary's fullness of grace and charity to the various missions of the Holy Spirit, who proceeds from the Father and the Son. This includes the gifts and fruits of every virtue, as well as the evangelical beatitudes and special charisms. Like a trousseau for a heavenly wedding, all of these adorned her who was predestined as the mystical Bride of the Divine Paraclete, and Mother of God's Word made flesh. Because of her privileges and exceptional gifts of grace, all of which come from the divine Spirit, Mary is greeted in the sacred Liturgy as '*Templum Domini, sacrarium Spiritus Sancti*', (Temple of the Lord, Sanctuary of the Holy Spirit)."[10]

The Pope then analyses the various interventions of the Spirit in Mary's life, from the moment of her conception through the episodes related in the gospels, in the synoptics and Jn, to the final moment when "the Holy Spirit burning with supreme ardour in Mary's heart as she continued her earthly pilgrimage, made her eager to join her Son in glory," thus preparing her for the Assumption.

Paul then turns to Mary's action in the Church. "But Mary's mission as partner of the Spirit of Christ in the mystery of salvation did not end with her glorious Assumption. While absorbed in joyful contemplation of the Blessed Trinity, she continues to be present spiritually to all the redeemed. And it is Uncreated Love himself, the soul and supreme mover of the Mystical body, who impels her to carry on this noble task."[11]

There is no question of putting Our Lady in the place of the Spirit: "We must consider, therefore, that the activity of the Mother of the Church for the benefit of the redeemed does not replace, or compete with, the almighty and universal action of the Holy Spirit. Rather, the former implores and prepares for the latter, not only by prayer of intercession, in harmony with the divine plans which Mary contemplates in the beatific vision, but also with the direct influence of her example, in particular the extremely important one of her supreme docility to the inspirations of the Divine Spirit. It is, therefore, always in dependence on the Holy Spirit that Mary leads souls to Jesus, forms them in her image, inspires them with good advice and serves as a bond of love between Jesus and the faithful."[12]

The Pope then adverts briefly to the patristic witness to Our Lady, that of the Fathers and Doctors of the eastern Church. To conclude he points to the gravity of the present hour in the history of the Church and the call for renewal and reconciliation with God and our fellow-men. "These can occur only if the soul of the faithful is dominated by the worship of the Spirit, who is the supreme source of charity, unity and peace. But in harmony with this worship, kindled and enlivened by the fire of Divine love, there must also be the veneration of the great Mother of God and Mother of the Church, the incomparable model of love for God and for our brothers."[13]

To sum up we may quote Pope Paul's teaching on the Spirit in his *Credo of the People of God*, promulgated to conclude the *Year of Faith* on 30 June, 1968. "We believe, therefore, in God, who from all eternity begets the Son, we believe in the Son, the Word of God, who is eternally begotten, we believe in the Holy Spirit, the uncreated Person who proceeds from the Father and the Son as their eternal Love. And so in the three divine Persons who are *co-eternal and co-equal with one another*, the life and beatitude of God, who is uniquely One, is realized and fulfilled in overwhelming plenitude in the supreme excellence and glory which is proper to him who is the uncreated Being, in such wise that *unity in the Trinity and Trinity in the unity must be humbly acknowledged*.... We believe in the Holy Spirit, the Lord and giver of life, who together with the Father and the Son is adored and glorified. He it is who spoke through the prophets. He it was who was sent to us by Christ after his resurrection and ascension to the Father. He enlightens, vivifies, guards and rules the Church whose members he purifies as long as they do not turn away from grace. His action, which reaches to the inmost centre of the soul, enables man, in the humility which he draws from Christ, to become perfect even as the Father in heaven is perfect."[14] A pithy precis of doctrine and spirituality. (See also article *Marialis Cultus*).

[1]Official sources *AAS, Insegnamenti, L'Osservatore Romano*; cf. also as source *La Documentation catholique*; cf. E. D. O'Connor, C. S. C., *Pope Paul and the Spirit*, Notre Dame, Indiana, 1978; [2]June 6, 1973, *OR* 7 June, 1973; [3]*OR* 30 November, 1972; [4]Address to the judges and officials of the Tribunal of the Sacred Roman Rota, *OR*, 29 January 1971; [5]*OR*, 14/15 February 1972; [6]*OR*, 19/20 May 1975; [7]*Contra Fabianum*, Fragment 28, *PL* 65, 791; [8]Cf. *Etudes Mariales, Bulletin de la Société française d'études mariales, Le Saint Espirit et Marie*, 1968, 1969, 1970; [9]*Estudios Marianos,* Spanish Mariological Society, 41 (1977), *Maria y el Espiritu Santo*, Madrid; *Lo Spirito Santo e Maria Santissima*, ed. Mgr. P. C. van Lierde, Vatican Press, 1976; *Maria Santissima e lo Spirito Santo*, ed. Centro Volontari della Sofferenza, Rome, 1976; further bibliography, M. O'Carroll, *Theotokos*, Wilmington, 1981, 332; [10]Apud E.D. O'Connor, *op. cit.;* [11]*Ibid.;* [12]*Ibid.;* [13]*Ibid.;* [14]A. Flannery, Vatican Council II, 389, 390.

PENTECOST[1]

"'And behold, I send the promise of my Father upon you; but stay in the city, until you are clothed with power from on high.'" (Lk 24:29).

"'Nevertheless I tell you the truth; it is to your advantage that I go away, for if I do not go away, the Counsellor will not come to you; but if I go, I will send him to you.'" (Jn 16:7).

"'It is not for you to know times or seasons which the Father has fixed by his own authority.

But you shall receive power when the Holy Spirit has come upon you; and you shall be my witnesses in Jerusalem and in all Judea and Samaria and to the end of the earth'" (Acts 1:7-8).

"When the day of Pentecost had come, they were all together in one place. And suddenly a sound came from heaven like the rush of a mighty wind, and it filled all the house where they were sitting. And there appeared to them tongues as of fire, distributed and resting on each one of them. And they were all filled with the Holy Spirit and began to speak in other tongues, as the Spirit gave them utterance" (Acts 2:1-4).

This is the event of Pentecost, as it was foretold, promised and occurred. The event of Pentecost was public. St. Luke, the author of Acts, tells of the impact on the multitude of the "other tongues". "'Are not all these who are speaking Galileans? And how is it that we hear, each of us in his own language?'" (2:7-8). The places of origin are listed with the summary remark: "'We hear them telling in our own tongues the mighty works of God'" (ibid., 11).

On that day Peter made his first public pronouncement. He rejected the interpretation of the phenomena by some bystanders, that the speakers in tongues were "filled with new wine." He appealed to the prophecy of Joel (qv), beginning with the words, "And in the last days it shall be, God declares, that I will pour out my Spirit upon all flesh, and your sons and daughters shall prophesy, and your young men shall see visions, and your old men shall dream dreams..." (Joel 2:28).

Peter then outlines the kerygma, the message of salvation, links the life and ministry of Christ which is the heart of it with the OT and announces the effective beginning of God's plan of salvation, with the evidence that makes it acceptable: "'This Jesus God raised up, and of that we all are witnesses. Being therefore exalted at the right hand of God, and having received from the Father the promise of the Holy Spirit, he has poured out this which you see and hear. For David did not ascend into the heavens; but he himself says, "The Lord said to my Lord, Sit at my right hand, till I make thy enemies a stool for thy feet." Let all the house of Israel therefore know assuredly that God has made him both Lord and Christ, this Jesus whom you crucified'" (Acts 2:32-36).

As to the response expected from the listeners Peter felt authorized to make an extraordinary promise: "'Repent, and be baptized every one of you in the name of Jesus Christ for the forgiveness of your sins; *and you shall receive the gift of the Holy Spirit*" (*ibid.*, 38, emphasis added). With the conversion of some three thousand souls, a new community was born.

Jewish Background

There is no patent link with the Jewish feast of Pentecost; yet the coming of the Spirit occurred on this day. It was a harvest festival, when the first fruits were offered to God. Variable possibly in date at first, dependent on the ripening of the crops, it was fixed when the celebration of the Passover was joined with the Feast of the Unleavened Bread (*massot*) seven weeks from the *massot*: "'And you shall count from the morrow after the sabbath, from the day that you brought the sheaf of the wave offering; seven full weeks shall they be, counting fifty days to the morrow after the seventh sabbath; then you shall present a cereal offering of new grain to the Lord'" (Lev 23:15).

A prescribed very full ritual marked the feast, (Lev 23:15-22; Nm 28:26-31) which eventually always fell on Sunday, the fifteenth day of the third month. The time between the combined feasts of Passover and Unleavened Bread and this feast of Pentecost was taken as equivalent to the time between the Exodus from Egypt and the arrival at Sinai. This prompted interpretation of Pentecost as a memorial of the giving of the Law on Sinai. The firm evidence for this is in the Book of Jubilees and since this calendar was followed by the Qumran community the monks celebrated Pentecost, a Covenant memorial, as the principal liturgical moment.

Christian Liturgy

For the first centuries Pentecost in Christian celebration was part of a whole fifty days commemoration in which all the mysteries of Christ's death, resurrection, apparitions, ascension and sending of the Spirit were absorbed.[2] No particular day, not even the eighth, fortieth or fiftieth, is privileged. This is a time of great joy (*laetissimum spatium*, Tertullian), especially suited to reception of the Sacraments, Baptism in particular, the Eucharist. It is not a time for fasting and in this context the parable of the "friends of the bridegroom" is recalled (Lk 5:34-35; Mt 9:15); prayer is said without prostration or kneeling. This is a time to recall that salvation is a free gift of God. The whole Paschal Mystery is relived. At least two days fast precedes the Fifty Days and in places it is followed by fast. A normal ending occurs in some oriental churches by the ceremony of "genuflexion"—now ordinary practices are resumed.

A change took place towards the last quarter of the fourth century. The fortieth and fiftieth days were now commemorations of the events reported in Acts, the Ascension and the Descent of the Spirit. The patristic homilies, especially those of St. Augustine (qv) bring out the Covenant theme, which was Jewish in the celebration of Pentecost, or again the restoration of the unity lost in the Tower of Babel. The parallel between Sinai and the event of Pentecost related in Acts merits study. The tongues of fire recall the rabbinical commentaries which speak of the word of God visible as lightning flashes. "There," says St. Augustine, "God came down on the mountain; here the Holy Spirit comes, manifesting himself through tongues of fire. There thunder and voices; here sinners are enlightened by the flames of different tongues."[3] St. Augustine draws attention to the fact that the Law on Sinai was written on tables of stone and the Holy Spirit is called the finger of God.[4]

The reversal of the incident at Babel is beautifully expressed by St. Gregory Nazianzen: "But as the old Confusion of tongues was laudable, when men who were of one language in wickedness and impiety, even as some now venture to be, were building the Tower; for by the confusion of their language the unity of their intention was broken up, and their undertaking destroyed; so much more worthy of praise is the present miraculous one. For being poured from one Spirit upon many men, it brings them again into harmony. And there is a diversity of Gifts, which stands in need of yet another Gift to discern which is the best where all are praiseworthy."[5]

With the development of Trinitarian theology especially at the hands of the great Cappadocians, the break-up of the Fifty Days was accelerated. The first week was to become a privileged octave and the day of Pentecost would be isolated by also having an octave, an innovation which would take place in seventh century Rome. In medieval times Pentecost had become a feast of the Holy Spirit, not a day ending the Paschal Fifty Days, the *clausum Paschae*. In the nineteenth century Leo XIII (qv) in the Encyclical *Divinum Illud Munus* (qv) proclaimed a special novena of preparation for the feast, which served to heighten the separate importance of the day.

Theoretically there is not a feast of the Holy Spirit but certain spiritual movements within the Church, the foundation of religious institutes with the Holy Spirit as special patron, and the Charismatic Renewal Movement (originally bearing the name Pentecostal Movement) serve to focus attention on a celebration of the Holy Spirit on the sacred day.

There has been, nevertheless, a recall of ancient observance in certain recent documents of the Church. In the *Normae universales de anno liturgico et de calendario*, 1969, no. 22 reads: "The fifty days of Pentecost are celebrated in joy and exultation, as if it were a unique festive day, or, better a 'great Sunday'. On these days especially the Alleluia is chanted."

Liturgy of the Day

The reforms consequent on Vatican II take account of the ancient traditions; the feasts of Easter, the Ascension and Pentecost remain, but there is encouragement to recall the unity of the period; to this end the octave of Pentecost is suppressed. The collect prayers for the Vigil are suggestive: "Father in heaven, fifty days have celebrated the fullness of the mystery of your revealed love. See your people gathered in prayer, open to receive the Spirit's flame. May it come to rest in our hearts and disperse the divisions of word and tongue. With one voice and one song may we praise your name in joy and thanksgiving." The alternative: "Almighty and ever-living God you fulfilled the Easter promise by sending your Holy Spirit. May that Spirit unite the races and nations on earth and proclaim your glory."

The collects for the day read: "God our Father let the Spirit you sent on your Church to begin the teaching of the gospel continue to work in the world through the hearts of all who believe." "Father of light, from whom every good gift comes, send your Spirit into our lives with the power of a mighty wind and by the flame of your wisdom open the horizons of our minds. Loosen our tongues to sing your praise in words beyond the power of speech for without your Spirit man could never raise his voice in words of peace or announce the truth that Jesus is Lord."

The preface of the day is evocative of historical development: "Today you sent the Holy Spirit on those marked out to be your children by sharing the life of your only Son and so you brought the paschal mystery to its completion. Today we celebrate the great beginning of your Church when the Holy Spirit made known to all peoples the one true God and created from the many languages of man one voice to profess one faith. The joy of the Resurrection renews the whole world, while the

choirs of heaven sing forever to your glory." The "completion of the paschal mystery" certainly echoes the ancient unified period as does the reference to the "joy of the Resurrection." There is possibly a further development ahead, in view of what has been noted in recent consciousness of the Spirit. Meanwhile the readings prescribed for the Vigil are of the Tower of Babel and the descent on Mount Sinai.

Theology

Vatican II (qv) links Pentecost with two other capital moments in salvation history: "To achieve this (that the salvation accomplished should have its universal effect) Christ sent the Holy Spirit from the Father to exercise inwardly his saving influence, and to promote the spread of the Church. Without doubt, the Holy Spirit was at work in the world before Christ was glorified. On the day of Pentecost, however, he came down on the disciples that he might remain with them forever (cf. Jn 14:16); on that day the Church was openly displayed to the crowds, and the spread of the gospel among the nations through preaching was begun. Finally, on that day was foreshadowed the union of all peoples in the catholicity of the faith by means of the Church of the New Alliance, a Church which speaks every language, understands and embraces all tongues in charity, and thus overcomes the dispersion of Babel. The 'acts of the apostles' began with Pentecost, just as Christ was conceived in the Virgin Mary with the coming of the Holy Spirit and was moved to begin his ministry by the descent of the same Holy Spirit, who came down upon him while he was praying."[6]

With Pentecost we have the opening of a new era. The Spirit had been "quenched" (qv) in the last days before the coming of John the Baptist (qv) and of Jesus. This phase had been closed by the coming of the two, was now totally past history. The great event of expectation, the coming of the Messiah, had taken place and Jesus, the Messiah, was now Lord and Christ at the right hand of the Father. Salvation is now a reality, sins are forgiven (Acts 2:38; 5:31; 10:43; 13:38; 26:18) and the gift of the Spirit is for all (Acts 2:4; 4:3 etc.).

But there is a social condition made clear on the very day, entry to the Church. Pentecost is the event which marks the beginning of the Church's recognisable existence among people; it validates the Church's call to them and claim to save them; it reveals whence the Church draws its power and the equipment necessary to its mission. (Acts 2:41;

9:31). The Church is the messianic community, the new Israel, universal, its apostolic thrust declared from the outset.

Thus the Spirit who had endowed the Messiah with his human nature in the Virgin's womb, equipped him at the Jordan with the array of gifts needed for his public ministry, was now offering the fruits of his life-work, his redemptive death, resurrection and ascension to each individual human person. The prophecies of Israel's new life in the Spirit were fulfilled: "the Spirit is poured upon us from on high, and the wilderness becomes a fruitful field and the fruitful field is deemed a forest" (Is 32:15); "I will pour my Spirit upon your descendants, and my blessing on your offspring" (ibid., 44:3); "And I will put my Spirit within you, and cause you to walk in my statutes and be careful to observe my ordinances" (Ez 36:27); "and I will not hide my face any more from them, when I pour out my Spirit upon the house of Israel, says the Lord God" (ibid., 39:29; cp. Is 59: 21; Ez 11:19; Jl 3:1-5).

As the geographical list in Acts 2:8-11 manifests the Church's universality, the break with Jewish exclusiveness, so Peter's reminder to the "men of Israel" of the "God of Abraham and of Isaac and of Jacob, the God of our fathers", emphasized the essential continuity between the Israel of God and the Church of Christ. As Vatican II says: "As Israel according to the flesh which wandered in the desert was already called the Church of God (2 Esd 13:1; cf. Num 20:4; Deut 23:1ff), so too the new Israel, which advances in this present era in search of a future and permanent city (cf. Heb 13:14) is called also the Church of Christ (cf. Mt 16:18). It is Christ indeed who has purchased it with his own blood (cf. Acts 20:28); he has filled it with his Spirit; he has provided means adapted to its visible and social union."[7]

[1]R. Dussaud, *Les origines cananéenes du sacrifice israelite,* Paris, 1921; S. Salaville, "La 'Tessarakoste', Ascension et Pentecôte au 4e siècle," *Echos d'Orient,* 28 (1929), 257-71; O. Casel, "Art und Sinn der ältesten christlichen Osterfeier," *Jahrbuch fur Liturgiegeschichte,* 14 (1934), 1-78; French tr. *La fête de Paques dans l'Eglise ancienne, Paris,* 1963; W. F. Albright, *Archaeology and the Religion of Israel,* Baltimore, 1953; G. Kretschmar, "Himmelfahrt und Pfingsten", *Zeitschrift für Kirchengeschichte,* 66 (1954/55), 209-53; Y.-M.J. Congar, O. P., *La Pentecôte, Paris,* 1956; id., *The Holy Spirit,* I 44-49; E. Flicoteaux, *Le rayonnement de la Pentecôte, Paris,* 1957; A. S. Herbert, *Worship in Ancient Israel,* London, 1959; Cl. Jean-Neamy, *La spiritualité de la Pentecôte, Paris,* 1960; J. Broeckh, "Die Entwicklung der altkirchlichen Pentekoste," *Jahrbuch für Liturgie und*

Hymnologie 5 (1960), 1-45; R. le Deaut, C. S. Sp., "Pentecôte et tradition juive," 7 (1961), *Spiritus* 127-44; id., "La 'Cinquantaine' et la Pentecôte chrétienne, *Svensk Exegetisk Arsbok,* 44 (1979), 148-70; P. Jounel, "Le temps pascal, La Tradition de l'Eglise," La Maison-Dieu, 67 (1961), 163-82; P. Evdokimov, "La fête de la Pentecôte dans la tradition orthodoxe," *Verbum Caro,* 16 (1962), 177-98; id., *L'Esprit Saint dans la tradition orthodoxe,* Paris, 2969; A. Brinkman, "The Literary Background of the Catalogue of the Nations (Acts 2:9-11)," *CBQ* 25 (1963), 418-27; esp., R. Cabie, *La Pentecôte. L'évolution de la Cinquantaine pascale au cours des cinq premiers siècles,* Paris-Tournai, 1965, bibl.; Collection—*Assemblées du Seigneur, Fête de la Pentecôte,* n. 30, 1970; H.-M. Legrand, "Inverser Babel. Mission de l'Eglise," *Spiritus,* 63 (1970), 323-46; J. H. E. Hull, *The Holy Spirit in the Acts of the Apostles,* London, 1967; K. Hruby, "La fête de la Pentecôte dans la tradition juive," *Bible et Vie Chrétienne,* 63 (1965) 46-64; J. Potin, *La fête juive de la Pentecôte* 2 vols, Paris, 1971; G. Haya-Prats, *L'Esprit force de l'Eglise. Sa nature et ses activités d'après les Actes des Apotres,* Paris, 1975; J. Lopez Martin, *El dono de la Pascua del Senor. Pneumatologia de la Cinquecentena pascual del Misal Romano,* Burgos 1971; H. Leclercq, *DACL,* XIV, 1939, 259-74; H. Haag, *Bibel-Lexikon,* Einsiedeln, 1951, I, 1324-27; A. Arens, N. Alder, VIII, 1963, 421-23; M. Delcor, *DBS,* VII, 1966, 858-79; B. F. Meyer, J. L. Ronan, *NCE* XI, 104-06; R. Cabie, *DSp,* XII, 1029-36; A.T. Lincoln, *Luke's Pentecost, Theology and History, Expository Times,* 96 (1985) pp. 204-209; [2]Patristic references, R. Cabie, op. cit., 1030-31; patristic references; [3]*Sermo* 186, ed. A. Olivar, *Sacris Erudiri,* 5 (1953), 139; references to the theme of Babel and Pentecost, Vatican II, Decree on Missionary Activity, 4, n. 6; [4]*Contra Faustum,* 32, 12 *CSEL* 25, 770-71; [5]*Orat,* 41, 16, *PG* 36, 449, *LNPF* VII, 384; [6]Missionary Activity, 4, Vatican II, ed. A. Flannery 816; [7]Constitution on the Church, 9, ed. A. Flannery, 360.

PENTECOSTALISM[1]

The beginnings of Pentecostalism were in the United States in the opening years of the present century. Revivalist or Holiness groups had created a favourable climate. An important event was the opinion formed by the students of Bethel Bible College in Topeka, Kansas, strongly influenced by its founder Charles Parham: Baptism in the Spirit must be evidenced in the phenomenon of speaking in tongues. A disciple of Charles Parham, a black preacher, William J. Seymour, was instrumental in the inception of the movement in California. From 1910 Pentecostalism was established and it grew fast. Already in the late sixties it was estimated that there were twenty million Pentecostals in the United States, Latin America, Africa, the U.S.S.R. and Indonesia. The movement was being carried into over ninety countries by over a thousand missionaries establishing Bible schools, and operating on an annual budget well over twenty million dollars. This is not to say that money is a dominant factor. There is continuous reliance on

Scripture, interpreted in a fundamentalist sense. Pentecostals aimed at organised structures, the two largest the Church of God in Christ and the Pentecostal Holiness Church. The Assemblies of God eventually came to prominence. Neo-Pentecostalism dates from the sixties and late in the decade the movement spread to the Catholic Church. Known by preference as the Catholic Charismatic or Renewal movement it originated at Duquesne University, Pittsburgh, in 1967, soon found an encouraging home in Notre Dame University. It has remained within the structure of the Catholic Church, has benefitted by advice and encouragement given in formal addresses by Paul VI (qv) and John Paul II (qv) and in official statements by national hierarchies, notably the Canadian and American. It is dealt with in a separate article (see Charismatic Movement, Catholic).

Pentecostal denominations are numerous, exhibiting the tendency to split. Certain features are common, acceptance of the main Christian dogmas, emphasis on speaking in tongues, with in this feature a minimal variation, belief in the presence of the gifts listed by St. Paul in 1 Cor 12, different forms of water baptism—immersion, generally preferred, pouring, sprinkling; some practice ritual foot-washing. An organisation of lay Pentecostals which has grown rapidly and has proved highly supportive is the *Full Gospel Business Men's Fellowship International.*

------

[1]Cf. N. Bloch-Hoell, *The Pentecostal Movement*, Copenhagen, London, 1964; P. Damborierna, *Tongues as of Fire. Pentecostalism in Contemporary Christianity*, Washington, 1969; F.D. Bruner, *A. Theology of the Holy Spirit*, Grand Rapids, 1970; V. Synan, *The Holiness-Pentecostal Movement in the United States*, Grand Rapids, 1971; D.W. Fraupel, *The American Pentecostal Movement. A Biblical Essay*, Wilmore, 1972; W. J. Hollenweger, *The Pentecostals*, London, 1972; F. A. Sullivan, DSp XII, 2027-2052;

PERSONAL FULFILMENT

The Christian instinct may feel that profound devotion, which may mean assimilation, to the Holy Spirit, leads to the highest possible degree of personal fulfilment. In this the Christian instinct is unquestionably right, though on the way concepts, mental categories and spiritual attitudes may have to change considerably. Personal fulfilment is thwarted, impeded, slowed by many things: impairment of mental or physical powers, defective education, lack of self-knowledge, lack of determination, sin of different kinds, sinfulness of different degrees. For reasons of space the subject is here narrowed to those who have the Christian faith and Christian commitment.

Complete personal fulfilment is achieved by the one who perfectly realizes the divine image to which every single human being was designed to conform. To achieve this conformity divine grace is necessary and divine omnipotence disposes of the infinitely varied resource which permits each human individual to attain the fulfilment intended for him or her. A test of conformity being progressivly achieved or attaining important summits is an increasing realization of happiness. Here again there is a problem, for happiness is not immediately understood. An integral part of complete personal fulfilment will be the full understanding, with concepts and experience firmly one, of happiness itself.

A major obstacle to such a final desirable result is fissure within the individual human being, due to lack of self-knowledge which is a universal unavoidable defect. These internal fissures are possible through the uncontrollable subconscious mind: it is not only existent within each single individual, but dynamic, thrusting into his sentiments, intellectual consciousness and volition elements which disrupt his conviction and motivation unpredictably. It is a spring not only of crude egoism and selfishness in its many forms, but of self-deceit, a permanent food for pride.

Spiritual writers, depth psychologists and psychiatrists meet on this unpleasant ground. How can the sincere, well-meaning Christian extricate himself from the pernicious forces crowding on him in this dimly lit area? St. Paul seems to have been conscious of the problem. "So I find it to be a law that when I want to do right, evil lies close at hand. For I delight in the law of God, in my inmost self, but I see in my members another law at war with the law of my mind and making me captive to the law of sin which dwells in my members. Wretched man that I am! Who will deliver me from this body of death? Thanks be to God through Jesus Christ our Lord! So then, I of myself serve the law of God with my mind, but with my flesh I serve the law of sin. There is therefore now no condemnation for those who are in Christ Jesus. For the law of the Spirit of life in Christ Jesus has set me free from the law of sin and death" (Rom 7:21-25; 8:1-2).

The Apostle then goes on to his well-known contrast between flesh and the Spirit: "For those who live according to the flesh set their minds on the things of the flesh, but those who live according to the Spirit set their minds on the things of the Spirit. To set the mind on the flesh is death, but to set the mind on the Spirit is life and peace.... But you are not in the flesh, you are in the Spirit, if in fact the Spirit of God dwells in you. Any one who does not have the Spirit of Christ does not belong to him" (Rom 8:5,6,9).

It will appear facile to suggest that the Spirit is the one indispensable ally, guide, overruling master in the struggle for internal harmony. Clearly available and adequate natural means must be used, as the proper professional therapy where personality disorders take on a dimension of illness. Even in the use of these natural resources, Christian virtues may exert a stabilising influence. It is increasingly admitted that strong faith and total Christian commitment may help solve what look like purely natural crises. Faith helps maintain equilibrium in face of unforeseen calamity; it sustains victims of torture, but especially if they are reduced to automata by beating or exhaustion or drugging, when the moment of recovery comes and they realize what they have been forced to do, and they have to regain their self-respect, faith is the anchor; it is a remedy for the disease of the affluent society, loneliness, which is not to be confused with living alone or being forced into isolation. Loneliness here is a desolation of the spirit, in natural terms practically incurable. It accounts for many suicides, for no issue is visible. To add to this list the effects of religious faith and practice on the mentally ill, in the way of hastening their healing, would be hazardous did we not have the testimony of a master. It was Karl Jung who said that in many cases of psychiatric illness he was powerless because he was faced with the effects of religious breakdown.

What is wanted to avert personality failure, to remove it or to eliminate its after effects, is a force or power outside the person which will attract, concentrate and draw its full resources, realize its potential, prevent neurotic introspection. The Christian must, with guidance for a while, by submitting to the necessary apprenticeship, discover this force which is outside him and by a divine paradox lives within him. This is the Spirit of God. He gives permanently what so many other secondary things in life give for a while and possibly piecemeal, strong personal love, dedication to a cause, ambition which is seen to be legitimate, in one or other walk of life, artistic, literary, political, social, economic.

He works in mystery. He works by stripping away the several selves which fetter and encrust the real self which can respond to him fully. What this process of cleansing can be when a mighty personality is involved may be studied in the works of St. John of the Cross (qv); the "Dark Night of the Soul" is no empty metaphor. All are not called to this profound purification.

The thrusting of the self beyond its own reach must have a discernible point of reference. It is risk, but risk which is covered. The name commonly given to the safeguard of personal identity is destiny, the ultimate eschatological answer to all life's questioning. When it is achieved, all the pieces of life's puzzle are in place, all tension is removed, the whole thrust of the individual is straight, unerring, consuming. The fulfilled person captures the divine irony, wholly focussed on another, and totally aware of spending his own inner power.

To discover personal destiny the person needs the enlightening Spirit, for the Spirit "searches all things", penetrates to the depths of man. Life is, with him as "the sweet Guest of the soul," a successful search for the destiny which gives meaning to all. A sense of destiny, naturally felt, can be transforming, though with natural resources alone this transformation is vulnerable. When the sense of destiny comes from the Spirit of God, it is immune to any such threat. Witness the martyrs, the striking instance of destiny fulfilled, equally striking as a manifestation of the Spirit's action. The martyr has at once, at times with little previous preparation, a full, instantaneous vision of what others see partially, through the mist of faith over many years. It is the same Spirit at work.

PERSONALITY

Is it theologically possible for us to grasp the personality of the Holy Spirit? One facile means is through a special study of the Blessed Virgin Mary, for an Orthodox theologian Bulgakov (qv) saw her as transparent to the Spirit and the Brazilian Franciscan, known in the world of Liberation theology, Leonardo Boff, O. F. M. speaks of her as the personification of the Spirit. Another means is to seek some reflection of the Spirit in the Church, (qv) which is so closely related to him for its existence, its continuity, its immunity from error as this is necessary to its mission among people. But the very phrases 'transparent to the Holy Spirit' and 'personification of the Holy Spirit' need very much analysis and very precise interpretation to prove acceptable. The Church may prove more helpful.

We have a means which does not always yield results if it is seriously tried: The Spirit is of the Father and the Son, proceeding from them. How can we learn about him from them? What does it mean to a personality, divine, omnipotent, omniscient, to exist by procession? What of the Father's power as a communication to the Spirit, whom he "breathes?" What of the Son's distinct property as the Only-Begotten? What has the Spirit from him?

What seems to halt speculation of this kind is the sense of mystery which surrounds the deity, One and Three. The way of analogy helps us in our attempt to reach knowledge of God's existence and his attributes. It is not easy to apply it to study of his Trinitarian existence. Appropriation is likewise quickly exhausted. We come to a point in the reflection where our intellectual curiosity convinces us of the poverty and inherent restriction of all our cognitive powers. How can we reconcile our faith in the Spirit, source of all that is illuminating, loving, renewing with our intellectual schema?

We need a totally new dimension and dynamism to our knowing equipment. We need in permanence innate mystical power, which would at one and the same time free us from the pitiful weakness of our equipment in cognition and experience and release a new set of powers not entirely inadequate to the mighty task. We should, to be totally satisfied, need the Light of Glory, that special lasting illumination which lifts the souls of the blessed to the level of things divine, and fills them simultaneously with God's life and his light. There the manifold frustration ends.

One form of this frustration is that our intellects are fettered for lack of images. The human mind needs images to initiate understanding. We seem to have no images on which our minds can work. This brings us back to the question whether we may, from the Church, as a reality embodying possible imagery, rise to some knowledge of the Spirit other than just assent to formulas of faith. Will our persons in some way reach this divine Person? See article: Kenosis.

PHOTIUS (c.810-897)[1]

P. a humanist and man of vast knowledge is better known to us through the scholarship of F. Dvornik. His erudition is evident in his *Myriobiblion*, a study of 280 books, with quotations. In a moment of church-state conflict while yet a layman he was made Patriarch of Constantinople. He was twice deposed and sent to a monastery. Pope Nicholas I excommunicated him in 863 and he in turn excommunicated the Pope in 867. He was condemned by a Council, Constantinople IV, which Pope John VIII refused to recognize. The measures there taken against P. were annulled solemnly by another Council, over which John's legates presided. P. died reconciled to Rome, and was canonized by the Orthodox Church while it was still in communion with Rome.

Within this career of vicissitude and fluctuation there was one hard doctrinal result of P.'s writing. It concerned the *Filioque*. By his concentrated, highly polemical, closely reasoned attack on the Latin doctrine he created a gulf which it has been, to this day, impossible to bridge. He is the quarry of all who are opposed to the Latin tradition. Already adumbrated in an Encyclical to his faithful and expressed in other texts, his argumentation is fully developed in the *De Sancti Spiritus Mystagogia*.[2]

P. proceeded from four assumptions: we must distinguish between properties which belong to the divine nature and those which belong to the hypostases; what is common in the Holy Trinity is so to all the hypostases, what is hypostatic is individual and belongs only to the hypostasis involved; hypostatic properties are incommunicable and singular; the Father is linked with the Son and Holy Spirit as unique cause of their existence, and by him they are caused. For the Latins the distinction of Persons in their perfect consubstantiality is derived from their relationship and the opposition of their relationship, which is one of origin and procession. The distinction, for P., was by personal properties that could not be communicated.

According to P. the procession of the Holy Spirit comes from a property in the Father which is of his hypostasis, not from the common divine nature. It cannot, therefore, belong to another Person of the Holy Trinity, for participation by another Person would be contrary to the fact that properties of the hypostasis are incommunicable and singular. Since the Father begets the Son and makes the Spirit proceed, any participation by the Son in the procession of the Holy Spirit would imply that the Son shares the hypostasis of the Father, takes his place or is a part of the hypostasis of the Father, which P. thinks, would reduce the Trinity to two Persons.

If, the argument goes on, the operation by which the Father makes the Spirit to proceed is not of his hypostasis, but springs from his nature, it would result that not only does the Son participate in the procession but the Spirit himself does. The double procession reduces the Father to a mere appellation, deprived of sense; the property designated by the word Father would not belong exclusively to him and the two divine hypostases would be merged into one and the same person: worthy of Sabellius or some semi-Sabellian monster, he thinks. From another standpoint he thinks that the double procession would lead to a plurality of hypostases; the divine Persons being equal, if the Son is begotten by the Father and the Spirit comes from the Father and the Son, then the Spirit must himself produce something: four or more hypostases.

P. insists that the Father must remain the unique cause of the mode of existence of the Son and of the Spirit. If the Son is with the Father, the cause of existence of the Spirit, there are two principles in the Trinity, irreconcilable with the divine monarchy of the Father. He sees all kinds of strange consequences. He thinks that the procession of the Spirit from the Father and the Son would mean that it was imperfect from the Father.

P. is not beyond charges of a very polemical kind, references to polytheism, Greek mythology, Gnosticism, an allusion to the Son as "grandson" of the Father, to the heresy of Macedonius—on the *Filioque*. He was convinced that the Bible and the Fathers were on his side. He argues from Jn 16:14 and Gal 4:4 to deprive them of any *Filioque* content. He dismisses the views of Ambrose, Jerome and Augustine as either based on falsified texts or explainable on grounds of human fallibility—noting too that they did not write dogmatically. He lists a number of Popes who were of a contrary opinion to Ambrose and Augustine and thinks that six of the seven Ecumenical Council declared likewise. He does not consider the Greek tradition "through the Son."

[1]F. Dvornik, *The Photian Schism*, Cambridge, 1948; id., *NCE*, XI, 326-29; Cardinal Hergenrother, *Photius, Patriarch von Constantinopel*, 3 vols, Regensburg, 1867-69; J. Slipyi, *Die Trinitätslehre des byzantinischen Patriarchen Photios*, Innsbruck, 1921; V. Grumel, "Le Filioque au Concile photien de 879-80 et le témoignage de Michel d'Anchiados," *Echos d'Orient*, 29 (1930) 257-264; id., "Le patriarche Photius, père du schisme ou patron de la réunion," *La Vie intellectuelle*, December, 1945, 16-28; L. Lohn, *Doctrina Graecorum et Russorum de Processione Spiritus Sancti a solo Patre, I,* *Photii temporibus*, Rome, 1934; M. Jugie, A. A., *Theologia Dogmatica Christianorum Orientalium ab Ecclesia Catholica Dissidentium*, I, Paris, 1926, 179-222; id., *De Processione Spiritus Sancti ex Fontibus Revelationis et secundum Orientales Dissidentes*, Rome, 1936, 282-386; id., "Origine de la controverse sur l'addition du Filioque au Symbole," *RSPT*, 28 (1939), 369-385; (against Jugie) V. Grumel, A. A., "Photius et l'addition du Filioque au Symbole de Nicée-Constantinople," *REB* 5 (1947) 218-234; R. Haugh, *Photius and the Carolingians, The Trinitarian Controversy*, Belmont, Mass., 1975; M. A. Orphanos, in "La Théologie du Saint Esprit," ed. L. Vischer, *Faith and Order*, 103, French tr., Paris, 1981, 29-33; De Régnon, *Etudes*, III, 241-383; E. Amann, *DTC* XII, 2, (1937), 1536-1604; [2]*PG* 102, 263-400; cf. also encyclical 867, *PG* 102, 721-741; letter to Walpert, of Aquileia, c.882, *PG* 102, 793-821; *Amphilochia*, q.28, between 867 and 876, *PG* 101, 205-209.

PIUS XII (1876-1958)

Pius XII's pontificate did not witness the increased consciousness within the Church at large of the Holy Spirit, nor the extensive literature about him which have been noted in recent years, broadly in the post-conciliar age.[1] He was not consequently, prompted to issue pronouncements which would meet a need either for encouragement or guidance. To such interventions Paul VI (qv) was called more than once.

There are, nonetheless, passages of some interest to the subject here and there in the vast corpus left by Pius XII. The great Encyclical on biblical studies, opens with the words *Divino Afflante Spiritu,* from which it takes its name: "Inspired by the Divine Spirit, the sacred writers composed those books which God, in his paternal charity towards the human race, deigned to bestow on them in order 'to teach, to reprove, to correct, to instruct in justice: that the man of God may be perfect, finished in every good work.'"[2] In the second doctrinal Encyclical, *Mediator Dei*, on the liturgy, the Pope wrote these words in defence of personal choice in regard to spiritual exercises: "As for the various ways in which such spiritual exercises may be conducted, it should be borne in mind that in the Church on earth, as well as in the Church in heaven, there are many mansions; and that ascetical doctrine is no one's monopoly. There is but one Spirit, but 'He breathes where he will,' and by various gifts and various paths leads to sanctity the souls that he enlightens. Their freedom, and the supernatural action of the Holy Spirit in them, are a thing sacrosanct, which no man may under any pretext hamper or violate."[3]

If we look in the writings of Pius XII for something more substantial than these statements, important though each is, we shall get it in *Mystici Corporis Christi*. Having dealt with Christ as founder of the Body and Head of the Body, the Pope goes on to consider Christ the Upholder of the Body. He is thus led to speak of the Church as animated by the Spirit of Christ: "If, now, we carefully consider this divine principle of life and power given by Christ inasmuch as it constitutes the very well-spring of every created gift and grace, we shall easily understand that it is none other than the Paraclete, the Spirit who proceeds from the Father and the Son, and who in a special manner is called the 'Spirit of Christ' or the 'Spirit of the Son' (Rom 8:9; 2 Cor 3:17; Gal 4:6). For it was with this Spirit of grace and truth that the Son of God adorned his soul in the Virgin's immaculate womb; he is the Spirit who delights to dwell in the Redeemer's pure soul as in his favourite temple; he is the Spirit whom Christ merited for us on the Cross with the shedding of his own blood; the Spirit whom he bestowed upon the Church for the remission of sins, breathing him upon the Apostles (cf. Jn 20:22). And while Christ alone received this Spirit without measure (cf. Jn 3:34), it is only according to the measure of the giving of Christ and from the fullness of Christ himself that he is bestowed upon the members of the Mystical Body (cf. Eph 1:18; 4:7). And since Christ has been glorified on the Cross his Spirit is communicated to the Church in abundant outpouring, in order that she and each of her members may grow daily in likeness to our Saviour. It is the Spirit of Christ who has made us adopted sons of God (cf. Rom 8:14-17; Gal 4:6-7), so that one day 'we all, beholding the glory of the Lord with open face, may be transformed into the same image from glory to glory'"[4] (cf. 2 Cor 3:18).

This passage is comprehensive certainly and every phrase is replete with meaning. The pope goes on to elaborate a truth already expressed by Leo XIII, that the Holy Spirit is the soul of the Mystical Body: "The Spirit of Christ is the invisible principle to which we must also attribute the union of all the parts of the Body with one another and with their exalted Head, dwelling, as he does, whole in the Head, whole in the Body, and whole in each of its members, and assisting those with his presence in divers manners according to their various functions and duties and their higher or lower degree of spiritual perfection. He, with his heavenly breath of life, is the source from which proceeds every single vital and effectively salutary action in all parts of the Body. It is he himself who is present in all the members and divinely acts in each, though he also acts in the lower members through the ministry of the higher. And, finally, it is he who, while by the inspiration of his grace giving ever new increase to the Church, refuses to dwell by sanctifying grace in members which are completely severed from the Body. This presence and operation of the Spirit of Jesus Christ has been vigorously and compendiously described by our wise predecessor of immortal memory, Leo XIII, in the following words: 'It is enough to state that, since Christ is the Head of the Church, the Holy Spirit is her soul.'

If, however, this vital force and power, through which the whole community of Christians is upheld by its Founder, is viewed not in itself but in the created effects which proceed from it, then it consists in those heavenly gifts which our Redeemer together with his Spirit bestows upon the Church, and of which he, giver of supernatural light and cause of sanctity, together with his Spirit is the author. Thus the Church, as well as all her holy members, may make her own the eloquent words of the Apostle: 'I live, now not I; but Christ liveth in me.'"[5] See also Encyclical *Haurietis Aquas,* 4.

---

[1]Cf. M. O'Carroll, C.S.Sp., *Pius XII, Greatness Dishonoured,* Dublin, 1980, esp. 198ff; *id., DSp,* XII, 1438-1442, bibl., R. Aubert, in *Catholicisme* XI, 300-311; R. Brunet, "L 'Encyclique Mystici Corporis Christi," *DSp* II,2, 2397-2403, in art. "Corps Mystique; C. Lialine, "Une étape en ecclésologie. Refléctions sur l'Encyclique Mystici Corporis Christi, *Irenikon* 19 (1946) 129-151, 283-317; 20 (1947) 34-54; S. Tromp, S.J. (generally thought to have written a draft of the Encyclical), *Litterae Encyclicae, Mystici Corporis Christi,* 3rd ed., Rome, 1958; *id., Corpus Christi quod est Ecclesia,* 2nd ed., 1946; *id., DSp,* IV, 1, 1296-1302; L. Bouyer, "*Où en est la théologie du Corps Mystique? RSR,* 22 (1948), 313-333; K. Rahner, S.J., "Die Zugehörigkeit zur Kirche nach der Lehre der Encyklika Pius XII Mystici Corporis Christi," ZKT 69 (1947), 129-188; L. Malevez, NRT 67 (1945), 397; [2]CTS ed.; [3]CTS ed.; [4]CTS ed.; [5]CTS ed.

PNEUMATOMACHI (4th century)[1]

Heretics who denied the equality of the Holy Spirit with the Father and the Son.[1] The historians Sozomen and Socrates as well as St. Jerome, Rufinus and others thought that Macedonius was their founder. Since he was no longer Bishop of Constantinople when they became really active, it is difficult to achieve certainty on this.

Evidence for the P.'s views is found in the writings of those who opposed them; they were unfortunate in meeting giants in their way:

Didymus the Blind (qv) in his two works, *De Spiritu Sancto* and De Trinitate, the first composed apparently before 362, the second some twenty years later, after the Council of Constantinople 381, (qv). In the first Didymus though hoping to convert his opponents, treats them as heretics; they seem to hold a position analogous to those against whom St. Athanasius (qv) wrote in the Letters to Serapion. They accept a binitarian formula, cannot see how the Holy Spirit could be other than a creature, for if he were begotten, we should have two Sons of the Father. They invoke Scripture, Jn 1:3 and Amos to show that the Spirit is a *Servus*, has a ministerial role.

The Alexandrian P. with whom Didymus was dealing, wished to avoid the errors of the Arians and the Sabellians, and they cultivated the spiritual life, maintaining that the Spirit's sanctifying mission was fitting in a creature; there must be close sympathy between the Spirit and those in whom he dwells, whom he fills with his grace. Thus the picture in the *De Spiritu Sancto*. In the *De Trinitate* the portrayal continues. But the positions are hardened: they think the Holy Spirit is but a creature nearer to angels than to God, with a substance altogether different from the *ousia* of the Father and Son. Didymus had access to a P. dialogue as a source. There are other testimonies which cannot be firmly linked with Egypt.

St. Epiphanius, St. Basil and his fellow Cappadocians, St. Gregory of Nyssa and St. Gregory of Nazianzus (qqv) fill in the picture for Asia Minor, Cappadocia and Constantinople. The heresy varied in the points emphasized, as in the backing it could summon. It could not sustain the massive criticism which came from the authorities named. Their analysis was sealed by the Council of Constantinople.

---

[1]Cf. *Trinitas*, s.v.; esp., C. Pietri, "Le débat pneumatologique à la veille du Concile de Constantinople (358-381), "*Atti del Congresso*, I, 55-87.

POULLART DES PLACES, CLAUDE-FRANCIS (1679-1709)[1]

What interests in this personality is that at the early age of twenty-four he laid the foundation of a work which would eventually become a religious missionary institute working in fifty-five countries. The beginning was a seminary founded in Paris on Pentecost Sunday, 27 May, 1703; the purpose was to educate seminarists not endowed with this world's goods, and willing themselves to devote their ministry to those most in need. The founder who was of a Breton noble family, had turned from a worldly career to the priesthood, enjoyed rapid progress in the spiritual life, with a distinctive *mystique* of poverty. Among his allies were St. John Baptist de la Salle and St. Louis Marie Grignion de Montfort (qv), the latter particularly close since their student days with the Jesuits in Rennes. Claude Poullart des Places chose the Collège Louis le Grand in Paris, also a Jesuit institution, for his theological studies. St. Louis visited him here, was probably present at the inaugural ceremony. Des Places promised to train the subjects for the saint's own society, the Compagnie de Marie, and this was done for years, even after the founder's death.

Why the choice of Pentecost Sunday and the title chosen, *Séminaire du Saint Esprit*? In Brittany and in Paris the founder had come under the influence of a spirituality centred on the third Person of the Holy Trinity. This current of enlightened piety was evident in man ways, was certainly increased by the recent publication of the work of Louis Lallemant (qv). At Louis Le Grand Des Places had been a member of the *Assemblée des Amis* (known as Aa), a secret society for promoting holiness among the students accepted as members. An extract from a meditation used in the Association will point to a source of Des Places' spiritual outlook: "On Pentecost Sunday and all the week I shall open my heart to the Holy Spirit that he may fill it, that he may intimately possess it and that he may be the mind of my mind and the heart of my heart. I shall offer it to him that he may consume it, as a victim with the flames of his love. . . . The practice must be to accustom myself to consider the Spirit of God dwelling intimately within me, that this is a Spirit of love who asks nothing more than to light in my heart the flames with which he, the Father and the Son, are one and thus to surrender soul and heart to him entirely, that it may breathe nothing else but the love of God. . . . I shall beseech the Holy Spirit, who prepared the soul and body of the Virgin to receive the divine Word, that he dispose my soul by charity, my body by purity, for this ineffable union which his love seeks in the Eucharist."

Influenced by such thinking Des Places was led to give the following directive in his General and Particular Regulations: "All the students will especially adore the Holy Spirit, to whom they have been specially dedicated. They will also have a singular devotion to the Blessed Virgin, under whose protection they have been offered to the Holy Spirit. They will choose the feast of Pentecost and of the Immaculate Conception as their principal feasts. They will celebrate the first to obtain from the Holy Spirit the fire of divine love, and the second to obtain from the Most Blessed Virgin angelic purity; two virtues which constitute the whole foundation of their piety."[2]

Ordained priest on 17 September 1707 des Places died on 2 October 1709, in his thirty-first year; he was buried in a pauper's grave. His work continued, formed hundreds of priests to serve at home and overseas, was joined with the Society of the Holy Heart of Mary founded by Francis Libermann in 1849, serves the Church in many countries, especially in the Third World. The Daughters of the Holy Spirit, a foundation made by Allenou de la Ville-Angevin, an immediate disciple of des Places, continue the inspiration derived from the latter.

---

[1]Cf. H. Le Floch, *Une vocation et une fondation au siècle de Louis XIV. Claude-Francois Poullart des Places, fondateur du Séminaire et de la Congrégation de Saint Esprit*, Paris, 1915; J. Michel, *Claude Francois Poullart des Places, fondateur de la Congrégation du Saint Esprit*, 1679-1709, Paris, 1962; H. J. Koren, *The Spiritual Writings of Father Claude Francis Poullart des Places. Founder of the Congregation of the Holy Ghost*. Duquesne Studies. Spiritan Series 3, Pittsburgh, 1959; *id.*, *To the Ends of the Earth*, Pittsburgh, 1983; *Claude-Francis Poullart des Places. Writings*, Introduced by J. Lécuyer, C.S.Sp., Spiritan Centre, Rome, 1988; *Les Fondateurs des Spiritains*, Spiritains aujourdhui, 4 Rome, 1985; [2]Spiritains aujourdhui, 20, article J. Michel, *Poullart des Places; les sources de sa spiritualité et la génèse de son oeuvre*, p. 20.

POWER[1]

Reflection on the power of the Spirit must be kept within a framework mysteriously fixed by divine revelation. A theism which did not include the concept of power, limitless in itself, as a divine attribute would deserve rejection. But since God revealed himself in an existence which comprised the comprehensive element of kenosis (qv) the mind, even when enlightened by faith, must wrestle with the mystery which envelops the divine manifestation of power. The basis of all divine power is God's creative act, which was Trinitarian; as creator he dominates by his power the creature issued from it. In the unfolding of salvation history, God exercises his might through those chosen as his instruments. In the Old Testament God's Spirit worked through the prophets. He was the embodiment of divine, as opposed to human power: "Not by might, not by power, but by my Spirit, says the Lord of hosts." (Zech 4:6). The idea is concentrated on the portrait of the future Messiah: "Wonderful Counsellor, Mighty God, Everlasting Father, Prince of Peace" (Is 9:6). On him will repose the Spirit of God (Is 11:2). When he comes he will be fashioned by the power of the Spirit: "The Holy Spirit will come upon you, and the power of the Most High will overshadow you" (Lk 1:35).

The miracles are Christ's way of showing his power; he had first been "anointed with the Holy Spirit and with power." (Acts 10:38); in his works the effects of the Spirit are seen, for on him the Spirit rested, and to him the Spirit was given without measure (Lk 3:22; Jn 1:32ff; 3:34f). His power is oriented to the Father's will (Jn 5:30; 17:4) and in his trinitarian existence to the accomplishment of this eternal living ordinance, he works by the Spirit, as he insists in a most challenging example of his might, the casting out of devils (Mt 12:28; Lk 11:20).

Jesus was raised by the Spirit, who thus becomes a universal source of hope: "If the Spirit of him who raised Jesus from the dead dwells in you, he who raised Christ Jesus from the dead will give life to your mortal bodies also through his Spirit which dwells in you." (Rom 8:11). This power of the Spirit Christ would share with his disciples: "but stay in the city until you are clothed with power from on high." (Lk 24:49) "But you shall receive power when the Holy Spirit has come upon you." (Acts 1:8). The story of Christian origins as related in Acts (qv) is the beneficial infiltration of society by this power conferred on the Apostles by the Spirit: "And with great power the apostles gave their testimony to the resurrection of the Lord Jesus, and great grace was upon them all" (Acts 4:33). Paul (qv) in his ministry is equally explicit on the Spirit as the source of power: "My speech and my message were not in plausible words of wisdom, but in demonstration of the Spirit and of power" (1 Cor 2:4); "May the God of hope fill you with all joy and peace in believing, so that by the power of the Holy Spirit you may abound in hope" (Rom 15:13).

This power of the Spirit is limitless, it is supremely free, it achieves at times the divine paradox of triumphing in the midst of human weakness; it is often hidden, being manifest only with the passage of time; it is clothed with mystery, but efficacious beyond human calculation; it confounds the judgement of men and women for it fashions through their poverty of mind and body, an enduring graceful fabric which sustains the universe. It does so because it is the work of the Spirit.

----

[1] Biblical dictionaries and encyclopaedias s.v., e.g. *Dictionary of Biblical Theology*, ed. X.Leon-Dufour, London, 1967, 388-392; J.Fitzmyer, S.J., *Jerome Biblical Commentary*, II, 79, p. 819.

PRAYER[1]

A capital text here is in Romans: "Likewise the Spirit helps us in our weakness; for we do not know how to pray as we ought, but the Spirit himself intercedes for us with sighs too deep for words. And he who searches the hearts of men knows what is the mind of the Spirit, because the Spirit intercedes for the saints according to the will of God." (8:26, 27). It is immediately after this text that St. Paul makes his affirmation on divine predestination: "We know that in everything God works for good with those who love him, who are called according to his purpose. For those whom he foreknew he also predestined to be conformed to the image of his Son, in order that he might be the first-born among many brethren. And those whom he predestined he also called; and those whom he called he also justified; and those whom he justified, he also glorified" (8:28-30).

Earlier in the same chapter Paul had given a basis for the Spirit's role in prayer: "So then, brethren, we are debtors, not to the flesh, to live according to the flesh—for if you live according to the flesh you will die, but if by the Spirit you put to death the deeds of the body you will live. For all who are led by the Spirit of God are sons of God. For you did not receive the spirit of slavery to fall back into fear, but you have received the spirit of sonship. When we cry 'Abba! Father!' it is the Spirit himself bearing witness with our spirit that we are children of God, and if children, then heirs, heirs of God and fellow heirs with Christ, provided we suffer with him in order that we may also be glorified with him" (Rom 8:12-17; cp. Rom 8:5).

Confirmation of this truth from another angle is given in Gal 4:4-6: "But when the time had fully come, God sent forth his Son, born of a woman, born under the law, to redeem those who were under the law, so that we might receive adoption as sons. And because you are sons, God has sent the Spirit of his Son into our hearts, crying 'Abba! Father!'" This Spirit can be sought in prayer, as Jesus tells us: "'If you then, who are evil, know how to give good gifts to your children, how much more will the heavenly Father give the Holy Spirit to those who ask him!'" (Lk 11:13).

Since the Spirit dwells within us (see Indwelling) personally, he leads us towards perfect personal prayer, teaching us who God is to whom we pray, enlightening us on ourselves who pray, unravelling the tangled skeins of our individuality. With the text from Rom 8 we must take this from Rom 11: "O the depth of the riches and wisdom and knowledge of God! How unsearchable are his judgements and how inscrutable his ways! 'For who has known the mind of the Lord, or who has been his counsellor?' 'Or who has given a gift to him that he might be repaid'" (Rom 11:33-35, cp. Is 40: 13-14; Job 35:7; 41:11)?

Along with this Pauline insight we must take the Apostle's teaching on the Spirit in communion with the individual, the author of intimate revelation, a stimulus and guide in prayer: "But, as it is written, 'What no eye has seen, nor ear heard, nor the heart of man conceived, what God has prepared for those who love him, 'God has revealed to us through the Spirit. For the Spirit searches everything, even the depths of God. For what man knows a man's thoughts except the spirit of the man which is in him? So also no one comprehends the thoughts of God except the Spirit of God. Now we have received not the spirit of the world, but the Spirit which is from God, that we might understand the gifts bestowed on us by God. And we impart this in words not taught by human widsom but taught by the Spirit, interpreting spiritual truths to those who possess the Spirit. The unspiritual man does not receive the gifts of the Spirit of God, for they are folly to him, and he is not able to understand them because they are spiritually discerned. The spiritual man judges all things, but is himself to be judged by no one. 'For who has known the mind of the Lord so as to instruct him?' But we have the mind of Christ" (1 Cor 2:6-16).

Prayer, as the thrust of the soul towards God, in this Pauline perspective, has all its riches from the Spirit. No wonder the author of Ephesians formally recommends: "Pray at all times in the Spirit, with all prayer and supplication" (Eph 6:18). The injunction is repeated in the epistle of Jude: "But you, beloved, build yourselves up on your most holy faith; pray in the Spirit; keep yourselves in the love of God; wait for the mercy of our Lord Jesus Christ unto eternal life" (v.20).

To hearken to this advice may mean a profound spiritual revolution or reorientation. It must lead to the final uncovering of our deepest self (see Personal Fulfilment), but that is a goal which even the greatest saints found daunting. We must strain to reach the "hour which is coming, and now is, when the true worshippers will worship the Father in Spirit and Truth, for such the Father seeks to worship him. God is Spirit and those who worship him must worship in Spirit and Truth'" (Jn 4:23,24).

Different spiritual techniques, methods as they are currently called, have been proposed to help the Christians in their prayer. Some allow a place for bodily movements or attitudes; others long in use in the West and highly honoured, prescribe a discursive mental sequence. Here personal freedom (qv) is paramount—unless it has been initially surrendered by the adoption of a particular way of life; in this act of surrender, this deliberate acceptance of a method as binding, freedom has been exercised. In the sequel to the decision it still remains, and may opt for change, including change in the way of life.

When spiritual writers speak of the "presence of God," they are really speaking of the presence of the Spirit, a condition of fruitful prayer. When failure in prayer is being diagnosed, rarely is the true attitude to the Spirit questioned. For some it would appear presumptuous to speak of the Spirit when it is the initial stage in prayer that is being planned, considered or judged. This objection is similar to that raised to early frequent and daily Communion. A degree of perfection was thought to be a prior necessity. But the Eucharist itself is the very source of Christian perfection; it is the imperfect who need it most.

In a different way the Holy Spirit is the source of all true prayer. To delay advertence to him, attention to the conditions of his presence and action, is to ignore the order laid down by God. This clearly implies apprenticeship, a learning process, as all masters of the spiritual life advocate. But not a learning process which will dispense with the essential Master.

This Master surrounds the soul with the necessary safeguards in the prayer of petition. We have the promises recorded in the gospels: "'Ask, and it will be given you; seek, and you will find; knock, and it will be opened to you'" (Mt 7:7); "'Therefore, I tell you, whatever you ask in prayer, believe that you have received it, and it will be yours'" (Mk 11:24); "'Whatever you ask in my name, I will do it, so that the Father may be glorified in the Son; if you ask the Father anything in my name, I will do it'" (Jn 14:13-14); "'Truly, truly I say to you, if you ask anything of the Father in my name, he will give it to you. Hitherto, you have asked nothing in my name; ask, and you will receive, that your joy may be full'" (Jn 16:23,24).

There is mystery in the way these promises are fulfilled. It is part of the Spirit's role to instruct the soul so that it may cope with this mystery. As the Spirit guides the soul in its practice of personal or shared prayer, in prayer groups of fixed pattern, or in more spontaneous gatherings, there is a deepening realization of God, and more perfect conformity to his will, the norm of perfection. This effects genuine communion with others.

The Spirit animates the Church, building it up, assisting it to maintain or recover unity; he is expressed in the Liturgy, not that every liturgical formula is perfectly chosen, but that his dynamic presence in the Body of Christ is the ultimate guarantee of validity. As St. Paul says: "But now in Christ Jesus you who once were far off have been brought near in the blood of Christ. . . . And he came and preached peace to you who were far off and peace to those who were near; for through him we both have access in one Spirit to the Father. So then you are no longer strangers and sojourners, but you are fellow citizens with the saints and members of the household of God, built upon the foundation of the Apostles and prophets, Christ Jesus himself being the cornerstone, to whom the whole structure is joined together and grows into a holy temple of the Lord; in whom you also are built into it for a dwelling place of God in the Spirit." (Eph 2:13, 17-27). "What we have here," says Fr. Congar, "is the worship of the new people of God, the Body of Christ and the Temple of the Holy Spirit offered to 'God' the Father. . . ." This holy worship is able to reach God through Christ, the only priest of the new and definitive covenant, because we are members of his Body—one new man—in the Holy Spirit, "for by one Spirit we were all baptized into one body, Jews or Greeks. . ." (1 Cor 12:13; Eph 4:4). That Body is a "holy Temple in the Lord". There is no longer any other true temple, but the one holy temple is truly a "house of prayer for all people." The Church's holy and precious Liturgy is the place where the Spirit and the Bride say "'Come'" to the Lord (Rev 22:17). The Lord does in fact come every day to make his Easter event present for us in the Church's holy Eucharist."

The ideal would seem to be choseknit harmony, even integration of personal and liturgical prayer. But wise spiritual directors refrain from imposing this ideal immediately in every aspect of worship. While disposition should correspond with the objective reality in the Paschal Mystery, it is conceivable that spiritual development does not always correspond to the sequence of liturgical seasons. Such flexibility is a tribute to the mode and pace of each individual's assimilation to Christ. The succeeding seasons, each with its distinctive spirit, may find a different response from some who are living out in their special situation one mystery of the Lord more than another. One who is entering a phase of terminal pain willingly modelled on Christ's Passion, may persist in this disposition at Christmastide. The Eucharist, which is the synthesis of all that is most precious in Christ's life, will still have the same rich meaning for such a one through one season. Liturgical observance has to attend to the mystery of Christ, and not overlook the mystery of his disciple. The very freedom (qv) bestowed by the Spirit comprehends the whole of life, and every form of prayer.

Prayer may benefit by the Spirit's charisms (qv). But it draws especially on the structure of the Gifts (qv) which are permanent, oriented to personal perfection whereas the charisms are directed to the good of others—this is not a rigid distinction, for the Gifts enlighten on the identity of the charisms and the charisms indirectly stir faith and love centered on the One who gives.

How the intellectual Gifts: Wisdom, Understanding, Knowledge, do foster progress in prayer is a subject awaiting fuller research. Whether there is a universal call to comtemplative prayer through the functioning of the Gifts, or whether this stage is reached only by the favoured few through an extraordinary communication of the Gifts has been much debated. It is a debate which may stray into mere abstract theory, with little factual evidence to draw on. A survey of great saints and saintly figures of the past would be inconclusive; investigation of those living presents obvious difficulties.

Solely by way of illustration one may point to the monastery of Helfta in the thirteenth century as a centre of contemplation of the highest kind, with a striking degree of intellectual culture. Interestingly though great charismatic moments occasionally marked the contemplative life of the members, especially that of St. Gertrude the Great, the Liturgy was the framework of the mystical experience.

---

[1]Cf. Y.-M.J. Congar, O.P. The Holy Spirit, II, *The Holy Spirit and our Prayer*, 112-118; L. Cerfaux, "L' Apôtre en présence de Dieu; Essai sur la vie d'oraison de saint Paul," Recueil Lucien Cerfaux , II, 469-481; J. Quinn, "*Apostolic Ministry and Apostolic Prayer*," CBQ 33 (1971) 479-491; D.M. Stanley, *Boasting in the Lord*, New York, 1971; G. P. Wiles, Paul's Intercessory Prayers (ENTSMS 24) Cambridge, 1974; Add bibl. E.A. Obeng, The Spirit Intercession Motif in Paul, *Expository Times* 84 (1985), 36-339.

PROCESSION OF THE SPIRIT, THE

Procession is the word used to signify that one divine Person takes his origin in another.[1] It must be fully understood that inequality of any kind is neither stated nor implied; and it must be recalled that all our language about the Holy Trinity is based on analogy. There is real distinction without cleavage or separation or discontinuity or cessation of circuminsession or of perichoresis. The Father does not proceed from any other Person. The Son proceeds from the Father (Jn 8:42). The Holy Spirit is said to proceed from the Father, "the Spirit of truth who proceeds from the Father" (Jn 15:26). Does he also proceed from the Son? That is the debate on the *Filoque* (qv).

---

[1]Cf. esp. St. Thomas (qv) *S.T.* I, q. 27; M. J. Scheeben (qv), *The Mysteries of Christianity*, St. Louis, London, 1946, 87-117; B. de Margerie, S.J., *La Trinité chrétienne dans l'histoire*, Paris, 1974, 205ff; W. J. Hill, O.P., *The Three-Personed God*, Washington,1982, 262ff; manuals of Theology, L. Billot, S.J., *De Deo Trino*; B. Lonergan, *De Deo Trino*; works popularizing theology, E. Hugon, O.P., *Le Mystère de la Sainte Trinité*, Paris, 1921, 141-171; V. M. Breton, O.F.M., *The Blessed Trinity*, London, 1934, 120ff.

PROPHECY[1]

St. Paul (qv) lists prophecy among the charisms (qv). Here we are dealing with prophecy as an important element in the history of salvation. It denotes a divine message convoyed with conviction. Scholars debate how the prophet communes with God to obtain God's message which he must publish or proclaim. It is not, despite plausible arguments put forward, the product of the prophet's own deep religious thinking; nor is it to be confused with ecstatic utterance. There must be a commission from God, a vocation. With this is granted a direct experience of God with the certainty that he wills the knowledge so acquired to be given in his name, to the people or to chosen individuals. Scholars have identified the content of the prophetic utterance and the stylized formulas used. The Spirit had a determining role in the bestowal of prophecy. When there was a consciousness of the "quenched Spirit" (qv), this was expressed equivalently in the words, there are no more prophets.

This is the the broad picture in the OT. Jesus appears, at the outset of his earthly existence, in a world wherein prophets figure: Zechariah (Lk 1:67), Simeon (Lk 2:25ff), Anna (Lk 2:56), especially John the Baptist (qv). The general sense of the NT is that the ancient combined prophetic revelation is now brought to fulfilment. And we have a clear teaching on the very meaning of prophecy. "The prophets who prophesied of the grace that was to be yours searched and inquired about this salvation; they inquired what person or time was indicated by the Spirit of Christ within them when predicting the sufferings of Christ and the subsequent glory" (1 Pet 1:11): "First of all you must understand this, that no prophecy of scripture is a matter of one's own interpretation, because no prophecy over came by the impulse of man, but men moved by the Holy Spirit spoke from God" (2 Pet 1:20,21).

Jesus, in traditional theological thinking, is given among many titles, especially three, prophet, priest and king. He did not speak of himself as a prophet, but never objected on the occasions when others so addressed him or spoke of him. In fact he completely surpassed the concept of prophecy, as it had been so far witnessed in the life of the chosen people. He bore a message from God primarily that he was God, that in him all that revelation could convey was personally embodied, for he was "the Mediator and the fullness of all revelation ... by his whole presence, by all that he manifests of himself, by his words, by his works, by his signs, by his miracles, but especially by his death and his glorious resurrection from the dead, by his sending finally of the Spirit of truth, he gives to revelation its final completion, confirming it by the divine testimony: Jesus Christ is God with us, that we should be delivered from the darkness of sin and death, and that we should be raised for eternal life." (Vatican II, Constitution on Divine Revelation, art, Q,4).

---

[1]Cf. R.H. Rowley, *The Nature of Prophecy in the Light of Recent Research,* HTR 38 (1945) 1-38; E. Jacob, *Le prophétisme israélite d'après les recherches récentes, Rev. d'Histoire et de Phil. Religieuses,* 32 (1952) 56-69; A. Neher, *L'essence du Prophétisme,* Paris, 1955; J. Schaubert, *Die prophetische Literatur. Der Stand der Forschung,* ETL 44 (1968) 346-406; R.E. Clements, *Prophecy and Tradition,* Atlanta, 1975; C. Trestomant, *Le prophétisme hébreu,* Paris, 1982; J. Blenkinsopp, *A History of Prophecy in Israel,* Philadelphia, 1984; J. Asurmendi, *Le prophétisme des origines à l'époque moderne,* Paris, 1985.

PROVIDA MATRIS CARITATE, 5 MAY 1895

An Apostolic Letter sent by Leo XIII (qv) to urge special prayer to the Holy Spirit during the novena preceding Pentecost. (qv) [1]The Pope first states the special intention for prayer which he feels so important "that the Christian people should have 'one faith in their minds, one devotion in their deeds,' that God should be glorified and the salvation of souls assured. To this duty of piety no time seems more appropriate than that when formerly the Apostles, after the Lord's Ascension into heaven were at the same time *perservering in prayer with ... Mary, the Mother of Jesus* (Acts 1:14), awaiting the power promised from on high and gifts of all charisms. For in that august Cenacle, and from the mystery of the Spirit coming upon it, the Church which was conceived by Christ had come forth as he died, began, with the help of divine inspiration, to take up its office among all the nations, who were to be led to one faith and the newness of Christian life."[2]

The Pope points to the summary phrase which says so much: "Now the company of believers had one heart and one soul." (Acts 4:32). He asks Catholics to implore the Holy Spirit, during the novena, especially with this prayer: *Send forth your Spirit and they shall be created; and you will renew the face of the earth.* Thereon the Pope gives a pithy message of praise of the Spirit: the Spirit of Truth, "who spoke the secrets of God in the Scriptures, confirms the Church by his continuous presence"; the source of adoptive sonship and of every grace. "The same Spirit, finally, so acts by his power in the Church that as Christ is the Head of this Mystical Body, he may be called its soul, through a likeness that is apt; for *the heart has a certain hidden influence; and therefore the Holy Spirit is compared to the heart, for invisibily he vivifies and unites the Church* (St. Thomas, III q. 8, art 1 ad 3)."[3]

The Spirit, says the Pope, is love; to him all works of love are attributed. He will, in answer to the prayer of Catholics, promote harmony among them. From such harmony the Pope hoped for something else very important in his eyes, the return of the dissidents, that they should want to have in themselves 'that mind which is in Christ Jesus,' sharing with us the same faith and hope, bound with the most desirable bonds of perfect charity."[4]

The papal letter was composed two years before his Encyclical on the Holy Spirit, *Divinum illud munus*, which it seemed to anticipate. The text from Acts 1:14 which he used as basic in his brief essay was to be lost in church or papal pronouncements until John XXIII (qv) and Vatican II (qv). John appealed to it frequently, when he spoke of his hopes that the Council would be a new Pentecost. It was used in the Marian chapter of the Constitution on the Church (art. 59). It has been subjected to exhaustive exegesis in recent years, although notably overlooked previously.

---

[1]*Lettres Apostoliques de SS Léon XIII, Encycliques, Brefs*, Paris, La Bonne Presse, Latin and French tr., IV, 206-211; [2]206, 8; 3. 208; [4]210.

Q

QUAKERS, THE SOCIETY OF FRIENDS[1]

The popular name was first used as a gibe; it is now a word that evokes admiration and respect. The origins, vicissitudes and activities of the body do not directly concern us, save in so far as the founder, George Fox, whose central idea and inspiration was the "Inner Light", did emphasize the influence of the Spirit in every Christian life. He thought that without this Spirit no one profits anything even if he were to know all the Bible from Genesis to Revelation. He deemed the fruit of the Spirit to be virtue and justice. Christ, he recalled, baptized in the Spirit and in fire, and his ministers would lead in the Spirit to all truth. He aimed at no elaborate, systematic theology of the Spirit, was preoccupied with receptivity to the Inner Light and the moral life. In the Society everyone is free to take an initiative and voice his or her conviction for the good life. The services of the Quakers in the cause of peace, of education, of international relief, in promoting a caring society are well known.

---

[1]Basic text, *Journal* by George Fox, ed. Norman Penney, London, 1911; cf. A. N. Bradshaw, *The Personality of George Fox*, London, 1933; H. J. Cadbury, *George Fox's Book of Miracles*, 1948; H. E. Wildes, *Voice of the Lord, A Biography of George Fox*, Philadelphia, 1965; L. G. Braithwaite, *The Beginnings of Quakerism*, Cambridge, 1955; R. A. Knox, *Enthusiasm, A Chapter in the History of Religion*, Oxford, 1950, 139-175; Elfrida Vigont, *The Story of Quakerism, 1652-1952*, London, 1954; J/ Sykes, *The Quakers, A New Look at their Place in Society*, 1958); P. Janelle, s.v. Fox, George, "*DSp*, V, 770-779; F. Frost, s.v. "Quakers," *DSp*, XII,2, 2684-2702.

QUENCHED SPIRIT, THE

Jesus was taken by his contemporaries as a prophet and was himself conscious of the fact that he was this.[1] As a prophet, he was a bearer of the Spirit. Behind this assertion lies much complex religious history. J. Jeremias sums it up thus: "The presence of the Spirit is a sign of the dawn of the time of salvation. Its return means the end of judgement and the beginning of the time of grace. God is turning towards his people. As bearer of the Spirit, Jesus is not only one man among the ranks of the prophets, but God's last and final messenger. His proclamation is an eschatological event. The dawn of the consummation of the world is manifested in it. God is speaking his final word."[2]

The reason why Jesus did not take "his place as a link in the chain of the many Old Testament messengers of God" was that the continuity had been broken. Israel was living in an age when the Spirit was "quenched." This was believed by the synagogue. It was an opinion possibly held already in later parts of the OT. Ps 74:9 for instance, says: "We do not see any signs; there is no longer any prophet, and there is none among us who knows how long." Again in 1 Macc 4:45-46: "So they tore down the altar, and stored the stones in a convenient place until there should come a prophet to tell what to do with them." Or 9:27: "Thus there was great distress in Israel, such as had not been since the time the prophets ceased to appear among them." Or 14:41: "And the Jews and their high priests decided that Simon should be their leader and high priest forever until a trustworthy prophet should arise." The view generally is supported by the apocalyptic and rabbinic literature and by Josephus.

The religious history of the Jewish people was thus understood. In the time of the patriarchs all the devout God-fearing and upright men benefitted by the action of God's Spirit: they did not have a theology of the Holy Trinity, did not understand the Spirit as a hypostasis. He was the dynamic power of God in their lives (see article Old Testament). Then Israel failed God, sinning with the golden calf (Ex 32:2; Ps 106: 19-20). Thereafter, the giving of the Spirit was restricted to certain people, categories as the judges, prophets, high priests and kings. When the last of the prophets who committed their thoughts to writing, Haggai, Zechariah and Malachi died, the Spirit was quenched, because Israel had sinned. God still spoke, men thought, but only through an echo of his voice.

There were some who thought that all was not lost. Qumran, (qv) in particular, is quoted as a community which benefitted by the Spirit. But Qumran was an exception. The generally accepted opinion among orthodox Jews was that the Spirit had been quenched. This is an assumption of the New Testament. It is borne out particularly by the narrative of John the Baptist's appearance, with all that followed from it (cf. Mk 1:8 par.). When the disciples of John made answer, "'No, we have not even heard that there is a Holy Spirit,'" (Acts 19:2) they were saying,'"we have not yet heard anything about his being present again'". The accepted view makes Mk 3:28ff understandable.

Humans lived then in a void, in darkness, with a sense that they were cut off from God—recognition of this fact may be helpful in understanding the place of the Spirit in OT dispensation. In the last days, they thought, the calamitous epoch of the Spirit's absence would end. That they longed for the coming of the Spirit is amply shown. A supreme advantage of John the Baptist's mission was to reassure them that one was coming who would baptize in the Spirit.

---

[1]Cf. R. Meyer, *Der Prophet aus Galiläa,* Leipzig, 1940; O. Cullmann, *The Christology of the New Testament,* London, 1959, 13-59; F. Hahn, *Christologische Hoheitstitel,* Göttingen, 1963; after 1963, English tr., *The Titles of Jesus in Christology,* London 1969; J. Jeremias, *The New Testament Theology,* I, London, 1971, 80-83. [2]*Op. cit.,* 85.

QUMRAN[1]

The important documents discovered in our time in the Judean desert shed some light on the beliefs, mentality and religious observance of a singularly devout community of Jews about the time of Christ; in existence, it is thought from about 140 B.C. to the destruction of Jerusalem after the Jewish revolt in A.D. 70. Two of the documents afforded some idea of how these sectaries thought of the Spirit. Taken out of context some passages may mislead: "I thank thee, O Lord, for thou hast upheld me by thy strength. Thou hast shed thy Holy Spirit upon me that I may not stumble."[2] Or again: "And I know that man is not righteous except through thee, and therefore I implore thee by the spirit which thou hast given me to perfect thy (favours) to thy servant (for ever), purifying me by thy Holy Spirit and drawing me near to thee by grace according to the abundance of thy mercies."[3]

These and similar passages must be interpreted in part in the light of the doctrine of the two spirits held by the Qumran community. When attention is focussed exclusively, however, on the two spirits, spiritual insights of value may be missed. The good spirit may be the creative self of each man. But especially it may be the spirit of holiness. "The holy spirit also effects cleansing and justification, making possible the perfect sacrifice of praise. Quite clearly man's ability to stand in God's gracious approval is an effect of God's grace. If the 'grace' aspect of Qumran is pushed to a pre-destinarian extreme, it at least provides a counterbalance to the kind of justification by works which viewed the holy spirit as something which very holy men might merit. For the Dead Sea covenanters the holy spirit is less the prophetic spirit than the spirit of inner revelation and understanding and the purifying spirit."[4]

---

[1]G.T. Montague, *The Holy Spirit,* 116-124; J. (Cardinal) Danielou, *Théologie du Judéo-Christianisme,* Paris, 1957, 192ff; [2]Hymn VII, G. Vermes, *The Dead Sea Scrolls in English,* 1962, Pelican ed., London, p. 173; [3]*Op. cit.,* Hymn XVI, 0. 197; [4]G.T. Montague, *op. cit.,* 123; P. Wernberg Moller, *A Reconsideration of the Two Spirits in the Rule of the Community. Revue de Qumran,* III, 11, 413-441; *ibid.,* M. Treves, *The Two Spirits of the Rule of the Community,* 449-452; cf. esp. art. John the Baptist; cf. esp. DBS, XI, 156-172, E. Cothenet.

R

RAHNER, KARL, S.J. (1904-1984)

The great German theologian did not give as much attention to the Holy Spirit as did his French Dominican contemporary, Fr. Y.-M.J. Congar. The Jesuit was drawn to exercise his speculative gift on many other areas of theology, returning often to Christology, expressing remarkable insights on the structure and life of the Church, on the nature and sources of theology itself, on themes of Christian living, the Eucharist notably and the Sacred Heart, the challenge of the present age. But if the subject of the Holy Spirit is not often dealt with in the extensive corpus, the topics considered are important and the insights are by no means insignificant. Notable are: the paper on uncreated grace, which revitalized thinking on the divine indwelling (qv); the contribution to the very necessary theology of charisms in the contemporary situation; a thought-provoking essay on the Sacrament of Confirmation (qv); useful reflections on such widely different subjects as the Spirit and the teaching authority, and visions and prophecies; and a singularly optimistic assessment of the existential and experiential dimension to the whole reality of the Spirit. A valuable anthology, which is not complete has been compiled from these writings.[1]

On the subject of charisms suddenly thrust into the forefront of thinking R. wrote: "All this is merely intended to make it clear that office and spiritual gifts in the Church cannot be conceived as two totally distinct elements which happen to be united more or less by chance in a person who is endowed with office and yet at the same time with a charisma. Office itself and not merely the actual man who in fact holds office must be characterized by charismatic gifts if the Church with its hierarchical constitution is to remain to the end the Church of the abiding Spirit, which through God's grace alone is incapable of falling in its totality from the grace, truth and holiness of God and of so turning the visible manifestation of grace (for that is what the Church is) into a synagogue devoid of the Spirit."[2]

R. rejects the view that the "hierarchy is the only portal through which the Spirit enters the Church," for he holds that it would be false "if one were to suppose that the charismatic element in the Church is reserved to her official ministry."[3]

---

[1]B.A. Finan, *The Mission of the Holy Spirit in the Theology of Karl Rahner, Ph.D.* Diss., Marquette University, 1986; *DSp* XIII, 45-48, with bibl. and information on bibliographies already published; R's contributions, *The Spirit in the Church*, Anthology, London, 1979; *The Dynamic Element in the Church*, Quaestiones Disputatae, 12, London, 1964; in *Theological Investigations*: I (1961), "Some Implications of the Scholastic Concept of Uncreated Grace," 319-346; III (1967) "The Consecration of the Layman to the Care of Souls," *Confirmation,* 274-75; VII (1971), "Do not Stifle the Spirit," 72-87; XVI (1979), "Experience of the Spirit and Existential Commitment," 24-34; XVII (1983) "Confirmation in the Practice of Faith," 51-53; XVIII (1984) "Experience of the Holy Spirit," 189-210; "Das Charismatische in der Kirche, *Stimmen der Zeit* 160 (1956-57), 181-86; *Foundations of the Christian Faith*, London, 1978, 316-318; *Confirmation Today*, Dimension Books, New Jersey, 1975; [2]*The Dynamic Element in the Church*, 47f; [3]*Ibid.,* 48.

RECENT WRITINGS

Bibliographies to the articles include all of recent literature that is relevant and enlightening. Separate articles deal with those who have worked, generally to effect, to secure theological and devotional awareness of the Holy Spirit, Père Congar, Fr. Hans Urs von Balthasar, Frank Duff, Fr. Heribert Mühlen, Paul Evdokimov, James D. G. Dunn to mention those still living or only recently deceased. In the previous generation one must note such figures as Karl Barth; H.B. Swete; S. Bulgakov; E. Leen, C.S.Sp.; V. Lossky, who are also considered.

The theme which arose from the teaching of Vatican II, Mary and the Spirit, has drawn a considerable literature, and continues to do so, at times quite surprising.[1] As intellectual curiosity and the ensuing research are maintained, new fields of interest are discovered, new insights gained in aspects thought fully explored. Light thrown on one aspect of the subject is reflected beneficially on others.

Authors with established reputations in other fields have at times published studies on one or other aspect of the theology of the Holy Spirit. Certain subjects such as the Trinity call for special treatment of the theme, which will now be more enlightened and extensive than it would have been formerly. The subject of divine grace will now prompt similar exposition.

Among the works of significance to note are the posthumous work of the Orthodox Nicolas Afanassief, *L'Eglise du Saint Esprit* (Paris, 1975), Louis Bouyer's *Le Consolateur* (Paris, 1980), which has interesting insights from the Fathers, *Ecclesia a Spiritu Sancto edocta, Mélanges G. Phillips*, (Gembloux, 1970), much of which deals with the Holy Spirit, becoming in a tribute to Mgr. Philips, the guiding spirit of the Constitution on the Church, Vatican II, a theologian of the Holy Spirit at Louvain, W. Kasper, *Die Kirche als Sakrament des Geistes* in *Kirche Ort des Geistes* (Freiburg, 1975).[2]

Certain themes have accumulated a literature, the *Filioque (qv)* understandably because of the ecumenical climate in which we live. The theology of the Church (qv) actively renewed since Vatican II has prompted considerable writing. So has the charismatic (or renewal) movement (qv). A profound subject calling for great subtlety and insight with a capacity for valid synthesis is the Spirit and the Eucharist. Here Louis Bouyer's *Eucharistie* is valuable. John S. McKenna in the collection *Alcuin Club* 57, 1975 has published *Eucharist and Holy Spirit*, with an immense bibliography. J. Moltmann has dealt with *The Church in the Power of the Spirit.*[3]

Studies to note also are: A. Orbe, *La teologia del Espiritu Santo*, Rome, 1966; K. McDonnell, O.S.B., *Vatican II (1962-1965) Puebla (1979) the Synod (1985): Koinonia, Communio as Integral Ecclesiology*, in *The Journal of Ecumenical Studies*, 25 (1988) 399-427; Wolf-Dieter Hauschild, *Gottes Geist und der Mensch, Studien zur fruhchristlichen Pneumatologie*, W. Kasper, ed., *Gegenwart des Geistes, Aspekte des Geistes*,

Freiburg 1. Brisgau, 1979; C. Hertmann and H. Mühlen (qv) ed. *Erfahrung und Theologie des Heiligen Geistes*, Munich, 1971.

---

[1]Bibl. on Mary and the Spirit in *Theotokos*, M. O'Carroll, C.S.Sp.; Noteworty also is B. Sesboue, *Bulletin de Pneumatologie*, RSR 76 (1988) 115-128; [2]Cf. *New German Catechism*, on the Church as Sacrament of the Spirit, influenced by W. Kasper; [3]London, 1975, English tr.

REVELATION, BOOK OF

Scholars wrestle with the complexities of this mysterious book, through which the Spirit of prophecy shows itself, amid the many symbols and general apocalyptic character.[1] Two texts are striking and well-known: "And I heard a voice from heaven saying, 'Write this: Blessed are the dead who die in the Lord henceforth.' 'Blessed indeed' says the Spirit 'that they may rest from their labours, for their deeds follow them'" (14:13). Here there is a thought that may be collated with the thesis expressed in the article on death (qv) in the present work: the Spirit manifesting his presence especially at the moment when eternal happiness is the issue. The second passage is not alien to the same line of thought. "The Spirit and the Bride say 'Come.' And let him who hears say 'Come.' And let him who is thirsty come, let him who desires take the water of life without price" (22:17). Fr. Montague comments: "There can be no doubt here that just as the Bride is one, so the Spirit is one." The Spirit here, however, is likewise the Spirit of prophecy we have met throughout. It speaks primarily through the prophets, so that the combined expression, "The Spirit and the Bride" is equivalent to "the prophets and the saints." The prophets inspired by the Spirit cry out to the Lord Jesus to come. Their "Come" is echoed by the whole body of believers, described in the preceding chapters as the Bride of the Lamb. Their chorus in turn is an invitation to all who are listening to the reading of this book in their churches (cf. 1:3) to interpose at this point their own "Come." The Spirit of prophecy bears witness to Jesus not only in worshipping him alone (cf. 19:10) but also in the cry for him to return."[2] The same author expounds convincingly the relevance to the Spirit of the passage on the river of life-giving water (22:1-5). "If, as is held by the majority of scholars, the Book of Revelation stands within the Johannine tradition, we are justified in calling on the Gospel of John to help us understand the Christian symbolism of this fountain of water."[3] Jn 7:38-39 speaks of the Spirit in terms of living water. The author thinks that this linking of ideas "gives perhaps the most profound image of the Spirit in the NT. It is no longer the prophetic Spirit, but the Spirit of life. And the Spirit flows jointly from God and the Lamb into the city of God." Here, as he says, is in embryo what later Trinitarian theology will say about the Spirit proceeding from the Father and Son. Thus a great doctrine emerges; so many other references in the work are in terms of angelology that it is most satisfying to see the shining central truth amid the symbols.

---

[1]Cf. F.F. Bruce, *The Spirit in the Apocalypse*, Christ and the Spirit in the New Testament, ed. B.Lindars, S.S. Smalley, for C.F.D. Moule, Cambridge, London, 1973, 333-344; esp., G.T. Montague, *The Holy Spirit*, 321-332; [2]*Op. cit.*, 327; [3]*Op. cit.*, 331.

RICHARD OF ST. VICTOR (d. 1173)

A Scot by origin V. entered the famous Abbey of St. Victor in Paris, eventually became its Prior. The Abbey was in its great age. His Trinitarian doctrine is expounded in the author's *Trinitas*.[1] He asserts the *Filioque*: "If the two (the Father and the Son) possess the same power in common, it must be concluded that it is from both that the third Person of the Trinity received his being and has his existence."[2] In the Trinity the third Person proceeds both from the one who was born, and from the one who cannot be born (*innascibilis*). This is not Augustine's idea of the Spirit as the love of the Father and Son for each other. No other Person proceeds from the Spirit. But through him God as Love is bestowed on the believer and grows in him. "Insofar as we enable the love that is due to our Creator to go back to him, we are quite certainly configured into the property of the Holy Spirit.... For the rest this gift is given to us, this mission is sent to us at the same time and in the same way by the Father and the Son. It is, after all, from the one and from the other that the Spirit has everything that he possesses. And because it is from the one and from the other that he has his being, power and will, it is right to say that it is they who send and give him, who has received from them the power and the will to come from them into us and to dwell in us."[3]

---

[1]Bibl. to article s.v. in *Trinitas,* 197, 198; [2]*De Trinitate* V, 13, *SC* 63, 321; [3]*Op. cit.* VI, 14, *SC* 63, 413, 417.

RITZ, MARIA JULITTA (1882-1966)

This sister of the Congregation of the Holy Redeemer lived a religious life not outwardly remarkable.[1] Born of farming stock, she entered the institute in Würzburg and, apart from a short stay in another convent due to the wartime destruction of the Würzburg house, spent her life there, first for thirty years in charge of postulants, then as portress. Her personal holiness did attract those who needed spiritual counselling. But her exceptional mystical experience was practically unknown until, after her death, her *Spiritual Testament* was published. She had been trained as a teacher, had studied the works of St. Teresa and of Blessed Elizabeth of the Trinity, but her knowledge was based on a direct experience of the Trinity, unique in modern recorded mysticism. Some illustration is all that can be given.

"I was granted a second intellectual vision by the most Holy Trinity manifesting itself to me in the mystery of the three Persons spatially outside my body. At first this vision only lasted a short time, but then it lasted longer without interruption throughout the day. Initially I perceived how the most Holy Trinity in its divine essence fills the surrounding air, penetrating everything and sustaining everything through its omnipotence, wisdom and goodness. Later the concept of the most Holy Trinity in its greatness and immensity was formed in my mind, and I saw it filling the universe by its immensity, penetrating and sustaining all things. From that time on I see creatures in the most Holy Trinity and see the most Holy Trinity in creatures."[2] "The nobility of the soul through divine adoption and its greatness through the splendour and reflection of the image of God fill me with tremendous reverence towards my body as the dwelling place of the soul and the living temple of the most Holy Trinity.... As though freed from and emptied of earthly impressions the soul is all attention, all love for the heavenly Father who lets my life be fused with his own through his divine Son in the love of the Holy Spirit.... The body serves the soul and both together serve their Creator without physical or moral clumsiness and hindrances. The body experiences the elevation of the soul to the most Holy Trinity as a joining in a hymn, blending its tune with the divine harmony; the praise of the adorable most Holy Trinity takes place without fatigue and without the experience of the passage of time: it is like a stationary movement.... Each minor or major task I am allowed to do in the Holy Trinity and by it also, for its glory fills me with indescribable happiness, particularly because the most Holy Trinity deigns to accept my paltry service lovingly.... Once again, God the Father, in union with the divine Son in the Holy Spirit, imprinted on my soul his holy and divine face through an intimate touch of his essence.... This sublime touch of the essence of the most Holy Trinity brought about in me a high degree of likeness to God, of peace and of happiness."[3]

These extracts give some idea of the quality of this spiritual record. Sister Mary Julitta speaks of the Holy Spirit in very distinctive terms: "The Holy Spirit, the essential divine love of Father and Son, and the bond of love of the most Holy Trinity, embraces my soul also, fusing with it through the touch of his essence, communicating himself as the fountain of peace, refreshing me, making me blissful in immutable peace and interior happiness, and does this in an increasing way according as the Father deigns to imprint his most holy face upon me, and as the more intimate become my mystical espousals with the divine Son."[4]

Sister Mary Julitta describes a more direct experience of the Holy Spirit, at a later stage in her spiritual journey: "Moved by the Holy Spirit, a fiery glow suddenly began within me. It immediately grasped my whole body. I saw the brightness and felt the heat, and in a moment my entire body was consumed by the fire of the Holy Spirit, vanishing into him as if it no longer existed. My soul was surprised and astonished as it was carried off by the force of the fire of the Holy Spirit. My body was overwhelmed and I feared it would collapse under such a force.... The Holy Spirit maintains in the soul a glowing, devouring longing for the blessing that is the most Holy Trinity everywhere and for everything in desire and achievement."[5]

The important quality of Sister Mary Julitta's testimony on the Spirit is to show her consciousness, firm and constant of all three Persons, the Spirit entering her life always in his recognisable Trinitarian relationship and property. Sister has written a case history, beautiful to the point of the sublime, on Fr. Karl Rahner's maxim that the economic Trinity is the immanent Trinity and vice versa: in so far as this affirmation is valid.[6]

---

[1]Cf. *Schwester Maria, Julitta, Ihr Geistliches Vermächtnis*, ed. P. Dr. Andreas M. Back, C.M.F., 4th ed., Würzburg, 1970; English tr. quoted here by sections, available Dominican Publications, Dublin, 1987; [2]34; [3]92,93, 96; [4]112; [5]198; cp. 142, 147; [6]Cf. *Trinitas*, M. O'Carroll, C.S.Sp., article "Economic Trinity," 94-96.

RUPERT OF DEUTZ, (c. 1075-1129 or 1130)

A Benedictine involved in the Church-State controversies of his time, R., challenged too in his Eucharistic doctrine, wrote at length on the ecclesiastical year, and in a work entitled *De Trinitate* expounded his ideas on the entire history of salvation.[1] The work comprises forty-two books: three books in the first part deal with the work of the Father, from the first appearance of light to the fall of Adam; thirty books follow the work of the Son through the Old Testament; then come nine books on the Holy Spirit. Seven ages of the world correspond to the seven days of creation, as do the seven Gifts of the Holy Spirit. As this works out, it may not satisfy either a scientific exegete or a systematic theologian. We have to try to understand R.

His general Trinitarian doctrine has first to be understood. It is conveyed in the work he wrote at the suggestion of the Pope's legate, *De glorificatione Trinitatis*, as well as in the major work under consideration. "Therefore, as has been said above, confessing three Persons, we are nevertheless rightly forbidden to speak of three gods, and whatever names refer to substance we must not use in the plural number. Only the persons we speak of as three, since we are properly bound to this by clear relation, that is by the relative names of Father, Son, and holy Spirit."[2]

R. thought that the dogma of the Holy Trinity was taught in OT all through. But it was reserved to the faithful who were to come, was an inaccessible secret to those then living who could not accept the idea of several persons in God. Even today it is a treasure hidden from those who have no faith, especially for the Jew who reads the law and the prophets and meets directly the warning: 'Hear, O Israel, the Lord your God is one God.'

R. proposes the traditional analogy of the "spring, the fountain and the water course"; he adds one of his own: "If there are three *spiramina* of a man, the heart and soul, and the strength of both, nor are there three spirits of man, but he is one spirit." From Ps 4 he borrows another: "The Lord himself is the Father, the countenance of the Lord is the Son of the Father, the light of the Lord's countenance is the Holy Spirit of the Father and the Son."[3] But he stays with St. Augustine's analogy.

In the ex professo exposition of the dogma in

the *De Officiis divinis*, which has been quoted, R. follows Augustine. He points out that the relations are not based on accidental inequality, but on substantial communication of the divine nature to the Son and the Holy Spirit; thus is ensured the unity of substance and the distinction of persons. Attached to Sacred Scripture R. is here in line with the Greek Fathers, going from the persons to the unique nature.

R. speaks, at the beginning of the *De glorificatione Trinitatis*, of the processions and states, "God has created through his Son, sanctifies by his Spirit: therefore the procession of the Son is in the past, *a Patre processi* (Jn 8:42), while that of the Spirit is actual: *Spiritus qui a Patre procedit* (Jn 15:26)." He writes thus because he thinks that the procession "is the result of an admirable work", but he leaves himself open to the charge that he confuses processions, missions and *opera ad extra*. On the last point he essays a clarification. "The operation of the whole Trinity is indivisible, but in the effect of the work, the difference must be recognized in the procession of each, that is of the Son and the Holy Spirit."[4] He does nonetheless see in the distinction of the works a basic indication of the distinction of the Persons; this is especially true of the Holy Spirit.

As the principle of fulfilment, of perfection, of fruitfulness, of sanctification, the Holy Spirit proceeds from the Father and the Son. As the debate with the Greeks was at the time active on the subject, R. develops the idea of the procession, following what he thought was the Athanasian Creed (qv), and the decrees of Rome. On the analogy of faith he thought that the Spirit being the *gratiarum divisio et peccatorum remissio*, must proceed from the Father, the Creator, as the distributor of free gifts and from the Son, the Redeemer, as the one who pardons sins. When R. seeks to justify this theory from Scripture he becomes somewhat original in exegesis. "When Christ says not *Pater meus* but *Pater*, he speaks not of the sole person of the Father, but of the Father, Son and Holy Spirit together, in their unique divinity."[5] Thus the words *Spiritus veritatis, qui a Patre procedit*. The words then in Jn 15:26, *Spiritus veritatis qui a Patre procedit*, are of the procession, rather than the temporal mission of the Spirit from the bosom of the Trinity, and *quem ego mittam a Patre*, are spoken of God the Son. At the instance of the papal Legate, R. published a special passage on the procession of the Holy Spirit; without adding anything

new, R. weaves his way through the Johannine texts with adroitness and confidence nonetheless.

R. becomes involved in some intricate speculation on the subject of the Spirit's role in the Incarnation. God the Father through the Son created the world; the Spirit recreates, reforms (the fallen creature) through the Son made man; no creature was made save through the Son as God, none is recreated save by the Son incarnate. The Spirit must first fashion the prototype and instrument he will use, the new man Jesus Christ must be the principal work of the Holy Spirit.

R. enters in some detail into the fact that the Holy Spirit, whose role he sometimes exaggerates, at other times minimizes, does not act as one who generates, but as one who operates. "Will he then be called the Son of the Holy Spirit? By no means. For the Holy Spirit will come upon you, *non ut pro semine sit, aut ut de substantia sit ejus caro filii quem concipis*. You will conceive of the Holy Spirit, not as from one who generates. This conception is *de Spiritu sancto*, is not through generation but operation. The flesh of the Word will be drawn from the flesh of the Virgin, not from the substance of the Holy Spirit. And let us note that the angel does not at all say 'He will be the Son of God, but he will be called the Son of God.' In fact what the Virgin conceived has always existed. And this everlasting essence was holy; it was the Son of God. It but remained to call him what he was. And in this very designation, Son of God, he was about to reveal God's true name, not as God but as Father of the Son.... Note also that the text does not have *Quod nascetur ex te sanctus* ... but *sanctum*. For there are many people who have been saintly or sanctified; only One is a holy reality, and his sanctity has sanctified others; he is the Saint of saints, essentially saintly whom the pure Virgin conceived of the Holy Spirit."[6]

The way in which R. speaks of the endowment of the soul of Christ by the Spirit could be misleading, though his Christology is ultimately, as elsewhere expressed, orthodox. "The human nature taken from the substance of the Virgin's flesh was like a white, well prepared parchment, ready to receive the work of a scribe; the Holy Spirit, acting for the Father covered it completely; he filled the entire substance of the Word, and left nothing empty, but he wrote all that was in the Father's heart, he wrote in this soul. It was the entire wisdom, the entire understanding ... of God which passed into Jesus, to the point that there was nothing he did not know, nothing he could not do, nothing in God the Father that the human nature of this Child did not receive."[7]

Only the Holy Spirit could enter the soul of Jesus, because he is God, and only God the Word could hypostatically take on human nature. "It is by these indissoluble links with the Holy Spirit, this inexpressible intimacy—this inestimable love between the Spirit and the human nature of Jesus, that the divinity of the Word was united to our flesh."[8]

Jesus received the plenitude of the Spirit's gifts.

[1]Works, *PL* 167-170; *CCCM* 7,9,21; *SC* 131, 165, *De operibus Spiritus Sancti*; cf. introduction *SC* 131 J. Gribomont, O.S.B.; L. Scheffczyk, "La doctrine trinitaire relative a l'économie du salut et son importance dogmatique chez Rupert de Deutz," J. Betz, H. Fries ed., *Eglise et Tradition*, Le Puy, 1963, 75-103; P. Sejourné in DTC XIV, 169-205; J.H.V. Engen, *Rupert of Deutz*, University of California Press, 1983, esp., 90-94, 339-341, 361-363; [2]*De divinis Officiis*, XI, 7, CCCM VII, 375, [3]*De Glor. Trin.*, bk. 1,ch14,PL 169, 131; [4]*Ibid.*, ch 16, PL 169, 28; [5]*De Trinit.*, bk. 42, I *De Spiritu Sancto*, ch. 5, PL 167, 1575; CCCM XXIV, 1826; [6]*Ibid.*, ch. 10, PL 167, 1580; CCCM XXIV, 1832; [7]*De Victoria Verbi*, XI, ch. 23, PL 169, 1458; [8]*De divinis Officiis*, I,24,PL 170, 24; CCCM VII, 20.

S

SACRAMENTS, THE[1]

The Sacraments, like authority, are a point where the individual, who may be charismatic, meets the institution. But the possibility of conflict or sharp divergence, is reducible to a minimum. One Sacrament, Confirmation, (qv) is directly related to the Spirit. But in all there is an intervention by him for the essential reason that all confer grace to the soul and he is the author of grace. One of the enemies of Christian perfection, legalism, has scope for its baneful intrusion in the administration of the Sacraments. Law (qv) has a necessary place in what the Church dispenses through the Sacraments. There are the essentials of the Sacraments, the matter and form, and to affirm these clearly is to make a binding legal statement. Personal, arbitrary choice is by the statement rejected.

To interpret the Spirit's special action in imparting divine grace with each Sacrament we need to appreciate the goal of each, the precise purpose fulfilled. In Baptism it is the first and necessary regeneration of the soul which is intended: union with Christ, in the saving moments of his death and resurrection (Rom 6:4). Thereby the sin which would impede God's grace is removed and the newly baptized person is incorporated into the Body of Christ (1 Cor 6:11; 12:13), open therefore to all the subsequent grace which membership brings. It is birth to a new life and this rebirth is described by Christ himself as of the Spirit. "'Truly, truly, I say to you, unless one is born of water and the Spirit, he cannot enter the kingdom of God. That which is born of the flesh is flesh, and that which is born of the Spirit is spirit. Do not marvel that I said to you, 'You must be born anew.' The wind blows where it wills and you hear the sound of it, but you do not know whence it comes or whither it goes; so it is with every one who is born of the Spirit'" (Jn 3:5-8).

The new birth here described has an origin, which determines its lineage, its ancestry. If we are to use the metaphor of genetics it is to the Spirit that we shall apply it. And his identifiable effect will be directly from the baptismal character. This seal on the soul is sometimes taken in a legalistic, certainly in a static sense. Since it comes from the Spirit it must be essentially dynamic. Everything creative in the new life to which the Spirit gives existence, is potentially contained within it, stirs from it under his impulse. Comparison with the gene pool which, by nature, each of us carries breaks down, as comparison between natural fatherhood and the fatherhood of God soon proves inadequate.

The more a son grows naturally, the more independent of his father he becomes; the more we grow spiritually, in grace, the more fully we come to be God's children. Likewise, our human inheritance is limited from within by its content initially established. Our divine inheritance, guaranteed by the sacramental seal, is not circumscribed once for all by fixed limits; it is rather the pledge of growth and increase which it will transmit, but has its constant source beyond itself.

M.J. Scheeben (qv) thought that the character must be analogous to the hypostatic union and grounded upon it. "Thus from every point of view the idea we expressed at the beginning is substantiated: that the character by which Christians are anointed and become Christians is analogous to the hypostatic union of the humanity with the Logos, which is what makes Christ what he is. Accordingly, when theologians declare that the sacramental character is a *signum configurativum cum Christo*, this is not to be understood of a similarity with the divine or human nature in Christ—for this is founded on grace—but of a similarity, or better, both similarity and connection, with the stamping of the seal of the divine Person upon the human nature."[2]

The great theologian also saw the link with the Spirit: "For normally the sealing contained in the character involves the sealing contained in grace, if no obstacle is present, and indeed that of the Holy Spirit himself, who comes to us with grace; the character receives its complement in grace. Conversely, it is only in the character that the grace of the Holy Spirit and the Holy Spirit himself are closely and firmly implanted in the soul and impress their seal upon the soul."[3]

It is evident that if the analogy here set forth is valid, then it must be seen in relation to the Spirit's action in the Incarnation. The Virgin Mary conceived the God-man through the power and operation of the Spirit. It is this same Spirit who, in the Sacrament of Baptism, imprints the character on the soul. It is another reminder that the Fiat of the Virgin Mary was the prototype and source of all else that would restore the creature to God's favour. Mary, as St. Thomas says, spoke for humankind. When the Spirit descended on her, he was setting a precedent for all his future action on the souls of the just.

In dealing with the character, therefore, we must avoid anything which would make it appear to make it a mere impersonal mark. Thus it is sometimes understood very wrongly. The fact of its permanence, its resistance to waywardness, sin or loss of faith does not imply deficiency on the personal level. Since, most frequently, Baptism, which first imprints a character, is received in the infant stage, the illusion of an impersonal, indelible

mark is understandable. But when the Christian consciousness awakens, the character also begins to respond to the Spirit, to manifest its true role. Its universal existence does not mean that the potential in each separate case is entirely unique; on that potential the Spirit in each case operates according to his mysterious design.

The same mystery is present in the other Sacraments which confer this character, Confirmation (qv) and Priesthood. In each the character has, in the theology of St. Augustine and St. Thomas, a relationship to divine worship. The fullness of this reality is found in the priestly character; the other two Sacraments have, through the character, a certain *configuration* with the priesthood. Of the latter Vatican II says: "Therefore, while it indeed presupposes the Sacraments of Christian initiation, the sacerdotal office of priests is conferred by that special Sacrament through which priests, by the anointing of the Holy Spirit, are marked with a special character and are so configured to Christ the Priest that they can act in the Person of Christ the Head."[4]

It will be noted that the Council, which in the fourth session was desirous in its teaching to stress the role of the Spirit, is more explicit here on the link between the Spirit and the priestly character than had been noted in previous statements from the Magisterium. That the Spirit's role in the priesthood should be taught is clear to those who reflect on the Spirit as the very life of the Church. There is much yet to be investigated theologically on the sacramental character as a vehicle of the Spirit, as there is on the deep meaning of the character in regard to the Church. Witness these words of Scheeben: "Thus the mystery of the sacramental character is essentially bound up with the mystery of the Incarnation and its continuation in the mystery of the Church. Truly, it is the character which interiorly stamps and organizes the Church as the mystical Body of Christ. It is the character which discloses to us the wonderful, supernatural sublimity of the sacramental order, and unites us with the great Sacrament of the God-man."[5]

If we turn to the other Sacraments we should bear in mind Scheeben's teaching: "Further, the high consecration and eminent rank which the character imparts to us is, as was shown in section 83, the foundation for the supernatural significance of those Sacraments that do not imprint a character. Particularly as regards matrimony, the fourth consecratory but non-hierarchical Sacrament, the character is the source from which matrimony derives its whole supernatural consecration, as well as the bond connecting it with the mystical marriage of Christ and the Church, and showing that it is not merely the image, but the offshoot of that mystical marriage. In matrimony, further, the character clearly manifests the full range of its power and meaning, since it brings out the fact that those who possess it belong completely to Christ, body and soul, as his members."[6]

The Saviour himself associated the Spirit with the Sacrament of Penance: "'As the Father has sent me, even so I send you,'" said the risen Jesus to the disciples. "And when he had said this, he breathed on them, and said to them, 'Receive the Holy Spirit. If you forgive the sins of any, they are forgiven; if you retain the sins of any, they are retained.'" (Jn 20:21-23). The same power of the Spirit to forgive and extirpate sin with its consequences is felt in the Sacrament of the Anointing of the Sick, Assuming that "the connection of the supernatural power of the Holy Spirit, the Spirit of Christ, with the organs of the Church has close connections with the Incarnation of the God-man and his union with the members of the race," Scheeben concludes that if the members of the Body perform the appropriate actions "the merits of Christ descend to us through such actions, and draw the vitalizing grace of the Holy Spirit down on us."

The ideas here assembled must be more fully developed to show how the sacramental system established by Christ was from all eternity designed by the Holy Trinity as a manifold means through which the sanctifying Spirit, sent by the Father and the Son, would operate characteristically and with total insight into the spiritual structure of each human person. The Spirit operates as he wills. In the Sacraments there is certainty of his operation, though not of the measure of his gift in each case. The charisms are not received with this certainty. The action of the Spirit is limited only by the Spirit, not by any ideas of ours. His action is mysterious; for our salvation it is an act of divine condescension to clarify, within that pervading mystery, certain moments when his power and its specific effects are recognisable.

----

[1]Cf. Y.-M.J. Congar, O.P., *The Holy Spirit III*, 217ff; [2]*The Mysteries of Christianity*, English tr., London, St. Louis, 1951, 586; [3]Op. Cit., 591; [4]*Decree on the Ministry and Life of Priests*, art. 2; [5]*Op. cit., 591;* [6]*Ibid.*

SATAN

The role of the Spirit in the reduction of Satan's power is explicitly stated by Jesus Christ.[1] "'And if I cast out demons by Beelzebul, by whom do your sons cast them out? Therefore they shall be your judges. But if it is by the Spirit of God that I cast out demons, then the kingdom of God has come upon you'" (Mt 12:27,28). "'But if it is by the Finger of God that I cast out demons, then the kingdom of God has come upon you.'" (Lk 11:20). The theme of the Spirit is not often elaborated in the literature of demonology. The well-known dualism of the Good Spirit, Prince of Light and the Bad Spirit, Prince of darkness, found in Qumram and Jewish-Christian literature (qv) is an imperfect reading of the truth: it is the Spirit of God everywhere, by his omnipotent power, by his entry into the very depths of the human being in grace with God, by his total dominion of the plan of salvation overall and in each single life benefitting by it, who evaluates human need, apportions the appropriate spiritual help, safeguards the treasure of divine life which is himself. The Spirit, who is the architect of the supernatural life of the soul, is alone powerful enough to ward off the adversary, to fortify the defences; he disposes of the manifold armoury of Gifts and charisms (qqv), which will divert or nullify the assailant's blows; he knows the path whereon the Christian must travel to attain the goal of life. If, in the considerable literature from ancient times on the subject of Satan, his wiles, his threat, his occasional seizure of the physical powers of individuals by possession, there is not extensive treatment of the role of the Spirit, this is certainly to be assumed as central and decisive.

----

[1]Cf. *Satan*, ed. Bruno de Jésus Marie, several authors, English tr. M. Carroll and others, New York, London, 1952; article "Démon," *DSp*, III, 141-238, S. Lyonnet, S.J., J. Daniélou, S.J., A. and C. Guillaumont, F. Vendenbroucke.

SCHEEBEN, MATTHIAS JOSEPH (1835-1888)

It is regrettable that some misgivings should be felt on S's theology of the Holy Spirit.[1] In reality in the developed synthesis wherein he expressed his mature theological thinking, *The Mysteries of Christianity*, the treatment of the subject is learned and profound. It may be supplemented by his reflections on the Spirit and Our Lady in his *Mariology* and on the Indwelling Spirit in book two of *The Glories of Divine Grace*. In this book he worked from a previous treatise, but book two is like book five "recast almost entirely from new material;" it contains his own learning and thinking. S's strength was in his knowledge of the Fathers; his final composition always shows his power of synthesis: his theology had a spiritual and pastoral orientation, which gives it survival value.

S. expounds the theology of the Holy Spirit by a considered study of the names the Third Person is given, an excellent pedagogic device. He can write like this: "There is another reason, closely connected with the foregoing, why holiness is not merely predicated of the Third Person in God, but is especially stressed as a characteristic note. As we have seen repeatedly, the Third Person, who is the common breath of love and life of the two other Persons, is also the pledge of their love as well as the bond and seal of their absolute physical and moral unity. What confers upon a pledge of love as also upon a bond and seal of unity, the value which enables them to fulfill their essential function? In the case of a pledge is it not the costliness of the gift, in the case of a bond its firmness, in the case of a seal its unquestioned genuineness? If the love and unity are divine, must not the infinite costliness of the pledge, the absolute sacredness and inviolability of the bond, the absolute authenticity and genuineness of the seal, be expressed and emphasized? But all these sublime attributes are expressed in simplest and noblest fashion by the single word, holiness."[2] S. goes on to essay a metaphor for the Spirit of the Father and the Son: "we behold him, as it were, in the guise of an infinitely precious diamond of unshatterable compactness and the most limpid purity, crystallized out of the breath of their love and life, a diamond in which in an inexpressibly sublime manner the Father and the Son pledge their love, and secure, seal, and crown their bond of union."[3]

Discussing the Trinity and the order of grace S. shows how our adoption as God's children is rooted in the procession of the Holy Spirit. "The relationship of the second procession in God to the grace of divine filiation is direct, to some extent even more direct than is the relationship of the first procession.... The Holy Spirit, as the first all-perfect, and innermost fruit of the self-communicating divine love, is the seed and root of all other fruits which God puts forth by way of his love. In the procession of the Holy Spirit we perceive, according to an aspect different from the generation of the Son, the basis for the possibility of a further communication of the divine nature through gracious love; and this is the perfect exemplar for the external outpouring of love in finite brooklets, and at the same time the motive for still further revealing to creatures, beyond the inner life of the Godhead, that love of the Father for the Son which has already shown itself to be so fruitful and beatifying in the Holy Spirit."[4]

S. deals also with the mission of the Spirit and he has two appendices to the section of his work on the Trinity: one on his proposed analogy between the mother in a family and the place of the Spirit in the Trinity, not successful; the other a lengthy quotation from the *Summa contra Gentiles* of St. Thomas Aquinas, two chapters from that work—the first deals with the effects which Scripture attributes to the Holy Spirit with regard to creation in general; the second with the effects attributed to the Holy Spirit in Sacred Scripture as regards the gifts bestowed by God on rational creatures. The interpretation is of course according to appropriation.

On the Spirit and the Eucharist S. writes profoundly and movingly: "Although the Holy Spirit is sent by the Son and comes to us in the Son, he is, by the strongest of all appropriations, also the channel through which the Son is brought to us. As the aspiration terminating the Son's love, he urges the Son to deliver himself up to us in the Incarnation and the Eucharist. As the flame issuing from the mighty ardour of the Son in his work of sanctification and unification, in the womb of the Virgin he brings about the origin, the hypostatic union, and the resulting holiness of the Son's human nature, and in the Eucharist effects the conversion of earthly substances into the Son's flesh and blood. After the hypostatic union and transubstantiation have been wrought, he lives on in the Son's flesh and blood with his fire and his vitalizing energy, as proceeding from the Son, and fills the sacred humanity with his own being to sanctify and glorify it. Particularly in the Eucharist he glorifies and spiritualizes the Son's human nature like a flaming coal, so that it takes on the qualities of sheer fire and pure spirit. Straightway he makes use of the Eucharist as an instrument to manifest his sanctifying and transforming power to all who come in contact with it, and as a channel to communicate himself to all who receive it and feast upon it. The body of Christ, as a spiritual gift which God presents to us, and which we offer in sacrifice, has its origin from the fire of the Holy

Spirit; it is permeated and encompassed by the Holy Spirit, who so transfigures and spiritualizes it that both the fire and the coal which the fire pervades with white heat seem to be one and the same object; and finally, it is flooded with the Holy Spirit, thus yielding up his fragrance in sacrifice, and his vitalizing energy in Holy Communion."[5]

S. recalls that the Eastern Fathers and liturgies like to use the figure of a glowing coal when describing the Eucharist. The Eucharist is the eminently good gift "conferred by the Holy Spirit as the eternal *donum per excellentiam*, the gift which contains the Holy Spirit himself, with his essence and his power," and he sees as singularly appropriate the ancient usage of reserving the Eucharist in a receptacle symbolic of the Holy Spirit, fashioned in the form of a dove, the *peristerium*. "How beautifully the Holy Spirit was thus symbolized as he who brings and fashions the gift contained in that receptacle...."[6] S.'s ideas on the Spirit in relation to the sacramental character are dealt with in the relevant article.

The great theologian gives special attention to the Spirit's role in the Church. "In the Incarnation the Son of God brings to his real and his mystical body the Holy Spirit who proceeds from him and who, because of this procession, is his own Spirit. And this Spirit is the Son of God's own Spirit. He now becomes the body's own Spirit. As he moves in Christ's own humanity, he must move in the (human) race, since this race is the body of him to whom the Spirit belongs and from whom he proceeds. 'The body of Christ' says St. Augustine 'is animated by the Spirit of Christ.' Inasmuch as the race is Christ's body it must be animated by no other spirit than the Spirit of God's Son."[7]

"In all its members the Church is a temple of the Holy Spirit, who dwells in it as the soul in its own body, and manifests his divine and divinizing power in it. He is active in the Church not only in the way in which, as the Spirit of eternal wisdom and order, he guides and directs all well-regulated societies, not merely by sustaining with special assistance individuals and the entire community in its religious pursuits, by granting the remission of sins, and by helping to heal our moral weaknesses and infirmities. No, he must be active in the members of Christ's body as he is in the real body of Christ, namely by filling them with the plenitude of the divinity. He must overshadow the bride of Christ as once he overshadowed Mary's womb, so

that in her the Son of God may be reborn in his divine holiness and majesty."[8]

S. links this idea to his theory of the Spirit present in the Eucharist—not as Christ is present, of course. "Since the Holy Spirit himself proceeds from the Son of God and as such belongs to him, he necessarily enters into the Son's humanity and into his whole mystical body, and belongs also to the latter. This is true all the more inasmuch as in the Eucharist the Son of God dwells bodily and essentially, with all the plenitude of his divinity, among his members in the bosom of the Church. In the Son and through the Son the Holy Spirit dwells there also, personally and essentially. He is the very Spirit and, as it were, the soul of the Church."[9]

Closely connected with this thinking is S.'s exposition of the parallel between Mary and the priest: "As Mary conceived the Son of God in her womb by the overshadowing of the Holy Spirit, drew him down from heaven by her consent, and gave him, the Invisible, to the world in visible form, so the priest conceives the incarnate Son of God by the power of the same Spirit in order to establish him in the bosom of the Church under the Eucharistic forms. Thus Christ is born anew through the priesthood by a continuation, as it were, of his miraculous birth from Mary; and the priesthood itself is an imitation and extension of the mysterious maternity that Mary possessed with regard to the God-man. The priesthood is for the Eucharistic Christ what Mary was for the Son of God about to become man."[10]

S. puts this view rather strongly: "Inexpressibly sublime is the dignity imparted to the priesthood, and in it to the Church: to the mother of the God-man in his sacramental existence, and of men in their higher, divine existence. Incomprehensible is the fruitfulness which the church reveals in this maternity, unspeakable is the union with the over-shadowing Holy Spirit, who in her bosom and through her brings about marvels similar to those that took place in the most pure womb of Mary. This supernatural motherhood is the central mystery of the Church as an organically constructed society."[11] The author briefly recalls the sanctification proper to each of the Sacraments and attributes these activities to the Church's motherhood: "With an ever-growing manifestation of the marvellous fertility she possesses by reason of her union with the Holy Spirit."[12]

Along with these passages S.'s pages must be read on the role of the Spirit in the Incarnation.

Though he states that since the Spirit is infused into the Virgin "as the substantial bearer or vehicle of the forming power radiating from the heavenly Father," "to that extent he takes the place of the *semen materiale* which in natural propagation issues from his power." S. adds: "For that reason the Fathers sometimes call Him *semen divinum.*"[13]

But the author distinguishes this influence totally from anything like "the paternal principle of the humanity of Christ." This for three reasons: (1) the Spirit does not constitute the flesh of Christ through his own substance; (2) Christ's humanity is not consubstantial with his nature or specifically similar to it; (3) the Holy Spirit works with the other divine Persons. The Spirit's influence is understood by appropriation for these reasons: the forming and vivifying of matter, the creating and producing of the first man, is attributed to the Spirit "the finger and breath of God"; the forming of the flesh of Christ under divine influence has the closest relation with the *actio unitiva*, which is attributed to the Holy Spirit; the very name of the Holy Spirit points to this singular role; this was a virginal conception and it was appropriate to think of him as its author.

S. adds an appendix to develop his ideas on the *actio unitiva* where we read: "As the Holy Spirit is produced last of the Persons in the Blessed Trinity, it is likewise he who appears as the natural author of the relations of God *ad extra.* And as he forms the crowning tie between the Father and the Son, so he effects the tie between the Son and his created nature."[14]

When S. comes to consider Mary's supernatural activity he relates this to the Holy Spirit, but all inset in his governing principle in Marian theology: the bridal motherhood, Mary is the bride of her divine Son. "The distinguishing mark of her person as bride of Christ is conceived fully in her capacity of bearer and temple of the Holy Spirit. Likewise, the foundation for this special power and dignity of her activity must be traced to this capacity of her person. Thus it must be found formally in the fact that Mary is the organ of the Holy Spirit, who works in her in the same way that Christ's humanity is the instrument of the Logos."[15]

S. had first laid down the principle that Mary's activity remains that of a created being. He then says that Mary is the dynamic and authoritative organ of the Holy Spirit. "Mary's flesh and blood in no wise possess a special, inherent, and vivifying power as is proper to the flesh and blood of the Logos. To the vivifying flesh of Christ hers is only

as the earth impregnated by the dew of the Holy Spirit. But her womb is and remains the original seat and her heart the living root of Christ's vivifying flesh, and to that extent every activity of Christ can be regarded as arising from her womb and especially from her heart, as the instrument of the Holy Ghost."[16]

S. says that "in respect to the effects of God's grace in others Mary does not possess that kind of dynamic activity exercised by the organs of the Church, as for instance the vicars of Christ in the dispensing of the Sacraments."[17] But "when the Apostle says of other living temples of the Holy Spirit, that the Holy Spirit 'prays in them with unutterable sighs', this statement is all the more true of Mary. For she is the prototype of the Church. In her public worship and prayers the Church possesses a specific and supernatural power and dignity in so far as she is the instrument of the Holy Spirit who works in and by her."[18]

S. deals at length in *The Glories of Divine Grace* with the indwelling Spirit. His thesis is thus enunciated: By grace we receive the Person of the Holy Spirit into our Soul. The Holy Spirit, he says, "stands, as it were, on the boundaries of the Blessed Trinity, and therefore the union of God with the creature, and of the creature with God, is primarily and principally attributed to him. Besides, he is the personal representative of the divine love from which he proceeds. But since the union of God with the creature is effected by his love, and on the other hand, our union with God in this life consists principally in our love for him, it is evident why it is the Holy Spirit who represents in this respect the whole Blessed Trinity. Of the Holy Spirit now we say, that he himself comes to us with grace, he gives us himself in grace, and that he really and essentially, in an unspeakably intimate manner, dwells in us by grace."[19]

It is the Spirit, S. thinks, who transforms us into the image of God. "He himself is the seal by which God impresses upon our soul the image of his divine nature and holiness. As the seal indeed only imprints its form in the wax, but in order to do this must be brought into most intimate connection with it; so the Holy Spirit, by impressing us with the seal of his image, enters into most intimate union with our soul. Thus the Holy Spirit cannot give us his grace without giving us himself, as the Apostle says. (Rom 5:5). S. thought that the Holy Spirit brings us grace and grace brings us to the Holy Spirit. The Spirit is the pledge of our blissful possession of the Most Holy Trinity: "But this distinguished guest comes not only to honour us with his presence; he brings us also a very rich treasure, and he himself is this treasure; or rather he himself is not only a treasure, but the pledge of a still greater treasure. For as we now are to experience and enjoy the Holy Spirit in the sweetness of his love, so we shall taste and enjoy hereafter the Father and the Son in their whole divine essence and glory. 'He is the pledge of our inheritance,' says the Apostle."[20] S. elaborated his theory, drawing out many consequences of it. He did not discuss fully the question of the personal indwelling by the Spirit in relation to the traditional doctrine of appropriation.

Taken with the doctrine expressed in S.'s other works, the theory on the indwelling gives depth and a relevance to spirituality which are in keeping with the personality as well as the immense erudition of this man. His preface to *The Glories of Divine Grace* in which he expresses the hope that his book may offer "a new and rich mine for the instruction of the people ... and that they may turn it to very profitable account," ends thus: "May the Author of grace realize it through the intercession of the Immaculate Virgin, the first-born daughter and Mother of grace, and especially also, through the intercession of the venerable Fr. Nieremberg, who in his time defended and glorified the Immaculate Conception of Mary in as brilliant and magnificent a manner as he praised and proclaimed the glories of divine grace."[21] (*See* art. *Indwelling* for Scheeben's distinction of Uncreated and created grace).

[1] *Gesammelte Schriften*, ed. J. Hofer, 8 vols, Freiburg I. Breisgau 1941-1967; English Tr. *The Mysteries of Christianity*, C. Vollert, S.J., St. Louis, 1946; English tr. *Mariology*, T. L. M. J. Geukers, 2 vols, St. Louis and London, 1946, 1953; English tr. *The Glories of Divine Grace*, A Benedictine Monk of St. Meinrad's Abbey, Indiana, New York, 1885; J. Hertkens, *Professor M. J. Scheeben, Leben und Wirken eines katholischen Gelehrten im Dienste der Kirche*, 1892; K. Feckes and others, *M.J. Scheeben*, Mainz, 1935; F. S. Pancheri, O. F. M., *Il pensiero teologico di M. J. Scheeben e S. Tommaso*, 1956; B. Fraigneau-Julien, *L'Eglise et le caractère sacramentel selon M-J Scheeben*, Paris, 1958; N. Hoffmann, SS.CC., *Natur und Gnade*, Die Theologie des Gotteschau als *vollendeter Vergöttlichung des Geistgeschöpfes bei M. J. Scheeben* (Analecta Gregoriana 160) Rome, 1967; E. Paul, *Denkweg und Denkform der Theologie von Matthias Joseph Scheeben* (Münchener theologische Studien. 2, Systematische Abteilung, 60), Munich, 1970, bibl.; G. Fritz, *DTC* XIV, 1 (1939), 1270-74; A. Piolanti, *EC* XI (1953) 33f, bibl.; J. Hofer, LTK IX (1964) 376-9; cf. esp. *M.J. Scheeben, Teologo cattolico nel centenario della morte*, Rome, Divinitas, 1988, 32 contributors, esp. A. Huerga, "La pneumatologia de M. J. Scheeben"; H. Schauf, "M. J. Scheeben de inhabitatione Spiritus Sancti"; A. Pedrini, "La dimensione carismatica della dottrina teologica di M.J. Sheeben"; F. Holböck, "Der Heilige Geist" als Seele des Mystichen Leibes Christi bei M. J. Scheeben, Munich, 1964; [2] *The Mysteries of Christianity*, IV, 18, p. 111; [3] *Ibid.*, p. 112; [4] *Ibid.*, [5] *Ibid.*, XVIII, 75; [6] *Ibid.*, 530; [7] *Ibid.*, XIV, m 58, 393f; [8] *Ibid.*, 544; XIX, 78; [9] *Ibid.*, 545; [10] *Ibid.*, 79, 546f; [11] *Ibid.*, 548; [12] *Ibid.*, 549; [13] *Mariology*, I, 73; [14] *Ibid.*, 247f; [15] *Mariology*, II, 185; [16] *Ibid.*, 187; [17] 187; [18] 189; [19] Bk II, ch. 1, 94f; [20] *Ibid.*, 95, 99; [21] Preface to the first ed., p. 8; on the Spirit and the indwelling cf. D. Coffey, *Grace, the Gift of the Holy Spirit*, Sydney, 1979.

SIMEON THE NEW THEOLOGIAN, ST. (c. 950-1022)

One of the greatest mystics in the history of the Church, S., trained for imperial service and already a senator, entered the monastery of Studios in Constantinople in 977: the decision came after he had had a singular mystical experience but was doubtless also due to the influence on him of his "spiritual father", Simeon the Devout, who may also have determined his choice of name: the disciple vowed a special cult through life to the master.[1] This very enthusiasm may have been his downfall, for the community refused his admission to vows. He was, however, accepted in the monastery of St. Mammas at Xirokerke by the *hegumenos*, (superior) Anthony.

Ordained a priest, S. became *hegumenos* and revitalized the monastery as well as giving it material stability. After twenty-five years the monks turned against him, complaining of his mystical tendencies—he had changed the monastic trend from mere asceticism to contemplation; they also objected to the public cult given Simeon the Devout (d.c. 986). S. was secure while the ecclesiastical authority supported him. When this, in the person of the *syncellus*, Stephen of Nicomedia, deserted him, he was forced into exile on the other side of the Bosporus. In Palonkiton he took up residence in the derelict oratory of St. Marina and soon this became a spiritual centre. S. rejected attempts to recall and reinstate him and died at St. Marina in 1022.

S. had been initiated by his spiritual father into the writings of Mark the Hermit (fl.c.431), an ascetical writer not without mystical insights. He was a stimulus perhaps rather than a teacher, for S's starting-point was experimental. His experience, like that of the great western mystics, John of the Cross and Teresa of Avila (qqv) was of the kind that directly motivated description and analysis. Like the Spanish theologians he saw

God's working in his soul as an objective reality, his experience but primarily God's action.

The great Byzantine mystic left a considerable body of writing. In all his thinking about the spiritual life the idea of the Holy Spirit is dominant. The Holy Spirit is the principle of all spiritual life. To seek the kingdom of God is to seek the Holy Spirit, who makes Christ present to the soul through the Church. The end and goal of the Incarnation is the communication of the Holy Spirit.

S.'s decisive mystical experience, the turning-point in his life, was of a divine light suddenly shining on him and filling the room where he prayed. "He was one with this divine light and it seemed to him that he himself had become light and left the world altogether. He was filled with tears and unspeakable joy."[2]

Understandably light is especially associated with the Holy Spirit in S's mystical doctrine.[3] He prays thus to the Spirit: "Come, true light. Come, eternal life. Come, hidden mystery. Come, name-less treasure. Come, inexpressible reality. Come, person who flies from human comprehension. Come, abiding gladness. Come, light that knows no dusk. Come, true hope of all the saved. Come, resurrection of the dead.... Come thou for whom my wretched soul has longed, and still longs. Come alone, to the alone; for I am alone, as thou dost see.... Come, thou who hast made thyself the object of my desire, and who hast caused me to desire thee—thou to whom none can aspire. Come, my breath and my life. Come consolation of my contemptible soul. Come, my joy, my glory and my delight forever. I thank thee that thou has made thyself one Spirit with me, without con-fusion, movement or change; and that though thou who art God art above all, thou hast become all in all for me."[4]

S. thought it normal that the Spirit should be the object of experience: "If someone were to say that each of us believers receives and possesses the Spirit without knowing it or being conscious of it, would he be blaspheming by making Christ lie when he said, 'In him there will be a spring of water welling up to eternal life' (Jn 4:14) and, 'He who believes in me, out of his heart shall flow rivers of living water(Jn 7:38)."[5] "The Lord who has favoured us with good things that transcend our senses will also give us a new sensitivity that transcends our senses through his Spirit, so that his gifts and his favours, which transcend our senses, will be supernaturally perceived in a clear and pure way by our very senses, and through them all."[6] "As for the power and effectiveness of his Holy Spirit, otherwise known as his light, no one can speak about it if he has not first seen the light with the eyes of his soul and has not become aware in himself of its illuminations and its ef-fective powers."[7]

Recalling the word of Christ, "'Woe to you lawyers, for you have taken away the key of knowledge, you did not enter yourselves and hindered those who were entering'"(Lk 11:52), he comments: "What is this 'key of knowledge' if it is not the grace of the Holy Spirit given by faith, which, by illumination, really brings about a state of knowledge and indeed of full knowledge? And I would say that the door is the Holy Spirit: 'Re-ceive the Holy Spirit. If you forgive the sins of any, they are forgiven; if you retain the sins of any they are retained. (Jn 20:22,23). What is more, the house is the Father: 'In my Father's house are many rooms' (Jn 14:2). Pay great attention then to the spiritual meaning of the word. If the key does not open—for 'to him the gatekeeper opens' (Jn 10:3)—then the door will not be open; but if the door is not open, no one will enter the Father's house. Christ himself said: 'No one comes to the Father, but by me' (Jn 14:6). Now that it is the Holy Spirit who first opens our spirit (see Lk 24:45) and teaches us about the Father and the Son, is what he himself has said."[8]

S. adds Johannine texts to his development of the idea: Jn 16:13 and 15:26; 16:13 and 14:26; 16:7; 14:15-17 and 20. He ends with the promise: "'John baptized with water, but ... you shall be baptized with the Holy Spirit'" (Acts 1:5; 11:16). S.'s comment is "This is normal, since, if one is not baptized in the Holy Spirit, one cannot become a son of God or a co-heir of Christ."[9] He expands thereon his idea of the Spirit as the key that opens for us our life as children of God: "If the Holy Spirit is called the key, then it is above all through and in him that our spirit is enlightened and that we are purified, illuminated by the light of knowl-edge, baptized from on high, born anew (cf Jn 3:3,5) and made children of God.... Paul himself said: 'The Spirit himself intercedes for us with sighs too deep for words' (Rom 8:26) and 'God has sent the Spirit of his Son into our hearts, crying 'Abba! Father!' (Gal 4:6). It is, therefore he who shows us the door and that door is the light."[10]

Important questions arise out of texts such as this in S.'s work: Who has the "power of the keys"?

Is it the monk or spiritual man, or is it the priest or ordained hierarchical minister? S. would hold a general view of the Sacraments whereby Baptism would be a dead reality if it did not give life in the Spirit, and the Eucharist, which he believed held Christ really present, must nonetheless be in communion, object of a *manducatio spiritualis*, to use the phrase of St. Thomas. S. does not deny the power of sacramental orders; he had been ordained himself. But without the Spirit he seemed to think the sacrament empty.

"Simeon," says Fr. Congar, "believed that it was not possible to communicate the Spirit by means of an external, visible and social process as such, even though it might be canonical, and therefore to open the door, bind or loose, in this human way with the key of the Spirit. This can only be given by the Spirit himself to the one who has opened himself or has responded to his coming by doing penance or practising ascesis."[11]

S. applied this principle to the celebration of the holy mysteries. He inveighed particularly against the ambitious for ecclesiastical office, made exacting demands on the true celebrant: "Not all those people have the right to officiate after all. Even if (someone) had received the whole grace of the Spirit ... so long as God did not give him a guarantee by his choice and his command by illuminating him with his divine light and embracing him with the desire of his divine love, it would not seem to me to be reasonable for him to offer the divine (sacrifice) and to be in touch with such untouchable and fearful mysteries."[12]

S. expressed his opinion in regard to the power of the keys in the treatise *Peri exomologeseos*, which was until recently attributed to St. John Damascene (qv), but which K. Holl has proved to be the work of S. A typical opinion would be: "In order to be reconciled to God's holiness, it is necessary to be holy. In order to give the Holy Spirit, it is necessary to have the Spirit because of the purity of one's own life. At the present time, those who satisfy these conditions are the monks and even then only those who live in accordance with their profession, not those 'monks who have become totally non-monks.'"[13]

S. appeals, in justification for this view, to Jn 20:22: "'Receive the Holy Spirit. If you forgive the sins of any they are forgiven; if you retain the sins of any, they are retained.'" Only those who have the Spirit and give evidence of this in their lives can bind and loose—this is his firm conviction. Some writers before S. had held similar views,

and some continued them after him. His position is summed up by Fr. Congar: "We may therefore conclude that Simeon did not sufficiently emphasize the importance of the sacrament of ordination, which is derived from the saving activity of the Incarnate Word. On the other hand he over-emphasized a certain autonomy of the Spirit and of experience of the Spirit with regard to this sacrament of order, which forms part of the structure of the Church."[14]

We leave S. with a notable text: "The resurrection of all men is brought about by the Holy Spirit. And I do not mean the resurrection of the body at the end of time ... but the spiritual regeneration and resurrection of dead souls, which takes place spiritually every day. By means of the Holy Spirit, this resurrection is given by Christ, who died once and rose again, and who is risen and rises up in all those who live worthily. With him there rise those souls who died with him, in intention, by faith; and he bestows on them the kingdom of God, even now and forever."[15]

---

[1]Critical ed. of his works: *Catecheses*, ed. B. Krivocheine, French tr. J. Paramelle, S.J., *SC 96, 104, 113*; *Chapitres, theologiques, gnostiques et pratiques*, tr. J. Darrouzes, *SC* 51; *Ethical and Theological Treatises*, ed. tr. J. Darrouzes, *SC* 122, 129; *Hymns* ed J. Koder, tr. J. Paramelle and L. Neyrand, *SC* 156, 174, 196; *Peri exomologeseos*, ed. K. Holl, *Enthusiasmus und Bussgewalt beim griechischen Monchtum. Eine Studie zu Symeon dem neuen Theologen,* Leipzig, 1898, 110-127; Cf. I. Hausherr, G. Horn, *Un grand mystique byzantin, Vie de Simeon le Nouveau Théologien par Nicetas Stathotos, Orientalia Christiana,* XII, Rome, 1928; V. Lossky, *Essai sur la théologie mystique de l'Eglise d'Orient,* Paris 1944; esp. B. Krivocheine, "The Brother-loving Poor Man," *Christian East,* 25 (1953-54), 216-227; id. "The Most Enthusiastic Zealot," *Ostkirchliche Studien,* Vol. 4, No. 2, Würzburg, 1955, 108-28; id., "The Writings of Saint Symeon the New Theologian", *OCP* 20 (1954) 298-328; L Bouyer, *A History of Christian Spirituality,* II, *"The Spirituality of the Middle Ages,"* London, 1968, 560-571; esp. Y.-M.J. Congar, *The Holy Spirit,* I, 93-103; S. Gouillard, *DTC* XIV, 2, 2941-2959 s.v.; on Mark the Hermit, cf. esp., J. Gribomont, *DSP*, X (1980), 274-83, s.v.; [2]*Catechesis 22, SC* 104, 273; [3]Y.-M.J. Congar, *op. cit.,* 94; [4]*Hymns, SC* 156, 151ff; [5]*Ethical Treatise, SC* 129, 297; [6]*SC* 51, 72; [7]*Ethical Treatise* V, *SC* 129, 99; [8]*Catechesis* 33, SC 113, 255; [9]*Ibid.,* 259; [10]*Ibid.,* 261; [11]Y.-M.J. Congar, *op. cit.,* 98; [12]*Hymn* 19, *SC* 174, 107ff; [13] I. Hausherr, *op. cit.,* 107; [14]*Op. cit.,* 101; [15]*Catechesis VI,* B. Krivocheine, The Most Enthusiastic Zealot, 115.

SWETE, WILLIAM BARCLAY (1835-1917)

The most prolific writer on the Holy Spirit in the Anglican communion in the late nineteenth and early twentieth centuries, S.[1] wrote from a rich biblical and patristic scholarly background.

Thought worthy to succeed B.F. Westcott as Regius Professor of Divinity in Cambridge, he participated in several projects of co-operative scholarship, influenced in particular the inception of the *Journal of Theological Studies* and the Cambridge patristic texts, inspired the prestigious *Greek Patristic Lexicon*, which appeared long after his death. His contributions to biblical scholarship include the edition of LXX and commentaries on St. Mark and Revelation.

S's first contributions to the subject of the Holy Spirit with Especial Reference to the Controversies were *On the Early History of the Doctrine of the Fourth Century*,[2] and *On the History of the Doctrine of the Procession of the Holy Spirit from the Apostolic Age to the Death of Charlemagne*.[3] These were followed by the article in Smith and Wace's *Dictionary of Christian Biography*.[4] S. had also edited a text, *Theodorus Lascaris Junior: De Processione Sancti Spiritus Oratio Apologetica*.[5] Somewhat later came *The Holy Spirit in the New Testament. A Study of Primitive Christian Tradition*,[6] and *The Holy Spirit in the Ancient Church. A Study of Christian Teaching in the Age of the Fathers*.[7] A short paper on *The Person of the Holy Spirit* from his early years brings his total output to over 1300 pp., probably unique quantitatively on this subject in his time. It was unique also that this subject should be studied and with a method which anticipated the modern "return to the sources"; no one else in that age undertook a separate, objective study of the scriptural and patristic witness to the Spirit; it was undertaken with remarkable scholarly equipment.

With recent scholarly progress some of S.'s findings are understandably revised. His patient analysis of the relevant NT texts ends with a series of brief essays in biblical theology,[8] on the Spirit of God, the Spirit of Jesus Christ, the Spirit in the Church, the Spirit and Ministry, the Spirit and the written word, the Spirit and Personal Life, the Spirit and the Life to come. "Nevertheless," he writes, "it is a fair inference from the teaching of the NT that the Spirit of God belongs eternally to the Divine Essence and that the Only-begotten Son, who as the Word was in the beginning with God, stands in a timeless relation to the Divine Spirit. If the Spirit of the Incarnate Son dominated the whole human life of the Word made flesh, who can doubt that it was also in the most intimate relation with that pre-existent Life which was with the Father before the world was. All this lies in the background of NT thought ready to be drawn into fuller light by the consciousness of the Church as she pondered on her inheritance of Apostolic truth."[9]

Turning to the virginal conception S. writes: "God working by his Spirit is the Father of the humanity of Jesus in the sense that its origination from the substance of the Virgin Mother was a divine act."[10] Of Christ and the Spirit he writes: "It was no conventional rule that guided him but the Holy Spirit working in the sphere of his human consciousness." "From the exalted Head the life of the Spirit flows down into all the members; there is vitality, and there is growth in every part which is in real union with the Lord and with the Body as a whole."[11]

The Spirit will always guide his Church: "No age of the Church can depart fundamentally from this experience. The same Spirit inspires the whole Body to the end of time. But each age receives its own manifestation of the Spirit's presence. Loyalty to the Apostles' teaching and fellowship does not exclude readiness to follow the guidance of the Spirit of truth when it leads into paths which the first generations were not called to tread. The NT marks out the great lines of Christian truth which can never be changed; but it leaves to successive generations the task and joy of pursuing them into regions of thought and life as the Spirit points the way."[12]

S. was attentive to the great Fathers who wrote on the Spirit in the East and the West, to heresies like that of the Macedonians, to creeds and councils. Though he made a specialized analysis of the testimony on the procession, noting the absence of conflict in the Church until the fourth century, he had in his biblical work expressed the judgement that "for the eternal Procession from the Son no direct support from the NT has ever been claimed." This overlooks St. Augustine, whom S. certainly had read.[13] S. applauds the efforts of Pope Leo III to withstand pressure from Charlemagne to insert the *Filioque* in the creed.

S. ends his patristic history with a summary of doctrine under these headings: the Godhead of the Spirit, his relations to the Father and the Son and his function in the life of God, the personal life of the Spirit, his work in creation, in inspiration, in the Incarnation and the incarnate Son, in the mission of the Paraclete, in th Sacraments and in the sanctification of life.

In the course of this summary interesting points are made. S. shows divergent views among the

Fathers on such points as whether, for example, the miracles of Christ were a direct effect of the anointing by the Spirit, whether at Pentecost the Spirit was given to the whole world or only to the Church. "Whatever individuals may have thought," S. writes, "the consensus of opinion in the ancient Church supported a brief in the personal subsistence of the Holy Spirit." He formulates his teaching thus: "But the Church did not attribute to him, as the Arians did, a personality separate from the personal life of God, The Holy Spirit is an eternally existing mode of the Being of God, and not a separate centre of consciousness and self-determination; the one God thinking, willing, and acting in one of his three eternal spheres of thought, volition and activity. The Holy Spirit is not, according to the doctrine of the ancient Church, a divine individual, but the indivisible Godhead subsisting and operating in one of the essential relations of his tripersonal life."[14] This is not the ancient heresy of modalism; it is not phrased in the technical language of scholastic theology, but is not too far from it. Both Karl Barth and Karl Rahner (qv) did use the word "mode" in regard to the Holy Trinity without incurring any charge of heresy or grave inaccuracy.

---

[1] Relevant works here named; cf. J. H. Strawley, *DNB*, 1912-1921, 320-322; bibl. of S., *JTS* 19 (1918), 1-19, by C. H. Turner-A. Rogers, repr. enlarged *Henry Barclay Swete, A Remembrance*, by 'M.B.K.'-'H.G.' 'J.F.B.B.' pp. 163-192; *DTC* Tables, 4191; [2] London, 1873; [3] London, 1876 [4] III, 1882, 113-133; [5] London, 1875; [6] London, 1909; [7] London, 1912; [8] *Op. cit.*, 283-360; [9] *Op. cit.*, 309 [10] *Op. cit.*, 29 [11] Op. cit., 40, 311;29, [12] *Op. cit.*, 360; [13] *De Trinitate*, IV, 20, *PL* 42, 908; *Ibid.*, V,14,15, PL 42, 921; *Tract 99 in Joannem*, 8, PL 35, 1890; [14] *The Holy Spirit in the Ancient Church*, 376.

T

TERTULLIAN (c. 160-c.225)

A convert to Christianity, T., educated in Carthage, produced a considerable amount of writing in Latin, diverse in motivation and in manner, all of theological interest.[1] Styled Father in Latin theology, his status was impaired by his decision to join the Montanist sect. His contribution to Trinitarian theology was notable, principally in providing the terminology: he was the first to use the word *Trinitas* and certain of his formulas have lasted. This does not mean, particularly in the use of the word *persona*, that there was not later development in the sense of the language.

There has been controversy about T.'s theology of the Trinity, and consequently of the Holy Spirit. Was he, at one stage of his career, a binitarian? In *De Praescriptione*, 36 and in *De Virginibus Velandis*, 1, there are phrases which appear to lend themselves to this interpretation, but careful examination of all the texts has exonerated him. Was he a subordinationist? A recent scholar revives plausibly this criticism occasionally heard in the past.[2] T. speaks of the Father and the Son, "the one commanding what is to be done, the other doing what has been commanded,"[3] and again, "This (the word '*portio*') does not properly mean 'part' (*pars*). The Son is not a 'part' of the divine substance but has a 'share' in it. The Father possesses the *substantiae plenitudo*, the Son is a *portio* and as such has a share in this fullness. The divine substance is essentially one; the Son is, as it were, an effluence of this one substance: *Pater enim tota substantia est, filius vero derivatio totius et portio*."[4] Defenders of T. seek to explain these statements by reference to the ensemble of his doctrine, and by the handicap of inadequate language and insufficiently developed concepts. T. also suffered from the restricting doctrinal outlook of the very opponents he sought to defeat, Praxeas notably. The latter's perspective did not include the eternal life of the Godhead before the beginning of the world.

More pertinent to our subject is the question raised about T.'s theology of the Holy Spirit. Adhemar d'Alès in his substantial work on T.'s theology writes: "One thing certain is that the personality of the Holy Spirit appears only in a very confused manner in the treatise against Praxeas."[5] It was in this work that T. set out to combat the modalism of his opponent, about whom, apart from his name not much is known for certain. The great Trinitarian theologian J. Lebreton is more severe: "Led astray by these materialistic conceptions (derived from Stoics), T. represents the divinity as possessed in totality by the Father, but only partially by the Son: 'The Father is all the substance, the Son is only a derivation from it and a part, as he himself affirms, saying "The Father is greater than I."' In this haze the theology of the Holy Spirit becomes even more confused and muddled than that of the Son."[6]

But the great African has defenders.[7] Let us see his writing at least in typical passages. "The rule of faith, which we profess that we may defend it, consists in believing that there is absolutely one God, who is none other than the Creator of the world; it is he who by his Word sent forth before all things, produced the universe from nothing; this Word who has been called his Son was seen in diverse forms by the patriarchs, was heard at all times by the prophets, and lastly was sent down from the Spirit of God the Father and his power to the Virgin Mary, was made flesh in her womb and being born of her was known as Jesus Christ. Then he preached a new law and the new promise of the kingdom of heaven, he worked wonders, was crucified and rose again on the third day; being taken up to the heavens he sat at the right hand of the Father; he sent in his place the power of the Holy Spirit to guide believers; he will come in glory to take the saints to the enjoyment of eternal life and the heavenly promises, and to condemn the wicked to eternal fire after the resurrection of all and the restoration of the flesh."[8] In a credal summary in the *Adversus Praxean* he speaks of the "one being all since all are from the one, namely through the unity of substance; while at the same time the mystery of the divine economy should be safeguarded, which of the unity makes a trinity placing the three, Father, Son and Spirit—three not in order of quality but of sequence, not of substance but of aspect, not of power but of manifestation—all of one substance, one quality and one power, for there is God from whom the phases and aspects and manifestations are in the name of the Father and of the Son and of the Holy Spirit."[9]

Again in his use of imagery T. seeks to show, using his mental categories to the best, the equality of the three in their diversity: "For God brought forth the Word, as also the Paraclete teaches, as a root brings forth the ground shoot, and a spring the river, and the sun its beam: for these manifestations also are projections of those substances from which they proceed. You need not hesitate to say that the shoot is son of the root and the river son of the spring and the beam son of the sun, for every source is a parent and everything that is brought forth from a source is its offspring—especially the Word of God, who also in an exact sense has received the name of Son. Yet the shoot is not shut off from the root nor the river from the spring, nor the beam from the sun, any more than the Word is shut off from God. Therefore according to the precedent of these examples I profess that I say that God and his Word, the Father and his Son, are two; for the root and the shoot are two things, but conjoined; and the spring and the river are two manifestations, but undivided; and the sun and its beam are two aspects but they cohere. Everything that proceeds from something must of necessity be another beside that from which it proceeds, but it is not for that reason separated from it. But where there is a second one there are two, and where there is a third there are three. For the Spirit is third with God and his Son, as the fruit out of the shoot is third from the spring, and the illumination point out of the beam third from the sun; yet in no respect is he alienated from that origin from which he derives his proper attributes. In this way the Trinity, proceeding by intermingled and connected degrees from the Father, in no respect challenges the monarchy, while it conserves the quality of the economy."[10]

T. was clear that the procession of the Spirit was from the Son. This must be seen in his manner of thinking, which is largely in the context of the economy. He is often quoted as the first witness to the procession *a Patre per Filium*: his full statement is *Spiritum non aliunde (de) puto quam a Patre per Filium.*[11] Here he was not thinking of the eternal origin of Spirit. He does not always consider *Spiritus Dei* and *Sanctus Spiritus* as identical; like a number of Fathers he sometimes uses *Spiritus Dei* for Christ.

T. is led to some interesting reflections when he considers Christian Baptism. "Not that the Holy Spirit is given to us in the water, but that in the water we are made clean by the action of the angel, and made ready for the Holy Spirit. Here also a type had come first. As John was Our Lord's forerunner, preparing his ways, so also the angel, the mediator of Baptism, makes the ways straight for the Holy Spirit who is to come next. He does so by that cancelling of sins which is granted in response to faith signed and sealed in the Father and the Son and the Holy Spirit. For if in three witnesses every word shall be established, how much more shall the gift of God? By the benediction we have the same mediators of faith, as we have sureties of salvation."[12]

The coming of the Spirit is thus described by T.: "Next follows the imposition of the hand in benediction, inviting and welcoming the Holy Spirit. Human ingenuity has been permitted to summon spirit to combine with water, and by application of a man's hands over the result of their union to animate it with another spirit of excellent clarity: and shall not God be permitted, in an organ of his own, by the use of holy hands to play a tune of spiritual sublimity? At this point that most Holy Spirit willingly comes down from the Father upon bodies cleansed and blessed, and comes to rest upon the waters of Baptism as though revisiting his primal dwelling-place."[13]

T. then elaborates a typology of the dove in the Baptism of Christ and in the "baptism," so to express it, as he adds, of the world by the flood, "by the same divine ordinance of spiritual effectiveness the dove who is the Holy Spirit is sent forth from heaven, where the Church is which is a type of the ark, and flies down bringing God's peace to the earth which is our flesh, after it comes up from the washing after the removal of its ancient sins."[14]

In ch. I of *De virginibus velandis* where he seems to limit the Godhead to "one God omnipotent, the Creator of the universe, and his Son Jesus Christ", T. goes on later to describe the role of the Spirit thus: "Actually the reason why the Lord sent the Paraclete was that, since human mediocrity was unable to take in all things at once, discipline should, little by little, be directed, ordained, and brought to perfection by that Vicar of the Lord, the Holy Spirit. 'Still,' he said, 'I have many things to say to you, but you are not yet able to bear them; when that Spirit of Truth shall have come, he will lead you into all truth, and will report to you the things which are to come.' (Jn 16:12-13). Thus he declared the work of the Spirit. This, then, is the Paraclete's guiding office: the direction of discipline, the revelation of the Scriptures, the reformation of the intellect, the advance towards the 'better things.'"[15] T. tried to justify the Montanist prohibition on a second marriage, even after the death of a spouse, by appeal to this kind of action by the Paraclete: a specious piece of argument.[16] In the same way he sought to justify the Montanist practice of excluding Christians who sinned after Baptism from communion with the Church.[17] Despite these vagaries he did, in the essentials of his teaching, help to further doctrinal development.

---

[1]Karl Adam, "Die Lehre v. Hl. Geist bei Hermas und Tertullian," *Theol. Quartalschrift.* 1906, 51ff; Works, *PL* 1,2; *CCSL* 1,2; *CSEL* 20, 47, 70, 75 etc.; cf. A. d'Ales, *La théologie de Tertullien*, Paris, 1905, 67-103; M. Kriebel, *Studien zur älteren Entwicklung der abendländischen Trinitätslehre bei Tertullian und Novatian*, Ohlau i. Schl. 1932 95ff; R.E. Roberts, *The Theology of Tertullian*, London, 1924; J. Morgan, *The Importance of Tertullian in the Development of Christian Dogma*, London, 1928; J. M. Restrepo-Jaramillo, "Tertullián y la doble fórmula en el simbolo apostólico," *Greg* 15 (1934), 3-58; T. L. Verhoeuven, *Studiën over Tertullianus' Adversus Praxean*, Amsterdam, 1948; G. Aeby, *Les missions divines de saint Justin à Origène*, Fribourg (Switzerland), 1958, 68ff; K. Wolff, *Das Heilswirken Gottes durch den Sohn nach Tertullian*, Rome, 1960; R. Braun, '*Deus Christianorum', Recherches sur le vocabulaire doctrinal de Tertullian*, Paris, 1962; B. Piault, "Tertullien, a-t-ilété subordinatien?" *RSPT*, 47 (1963) 181-204; J. Moingt, *Théologie trinitaire de Tertullien*, 4 vols, Paris, 1966, esp., vol III, *La procession de l''Esprit Saint*, 1062-69; W. Bender, *Die Lehre über den Hl. Geist bei Tertullian*, Munich, 1961; Quasten II, 266-340; Kelly, *Doctrines*, 111-115; Fliche-Martin, III, 680-683 (J. Lebreton); A. Qulquarelli in *Semanas de Estudios Trinitarios*, VII, Salamanca, Secretaria Trinitaria, 141-187; M. O'Carroll, *Trinitas*, 208-209; *Message*, 47-60; [2]G. Aeby, *op.cit.*, [3]*Adversus Praxean*, 12, *PL* 2, 168; [4]*Ibid.*, 9, 164; [5]Op. cit., 99; [6]Op. cit., 682; [7]Cf. J. Moingt, op. cit., especially 1063, n.6, with refutation of A. d'Ales [8]*De praescriptione haereticorum*, 13, *PL* 2, 26; [9]*CSEL* 47, 229; *PL* 2, 156; [10]*Adv. Prax.*, 8, *CCSL* 2, 1167, 68; [11]*Ibid.*, 4, *CSEL* 47, 232; *PL* 2, 159; [12]*De baptismo.*, 6, *CCSL* 1, 282, tr. E. Evans, London, 1964, 15; [13]*De baptismo*, 8, *CCSL* 1, 283; tr. E. Evans, London, 1964, 17; [14]*Ibid.*; [15]*De virginibus velandis*, 1, *CCL* 2, 1210; *ANF* IV, 27-28; [16]*De monogamia*, 2, *ACW* 13, 71-72, *CCSL* 2, 1229,30; [17]*De pudicitia*, 21, *PL* 2, 1024.

THEOPHANES OF NICAEA (d.c. 1381)

Little is known of T. save that he was Bishop of Nicaea in the fourteenth century, and left a corpus of writing, part of which is unpublished. One published work is altogether outstanding, the *Sermo in Sanctissimam Deiparam,* the most remarkable treatise in any language on the universal mediation of the Blessed Virgin Mary.[1] To the editor of this text, Martin Jugie, A.A., we are also indebted for a credible account of the life and work of T. As Bishop of Nicaea c. 1369 he was theologian to the ex-emperor John Cantacuzenus. His published works are three pastoral Letters,[2] a short *Oratio eucharistica*,[3] in addition to the *Sermo*. Two of his unpublished works would be of interest to our theme: *Against the Barlaamites and Acindynists*, (Paris MS 149, 15th century, fol 26-112 and Pantteleim Athonensis 567, 18th century, fol 1ff), a long treatise containing the answers to questions put to John Cantacuzenus by Paul, the Latin Patriarch of Jerusalem on the Palamite controversy; *Against the Latins*, a treatise in three books, with two shorter works, on the disputed question of the *Filioque (Baroccianus Oxoniensis* 193, 14th century, Mosquensis 246, 16th century).

There is a brief passage in the most theological of the pastoral Letters, one addressed to the clergy, dealing with the Holy Spirit: "Hence (the Lord) generously bestowed on his Apostles that operative grace of the Holy Spirit by which the new creation and the regeneration of those who are and who will be to the end of the age, was to take place, and he granted them his own office and function to be exercised by them, and accordingly he created them, as it were gods and creators, powerful with the force of the omnipotent Spirit, to achieve the greatest works of divine power.... For taking bread and wine, by the power of the Holy Spirit, they change them, O wonder, into the Lord's body and blood, and they also received the power of loosing and binding sins, which is a work of God alone."[4] T. considers Baptism, where "man is made a god," goes on, "for it is greater to change bread and wine into the divine body and to make man God according to grace, than to create heaven and the angels."

T. repeats his idea on the Spirit's role, characteristically eastern: "Therefore, dearly beloved, this operative and divinizing grace and power, which can be created in the twinkle of an eye, without doubt the priest, who is the greatest of creatures, receives."[5]

It is, however, in the sublime masterpiece, the *Sermo* that T. has most to say about the Holy Spirit. He considers the *Theotokos* in relation to each divine Person. In dealing with the third Person he begins by taking up an idea frequently found in Byzantine literature: Mary was miraculously born of sterile parents, which T. sees as an intervention of the Spirit. "Therefore from the beginning she was united to the Spirit, the source of life; nor did she have the slightest participation in existence itself without his partner-

ship. For that partnership of the Spirit became for her participation in existence, and her conception was an image and prelude of the conception of her Son. For if virginal conception is an awesome and incomparable prodigy, nonetheless that a sterile and deadened womb should bring forth is something really new, the work of divine power alone. Consequently, after this prodigy and gift truly worthy of God had taken on life, of her who was chosen before the ages and consecrated for the ministry of the venerable mystery of God's becoming man, the Holy Spirit was the guardian, guide, and, as it were, her sponsal beautifier. He prepared her as a pleasing spouse for God and Father, and a most pleasing Mother for his beloved Son, the beautiful beloved, as the mystical Song (6:3) says, that is suited and adapted to the will of the Father. *For it pleased him that in her should dwell all the fullness of the Godhead.*" (Col 1:19 adapted).[6]

Mary was so prepared and formed for the ministry of the awesome mystery that the archangel "Gabriel, bearing to her the auspicious news of our salvation, found the Paraclete, who had sent him from heaven, dwelling more in her than in heaven, for he had prepared her a minister and dispenser of those mysteries *into which angels long to look* brighter and holier than heaven or those in heaven."[7]

T. goes on to consider the "ineffable union of the Paraclete and the Virgin." "For God the Word, Son of the virgin, not only by his own Spirit, the purifying and sanctifying power, purified and sanctified her, making her ready to become his ineffable abode, but in the Incarnation itself he touched her flesh directly by his Spirit, as by his own finger, and made it thus to subsist in him."[8]

T. here inserts a reflection on Mary's role in spreading God's gifts. He goes on: "Of such a kind and so great are the union and coalition of the Paraclete with the most holy Virgin that no language can explain them, no mind grasp them, although in an excess of kindliness the mystery is a little disclosed to us by divine words and their interpreters and master."[9] T. then summarizes the life of Mary, all as a "participant in the Spirit," to the wonder of the Incarnation, which united her ineffably with the Son and through him with the Father: "all these realities were accomplished by the divine Spirit, and by his total presence in her by a kind of circuminsession, when without the divine Spirit and his partnership it is impossible for a created nature in any way to approach the

Son, to be found worthy of such an ineffable union and coalition, just as no one can have access to the Father without the Son and his presence."

Mary, T. then says, has a special relationship with the three Persons of the Trinity. "Accordingly, as the Son is the natural image of the Father, and consequently an image altogether similar, the Paraclete in the same way is the image of the Son, thus also the Mother of this Son is the image of the Paraclete, certainly not a natural one, but by participation and grace, but nonetheless so that incomparably in a way superior to all creation she stands for him as a prototype, and in her alone all the graces and distinctions of the Spirit which pertain to her Son, shine afar and are perceived; for the appearance and beauty of the two are one; whence she is, as it were, a kind of stele manifesting the hidden treasures of the Spirit, who himself is the power manifesting the secrets of the divinity."[10]

The idea of Mary as the image or icon of the Spirit is found elsewhere, notably with S. Bulgakov (qv); it is brought to an extreme by those who maintain that Mary is the personification of the Spirit. T.'s suggestion of circumincession would be understood analogically on this reality with the Holy Trinity: "the mutual immanence of the three divine Persons, their reciprocal interiority, their ceaseless vital presence to each other, interpenetration. Circuminsession emphasizes the abiding reality; circumincession the dynamic circulation of Trinitarian life from each to the others."[11]

This is the fullest exposition of the theme of Mary and the Spirit found in Christian literature to the time of T. and for long after. Besides this section of his sermon he adverts elsewhere to the Spirit in other contexts. And when he comes to formulate fully his doctrine of Mary's mediation these are his words: "The Mother of him who through his unspeakable kindess, wished to be called our Brother is the dispenser and genuine distributor of all the outstanding and uncreated *gifts of the divine Spirit* which are now given and are still being dispensed, by which we are made brothers and co-heirs of Christ, not only because she shares out the gifts of him who is truly her Son to his brothers according to grace, but also because she bestows them on those who are her own true sons not by a relationship of nature but of grace."[12]

Here T. links Mary's universal mediation and her spiritual motherhood, on which Byzantine writers—with exceptions like John the Geometer—say little, with his vast cosmic scheme within which Mary is so near to the Spirit.

---

[1]Works *PL* 150; *Sermo in sanctissiman Deiparam*, ed, M. Jugie, A.A. *Lateranum* (nova series), 1935; P. Aubron, "Le discours de Theophane de Nicée sur la très sainte Mère de Dieu, *RSR* 27 (1937), 257-279; G. Pinna, O.F.M. *De praedestinatione Christi et Deiparae secundum Theophanum Nicaenum*, Dissert., Antonianum, n. 49; S. Zardoni, "Teofano di Nicea e il dogma dell 'Immacolata Concezione nel discorso sulla Madre di Dio," *Euntes Docete* 10 (1957), 211-35; M.S.J. Candal, S.J. "El 'Sermo in Deiparam' de Teofanes Niceno," *Marianum*, 26 (1965), 72-103; esp. M. Jugie, *DTC* XIV, 513-517 s.v.; *id. DTC* VII, 893-975, "Immaculée Conception dans l'Eglise grecque"; *id., L'Immaculée Conception dans l'Ecriture Sainte et dans la Tradition orientale*, Rome 1952, 240-246; B. Schulze, S.J., in *De Mariologia et Oecumenismo*, ed. K. Balic, O.F.M., Rome, 1962, 389-406; H. Graef, *Mary: A History of Doctrine and Devotion*, London, 1963, 334-39; M. O'Carroll, C.S.Sp., *Theotokos*, Wilmington, 1982, 340-341; *id., Trinitas*, Wilmington, 1987, 209-210. [2]*PG* 150, *Epist. III*, 6, 336C-337A; [3]Epist. III, 7, 337C; [4]*Op. cit.,* XIII, p. 180; [5]*Ibid.*, p. 184 [6]*Ibid.*, 189; [7]*Ibid.*, 189; [8]190; [9]192; [10]XV, 204. [11]M. O'Carroll, *Trinitas*, 69; [12]XV, 205.

THOMAS AQUINAS, ST., DOCTOR OF THE CHURCH (1225-1274)[1]

It is necessary to recall the great theses of Trinitarian theology as laid down by St. Thomas. He is indebted to Augustine (qv), and to Hilary (qv) and Boethius, whose definition of person he quotes, *substantia individua rationalis naturae*, though he was prepared to consider Richard of St. Victor's substitute, *divinae naturae incommunicabilis existentia*. For T. subsistent relation was the basis of divine personality. "Person in any nature signifies what is distinctive in that nature; as in human nature it signifies this flesh, these bones, this soul, the individuating principles of man; which though they are not intrinsic to the meaning of person in general, are so to the meaning of person in man. But in divine realities distinction only occurs by the relations of origin as has already been said. But relation in divine realities is not as an accident inhering in a subject, but is the very divine essence. Therefore it is subsisting as the divine essence subsists. Just then as the godhead is God, so the divine fatherhood is God the Father, who is a divine person. Therefore a divine person signifies relation as subsistent; and this is to signify a relation in the manner (*per modum*) of substance, which is a hypostasis subsisting in divine nature, though the one subsisting in the divine nature is not anything other than the divine nature."[2]

This is a basic passage in T.'s treatment of the Trinity. It comes in the question where he treats of the divine persons; he had previously dealt with processions and relations. Here he was heir to a body of thought from previous ages, and this he carried forward to clearer more coherent statement. He distinguished firmly the procession of generation, the origin of the Son and the procession of love, the origin of the Spirit. He was following the thought of Augustine (qv), but also benefitting from the intuition of St. Anselm (qv). He welcomed the idea of the Spirit bond of love between Father and Son, but would not use it as an essential element in ordering the intellectual structure of the treatise on the Trinity.[3]

It must also be borne in mind that T. was not an essentialist, thinking of the Persons on the basis of the essence, as modes or faculties. This, however, is not the case, as E. Bailleux, A. Malet, and others have shown. Everything active in God was, for Thomas, done by Persons (*actiones sunt suppositorum*). The essential knowledge and love of self exist only as hypostatized in personal subjects, which can be distinguished only by the opposition in the relationships which constitute them. These relationships are established in the divine substance, which is absolute existence, and are therefore themselves subsisting, in other words, they make the Persons exist according to the divine substance, the first *sub ratione intellectus*, under the aspect of knowledge (although the Word is *spirans amorem*; see *Comm. in ev. Joan.* c.6, *lect. 5, no.5*) and the second *sub ratione voluntatis*, under the aspect of will or love."[4]

Fr. Congar here quoted rightly thinks that T.s theology of the Spirit would demand a whole book. "Thomas Aquinas' consideration of the role of the Holy Spirit in the whole economy of grace and in his view of the Church, has, however, still to be discussed with the full and precise attention that it deserves."[5] Fr. Congar thinks that a monograph on the saint's doctrine of the Spirit should comprise four chapters: (1) the great principles of the theology of faith in the Trinity; (2) the procession of the Holy Spirit *a Patre et Filio tanquam ab uno principio*; (3) the theme of the Spirit as the mutual love of the Father and the Son; (4) the part played by the Holy Spirit in the life of the Christian and the Church. The last chapter has not been greatly studied, except for the question of the indwelling (qv) of the Holy Spirit and that of the Gifts (qv) of the Spirit."[6]

T. preserved Augustine's analogy derived from the structure of the Spirit as this passage from the *Compendium Theologiae* illustrates: "Three aspects of man can be considered here: man existing in his nature, man existing in his intellect and man existing in his love. These three aspects are, however, not one, since thinking here is not being, nor is loving; and only one of the three is a subsisting reality, that is, man existing in his own nature. In God, however, being, knowing and loving are one, with the result that God existing in his own natural being, God existing in his intellect and God existing in his love are only one, each of the three being one subsisting reality."[7]

On the procession of the Spirit T. writes as follows: "it is necessary to state that the Holy Spirit proceeds from the Son. If he did not proceed from him, it would not be possible to distinguish one from the other.... It is clear, then, that the divine Persons can only be distinguished from each other by their relationships. These relationships, however, can be used to distinguish the Persons only in so far as they are opposed. The evidence of this is that the Father has two relationships; he is related by the one to the Son and by the other to the Spirit. As these relationships are not opposed to each other, however, they do not constitute two Persons, but only belong to one Person, that of the Father. If then it is only possible to find in the Son and the Holy Spirit these two relationships, each of which refers to the Father, these relationships will not be mutually opposed, just as the two relationships between the Father and each of them are not opposed. Just as the Father is only one Person, then it would follow that the Son and the Holy Spirit would only be one Person possessing two relationships opposed to the two relationships of the Father. This, however, is a heresy, since it destroys faith in the Trinity. It is therefore necessary for the Son and the Holy Spirit to refer to each other by opposed relationships. In God, however, the only opposed relationships there can be are relationships of origin, and these opposed relationships of origin are, on the one hand, relationships of principle and, on the other, of term resulting from that principle. It is therefore necessary to say either that the Son proceeds from the Holy Spirit—but no one says this—or that the Holy Spirit proceeds from the Son—which is what we confess.

"The explanation that we have given above of their respective procession is in accordance with this teaching. It has been said that the Son proceeds according to the mode that is peculiar to the intellect, as Word, and that the Holy Spirit proceeds according to the mode that is peculiar to the will, as Love. Love, however, has of necessity to proceed from the word, since we can have nothing but what we can apprehend in a conception of the mind. On this basis, then, it should be clear that the Holy Spirit proceeds from the Son."[8]

It would be recalled at the Council of Florence (qv) that T. taught that the Holy Spirit proceeded from the Father through the Son (*per Filium*), which is the traditional eastern view. T. put it succinctly: "Since therefore the Son has from the Father that from which the Holy Spirit proceeds, it can be said that the Father through the Son spirates the Holy Spirit, or that the Holy Spirit proceeds from the Father through the Son; which is the same thing."[9] T. develops the point that the Father and the Son are one principle.

T. likewise develops the idea that the proper name of the Holy Spirit is Love, taking this in a personal sense. Here he quotes St. Gregory the Great (qv), as he quotes St. Augustine (qv) when demonstrating that the Holy Spirit is also rightly called Gift.

Consideration of T.s doctrine of the Holy Spirit calls for special study of his explanation and analysis of the Gifts (qv). He is quite expansive on this theme, in general and in particular.

---

[1]Principal texts of St. Thomas: *I Sent.* d. 3 to 31; *Contra Gentiles* IV c. 1 to 28; *Contra errores Graecorum*; Quaest. disp. *De Potentia*, q. 8 to 10; *Summa Theol.* I, q. 27 to 43; French tr. H.-F. Dondaine, O. P., 2 vols, Paris 1943; Cf. Th. de Regnon, *Etudes de théol. positive sur la S. Trinité*, vol II, Paris, 1892; M. Grabmann, *Die Lehre des hl. Thomas von der Kirche als Gotteswerk*, Regensburg, 1903; G. Bardy, "Sur les sources patristiques grecques de S. Thomas dans la Ie partie de la Somme Theologique," *RSPT* 12 (1923) 493-502; J. Slipyi, *De Principio Spirationis in SS. Trinitate*, Lwow, 1926; M.-T. L. Penido, "Cur non Spiritus Sanctus a Patre Deo Genitus? S. Augustin et S. Thomas," *RT* 13 (1930) 508-527; *id.*, "La valeur de la théorie psychologique de la Trinité, *ETL* 8 (1931); 5-16; *id.*, "Gloses sur la procession d'amour dans la Trinité, *ETL* 14 (1937) 33-68; *id.*, *Le rôle de l'analogie en theʲologie dogmatique*, Paris, 1931, 295-311; M. Rackl, "Der hl. Thomas von Aquin und das trinitärische Grundgesetz in byzantinischer Beleuchtung", *Xenia Thomistica*, ed. S. Szabo, Rome, 1925, III, 363-389; P.V. Grumel, "St. Thomas et la doctrine des Grecs sur la procession du Saint Esprit", *Echos d'Orient*, 25 (1926) 257-280; E. Candal, *Nilus Cabasilas et theologia S. Thomae de Processione Spiritus Sancti (Studi e Testi)* Vatican, 1945; H.-F. Dondaine, "La théologie latine de la procession du Saint Esprit, in *Russie et Chretiente*, 1950, 211-218; S.J. Dockx, "Note sur la procession de terme dans la volonté'", *Angelicum* 15 (1938) 419-428; A. Krapiec, "Inquisitio circa Divi Thomae doctrinam de Spiritu Sancto prout amore, *Divus Thomas* (Piacenza) 55 (1950) 474-495;

H. D. Simonin, "Autour de la solution thomiste du problème de l'amour," *Archives d'Histoire doctr. et litt. du Moyen Age* 6 (1931) 174-276; A. Malet, "La synthèse de la personne et de la nature dans la théologie trinitaire de St. Thomas," *RT* 54 (1954) 483-522 and 55 (1955) 43-84; *id.*, *Personne et amour dans la théologie trinitaire de St. Thomas*, Paris, 1956; C. Vaggagini, O.S.B., "La hantise des 'rationes necessariae' de St. Anselme dans la théologie des processions trinitaires de St. Thomas," *Spicilegium Beccense*, I *International Congress for the IXth Centenary of the arrival of Anselm at Bec*, Le Bec-Hellouin and Paris, 1959, 103-139; E. Bailleux, "Le personnalisme de St. Thomas en théologie trinitaire," *RT* 61 (1961) 25-42; J. Pelikan, "The Doctrine of the Filioque in Thomas Aquinas and its Patristic Antecedents, An Analysis of Summa Theologica I, q. 36 in *St. Thomas Aquinas Commemorative Studies*, I, Toronto, 1974, 315-336; Y.-M.J. Congar, O. P., *The Holy Spirit*, I, 88-92; III, 116-127; M. O'Carroll, *Trinitas*, 210-212; [2]Ia, q. 29, a.4; [3]Y.-M.J. Congar, *op. cit.*, 88; [4]*Ibid.*; [5]*Op. cit.*; [6]*Op. cit.*; [7]*Compendium Theologiae*, ch., 50 [8]Ia, q. 36, a.2; [9]q.36,a.3.

TONGUES, SPEAKING IN[1]

Two passages principally in Sacred Scripture narrate or discuss speaking in tongues. Acts 2:4-11: "And they were all filled with the Holy Spirit and began to speak in other tongues, as the Spirit gave them utterance. Now there were dwelling in Jerusalem Jews, devout men from every nation under heaven. And at this sound the multitude came together, and they were bewildered, because each one heard them speaking in his own language. And they were amazed and wondered, saying, 'Are not all these who are speaking Galileans? And how it is that we hear, each of us in his own native language? Parthians and Medes and Elamites and residents of Mesopotamia, Judea and Cappadocia, Pontus and Asia, Phrygia and Pamphylia, Egypt and the parts of Libya belonging to Cyrene, and visitors from Rome, both Jews and proselytes, Cretans and Arabians, we hear them telling in our own tongues the mighty works of God.'"

1 Cor 14: "For one who speaks in a tongue speaks not to men but to God; for no one understands him, but he utters mysteries in the Spirit. On the other hand, he who prophesies speaks to men for their upbuilding and encouragement and consolation. He who speaks in a tongue edifies himself, and he who prophesies edifies the Church. Now I want you all to speak in tongues, but even more to prophesy. He who prophesies is greater than he who speaks in tongues, unless some one interprets, so that the Church may be edified. Now brethren, if I come to you speaking in tongues, how shall I benefit you unless I bring you some revelation or knowledge or prophecy or teaching?.... if you in a tongue utter speech that is not

intelligible, how will anyone know what is said? For you will be speaking into the air.... Therefore, he who speaks in a tongue should pray for the power to interpret. For if I pray in a tongue my spirit prays but my mind is unfruitful. What am I to do? I will pray with the spirit and I will pray with the mind also; ... I thank God that I speak in tongues more than you all; nevertheless, in church I would rather speak five words with my mind, in order to instruct others, than ten thousand words in a tongue.... In the law it is written, 'By men of strange tongues and by the lips of foreigners will I speak to this people, and even then they will not listen to me, says the Lord. Thus tongues are a sign not for believers but for unbelievers, while prophecy is not for unbelievers but for believers. If, therefore, the whole church assembles and all speak in tongues, and outsiders or unbelievers enter, will they not say that you are mad.... What then, brethren? When you come together, each one has a hymn, a lesson, a revelation, a tongue, or an interpretation. Let all things be done for edification. If any speak in a tongue, let there be only two or at most three, and each in turn; and let one interpret. But if there is no one to interpret, let each of them keep silence in church and speak to himself and to God" (2-6; 9; 13-15; 18-19; 21-23; 26-28).

The first passage from Acts relates a unique phenomenon suited to a unique event. In its literal sense the text tells of a gift of tongues which was on the spot intelligible. There may also be a latent symbolism: here was the reversal of Babel which signified division and dispersion; now it is through unity in the understanding of the message by people of different tongues that the spiritual unity is manifest.

In the passage from 1 Corinthians we have a set of contrasts and directives drawn up by Paul to secure the good of the Church from the charismatic action of the Spirit on the faithful.

The account in Acts of the strangers comprehending the words spoken each in their own language (Acts 2:8) is differently explained by scholars. People speaking four different languages have been identified among the crowd assembled. Was it really a miraculous, simultaneous translation? There is nothing against believing this, though the context may be recalled. The gift of tongues, mentioned by Paul in regard to the first Christian communities, glossolalia, was not xenoglossia, that is speaking in a foreign language. Such a happening would be miraculous, but has never been scientifically verified. Glossolalia is a phenomenon much studied lately, as it is a fairly common feature of charismatic (qv) meetings. It is a kind of return to the unsophisticated, untroubled, language of childhood, not rational, not expressive of clear ideas, a muttering or murmuring which has a strongly therapeutic, liberating effect. It may be simulated, or be artificial, but that is not the genuine glossolalia. Everything is open to abuse, and abuse must not be taken as evidence. It lasts only for a few minutes, is not necessarily accompanied by trance or ecstasy, is under the control of the true charismatic. Commentators note that as a charismatic group grows in maturity, as its life becomes increasingly interior, speaking in tongues tends to diminish.

---

[1]Bibl. in R. Laurentin, Chronological Bibliography on Glossolalia, in *Catholic Pentecostalism*, London, 1977; prehistory; 1829-1899; 1901-1963; 1964-1973; pp. 213-221; cf. R. Laurentin ch IV, *Speaking in Tongues*, 58-99.

TWELVE APOSTLES, THE

"The Church was founded on the college of the Twelve, which was instituted by Christ. But this college only received its definitive mandate when the risen Christ charged its members to bear witness to the resurrection, and when the Holy Spirit constituted them as an instrument of revelation to conserve and complete the teaching of the gospel. It was at that moment that Paul, by the divine will expressed through the risen Jesus who gives the Holy Spirit, took his place with the Twelve."[1] Thus the great Pauline scholar, Mgr. Lucien Cerfaux, summarizes his response to the various questions raised about the meaning of the word 'apostle', the special status of the Twelve in the first days of the Church, and the fact of Paul's (qv) admission to their number. Scholars debate different aspects of the matter, the difference between three different but inter-related categories, the disciples, the apostles and the Twelve. Here the view defended by D.M. Stanley and R.E. Brown, with their customary erudition and acumen, is followed. The Twelve were apostles from the first post-resurrectional days: they had been companions chosen by Christ; they had the vision of the risen Jesus (1 Cor 15:5); they were commissioned to preach by the Lord himself.

Vatican II remarkably associates them with the work of the Spirit: "Before freely laying down his life for the world, the Lord Jesus organised the apostolic ministry and promised to send the Holy Spirit in such a way that both would be always and everywhere associated in the fulfilment of the work of salvation."[2]

John Paul II expresses a similar idea in the Encyclical *Dominum et Vivificantem*: "The era of the Church began with the 'coming', that is to say, with the descent of the Holy Spirit on the Apostles gathered in the Upper Room in Jerusalem, together with Mary, the Lord's Mother (Acts 1:14). The time of the Church began at the moment when the *promises and predictions* that so explicitly referred to the Counsellor, the Spirit of truth, began to be fulfilled in complete power and clarity upon the Apostles, thus determining the birth of the Church. The Acts of the Apostles (qv) speak of this at length and in many passages, which state that in the mind of the first community, whose convictions Luke stresses, *the Holy Spirit assumed the* invisible—but in a certain way 'perceptible' guidance of those who after the departure of the Lord Jesus felt profoundly that they had been left orphans. With the coming of the Spirit they felt capable of fulfilling the mission entrusted to them. They felt full of strength. It is precisely this that the Holy Spirit worked in them, and this is continually at work in the Church, through their successors. For the grace of the Holy Spirit, which the Apostles gave to their collaborators through the imposition of hands, continues to be transmitted through episcopal ordination."[3]

The significance of the founding fathers, the Twelve dominant among them, was twofold, as Mgr. Cerfaux explains: "The apostolate of the Twelve and of Paul may be called institutional or charismatic. Institutional because founded by Christ during his life on earth, and then strengthened by the power of the Spirit, by the mission which the risen Christ entrusted to the apostolic group. Charismatic if we take into account either the apparitions of the risen Christ, or the spiritual benefits granted to the Apostles for carrying out of their tasks."[4]

That the Twelve were so dominant is clear from the role assumed by their leader, Peter, in decisive moments. He was explicit on the relationship they had with the Spirit. When Ananias cheated over the profit of his sale, Peter addressed him thus: "Ananias, why has Satan filled your heart to lie to the Holy Spirit and to keep back part of the proceeds of the land?" To his wife he said, "How is it that you have agreed together to tempt the Spirit of the Lord?" (Acts 5:3,9). Here Peter is assuming immediate access to the mind of the Spirit.

Peter too undertook the defence when with others he was arraigned before council: "We must obey God rather than men. The God of our fathers raised Jesus whom you killed by hanging him on a tree. God exalted him at his right hand as Leader and Saviour to give repentance to Israel and forgiveness of sins. And we are witnesses to these things, and so is the Holy Spirit, whom God has given to those who obey him" (Acts 5:29-32). In the same vein is the daring formula from the council of Jerusalem: "For it has seemed good to the Holy Spirit and to us to lay upon you no greater burden than these necessary things" (15:28).

Before the descent of the Spirit the place in the Twelve left vacant by the defection of Judas had been filled. But after the descent, there was no question of a replacement when Herod "killed James, the brother of John with the sword" (Acts 12:2). The initial act of consecration had made the Twelve sacrosanct: chosen and formed by Jesus they were anointed by the Spirit.

When a new ministry was to be created we read that the Twelve summoned the body of the disciples and said: "It is not right that we should give up preaching the word of God to serve tables. Therefore, brethren, pick out from among you seven men of good repute, full of the Spirit and of wisdom, whom we may appoint to this duty." And the first chosen was Stephen, "a man full of faith and of the Holy Spirit." (6:2-3,5).

The Spirit was of course independent: "(The Spirit) sometimes visibly anticipates the Apostles' action," says Vatican II, "just as he unceasingly accompanies and directs it in different ways."[5]

This idea of the Spirit's independence is clearly affirmed by Y.-M.J. Congar (qv), in a study, *The Holy Spirit and the Apostolic Body*, which elaborates a thesis similar to that of the Council. The great Dominican ecclesiologist served on the drafting committee for the text in question on the Missionary Activity of the Church; it is therefore reasonable conjecture that he influenced the ideas and words chosen. Fr. Congar explains with examples how the "Spirit acts by himself for the building up of the Body of Christ."[6] This brings us back to the mission of Christ and of the Spirit. They are distinct, but, in purpose and content, complementary and, in the final outcome, homogeneous.

[1] Ample bibl., L. Cerfaux, *The Christian in the Theology of St. Paul*, London, 1967, 109ff; here quoted 124; cf. from among the works listed, H. Monnier, *La notion de l'apostolat des origines á Irénée*, thesis, Paris, 1903; Kirsopp Lake, *The Twelve and the Apostles*, in *The Beginnings of Christianity*, V. London, 1933, 37; A. Fridrich, *The Apostle and his Message, Inbjuddning till Theologie Doktorspromotionen vid Uppsala Universitat*, Uppsala, 1947; H. Mosbech, *Apostolos in the New Testament, Stud. Theol.* 2 (1949-50), 166-200; C.K. Barrett, *Paul and the 'Pillar' Apostles, Studia Paulina. In honorem J. de Zwaan* (Haarlem, 1952), 1-19; L. Cerfaux, *L'unité du corps apostolique dans le Nouveau Testament*, in *L'Eglise et les Eglises (Mélanges Lambert Beauduin.)* Chevetogne, 1954, 99-110 (=*Recueil Lucien Cerfaux* II, Gembloux, 1954, 227-37); id., *Pour l'histoire du titre Apostolos dans le Nouveau Testament, RSR* 48 (1960), 76-92; H. von Campenhausen, *Der urchristliche Apostelbegriff, Stud. Theol.*, I (1947), 96-130; id., *Kirkliches Amt und geistliche Voltmacht in den ersten drei Jahrhunderten*, Tübingen 1953, 13-91; J. Dupont, *Le nom d'Apôtres a-t-il été donné aux Douze par Jésus?, L'Orient Chrétien*, 1 (1956), 267-290; 425-444; L. Cerfaux, *Le message des Apôtres à toutes les nations, Scrinium Lovaniense (Mélanges historiques Etienne Van Cauwembergh*, Gembloux, 1961, 99-107; esp. Y.-M.J. Congar, O.P. *The Holy Spirit and the Apostolic Body, Continuators of the Work of the Church*, in his work *The Mystery of the Church*, Helicon, 1960, repr. in *Mission and Witness, The Life of the Church*, London, 1965, 275-312, here quoted; esp., R.E. Brown, S.S., *Priest and Bishop: Biblical Reflections*, New York, 1970; id, with D.M.Stanley, in *Jerome Biblical Commentary*, II, *The Twelve and the Apostles*, 795-799; [2] *Decree on the Missionary Activity of the Church*, art. 4: [3] No. 25, tr. *L'Osservatore Romano*, English ed., 9 June, 1986; [4] *Op. Cit.*, 127; [5] *L. cit.*, footnote reference to Acts 10:44-47; 11:15; 15:8; [6] *Op. cit.*, esp. 309f.

V

VATICAN II[1]

Pope John XXIII thought that Vatican II would be a new Pentecost; he liked to recall the expectation of those who would receive the Spirit, spoken of in Acts 1:14, "with Mary the Mother of Jesus." The Holy Spirit was doubtless active in the Council. What historians of its sessions and documents investigate is conciliar teaching on the third divine Person. Some background must be filled in. Catholic theologians and spiritual writers in the decades preceding Vatican II did not give very great attention to the Holy Spirit. It was not too long since Mgr. Landrieux's *Le divin Méconnu* (tr. *The Forgotten Paraclete*), or since Dom Columba Marmion would, in retreat lectures, recall Paul's question reported in Acts 19:2, "'Did you receive the Holy Spirit when you believed?'" and the reply, "'No, we have not even heard that there is a Holy Spirit.'" The great Benedictine would go on to say that today many lived as if they were in the same plight.

The results of Cardinal Tardini's inquiry on a conciliar agenda among the world episcopate yielded no relevant suggestion. No one among the bishops or in the Catholic universities saw the need for a statement about the Holy Spirit; over 600 had asked for teaching on Our Lady. The Council was attended by Observers from the different Orthodox and Protestant churches and communions. Something like a briefing session was organised for them weekly by the Secretariat for Christian Unity. A frequent complaint from them was the lack of a pneumatology in the Council texts. During and since the Council some of them have put this criticism in writing. One article, in the *Ecumenical Review* between the third and fourth sessions, may have had a notable impact.[2] The author, Nikos Nissiotis, of the Greek Orthodox Church, editor of the review, asserted that the Constitution on the Church, then promulgated and the Constitution on Divine Revelation, circulating in draft form, would find little response in the Orthodox churches, because the role of the Spirit was not adequately expounded.

We touch here problems which need scientific investigation: was the drafting of conciliar documents subsequent to this article influenced by the author's thesis, and to what extent? Was there a "development of doctrine" within Vatican II? What were the determining factors? Those who think the questions otiose should compare the doctrine expressed in the Decree on the Church's Missionary Activity (see article "Annunciation") with the Constitution on the Sacred Liturgy, the first promulgated text of Vatican II, admittedly deficient in regard to the Spirit and the Eucharist; the Decree on the Church's Missionary Activity was issued on the last day of the fourth session.

Paul VI drew attention in public to what is now often repeated that there are 258 references to the Holy Spirit in the conciliar documents. But the same Pope said on 6 June, 1973: "The Christology and especially the ecclesiology of the Second Vatican Council should be followed by a new study and a new cult of the Holy Spirit, as an indispensable complement of the conciliar teaching."[3] In the following year, in the Apostolic Exhortation, *Marialis Cultus*, he urged the faithful "to deepen their reflection on the Spirit's action in the history of salvation." (No. 27). It was in the context of the Spirit's role in the mystery of Mary. The Pope was well aware that the immense revival and renewal of the theology of the Spirit within the Catholic Church had one singular aspect, a stimulus and a result, the search for understanding of Mary's relationship with the Spirit. Already by the year of *Marialis Cultus* the relevant bibliography was immense.

Not all the 258 references to the Spirit in the documents of Vatican II have substantive value. The texts should be taken chronologically to appreciate development. SC speaks of Christ, the Son sent by the Father, anointed by the Holy Spirit (art. 5) and of Christ sending the Apostles, filled with the Holy Spirit (art. 6). LG, promulgated in the third session, has a notable passage on the Trinitarian origin of the Church. Thus it treats of the Holy Spirit: "When the work which the Father gave the Son to do on earth (cf. Jn 17:4) was accomplished, the Holy Spirit was sent on the day of Pentecost in order that he might continually sanctify the Church, and that, consequently, those who believe might have access through Christ in one Spirit to the Father (cf. Eph 2:18). He is the Spirit of life, the fountain of water springing up to eternal life (cf. Jn 4:47; 7:38-39). To men, dead in sin, the Father gives life through him, until the day, when, in Christ, he raises to life their mortal bodies (cf. Rom 8:10-11). The Spirit dwells in the Church and in the hearts of the faithful, as in a temple (cf. 1 Cor 3:16; 6-19). In them he prays and bears witness to their adoptive sonship (cf. Gal 4:6; Rom 8:15-16 and 26). Guiding the Church in the way of all truth (cf. Jn 16:13) and unifying her in communion and in the works

of ministry, he bestows upon her varied hierarchic and charismatic gifts, and in this way directs her; and he adorns her with his fruits (cf. Eph 4:11-12; 1 Cor 12:4; Gal 5:22). By the power of the Gospel he permits the Church to keep the freshness of youth. Constantly he renews her and leads her to perfect union with her Spouse (St. Irenaeus, *Adv. Haer.*, III, 24,1) For the Spirit and the Bride both say to Jesus, the Lord: 'Come!' (cf. Apoc 22:17)" (art.4).

Further on, this account is given of the equipment of the Body by the Spirit: "Also in the building up of Christ's Body there is engaged a diversity of members and functions. There is only one Spirit who, according to his own richness and the needs of the ministries, gives his different gifts for the well-being of the Church (cf. 1 Cor 12:1-11). Among those gifts the primacy belongs to the grace of the Apostles, to whose authority the Spirit himself subjects even those who are endowed with charisms (cf. 1 Cor 14). Giving the body unity through himself, both by his own power and by the interior union of the members, this same Spirit produces and stimulates love among the faithful" (art. 7).

In ch. II on the People of God the Council exposes its teaching on charisms (qv); in ch. III on the hierarchy the Council deals with infallibility (qv), showing that the Holy Spirit is its ultimate guarantee. In the section of this chapter dealing with priests there is a paucity of teaching on the Spirit—it will be made up in the Decree on the Ministry and Life of Priests. On the laity we read: "Hence the laity, dedicated as they are to Christ and anointed by the Holy Spirit, are marvellously called and prepared so that even richer fruits of the Spirit may be produced in them. For all their works, prayers, and apostolic undertakings, family and married life, daily work, relaxation of mind and body, if they are accomplished in the Spirit—indeed even the hardships of life if patiently borne—all these become spiritual sacrifices acceptable to God through Jesus Christ" (cf. Pet 2:5).

One of the draftsmen of Ch VIII on Our Lady, Mgr. G. Philips of Louvain, admitted sometime after the Council that they had not taken sufficient account of the Spirit in the Lucan infancy narrative. He is not mentioned in art. 57 which deals with the Visitation and the Presentation in the Temple.[4] Mary in art. 56 is spoken of as "fashioned by the Holy Spirit into a kind of new substance and new creature." There was, regrettably, no effort made to solve the problem of Mary's mediation by showing her relationship with the Spirit; the assembly was, for a while, in a deadlock on this matter.

The Mary Church typology was seen, to some extent, in the context of the Spirit: "The Church, moreover, contemplating Mary's mysterious sanctity, imitating her charity, and faithfully fulfilling the Father's will, becomes herself a mother by accepting God's word in faith. For by her preaching and by baptism she brings forth to a new and immortal life children who are conceived of the Holy Spirit and born of God. The Church herself is a virgin, who keeps whole and pure the fidelity she has pledged to her Spouse. Imitating the Mother of her Lord, and by the power of the Holy Spirit, she preserves with virginal purity and integral faith, a firm hope, and a sincere charity" (art. 64). And there is this passage on which Cardinal Suenens insisted: "Hence the Church in her apostolic work also rightly looks to her who brought forth Christ, conceived by the Holy Spirit and born of the Virgin, so that through the Church Christ may be born and grow in the hearts of the faithful" (art. 65). The Belgian Cardinal was here echoing much of what he had written in *The Theology of the Apostolate*. The Decree on Ecumenism (qv) promulgated the same day as LG repeats that the Holy Spirit is the principle of the Church's unity (art. 2), it reminds us that his interior gifts may be found "outside the visible boundaries of the Catholic Church" (*ibid.*) and teaches: "Nor should we forget that anything wrought by the grace of the Holy Spirit in the hearts of our separated brethren can contribute to our own edification." (art. 4) The Council saw the ecumenical movement as fostered by the Holy Spirit (art. 1,4).

Three documents from the fourth session of the Council have major interest to our theme, the Constitution on Divine Revelation, The Decree on the Missionary Activity of the Church and the Decree on the Ministry and Life of Priests. In the latter occurs an idea which should have been expressed in SC: "For the most blessed Eucharist contains the Church's entire spiritual wealth, that is Christ himself, our Pasch and the living Bread which gives life to men through his flesh—that flesh which is given life and gives life through the Holy Spirit" (art 5). There is also an idea which should have been found in LG: "Hence the priesthood of priests, while presupposing the sacraments of initiation, is nevertheless conferred by its own

particular sacrament. Through the sacrament priests by the anointing of the Holy Spirit are signed with a special character and so are configured to Christ in such a way that they are able to act in the person of Christ the Head" (art. 2).

The Spirit in the life of the priest is brought to mind. After comparing the priest "consecrated by the anointing of the Holy Spirit and sent by Christ" to Christ in his self-giving, the Council goes on: "In this way they are made strong in the life of the Spirit by exercising the ministration of the Spirit and of justice, provided they are prepared to listen to the inspiration of the Spirit of Christ who gives them life and guidance . . . God ordinarily prefers to show his wonders through those men who are more submissive to the impulse and guidance of the Holy Spirit, and who, because of their intimate union with Christ and their holiness of life, are able to say with St. Paul: 'It is no longer I who live, but Christ who lives in me' (Gal 12:20)" (art. 12). There are other references to the Spirit and priests are reminded that "the divine task for the fulfilment of which they have been set apart by the Holy Spirit transcends all human strength and human weakness; for God chose what is weak in the world to shame what is strong (1 Cor 1:27)" (art. 15). The Spirit is thought of when celibacy is urged (art. 16). Bishops and priests in dealing with the poor should be "guided by the Spirit of the Lord" (art. 17).

Finally there was the question of Our Lady and priests. For some reason not yet clarified, there was a lobby against Our Lady within certain influential circles at about the time of the third session. No mention of her was made in draft texts where it might be expected; in some where such mention had existed it was deleted. Thus it was with the text on priests. But demand for a better draft and explicit demand for a passage on Our Lady reached the commission responsible. The final result was this passage: "Under the light of faith that has been nourished by spiritual reading, priests can diligently search for God's will and the inspirations of his grace in the varied events of life. In this way they will become daily more docile in the demands of the mission they have undertaken in the Holy Spirit. They always find a wonderful example of such docility in the Blessed Virgin Mary who under the guidance of the Holy Spirit totally dedicated herself to the mystery of man's redemption" (art. 18). In urging docility to the Holy Spirit on priests the Council expressed a new idea: nowhere in LG is it said that Mary "under the guidance of the Holy Spirit" served the mystery of the redemption. An irony remains: SC, acclaimed as a major triumph of Vatican II, is deficient in face of the immense demand to be thrust forward in the aftermath of the Council.

The significant teaching of the Decree on the Missionary Activity of the Church is dealt with in the articles on the Annunciation and on Pentecost. The Constitution on Divine Revelation is of interest for three reasons. First the structure of revelation is taught to be Trinitarian: "It pleased God, in his goodness and wisdom, to reveal himself and to make known the mystery of his will (cf. Eph 1:9). His will was that men should have access to the Father through Christ, the Word made flesh, in the Holy Spirit, and thus become sharers in the divine nature (cf. Eph 2:18; 2 Pet 1:4)." The text then goes on to show how concretely revelation was realized in Christ "the Mediator and fullness of all revelation."

The Holy Spirit is next mentioned when human assent to revelation is considered, the "obedience of faith." "Before his faith can be exercised, man must have the grace of God to move and assist him; he must have the interior help of the Holy Spirit, who moves the heart and converts it to God, who opens the eyes of the mind and 'makes it easy for all to accept and believe the truth.' The same Holy Spirit constantly perfects faith by his gifts, so that Revelation may be more and more profoundly understood" (art. 5).

In ch. II of the Constitution the Council deals with the transmission of divine revelation. We learn that the "Apostles handed on, by the spoken word of their preaching, by the example they gave, by the institutions they established, what they themselves had received—whether from the lips of Christ, from his way of life and his works, or whether they had learned it at the prompting of the Holy Spirit; it was done by those Apostles and other men associated with the Apostles who, under the inspiration of the same Holy Spirit, committed the message of salvation to writing" (art. 7).

In the transmission of divine revelation "sacred Tradition, sacred Scripture and the Magisterium of the Church are so connected and associated that one of them cannot stand without the others. Working together, each in its own way under the action of the same Holy Spirit, they all contribute effectively to the salvation of souls" (art. 10). Each of the three is explicitly referred to the Spirit by the Council. "The Tradition that comes from the Apostles makes progress in the Church, with the help of the Holy Spirit. . . . Sacred Tradition and sacred Scripture, then, are bound closely together, and communicate one with the other. For both of them, flowing from the same divine well-spring, come together in some fashion to form one thing, and move towards the same goal. Sacred Scripture is the speech of God, as it is put down in writing under the breath of the Holy Spirit. And Tradition transmits in its entirety the word of God which has been entrusted to the Apostles by Christ the Lord and the Holy Spirit. It transmits it to the successors of the Apostles so that, enlightened by the Spirit of truth, they may faithfully preserve, expound and spread it abroad by their preaching" (art. 9).

In the other documents promulgated during the last session, there is mention of the Holy Spirit, sometimes, as in the Constitution on the Church in the Modern World, much more than once, but scarcely anywhere a substantial teaching. What has been here exposed indicates what was at the time, under the influence of the forces then operative, fully grasped. Further development will come in the new age when the Spirit will increasingly dominate life, thinking and action in the Church and the world.

---

[1]Cf. G. Barauna, Ed., *Vatican II: L'Eglise de Vatican II* (Unam Sanctam 51b), various articles ; C. Moeller, in *Theological Issues of Vatican II*, Notre Dame, Indiana, 1967, 125-126; H. Cazelles, "Le Saint Esprit dans les textes de Vatican II", in H. Cazelles, P. Evdokimov (qv), A. Greiner, *Le Mystère de l'Esprit Saint*, Paris, 1968, 161-186; H. Mühlen (qv), *L'Esprit dans l'Eglise*, II (Bible Oecum., 7), Paris, 1969, 9-114; A. Charue, "Le Saint Esprit dans 'Lumen Gentium'", in *Ecclesia a Spiritu Sancto edocta. Mélanges théologiques, Hommage à Mgr. G. Philips*, Gembloux, 1970, 16-39; J. G. Geenen, "Ecclesia a S. Spiritu edocta. Heilige Geest en Heilige Kerk in die transmissie der Openbaring volgens de dogmatische Constitutie, 'De divina Revelatione' van Vaticaan II, *Ibid.*, 169-199; G. Philips, "Le Saint Esprit et Marie dans l'Eglise, Vatican II et Prospective du Problème," in *Etudes Mariales*, BSFEM 25 (1968), 7-37; Y. -M. J. Congar, O.P., *The Holy Spirit*, I, 167-173; id., "Actualité de la Pñeumatologie, *Atti del Congresso*, I, 1528f; M. C. Boulding, O. P., "The Holy Spirit in the Texts of Vatican II," *ITQ* 51,4 (1985), 253-267; G. Chantraine, "L'Enseignement du Vatican II concernant l'Esprit Saint." *Atti del Congresso* II, 993-1010; N. Silanes, O.SS.T., "El Espiritu Santo y la Iglesia en el Concilio Vaticano II", *ibid.*, 1011-1024; C. Marmion, O.S.B., *Christ, the Life of the Soul*, London, 10th ed., 99-100; [2] N. Nissiotis, "The Main Eccelsiological Problems in the Second Vatican Council and the Position of the Non-Roman Churches Facing it," *The Ecumenical Review*, 2 (1965), 31-62, esp. p. 48; cf. *id.*, "Critique of Vatican II," in *Journal of Ecumenical Studies*, 2 (1965), 38-40; [3]*DocCath*, 1 July 1973, 1635; [4]*Op. cit.*, p. 16.

VENI CREATOR SPIRITUS

Along with the *Veni Sancte Spiritus* (qv) this is the best known hymn to the Holy Spirit.[1] It is singularly rich in doctrine. The key words in the first stanza, *veni, visita, imple* are developed through later stanzas. The Spirit is the author of the new creation, *quae tu creasti pectora*, the source of sanctifying grace, *imple superna gratia*, the Gift of God (qv), *Altissimi donum Dei*, coming in a symbol of fire, *fons vivus, ignis*, author of the sevenfold gift, *tu septiformis munere*, symbolized in the biblical image on the Saviour's own lips, the "finger of God" *digitus paternae dexterae*, spreading the charity of God, as St. Paul says, *infund" amorem cordibus*, supplying for weakness, *infirma nostri corporis virtute firmans perpeti*, protecting the soul from harm with his presence marked by peace, *hostem repellas longius, pacemque dones protinus*, the Light of true Trinitarian revelation, *Per te sciamus da patrem, noscamus atque Filium, teque credamus*.

The hymn was since the tenth century used at Whitsuntide Vespers, from the twelfth century during the Whitsuntide Octave and for the hymn at Terce, replacing *Nunc Sancte nobis Spiritus*. Its authorship has been variously attributed, to St. Ambrose, St. Gregory the Great, Charlemagne and Rabanus Maurus. The evidence, in the case of Charlemagne, is of the slightest, the emperor's known devotion to the Holy Spirit, and his insistence on the *Filioque, Teque utriusque Spiritum*, a clear statement in this sense. Opinion latterly settles on Rabanus Maurus, a tenth-century MS in Fulda and his own writing.[2]

---

[1]Text, *Analecta Hymnica Medii Aevi*, I, 1907, 193f; cf. S. G. Pimont, *Les Hymnes du bréviaire romain*, II, 1884, No. 20, pp. 125-43; A. J. Walpole, *Early Latin Hymns*, Cambridge, 1922, 373-76; A. Wilmart, O.S.B., "L'Hymne et la Séquence du Saint Esprit" in *Auteurs spirituels et textes dévots du moyen-âge latin*, Paris, 1932, 37-45; F. J. E. Raby, *A History of Christian Latin Poetry*, 1953, 183; M. J. Rousseau, NCE, *XIV*, 600; [2]PL III, 23-26.

VENI SANCTE SPIRITUS[1]

Called the 'Golden Sequence', this composition marks a high point in Latin hymnody, the most perfect realization of the Sequence form. The verse form and phrasing are flawless and the sentiment so strong and pure matches doctrinal insights that are sure and uplifting. The Spirit is the author of charisms—*dator munerum*—, he abides in the soul of the just —*dulcis hospes animae*,—Sweet Guest of the soul—, he is the Consoler, the Source of holiness—*Sine tuo numine, nihil est in homine*—, he purifies from sin —*lava quod est sordidum*—, he gives Christian meekness and resilience—*flecte quod est rigidum*—, is the author of the seven Gifts—*sacrum septenarium*—he will ensure the reward of a faithful life—*da perenne gaudium*.

Pope Innocent III has been mentioned as the author of this noble liturgical poem. The evidence is scant, unreliable. That supporting the attribution to Cardinal Stephen Langton (d. 1228), Archbishop of Canterbury, is much stronger and was deemed conclusive by the Jesuit historian, hagiographer, Fr. Herbert Thurston. In 1915 he argued the case for Stephen with acumen and impressive erudition. The document in the case is in the *Distinctiones Monasticae*, published by the great Benedictine scholar, Cardinal Pitra of Solesmes Abbey in his *Spicilegium Solesmense* in 1855. Pitra was convinced that the author was a Cistercian and an Englishman, and Fr. Thurston, having examined the text minutely, concurs. As Julian's *Dictionary of Hymnology* shows, whenever the *Veni, Sancte Spiritus* is found in an eleventh or twelfth-century MS, it is an interpolation. Moreover, the rhythmical pattern could not have been before the twelfth century.

The exact relevant words of the unknown author of the *Distinctiones Monasticae* are: "I say consoler because it is proper to the Holy Spirit to console those who mourn and are sorrowful. I might prove this by many passages of Holy Scripture, but I prefer to cite what has been said in praise of the Holy Spirit by a man venerable both for his life and his learning, Master Stephen de Langton, by the grace of God Archbishop of Canterbury, in a certain splendid sequence which he composed upon the Holy Spirit, using the following words, *Consolator optime, dulcis hospes animae, dulce refrigerium*, etc."[2]

Langton had studied in Paris, where he was friendly with the future Innocent III. The latter it was who made him Cardinal and Archbishop of Centerbury. Impeded for a while in taking his office, Langton resided in Pontigny. On his return to England he played a part in the *Magna Carta* story. His stay in France accords with the early manuscript tradition of the *Veni Sancte Spiritus*.

---

[1]Text *Analecta Hymnica Medii Aevi*, 54, 1915, 234-39; cf. M. Dulong in *Mélanges Mandonnet*, 2 vols., *Bibliothèque thomiste*, 13-14, II, 183-90; F. J. E. Raby, *A History of Christian Latin Poetry*, 1953, p. 342-4; F. M. Powicke,

Stephen Langton, "Ford Lectures for 1927, 1928"; A Wilmart, O.S.B., *Auteurs spirituels et textes dévots du moyen-âge latin*, Paris, 1932, 37-45; esp. H. Thurston, S.J., "The Veni Sancte Spiritus" in *Familiar Prayers*, ed. P. Grosjean, S.J., London, 1953, 54-72. [2]*Spicilegium Solesmense*, III, 130, tr. H. Thurston, op. cit., 60f; reference to Julian, *Dictionary of Hymnology*, ed. 2, 1721.

VON BALTHASAR, HANS-URS (1905-1988)[1]

The great theorist of *Theodramatik* made a dramatic exit from his life, surely had a still more dramatic entry to the next. His encounter with Adrienne von Speyr, in the light of all that he wrote about her and her influence on his varied apostolate, notably as a theologian, may have surprised even heaven! Eventually persuaded to accept the cardinalate, he died suddenly as he was preparing to leave for the conferring ceremony in Rome. He had written a book on the secular institute, he and Adrienne had founded. It opened with these words: "This book has a primary purpose: to prevent anyone attempting after my death to separate my work from that of Adrienne von Speyr. It will prove that this is in no way possible, either in regard to theology or even the community which was begun." B's literary production: over 70 works translated, over 80 books and about 300 articles, is more varied in subject-matter than that of any Catholic writer in this or possibly any century; he was awarded the Paul VI prize for Theology by John Paul II in 1984. University courses are devoted to him; over 20 books, many of them university dissertations, have been written on his thought. His friend, Cardinal de Lubac, declared him the most cultured man of his time. He has been called the greatest theologian of his age.

This means that B. is himself an excellent case-history of the Spirit's action in the Church, for his life was consumed in the Church. He wrote much on the Holy Spirit, in essays and passages found widely in his works. In his last year he published a substantial work on the subject. His reflections on the Spirit and Mary, found likewise throughout his writings, provide material for two important studies on the decisive moments and meaning of the Spirit's relationship with the Mother of God.

B. once wrote that the Holy Spirit is the most mysterious of the three divine Persons. But in his twofold aim of opening theology to life and demonstrating the unity of theology and spirituality he was rarely without some advertence to this mysterious one. Among ideas which must be noted and investigated by those pursuing the great theme through B's writings is that in the Annunciation (qv) the Holy Trinity was revealed: to this he returns. In the scene for the first time the differentiating elements in Trinitarian belief are manifest: the transcendent Father who sends, the eternal Son allows himself to be sent, the Holy Spirit operates the Incarnation of the eternal Word.[2] Elsewhere B. says: "At the origin of the revelation of the Word, there was already the Holy Spirit. 'God sent his Son' (Gal 4:6). He alone can produce the entry of the Word of God into man, nature and history, and that is also why man cannot receive, contemplate, understand the Word save in the Spirit.... The Spirit which leads us into all truth is thus inseparably a Christological and Trinitarian Spirit. He realizes the Incarnation of the Word, but wishes thereby that Christ should be believed and understood as a divine Person, inseparable from the Father and the Spirit. Finally he brings the Son back to the Father, in such wise that this return should be the establishment of the Son as Head and principle of life of the Church, of the outpouring of his life in the Sacraments, Scripture, the Liturgy, preaching, the whole Christian life.... As our view passes from the unknown God to the revealed God, to reach, through the latter, the heart of the Father, we cannot still discover the property of the Holy Spirit, save through the property of the Son and the property of the Father."[3] B. calls the Holy Spirit "the Unknown one beyond the Word."

The role of the Spirit, according to B. is to make interior and at the same time universal the Redemption operated by Christ. He has a highly singular idea of the kenosis of the Word, as pre-existing, not merely in his humanity, and a somewhat similar idea of the kenosis of the Spirit, though the term is not used.

The Spirit, B. maintains, has the distinctive mission to show us the mystery of the power of the love of the triune God. He sees the same Spirit announced with the Father and the Son as creating the world; the Spirit goes before the chosen people in their wanderings, overshadows the Christ-event, from the Annunciation to the death of Christ on the Cross, is given to the Church in view of its eschatological pilgrimage to the heavenly Jerusalem. But always as "the unknown one beyond the World," the Spirit does not make himself known to us directly, sending us always to the Father and the Son. But he enters into the very depth of our being, and as he purifies our freedom he becomes the last subject of all that we are: "Our most intimate actions of believing, hoping, loving, our states of soul and our attachments, our most personal and freest resolutions, all the non-transferable reality that we are, is so much animated by him that he is the last subject making us."

In an article for *Communio* some years before his death B. gave a highly original series of reflections on the Spirit: "He who covered Mary with his shadow, who was then the author of the first interpretation of God in Christ, who had endowed Jesus in his baptism (qv) with the Spirit of mission and had ceaselessly guided and driven him, had finally to be 'handed over' to the Father by the dying one, so that risen he should from the Father breathe him on the Church. The Spirit is not a second interpretation of God, but only the completion of the first and unique interpretation, for 'he will not speak on his own authority, but whatever he hears he will speak, and will declare to you the things that are to come. All that the Father has is mine; therefore I said that he will take what is mine and declare it to you' and 'he will guide you into all truth' (Jn 16:13-15). The unity of God's auto-interpretation could not be more clearly expressed; it is also manifested by the Spirit diffused in the hearts of believers who cries, 'Abba, Father' which is the cry of the Son to the Father."

Here there is a feature of B's writing, one of his strengths, closeness to Scripture—another is, of course, his immense knowledge of the Fathers. In the same article he has other interesting insights: "The guidance of the disciples by the Spirit 'into all truth' is now, truth to tell, an indefinite process, impossible of achievement on earth and at the heart of history. That this process should not sink into what is formless it must take place within certain fixed structures which correspond exactly to the incarnation of the word in the corporal and spiritual structure of a man. And the fundamental tendency of the authentic Spirit of interpretation will always be recognisable by its power for incarnation. It sculptures the image and being of Jesus in the believer.... Interpretation under the influence of the Spirit takes place within structures established and protected by him: the Church, with Sacred Scripture and Tradition both attached to it, with its charactertistic distinction between 'pastor' and flock. These factors are the preliminary condition of an interpretation ever advancing further, inspired by the Spirit; in the deep

insights of the saints, which are ever new, in the increasingly perfect purifying process which separates what is genuinely Christian from additions alien to it, as this pure good thing takes root simultaneously in a multiplicity of civilizations and traditions (cf. the miracle of Pentecost; all peoples understand, each in their own language, the same thought-content), in the permanent, living testimony of Christians up to martyrdom, which Jesus predicted to them, in the constantly deepening prayer through which the truth of God in Christ can enter each individual in a new and original way, in the renewed efforts of Christian theology seeking to penetrate the mystery of the Trinitarian self-giving, which is open to the world." There is no danger of the stream drying up for the Spirit and Jesus are ever present. Nor are there grounds for dividing history into phases corresponding to the Three Divine Persons, for God in the three hypostases is always one, and cannot consequently be interpreted save as one. "The Fathers of the Church always saw the Trinity of God already in the first verses of Genesis: God the Father spoke his Word in the beginning, and his Spirit moved over the deep."[4]

B. saw the Spirit ruling the life of Christ and he wrote beautifully of the Spirit as the one understood by saints. Still more so of the relationship between Mary and the Spirit. As he saw all true contemplation as ultimately returning to the Incarnation, so Mary's fiat, her 'Yes' to God, in the Spirit, was the original cell which would develop organically into the entire Catholica while the Church, on its side, seeks constantly to match its hidden origin, this 'Yes' without stain pronounced in Nazareth. B. shows how, on Mary's side, every moment of a decisive kind, is lived in the Spirit, until, on Calvary she fully embodies the Church, as the Spouse of Christ, and fully justifies her title as "vessel" of the Spirit. "We are here faced with a double truth: the Church is born when Jesus, dying, pours out the Spirit, when his side opens; but it is born too when the feminine "Yes" to all that God wills is transformed into the inexhaustible fruitfulness of the new Eve. The Church is called 'immaculate' by Paul (Eph 5:27), though on earth it is not truly and literally immaculate save in its Marian archetype. The Cross (with which Easter and Pentecost are linked indissolubly) is the accomplishment of every conjugal relationship between man and woman, between heaven and earth."[5] For B. there is continuity between the "Marian experience" and the "maternal experience" of the Church. B. also speaks of the "Marian dimension of the Church," even the "Marian Church."

B's contribution to the theology of the Spirit, as to so much else, is a stimulus of powerful renewal, a reassurance of worlds of thought still to be explored. "The doctrines of the Trinity, of the Man-God, of redemption, of the Cross and the resurrection, of predestination and eschatology, are literally bristling with problems which no one raises, which everyone gingerly sidesteps." Theology is ongoing. What has been defined must not be lost, but definitions are "less an end than a beginning." "Whatever is transmitted without a new personal effort, an effort which must start *ab ovo* from the revealed source itself, spoils like the manna. And the longer the interruption of living tradition caused by a simply mechanical tradition, the more difficult the renewed tackling of the task."

B's advice to scholars on the need for a spiritual intelligence in the study of Scripture, his strictures on the historico-critical method when there is question of the history of Israel and the person of Jesus have had wide validity. "The Holy Spirit is a reality which the philologists and philosophers ignore or at least 'provisionally put into parentheses.'" B's friend and fellow-theologian, Cardinal de Lubac adds. "B. removes the parentheses, or rather, he shows us how the Holy Spirit himself removes them."[6]

[1]For works cf. bibliographies issued by Johannesverlag, Einsiedeln, 1975, 1980; particularly relevant here, *Spiritus Creator*, 1965; *Pneuma und Institution*, 1974; "Empfangen durch den Heiligen Geist, geboren von der Jungfrau Maria," in *Ich glaube, Vierzehn Betrachtungen zum apostolischen Glaubensbekenntnis*, ed. W. Sandfuchs, Würzburg, 1975, 39-49; *Das betrachtende Gebet*, 4 ed., 1977; *Der driefache Kranz, Das Heil der Welt im Mariengebet*, 2 ed, 1977; "Maria in der kirchlichen Lehre und Frömmigkeit" in J. Ratzinger-H. U. von Balthasar, *Maria Kirche im Ursprung*, Freiburg I. Breisgau, 1980, 51-79; *Klarstellung. Zur Prüfung der Geister* 4 ed., 1978; "Maria und der Geist" in *Geist und Leben* 56 (1983) 173-177; "The Spirit Interpreter of Jesus" in *Does Jesus know us? Do we know him?*, San Francisco, Ignatius Press, 1983, 85-99; *Theologik*, Band III, 1987, *Der Geist der Wahrheit*, 1987; (Einsiedeln save where mentioned); *The Von Balthasar Reader*, Ed. M. Kehland and W. Loser, tr. R. J. Daly and F. Lawrence, Edinburgh, 1982, 175-181; esp. "Prayer to the Spirit, 426-431; Works on B. cf. esp. H. (Cardinal) de Lubac, S.J., "He chose Beauty as a Way to God," in *Thirty Days*, 1988, 4, 25-32; K.K.J. Tossou, *Strehen nach Vollendung. Zur Pneumatologie im Werk Hans Urs von Balthasars*, Freiburg, Basel, Vienne, 1983; J.R. Sachs, *Spirit and Life. The Pneumatology and Christian Spirituality of Hans Urs von Balthasar*, Tübingen, 1984; M. T' Joen, *Maria, Kerk-in-oorsprong. De Mariavisie van H.U. von Balthasar tegen de achtergrond van de mariologischeontwikkelingen in de twintigste eeuw*, Dissertation, Louvain-la-Neuve, 1986; on the Spirit and Mary cf. A. Peelman, "L'Esprit et Marie dans l'oeuvre théologique de Hans Urs von Balthasar," *Science et Esprit*, 30 (1978) 279-294; M. T'Joen, "Marie et l'Esprit dans la théologie de Hans Urs von Balthasar," *Marianum* 49 (1987), 162-195; [2]*Theologik* III, 220; *Das betrachtende Gebet*, 170; *Spiritus Creator*, 107; [3]*La prière contemplative*, 73, 77; Paris, 1964; English tr., p. 71; Prayer, [4]*Communio*, French ed., XI, February 1986, 10f; Cf. *Does Jesus know us*, l. cit.; [5]*Kleine Fibel für verunsicherte Laien* (Kristerien 55), 1980, 72; [6]H. de Lubac, *op. cit.*, *Communio*, XIII, 5 *Prière por recevoir l'Esprit Saint*, 5-13, repr. *Von Balthasar Reader*; cf. esp. *Communio*; XIV, 7, special issue, *The Life and Work of Hans Urs von Balthasar*.

WESLEY, JOHN (1703-1791)

The founder of Methodism, W. after different attempts to find his vocation, had his moment of conversion on 24 May, 1738 at a meeting in Aldersgate Street, London, after he had heard the reading of Martin Luther's preface to the Epistle to the Romans.[1] His course was now set on wholehearted evangelism and his splendid qualities, especially his immense capacity for work, his perseverance and personal magnetism ensured immeasurable results in this Christian task. The Holy Spirit considered in the light of experience was essential to the outlook which W. fostered. His religion, as he thought of it, was that of the Articles, Homilies and Liturgy of the Church of England, but with a difference from that religion as it was understood at the time. "The Holy Spirit had brought this doctrine and devotion home to the heart with such intensity that it was now much more than a sincerely approved system. The sense of the presence of Christ dwelling in the heart as Judge and Saviour was so vivid that he reigned there the unquestioned Master of the mind, of the will, of the affections."[2] Entry to the Methodist church involved a "new birth," described as "a vast inward change, a change wrought in the soul by the operation of the Holy Spirit, a change in the whole manner of our existence,"[3] making the one newly born sensible to the graces which the Spirit of God works in his heart, giving him fellowship with the Father and the Son.

A vital element in the Methodist way of life is the witness of the Spirit, an idea drawn from Rom 8:16, "This Spirit bears witness with our spirits that we are God's children." W. explained it thus, defending the same view over a period of time, "an inward impression on the soul, whereby the Spirit of God immediately and directly witnesses to my spirit that I am a child of God, that Jesus Christ hath loved me and given himself for me, that all my sins are blotted out, and I, even I, am reconciled to God."[4] One must applaud the fidelity shown to this intuition, which must in day to day practice call for sure exercise of the discernment of spirits (qv). W. supported his theory by appeal to Gal 4:4. The importance of experience is always recognised by W.

[1]Excellent bibl. in *Oxford Dictionary of the Christian Church,* 2nd ed., 1983, 1467; cf. C. W. Williams, *John Wesley's Theology Today,* 1960; H. Lindstrom, *Wesley and Sanctification,* A Study in the Doctrine of Salvation, Stockholm, 1946; R. Davies and G. Rupp, ed., *A History of the Methodist Church in Great Britain,* London, 1965; A. C. Outler, ed., *John Wesley,* in A Library of Protestant Theology, Oxford, 1964; [2]J. Lawson in *A History.,* ed. R. Davies and G. Rupp, 185f; [3]R. Davies, *op. cit.,* 164; [4]A. C. Outler, *op. cit.,* 211; full text of discourse, 210-220; cf. C. W. Williams, *op. cit.,* 98-125; R. A. Knox, *Enthusiasm* London, 1950, 422-488, and 513-548.

WISDOM LITERATURE[1]

With the final state in the growth of Wisdom literature we are brought very near to the NT revelation of the Spirit. This body of writing comprises Job and the Proverbs (between 450 and 400 B.C.), numerous psalms, Qoheleth or Ecclesiastes (c.250 B.C.), Ben Sira or Sirach or Ecclesiasticus (190-180-B.C.) and Wisdom of Solomon (c.50 B.C.). Only Yahweh is wise in the strict sense. His wisdom is shown in creation (Pr 3:19; Jb 38-39; BS 42:15-43). Wisdom is personified: "Wisdom cries aloud in the street; in the market she raises her voice; on the top of the walls she cries out; at the entrance of the city gates she speaks: 'How long, O simple ones, will you love being simple? How long will scoffers delight in their scoffing and fools hate knowledge? Give heed to my reproof; behold I will pour out my thoughts (Heb "spirit") to you; I will make my words known to you'" (Pr 1:20-23). "I, wisdom, dwell in prudence, and I find knowledge and discretion.... I have counsel and sound wisdom, I have insight, I have strength. By me kings reign, and rulers decree what is just; by me princes rule, and nobles govern the earth.... The Lord created me at the beginning of his work, the first of his acts of old ... and I was beside him like a master workman; and I was daily his delight, rejoicing before him always, rejoicing in his inhabited world and delighting in the sons of men.... Happy is the man who listens to me, watching daily at my gates, waiting beside my doors. For he who finds me finds life and obtains favours from the Lord; but he who misses me injures himself; all who hate me love death." (Pr 8:12,14-16,22,30-31,34-36).

Ben Sira places wisdom within the divine reality, quasi-hypostatized: "Wisdom will praise herself, and will glory in the midst of her people. In the assembly of the Most High she will open her mouth, and in the presence of his host she will glory; I came forth from the mouth of the Most High, and covered the earth like a mist.... From eternity, in the beginning, he created me, and for eternity I shall not cease to exist.... Whoever obeys me will not be put to shame, and those who work with my help will not sin." (BS 24:1-4,9,22).

Of particular interest to us are the passages in Wisdom of Solomon where wisdom is almost identified with spirit: "For the holy spirit of discipline flees deceit and withdraws from senseless counsels; and when injustice occurs it is rebuked. For wisdom is a kindly spirit, yet she acquits not the blasphemer of his guilty lips; because God is the witness of his inmost self and the sure observer of his heart and the listener to his tongue. For the Spirit of the Lord has filled the world, is all-embracing and knows what man says." (1:5-7).

The final text appears like a junction of OT theologies of wisdom and the Spirit; it contains a litany of praise in regard to wisdom: "I learned both what is secret and what is manifest, for wisdom, the fashioner of all things, taught me. For in her there is a spirit that is intelligent, holy, unique, manifold, subtle, mobile, clear, unpolluted, distinct, invulnerable, loving the good, keen, irresistible, beneficent, humane, steadfast, sure, free from anxiety, all-powerful, overseeing all, and penetrating through all spirits that are intelligent and pure and most subtle. For wisdom is more mobile than any motion; because of her pureness she pervades and penetrates all things. For she is a breath of the power of God, and a pure emanation of the glory of the Almighty; therefore nothing defiled gains entrance into her. For she is a reflection of eternal light, a spotless mirror of the working of God, and an image of his goodness. Though she is but one, she can do all things, and while remaining in herself, she renews all things; in every generation she passes into holy souls and makes them friends of God, and prophets; for God loves nothing so much as the man who lives with wisdom. For she is more beautiful than the sun and excels every constellation of the stars" (7:21-29). It is noteworthy that Wisdom 1:7 has been taken into the Church's liturgy for the feast of Pentecost. There are similar passages in Ps 139:7-12 and Job 28:20-27.

So much do wisdom and spirit finally converge that one can understand the judgement of a scholar: "Wisdom and Spirit are identified in so many respects that Wisdom appears above all as a sublimation of the part played by the Spirit in the Old Testament."[2] Wisdom has a cosmic role, she stirs the prophets, guides men, especially God's chosen people, is the spiritual master of individuals. The language used about her and the concepts formed would be an intellectual preparation for the formulation later needed in regard to doctrine about the Holy Spirit. What is said about Wisdom, especially in the Wisdom of Solomon, will be, with the required alteration or amendment, applicable to the Holy Spirit. It is a striking example of divine use of the particular Jewish genius, enlarged, it may be admitted, by Hellenistic influence, to open intellectual paths whereon the full divine message would smoothly pass. It helps us possibly to answer a question prompted by the dialogue of the Annunciation: How could Our Lady as a Jewess, one admittedly steeped in the religious traditions and outlook of her people, reach out to grasp a divine word which appeared to assume her understanding of the Spirit as one who would overshadow her?

We touch here the problem of personal traits and status attributed to Wisdom and the Spirit in the OT. This is still more marked in the Rabbinic writings where the Spirit is spoken of as speaking, crying, admonishing, sorrowing, weeping, rejoicing, comforting etc. How near was the OT to the NT in the matter? Could one with exceptional, unique, spiritual genius bridge the gap? It is one of the problems in regard to the Annunciation (qv).[3]

---

[1]Cf. P. van Imschoot, "Sagesse et Esprit dans l'Ancien Testament," *RB* 47 (1938), 23-49; D. Colombo, "Pneuma Sophias ejusque actio in mundo in libro Sapientiae," *Studii Biblici Franciscani: Liber Annuus* 1)1950-51) 107-160; C. Larcher, *Estudes sur le livre de la Sagesse*, Paris, 1969, pp. 329-414 "La Sagesse et l'Esprit"; M. Gilbert, "Volonté de Dieu et don de la Sagesse, (Wis 9:17f)," *NRT* 93 (1971), 145-166; G. T. Montague, *The Holy Spirit*, 91-110; Y.-M.J. Congar, O.P., *The Holy Spirit*, I, 9-12; [2]C. Larcher, op. cit., 411; [3]J.M. Reese, *Hellenistic Influence on the Book of Wisdom and Its Consequences* (Analecta Biblica), Rome 1950; D. Winston, *The Wisdom of Solomon*, Garden City, New York, 1975.

About the Author

Michael O'Carroll, C.S.Sp., is an internationally respected theologian and educator. He has written widely and well, over the past three decades, on theological and ecumenical topics. He is also the author of the much acclaimed works *Theotokos: A Theological Encyclopedia of the Blessed Virgin Mary; Trinitas: A Theological Encyclopedia of the Holy Trinity;* and *Corpus Christi: An Encyclopedia of the Eucharist,* all of which have been published by Michael Glazier.

Other reference works by Michael O'Carroll,
C.S.Sp. available from The Liturgical Press:

Theotokos:
A Theological Encyclopedia of the Blessed Virgin Mary

Trinitas:
A Theological Encyclopedia of the Holy Trinity

Corpus Christi:
An Encyclopedia of the Eucharist